Ernest Newman

WAGNER NIGHTS

PICADOR
Published by Pan Books

First published 1949 by Putnam and Co Ltd
This edition published 1977 by Pan Books Ltd,
Cavaye Place, London SW10 9PG
Copyright Ernest Newman 1949
ISBN 0 330 25070 1
Printed and bound in Great Britain by
Richard Clay (The Chaucer Press) Ltd, Bungay, Suffolk

Born in Liverpool in 1868, Ernest Newman was successively music critic of the *Manchester Guardian*, the *Birmingham Post* and (from 1920) the *Sunday Times*.

His writing is distinguished for its wit, elegance and factual accuracy. His books include *Opera Nights*, studies of Gluck and Hugo Wolf, and a four-volume biography of Richard Wagner.

It is for his extensive studies and profound understanding of Wagner opera that Newman is best remembered. *Wagner Nights* is widely regarded as the standard work on the Wagner operas.

Ernest Newman died in 1959.

to Vera

CONTENTS

WAGNER NIGHTS

OVERTURE

When the first volume of this series was published—the *Opera Nights* of 1943—those great and good men the reviewers, from whose lynx-eyes nothing can remain hidden for long, reproached me tenderly for what they regarded as my arbitrary choice of operas. *Falstaff*, for instance, was there, but not *Otello* or *Aïda*, *Turandot* and *Gianni Schicchi* but not *Tosca* or *La Bohème*, *Così fan tutte* but not *Don Giovanni* or *Figaro*, and so forth. Berlioz and Tchaikovski and Johann Strauss were among the chosen company, but not Weber or Rossini or Wagner and a few others in whose company the music lover looks to spending an occasional night at the opera. In their grieved perplexity at this seeming aberration on my part there went up a wail from the reviewers like that of Mr. Wodehouse's Monty Bodkin when Miss Butterwick broke off the engagement—"Gertrude, your conduct is inexplicable." My own conduct, however, can be explained.

A good many years ago I dashed off, at the request of an English firm of publishers, a fortnightly series of analyses, in popular style, of some of the best-known operas, together with brief biographies of the composers. Although this matter did not, in my opinion, in any sense constitute a "book", it was issued as such, in three volumes, under the general title of *Stories of the Great Operas*, in the United States, where, if hearsay is to be trusted, it had a considerable sale. As the English copyright was mine, Messrs. Putnam and Co. suggested, during the late war, that the American volumes should be reprinted here. From this suggestion I recoiled in horror. In the first place I saw no sense in reprinting the elementary biographies, while in the second place I felt that if the opera analyses were to be collected in volume form I would prefer to revise them all thoroughly, enlarge the scale of treatment, and altogether try to make a better job of it. On these terms agreements were ultimately made with Messrs. Putnam on this side of the Atlantic and Mr. Alfred Knopf on the other.

While these negotiations were proceeding I arranged with Mr.

Knopf for a volume dealing with twenty-nine operas that had not been included in the fortnightly series to which I have referred. This entirely new volume appeared in this country in 1943 under the title of *Opera Nights*; but as the analyses of twenty-odd years ago had been issued in the U.S.A. under the title of *Stories of the Great Operas*, Mr. Knopf brought out the new volume as *More Stories of the Great Operas*, a procedure calculated, I am afraid, to give a little trouble one of these days to library cataloguers and bibliographers. However, that was no concern of mine. I then set to work to rewrite all the original analyses (*Stories of the Great Operas*), one volume to be devoted to Wagner, the other to deal with all the famous works by other composers not included in *Opera Nights* (*More Stories of the Great Operas*). The present volume is the first stage in this process of reincarnation. It has no connection whatever with the Wagner volume of *Stories of the Great Operas*; it is an entirely new work from cover to cover. A further volume, similarly rewritten, dealing with the standard works of Mozart, Verdi, Puccini, Gounod, Rossini etc. not included in *Opera Nights*, will follow, I hope, before long.

At first sight there may appear to be no great necessity today for yet another book on the Wagner operas. Sooner or later, however, such a work would have had to be written by someone or other, for our knowledge of Wagner has been so vastly increased during the last few years that the close student of him has a score of lights on him that were denied to our fathers. The recent publication in Germany of his full-length prose sketches for some of his works has taught us a great deal we had never suspected before about him and them; for example, we are now able for the first time to trace every smallest step of his that led, over so many years, to the building up of the present *Ring*. We see how drastically his original scheme was changed in the course of time, and not always, perhaps, for the better; we see, too, that, as was the case with Vergil and the *Aeneid*, he has sometimes made an alteration in his plan without noticing that the new feature is inconsistent with something he has left in its first form elsewhere in the poem.

My own study of him has convinced me that it is impossible to understand fully the works of his maturity without having traversed on our own account the extensive and often difficult country over which he himself had to travel before he reached his distant goal. Often a point that is obscure or even inconsistent in the opera poem is elucidated for us by his sketches. Sometimes the psychological motivation of an episode becomes clear to us only in the light of our knowledge of the mediaeval legend that was his starting-point. Sometimes, in the *Ring*, the clue to his procedure is unexpectedly discovered in such works as the *Deutsche Mythologie* of the brothers Grimm, which we know him to have studied closely in the late 1840's.

I venture to lay it down, then, that a clear picture of Wagner's mind-processes during the conception and realisation of a work is to be obtained only by following him step by step through the literature, ancient and modern, out of which it grew. It may be objected that a work of art should be its own sufficient explanation. But there are cases, some of them the most notable in literary history, in which that simple proposition obviously does not hold good. The *Aeneid* is one of them; the *Divina Commedia* is another. No student of today can hope to get quite inside the mind of Dante by a mere reading of his text; he requires to be told a great deal about many things which are implicit in the text but not self-revelatory in it, such as the mediaeval conception of the universe, the mediaeval attitude towards religion, the contemporary characters who figure in the poem, and so on. Coming down to our own epoch, Albert Thibaudet, in his searching study of Flaubert, has told us that in *Salammbô* the great novelist "has for the most part followed the history of Polybius, and the reader assuredly needs to be acquainted with this." So it is again with Henry James: his own retracing, in the prefaces to one of the later editions of his works, of his mental processes when he was working out the characters and the situations of this novel or that is of fundamental importance to the serious student of him; after reading one of these prefaces we re-read the novel itself in quite a new way, with many a new and revealing light on things.

It would be surprising, indeed, if the case were otherwise: since the whole mind of a great artist has gone into the making of one of his major works, the more we know about the nature and the operations of that mind the more profound will be our under-

standing of the work; and since the inner world from which it
came was built up by the slow unconscious coalescence within the
man of influences and impulses from many quarters, it is of the
first importance that we, for our part, shall re-live, to the best of
our ability, his own inner life during the years when the work
was shaping itself within him.

I have accordingly devoted a considerable amount of space not
only to Wagner's prose sketches for some of his works but to the
mediaeval poems that were the prime generators of them; we
listen to *Tristan* and *Parsifal*, for instance, in a new way—and I
venture to say, a way that is more like Wagner's than any opera
house ever conveys to us—after we have read Gottfried of Strassburg and Wolfram von Eschenbach. The *Ring* is a peculiar case.
The Wagnerian mental complex that went to the making of the
great tetralogy was built up slowly out of not only the Nibelungenlied and the Volsunga and other sagas but also out of the store-
house of facts relating to the Teutonic past that was thrown open
to Wagner by the Grimms and other scholars of the first half of
the nineteenth century. For this reason, among others, I have
gone at considerable length into the history of Wagner's prose
sketches for the *Ring*. The reader need not necessarily plough
doggedly through all this right away, for its complexities may
sometimes discourage him: he will probably find it more convenient to keep these pages for reference after he has worked at
the poems and the scores and read the present analyses. Some
knowledge of it all is indispensable to a full understanding of the
Ring; and a reader or two here and there may at any rate be grateful to me for having spared him the labour of hacking his way
through the jungle on his own account.

The need for a clearer view on our part of the Wagner operas
as Wagner himself saw them is all the greater because it is the sad
lot of the ordinary opera-goer, who is almost entirely dependent
for his impressions of them on what he sees and hears in the theatre,
to have them put before him, in even the best of present-day performances, in a way that often does them the minimum of justice.
In the Overture to *Opera Nights* I pointed out how much worse
off the opera-lover is than the ordinary theatre-goer in the matter
of casting. Care is taken when casting Hamlet, for instance, that by

the grace of the gods there is some correspondence between the actor's own appearance and build and voice and mentality and those we associate with the character; whereas in the opera house a woman with neither the face nor the figure nor the mind for a Gilda or a Lakmé is set down to play the fragile part merely because she has the right range and timbre of voice and the coloratura technique for it; or a man who physically and intellectually might have made the ideal Des Grieux or Parsifal is forced to play the Conte di Luna or Germont *père* merely because nature has stupidly seen fit to make him a baritone instead of a tenor.

Seldom indeed do we find a Wagnerian part played by a man or woman who looks and thinks—or mimics the apparatus of thinking—like the character he or she is supposed to be representing. Wagner himself, after working himself to death trying to knock some understanding of a part into one of his male singers, asked the gods piteously by what primal curse laid upon him it came about that he had to allot his most intellectual parts to a tenor. Think of the young Siegfried as Wagner imagined him, the incarnation of youthful health and beauty and active joy in life, or the metaphysical Tristan, or the spiritual Parsifal, and then recognise these creations, if you can, in some amphora[1] Heldentenor or other who looks and behaves like an overgrown Boy Scout, and gives the spectator the impression of a man whose mental development was arrested at the age of twelve and has been in custody ever since. Or take the case of Brynhilde. "That is no man!" Siegfried ejaculates when he has removed the breastplate from the form of the sleeping Valkyrie; and a smile goes round the house, for what we see is a matron who could serve anywhere for a demonstration of the physical possibilities of the higher mammalia. And only the other day I found a French critic complaining that while some German lady or other had sung beautifully in *Lohengrin* her Elsa "manquait de virginité". Well, one can't have everything.

[1] An amphora is defined by the classical dictionaries as "a two-handled, big-bellied vessel, usually of clay, with a longish or shortish neck and a mouth proportioned to the size, sometimes resting firmly on a foot, but often ending in a blunt point . . ."

My main object in the present volume has been to help the opera-goer to see the Wagnerian works as nearly as possible as Wagner must have seen them, and so to get more value out of his listening in the theatre and by radio. It is unfortunately impossible to make an analysis of them clear except by frequent reference to the leading motives. But I have tried to reduce that reference to the minimum, for two reasons: in the first place, if there is too much of it one's text comes to resemble a series of mathematical formulae; in the second place, it is a cardinal error to suppose either that the musical tissue of a Wagner opera is made up simply of a pinning together of motives, or that, in most cases, any one label can be found that will cover all the uses and meanings of any one motive. The practice of the commentators has been to make out the label in terms of the words that have accompanied a given motive at its first appearance in the score. But that is pure fallacy: for Wagner himself his motives had no such fixity or limitation of meaning, a point which the reader will find insisted upon again and again in the course of these analyses.

I have made *The Flying Dutchman* my starting-point because the central purpose of the volume is to be practically helpful, and the reader is hardly likely ever to see a performance of *Die Feen, Das Liebesverbot* or *Rienzi*.

As often as was possible I have allowed Wagner the poet to speak for himself, using my own translations in the Breitkopf and Härtel edition of the operas. (The one exception is *Lohengrin*, which I never translated).

E. N.

THE FLYING DUTCHMAN

CHARACTERS

DALAND, A NORWEGIAN MARINER	*Bass*
SENTA, HIS DAUGHTER	*Soprano*
ERIK, A HUNTER	*Tenor*
MARY, SENTA'S NURSE	*Mezzo-soprano*
DALAND'S STEERSMAN	*Tenor*
THE DUTCHMAN	*Baritone*

Scene: The Norwegian Coast

I

The story of the Flying Dutchman may be a modern variant of the ancient one of the Wandering Jew; but when it first took its present form we do not know. In *Blackwood's Magazine* for May 1821 there appeared an anonymous short story entitled *Vanderdecken's Message Home; or The Tenacity of Natural Affection*, which, on the face of it, could be taken for an episode detached from a novel. The narrator is on a vessel that has just left the Cape of Good Hope. The conversation on board turns to the story of the Flying Dutchman, which is assumed to be known, more or less, to everyone present. Seventy years earlier, it appears, one Vanderdecken, captain of an Amsterdam ship, had sworn to round Table Bay in spite of wind and weather, "though I should beat about here until the day of judgment"; and beating about those seas he is still, always bringing foul weather to any ship that sights him. He has an embarrassing habit of hailing other vessels, sending out his jolly-boat to them, and asking them, if they are homeward bound, to take charge of a bundle of letters for delivery to his friends and relatives in Holland; "but no good", says one of the seamen who are discussing the matter, "comes to them who have communication with him".

Soon the Flying Dutchman's ship comes into sight, its boat is lowered, and a sailor appears with letters from the captain for Holland; but he is considerably put out when the crew of the

English ship, after glancing at the letters, inform him that this and that addressee—including the wife of Vanderdecken—has long been dead, such-and-such a banking house went bankrupt forty years ago, and so on. He insists on leaving the letters on the deck, however, though none of the English seamen will touch them. In the end, to everyone's relief, a gust of wind blows them into the sea; "there was a cry of joy among the sailors, and they ascribed the favourable change which soon took place in the weather to our having got quit of Vanderdecken".

The writer, as has just been said, seems to take it for granted that his readers have already heard of the Flying Dutchman. But there is nothing elemental or eerie in the story as he tells it—no compact with the Devil, no landing of Vanderdecken every few years to find, if he can, some woman whose love will lift the burden of the curse from him. All the *Blackwood's Magazine* writer is concerned with is the touching evidence of "the tenacity of natural affection" afforded by Vanderdecken's still writing home to wife and friends after seventy years.

2

We next meet with the story, so far as England is concerned, in a play by an industrious theatrical man-of-all-work of the period, calling himself Edward Fitzball, which was produced at the Adelphi Theatre, London, under the title of *The Flying Dutchman, or the Phantom Ship, a Nautical Drama in three acts*, on the 4th December 1826. We need not have concerned ourselves with Fitzball at all had it not been conjectured at one time that Heine may have seen the play in London in 1827 and derived from it some hints for his story of a play in his *Memoirs of Herr von Schnabelewopski*, to which we shall come shortly. No one who had ever read Fitzball's farcical tragedy could have entertained such a notion. The drama has the minimum of connection with the Flying Dutchman story as we all know it now, and that minimum it derives from the fact that, as the author tells his readers in a fore-word to the play, it was founded on the *Blackwood's* article of 1821.

Evidence of the currency of the legend just then is afforded by a passage in De Quincey's *Murder as a Fine Art*, which appeared in 1827. Speaking of the cool intrepidity by which the philosopher Descartes was said to have saved himself, in 1621, from the seamen who were plotting to kill him, De Quincey says that "he could not possibly have brought the vessel to port after murdering the crew; so that he must have continued to cruise for ever in the Zuyder Zee, and would probably have been mistaken for the Flying Dutchman, homeward bound." The casual nature of the reference implies that knowledge of the legend on the ordinary reader's part can be taken for granted.

3

Captain Marryat's full-length novel *The Phantom Ship*, which is still a capital yarn of the sea, appeared in 1839. Here again the Dutch captain bears the name of Vanderdecken, but there is still no suggestion either of the periodical permission of the mariner to seek salvation on shore or of the Devil having had a hand in the business. It is the celestial, not the infernal powers that pounce upon the Dutchman's oath and take the bold blasphemer at his word. His vow to round the Cape even if he had to beat about until the Day of Judgment "was registered", he writes to his wife in Amsterdam, "in thunder and in streams of sulphurous fire. The hurricane burst upon the ship, the canvas flew away in ribbons; mountains of seas swept over us, and in the centre of a deep o'erhanging cloud, which shrouded all in darkness, were written in letters of vivid flame these words—UNTIL THE DAY OF JUDGMENT!" He had sworn his impious oath by a sacred relic, a fragment of the Holy Cross, which his wife was accustomed to wear on her neck; and the only thing that can put an end to his sufferings is a sight of this, if it can be brought to him. His son Philip brings it to him after many marvellous adventures by sea and land; at the moment of reunion his vessel breaks into fragments, father and son sink beneath the waves, and "all nature smiled as if it rejoiced that a charm was dissolved for ever, and that THE PHANTOM SHIP WAS NO MORE."

Marryat has an eerie character of the name of Schriften, a little wizened old sailor who turns up like a bad penny wherever

Vanderdecken junior goes, always bringing disaster to him and the ship on which he happens to be, but always being miraculously saved from death himself. It appears that when Vanderdecken senior was persisting in his blasphemous resolve to round the Cape he was remonstrated with by his pilot, whom the captain knocked overboard in a scuffle and left presumably drowned. Schriften was this pilot: like the Flying Dutchman, he is death-proof, and he lives only for the exquisite revenge of enticing the son to destruction and so preventing the father from ever getting a sight of the holy relic. Just before the final catastrophe to Vanderdecken and Philip, however, Schriften is redeemed and released from his own particular curse by the magnanimous forgiveness of the son.

Though Wagner makes no use of this Schriften, a character corresponding to him comes into the Wagnerian record later in a curious way. The reader will know that while Wagner was working at his *Flying Dutchman* in Paris in 1841 he tried to get the work accepted at the Opéra. The Director, Léon Pillet, would not promise this; but he liked the scenario so much that he offered to buy it from Wagner, meaning to have it made into a libretto for one of the composers on the Opéra's waiting-list. As Wagner could claim no proprietary rights in the story itself he wisely, though much against the grain, accepted Pillet's offer; he was not in a position at that time to turn his back contemptuously on a few hundred francs. A new text was therefore put together by two theatre hacks of the day, Benedict-Henri Révoil and Paul Foucher; it was set to music by Pierre Dietsch, and the opera, which proved a dismal fiasco, was produced in 1842. The French librettists altered Wagner's plan so radically that the two plots are hardly the same. It is interesting to note, however, that in their version the phantom seaman—not Vanderdecken and a Dutchman now but a Norwegian of the name of Troïl—has added to the sin of impiety the crime of killing the pilot when the latter tried to persuade him not to persist in his mad purpose. Now this pilot motive, as we may call it, is not found either in Wagner or in Heine, who was Wagner's source for at any rate part of the story. It appears, however, as we have seen, in Marryat, so that it looks as if Révoil and Foucher may have read *The Phantom Ship*; as a matter of fact their opera was entitled not *The Flying Norwegian* but *Le vaisseau fantôme*. (The pilot motive, of course, may have existed already in some popular version of the legend, unknown to us today, that was in circulation at the time).

4

In view of the fact that Marryat, De Quincey and the *Blackwood's* writer all imply that the legend of the Flying Dutchman was known to their readers we can take it for granted that a popular version of it was already current to some extent. We find the same implication again in the next literary form of the story that comes within the scope of our enquiry.

In 1834 Heine published in his *Salon* a series of papers with the title of *Memoirs of Herr von Schnabelewopski*. In Chapter VI the supposed memoirist tells how in Hamburg he saw one night "a big ship looking like a sombre giant in a great scarlet cloak. Was it the Flying Dutchman?" he asks. "This fable of the Flying Dutchman", he continues, "you surely know." After leaving Hamburg the itinerant Herr von Schnabelewopski had gone to Amsterdam; and in his next chapter he tells how he there saw "the dread Mynherr", as he calls him, on the stage. Heine outlines the action of the play thus. The Dutch captain had sworn by all the devils in hell that he would round a certain cape if he had to keep on sailing until the Day of Judgment. "The Devil took him at his word; he would have to sail the seas until the Last Judgment, unless he was redeemed by the fidelity of a woman's love. Donkey as the devil is, he doesn't believe in female constancy; so he allows the accursed captain to land once every seven years, take a wife, and thus achieve his salvation. Poor Dutchman! Time after time he is glad enough to be saved from matrimony itself and escape from his saviour; so back he goes to his ship again."

Heine continues with the action of the play up to the point where the Dutchman has met Katharina, the daughter of a Scottish skipper, and received her promise to be "true unto death". Then Herr von Schnabelewopski's attention is diverted to a pretty blonde in the audience. He makes her acquaintance: she is of an obliging disposition, and by the time the pair return to the

theatre the drama is in its final stage, with the Dutchman gener-
ously warning Katharina of the doom that awaits her if she links
her fate with his, Frau Flying Dutchman, as Heine calls her, leaping
into the sea, true to death, the accursed seaman being well and
truly redeemed at last, and the spectral ship being engulfed by the
waves. "The moral of the piece", Heine concludes, "is, for women,
to be careful not to marry Flying Dutchmen, while we men may
learn from it how even at the best we founder through women."

As this important motive of redemption by a woman is found
only in Heine, it has been universally assumed that it was from
him that Wagner derived the idea of an opera on the Dutchman
theme. Wagner, of course, had read the *Memoirs of Herr von
Schnabelewopski*, and never made any secret of that fact. But that
does not necessarily mean that he made his first acquaintance with
the story itself through Heine; from his own various accounts of
the matter it is evident enough that he, like thousands of other
people, was already familiar with the legend *as* a legend. Eight
years before the publication of the Schnabelewopski memoirs
Heine himself had referred to the story in a letter from the island
of Nordeney which formed part of his *Travel Pictures*. He often
strolls along the shore, he says, and turns over in his mind the
yarns the sailors have told him. "One of the most attractive of
these is that of the Flying Dutchman, whom one sees sailing by
with sails spread, and who occasionally sends a boat out to a ship
with a bundle of letters, which the men of the ship can do nothing
with, however, for they are addressed to people who have long
been dead." For the legend itself, then, Wagner need not have
been indebted in any degree to Heine's account of the supposed
play at Amsterdam.

5

The impression we receive from his autobiography is that he
had conceived the idea of an opera on the subject even before he
embarked on the "Thetis", in July 1839, on his famous voyage
from Riga to London, *en route* to Paris, where he arrived in the
following September. While the ship was passing through the
Norwegian fjords to escape a storm, he says, "a feeling of in-

describable contentment came over me when the enormous granite walls echoed with the hail of the crew as they cast anchor and furled the sails. The sharp rhythm of the call struck into me like a mighty consoling omen, and soon shaped itself into the theme of the sailors' song in my *Flying Dutchman*,[1] *the idea of which was already at that time continually in my mind*[2]; now, under the influence of these new impressions, it took on a definite poetic-musical colour." This was written about 1866. More than twenty years earlier, when writing his short *Autobiographical Sketch* in 1842, he had been equally definite. A storm, he said, had compelled the captain of the "Thetis" to put into a Norwegian haven: "The passage among the crags made a wonderful impression on my fancy; the legend of the Flying Dutchman, *as I heard it confirmed from the seamen's mouths*,[3] took on within me a distinct and peculiar colour, which only the sea-adventures I was experiencing could have given it." Once more, then, we gather that he had no need to go to Heine for an introduction to the legend. He knew it before he stepped on board the "Thetis". He did not even learn it from the seamen; he talked about it to them, and they "confirmed" it.[4]

That he had previously read Heine's account of the Amsterdam play is proved by a letter of his of July 1843 to Ferdinand Heine, the costume designer at the Dresden theatre. "When I wrote my *Flying Dutchman*", he said, "it was in the firm conviction that I could not proceed otherwise than I did. During my famous sea-voyage and amid the Norwegian cliffs the subject—already long known to me through your namesake—acquired for me a quite peculiar colour and individuality, gloomy, it is true, but deriving from the nature common to all of us, not at all from the speculations of a gloom-sick enthusiast. But the vast wild ocean, with the legends woven about it, is an element that does not lend itself obediently and willingly to being trimmed into a modern opera; and I saw that the whole story of *The Flying Dutchman*, filled as

---

[1] See musical examples Nos. 10, 14, 15, 16.
[2] Italics mine.   [3] Italics mine.
[4] Ashton Ellis, in his English translation of the *Autobiographical Sketch*, unwittingly kept this fact from the reader by omitting the important word "bestätigt" (confirmed).

it is with the roar of the sea—which now took such complete possession of me that it cried out for artistic reproduction,—would have to be atrociously cropped and mangled to be made into an opera text with the piquant suspenses, surprises and so forth which the modern taste demands. Therefore I preferred not to modify the material, just as it lay to my hand, to any further extent than is required by a dramatic action, leaving the full aroma of the legend entirely free to spread itself over the whole. Only in that way, I believed, could I cast upon the spectator the full spell of that strange mood in which anyone with a feeling for poetry can take to his heart this gloomiest of legends."

6

Wagner, it will be noticed, speaks of the "subject" as being "already long known to me through your namesake". Does this mean that he had never heard of it until he had read Heine? That is an unwarrantable assumption. The "subject"—*der Stoff*, the raw material—was of course to be found in Heine, as it had been in Marryat and the others. But this does not forbid our believing, on the strength of the evidence as a whole, that Wagner had met with this "material" independently, as the crew of the "Thetis" and the mariners with whom Heine had talked at Nordeney had manifestly done. The point to be observed in Wagner's letter to Ferdinand Heine is his threefold use of the term "legend". We meet with it again in a letter of his of January 1843 to one Philipp Samuel Schmidt of Berlin, who had asked him for particulars of the new opera, which had just had its third performance in Dresden. He is sending him, he says, a copy of the text-book, from which Schmidt will see for himself that his *Flying Dutchman* is an entirely different genre from that of *Rienzi*, and how far it departs from the conventions expected of an opera composer by the public. "You will see that I have allowed the simple legend to tell itself purely in its own way, without adding this or that modern accessory to make it 'operatic' in the sense which everyone deems necessary nowadays;" and he goes on to speak of the way in which "the marvellous fragrance of the legend" has been completely destroyed in the French perversion of the subject by Foucher and

Dietsch, where "effective" episodes of the kind without which no French opera is considered complete have been introduced.

Liszt, in an article on *The Flying Dutchman* written in 1854, told his readers that "during a sea voyage Wagner read Heine's version of the legend of the Flying Dutchman: the coincidence of this reading with a violent storm aroused in him, swept as he was himself by so many inner tempests, the idea of a dramatic treatment of the material. He worked this out without making any essential changes in Heine's moving narration." This account of the genesis of the opera is not strictly accurate: from Wagner's own testimony, both at the time and later, it is clear that not only had he known the Schnabelewopski story before sailing from Riga but he had already formed the idea of turning the subject into an opera; his experiences in the Norwegian fjords had merely quickened his interest in the theme. All this, however, is of minor importance; the point vital to our present discussion is that Liszt, like Wagner, distinguishes between the "legend"—which, he says, is well known—and Herr von Schnabelewopski's account of the play he alleged he had seen in Amsterdam.

7

One other source may possibly have contributed a trifle to Wagner's poem. In Wilhelm Hauff's *Die Karawane*—the story of an Oriental caravan the members of which entertain each other with adventures in their own lives—one of them, Achmet, contributes "The Story of the Phantom Ship". During a voyage he had made in his youth his own ship had sighted a ghostly vessel from which came sounds of uncanny merriment, although a storm was threatening. "The captain, who was standing by my side, went deathly white. 'My ship is lost', he cried; 'there sails Death!';" and sure enough they were wrecked that night, only Achmet and his old servant Ibrahim being saved. The stranger ship comes clearly into sight, and they recognise it as the spectral one they had seen just before the storm. They board it and find it manned only by dead men; the decks are red with blood; the captain, sword in hand, is nailed through the head to the mast. Achmet and Ibrahim cannot sleep o' nights because the captain and the crew have an unpleasant habit of coming to life again then and going about their ordinary ship's occasions, while in the day-time they are once more as dead as when Achmet first set eyes on them. In the end, with the assistance of a magician, the ghostly crew are taken ashore and buried, while the captain, after earth has been placed on his head, comes to life again long enough to tell them his story. Fifty years ago he had been a pirate operating from Algiers. On one of the ships he had captured was a holy dervish who annoyed him by trying to get him to see the error of his ways. He plunged his dagger into the breast of the good but pestiferous old man, who thereupon cursed him and his ship with his last breath: he and his crew should henceforth neither die nor live un-til their heads were laid in earth. That same night his crew began to massacre each other; soon they were all dead men by day and live men again by night; and so it had gone on for fifty years, for how, in circumstances such as these, could the ship ever reach land?

Obviously this is one more variant of the Flying Dutchman legend. Wagner, who was an omnivorous reader and had a most retentive memory, must have read Hauff's story in his youth; and a few phrases from it may have sunk into what Henry James called "the deep well of unconscious cerebration", to come to the surface later in the way that so many fragments from Coleridge's reading emerged to make up the story and even the wording of *The Rime of the Ancient Mariner*. "With insane joy", says the captain to Achmet when telling him the story of his crime and its punishment, "we would plunge again and again, with sails full set, into the teeth of a storm, hoping we might be dashed to pieces on some cliff or other and so lay our heads on earth." Did some dim memory of all this re-emerge in Wagner when he made his Dutchman soliloquise thus when he sets foot on land once more after another seven years?:

> *How oft in ocean's seething deep*
> *Death have I sought, eternal sleep:—*
> *Yet ah! sweet death, I found it ne'er!*
> *Upon the cliffs my ship I drave,*
> *In hope to find the longed-for grave:*
> *But ah! no grave for me was there.*

In scorn on pirates would I fling me,
Their utmost fury I would dare:
"Here", cried I, "bitter death come bring me,
My ship is filled with treasure rare!"
But ah! the scourge of every sea
Would cross himself, and shrink and flee!

Stranger things have happened in the creative subconscious than that Hauff's captain's talk about pirates and driving his ship on to the cliffs in the hope of finding a grave in earth should have suggested the above lines to Wagner. We may further note the passage in Hauff in which sounds of uncanny merriment are heard coming from the phantom ship just before the storm breaks. This has its direct counterpart in the grisly episode at the end of the first scene of the third act of the opera, where the crew of the Dutchman's vessel, after their long silence, terrify the Norwegian sailors by breaking into a grim chorus as the storm begins to shake their ship. There cannot be much doubt that Wagner had read Hauff.

8

We can now address ourselves to the vexed question of the extent of Wagner's indebtedness to Heine. The motive of redemption by female fidelity, as we have seen, appears only in the poet's story of the Amsterdam play. Was there really such a play, or was the motive Heine's own invention, the "play" being only a fictive way of introducing it?

If the reader will turn to the relevant passage in Wagner's *Autobiographical Sketch* (written not long after he had returned from Paris, where he had met Heine), he will find the following account of the processes by which *The Flying Dutchman* came into being:

"I had already provided myself with a scenario for this emergency [i.e. the possibility that Pillet might commission an opera from him]. The Flying Dutchman, whose intimate acquaintance I had made on the ocean, fascinated my imagination unceasingly. In addition I made the acquaintance of Heine's particular version of this legend in a section of his *Salon*; and it was especially his treatment—borrowed from a Dutch play bearing the same title—of the redemption of this Ahasuerus of the sea that furnished me with all I needed to turn the story into a subject for opera. I came to an understanding [the German may mean also "an arrangement", or "terms"] with Heine himself on this matter, drafted a sketch, and gave it to M. Léon Pillet."

While making it clear, then, as he did in various other places at various other times, that the idea of his opera was born of his fascination with the legend, he acknowledged that it was the redemption motive that enabled him to round off his plan, and that he had found that motive in Heine, who had "borrowed" it from a Dutch play.

But this *was not the original wording of the passage* in the *Autobiographical Sketch* as it appeared in the *Zeitung für die elegante Welt* of February 1843. There the sentence relevant to our enquiry had run thus: "Heine's truly dramatic treatment—his own invention—of the redemption of this Ahasuerus of the sea gave me all I needed to utilise the legend for an opera subject." Originally, then, Wagner had given Heine credit for having "invented" (*erfundene*) that motive; later he said that it had only been borrowed (*entnommene*) by the poet. It may be added that before the publication of the *Sketch* in the *Zeitung für die elegante Welt* there had appeared in the first number of that journal a despatch from its Dresden correspondent, giving its readers some advance information—which could only have been derived from an interview with Wagner—about the young composer who had so suddenly sprung into fame. "A second opera by Richard Wagner, who has become famous overnight through his *Rienzi*, is being energetically rehearsed for production this month [December 1842: actually the production did not take place until the 2nd January 1843]. It is entitled *The Flying Dutchman*, and Wagner has combined Heine's fantastic story *and the English narrative*,[1] with some additions of his own." Once more, then, we see that for the legend in general Wagner had had other sources open to him than Heine. What "the English narrative" may have been we can hardly even conjecture: from the casual way the words flow from the Dresden writer's pen, and the fact that he

[1] Italics mine.

speaks not of *an* but of *the* English narrative, it looks as if either the *Blackwoods'* story or the Marryat novel may have been translated into German; the journalist appears to be speaking of something which he takes it for granted his readers will understand without explanation. But neither *Blackwood's* nor *The Phantom Ship* can be seen to have contributed anything to Wagner's scenario, which makes the situation still more puzzling. What is in neither of the English stories, but is in both Heine and Wagner, is the motive of redemption through a woman's love; and in 1842/3 Wagner credited the "invention" of this motive to the poet.

9

All the modern reprints of the *Autobiographical Sketch* reproduce the text as it appeared in the first edition of Wagner's Collected Writings, issued by himself from 1871 onwards. Why did he make at that time the radical alteration in his original text of 1843 to which I have drawn attention above, and further omit all reference to Heine's supposititious contribution to the *Dutchman* plan in *My Life*—the large-scale autobiography on which he was engaged at that time? The customary and most facile explanation of his cold-shouldering of Heine in *My Life* is that Wagner was giving way to a prejudice against him both as a personality and as a Jew. But we may reasonably doubt whether that is a correct explanation; while it is a still more dubious explanation of his substituting "borrowed" for the original "invented" when reprinting the Sketch of 1842/3 in 1871.

Had his object been to edge Heine out of the picture he would surely have expunged all reference to him in his account of the genesis of *The Flying Dutchman*. But he does not do so. Even here he makes no secret of the fact that it was his reading of the *Memoirs of Herr von Schnabelewopski* that had furnished him with the ideal motive for rounding off the dramatic action of the opera upon which he had long been brooding. All he does in 1871 is to say that Heine did not invent but only borrowed that motive. What lies behind that change of wording?

Had he found reason in the after years to doubt Heine's originality in the matter? Do we not come upon at least a hint of that scepticism as early as 1851, when, in *A Communication to My Friends*, he once more set forth the genesis of his early works? Here he already as good as ruled Heine out as an *original* contributor to the Dutchman subject. All he said was this: "During this [Riga] period I first became acquainted with the story of the Flying Dutchman: Heine tells it incidentally when speaking of a performance he had seen in, I believe, Amsterdam." The point-blank declaration in 1871 that Heine had merely borrowed the redemption motive he had claimed to have invented is only a more emphatic nuance of what looks like the irony of the "seen, I believe" in the sentence of 1851.

I would suggest the following possible interpretation of the matter. In their conversations in Paris in 1840/1 Heine had told him that the alleged "Amsterdam play" was pure fiction on his part, and claimed in particular that the redemption motive, to which he could see that Wagner was attaching the greatest importance as a factor in his opera, was entirely his own invention. Only on some such hypothesis as this can we account for that sentence in the *Autobiographical Sketch* in which Wagner said that he "came to an understanding [or "arrangement", or "terms"] with Heine himself on this matter." What was there to come to an understanding about with Heine or anyone else? Certainly not the use of the Flying Dutchman subject in general, for that was well known and was no one's literary property. Nor even a redemption motive *per se*; for it was of the poetic essence of the legend that the Dutch skipper, who had everyone's sympathy, should be redeemed from the curse in some way or other at the finish; he had been so, in fact, in Marryat's novel—by the devotion and pious labours and sufferings of his son. The only feature of the Schnabelewopski story in which Heine could have claimed the shadow of a proprietary right in his conversations with Wagner was this little matter of having the Dutchman saved by "a woman true unto death". It seems, then, a workable hypothesis that Heine had demanded from Wagner an "understanding" or "arrangement" of a pecuniary kind with regard to that motive, and that Wagner had reason, or thought he had, to doubt, in later years, whether the poet had played quite straight with him on that point. Heine was rather given to levying a quiet kind of financial blackmail on his friends, as Meyerbeer and Liszt and others knew to their cost.

10

So the question arises, *did* he, as has been universally taken for granted, invent the redemption-by-a-woman motive, or had he really seen some play or other, or heard some version or other of the story, of which it formed a part? Let us glance critically at his account of the matter.

He begins, as we have seen, by saying that his readers will already be familiar with the tale of the Flying Dutchman: it tells, he says, of a ship condemned to sail the seas for ever because its Dutch captain had sworn by all the devils that he would round a certain cape even if it took him until the Day of Judgment. The Devil had taken him at his word; his only chance of redemption from the curse would be by the love of a faithful woman. Whenever the phantom ship sights another vessel, Heine goes on to say, the Dutch crew send out a boat with letters which they desire to be carried to Holland; but these letters are always addressed to people who have long been dead.

Heine, then, is confessedly telling a story already known to his readers; and—a point of some importance—he makes no distinction between one item in the tale and another, or between the familiar legend and the play. The legend of the Flying Dutchman *per se* was widely current; the evidence as to that is copious. The "letters motive" had formed the core of the *Blackwood's* story of 1821; and Heine himself had included it in his summary, in the *Travel Pictures* of 1826, of the Dutchman legend as, according to him, it had been told to him by the seamen at Nordeney.[1] In the Schnabelewopski account of the Amsterdam play Heine makes no claim whatever that whereas all the other elements of the drama are already in general circulation the motive of redemption by a woman was peculiar to the play. He begins with the words "The legend of the Flying Dutchman will be known to you". He tells

[1] Years later, in chapter 6 of the Schnabelewopski *Memoirs*, he said that the legend had been told him of old by his grand-aunt. It is always difficult to distinguish between truth and fiction in Heine.

it from start to finish *as* a legend; and having done so he begins his next paragraph with the words "It was on this legend that the play was based which I saw in the theatre at Amsterdam." In face of these plain facts, what warrant is there for assuming that one feature of the play—the redemption motive—was not part of the legend but Heine's personal contribution to it?

And how does he handle this motive? He mentions it only to gibe at it as a piece of romantic tarradiddle. After having told his readers how, *in the legend*, the Devil had taken the impious seaman at his word and condemned him to sail the seas to all eternity unless he could find a woman faithful enough to redeem him, he speaks *in propria persona*; the Devil is not such a fool as to believe in female constancy, and the perennially disillusioned Dutchman is always glad to escape from his redeemer and go off to sea again.

Next we have an account of the action of the play, beginning with the Dutchman's meeting with the daughter of a Scottish skipper who is willing to play the part of redemptress, and ending with the Dutchman's lament to her over his sad lot—life maltreats him and death rejects him; "his grief is as deep as the sea, his ship without an anchor, his heart without hope." "These", says Heine, "were virtually the words with which the bridegroom concluded" —a little touch which seems to suggest that he was in truth describing some play he had seen.

It is at this point, after Katharina has sworn eternal fidelity, that Heine tantalisingly breaks off to tell, with great gusto, that adventure of his with the light-o'-love in the audience that took him away from the theatre for a while—an episode which was probably the real reason for the writing of that chapter. When he returns, the play is in its last moments, with the ending we all know so well. And now again Heine speaks *in propria persona*; the moral is for women not to marry Flying Dutchmen and for men to beware of women. Once more, it will be observed, he touches on the motive of redemption by a woman's fidelity only to drench it with the acid of his irony. Is it not making a rather heavy demand on our credulity to ask us to believe that he "invented" that motive only to deride it? As has been pointed out already, it was of the poetic essence of the legend that the curse should be lifted from the Dutchman some time or other. Marryat had found one way to do that. Another way—through the self-sacrificing devotion of a woman—was one so wholly in keeping with the romantic sentiment of that generation that even if it had not figured in some current version of the legend, even if it had not appeared in an Amsterdam or some other play, it was certain, we feel, to have occurred at some time or other to some German romantic or other. But no one, surely, after having been so fully sympathetic to the Dutchman as to depict his unending sufferings, would have invented that charitable ending merely to make ribald fun of it. One's final impression of it all is that the ribaldry alone was Heine's, that he was indulging his satirical bent at the expense of a romantic invention of someone else—that, in fact, he actually had met with that particular ending to the legend somewhere or other, and as likely as not in a play. And perhaps the explanation of Wagner's coolness towards Heine in 1851, and of his substitution of "borrowed" for "invented" in 1871, is that by then he had found good reason, or thought he had, for doubting the poet's claim to originality in the matter of the redemption motive, and felt that the "arrangement" of 1841 with him had really been unnecessary.

To complete the factual record it may be added that in one of his letters (to Ewald) about the French stage (1837), Heine had spoken of himself as homesick in Paris, "like the Flying Dutchman and his shipmates... Poor Vanderdecken!" He refers to the Dutch crew writing letters home to people long since dead, but does not say a word to suggest that in the Schnabelewopski of 1834 he himself had contributed any new feature to the well-known story. Finally in one of his articles (March 26th 1843) for a German journal on "The [Paris] Musical Season of 1843" he refers to the failure of the Foucher-Dietsch opera in these terms: "Dietz's (sic) Flying Dutchman has suffered woeful shipwreck. I did not hear the opera, but I saw the libretto, and I was disgusted to see what a mess had been made in the French text of the beautiful story which a well-known author, Heinrich Heine, had imagined in a form completely suitable for the stage." Here he certainly appears to be implying that the "Amsterdam play" was his own invention. But even at that he only claims to have given a stage form to the "beautiful story" which everyone knows: he makes no claim whatever that the redemption motive was a contribution of his own, a crowning touch, to the legend.

II

The legend of the Flying Dutchman and the motive of redemption through love appealed so strongly to the buffeted young Wagner because he could read his own melancholy story into it: he too was a homeless wanderer on the face of the earth, he too longed for the sympathy and self-sacrifice of a woman who would understand and pity and comfort him. He shared the passion of most of his poetic compatriots of that romantic epoch, nourished as they were on Goethe, for idealising woman into the *Ewigweibliche*. In *A Communication to My Friends* (1851) he described his "utter homelessness in Paris" between 1839 and 1842 and his "yearning for the German homeland"—not the political entity known at that time as Germany, however, but a new Germany of his dreams, "in connection with which I was certain only of one thing, that I would never find it here in Paris". "It was the longing of my Flying Dutchman for *the woman*—not . . . the wife who waited for Odysseus but the redeeming Woman whose traits I did not see in any definite outline but who only hovered before my vision as the element of Womanhood in general"; "the quintessence of womankind, and yet still the longed-for, the undreamed-of, the infinitely womanly Woman; let me say it in one word, *the Woman of the Future*."

Immature as it is, dramatically and musically, *The Flying Dutchman* foreshadows in various ways the Wagner of the later years. He himself was objectively critical of it as early as 1851. There was much in the poem, he said, that "is as yet inchoate"; "the joinery of the situations is in the main so loose, the poetic diction and versification so often lack the stamp of individuality", that he would not be surprised to find the professional playwrights treating it all as "a piece of impudence that calls for severe castigation". But for all that he always had a soft spot in his heart in later life for this ardent if cubbish work of his prentice days, because he could see in it an aspiration, however imperfectly realised, towards the logically-knit musical drama—the antithesis of "opera"—that had haunted his imagination almost from the first. In the last months of 1864 he had to prepare a "model" production of it for King Ludwig in Munich; and on the 2nd September he wrote thus to the King: "It is by a good dispensation that it is this early, unassuming work—which, for all that, is in my true style—that constitutes the occasion for my renewing my connection with the queer world of the theatre."

For he had been conscious from the first that here he had made his first big step, small as it may seem to us now in the light of the *Ring* and *Tristan* and the *Mastersingers*, from opera to music drama. He was right when he said in later life that "so far as my knowledge goes I can find in the life of no artist so striking a transformation, in so short a time, as is evident between *Rienzi* and *The Flying Dutchman*, the former of which was hardly finished when the latter was begun." His creative imagination had seen the subject from the beginning in terms of a new plastic form; though he was not sure enough of himself as yet to build up his work without the usual apparatus of arias, duets, ensembles and so on, he had begun not with these for their own sake but with a central conception from which the whole drama was to evolve as an organism from a germ. This was Senta's ballad in the second act, which is not only the central psychological point of the action but the musical core of the work.[1]

The poem was written in Paris between the 18th and 25th May 1841. Wagner began the musical composition with the ballad; next came the song of the Norwegian sailors and the "Phantom Song" of the Dutchman's crew, then the Helmsman's song and the Spinning Chorus; and so possessed was he by the subject and so easily did his ideas flow that the whole work was completed in seven weeks, the overture being written last. According to Glasenapp the title-page bears the inscription "In Nacht und

---

[1] In his letter of the 9th January 1843 to Schmidt he stressed the fact that he had worked out his opera without any "resounding, effective finales", trusting to his audiences, who expected that kind of thing as a matter of course, to get over their first disappointment after seeing the work a few times and realise that his simple treatment of the moving legend was the right one.

Elend ["In Night and Wretchedness"]. Per aspera ad astra. Gott
gebe es! ["God grant it!"]". It has recently been established,
however, that Glasenapp was in error on this point. After the
Munich performance of the 4th December 1864, which was conducted by Wagner himself, he presented King Ludwig with the
complete orchestral sketch of the work. His jottings on this give
us a glimpse into the misery of soul in which the opera was conceived; he was generally on the verge of starvation in Paris, and it
seems certain now that he spent a few days in confinement for
debt. At the end of the second act he wrote: "13 August. Tomorrow the money difficulties start again!"; at the end of the third act,
"Finis, Richard Wagner. Meudon, 22 August 1841"; and at the
end of the overture, "Paris: 5 November 1841. Per aspera ad astra.
Gott geb's!" The words "In Nacht und Elend" do not appear in
the manuscript.

Wagner's intention had been from the first that the opera
should be in one act only; by this means, he tells us in *My Life*,
he hoped to be able to cut out all the conventional "operatic"
accessories and concentrate on the psychological involutions and
evolution of the two principal characters. But the practical
exigencies of the German stage of the period compelled him to
cast it into the customary three acts, which fact no doubt accounts
in part for the weakness of some of the more obviously padded
parts of it. In later years he often thought of revising the opera
and compressing it into a single act; he promised King Ludwig,
indeed, in 1865 that he would do this, and had his life been prolonged for a few years after 1883 he would certainly have included
a re-shaped *Flying Dutchman* in the Bayreuth programmes. As it
was, the plan came to nothing. What he actually did in the way of
revision was to tone down the original orchestration, which, in
the inexperience of youth, he had made excessively noisy, and to
re-write the ending of the last act and that of the overture, points
with which we shall deal later.

12

The Flying Dutchman has been made to look so old-fashioned
by Wagner's later works that it is difficult for us now to realise the

many ways in which it leaped ahead of contemporary operatic thinking, and the problems it created for the actors and stage managers and machinists. It was to assist all these people to present the opera more intelligently that he wrote in 1852 his *Remarks on Performing the opera 'The Flying Dutchman'*, which singers and producers of today would do well to study. Every theatre specialist who came into contact with Wagner agreed that if he had had sufficient voice and stature he would have been the greatest German actor of his time; again and again at rehearsals he would not merely tell his singers how a given scene should be acted but show them in his own person how to do it. In the *Remarks* he devotes three pages of print to analysing the opening monologue of the Dutchman, describing every nuance of voice he expected of the singer, every gesture and posture he demanded of the actor. He warned the singer of Senta's part against turning her into a soft, sentimental *ingénue* of the conventional stage kind; on the contrary, while she was to be naive she was also to give the impression of a sturdy Northern maiden with the strength of the salt sea in her; her obsession with regard to the Dutchman whose story she had so often heard should be the monomania of a strong nature, not of a sickly one. And Erik, her lover, should not be a futile "sentimental whiner" but "tempestuous, vehement, sombre, like every solitary, especially in the highlands of the North. Whoever sings Erik's cavatina in the third act in sugary style does me a sad disservice; it ought to breathe sorrow and affliction". (Unfortunately the part is generally given to what is called a "light lyrical tenor", whose voice is incapable of the sombre tints that Wagner required, and whose notions of acting are rudimentary). Wagner insisted, too, that the part of Daland should not be played in the conventional key of the comic stage sailor. "He is a tough, blunt figure of everyday life, a seaman who defies tempests and dangers for the sake of gain, and with whom the sale—as it appears to be —of his daughter to a rich man would not seem at all reprehensible; he thinks and acts, like a hundred thousand others, without the least suspicion that he is doing anything wrong." Wagner, it will be seen, made heavy demands on the intelligence and the technique of his actors, especially those of the second line. It all seemed so easy to him because he had no difficulty in doing it

himself: one singer who had watched him producing *Tannhäuser*
in Vienna declared in later years that he had never afterwards
seen a performance of the opera in which he was not constantly
reminded of Wagner's acting in this or that situation—to the
great disadvantage of the singers who were supposed to be
representing this character or that.

To the staging of *The Flying Dutchman*, and more especially
of the scenes in which the phantom ship appears, Wagner
attached the greatest importance. He gives a good deal of attention
to this matter in the *Remarks*; and there have recently been published in Germany some excerpts from his numerous jottings in
the margin of the vocal score used for the production of the opera
in Munich in 1864. (That score is still in the archives of the Munich
Theatre). The notes were intended for the guidance of the stage
designers and machinists; and it is interesting to see Wagner
insisting on the sharpest differentiation between the appearance of
the Dutchman's ghostly ship and that of Daland, and on it being
made perfectly clear to the spectator that while the latter was calm
at its moorings, the former seemed to be still tormented and tossed
about by something evil and eerie in it, as if it carried the storms
of the Cape about with it wherever it sought shelter.

13

The opera was first performed in Dresden, Wagner himself
conducting, on the 2nd January 1843, with the following cast:

Senta:	Wilhelmine Schröder-Devrient.
The Dutchman:	Michael Wächter.
Daland:	Karl Risse.
Erik:	Reinhold.

(In Wagner's first sketch for the opera the heroine bore the name
not of Senta but of Minna).

When *The Flying Dutchman* was being rehearsed in Munich in
1864 the conductor, Franz Lachner—a capable, sober routinier of
the older school—used to grumble about "the wind that blew out
at you wherever you opened the score". He was right: *The Flying
Dutchman* was born on the sea and still has its home on it. The

overture is the first real sea-picture in music, and to this day the best of its kind.

It opens with reiterated hollow fifths and octaves in the strings, against which, in the third bar, the stark motive always to be associated later with the Dutchman stands out challengingly in bassoons and horns. (It will be observed that it too consists simply of the tonic and dominant of the scale of D):

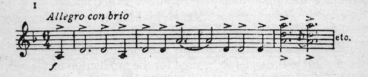

We hear the whistle of the wind in the rigging and a roar from the depths of the sea, then another statement of the Dutchman motive. It all culminates in a great crescendo on a diminished seventh chord in the full orchestra:

after which we hear, in the orchestral winds, a succession of calls that will always be associated later with the spirits of the ocean:

Then comes a hint of the motive of the Dutchman as perpetual wanderer over the seas:

followed by a descending sequence of those chords of the diminished seventh which even composers of the present day, however much they may affect to look down their noses at them, find extremely useful for the expression of horror and terror:

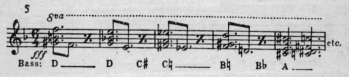

Gradually the fury of the wind and waves dies down into an exhausted muttering in the lower strings, with an occasional throb in the kettledrums; the tempo slows down to andante, and one of the main motives of the opera, that of the Redemption of which Senta is the predestined instrument, is heard in the wood wind, with the melody sung by the cor anglais:

It is the theme of the refrain of Senta's ballad in the second act. At this point in the overture, however, the melody, significantly enough, does not come to any kind of formal end, but, at the point where we would expect it to do so, shades off into a figure:

that will be associated later with the Fate that eternally overhangs the Dutchman.

This episode is a kind of inset in the great sea-picture, marked
off from that by both its tempo and its colouring. With a resumption of the original tempo we are back on the sea once more, with
the motive of Wandering (No. 4), that of the ocean spirits (No. 3,
with the figure of the restless sea shown in the bass of that quotation), the motive of Fate (No. 7), the characteristic theme of the
Dutchman (No. 1), and a new motive, that of his Longing for
Death:

all woven into one symphonic web. In the course of this development we find No. 1 answered by a theme in the wood wind which
Wagner has marked *espressivo*:

This episode ends with a melody that will be recognised later as
that of the sailors on the Norwegian ship:

Then the storm picture is resumed, with the various motives
associated with the Dutchman and Senta. No. 6 asserts itself more
and more insistently until we come to the final vivace section,
with No. 6 in a new and more exuberant form:

Now, too, the Redemption motive is given for the first time the ardent ending it has when Senta sings her ballad in the second act:

This Redemption motive dominates the remainder of the overture. Wagner, however, elaborated the final section considerably in later years, drawing more and more expression out of the repetitions and metamorphoses of No. 6; and he changed the coda completely. In the original edition of the score he had introduced the Dutchman's motive (No. 1) for the last time, in D major, at a point seventeen bars before the finish, rounding it all off rather conventionally with a scale passage and a few final emphatic chords. But his artistic sense must have told him later that logically the last word should be not with the Dutchman but with Senta; so now, after the thunderous re-statement of the Dutchman motive in D major in the brass, he suddenly switches for a moment into G major, tones the orchestral mass down to wood wind and harp, and finally reaches a restful D major in this way:

The effect is the one of "transfiguration" with which Wagner was later to end *Tristan* and the *Twilight of the Gods*.[1]

14

The curtain rises on a sea coast with steep and rocky cliffs: those in the foreground form gorges on either side which from

[1] The reader will find *The Flying Dutchman* overture in its first form in the Novello edition of the opera.

time to time give back echoes. A violent storm is raging; on the open sea the wind is lashing the waves, but between the rocks it is calmer, except for an occasional gust. Close to the shore lies a Norwegian ship, driven to take refuge here from the storm when already near home. It has just cast anchor, and the seamen are energetically occupied in furling sails, throwing out ropes, and so on, singing their "Hojohe! Halloho!" to typical sailors' calls of this kind:

and this:

and this:

the while the sea surges and the wind howls or mutters in the distance. The little figure shown in the second bar of No. 14 is echoed from time to time first by the cliff-hollows on one side, then by those on the other. For not only the stage action but the music of this scene Wagner drew upon his experiences in the "Thetis" during his voyage from Riga to London, when, as he tells us, a violent storm in the Skagerrack had forced the captain to run for shelter into one of the Norwegian fjords.[1]

[1] See the quotation on page 15. Four pages have survived of the pocket-book in which Wagner jotted down his day-to-day experiences during the voyage. There were evidently more storms than the one in the Skagerrack. Wagner's entries from the 27th July to the 11th August (1839) run thus: "27th in Skagerrack storm. 28 storm. 29 stormy west wind: had to run into a small Norwegian harbour near Arendal. Evening on shore with Minna. Mar-

The captain, Daland, has gone ashore; he has climbed one of the cliffs and is gazing landwards, trying to recognise the locality. At last he descends to the shore again; the storm, he says, has blown them a good seven miles out of their course, just as they were hoping to make their own port. The steersman assures him that all is well with the ship, in spite of the buffeting it has had. "Sandwike it is", says Daland; "full well I know the bay." [Sandwike, as we have just seen, was the little fishing village in the fjord to which the "Thetis" had run for safety]. He breaks into one of those four-square melodies, with the stresses falling in the same place in bar after bar, which Wagner himself was to recognise later, with a certain amount of amusement, as a mannerism of his melodies in his earlier years:

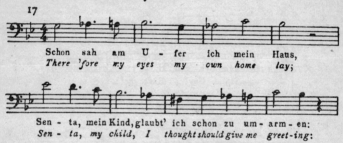

17

Schon sah am U - fer ich mein Haus,
There 'fore my eyes my own home lay;

Sen - ta, mein Kind, glaubt' ich schon zu um - arm - en:
Sen - ta, my child, I thought should give me greet-ing:

There, before Daland's eyes, had actually lain his own house, where his daughter Senta was waiting to embrace him; then this infernal storm had sprung up and driven him out of his course. "Who trusts in the wind trusts to the mercy of Satan!" he remarks sagely.

However, there is no help for it now, and a tempest of this ferocity cannot last long. At his bidding the crew go below; he himself goes into his cabin after telling the Steersman to take his watch for him that night and keep a sharp look-out, which the

vellous rocks out at sea. Place, Sand-Wigke. On the 31st we tried to sail again; going out of the harbour the ship strikes an invisible rock: 2 shocks. Back again . . . 1 August safe on sea again. Sunday evening, 4th, stormy north wind: favourable. 6th, evening, contrary storm. Wednesday, the 7th, bad day: storm at its worst 2.30 in the afternoon. 8th, mild contrary wind. 9th, evening, off English coast at Southwold . . . Evening 10th to evening 11th, fierce storm from the west between the sandbanks . . ."

man promises to do. Left alone, the Steersman paces up and down
the deck for a while: the storm has abated somewhat in the haven,
but out on the open sea it is still rough. A fragment of what we
shall discover later to be a dance-tune of the sailors:

runs through his mind. He is tired; he sits down, yawns, and, by
way of fighting down his desire for sleep, begins a song to the
maiden of his fancy:

with a prayer to the south wind to carry him soon to her:

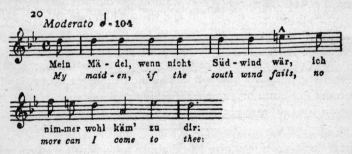

He ends with a long "Halloho! Holloho!" Just then there is an
ominous upward surge from the depths to the heights of the
orchestra (the "Waves" motive seen in the bass of No. 3), as a
bigger wave than ordinary mounts and hurls itself against the

ship, shaking her violently. The Steersman looks round with a start; assuring himself that all is well with the vessel he sits down again and resumes his song. But it is broken by yawns which he cannot suppress, and before he can finish his "Hoyohe! Halloho!" cadenza he falls asleep from sheer weariness.

15

By now it has grown darker and the storm has increased: the Dutchman's motive (No. 1) is heard thundering through the whistling wind as another ship (that of the Flying Dutchman) is seen approaching. Its masts are black, its sails blood-red: it makes swiftly for the shore on the side opposite the Norwegian vessel and casts anchor with a tremendous crash that wakens the Steersman. But only for a moment, so tired is he; he glances at the helm, sees that all is right, begins the refrain of his song once more—and falls asleep again.

The spectral crew of the Dutch ship is now seen furling the sails in uncanny silence, while the orchestra gives out the sombre, fate-laden theme associated with the Dutchman's endless submission to the behest of Fate (No. 7). He steps on shore, a sinister figure in a black costume of Spanish type: the orchestra accompanies him with a phrase that is not used often enough in the work to be ranked as a motive, but which is heard several times in the course of the monologue that now follows; it symbolises his weariness of life:

In an expressive recitative he describes how, another seven years having passed, the author of his curse allows him to set foot on land again, in quest of a grace which he knows he will never find: to the sea he is condemned to be true until its last wave is spent and it itself has been swallowed up. Then, over the undulating motive

(No. 4) that symbolises the endless wandering to which he is
doomed, he begins an aria—"How oft, in ocean's seething deep,
Death have I sought, eternal sleep", that has lost none of its
vitality after a hundred years of operatic development. The
second phrase of the aria, sung to the words "Yet ah! sweet
death I found it ne'er!" has already been heard in the overture
(No. 8). In despair he has driven his ship on to rocks that have
been the grave of other vessels, but in vain; he has tempted pirates
with his wealth, but the terror of the seas has only crossed himself
and fled. His curse he must carry to all eternity.

For a moment he turns again to heaven with the hope in his
heart that has been so often mocked—the hope that some day the
promised absolution and salvation will come to him:

This impressive section of his aria is sung over a succession of
tremolando chords in the lower strings, through which pierce
from time to time the solemn tones of the trombones.

But this is all delusion, he cries; where upon the earth is eternal
faithfulness to be found? And to a broad, sweeping melody:

he sings of the one real hope still left to him—that to the earth itself an end must some day come, the "Day of Judgment, last great Day", when the trumpets of God will peal forth and the universe will collapse in ruin, and all the dead will rise again: then will he too know the mercy of annihilation. For that fate he longs: "Ye worlds, end your course! Eternal destruction fall on me!" And as the spectral crew of the ship echo these last words of his in sepulchral tones, the Dutchman, with folded arms, leans gloomily against a cliff in the foreground.

16

At this moment Daland comes up on deck to take the direction of the wind. He sees the strange vessel, which had not been there when he had gone below, and turns to the Steersman for information about it. The Steersman, still half-asleep, makes another attempt at his love song; but Daland takes hold of him and shakes him awake. Then he takes up the speaking-trumpet and hails the stranger ship. There is no answer—only, after a long pause, an eerie double echo of the "Ahoy!" from the two sides of the bay. Neither another hail from Daland nor one from the Steersman brings any response. At last Daland perceives the Dutch captain on the shore, hails him again, and asks the name of his ship and whence he comes. A gloomy figure in octaves in the violas and 'cellos:

anticipates his reply—"Far have I come: wouldst thou deny me anchorage here while the storm doth rage?" The genial Daland, who has now joined him on the shore, assures him he is welcome. His own ship, he says, has been driven on this rocky coast by the same foul weather, only a few miles from his home. After a laconic statement that he is Dutch and his ship has escaped damage, the stranger tells Daland that for more years than he can measure he has been buffeted about by wind and wave: many lands have harboured him, but the land he longs for he can never find. Will Daland take him into his house for a while as his guest? He will not repent it, for the Dutchman's vessel is filled with treasures from every zone. He makes a sign to the watch of his ship, and the crew bring on shore a chest which, when opened, is seen by the dazzled Daland to be crammed with pearls and precious stones; and he becomes really interested when the strange captain assures him that all these and more are his in return for shelter for a single night; for the Dutchman, alas, has neither home nor wife nor child (No. 24).

It takes a little time to convince Daland that the Dutch captain is in earnest; but the latter clinches matters by asking him "Have you a daughter?", and, on being told that he has, by saying eagerly "Let her become my wife!" Daland, though he can hardly believe his ears, is overjoyed at the prospect of having this rich mariner for a son-in-law. Remarking in a lengthy sotto voce that he had better close with the offer before it is withdrawn, he decides to accept him. Turning to the Dutchman again, he assures him that he really has a daughter, a good and lovely girl who is his pride, his treasure, his consolation in adversity, his joy in happiness. All this the Dutchman finds very reassuring: so good a daughter, he comments, is bound to prove a faithful wife. Not to be outdone in noble sentiments, Daland tells him that he cannot help pitying the lot of a man who has suffered so much as the Dutchman has, for his large-handedness in the matter of gold and jewels is proof enough for anyone that he has a good heart—not, Daland hastens to add, that he would decline him as son-in-law were his fortune only half as great.

So it is arranged that with the first fair wind they shall make for Daland's home, where the Dutchman shall see the maiden who, he now fervently hopes, will prove to be his long-sought "angel" of redemption. Daland's contribution to the duet that follows is a song of thanks to the storm that has brought him this astonishing piece of good luck, and a promise to himself that he will not let this unexpected fortune slip through his fingers. The episode is excessively long, and the young Wagner is quite incapable of finding music for the situation that will rise above the routine commonplaces of the opera of the epoch. He would have done

better, we sometimes feel, to have dispensed almost entirely with
Daland; but operatic exigencies, of course, made that difficult.

By this time the weather has cleared, the sea is calm, and the
Steersman and the Norwegian crew give a shout of welcome to the
south wind that has sprung up. Daland also is rejoiced. He
suggests their raising anchor together at once; but the Dutchman
begs him to put to sea first, for he wants to give his own crew a
rest. (The real reason for postponing his own sailing is of course
a matter less of humanitarianism than of practical operatics.
Were Daland and the Dutchman to reach land again at the same
time Wagner would lose the opportunity for one of the most
impressive moments of the opera—the Dutchman's unexpected
entry into the spinning scene of the second act).

So Daland goes on board his ship, pipes the crew, and bids them
cast loose, which they do to the strain of the Steersman's song
(Nos. 19 and 20). The Dutchman returns to his own vessel, and the
curtain falls with the orchestra giving out some of the tunes associated with a life on the ocean wave, especially Nos. 3, 15 and 18.

17

The orchestral introduction to the second act begins with a
vigorous statement of the second part of the Steersman's song
(No. 20), which is followed by suggestions of the sailors' dance
(No. 18) and of other motives (Nos. 3, 15) already associated with
the seamen and the sea. This repetition was imposed on Wagner
by the enforced casting of his drama into three acts. When, at
Bayreuth in 1901, the work was played in one continuous act (in
accordance with his original intention), a cut was made from bar
26 before the end of the orchestral postlude to the first act to bar
19 of the prelude to the second. These bars are really superfluous,
and the work gains in organic unity by their omission.

The curtain rises on a large room in Daland's house—un-
mistakably a sea-captain's room, for on the walls hang sea-pictures,
charts and so forth. Prominent on the back wall is a portrait of a
pale man with a dark beard, wearing a black Spanish costume.
Round the fireplace are seated Senta's old nurse, Mary, and a
number of maidens engaged in spinning; while Senta sits a little

apart from the others, leaning back in a long chair with her arms crossed. She is lost in dreamy contemplation of the portrait.

Motive No. 15, which in the orchestral transition from the first to the second act was associated with the Norwegian sailors as they hoisted the sails and pulled at the ropes, now becomes associated in Wagner's mind, in some curious way or other, with another kind of work, that of the maidens. It becomes an integral part of the main phrase of their Spinning Chorus:

The humming of the wheels is suggested in the strings. (The piece soon became very popular in Germany; Liszt made a brilliant transcription of it for the piano in 1860). The burden of the girls' song is a prayer to the wind to bring their seafaring lovers home to them soon. Mary gently reproves Senta for not spinning with the others: this idleness, she tells her, is not likely to bring her a gift from her lover. The other girls twit Senta with the fact that she has no need to spin as they do, for *her* lover does not, like theirs, sail the seas in quest of treasure; instead of gold he brings her game, for Erik is a hunter.

Senta apparently does not hear their chatter. She remains immobile: the orchestra gives out a quiet suggestion of a phrase (No. 6) from the ballad into which she will launch later; and we are to understand from the stage directions that she is singing the ballad of the Flying Dutchman softly to herself. Mary asks her, with motherly solicitude, why she wastes so much of her young life brooding on the portrait on the wall. Senta's reply is "Why did you tell me of this hapless man, and fill my soul with pity for him?" The maidens, unable to comprehend this obsession of hers, mockingly hope that Erik will not become jealous and do something desperate; and they turn to their spinning again with more zest and noise than ever, until Senta begs them to stop. All this humming and buzzing, she says, distracts her; if they wish to interest her with their singing they must try with something better than this. We have arrived, it is evident, at the old-

fashioned opera "cue for song", a device which the young
Wagner did not as yet know how to dispense with, or at all
events how to disguise. Senta suggests that, for distraction's sake,
Mary shall sing them the ballad of the Flying Dutchman; but as
the older woman recoils in horror from the uncanny idea Senta
says she will sing it herself, in the hope of winning their sympathy
for the wretched man who is the subject of it. So the others—
except Mary, who goes on spinning peevishly by the fire—put
their wheels aside and gather round Senta, who begins the ballad
still sitting in the armchair.

18

The song tells of a phantom ship, with black masts and blood-
red sails:

On her deck stands a pale captain, whose watch is without end.
One thing alone can redeem him from the curse that lies on him—
the love of a woman faithful unto death (No. 6). But when and
where will he find her?

"Pray ye all that heaven will grant him this boon!" As she says
this, Senta turns towards the picture on the wall. The maidens
listen sympathetically, and even Mary has now ceased to spin.
The second stanza of the ballad tells of the seaman's rash vow

to round a certain cape if he had to sail the seas until Judgment Day, and of how Satan took him at his word. The third stanza, which Senta sings with febrile exaltation, describes the Dutchman's landing once in every seven years, his vain quest of a faithful woman, and his flight in despair to the sea again. The maidens —this is an effective dramatic touch—are so deeply moved that almost unconsciously they become first of all co-singers of the ballad with Senta, and then, when she falls back exhausted into the chair, continue it softly alone. Then, in a sudden access of enthusiasm, Senta springs up from the chair and vows that if God's angel will bring the Dutchman to her she will save him by her loyalty: at this point we hear the melody from which the motive of Redemption by Love (No. 12) in the overture had stemmed.

The maidens rise to their feet in terror at this fanatical outburst, and just then Erik appears in the doorway: he had heard Senta's closing words, and gives a startled cry of "Senta! wilt thou destroy me?" Gloomily he announces that Daland's ship has been sighted—news that fills the others with joy. The girls, in spite of Mary's appeal, will do no more work that day: they will be off to the shore to greet their men-folk and take them food; all which is made clear to the audience, after the operatic manner of the 1830's, by a great deal of repetition of the same words and musical phrases. It ends in Mary driving the girls out of the room and following them, for of course the stage must be free now for the big scene between Senta and Erik.

She would have followed the others out, but Erik restrains her. He implores her to give him an explanation. Before her father sails again the old man will keep his promise to give Senta in wedlock; and Erik speaks passionately of his own unrequited love for her:

Will she not be content to share his humble lot? He knows that her father's mind runs on wealth alone. Can he rely on Senta to speak for him, or is her whole affection, as he fears, centred in the portrait on the wall, and her whole heart in the morbid ballad she has just sung? When he speaks of his own grief she leads him up to the picture, points to it, and asks if he can be blind to the look it turns on her, imploring her pity for the doomed seaman and the redemption of him from the curse.

Exhausted by her conflicting emotions she sinks back into her chair as Erik begins to tell her of a vision he has lately seen. He had been lying dreaming on a high cliff that overhung the sea. He saw a strange ship nearing him, and then two men coming along the shore together. One of them was her father: the other he did not know, but recognised him, by his black garb and gloomy face, as the original of the portrait. From the house Senta had come running to greet her father; but catching sight of the stranger she turned to him and fell on her knees before him. He raised her up; she sank on his breast and kissed him, and then the two sailed away together. It was an excellent dramatic device on Wagner's part thus to introduce first as a figment of the imagination an episode that would become actuality a little later: he afterwards employed the same technique in *Lohengrin*, where Elsa, in a trance, sees her rescuer Lohengrin approaching some time before the swan-drawn boat appears on the river.

While Erik has been speaking, Senta has fallen into a cataleptic state, in which she not only sees incident after incident as her lover describes it but at times, by the force of her imagination, anticipates him. At the climax of his story she comes back suddenly to real life again with an enthusiastic cry of "'Tis I he seeks! To him must I go! His fate shall be mine!". "My dream was true, then!" ejaculates Erik; and he rushes out in horror and dismay.

19

Senta, her visionary excitement having spent itself, relapses once more into immobility and brooding silence, her eyes riveted on the portrait; then she murmurs softly to herself the refrain of the ballad (No. 27). Just then the door opens, and Daland and the

Dutchman appear. Daland pauses on the threshold, as if waiting for Senta to come forward and welcome him as usual; but the Dutchman, with his eyes fixed on Senta, comes slowly towards her, while she, for her part, stands motionless, gazing at him as if spellbound. Wagner creates a feeling of suspense by means of those throbs in the kettledrums and lower strings of which he was to make such good use for a similar purpose in his later operas. There appears, too, in the strings, a tender little figure, the parallel thirds of which are also characteristic of the later Wagner:

as Daland comes forward at last with a gentle reproof to his daughter for her seeming coldness towards him. She takes him by the hand, draws him closer to her, and asks "Who is this stranger?" He smiles affectionately at her, the orchestra launches the bluff motive characteristic of him:

and in a set aria—for in an opera of 1840 the bass, like the soprano, the tenor and the baritone, had to have his aria:

Mögst du, mein Kind, den fremden Mannwill-kommen hei-ssen!
Wilt thou, my child, ac-cord this stranger friendly greet-ing?

he urges her to give the newcomer friendly greeting. "A seaman he is, like myself", he says, "long without a home, a constant wanderer over the seas. Great wealth he has won him in foreign lands, and much of it he would give to find a home. Tell me, Senta, wilt thou give him welcome here?" She nods assent. Daland turns joyously to the stranger. "Did I overpraise her?" he asks.

"You see her yourself; is she not an ornament to womankind?"
The Dutchman, still silent, makes an assenting gesture, and, with
No. 29 in the orchestra expressing his tenderness for his daughter,
the bluff old captain, whose heart, after all, is in the right place,
turns to her again and urges her to consent to marry the stranger
on the morrow. Senta makes a convulsive movement:

but remains silent and soon regains her composure. Interpreting
her silence in the wrong way, Daland shows her a quantity of
jewellery which, he assures her, is the merest trifle compared with
what the stranger owns; and all this will be hers when she becomes his wife.

But the principal pair, wholly absorbed in each other, pay no
attention to his chatter. At last it dawns on him that he is not
wanted there; so with a parting word of advice and warning to
his daughter, and another singing of her praises to the stranger,
he departs, observing them narrowly all the while, obviously hard
put to it to understand what can be in their minds.

20

When at last they are alone they "remain motionless" for a
time, as the stage directions put it, "lost in contemplation of each
other"; and Wagner—rather helplessly, for he is unskilled as yet
in the art of ringing ever-new psychological changes on his
leading motives—fills in their silence with simple enunciations
of the Dutchman motive (No. 1) and that of Redemption (No. 27
etc.) in the orchestra. But he soon finds himself again when the
Dutchman begins to speak, which he does at first in a long unaccompanied line of quasi-recitative:

Up from forgotten depths of years long vanished
Beams now this maiden's face on me:
Dream-visions seen in days and nights unending
Now turned to substance here I see.

Then he launches into the first cantilena of the duet:

He speaks of his eternal longing, not so much for love itself as for release through love from his suffering. Senta answers him quietly at first, as if musing within herself rather than speaking to him:

Is all a dream, a vision fair and fleeting?
Can sight and hearing thus betray?
Was all till now illusion born of darkness?
Now dawns at last the glorious day?

Then, in more impassioned tones, she takes the lead in a combination of the two voices:

Before her, she says, stands at last in the flesh the man of whom she had so often dreamed, pouring his tale of sorrow into her pitying ears. She will bring him salvation and peace, she assures him—an assurance none the less sincere on her part, and accepted with none the less sincerity on his, because it ends weakly with one of those conventional cadenzas which the young Wagner could not help taking over from the opera of the period:

36

The Dutchman takes a few steps nearer to Senta, and earnestly asks her if she is willing to make good her father's word—will she give him the love and faith that alone can redeem him from the curse? She pledges her word, and he kneels before her, imploring heaven's help for her and for himself. Then, rising in great agitation, he asks her if she realises the fate that awaits her if she casts in her lot with his. If she gives him her word it will be beyond recall; does she not shrink from the abyss that opens before her? "Well know I woman's sacred duty", she replies, in the authentic vein of the German romanticism of the epoch. "Take heart, O hapless one: I know full well what is demanded of me: but he to whom I dedicate myself, his am I only, true to death!" And the duet ends in a glow of exaltation on both sides, Senta especially rejoicing in the new spiritual power that has taken possession of her:

Daland re-enters to the accompaniment of a festive melody in the orchestra:

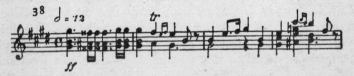

to ask, in his blunt way, if they are plighted yet, as the villagers are anxious to begin the junketing that celebrates the ending of each voyage. Senta assures him that her resolution has been taken and she will never rue it; and the act ends with a trio in which Senta and the Dutchman, entirely absorbed in themselves and each other, pay no attention at all to the simple Daland, whose one idea is that they shall come with him and "join the merry maze".

21

When *The Flying Dutchman* was given as a one-act opera in Bayreuth, nothing more in the way of compression and linking-up was necessary at this point than to slice off a dozen bars from the orchestral postlude to act II, for the introduction to the third act is merely a repetition of these. The one-act form is particularly preferable here, for obviously Daland is to be imagined as going straight out of the house to the popular merry-making of which he has spoken.

The joyous atmosphere of the next scene is established in a brief orchestral prelude, which consists mainly of motives and phrases familiar to us by this time—No. 37, No. 12, No. 18, No. 15 and No. 10 (the sailors' song), which last comes to the forefront as the curtain rises, showing a creek on a rocky strand. In the foreground, to the side, is Daland's house, while in the background we see Daland's ship and the Dutchman's, lying fairly close to each other. It is a clear, bright night. The Norwegian vessel is ablaze with light, and on the deck the sailors are singing a merry chorus in praise of the joys of home-coming from the sea (No. 10), and dancing clumsily. The Dutch ship, however, presents a strange and sinister contrast: it is enveloped in an unnatural gloom and a deathlike stillness.

The Norwegian maidens, who have entered carrying baskets of provisions and drinks, are the first to sense this grisly silence and darkness. They draw their own men's attention to it. The Norwegians, concluding that the others are dumb from fatigue after their voyage, decide to take them some of their own food and drink. They go close to the waterside and hail the Dutch crew again and again; but still no sign of life comes from the mysterious vessel:

Finally they come to the conclusion that these strange beings

are old and grey, with hearts of lead,
and all their sweethearts long since dead.

The maidens are terrified and perplexed, and become more so when the men suggest that the other ship must be the notorious Flying Dutchman's, of whom they should beware—for if it is, the crew are not flesh and blood but ghosts. It is evident that the legend of the Dutchman is known to them all, for they jocularly call out to the Dutch crew that if they have any letters to be delivered to friends or grandparents on land they will be delighted to take charge of them. When the Norwegian sailors further suggest that the others might hoist sail and show them how the Flying Dutchman can scud the sea, the girls run away in terror.

At last the seamen philosophically decide that the best thing to do with the dead is to leave them to death; they themselves, being alive, will feast and dance. The girls, after handing their baskets on board, leave the stage: the men fill their glasses and propose to drink their queer neighbours' health. At their cry of "Wake up and join our feast!" a sombre statement of No. 1 is heard in the bassoons and trombones of the orchestra, and a first faint sign of life is observable on the Dutch ship. The Norwegians resume their lively No. 10 in chorus, and the Dutchman's motive rings out more and more assertively in the orchestra.

The water round the Dutch vessel now begins to move, though everywhere else the sea remains calm. A violent wind shrills through the rigging, and on the deck a watch-fire—a blue flame— appears; this seems to call the invisible crew to life, for they are heard hoarsely shouting their "Yo-ho-hoe! Huissa!" (through speaking trumpets). While the wind whistles and the sea roars they sing an ironical song to their captain:

> *Gloomy captain, go on land!*
> *seven more weary years have flown!*
> *Seek a youthful maiden's hand!*
> *Faithful maid, be his alone!*
> *Merry be, hui!*
> *Bridegroom bold! Hui!*

prophesying cynically the usual end of it all—one more faithless maiden, and yet another voyage for the luckless wooer:

Howl then, storm-wind, blow thy worst!
Our good sails thou'lt never burst!
Satan blessed them ages back:
Blow until the heavens crack!
Hohoe! Hoe!

The Norwegian seamen have listened to all this with growing horror; and now they see the Dutch ship tossed about by the waves, while a furious wind whistles through the rigging, though everywhere else the sea is still calm and the air quiet.

The two choruses now contend with each other for a while. Gradually the Norwegians, frightened by this crazy kind of storm and the shouts of the other sailors, leave the deck and go below, making the sign of the Cross; whereupon the phantom crew burst into shrill, mocking laughter. And then, with startling suddenness, darkness and the silence of death descend upon the vessel once more, the wind dies down, the sea becomes placid. The Dutchman's motive (No. 1) comes out quietly in the horns over a string tremolando, and is answered by the Redemption motive.

22

The momentary calm is broken by an agitated figure in the strings, to the accompaniment of which Senta comes hurriedly out of the house, followed by Erik, who is in a state of wild excitement. Something she has said to him within doors has made him fear the worst. He asks her if it is true, or is he dreaming? She turns away, deeply moved, but unable to answer. Two motives, complementary to each other, each of them expressive of perturbation:

and:

dominate this episode. Erik reproaches her bitterly for having forsaken him and thrown herself into the mysterious stranger's arms at the bidding of her father. Has she forgotten, he asks her, that she had plighted her eternal troth to him? Senta is aghast. "Eternal troth?" she repeats helplessly. We are not surprised that Erik should stare at her in blank astonishment at this: "O Senta!" he cries; "hast thou forgotten?" But we soon realise that this piece of dubious psychology on Wagner's part is due to the necessity he was under to give the tenor of the opera another aria to sing before he bids not only Senta but the audience farewell for the night: this lame little bit of dialogue, in fact, is merely another "cue for song".

Erik's aria is a mellifluous reminder to Senta of the days when she had given him reason to believe she was not indifferent to him:

How often, he asks her, had they stood on the hill together and watched her father's sail disappearing in the distance, after Daland had placed her hand in his and entrusted her to his protection; and then she had twined her arms round his neck and pledged her troth to him anew. "Sure was I then, Senta, that thou would'st faithful be!"

All this has been overheard by the Dutchman, who now rushes forward in great agitation, crying despairingly, "Lost!

Lost! All hope of salvation lost!" She places herself in his path, imploring him to stay; but as the storm-wind begins to rise again he pipes on his whistle to his crew, bidding them hoist sail, raise anchor, and take their last farewell of land.

No. 41 becomes the main thematic material for a trio in which Senta protests that she is true to her vow, the Dutchman swears that he has no faith any longer in her or in God, and Erik sees the hand of the Devil in it all and begs Senta to come to her right mind before it is too late. At last the Dutchman tells her, to the accompaniment of a motive that has been gradually asserting itself more and more since the commencement of the trio:

of the awful fate from which he now voluntarily saves her. He is condemned to carry a grievous curse, from which only a woman who will be faithful unto death itself can redeem him. He has had Senta's promise; but it was not sworn before God, and so he will not hold her to it. For the fate of those who swear their troth to him and do not abide by their oath is eternal damnation. "Victims unnumbered I have brought beneath this curse; but thou, Senta, shalt escape it. Farewell! Hope has fled from me for ever!"

He turns to go: Senta holds him back, while Erik, in the grip of a new terror, calls to the house and the Norwegian ship for help. Daland, Mary and the maidens from the house and the seamen from the ship come out in response to his cry. "Well do I know thee!" Senta assures the Dutchman ecstatically. "Well do I know thy doom! Thy face I knew when I beheld thee first. The end of all thy woe is come: my love, true to death, shall bring thee redemption from the curse!" "Thou know'st me not, nor dreamest who I am!" he replies. He points to his ship, the red sails of which are now spread, while the crew, with uncanny movements, are making preparations to depart. "Ask thou the ocean and the tempest; ask thou the seamen of all the seas; they know my ship, of all good men the terror; the Flying Dutchman am I named!"

He rushes on board his ship, which immediately leaves the shore and reaches the open sea, the phantom crew singing their maniacal "Yo-he-hoe!" (No. 1). Senta tries to follow him, but is held back by Daland, Erik and Mary. She manages to tear herself away and reach a rock that overhangs the water. From there she cries with all her strength after the departing Dutchman: "Praise thou thine Angel with thy last breath! Here stand I, faithful unto death!" She leaps into the sea. The Dutch ship at once sinks and disappears with all her crew, engulfed in a wave that becomes a whirlpool. Then, in the glow of the setting sun, the glorified forms of the Dutchman and Senta, clasped in each other's arms, are seen rising above the wreck, soaring heavenwards.

The present orchestral postlude to the opera takes, of necessity, the same course as the revised version of the overture, the older, rather trite ending being replaced by the appearance of the Redemption motive in the transfigured form it had assumed in the overture (No. 13).

TANNHÄUSER

PRINCIPAL CHARACTERS

HERMANN, LANDGRAVE OF THURINGIA	*Bass*
TANNHÄUSER	*Tenor*
WOLFRAM VON ESCHENBACH	*Baritone*
WALTHER VON DER VOGELWEIDE	*Tenor*
BITEROLF	*Bass*
HEINRICH DER SCHREIBER	*Tenor*
REINMAR VON ZWETER	*Bass*
ELISABETH, NIECE OF THE LANDGRAVE	*Soprano*
VENUS	*Soprano*
A YOUNG SHEPHERD	*Soprano*

I

Wagner drew up his first plan for an opera on the subject of Tannhäuser in Teplitz in the summer of 1842, and wrote the poem in the following spring. The title originally planned for the work was *Der Venusberg*, but this he abandoned in deference to the wishes of his publisher Meser, who feared that it might provoke ribald comment—as, indeed, the location of the action in the Mountain of Venus did later in the brighter circles of Germany and Paris. According to his own account, it was with the Venusberg scene that he began the composition of the music. The first act was finished in January 1844, the second on the 15th October of that year, and the third on the 29th December: the orchestral score was completed on the 15th April 1845. Wagner's ultimate title for the work was *Tannhäuser and the Contest of Song on the Wartburg*. This fusion of two quite different stories, that of the Wartburg Contest and that of Tannhäuser, aroused the ire of some German scholars of the period, the great Simrock in particular, for reasons which will become clear to the reader when we have surveyed the stages by which the opera poem came into being.

Wagner tells us that when the subject first took hold of him he was not as well versed in mediaeval German poetry as he became later, by which he probably meant that as yet he had not put in much first-hand work upon the ancient texts. He had already, however, a good knowledge of the basic facts. One of his cronies in Paris (1839–1842) had been a philologist of the name of Lehrs, whose brother, a professor in Königsberg, specialised in German mediaeval literature. Lehrs himself was an accomplished Germanic scholar, and to him Wagner owed a great deal of the impulse that drove him during the next few years to make an ardent study of the ancient history and culture of his race. But there were other sources open to him. Like every other German of his day he must have known from childhood E. T. A. Hoffmann's collection of stories entitled *The Serapion Brethren*, out of which the poets and the librettists of the Romantic epoch dug so much of their material.

In one of these stories, *The Singers' Contest*, the tale is told of the Minnesinger Heinrich von Ofterdingen. The teller of the tale, it appears, has been reading Wagenseil's *Nuremberg Chronicle*, of which we shall hear more when we come to the *Mastersingers*. Fascinated by the old book, he dreams himself out of his lonely chamber into a lovely forest, where, at the pealing of a hunting horn, the animals peep shyly out of their lairs. The music of the horns gives way to that of harps, and as the sounds draw nearer there comes into view a gallant company of knightly hunters, laden with game, with boar-spears in their hands and bright horns slung over their shoulders. At the head of six noble cavaliers rides a man of princely mien, in old German costume, accompanied by a lady of dazzling beauty; at the end of the gay and happy procession comes a train of pages and servitors. We may fairly assume that Wagner remembered this episode when he came to write the fourth scene of his first act, in which the Landgrave and his knights, hunting in the forest, come upon their former comrade Tannhäuser after his flight from the court of Venus.

2

While the student of Wagenseil is musing upon this entrancing vision he is accosted by an old man—none other than Wagenseil himself—who obligingly explains the scene he has just witnessed and tells him the full story of Heinrich von Ofterdingen and the Contest of Song on the Wartburg. In the first decade of the thirteenth century, he says, there were six famous Minnesingers at the court of Thuringia—Heinrich von Ofterdingen, Wolfram von Eschenbach (whom we shall meet again in connection with Wagner's *Parsifal*), Walther von der Vogelweide (who comes into the story of the *Mastersingers*), Reinhart von Zweckstein, Heinrich der Schreiber, and Johannes Biterolf,—all of them of knightly birth except Heinrich von Ofterdingen, who was a burgher of Eisenach. While the others sang songs of purity and gladness, Heinrich's were filled with a pain and longing that made them strange and harsh. In time he separates himself from the noble company and goes back to his native town, where he is sought out by the gentle Wolfram, who, like the others, is distressed by the unhappiness that seems to be eating out his confrère's heart. Heinrich confesses that he has a hopeless passion for the beautiful Countess Matilda, the young widow of Count Kuno von Falkenstein. This was the lady whom the dreamer had seen riding by the Landgrave's side: she was the beloved of Wolfram, who had won her by the sweetness and moral elevation of his songs. Never will he return to the Wartburg, Heinrich assures Wolfram. But one day he finds himself again in the forest near the castle, and, overcome by sad memories, he takes up his lute and pours out his soul in a song in praise of Matilda. He is accosted by a sinister stranger who jeers at his song and at the whole poor craft of the Minnesingers, and offers to teach him the mysteries of a greater art known only to himself, for he is a pupil of the great master Klingsor, who is in bad odour everywhere because he is suspected of trafficking in magic; and the stranger hands Heinrich a little book in which a few of the master's secrets of song are set down.

In the following spring the Minnesingers and their ladies, among them Matilda, are assembled in the great hall of the Wartburg; and just as Wolfram is about to begin a song a young man comes forward whom they joyfully recognise as their long-lost Heinrich. He is given his old place between Wolfram and Walther von der Vogelweide, and permitted by the Landgrave to share in the singing. It is soon evident to all that he is a changed man, proud, confident and scornful; and after Wolfram has sung in praise of the Landgrave and congratulated the company on the return of their old companion, Heinrich seizes his lute and breaks into a song so unprecedented in its manner and so uncanny in its matter that at first the others do not know what to say about it. Then they break into applause, and the fair Matilda crowns him with the victor's garland. When twilight falls Heinrich and Wolfram find themselves alone together. The latter confesses that his friend has proved himself the greatest master of them all, but feels that this mastery has been dearly bought in some way which he does not understand. Heinrich listens in silence, then, covering his face with his mantle, rushes sobbing into the night. In all this, and in part of what follows, we have the basis for Wagner's second act.

As time goes on the other Minnesingers become critical and suspicious of Heinrich's new-found art. Matilda, however, whose praises he is always singing, becomes his advocate. Gradually her character changes as his had done; "she looked down upon the other masters scornfully and arrogantly, and even withdrew her favour from the unfortunate Wolfram von Eschenbach." She herself begins to compose Minnesongs in the new and suspect style of Heinrich. "From that time onward the charm and sweetness of the deluded lady seemed to desert her. Turning her back on everything that is the adornment of noble ladies, on everything, indeed, that is womanly, she became an uncanny something that was neither woman nor man, hated by her own sex and derided by the other." She leaves the court and goes to a castle near Eisenach, whither Heinrich would have followed her had not the Landgrave ordered him to remain and meet the challenge the other masters had thrown out to him. He censures the false brilliance of the young man's art, which Heinrich now confesses he had learned first of all from the little book which the stranger had given him, then from the sinister Klingsor in person.

3

At the Contest of Song he is surpassed by the others, whereupon, mortified and furious, he breaks into a series of lays in which he insults the Landgrave and all the ladies of the court except Matilda, whom he praises in a heathenish style which the others find unbecoming. The knights, as in Wagner's opera, turn upon

him with drawn swords, and his life is in danger. He appeals to the
Landgrave for protection, and begs for a new contest in which
Master Klingsor shall be arbiter. The Landgrave consents, but
with the proviso that the executioner shall stand beside Heinrich
as he sings, and behead him if he loses. The contest is to take place
within a year and a day, and Heinrich is sent out in search of
Klingsor.

After a number of episodes that do not concern us here, the
contest duly takes place. Wolfram, inspired by the presence of the
Lady Matilda, who has returned in all her former grace and
innocence, is adjudged victor by all the knights. (Klingsor is
present, but he refuses to act as judge, for fear of offending his
powerful patron King Andreas of Hungary; he prefers the decision to be left to the Landgrave and the assembly). The executioner advances to mete out justice to the vanquished Heinrich,
who, however, suddenly disappears in a cloud of black smoke—
a sure sign that he had sold his soul to the powers of evil. Klingsor
had imposed on the Landgrave for a while by telling him that a
daughter is about to be born to King Andreas whose name will be
Elisabeth; she will be of such surpassing piety that the Pope will
canonise her, and she will become the wife of the Landgrave's son
Ludwig. But now Klingsor is in as bad odour at the Wartburg as
Heinrich himself, and he too vanishes. "Some of the warders of the
castle said that at the very time when Wolfram von Eschenbach
had vanquished the supposed Heinrich von Ofterdingen a figure
very like that of Master Klingsor had been seen to dash out of the
gateway on a snorting black steed." The story ends with the reunion of Wolfram and Matilda, and a letter from Heinrich in
which he confessed that he had been corrupted by the magician,
but that his friend's pure song had torn the veil from his eyes and
restored him to life and happiness. He sent greetings to the
masters, and after a while news reached the Wartburg that he was
at the Court of Duke Leopold of Austria, singing inspired songs,
some of which he sent to the Landgrave. "Thus it was", the story
concludes, "that Wolfram von Eschenbach's noble art of song,
welling as it did from the purest depths of his soul, won a glorious
victory over the enemy and rescued his beloved and his friend
from perdition."

In Hoffmann's story, it will be seen, there is no mention of Tannhäuser. The central figures of it are the authentically historical Minnesinger Wolfram von Eschenbach and the dubiously historical Heinrich von Ofterdingen; but the latter is not associated in any way with the court of Venus, and therefore there is no question, at the end, of either his damnation on that account or his repentance and salvation. The nucleus of the story is the Contest of Song. Hoffmann had gone back, under the guidance of Wagenseil, to a long fourteenth century poem which tells of a "Contest of Song at the Wartburg", during the reign of the art-loving Landgrave Hermann of Thuringia (1190–1217), between six Minnesingers, Wolfram von Eschenbach, Walther von der Vogelweide, Heinrich der Schreiber, Reinmar, Biterolf and Heinrich von Ofterdingen; the last-named, who relied on the support of the Hungarian magician Klingsor (who is probably entirely mythical), gave offence to the others by praising Duke Leopold of Austria above all other princely patrons of the Minne-song. Whether such a contest ever took place we cannot be sure. But even if it did, the competitors must be conceived as having expressed their sentiments in verse alone, without the aid of music; this is inferable from the fact that in an old illuminated manuscript the contestants are depicted without any musical instruments in their hands.

4

From Hoffmann, then, Wagner could have derived, at most, only the basic conception of an opera with a contest of Minne-singers at its core, plus a striking incident here and there. No doubt he read later the old poem of *The Contest of Song at the Wartburg* for himself, for once a subject had taken root within him he never rested until he had learned all there was to be known about it. But here again, of course, as in Hoffmann, he would find himself with Heinrich von Ofterdingen, not Tannhäuser, as his hero; and it was Tannhäuser to whom, for some reason or other, he found himself being particularly drawn during the early 1840's. He was well acquainted with the rich treasury of German legend given to the world by Jacob and Wilhelm Grimm in their

Deutsche Sagen (1816–8). There he would have found an old
folk-tale of "the noble Tannhäuser"—a great traveller, who in
the course of his wanderings through the world had spent some
time with Frau Venus in her famous mountain of ill repute. After
a while his conscience had pricked him; wearying of all these
beautiful women and the delights of the flesh he had told Venus
that he must leave her court. As in Wagner's opera, she tried
every blandishment to retain him, but at last he won his freedom
by calling on the name of the Virgin. Filled with repentance he
went to Rome, hoping for absolution and the salvation of his soul.
But the Pope, after hearing his confession that he had spent a year
in the Venusberg, replied harshly, "When the dry staff I hold in
my hand puts forth green leaves shall your sins be forgiven you,
but not before". Tannhäuser, heart-broken at this repulse, left
Rome and returned to the Venusberg, where Frau Venus gave
him a hearty welcome; but on the third day, the staff having
miraculously burst into leaf, the Pope sent messengers through
every land in search of him. "But it was too late: he was back in
the mountain again, with his old love, and there he must remain
till the Day of Judgment, when no doubt God will send him elsewhere." And the growing dislike of the mediaeval German world
for the Papacy comes out in the final sentence of the story: "No
priest ought to withhold solace from any sinful creature, but forgive him when he comes to him penitent and desirous of making
atonement."

In Grimm also Wagner must have read the ancient legend of a
contest at the Wartburg in 1208 (or thereabouts) between "six
wise and virtuous men", of whom Heinrich von Ofterdingen was
one. The story as told there is in essentials that of the Wartburg
poem. One feature of it may have struck root in Wagner's
imagination, to emerge again, in a slightly different form, in the
second act of the opera—when the other knights turn in anger
upon Heinrich, clamouring for his death, he runs to the Land-
gravine Sophie and takes refuge beneath her cloak; and under her
protection he obtains a year's grace.

Wagner was acquainted also with Ludwig Bechstein's collection of the legends of Thuringia (1835); in this he would find
ancient versions of the Tannhäuser story and that of the Wartburg

Contest of Song. In the library of his learned Uncle Adolf he had found, when a boy, La Motte Fouqué's pseudo-drama *The Contest on the Wartburg* (1828). But, he assures us, it was not until he read "the homely Tannhäuserlied" and an old German Volksbuch of Tannhäuser that his interest in the theme was really aroused. The Tannhäuserlied is a charming poem of the fifteenth or sixteenth century, excellent English translations of which have been given us by Jethro Bithell[1] and Miss Jessie L. Weston.[2] In this we have the dialogue between Tannhäuser and Venus in the form of dramatic give-and-take. After his repulse by (it was alleged) Pope Urban IV (1261–4)—a dignitary in bad odour in Germany because of his opposition to the Hohenstaufen dynasty—Tannhäuser goes back to the Venusberg, where, after the sprouting of the staff on the third day, the papal messengers lose track of him:

> But he was in the mountain ben
> With his sweet love to be;
> And Urban that fourth Pope is damned
> To all eternity.

This piquant but not unattractive ending did not commend itself to Wagner.

5

So far, then, we can retrace the steps by which he was gradually led to the story of Tannhäuser and Venus and that of the Contest on the Wartburg. But what impelled him to combine the two, for the Tannhäuser of the legends had nothing to do with the Contest, the leading figure of which was Heinrich von Ofterdingen, while the latter was not associated in the popular imagination of a later day with either Venus or the Pope? In *A Communication to my Friends* (1851) Wagner said that after reading Hoffmann and "the homely Tannhäuserlied" he happened to come upon an old Volksbuch in which he "found established, however loosely, the connection between Tannhäuser and the Contest of Song at the Wartburg". Thereupon he set himself to study Middle-High-

[1] In *The Minnesingers* (1909), pp. 144–7.
[2] In *The Legends of the Wagner Drama* (1896), pp. 338–342.

German in order to read the massive old poem of the Contest in the original, a copy of which was in the possession of Lehrs. No Volksbuch combining the two legends, however, is known to German scholars, most of whom doubt whether such a thing ever existed. Wagner's memory seems to have been at fault. The idea of fusing the Tannhäuser and the Contest legends probably came to him from an essay of 1838 by one C. J. L. Lucas, a professor in Königsberg, who had put forward the suggestion that in the same way as the historical Minnesinger Tannhäuser and the legendary Tannhäuser of the old poem had become one in the popular imagination, so the Folk may have effected a further fusion between these two and Heinrich von Ofterdingen. Wagner heard of Lucas's theory through Lehrs, who, as we have seen, had intellectual contacts with Königsberg.

The German scholars in general resented what seemed to them Wagner's high-handed way of dealing with the mediaeval records; perhaps they could hardly be expected to see all at once that what is dubious history may be excellent opera, and in the theatre it is opera, not history, that matters. One learned authority, J. G. Theodor Grasse, the head of the Dresden Library during Wagner's residence in the town, did indeed, for a while, take the side of the composer. In 1846 he published a book in which the Tannhäuser legend and that of the Wandering Jew were "traced and elucidated", as he put it with Teutonic concision, "historically, mythologically and bibliographically". This book he dedicated to "his dear friend the Royal Saxon Chief Kapellmeister Richard Wagner, whose admirable tone-creation, by reason of its lofty poetic text—his own work—will attract afresh the attention of many people to this legend." But Wagner must have done something later to annoy the good gentleman—perhaps by taking so active a part in the Dresden rising of 1849,—for in 1848 another *Tannhäuser* had been produced, with a text by Eduard Duller and music by the now forgotten Karl Mangold; and in the second edition of his book (1861) Grasse not only cut out the earlier dedication to Wagner but said unkindly that "the opera composed by Mangold to a libretto by E. Duller is more sensible than the sanctimonious emendation of the sublime and highly poetic return of Tannhäuser to Frau Venus (as we have it in the German folk-ballad) perpetrated by Wagner in the text of his well-known opera." Duller and Mangold had given their opera a happy ending, with Tannhäuser being married to his Innigis and the naughty Venusberg collapsing in ruins. This charming piece of work was actually revived in Darmstadt in 1892.

6

Wagner had indeed made liberal use of the poet's privilege to deal with history in his own way for his own purposes. He substituted the Tannhäuser who was the lover of Venus for Heinrich von Ofterdingen as the central figure in the Wartburg Contest of Song, though by way of compensation to the latter he gave his Tannhäuser the Christian name of Heinrich. He flouted history by making *his* Tannhäuser one of the singers at the court of Landgrave Hermann in 1207 or thereabouts, when the real Tannhäuser would have been only a tiny boy. According to the poem of the Wartburg Contest, Klingsor had announced the birth of the saintly Elisabeth (daughter of the Hungarian King Andreas II), who would marry the Landgrave's son, the later Ludwig IV of Thuringia. This was the famous St. Elisabeth of history (1207–1231), the heroine of Liszt's oratorio, who went to the Thuringian court at the age of four, was married to Ludwig at fourteen, and was left a widow at twenty. We have seen that in Hoffmann the object of Wolfram von Eschenbach's adoration was the young Matilda, widow of Count Kuno von Falkenstein. We have seen also that in the Wartburg poem Tannhäuser, when the indignant knights are about to wreak vengeance on him, takes sanctuary under the mantle of the Landgrave's wife Sophia. Wagner creates an Elisabeth of his own, the *niece* of Landgrave Hermann, who is as saintly as her historical namesake of Hungary. It is she whom, in the opera, the pure and ardent Wolfram worships from afar; and it is she who saves Tannhäuser from punishment in the second act of the opera by standing between him and the angry knights. And in Wagner the old story of the knight and the Venusberg undergoes a drastic change at the finish. In the legend, the Pope's messengers having arrived too late, Tannhäuser returns to the arms of Venus, where he will remain until the Judgment Day.

Had the German scholars, after all, some excuse for jibbing at the
rejection of this colourful ending of the story? Could it perhaps
be restored in some future opera on the subject, supposing anyone to be bold enough to attempt one after Wagner? He had his
own good dramatic and ethical reasons for having Tannhäuser
"saved" by the saintliness of Elisabeth, though, as we shall see
later, he was not always of the same mind with regard to the
handling of the closing scene of his work.

7

Readers of John Livingstone Lowes's masterly book *The Road
to Xanadu,* in which the magic of Coleridge's *Ancient Mariner* is
shown, almost verse by verse, to be the result of the subconscious
coalescence of a host of tag-ends, many of them of the most un-
likely kind, from the poet's reading, will not be surprised to find
that a process of a similar kind contributed to the making of more
than one of the Wagner texts, particularly those of *Tannhäuser*
and *The Mastersingers*. Many a passage he had lighted upon in
his voracious reading must have sunk deep into his subconsciousness, remained dormant there perhaps for years, and then come
to the surface in obedience to the urge of a dramatic conception
of his own. It has already been pointed out that there is a broad
resemblance between the scene in the forest in Hoffmann's story
and the meeting of Tannhäuser, the Landgrave and the knights in
the first act of the opera. Possibly, too, some fragments had remained in Wagner's subliminal memory from his reading of
Tieck's story, told partly in prose, partly in verse, of *The Faithful
Eckart and the Tannhäuser*, which had first seen the light in 1799
and was reprinted in 1828. The story as told by Tieck is typical of
German romantic fiction at its most absurd.

A certain Friedrich encounters one day a pilgrim on his way to
Rome, in whom he recognises his long-lost friend Tannenhäuser,
who had mysteriously disappeared some years before. The pilgrim, who is obviously not quite in his right mind, gives Friedrich
an account of all that has happened to him. From his childhood, it
appears, he had not been as other children were. As a youth he had
loved a maiden who preferred another swain. On the eve of the

wedding he had killed his rival and then fled to the Venusberg, against entering which he was warned in vain by the Faithful Eckart, who had been posted there centuries earlier in order to save men from giving their souls to the powers of evil. After a while the sensuous pleasures of the Venusberg had palled on Tannenhäuser; he had escaped from the mountain and was now on his way to Rome. Friedrich tries to restore him to reason; *he* is the one-time rival, he assures him, and, far from having been murdered, he had married his Emma and is now living happily with her. But Tannenhäuser is not to be convinced that he has not been doing the Devil's work all these years; to Rome he must go and seek absolution of the Pope. One night some years later he returns to Friedrich, pale, wasted, in rags, and informs him that, the Pope having repulsed him, nothing remains now but for him to return to the Venusberg. He rushes out into the night, after having murdered Emma en route. Nor had Friedrich himself escaped: Tannenhäuser had pressed on his lips a kiss the burn of which will never leave them until the giver of the kiss has been found again. Friedrich runs out wildly in quest of Tannenhäuser, arrives at the Venusberg, enters it, and is seen no more by mortal eyes.

Even this absurd romantic farrago may possibly have left a trace or two in Wagner's imagination. In the scene of the meeting of Tannhäuser and Wolfram in the third act of the opera there may be a faint reminiscence of the corresponding scene between Friedrich and Tannenhäuser. When Wolfram asks to be told about the journey to Rome Tannhäuser replies: "Nun denn, hör' an! Du, Wolfram, *du sollst es erfahren!*" ("Be it so! Listen, Wolfram, and you shall learn what happened"). In Tieck the corresponding passage runs thus: "Nun, so mag dein Wille erfüllt werden, *du sollst alles erfahren*; mache mir aber nachher keine Vorwürfe, wenn dich die Geschichte mit Bekümmernis und Grauen erfüllt." ("Your wish shall be fulfilled: you shall learn all that happened, but reproach me not afterwards if the story fills you with grief and horror"). The words italicised are perhaps a trifle too definite for their occurrence in both episodes to be entirely accidental.

There may have been a faint hark-back of Wagner's memory

to Tieck, again, at the point in the opera where Wolfram tries to restrain Tannhäuser from returning to Venus, just as Eckart had tried to warn Tannenhäuser against entering the mountain. Finally, the scene in Wagner's first act where Tannhäuser escapes from Venus by calling on the Virgin, is suddenly transported back to earth, and pours out his gratitude to God when he hears the hymn of the pilgrims on their way to Rome, may be unconsciously indebted for a word or two to Tieck. "Ich war von dem Glanz gesättigt und suchte gern die vorige Heimath wieder. Eine unbegreifliche *Gnade des Allmächtigen* verschaffte mir die Rückkehr, ich befand mich plötzlich wieder in der Welt", etc., says Tannenhäuser to Friedrich. ("I was cloyed with all these splendours and fain would see my old home once more. An inconceivable *grace of the Almighty* effected my return; I suddenly found myself in the world again", etc.). It may not be pure coincidence that Tannhäuser in the opera cries out, on his release from his captivity in the Venusberg,

> Allmächt'ger, *dir sei Preis!*
> *Gross sind die Wunder deiner* Gnade!
>
> ("*Praise to thee, Almighty!*
> *Great are the marvels of Thy grace!*").

There is no conscious plagiarism in cases of this kind; examples of similar tricks of the subconscious memory can be culled by the thousand from the poets from Vergil to Shakespeare and from Shakespeare to Coleridge.

8

The genuine Tannhäuser legend itself, as we have it now, is a pastiche gradually constructed by the imagination of the Middle Ages out of a number of pre-existing and non-correlated elements. The historical Tannhäuser (Tanhuser, Danhuser, etc.) was a knightly Minnesinger of the thirteenth century, hailing from Salzburg and born about 1200; we lose authentic sight of him before 1270. A few of his poems have been preserved: from these we can learn something, and conjecture a trifle more, about the man himself and his career. More interested in poetry and song than in the ordinary pursuits of the knight and the small land-owner, imprudent in the management of his affairs, he lived for a while under the patronage of Duke Friedrich of Austria. After the Duke's death he seems to have been at a loose end. In 1228 he went on a Crusade to the Holy Land, and then and later saw a good deal of Italy and Sicily and had many strange adventures by land and sea. His poems give us the impression of one who lived not wisely but too well, squandering his patrimony, as he penitently says, on "fair women, good wine, dainty meats, and baths twice a week", with the result that he was reduced in the end to dire poverty, having "no roof to his house, no door to his chamber, his cellar fallen in, his kitchen burnt out, his barn empty". He drifted about from one court to another in search of shelter and support, but found that few of his old friends were as glad to see him now as they had been in the days of his prosperity.

We may conjecture that, his name being dimly remembered as that of a poet with a strong bent towards the sensual, he had gradually become, during the later Middle Ages, a semi-mythical character about whom there crystallised one of those legends-with-a-moral of which that epoch was so fond. By the end of the thir-teenth century the great period of the Minnesong was virtually over. It had declined with the worldly fortunes of the aristocratic class from which it had mostly flowered. The face of German society was changing: many of the nobles were or were becoming impoverished, as a consequence partly of wars, partly of too lavish expenditure on luxuries, partly of the alienation of the estates of many of them to the Church; and among the greater lords there were few now able and willing to support the smaller ones for their mere songs' sake. And while the aristocracy was thus declining the towns were rising; wealth and power were passing into the hands of the merchants, the burghers, the guilds of craftsmen. Along with all this went a democratisation of ethical standards; the old ideals of the knightly order were not those of the townspeople and the peasant. So it may well have come about that the Minnesinger Tannhäuser began to figure as a symbol of a moral licence upon which the new bourgeois society frowned; it may even be that the new age was scandalised not merely by the references to wine and women in his songs but by his reckless unorthodoxy in the matter of baths. Anyhow he was singled out as the most appropriate figure from the past on which to pin the many old legends then current of a mortal who had forsaken the simpler joys of earth for those of an enchantress reigning over an earthly paradise of her own in the heart of some mysterious mountain or other. So there came into being, in time, the fully-formed story of Tannhäuser and Venus that has been so charmingly told by an unknown fifteenth or sixteenth century poet that Heine, in a passage with which Wagner must have been acquainted, could hail it as worthy to stand by the side of *The Song of Songs*.

9

The legend of the Venusberg had originally no connection with Tannhäuser. Wagner boldly describes his opening scene as representing "the interior of the Venusberg (the Hörselberg, near Eisenach)". The brothers Grimm, in their *Deutsche Sagen*, tell an ancient folk-tale of this Hörselberg, "in which the Devil lives and to which the witches make pilgrimages. Sometimes fearful shrieks and howls come from it, made by the devils and the poor wretched souls. In the year 1398 three great fires broke out in broad daylight near Eisenach, burned for a long time, joined together, then separated again, till at last all three made for this mountain. Country people who were later passing by with a load of wine were enticed into the hill by the evil fiend, and there they were shown several well-known characters who were already sitting among the flames of hell." The place became known as Satans-stedt, which name was gradually transformed into Sattelstadt. So much for the Hörselberg as the Middle Ages saw it. The modern identification of this fearsome mountain with the Venusberg, however, was a mere flight of fancy on the part of some nineteenth century German scholars. There is nothing in the Hörselberg legend connecting it with either Venus or Tannhäuser; and it is not an earthly paradise, like the Venusberg, but the haunt of devils.

Classical antiquity had loved to dream of mountains or caves inhabited by beings whose life was one long round of delights, and of favoured mortals who had been permitted to taste of these. Naturally the longer these stories were in circulation the more circumstantial the details of them became. One mediaeval Italian legend, which was possibly the source of that of the German Venusberg, was associated with a Sibyl who reigned over an earthly paradise in what is still known as the Monte della Sibilla, a peak in the Apennines between the modern Norcia and Ascoli. We have a romantic description of the place by an adventurous Frenchman, Antoine de la Sale, who essayed, though he was finally beaten in the attempt, to penetrate to the innermost depths of the mysterious cave of the Sibyl. From the people of the neighbourhood he learned the legends connected with the place, and particularly the story of a German who had actually succeeded in penetrating to the recesses of the mountain, where he found the queen of this paradise seated on a magnificent throne, surrounded by nobles and ladies richly dressed; the felicity of these people, who never lost their beauty and never grew old, would endure, he was told, to the end of the world itself.

The rule of the place was this: a visitor could stay eight days and depart of his own free will on the ninth, but if he did not leave then he would have to remain until the thirtieth, and so on until the three hundred and thirtieth day; if he did not depart then he must stay there for ever. There was only one little blot on this captivating picture: from every Friday at midnight until midnight on Saturday the queen and the other charming ladies transformed themselves into snakes and serpents. Strangely enough, it was only on the three hundred and thirtieth day that the German gentleman discovered this. It made him suspect that he had been guilty of mortal sin in taking up his abode in such a place; so on the three hundred and thirtieth day he bade his charming hostesses adieu and went off to Rome to confess. The Pope was secretly willing to absolve him, but thought it necessary, to discourage others, to pretend to take a very serious view of his case. So he spoke to him harshly and drove him from his presence; and when he changed his mind and sent for him again he found that the poor German, having decided on reflection that if he were going to lose the joys of heaven he might as well make sure of those of earth, had gone back to the paradise of the Sibyl, where, presumably, he still is.[1] This Italian legend was evidently very ancient; and modern French scholars have maintained that it was from Italy that it passed into Germany, there to become, in time, the story of Venus and her magic mountain, and of a repentant Tannhäuser who craved absolution of the Pope and was refused. As Gaston Paris has pointed out, the journey to Rome would have been a natural and easy matter; the German gentleman could have walked there very comfortably from the Monte della Sibilla.

10

These then are the heterogeneous elements, deriving from many sources, that went to the making of Wagner's *Tannhäuser*. He began his composition, as already mentioned, with the music for the Venusberg scene; a sketch-book of his that happens to have survived contains also jottings made in the summer of 1842 for the Pilgrims' hymn, the end of the first act, the prelude to the third act, etc. In his autobiography he tells us that during that summer holiday in Teplitz he was climbing the Wostrai one day when, "turning the corner of a valley, I was surprised to hear a merry dance-tune whistled by a shepherd reclining on a hillock. I was at once transported to my scene of the chorus of pilgrims filing past the shepherd in the valley. Later, however, try as I would, I could not recall the melody, so I had to make one for myself in the usual way." But in the sketch-book just mentioned there is noted a melody for the shepherd boy in the first act which, we are told, is entirely different from that in the opera. It looks therefore, as if Wagner's memory was a trifle at fault when he was writing *My Life*: presumably he *had* jotted the tune down at the time, or shortly after, and decided later that it was not suitable for his purpose.

The original poem and score of *Tannhäuser* underwent many changes before they assumed their present form; with some of

[1] Antoine de la Sale was writing in the early part of the fifteenth century. He had had a predecessor, as regards the Sibyl story, in one Andrea da Barbarino, in 1391.

these, however, we shall deal at the end of our analysis of the work as we now have it. The final page of the score in its first form is dated by Wagner 15th April 1845.

The first performance took place in Dresden, under Wagner himself, on the 19th October 1845, with the following cast for the principal rôles:

Tannhäuser	Tichatscheck.
Venus	Wilhelmine Schröder-Devrient.
Elisabeth	Johanna Wagner (a niece of the composer).
Wolfram	Mitterwurzer.
The Landgrave	Dettmer.
Walther	Schloss.
Biterolf	Wächter.
Heinrich der Schreiber	Curti.
Reinmar von Zweter	Risse.

In the late summer of 1859, having completed the score of *Tristan*, Wagner decided to try his fortunes in Paris, where he arrived in September of that year. His plan for a production of *Tristan* came to nothing; but in March 1860 the Emperor Napoléon, for political rather than artistic reasons, gave orders that *Tannhäuser* was to be produced at the Opéra. Three performances were given, on the 13th, 18th and 24th March 1861; the conductor was the incompetent Dietsch, the statutes of the Opéra not permitting the composer to conduct his own work. The following were the principal singers:

Tannhäuser	Albert Niemann.
Venus	Fortunata Tedesco.
Elisabeth	Marie Sax.
Wolfram	Morelli.
The Landgrave	Cazaux.

The present analysis is of the Paris version of the opera: some details of the respects in which the later score differs from the earlier one will be given at the end of this chapter.

11

The orchestral introduction proceeds for a while on the lines of the original overture of 1845, which told, in its own way, the story of the opera, by means of a succession of motives drawn from the work itself. The term "motives", however, must not be taken to mean what it does in Wagner's later works. In *The Flying Dutchman*, *Tannhäuser* and *Lohengrin* the motives are solid blocks of masonry, as it were, which, whenever they appear later in the score, at once recall the character in his entirety; it is very much as if a piece on a chessboard had moved into a new position. Even in *Tristan* a whole section is now and then transported almost *en bloc* to another part of the work, as when a slice from the duet in the second act becomes the material for the Liebestod in the third. It was only by degrees that Wagner mastered the craft of working with motives of only a few notes that are capable of infinite melodic, harmonic and rhythmical mutations, can be employed referentially at any moment, and are capable of contrapuntal combination with each other.

The "solid block" system of motives comes into use at the outset of the *Tannhäuser* overture, in a full-length statement of the song of the Pilgrims:

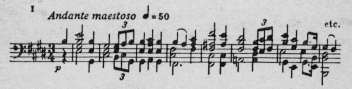

which, with its second strain:

runs on without a break for thirty-seven bars. No. 1 is then repeated *en bloc* in virtually the full orchestra, accompanied by a

febrile figure of broken triplets in the violins;[1] after which No. 2
is similarly treated at corresponding length, but in quieter colours.
(In the opera the Pilgrims sing No. 2 to the words "My heart is
sad, by sin oppressed", etc.) This exposition of the religious
element of the opera extends to eighty bars in all; in its totality it
presents us with a picture of the Pilgrims coming gradually into
sight, and as gradually disappearing in the distance as night falls.

Next comes a section depicting the seductions of the Venusberg
—first of all a feverish phrase in the violas:

then various suggestions of revelry:

---

[1] For Wagner this figure symbolised "the Pulse of Life".

This last culminates in a stanza of Tannhäuser's song in praise
of Venus:

which covers virtually the space allotted to it in the opera.

Then the bacchanal is resumed, in conjunction now with
Venus's cajoling invocation to the lover who desires to leave her:

This is followed by a second stanza of Tannhäuser's song, in a
higher key than formerly; and after a fortissimo statement of the
wild No. 5 we part company with the original overture and
plunge into the Paris version of the Venusberg music. The curtain rises, showing the interior of the Venusberg—"the Hörselberg, near Eisenach", as Wagner too confidently assures us. A
wide grotto curves round towards the right until it is lost in the
background distance; a dim light filters through an opening in the
rocks, from which a foaming greenish waterfall plunges down into
a basin; it then flows out to the background as a brook, which
broadens into a lake in which Naiads are bathing, while Sirens
recline on its banks. The cliff walls of the grotto are covered with
marvellous coral-like tropical growths. Venus reclines on a couch
in the foreground, which is bathed in a soft roseate light; round
her are grouped the three Graces, while numerous sleeping
Cupids are huddled together in a confused tangle, "like tired
children", say the stage directions, "who have fallen asleep after
play". Tannhäuser, his harp by his side, is half-reclining before
Venus, with his head in her lap. The foreground, with its rosy
light through which break the emerald green of the waterfall and
the white foam thrown up by its waves, contrasts with a clear blue
vapour that fills the background.

Youths with goblets in their hands come down from the heights in response to the signs of the Nymphs, who have begun an alluring dance: there are pursuits, flights and coquetries of all kinds while the dance continues.

To joyous reiterations of No. 4 and No. 5A, which latter has now an exuberant pendant that was not in the score of 1845:

a swarm of Bacchantes comes from the far background and breaks through the ranks of the amorous couples, urging them on to further abandonment "with gestures of exalted intoxication", as Wagner puts it. The dance grows ever wilder, till at last the revellers embrace each other passionately, to a new strain:

that is evidently an offshoot from *Tristan*.

12

Fiery developments of No. 11 are followed by a return to No. 3, with castanets adding a new and exotic touch of colour to it. Satyrs and Fauns, emerging from the clefts in the rocks and intruding their own wild dance into that of the Bacchantes and the pairs of lovers, increase the confusion by pursuing the Nymphs. Wilder and wilder still grows the tumult, until, as it rises to a delirious climax, the three Graces rise to their feet, horror-stricken, and try to restrain the dionysiac rout. Impotent to do so, and fearing that they themselves will be drawn into the whirl, they turn to the sleeping Cupids, awake them, and drive them up the heights, where they scatter for a while, then draw themselves up, as it were, in battle array, and rain down a shower of arrows on the tumult beneath them. A trumpet call rings out; then the music slows down in pace and decreases in volume as the Graces take possession of the wounded and try, with gentle force, to disperse the revellers towards the background. The Bacchantes, Fauns, Satyrs, Nymphs and Youths withdraw, pursued in part by the Cupids from the heights.

The music softens still further as a rosy mist settles upon the scene, growing thicker as it descends. First of all, while No. 5 comes out softly and graciously in the flutes and clarinets, the Cupids disappear; then, as the mist slowly envelops the background, the languorous song of the Sirens:

steals in and is developed in a "symphonic" way that would have been impossible to the Wagner of 1845.

Only Tannhäuser, Venus and the three Graces remain on the stage. The latter, according to Wagner's stage directions, "now return towards the foreground; gracefully interlocked they draw near to Venus, and apparently tell her of the victory they have won over the mad passions of the subjects of her kingdom. Venus gives them a grateful glance. The mist in the background dissolves, revealing a cloud-picture of the Rape of Europa; she is being carried across the blue sea on the back of the garlanded white bull, escorted by Tritons and Nereids." And now we hear the quiet song of the invisible Sirens—"Come to this strand, come to this land,[1] where your yearning shall be satisfied in glowing love":

[1] The current translations, of the type of "Come to these bowers, fragrant with flowers", are dictated by the necessity of finding two double-syllabled rhyming English words for "Strande" and "Lande".

The orchestra develops the strain in luscious Tristanesque fashion:

while "the rosy mist gathers again, obliterating the picture, and the Graces interpret in a graceful dance the mystic meaning of the picture as a work of love".

The Sirens' voices (No. 14) are heard again as once more the mist dissolves, revealing, in the half-light of the moon, Leda reclining on the banks of a woodland lake, with the swan fawningly laying its head on her bosom. Slowly the voluptuous melodies and harmonies sigh themselves out in the orchestra; the picture fades away and the mist entirely disappears, showing the grotto lonely and still. The smiling Graces make obeisance to Venus and retire to the inner grotto of Love. Venus and Tannhäuser maintain their attitudes unchanged.

13

At last the silence is broken by Tannhäuser, who raises his head suddenly as if waking from a dream, which he seems to be trying to recapture as he draws his hand across his eyes. Venus caressingly asks her beloved to tell her what is troubling him. He had thought he heard, he replies, a sound that had long been strange to his ears, that of bells pealing joyously. How long he has dwelt with her in the Venusberg he cannot say, for days and months have become all one to him; sun and stars and grass he sees no longer, nor hears the nightingale singing that spring is nigh. Will he ever see and hear all this again?

In quietly seductive tones she asks him why he complains thus. Is he weary of the wonders her love has lavished on him? Does he long to be a god? Has he forgotten his one-time suffering and his present transports? Holding out his harp to him she exhorts him to sing of love as he had done in the days when he had won her by his singing. His mood changing suddenly, he rises to his feet, seizes his harp, and sings the first stanza of his song, to the melody of No. 8. He praises her and all the godlike delights she has brought him, a mortal. But, he continues, his mood clouding over once more, such joys as these are for gods alone: he longs to be a man again and know the sufferings of men: and he implores her to set him free.

Venus herself now seems to waken from a dream. What has changed him? she asks anxiously: in what has her love been lacking? how has she deserved this lament? In a second stanza, in a key a semitone higher, he sings again in praise of her love and grace; enviable the man who has known the enchantments of her domain and has tasted joy in her arms! Yet—his mood darkening again—he longs to fly from her rosy bowers to the green woodlands, fresh with dew, and see the blue sky above him, and hear the song of birds and the chiming of bells; and once more he ends with an appeal to her to set him free.

Springing from her couch, she reproaches him for his ingratitude and refuses him his liberty; she turns away from him with a cry and buries her face in her hands. Then, after a long pause, she points to a magic grotto that has appeared in response to a sign from her, and turns to him again with a seductive smile, while the orchestra gives out a luscious strain:

that might have stepped straight out of the second act of *Tristan*. It is a far cry from the Wagner of 1845 to the Wagner of 1860; and there is no rebutting the charge that here, as in many other places in this opening scene, his new style is incompatible with the old fabric into which it has been woven.

Venus cajolingly invites Tannhäuser to come with her into the grotto, where she will lavish new enchantments of the senses on him. Wagner uses the original material of this episode to some extent, but presents it in more captivating forms, and inlays it with the finer and richer woods of the Paris score. Completely carried away, Tannhäuser seizes his harp once more and sings, again a semitone higher, the third verse of his song. It would have made for greater unity of style, of course, if Wagner had rewritten this song along with so much of the music of the scene. But that was hardly practicable; for one thing it would have meant a total recasting of the overture, while if he had changed the melody of the song the only logical course would have been to re-write the opening scene from first to last; and if he had done that, logic would have further dictated a re-writing of a good deal of the remainder of the opera. His admirers in 1861 were even more conscious than we of today are that his new style did not cohere with his old, for, it has to be remembered, they listened to all this Tristanesque music without knowing anything of *Tristan* beyond the prelude,[1] or anything at all of the *Ring*. Wagner himself must have been fully conscious of all this, but his musical daemon drove him on inexorably: he had long felt that he could make a

[1] This had been given at one of Wagner's Paris concerts in February 1860, and had provoked Berlioz into a wild denunciation of it in his *Débats* article of the 9th February.

better thing of the Venusberg scene than he had done in his original score, and his experiences of the Paris Opéra in 1859 and 1860
had enlarged enormously his conception of the possibilities of
ballet. So he abandoned himself luxuriously to the joy of writing
something more correspondent to his heart's desire than the
meagre capacities of the Dresden stage and his own relative
immaturity as a musician had made possible for him in 1845, and
cheerfully threw stylistic consistency to the winds.

14

Tannhäuser's third stanza ends, as its predecessors had done,
with an appeal to Venus to set him free. This time she rises in
anger and bids the "madman and traitor" go. In the original score
she had done so to rather conventional vocal and orchestral
phrases; but now, with *Tristan* and much of the *Ring* behind him,
Wagner puts a new fire into it all. A figure symbolical of Venus's
wrath:

dominates her furious harangue, though for a moment she reverts
to the lyrical Wagner idiom of the *Tannhäuser-Lohengrin* period:

as she tells him to sate his new desire if he will—to fly from her into the cold and loveless world of men and seek there for grace, though he will seek it in vain.

The episode is greatly extended in the Paris version, Venus becoming a more definite dramatic personality than she had formerly been. She bids Tannhäuser go back to the knightly company whom in his pride of old he had derided and antagonised, reveal his dishonour to them, and bear their scorn. They will curse him and cast him out, and then he will return to her downcast, moaning, "Oh, could I once more find her who once smiled on me! Would she but open again the door that leads to rapture!" For pity, not for love, he will then beg. Let him go from her, then; her kingdom is open only to heroes, not to slaves.

Wagner prolongs the original scene by making Tannhäuser show defiance—out of pride, he now says, he will never return to her—and Venus then breaks down. Her anger having exhausted itself, she loads him with tender reproaches:

What has she done, she asks, how has she offended, that her beloved will not forgive her? To the Queen of Love alone, then, it is denied to bring solace to her friend? How often, smiling through her tears, she had listened to his song! Were she to hear his sighs and laments again would she not comfort him as of old? But if her pleas are unavailing, she breaks out again despairingly, then her curse shall lay the whole world waste; and she beseeches him not to leave her but to trust in her love and grace.

But he is unyielding: he who is resolved to leave her "flies from all grace for aye". He is weary of soft enchantments; he longs for the world, for combat, even for death. "Then return to me", she implores him, "when even death shall fly from thee, and the grave be closed to thy bones." But death, he replies, is already in his heart; only in penitence and atonement shall he ever find rest. Once more she assures him that rest and peace will for ever escape him except in her arms: "return to me if thou wouldst be saved". He gives a great cry of "Goddess of all delights, not with thee shall my soul find its peace! My salvation lies in Mary!" Venus disappears, and the scene changes.

Tannhäuser, who has not changed his position, suddenly finds himself in a beautiful sun-bathed valley, with the old castle of the Wartburg showing in the background, while the Hörselberg is visible through an opening in the valley on the left. On the right a mountain path runs down from the Wartburg to the foreground, where it turns aside; and near the bend, on a slight eminence, is a shrine to the Virgin. From the heights on the left comes the sound of sheep-bells, while on the high cliffs sits a young shepherd blowing a pastoral strain on his pipe:

(The melody begins in the clarinet and is continued by a cor anglais behind the scenes). Then the shepherd sings a little song in praise of Holda, the goddess of spring:

Between the first two stanzas there comes, in the Paris score, an effective little interlude on the pipe that was not in the original version:

The song tells how at Holda's coming the woods were filled with music and the shepherd woke from his dreams to find that May had come; and once more he blows lustily on his pipe, the melody of which continues through the first part of the song of the elder Pilgrims:

who are making their slow way down the mountain path from the Wartburg. Their song takes a graver turn as they sing of their sense of sin (No. 2) and their hope of pardon, and hearing this the shepherd silences his own joyous melody, waves his cap to them, and cries "God speed to Rome! There for my soul to ask a blessing!"

Tannhäuser, into whom the song of penitence has struck deep, sinks on his knees with a great cry of gratitude to God for mercy. The pilgrims reach the stage and pass across it in slow procession, continuing their song until it dies away with them in the distance, the shepherd joining in occasionally with his melody before leaving the scene. Tannhäuser, as if sunk in fervent prayer, takes up the pilgrims' strain of No. 2; he too will never rest until his sin has been forgiven. Tears choke his voice: he bows his head and appears to weep bitterly.

15

By an admirable piece of transition the music merges almost imperceptibly into the horn fanfares of a hunting party in the distance:

and soon the Landgrave and the minstrels enter one by one from the eminence on the left of the stage. They see what they take at first to be a penitent of noble bearing, whom, however, they soon recognise and greet with joyous cries of "Heinrich!" Has he come back to them in friendliness, they ask, or is he still their foe? The gentle Wolfram reproves them for even suspecting him of hostility; is Tannhäuser's demeanour, he asks them, that of pride? He welcomes his return in phrases wholly characteristic of the melody of the early Wagner:

Walther, Heinrich der Schreiber, Reinmar, and even Biterolf, who is from first to last the least friendly towards Tannhäuser, echo Wolfram's welcome. The Landgrave joins in, but asks where the minstrel has tarried so long. Gravely and wearily Tannhäuser turns the question aside; all he will tell them is that he has been wandering in a distant land where he could never find rest or solace. Let them question him no more: he has not returned to contend with them; let them forget his leaving them and permit him to go his way. In a broad ensemble the others implore him to stay with them, but the gloomy man reiterates that it is impossible: his doom is to wander on for ever, not daring to look behind him again.

The knot is cut by Wolfram standing in front of him and exhorting him loudly to "stay for Elisabeth". The name awakens long-slumbering memories in Tannhäuser's bosom: deeply but joyfully agitated, he stands as if spellbound while Wolfram, at the Landgrave's request, tells him how the magic of his song among them in days of old had not only earned the praise of them all but won him the prize of Elisabeth's love:

26

Lento ♩ = 54

War's Zau - ber, war es rei - ne Macht, durch
Was't ma - gic, or some power di - vine, That

die solch Wun - der du voll - bracht,
wrought for thee that won - der fine,

The song is a moving one, in spite of several little evidences in it that as yet Wagner had not shaken himself quite free of the conventional melodic lines of his early days.

Since he had left them in his pride, says Wolfram, Elisabeth had closed her heart against their song; her cheek had grown paler, and she had come no more to the meetings of the minstrels; and he exhorts him to return among them and once more raise his song with theirs. The appeal is built up into a fine ensemble, with a captivating afterstrain that lends itself well to imitative interlocking:

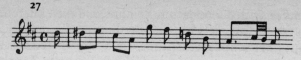

Tannhäuser, profoundly affected, throws himself into Wolfram's arms, then greets the other minstrels in turn and bows in gratitude to the Landgrave. "Lead me to her!" he cries, and his voice takes the lead:

in an animated ensemble that brings the first act to a close. Tannhäuser sees a new life opening out before him:

> *'Tis Spring! 'Tis Spring! a thousand tender voices*
> *With calls to gladness fill the air.*
> *My eager heart once more rejoices,*
> *And cries aloud: "To her! To her!"*

During the ensemble the stage gradually fills with the hunting retinue of the Landgrave. The hunters execute an exultant fantasia on their horns. At the end the valley is thronged with people: the Landgrave sounds his horn, and is answered by sonorous horn-blasts (No. 24) and the baying of hounds. The Landgrave and the minstrels mount the horses that have been brought to them from the Wartburg, and the curtain falls on an animated scene, with Tannhäuser's joyous cry (No. 28) ringing out in almost the full power of the orchestra.

16

It is in the orchestral introduction to the second act that we get, already in 1845, a foretaste of the later Wagner. The introduction presents us with a tone-picture of Elisabeth in happy mood after the return of Tannhäuser to the Wartburg. A preliminary mounting figure in the strings:

29

sets the general tone of the piece. It is succeeded by an energetic reminder of Tannhäuser's joyous greeting to the new world that had opened out before his imagination after Wolfram's appeal to him (No. 28). For a moment—and here we get a touch of the real Wagner—the sunny picture is darkened by a harsh reference:

30

to a phrase from Venus's warning to Tannhäuser in the episode the beginning of which is shown in our No. 18: after bidding the ingrate return to "the loveless world of men" the goddess had warned him that there he might seek for grace but would never find it. But when this cloud has passed the music regains its first sunny aspect, and after another reference to the joyous No. 29 Elisabeth herself bursts into song.

The curtain has now risen, showing the hall of song in the Wartburg, with an open background giving a view of the court-yard and the valley beyond. Elisabeth enters with a glad greeting to the beloved hall:

31

She tells of the dreariness that had descended on it and on her
when Tannhäuser had forsaken them, and—to the accompaniment of the exuberant No. 29—of her happiness at his return,
never, she hopes, to leave them again; and the aria ends with the
orchestra repeating the joyous No. 28 as Tannhäuser, accompanied
by Wolfram, enters by way of the staircase in the background.
The faithful Wolfram remains at the back of the stage as Tannhäuser advances and throws himself impetuously at Elisabeth's
feet. In modest confusion she is about to leave him, but turns
graciously to him at his appeal to her to stay, and, to the accompaniment of a typical early-Wagner melody in the clarinet:

urges him to rise and take her thanks for returning to the scene of
his many triumphs. But where has he been so long? she asks. The
music becomes clouded over once more as he replies, in sombre
tones, "Far from here, in distant, distant lands, and dark oblivion's
cloud between today and yesterday has rolled". His memory of it
all is dimmed; he remembers one thing only—that he had lost all
hope of ever raising his eyes to her again. A "mighty and mysterious wonder" has brought him back to her:

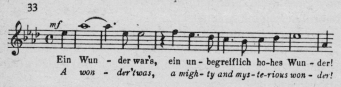

Ein Wun - der war's, ein un - begreiflich ho-hes Wun - der!
A won - der 'twas, a migh- ty and mys-te-rious won - der!

She praises this wonder for the happiness it has brought her; and
Wagner proceeds to paint, as well as it was possible for him to do
at that time, the musical portrait of the imaginative but as yet
unawakened girl as he saw her.[1] Quietly and modestly she tells

[1] The spectator must bear in mind that the matronly Elisabeth one generally sees on the stage is at the furthest remove imaginable from the Elisabeth of
Wagner. He visualised her as the St. Elisabeth of history and legend, still in
her girlhood, ignorant of the world, with a soul divided between vague
promptings of human affection and the call of a latent mysticism.

him of the joy the minstrels' songs, and his more than any, had given her in bygone days: his singing had brought her a rapture that was half a mystic pain, stirring in her longings which her childish heart could not comprehend. Then he had left them, and her heart had gone silent, cold and dead; and she ends with a poignant cry of "Heinrich! Heinrich! what hast thou done to me?" Tannhäuser answers her with a rapturous assurance:

34

Den Gott der Lie - be sollst du prei - sen!
The God of Love be praised for ev - er!

that it was the god of Love who had then inspired him and who has now brought him back to her; and their voices blend in a glad duet: "Oh blessed hour of meeting, oh blessed power of love":

35

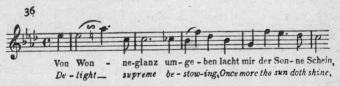

Ge - prie - sen sei_____ die Stun - de,
Oh bless - ed hour_____ of meet - ing,

the technical handling of which seems to have appealed more to Mendelssohn than anything else in the opera. In its latter half it opens out into a new strain:

36

Von Won - ne-glanz um - ge - ben lacht mir der Son - ne Schein,
De - light__ supreme be - stow-ing, Once more the sun doth shine,

as the pair sing of the power of love to re-create the world for lovers. At the climax Tannhäuser leaves Elisabeth and embraces Wolfram passionately: the pair disappear, and Elisabeth, from the balcony, looks fondly after Tannhäuser as the orchestra repeats No. 32 in soft tones.

17

The Landgrave now enters through a side door; Elisabeth runs
to him and hides her face on his breast. The dialogue that follows
shows Wagner still unable, as he had been in the Daland scenes
in *The Flying Dutchman*, to give musical life to some episode
or minor character that had to be there for constructional purposes but did not lend itself easily to musical delineation. The
kindly Landgrave reads his niece's secret in her eyes and spares
her the telling of it: as for the marvels that the minstrels' song had
once awakened in her, these shall be renewed today. The brief
dialogue is obviously there only as a device for introducing the
scene that is to follow; and Wagner is very far as yet from full
mastery of that art of imperceptible logical transition on which
he rightly prided himself in his later works.

"Even now", the Landgrave concludes, "arrive the nobles of
my land, whom I have bidden here to solemn festival; larger the
concourse will be than of old, for they have heard that thou the
victor's brow wilt crown." A trumpet fanfare peals out from the
courtyard:

succeeded by a quieter strain:

as the Landgrave and Elisabeth ascend the balcony to watch the
arrival of the guests. Knights and Counts, with their ladies and
retinues, gradually fill the hall, being received and formally
announced in turn by four noble pages; the ladies and attendants,
after doing honour to the Landgrave, remain in the background,
while the nobles take the places allotted to them. The ceremonious
processional music begins quietly:

This is followed by the equally quiet:

which, however, soon rises to a climax with:

and a repetition of No. 38.

At last brilliant trumpet fanfares introduce the big chorus in praise of the hall of song, "where art and peace alone prevail under the wise rule of Landgrave Hermann, Prince of Thuringia": the chorus is built up out of the material shown in No. 39 (all the voices)[1], No. 40 (the women's voices), No. 41 (the men), and finally the whole company as more and more nobles arrive with their retinues. One needs to have seen the Bayreuth setting and management of this scene to realise the full splendour of it.

18

Some final fanfares ring out at the conclusion of the chorus, by which time the guests have seated themselves in a large semicircle with the Landgrave and Elisabeth occupying seats of honour under a canopy in the foreground. To the accompaniment of a new and quieter strain:

[1] Wagner had anticipated this melody in a choral "Greeting of his Faithful Subjects to the Beloved Friedrich August" (King of Saxony) in August 1844.

the minstrels now come forward, greet the assembly with dignified bows, and take their seats in a narrower semicircle in the
centre of the hall, with Tannhäuser in the middle to the right and
Wolfram at the end (left) opposite the guests. The Landgrave
rises and addresses the assembly. He reminds them how, after the
land had been saved by their swords from the savage hordes that
threatened it, they had turned to the cultivation of the arts of
peace, the singing of the praises of grace and beauty, faith and
virtue. Today they celebrate their divine art once more, in a contest of song that will include the minstrel from whom they had
been too long parted. Where he has been, how and why he has
returned, has not been told them; perhaps the secret may be revealed to them in song. He gives them their theme—the true
nature of love: and the singer of the best lay on that theme will be
awarded the prize by Elisabeth; whatever his demand may be the
Landgrave pledges his word that she will grant it. The fanfares
ring out once more, the assembly hails the Landgrave as the protector of the arts, and the contest of song begins.

The choosing of the order of the singers is carried out to the
accompaniment of the minstrels' motive (No. 42). Each contestant
places a small roll of paper bearing his name in a golden bowl
borne by the four noble pages: they present the bowl to Elisabeth,
who takes out one of the papers and hands it back to them: they
read the name, advance ceremoniously into the centre of the stage,
and call out "Wolfram von Eschenbach, begin thou!". Then they
seat themselves at the feet of the Landgrave and Elisabeth.

Tannhäuser, leaning upon his harp, seems to be lost in dreams
as Wolfram rises to the accompaniment of some solemn chords in
the lower strings. He begins quietly with a courtly address to the
knights and ladies, whose nobility and virtue, he humbly feels,
will dazzle his eyes and make him dumb:

Blick' ich um - her in die - sem ed - len Krei - se,
Ga - zing a - round on this au - gust as - sem-bly,

welch ho - her An - blick macht mein Herz er - glühn!
How grows my heart to see so fair a scene!

But above them all sits throned one pure spirit like a star, before which his soul abases itself in prayer. His vision is of a fountain of stainless joy, from which flows a flood that allays the fever of his spirit: may he never dim that fountain's pure waters with the taint of thought impure:

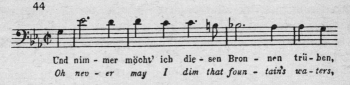

Und nim - mer möcht' ich die - sen Bron - nen trü - ben,
Oh nev - er may I dim that foun - tain's wa - ters,

In humble devotion he kneels before it, glad to give for it his heart's last blood. That, he concludes quietly, is his song, into which he has put all he knows of the purest essence of love.

Acclamations break from them all as he resumes his seat—from all but Tannhäuser, who now seems to waken from his dream. What that dream has been is told us by the orchestra, with its reminiscences of the wild Venusberg music (No. 10, No. 3 etc.). (For the Paris version the scene that immediately follows was changed considerably by Wagner). Gradually his demeanour had assumed the haughty tone that had led to his first separation from the court; now his expression changes to one of ecstasy as visions of the Venusberg rise before him. Unconsciously his fingers seek the strings of his harp. An uneasy smile plays for a while over his features; then, as if possessed by a demon, hardly knowing where he is, he bursts out into a scornful denunciation of Wolfram, whose tepid song, he says, shows that he has never known what love is: "were all men's hearts as chill as thine is, the world were lifeless as a stone!" Let him praise God and the stars of heaven if he will; but of life and love as Tannhäuser has experienced them he knows nothing. He himself will go to the fountain that alone can rekindle desire as fast as it quenches it; for of eternal desire he would drink eternally. This, and this alone, is love as he conceives it.

19

There is general consternation. Elisabeth "is a prey", say the stage directions, "to conflicting emotions of rapture and anxious astonishment". Biterolf, in a song that is still early Wagner, rises angrily, denounces the blasphemous pride of Tannhäuser and defies him to mortal combat. His outburst meets with the approval of the knights and ladies; and when Tannhäuser, in a gust of anger, calls his critic a poor starveling who, for all his virtuous sentiments, has never known what real love is, the knights rise in wrath and refuse to hear any more. The tumult is quelled by the Landgrave, who bids Biterolf put back the sword he has drawn, and still more effectively by Wolfram, who rises to implore heaven to send them peace of soul and banish all sinful thoughts from them. His song in praise of the higher love has the regularity of metrical accent which Wagner himself was to note with amusement, in later years, as a characteristic of his early vocal style:

By now Tannhäuser has lost control of himself. Madly he sings his song from the first act in praise of the goddess of earthly love, the fountain of all grace and beauty and joy (No. 8); he ends with a cry to all poor mortals who have never known her love to fly with him to the hill of Venus. At this unblushing revelation of where he had spent the time of his absence from them the assembly breaks up in horror. The ladies leave the hall with gestures of dismay. The Landgrave, knights and minstrels have left their seats and formed into a hostile group. Elisabeth, pale and anxious, trying desperately to preserve her self-control, supports herself against one of the wooden pillars of the canopy. Tannhäuser, throughout the first part of the chorus of denunciation of him that follows, remains isolated at the extreme left of the stage, still intoxicated with the vision he has conjured up in his memory. As the men advance on him with drawn swords he places himself in an attitude of defiance.

The crisis is averted by Elisabeth, who steps forward and shields Tannhäuser with her own body. If he is to die, she says, let her die with him, for no wounds that their swords could give her could match the one that has been dealt her by him. Gradually all the leading threads of the action pass into her hands, and not only psychologically but musically she raises it all to a higher plane. In a long passage commencing thus:

46

Andante ♩ = 56

Der un - glück-sel' - ge, den ge - fan - gen ein füreht-bar
This er - ring soul that now is cap - tive To some mys -

mächt'-ger Zau - ber hält,
- ter - ious power of sin,

and culminating in an impassioned plea to them for mercy on the sinner:

47

Adagio ♩ = 58

Ich fleh' für ihn, ich fle - he für sein Le - ben,
I plead for him, oh spare him I im - plore you:

she tells them that it is she, not they, who has been most grievously hurt by Tannhäuser's impious song, for she had loved him. Now she pleads that he shall be allowed to live and repent, for it was for such as he that the Redeemer died.

Tannhäuser, who has gradually lost his truculence of demeanour as Elisabeth's plea proceeded, at last sinks down, overwhelmed with contrition, as the minstrels, led by Walther, launch a massive choral ensemble in praise of Elisabeth:

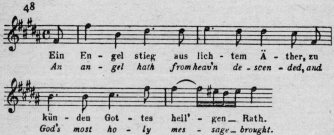

Tannhäuser breaks in with an appeal to heaven to grant him grace for the sake of the angel who has interceded for him, an appeal that reaches its culminating point in a poignant cry for mercy:

Finally Elisabeth takes hold of a phrase that had been begun by the knights, and between them they build up with it the climax of a long and impressive ensemble:

We sink to a lower musical plane again when the Landgrave steps forward, reproves Tannhäuser sternly, and pronounces sentence on him of banishment from their midst. One course alone remains open to him to avert God's anger. Some pious pilgrims (here No. 23 is given out in the wood wind) are now making their way to Rome, to lay the burden of their sins, light as it is in comparison with his, at God's feet. The knights and minstrels, to the strain of the motive of Atonement:

bid Tannhäuser repair to Rome with them and never return till his sin has been forgiven. For Elisabeth's sake they will restrain their wrath now, but their swords will take vengeance on him if he refuses to follow the path of salvation opened out to him. Elisabeth raises her voice above them all in a last plea to him and to them, Tannhäuser stammers his contrition:

and at the height of the turmoil the song of the younger pilgrims strikes in from the depths of the valley—"To God's high feast of grace I go, My burden at His feet to throw". All involuntarily moderate their gestures; Elisabeth, who has made a movement as if to protect Tannhäuser from the knights, calls his attention to the promise of comfort held out by the song; Tannhäuser, suddenly calmed, listens intently to the song as it soars to its climax and then dies away. A ray of hope lights up his face: he throws himself convulsively at Elisabeth's feet, kisses the hem of her garment, and rushes out with a cry of "To Rome! To Rome!" The others echo the cry, and the curtain falls to the strain of No. 51 in the orchestra.

20

The orchestral introduction to the third act is an expressive tone-painting of Tannhäuser's pilgrimage. First we hear (now in the key of E flat) the pilgrims' solemn song (No. 23), into which breaks, in the soft tones of oboe and clarinet, the melody of Elisabeth's pleading for Tannhäuser (No. 47), as it were a thought, at once sad and consoling, passing through the penitent's mind as he trudges along with the others. Then a second phrase of the pilgrims' song is followed by a motive of Tannhäuser's wretchedness that will play a considerable part in his own later story of his pilgrimage:

Further elaborations of these contrasting motives lead into a return of the motive of the Pulse of Life from the overture: this is twice broken in upon by the motive of the Feast of Grace in Rome of which Tannhäuser will tell Wolfram later; it takes first of all this form:

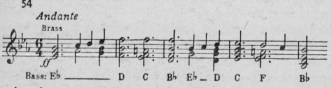

then thunders out in greater majesty still:

55

Then, after another brief reference to Tannhäuser's despair, the music slowly settles down into another statement of No. 47 and dies away in a soft E flat chord in the high wood wind.

At this point the curtain rises, showing the valley in front of the Wartburg, as at the end of the first act, but now in sad autumnal colours. Evening is falling. On the slight eminence to the right we see Elisabeth prostrate before the shrine of the Virgin, deep in prayer. Wolfram comes down slowly from the wooded heights on the left, catches sight of her, and pauses. Gravely he sings to himself of her constant praying day and night for Tannhäuser: now she is awaiting the home-coming of the pilgrims, whose return surely cannot long be delayed now that the sere leaves are falling. Will *he* be among them, pardoned and redeemed? For that mercy he prays for Elisabeth's sake, or for some solace for her if her heart's desire should not be granted.

As he is about to descend further into the valley he is arrested by the song of the returned pilgrims (No. 1) welling up from the valley, greeting gladly the home they are soon to see again. Elisabeth too has heard the song, and a tremor passes through her as she murmurs "'Tis they! They have returned! Show me, ye saints, my task, that I may worthily fulfil it!". Gradually the chanting pilgrims reach the stage and go slowly past the rocky eminence down the valley to the background, their song festooned with the broken triplet figure of the Pulse of Life. The song rises to a great "Hallelujah!"; then, to the strain of No. 1 again, the procession passes out of sight in the now setting sun. Tannhäuser is not among them.

As her last hope has died within her Elisabeth has poured out her grief in one of the great phrases of the opera, in which the throbbing strings add an extra poignancy to the simple words and as simple melodic line:

56

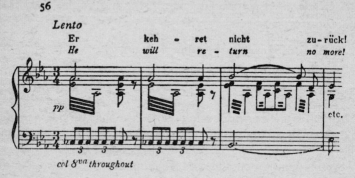

When she is left alone she falls on her knees in an ecstasy of grief and resignation: for the first time the mysticism of her young being finds full expression in a prayer to the Virgin to take her from this world of care:

57

Through the quiet plaint a figure in the bass clarinet—a typically later Wagner touch, this—keeps winding its melancholy way:

58

She ends with a quiet prayer to the Virgin to give ear to her pleading and pardon the sinner his great sin:

after which an orchestral postlude in the pure tones of the higher
wood wind seems to carry her supplication aloft.

As she rises slowly to her feet she perceives Wolfram approaching her. May he not lead her homeward? he asks. With a silent
gesture of refusal she conveys to him an expression of her gratitude and affection and a request that he will leave her to traverse
alone the path she has marked out for herself for the short remainder of her days. She ascends the height and gradually disappears in the direction of the Wartburg, the faithful Wolfram
following her with his eyes, and the orchestra dwelling sweetly
and sadly on phrases from his song in the second act in praise of
spiritual love (No. 45 and

21

The stage has by now grown darker, and with the disappearance of Elisabeth the orchestra, with a chord or two in the quiet
tones of trombone and tuba, tunes us in, as it were, to the gloom
that will envelop the remainder of the dramatic action. Wolfram
seats himself at the foot of the rising ground to the left and begins
to improvise on his harp. Evening, he muses, is falling on the

valley like a foreshadowing of death, terrifying and beating back
the soul that would fain ascend to the heights:

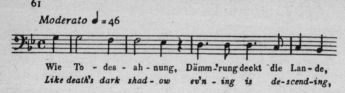

But one fair star there is whose friendly beams beckon a way
through the vale; and he begins that song to the evening star that
may seem old-fashioned to us now, but in its own day was rich
in new harmonic suggestions:

His song ended, the orchestra continues to muse upon the theme
of it while Wolfram raises his rapt eyes to heaven.

The stage is now quite dark. Suddenly a troubled figure in
horns and bassoons:

cuts harshly into the serene atmosphere as Tannhäuser appears in
the tattered garb of a pilgrim: his face is pale and tortured: he
walks falteringly, leaning heavily on his staff. He is at first not
recognised by Wolfram, but Tannhäuser knows the latter at once
and describes him scornfully as "the practised minstrel". The

gentle Wolfram runs to him eagerly, but cannot refrain from wondering that he should venture again, unabsolved, into the domain of the Landgrave. Tannhäuser acidly bids him calm his fears: he seeks the company of none of them—his one consuming desire, he adds feverishly, is to find again the path that leads to the Hill of Venus; and the orchestra entwines the dialogue with the wild strains of No. 3 and No. 10. The trembling Wolfram tries to hold the madman back. Has he not been then, to Rome? he asks; did he not sue for pardon? Yes, replies Tannhäuser bitterly; he has been to Rome. Wolfram pours out his heart's compassion for him, while the wood wind breathe softly the phrase (No. 47) of Elisabeth's intercession. Wolfram's sympathy surprises and touches Tannhäuser; he had thought the minstrel his foe like the others. Exhausted, he seats himself at the foot of the rock: Wolfram is about to join him there, but Tannhäuser motions him back; "Away from me! Wherever I rest me is accursed!", and the grievous No. 63 wells up in the orchestra once more.

Wolfram shall hear his story, he says; and he breaks into that long recital of his pilgrimage that placed Wagner, in 1845, on a musical height to which none of the Marschners of the epoch could ever hope to rise. To the accompaniment of the tortured No. 53 Tannhäuser tells how he had gone to Rome with an ardour in his soul such as no pilgrim had ever known, his old arrogant pride chastened, his heart set on justifying Elisabeth's appeal for grace for him. To that end he had pitilessly multiplied the mortifications of his flesh, always taking the rough road rather than the smooth, refusing to quench his thirst in the burning heat, shunning the friendly hospice and sleeping in ice and snow, his eyes blind to the beauty of everything around him—all that Elisabeth's grief might find an end. At last he had reached the holy city, where the bells were pealing from every steeple and every soul was filled with joy (No. 54). With the others he had knelt before him who holds the keys of heaven, and thousands were shriven, thousands went on their homeward way rejoicing. No. 53 reappears as Tannhäuser goes on to tell how he in his turn approached with head bent to earth, confessed his sin, and begged for deliverance from the fetters of earthly longings. The Pope's harsh reply—that if he has felt these vile desires, warmed himself at the fires of hell, dwelt in the Venusberg, he is eternally accursed:

> *As on this dead staff in my hand*
> *never a leaf again shall grow,*
> *so from hell's all-consuming brand*
> *salvation canst thou never know!*

—is punctuated by orchestral ejaculations of the tortured No. 63. Tannhäuser had fallen to the ground, crushed and confounded. When he awoke night had fallen and he was alone, but from afar he could still hear the happy song of the other pilgrims (No. 54). With horror in his heart he had fled, possessed now by only one desire, to feel again the transports he had known in the Venusberg, the themes of which now leap into flame in the orchestra as he sings, to the melody of No. 9, a frenzied appeal to Venus to take him to her bosom once more. The Venusberg music takes full possession of the orchestra as the frenzy of Tannhäuser and the horror of Wolfram increase.

22

A thin vapour spreads over the stage and soon begins to glow with a rosy light, and as the infernal rout grows madder in the orchestra first a confused whirl of dancing figures becomes visible, then Venus herself is seen reclining on her couch. To the melody of No. 14 she welcomes Tannhäuser again, reminding him of her warning that the cruel world of men would reject him and he would be glad to take refuge in her arms once more. The three voices unite for a while, Venus renewing her seductions, Tannhäuser straining towards her for a sign of pity, Wolfram vainly endeavouring to hold him back. He reminds the madman of one who is now an angel pleading for him in heaven and giving him her blessing; and the knot is cut, as it had been in the first act, by Wolfram crying "Elisabeth!" At the sound of that name Tannhäuser, who had struggled free of Wolfram, stands as if rooted to the spot; and at the same time there comes from behind the scenes a choral song of the minstrels and other mourners commending to God the soul of the pure Elisabeth. "Her prayer is heard! Heinrich, thou art redeemed!" cries Wolfram. Venus disappears with a cry of "Woe! he is lost to me!" The vapours dissolve, morning dawns, and from the Wartburg a funeral procession, with torches, comes down into the valley, singing a hymn of the blessing of Elisabeth:

64

Hei — lig die Rei — ne, die nun ver - eint
Blessed be the pure one, who now ap - pears,

gött — li - cher Schar vor dem E — wi - gen steht!
One — with the saints round the throne — of the Lord!

Tannhäuser has been led by Wolfram to Elisabeth's bier; he bends over it in a quiet prayer, "Sainted Elisabeth, pray for me!", and falls dead to the ground. All invert their torches and so extinguish them, the only light now coming from the red glow of the dawn. A band of younger pilgrims enters from the rocky eminence in the foreground, bearing in their midst a staff covered with fresh green leaves, and singing a chorus of praise for the miracle:

The barren staff the priest did bear
with tender green is clothed again:
the sinner need no more despair;
for God shall cleanse him of his stain.
High over all the Lord doth reign,
no man doth call on Him in vain.

The whole assembly unites with the orchestra in a sonorous statement of the Pilgrims' song (No. 1), which is once more accompanied by the triplet figure we had heard festooning it in the overture.

23

A good deal of confusion seems to exist as to the date of origin of what is known in the concert room as "the *Tannhäuser* Overture and the New Venusberg Music". We read, for example, that "in the original form of the overture, which is the one usually played at concerts, the Salvation motive re-enters and gradually overcomes the [old] Venusberg music, coming to a triumphant full close in the usual manner. When, however, Wagner made his preparations for the ill-starred production at Paris in March 1861 he omitted the last part of the overture and made the Venusberg music run straight on, without a break, into the first scene." This is quite wrong. It was not the present coalesced form of the old matter and the new that was given in Paris: the original overture was played intact, and followed, after the usual brief interval, by the new Venusberg scene in place of the old one. Both Wagner and Malwida von Meysenbug say definitely that the house broke into applause "after the overture". There is other contemporary evidence to the same effect—that of Marschner, for instance, who was present on that occasion. It is clear, again, from passages in Bülow's contemporary letters from Paris, in which he sets forth the alterations Wagner was making in the opera, that no change was contemplated as regards the overture.

For brevity's sake let us refer to the original overture of 1845 as A, the Venusberg ballet scene that followed it as B, and the re-cast Paris version of this last as C. In the 1845 version of the opera, after the usual interval for applause after A, act one began with a scene described in the score as "the Venusberg". The stage showed the interior of the hill of Venus: the enchantress reclined on a couch, with Tannhäuser half-kneeling by her side; nymphs and bacchantes indulged in a bacchanal during the course of which a chorus of sirens was heard in the background. When the music finally died away the vocal portion of the opera began with Tannhäuser's words "Beloved, say, where stray thy thoughts?"

Both Wagner's musical and his dramatic sense told him later that this procedure was faulty, for two reasons—it involved a certain amount of repetition of the same musical matter in A and B, and B was insufficiently orgiastic. As early as March 1852 he told Uhlig that he now saw that the "proper place" for the 1845 overture was "in the concert room, not the theatre". If the decision rested with him he would now play, in the theatre, only "the first tempo of the overture"—i.e. as far as the end of the pilgrims' chorus; the remainder is "too much to be given in front of the drama".

Later he became dissatisfied with B. It was plainly the weak spot in the opera, he wrote to Frau Wesendonk from Paris in April 1860. What was needed was something much wilder, more voluptuous, to serve as background to the spiritual tragedy of Tannhäuser. He had long been aware of this, he said, but only after he had completed *Tristan* did he feel that he was musically equal to such a task. He accordingly intended to write a new B in a style that would "astonish" the Parisians. He gives no hint, however, of any intention to modify the overture. That, in a sense, had by now passed out of the hands of its creator; it had become immensely popular both in the theatre and in the concert room, and opera directors, conductors and audiences alike would have been horrified at the suggestion that it should be curtailed. All that Wagner had in his mind now, in Paris, was a new and better version of B, the expanded scenario for which he sketched for Frau Wesendonk.

The further question now arises, when was the dovetailing of A and C effected?

In the summer of 1867 the opera was given in Munich, under Bülow, for the gratification of King Ludwig. This was simply the Paris version of 1861 again, with C following A, and, of course, with all the changes in, and additions to, the vocal parts made in 1861. The coalescence of C with a curtailed A was probably effected about 1871/2, for on the 12th May 1872, at a concert given by Wagner in Vienna in aid of his Bayreuth plan, he conducted the first performance of what we now know as "the *Tannhäuser* overture and the New Venusberg Music". The new arrangement was first heard under *operatic* conditions in Vienna on the 22nd November 1875, at a performance of the work under Wagner. But after he had left the town the Vienna Opera reverted to the original version—A followed by B: the overture—the most popular work of the period—was a *bonne bouche* of which the public objected to being deprived, while the new bacchanal (C) was frowned upon by many pundits, among them Hanslick, as a glorification of sensuality in music. Another Vienna critic, Ludwig Speidel, informed his readers that the New Venusberg Music was made up of "howls and shrieks, an endless succession of piercing dissonances. We hear the Spanish flies [cantharides] buzzing, and the draught served up by the satyrs is simply gin laced with cayenne pepper. Even in Wagner it would be difficult to find so horrible, so foul a musical daub."

24

Apart from the re-modelling of the overture and the bacchanal scene Wagner made several changes in *Tannhäuser* in the course of the years. The work had become so popular in Germany, and was always so badly performed—as, indeed, it still is—that in the summer of 1852 he was driven to write a brochure *On the Performing of Tannhäuser*, in which he tried to set the theatre directors and producers and singers on the right path with regard to it. Owing to the imperfections of some of the singers and of the stage management in Dresden in 1845 he had been compelled to make various cuts for the first few performances; the other theatres, to suit their own convenience, chose to regard these cuts as "authorised by the composer", and they faithfully reproduced them, to his great annoyance, in their own productions. Wagner's brochure was partly intended to correct misconceptions of this kind. But in addition there were several variants between the earliest published scores in use in the theatres and the later ones, the result of second thoughts on his part; and he wanted to impress it on the German theatres in general that it was the second version which they were to follow.

This was particularly the case in connection with the long orchestral introduction to the third act. A comparison of this as it stands in the earliest and in the present scores reveals several changes and curtailments. The final version runs only to 92 bars; the original ran to 155, and told the story of Tannhäuser's pilgrimage at rather greater length than was necessary, as Wagner himself recognised later. "The long instrumental introduction to the third act", he says in the brochure, "I wish to be performed in the re-modelled and abridged form in which it appears in the scores now supplied to the theatres. When first writing this piece I allowed the subject matter which I was describing to betray me into recitative-like phrases for the orchestra; but when we came to perform it I felt that while it made its meaning clear enough to me, because I could follow in my imagination the episodes with which it dealt, it could not be equally intelligible to others"—a point to which the composers of symphonic poems who are coy of revealing their "programme" to us might take note. "Nevertheless", continues Wagner, "I must insist on the *complete* performance of this introduction in its new form, as I deem it indispensable for establishing the mood necessary for the reception of what follows."

The most drastic change of all was made in the ending of the opera, which seems to have given Wagner some trouble from the beginning. In the original version of the final scene Venus did not appear in person; she was to be conceived by the spectator merely as a figment of the frenzied imagination of Tannhäuser, with the Hörselberg showing in a red light in the distance, and bells tolling from the Wartburg announcing the death of Elisabeth there. Evidently the spectators of 1845 did not grasp the full meaning of all this; yet, perversely enough, when Wagner improved it for them they resented being deprived of the dénouement to which they had grown accustomed. When originally writing this final scene, Wagner said in the brochure, his conception of it was just as clear to him inwardly as it became in the later version, but he had not been able to express it in terms of the theatre. "I had banked too completely on certain scenic effects, which, however, proved inadequate when put into actual practice: the mere glow from the Venusberg in the back distance could not produce the disquieting impression that was to lead up to the dénouement; still less could the far-away dirge and the lighting up of the windows of the Wartburg bring home instantly to the uninformed spectator the sense of the catastrophic stroke which Elisabeth's death brings into the action." The only way to make it all clear to the audience beyond any possibility of misunderstanding was by bringing Venus in person upon the stage to make a last effort to draw Tannhäuser into her coils again, while instead of Elisabeth's death being only suggested by the sights and sounds from the distant Wartburg, Tannhäuser was now to sink dead upon her actual bier. It seems probable, from certain fragments of indirect evidence, that Wagner made a tentative change of this kind as early as 1846. The work was played with its original ending, however, as far as the thirteenth performance, on the 7th February 1847, and with the new ending, for the first time, on the 1st August following.

It is unnecessary to set forth here all the details of the Paris re-casting of the opera. The most important of the changes appear in the first act. Not only was the bacchanal extended and intensified but the colloquy between Venus and Tannhäuser was worked out on a larger scale. This landed Wagner in some difficulties later. He wrote the new music for this episode to a French version of his new German lines; consequently when he came later to prepare a definitive German edition of the score he had to translate the French text back again into German. This of necessity compelled him sometimes to replace the regular metrical scheme of his German text by a sort of free verse in order to make the words fit the melodic line. A single example will suffice to give the reader an idea of what happened. At one point he had written the following lines for Venus:

> *Da liegt er vor der Schwelle,*
> *wo einst ihm Freude floss:*
> *um Mitleid, nicht um Liebe,*
> *fleht bettelnd der Genoss.*

In the process of fitting German words to the melody that had been composed to the French text these lines lost their metre and their rhyme and became these:

> *Auf der Schwelle, sieh' da!*
> *ausgestreckt liegt er nun,*
> *dort wo Freude einst ihm geflossen!*
> *Um Mitleid fleht er bettelnd,*
> *nicht um Liebe.*

It is not to be wondered at that occasionally the new words fall awkwardly from the tongue.

Other changes from the text of 1845 to that of 1861 have been indicated in the foregoing analysis of the opera.

LOHENGRIN

Principal Characters

LOHENGRIN	*Tenor*
ELSA OF BRABANT	*Soprano*
FRIEDRICH VON TELRAMUND,	
A COUNT OF BRABANT	*Baritone*
ORTRUD, HIS WIFE	*Soprano*
HENRY THE FOWLER, GERMAN KING	*Bass*
THE KING'S HERALD	*Bass*

Time and place of the action: Antwerp, first half of the 10th century.

I

Wagner has told us how, during a holiday and "cure" in Marienbad in the summer of 1845, the subjects of *Lohengrin* and *The Mastersingers* engrossed him almost simultaneously. He had been sadly overworked in Dresden, and his doctor had ordered him a complete rest. To this end he had taken with him, by way of light reading, the poems of Wolfram von Eschenbach and the old anonymous German epic of *Lohengrin*. But as he pored over these in the neighbouring woods, he says, "an ever-increasing excitement" took possession of him. Memories revived in him of the Paris days when he had read an article by the Königsberg Professor Lucas on the Lohengrin epic. "Thus", he said in his account of that Paris period, "a whole new world opened out before me, and though I could not find then and there the form in which to cast this *Lohengrin*, yet the image of it persisted undimmed within me." In Marienbad, as a result of his making acquaintance with the epic at first-hand, "there suddenly sprang up before my eyes a *Lohengrin* complete in every detail of dramatic form: in particular the saga of the swan, which forms so significant a feature of the whole complex of myths with which my studies had familiarised me, exercised an enormous fascination on my imagination."

Remembering his doctor's injunction not to do any writing during his "cure" he fought hard at first against this fascination and tried to drive Lohengrin out of his mind by thinking of Hans

Sachs and the Mastersingers of Nuremberg, about whom he had been reading in Gervinus's *History of German National Poetry*. The result was that the whole ground-plan of an opera on the subject of the Mastersingers at once took shape within him. As it was a comedy theme, he says, and therefore not likely to tear his exhausted nerves to tatters, he thought he could commit the plan to paper without really disobeying the doctor's orders; he hoped, indeed, that it would drive out the desire to set to work at *Lohengrin*. But in this he was mistaken: no sooner had his mind got into full working order again under the influence of the Nuremberg subject than that of Lohengrin clamoured more and more insistently for realisation. A similar thing was to happen to him more than once in later life; when the mighty dynamo of his imagination got really to work on one theme the sheer energy of it would force to the forefront some other subject which until then had been only hovering about in the hinterland of his consciousness. Getting into his bath at Marienbad at noon one day, he tells us, "I was suddenly overcome by so powerful a longing to commit *Lohengrin* to paper that, unable to stay in the bath the regulation hour, I jumped out impatiently after the first few minutes, and, hardly giving myself time to dress, ran back like a madman to my lodging to write out what was pressing so heavily on my mind. This went on for several days, until I had set down the detailed stage plan for a *Lohengrin*." It is not to be wondered at that his doctor gave him up as hopeless, the sort of man on whom a water-cure was wasted: Wagner was now so excited that he sometimes spent the night wandering about instead of sleeping.

Back in Dresden again in August, his time during the next few months was fully taken up with his duties at the theatre and the rehearsing of *Tannhäuser*, the first performance of which took place on the 19th October 1845. With that off his hands he could settle down in good earnest to turning his Marienbad Prose Sketch for *Lohengrin* into verse. This first form of the poem, the existence of which was unknown to the world in general until 1912, when the original manuscript came into a Berlin auction sale, he at once read to some of his Dresden friends. It met with their general approval, though Schumann was unable to see how the plan could be carried out musically, there being no provision for the usual operatic "numbers"; and Wagner found an impish delight in reading detached portions of it to him as if they were arias and cavatinas, whereupon Schumann smilingly declared himself satisfied.

2

The preliminary Prose Sketch, which bears the end-date "Marienbad, 3 August 1845", runs to nearly thirty pages of print.[1] In most essentials it corresponds to the present poem. When Wagner came to cast it into verse he of course kept a more observant eye on the stage picture as it would work out in an actual production; consequently we find him here and there expanding a detail or making some little change or other to throw it into higher relief. The musician in him also took a larger part in the planning now, providing opportunities at this point or that not only for emotional elaboration or intensification but for a deeper psychological probing of character.

For instance, in the Prose Sketch Telramund, after his account of Elsa's alleged murder of her brother Gottfried, tells the assembly that she is a "haughty visionary" who had behaved highhandedly towards him, her rightful wooer, as soon as she had disposed of Gottfried; she now saw the way clear to making herself the mistress of Brabant and marrying some secret lover. When Elsa is called upon by the King to meet the charges against her she merely replies that she is innocent and looks to some one whom she does not know and cannot name to come forward as her defender. The trumpets are sounded, and soon there comes into sight a swan-drawn boat with a knight in silver armour in it, leaning on his sword, helm on head, shield on arm, a horn hanging at his side. Both the dramatist and the musician in Wagner saw later how all this could be made more effective in the theatre than it had been in the Prose Sketch. So in the poem we are not merely *told* by Telramund that "traumselig ist die eitle Magd, die meine Hand voll Hochmuth von sich stiess" ("Given over to ecstatic

[1] It was published in full, for the first time, in the Bayreuth *Festspielführer* for 1936.

dreaming is the vain maid who so arrogantly rejected my hand"); we now actually *see* her, at her first appearance on the stage, in one of her semi-trances. "Speak, Elsa", says the King; "what have you to confide to me?", whereupon Elsa, "gazing fixedly and tranquilly before her, as if transfigured", describes, more to herself than to the others, how once, during her dark and lonely days of prayer, she had fallen into a trance in which she saw a knight approaching her who seemed the very symbol of purity, a golden horn at her belt, leaning upon his sword. This new handling of the situation served a triple purpose: it allowed for the insertion, in what before and after is only sober narrative, of the lovely monologue of Elsa ("Einsam in trüben Tagen"), it *shows* her, before them all, as a visionary, instead of her merely being *described* as one by Telramund, and, best of all, it added tenfold to the dramatic force of the later appearance of Lohengrin at the bend of the river—the King and the nobles can have no doubt now of her innocence and her supernatural protection, for here, in the flesh, is the very knight she had seen in her trance, the deliverer sent to her from heaven, garbed and accoutred exactly as she had described him.

3

In the Prose Sketch the first act ends thus, after Lohengrin has spared the life of the defeated Telramund: "Outburst of jubilation on all sides. Lohengrin is enthusiastically praised; Elsa falls on his breast in ecstasy; the King[1] blesses her. Despair of Friedrich and Ortrude." That Wagner already had his doubts about the effectiveness of this ending is shown by two interrogative jottings in the margin of the Sketch: "??Friedrich and Ortrude pronounced to have forfeited honour and banished: the King wants to invest Lohengrin with the kingdom of Brabant; he declines it, declaring

---

[1] In the Sketch he figures as "the Emperor". No doubt some one in Dresden pointed out to Wagner that this was historically inaccurate, Henry the Fowler never having formally assumed that title; so in the poem he is given his proper rank of "German King". Elsa, by the way, appears in the Sketch as Elsam, Ortrud as Ortrude, and Telramund as Count Friedrich von Telramunt.

that he wishes to be called merely Brabant's protector??". Wagner must soon have realised that all this would have lowered the emotional tension to the verge of anti-climax: the right ending was the one adopted later in the poem—a great ensemble of jubilation, flecked here and there by the despair of Telramund and the fury of the indomitable Ortrud.

We see the same keen sense of the stage at work in some portions of the second act, the same unerring perception of the best moment at which to bring in a particular stroke. The scene, for example, in which Ortrud tries to instil the poison of doubt into Elsa's mind is handled far more subtly in the poem than in the Sketch. In the latter we are shown the processes of Ortrud's plot-spinning in too great detail. Professing gratitude for Elsa's kindly treatment of her after her downfall, she throws out a hint of how she may be able to repay her; " 'she has been endowed with a peculiar gift of seeing more than ordinary mortals do; perhaps she may warn Elsam to be on her guard and not trust too blindly to her good fortune'. *Elsam:* 'What mean you by that?' Ortrude tries, by means of vague suggestions, to arouse doubts in her regarding the stranger: may she never regret having given him her trust, etc. Elsam counters with the expression of unconditioned confidence in him whom God has sent to her; his prohibition [with regard to her asking who he is and whence he came] is dear to her; never will she disobey it. *Ortrude:* 'O fortunate one, so will you never experience what may seem to you evil; may he reward you with the same trust, and never leave you in the same incomprehensible fashion in which he came'. Elsam, after a momentary shudder, quickly repeats her assurance of rapturous confidence. Ortrude checks herself and now takes the line of flattery, praise of her goodness, etc. Elsam invites her in; she will give her splendid garments, and they will go to Mass together, where Elsam will await the bridegroom to whom she is to be joined for ever. *Ortrude:* (to herself) 'Perhaps I can work upon her better through her pride' ". Whereupon the two go into the kemenate."[1]

All this, as Wagner must have seen when he came closer down to the problem of the actual staging, is not only too elaborate in

[1] The women's quarters in the palace.

itself but anticipates too much the dramatic later scene at the
minster, in which Telramund tries to stir up general suspicion
against Lohengrin. So in the poem he cuts the scene between
Ortrud and Elsa down to its barest essentials. Ortrud now merely
throws out a vague suggestion that she may be able, by her gift of
second sight, to preserve Elsa from some future evil—may not
this Lohengrin leave her by the operation of the same magic as
had brought him to her? That is all. Elsa answers her in kindly
wise, hoping that Ortrud too will one day find such happiness as
hers; and the further workings of Ortrud's mind are sufficiently
revealed in an aside of hers that accompanies the quiet raptures of
Elsa:

> *Ha! dieser Stolz, er soll mich lehren,*
> *wie ich bekämpfe ihre Treu':*
> *gen ihn will ich die Waffen kehren,*
> *durch ihren Hochmut werd' ihr Reu'!*

("Ha! From this pride of hers will I learn how to break down her
faith: against it I will turn my weapons, and her own arrogance
will be her undoing").

4

In the third scene of the second act Wagner's riper judgment
dictated the elision of an episode which, in the Prose Sketch,
smacks too much of conventional opera. There the Herald, after
having announced (as in the present opera) the degradation and
outlawry of Telramund and the wedding of Lohengrin and Elsa,
had launched out into a description of the coming festivities and
an enumeration of the benefits that will come to Brabant through
its new ruler—"Blessings and peace will come upon the land.
Every home shall know security; the fields will bear richly, so that
all the poor can dedicate themselves to the King for resistance to
the Huns; on the morrow, the day of the wedding, all shall be
armed for the march. The people express their delight, and praise
Lohengrin's coming and the blessings to be expected from his
rule: this hope for happiness under the saviour who has come to

them from afar assumes an exalted form; they see in him the wonder-worker, sent to them to create a heaven on earth for Brabant. The infirm and the blind are brought in, begging to be healed by him on his way to the church." All this, which would have been well enough in a Meyerbeer opera or in *Rienzi*, would have been out of place in *Lohengrin*, coming as it would at the point when the psychological tragedy inherent in the situation was just about to develop to its climax. By 1845 Wagner had travelled too far as a dramatist to revert to machine-made operatic conventions of this sort. So when he came to write his poem he dealt ruthlessly with this section of the Sketch, compressing it all into a few lines for the Herald and an answering cry of jubilation from the male chorus; and the action moves straight on to the meeting of Telramund and the four Brabantine knights who are not ill-disposed towards him in his disgrace.

Towards the end of the second act, at the point where Lohengrin, turning with an expression of confidence to Elsa, is dismayed to read in her face that Telramund and Ortrud have instilled something of their poison into her, Wagner has written in the margin of his Sketch "adagio"—a clear sign that even when he was engaged on the first draft of the scenario he saw it all in terms not only of stage action but of music. (Actually, in the opera, the tempo becomes andante moderato, after two or three pages of presto, at the point in question). And at the very end of the act we see once more how his imagination must have been constantly playing upon his material, moulding it, improving it, making every detail co-operate to the one great dramatic end. The final lines of the second act run thus in the Sketch: "*Lohengrin:* 'Hail, Elsam! Now let us go before God's altar!' All doubt is suddenly dissipated; with renewed enthusiasm they all cry, 'He is a knight of God!' The procession moves towards the church." But in the poem we have the touch which, the reader will remember, is so effective on the stage. The directions now run: "To the solemn sound of bells the King ascends the steps of the minster, Lohengrin on his left hand, Elsa on his right. As she reaches the top step her gaze falls on Ortrud below, who stretches out her hand to her threateningly; horrified, Elsa turns away and anxiously presses close to Lohengrin. He leads her into the minster as the curtain falls."[1]

5

In the third act Wagner made several changes with a view to tightening up the action. The more important of these are in the final scene. The reader will be acquainted with what is known in the concert room as "Lohengrin's Narration", in which the hero tells the King and the others of Monsalvat and his father Parzival and the brotherhood of the Grail. In the Prose Sketch he had made Lohengrin continue with a long account of how news had come to the brotherhood that a maiden was in distress; how they saw a swan approaching down the stream, drawing a boat by a golden chain; how, after Parzival had consulted the Grail for guidance, they learned that the swan was a human being, the victim of an enchantment, who would remain with them for a year; and how Lohengrin was sent out in the boat, with the Grail's blessing, to

[1] In the score of the opera the sense is the same as in the separate editions of the poem, but the wording is different: "Here the King and the bridal pair have reached the highest step of the minster; Elsa, deeply moved, turns to Lohengrin, who takes her in his arms. Still in his embrace, she looks timidly and anxiously down the steps to the right and perceives Ortrud, who raises her arm against her as if in triumph. Elsa averts her face in terror."

As regards both the text and the stage directions Wagner's scores often differ considerably from the poem as he printed it later in his Collected Works. The discrepancies, especially in the case of the *Mastersingers*, run into hundreds; and the question has frequently been debated which of the two versions should be taken as the definitive one. Do the variants in the scores represent the composer's second thoughts which override the first ones? If so, why, when he published the poems later in the Collected Edition, did he print these in their earlier form? The subject has been discussed at great length during the last forty years or so, with a copious quotation of instances and a vast amount of insistence on the superior claims of this reading or that. Ever and anon there goes up the cry for a "definitive edition" of the poems and the scores, to be achieved by the co-operation of a committee of experts. But the experts are in irreconcilable disagreement with each other on almost every point. The problem bristles with difficulties of all kinds, and, it is safe to say, will for ever remain insoluble. As it is, the text and the stage directions as they stand in the scores need to be constantly studied in connection with those of the poem in its "literary" form.

champion distressed innocence. Here Wagner was following closely the old epic of *Lohengrin*. But drama cannot indulge itself in the leisurely descriptions of epic; and so not a word of all this appears in the poem of the opera. But Wagner had not only worked it out in detail in the original version of the poem but actually set it all to music. On the 2nd July 1850, however, we find him writing to Liszt, who was making preparations for the first performance of the work in Weimar, "Give my opera as it is without cuts! Just one cut I myself prescribe: I want you to take out the second part of Lohengrin's Narration in the big final scene of the third act. After Lohengrin's words, 'Sein Ritter ich, bin Lohengrin genannt' ('Its knight am I, and Lohengrin my name') fifty-six bars are to be omitted, down to 'Wo ihr mit Gott mich alle landen saht' ('Where all of you saw me land in God's name'). I have many times performed the whole work to myself, and I am now convinced that this second section of the Narration can have only a chilling effect. The passage must also be omitted from the text-books."

He had already effected a similar piece of compression, to the decided benefit of the work, at the point immediately after the solo in the last act in which Lohengrin hands his sword, horn and ring to Elsa, bidding her give them to her brother if he returns. In the Sketch this had been followed by a long monologue for Ortrud, in which she vaunts her triumph over Elsa, for now that her rescuer is returning to Monsalvat her brother, transformed into a swan, can never shake off the enchantment Ortrud has laid on him. In the poem all this is compressed into a few lines. Then comes an episode that aptly illustrates a fact that has often to be borne in mind when we are listening to a performance of a Wagner opera; in the final process of alteration or compression he has omitted, or touched upon too lightly, some little point or other that only becomes fully clear to us after we have read his first Sketch. In the final version, after Ortrud's last jubilant cry of "Erfahrt, wie sich die Götter rächen, von deren Huld ihr euch gewandt!" ("Learn from this how the gods from whose protection ye have turned avenge themselves"), we have the stage direction, "Lohengrin, who has reached the bank, has heard what Ortrud says. He now sinks on his knees in silent prayer. The eyes

of all are riveted on him in tense expectation. Suddenly he perceives a white dove hovering over the boat; with a look of gratitude he springs up and loosens the Swan's chain, whereupon it
immediately sinks; in its place appears a beautiful youth garbed in
gleaming silver—Gottfried—whom Lohengrin lifts to the bank."[1]
To understand what was the nature of this silent prayer of Lohengrin we have to turn to the Sketch, where we read: "Lohengrin
kneels on the shore. 'Give me a sign, eternal God, that shameless
evil shall not mock at Thee! A sign of propitiation let me have
from Thee that I may lay as balsam upon the wound dealt to the
purest of beings by the sin of doubt. O Lord my God, hear me in
my humility' . . . Here his voice sinks to so soft a whisper that it is
hardly audible. Again he prays silently. Intense concentration [on
the part of the beholders]." It is out of love for Elsa, then, to
spare her the bitterest consequences of her sin of doubt, that in
the opera he "silently" prays for a sign from heaven; and the
spectator should bear this in mind as he watches the action.

Then comes a very curious feature of the Sketch. In the opera,
after his prayer Lohengrin calls out "Behold the Duke of Brabant,
who shall be your leader", and then leaps into the boat, which is
led away by the Swan. But in the Sketch we find this: "A soft
melody is heard, coming from the Swan:

> *Leb wohl, du wilde Wasserfluth,*
> *die mich so weit getragen hat;*
> *leb wohl, du Welle blank und rein,*
> *durch die mein weiss Gefieder glitt:*
> *am Ufer harrt mein Schwesterlein,*
> *das soll von mir getröstet sein.*

('Farewell, wild flood that has carried me so far. Farewell, pure
bright waves over which my white feathers have glided. On the
shore my sister awaits me; by me she shall be consoled'). A white
dove suddenly hovers over the boat", etc.

Wagner not only cast this episode into verse at the very time
when he was writing the Prose Sketch but set it to music later.

[1] There are a few trifling differences between the stage direction in the
poem and that in the score. For greater clearness' sake I have combined the
two.

But in the Composition Sketch the page in question bears the following note in his handwriting: "For reasons of dramatic economy I could not make use of this song of the Swan in my *Lohengrin* . . ." This jotting was evidently the draft of an inscription to his friend Frau Lydia Steche, into whose album he copied the discarded words and music of the song in August 1853. There can be no question that he was right in deleting this episode from his score; it could only have relaxed the dramatic tension just as it was mounting to its climax.

6

Though few of those connected with an ordinary performance of *Lohengrin*—spectators, conductor, singers, producer and so on—appear to be aware of it, the opera is rather more than the story of a virtuous first soprano, a noble tenor, a wicked second soprano, and a baritone of good intentions but easily led astray by his wife. To the average performer and opera-goer the King, the nobles and all the rest of the ensemble are merely lay figures, theatrical devices for padding out the drama in the moments when the principal characters are not in action, pretexts for a little solo or two and a big chorus now and then, especially at the end of an act—all in the accredited style of opera construction. Wagner's background to the Lohengrin-Elsa story, however, is not simply so much operatic machinery. It is historical, and the interest of the action is increased if this is realised by the producer and borne in mind by the audience.

Henry I of Saxony (Henry the Fowler) reigned from 919 to 936. He was an energetic upholder of German rights and a fighter for German unity, features that commend him to the affections of the Germans of our own epoch. He set his face against the pretensions of the Roman Church to interfere in German politics, refused to accept his crown from the hands of the Archbishop of Mainz, and reserved to himself the right of appointing bishops. Saxony at that time was the most considerable of the German states. By wise rule and power of arms he made his own duchy internally strong, while externally he fought to save Germany from being overrun by alien hordes, in particular the Hungarians, who at that time were a formidable military power. Saxony was a relatively new state, based largely on the village community. Henry persuaded his people to aggregate into towns, and then to fortify them; and to win time for the realisation of these and other plans, such as the building of a number of strongholds, he concluded a nine years' truce with the Hungarians in 924, at the cost of an annual tribute. Then he brought in a new system of conscription for national defence and trained his men in the latest developments of the art of war; so that when the truce expired in 933 he was able to face the dreaded Hungarians on equal terms and defeat them, thus saving the German lands from the eastern menace of that period. Secure on this frontier, Henry now turned his attention to the west, extending his rule over the territories round and beyond the mouth of the Elbe. He was, in fact, not a king of opera but a very important historical person; though Wagner was incorrect in describing him, in his Prose Sketch, as the Kaiser, he was given the unofficial title of "Pater Patriae et Imperator Romanorum", and in point of fact he was "German Emperor" in everything but name.

In the opening scene of the opera we see him in Brabant; the pact with the Hungarians is nearing its end, war is imminent, and Henry has come to Antwerp to try to persuade the Brabant nobles and people, in their own interest, to take up arms with him against the eastern peril. They receive him cautiously; it is only after Lohengrin has appeared miraculously among them and been accepted as their protector that they range themselves enthusiastically on the side of the Saxon king. Wagner gives us in the third scene of his second act a hint of this holding back, a hint which always passes unnoticed by the spectator who is not thoroughly familiar with the text. After the Herald's proclamation of the ban upon Telramund and the appointment of the Knight of the Swan as Protector of Brabant, four nobles detach themselves from the jubilant crowd and discuss the new régime furtively and without enthusiasm. "You hear?" says one of them; "he [the King] means to take us outside our own borders." "To march against an enemy", says the second, "who has never yet threatened us!" "So bold a venture may not turn out well for him", says the third; and the fourth, "But who can hold out against him if he orders us to

march?" Telramund overhears them and succeeds in working
upon them; these indeed, are the four disaffected nobles who make
the attempt upon Lohengrin's life in the third act. This little
episode, which occupies only some eleven bars, is often omitted
in performance. This is typical of the measure of understanding
the average modern producer has of the drama of the Wagnerian
work he is supposed to be producing.

7

The antithesis of the Saxon and the Brabantine worlds, then, is
a dramatic point that should be made as clear as possible to the
spectator. Apparently this was never properly done, or perhaps
even attempted, until the Bayreuth performances of 1894, which
set the model, in many ways, for the impressive production of
1936. In the first and the final scene of the opera there should be
the clearest distinction to the eye between the costumes and the
weapons of the Saxons and those of the Brabantines. One need
not press the point too far; perhaps some of the historical niceties
of the 1894 production would have escaped the notice of all but
specialists in the manners and costumes of the tenth century. But
that a visible differentiation shall be made, and perceived by the
spectator throughout the opera, is essential to a real understanding
of the milieu of the drama. The importance which Wagner himself attached to this matter is shown in various little ways.

In the final scene the King, the nobles and the people are
assembled once more in the same setting as that of the opening of
the first act. Among the stage directions for the final scene we
find this: "Gradually, from various quarters, the Brabantine
Heerbann[1] pours upon the stage. Each section is headed by a
Count, whose banner-bearer plants his standard in the ground,
about which the others gather; children carry the shield and spear
of the Count; servitors lead the chargers aside. When the Brabantines have all entered, King Henry comes in from the left with his
Heerbann; all are in full war-equipment." These are the directions
in the poem. In the score they read thus: "A Count enters with
his adherents, dismounts, and gives his horse to a servitor; two

[1] The "arrière-ban", or levy.

noble youths carry his shield and spear. He plants his standard, round which his adherents take up their positions." This procedure is repeated several times while the martial music goes on, until finally the King enters with his Saxon troops. These earlier arrivals are in fact the Brabantines, who, after the triumphal advent of Lohengrin, have responded to the King's call to arms: one significant sentence in the stage directions as given in the score runs thus: "The Counts and nobles greet each other, examine and praise their weapons, and so forth". The intention of it all is to make it clear to the spectator that the Brabantines have at last come in on the Saxon side. But Wagner's fidelity to history does not end here. The horses which the Brabantines bring with them are not merely there for stage effect: they are meant to give a touch of real history to the action. The Hungarians had been formidable by virtue of their light cavalry; Henry had defeated them, in the last trial of strength between them, by the heavy cavalry he had trained during the nine years' truce.

Should there be any doubt in the reader's mind whether Wagner attached so much importance as this to the historical point, he has only to look at a letter from the composer to Hans von Bülow of June 1867. On the 16th of that month there had been a grand new production of *Lohengrin* in Munich, under Bülow, by command of King Ludwig. The work was to be given exactly as Wagner had planned it. On the 27th we find him writing to Bülow: "I hear, incidentally, that his Majesty has given orders that horses are not to appear in the third act. You are acquainted with my reasons for insisting on these in a gathering entirely of mounted men. I should have desired these horses to be caparisoned in conformity with the manner of the period. Since not only has there been no royal command to that effect but the horses are to be cut out altogether, I now request you to omit also the whole of the music that accompanies this gathering, for now it ceases to have any meaning; and as the royal command was that the score should be given complete, this omission must in duty bound be notified to his Majesty." He was prepared, then, to face the risk of offending the King by omitting the long orchestral introduction to the final episode of the opera if the scene of the Heerbann were not staged as he had originally planned it—with horses, or at least with a suggestion of them as part and parcel of the Brabantine contribution to Henry's army. So important did it appear to him that the spectator should grasp the significance of the contemporary political background of the story he was telling!

8

The legend of Lohengrin and the Swan has a long and interesting history, but as most of it has no bearing on Wagner's opera we need not trace the evolution of it in detail here. The essential points are these. From time immemorial there had existed stories of heroes who came to the aid of virtuous maidens in distress, stories of mysterious swans coming from afar, stories of children who had been transformed by magic into swans, stories of knights whose device was a swan, stories of children or heroes or gods who drift to some land or other in a boat (sometimes, but not necessarily, drawn by a swan), and so on. Episodes from all these stories gradually coalesced, and, as the final stage in the process, some time in the twelfth century the figure of a Swan-Knight was worked into the legend of the Grail. We first find this done in the concluding pages of Wolfram von Eschenbach's epic *Parzival*, which dates from about the beginning of the thirteenth century[1]; but there are grounds for conjecturing that this particular coalescence may have been effected in the lost poem on the Parzival subject which Wolfram alleges to have been the source of his own.

In the final section of Wolfram's poem we see Parzival, now the custodian of the Grail, appointing his son Kardeiss to rule over his territory of Brobarz, while he himself retires with his other son, Loherangrin, to Monsalvat.[2] Loherangrin "is chosen to serve the Grail", Parzival tells the boy's mother Kondwiramuir; "to it he shall be dedicated". One day there comes to Monsalvat news of a princess of Brabant, pure and unworldly, who had many kingly and knightly wooers, and was blamed by her people for not choosing one of them for consort and ruler of the land. At

[1] The epic will be discussed in the chapter on *Parsifal*.
[2] The name Loherangrin (elsewhere Lorangrime, Lohengârin, etc.) seems to have been taken from a French epic: "Loherens Garin" signifies Garin of Lorraine (Lothringen).

last she called them together and declared that she would give her hand only to one sent to her by God. Such a one, the brave, handsome, spotless young Loherangrin, comes to her from Monsalvat; a swan bears him across the waters to Antwerp in a boat. At his first meeting with the princess he had told her, before them all, that he would have to leave her if ever she sought to learn who he is and whence he came, a condition which she accepted. They had many fair children, and for years he ruled the land wisely and defended it against its enemies. But one day the princess asked the fatal question, whereupon the swan appeared again, and Loherangrin, in great distress, departed as he had come, leaving with her a horn, a ring and a sword. The whole story occupies no more than a few score lines of the *Parzival* epic; and Wolfram neither gives the Brabant princess a name nor associates her in any way with a brother who had been laid under an enchantment. Loherangrin goes to her aid simply in accordance with the Grail's rule of service, and when she sins against the divine nature of the Grail by bringing its chosen representative down to common earth through her question, his mission is at an end and he must leave her.

The later adventures of Loherangrin are set forth in another poem, *Der jüngere Titurel*, which was formerly attributed to Wolfram von Eschenbach, but is now credited to one Albert von Schaffenburg. In this poem, Loherangrin goes to Lyzaborie (Luxemburg?) and marries one Belaye, who loves him so much that she cannot endure separation from him. One of her maids tells her that she can secure his constancy by cutting off a morsel of his flesh and eating it. This the horrified Belaye cannot bring herself to do, so her parents, to whom the maidservant has slandered Loherangrin, plot to mutilate him for the purpose. One night he dreams of a thousand swords being brandished over him. He awakes and slays more than a hundred of his assailants. But they are too many for him; he is wounded in the left arm and dies; and Belaye too dies of grief for his loss.

9

Wagner must have been familiar with most of the twelfth and thirteenth century variants of the Lohengrin legend, for his poem is a skilful amalgam of incidents and motives from various quarters. We need consider here only two of the main sources, the Walloon-French epic of *Le Chevalier au Cygne,* belonging to the second half of the thirteenth century, and the German epic *Lohengrin,* which dates from about 1260 and the author of which is unknown. In the former, Oriant, king of the island of Lillefort, marries the beautiful Beatrix, who, during his absence, gives birth to a daughter and six sons: these the King's mother, the sorceress Matabrune, who hates Beatrix, sends by a servant into the forest to be murdered; and on the King's return she accuses Beatrix of having been unfaithful to him. The children, however, have not been killed but only abandoned. They are cared for by a hermit, who gives the eldest boy his own name, Helyas. The King, out hunting one day, finds these seven children, and on his return speaks of them to Matabrune, who, realising who they are, sends another of his men to make away with them. When he arrives, the young Helyas is absent with the hermit; pitying the others, the emissary merely takes away with him the silver chains they wear upon their necks, whereupon they change into swans and fly away. Matabrune now makes fresh charges against Beatrix, who is condemned to death by the King unless some champion comes forward to vouch for her innocence. In response to her prayers God sends the young Helyas to Lillefort, where he vanquishes the accuser put forward by Matabrune. (Before he leaves the forest the hermit predicts that from the line of Helyas shall spring Godfrey of Bouillon). Six swans alight on the water near the castle, and when Helyas puts round their necks the chains the servant had taken, five of them are transformed into King Oriant's children again; the sixth, however, Esmeré, whose chain had been melted down by the King's goldsmith and made into a cup, remains a swan.

One day Helyas sees a swan—his brother Esmeré—approaching the palace, drawing a boat; and he knows that this is a summons to him from heaven to depart with the swan in search of adventures. This he does after his father has given him a magic golden horn. Drawn by the swan he makes his way to Nimwegen, where, at the court of the Emperor Otto, the Count of Blancquebourc (Blankenbourg) is claiming the heritage of the Duchy of Bouillon, alleging that his brother, the previous Duke, has been poisoned by his Duchess, Clarisse. As usual, the issue is to be decided by combat. The swan and the boat appear in the river: Helyas champions the innocent Duchess's cause, weds her daughter Ydain, and becomes the ruler of Brabant; their daughter Ydain, we are solemnly assured, was the mother of the famous crusader Godfrey of Bouillon. It is not until seven years after the wedding of Helyas and Ydain that the latter asks the forbidden question about her husband's name and lineage; then the sorrowing Helyas gives her into the care of the Emperor and departs to Lillefort with the swan Esmeré, who is restored to human form again and baptized. After various strange adventures Helyas becomes a monk, is discovered by some of his vassals from Bouillon, and dies in his wife's arms. (It is conjectured that this association of the house of Bouillon with the Chevalier of the Swan was invented to fill up an awkward gap, due to a misalliance, in the pedigree of the Counts of Bouillon).

10

Comparatively little of this naive story, of course, could be of any use to Wagner: it will be observed, too, that in *Le Chevalier au Cygne* it is not the injured Duchess but her daughter whom the hero marries, there is no association of Helyas with Monsalvat, and the union of the pair lasts seven years. Wagner found material more to his purpose in the German epic *Lohengrin*, where the long story is supposed to be told by Wolfram von Eschenbach as his contribution to the routing of Klingsor at the Contest on the Wartburg. It was here that Wagner found the names of Elsa and Count Friedrich von Telramund, and the association of Lohengrin with King Henry the Fowler. In the German poem the dying Duke of Brabant has entrusted the guardianship of his kingdom and of his daughter Elsa to the brave and respected Telramund; but when she refuses his hand he claims the kingdom and appeals to the Emperor for judgment in his favour. Attached to Elsa's rosary is a little golden bell which she had taken from the leg of a lamed falcon that had alighted near the castle; and whenever she wept for grief this bell would ring. One day the sound of it came to the court of King Arthur at Monsalvat, and it rang without ceasing until the knights learned from a writing on the Grail that in Brabant there was a pure maiden in great distress, to whose aid the young and spotless Lohengrin must be sent. As he is about to mount his horse a wild swan appears, drawing a boat; and in this Lohengrin embarks, taking with him neither horse nor food. After some days he arrives at Antwerp, where the swan departs.

Lohengrin is received with great honour by Elsa and the people of Brabant, and after many festivities they go to Mainz, where, before the Emperor, Lohengrin vanquishes Telramund— who is condemned to execution—and marries Elsa, having first exacted from her a promise that she will never seek to know who he is and whence he came. They live happily together for many years, during which Lohengrin fights with the Emperor against first the Hungarians, then the Saracens. The catastrophe comes at a great jousting at Cologne after the Emperor's return, in which Lohengrin defeats the Duke of Cleves and breaks his arm. Thirsting for revenge, the Duchess stirs up the people's suspicions with regard to this mysterious hero from afar: who is he? whence comes he? is he of noble origin? The poison works in Elsa, who at last, disregarding Lohengrin's warnings, asks him the fatal question. Thereupon, before the Emperor and the court at Antwerp, he declares that he comes from Monsalvat, that his father Parzival is the custodian of the Grail, that his own name is Lohengrin, that he had been sent to Brabant by the Grail's command, taking with him a sword and horn given him by his father, and a ring, the gift of his mother, that Elsa has broken her promise not to question him about these things, and that now he must leave her for ever. The swan appears in the river: Lohengrin commends his wife and children and kingdom to the Emperor's care, steps into the boat, and is seen by them no more.

II

Here also, it will be seen, Wagner's mediaeval source supplied him with nothing more than the general outline and the raw material for a possible dramatic subject. He had to do a great deal in the way of selection, condensation and adaptation before the shapeless mass could take operatic form. In particular he had to create entirely the striking figure of Ortrud out of the faint hint afforded him by the character of the Duchess of Cleves in the German epic. Ortrud becomes the *fons et origo* of the ultimate disaster. Wagner makes her the antithesis of all that Elsa stands for—the woman incapable of love set over against the woman who is all love, the old Germanic paganism in implacable opposition to the new Christianity. Telramund, weak but not in himself evil, is only a pawn in the great game the masterful Ortrud is playing.

And there is one point that is not made entirely clear in the Wagnerian poem but should never be lost sight of by the spectator. Humourists have made delighted play with the notion of a woman simple enough to marry a man without knowing his name or antecedents and being coldly abandoned by him because in the end her curiosity gets the better of her discretion. But to look at the matter in that simple unimaginative way is to betray one's ignorance of the nature and the reason of the prohibition laid by Lohengrin upon Elsa. In Wolfram von Eschenbach's epic grief immeasurable had come upon the young Parzival and upon the land because the untutored boy, on his first entry into the castle of the Grail, had failed to ask a simple question of the suffering Amfortas.[1] From that event has come a double reason for Lohengrin's silence about himself. In the first place, since that prime failure of Parzival the Grail brooks no questioning of those consecrated to its service. (Wagner has to pass that point by in silence because to have made it clear would have meant a great deal of explanation—the telling, indeed, of the whole previous story of Parzival and the Grail). In the second place, it is a condition of the Grail's service to the unhappy world of men that while its emissaries may descend to it for noble ends they shall not become part of it. They represent a spiritual order whose service and whose motives must be accepted with unquestioning faith.

The motive of trouble ensuing from the indiscreet asking for a name occurs frequently in ancient myths; for primitive humanity the name was part of the man or the thing, and to learn the one

[1] For the meaning of this see the introduction to the chapter on *Parsifal*.

was to acquire a certain power over the other. But Wagner is not using the motive with any such primitive connotation as this. He himself has told us, in *A Communication to my Friends*, that he saw in the Lohengrin prohibition the counterpart of that in the story of Zeus and Semele. The god, for love of the mortal woman, had assumed human shape. But when, having realised that for all his love and hers she does not know him in his true being, Semele asks the god to reveal himself to her as he really is, Zeus knows, as Wagner puts it, that on the revelation of his true substance he must leave her; "he himself suffers from this knowledge, from the compulsion to destroy her the moment he complies with her desire", and when he shows himself to her in all the splendour of his godhead he signs not only his own death-warrant but hers. We need not follow Wagner in all his ingenious elucidations of the meaning of the myth and his psycho-analysis of love and woman as he conceived them to be: it is sufficient for us to have a better understanding of what Lohengrin's prohibition really means than those do who regard it as only a rather childish relic of a fairy tale.

12

As we have seen, Wagner completed the Prose Sketch for the opera in Marienbad on the 3rd August 1845, and set to work at the poem in Dresden towards the end of October. The first draft of this (dated 27th November 1845), which is now in some private collection or other, has not yet been published in its entirety; but extracts from it, showing some of the variants between it and the final poem, were given in an article by Julius Kapp in *Die Musik* in 1912, at the time when the manuscript was offered for sale by auction in Berlin. It is clear that the poem in its first form followed precisely the scenario of the Prose Sketch, which was printed for the first time in 1936; and the main differences between Wagner's first conception of the subject and his final handling of it have been set forth in the preceding pages of the present chapter.

The manuscript of the Sketch supplies one more proof of the fact, vital to our understanding of Wagner, that even while drafting the first prose outline of an opera he was already seeing the situations and the characters in terms of music. On the margin of one of the pages of the manuscript we find the following musical jotting :

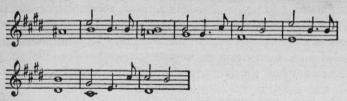

for an episode in the duet between Lohengrin and Elsa in the third act, which in the opera takes the shape shown in our example No. 46. It is a mistake to assume, as is generally done, that the sometimes crude form in which certain Wagnerian themes make their first appearance in some sketch or other indicates that this was a form that seemed to him adequate at the time, and that he gradually hammered it into a better shape later. The truth is that the first jotting was intended merely as a shorthand memorandum of the line and the harmony in general to be followed by the music in its final elaboration. In the present instance the A sharp in the first bar is clearly to fix a modulatory point; the theme was to begin in bar two as a return to the main key of E major after a hint of a modulation away from it. At the time the musical jotting was made not a line of the poem had been written; all that Wagner had before him in the Prose Sketch was an outline of Elsa's response to Lohengrin: "Elsam schildert ihm in entzückter Rührung das unaussprechliche Glück, das ihr durch ihn zu Theil geworden; wie sie vor Dank, vor gränzenloser Liebe vergehen möchte". ("Elsa, deeply moved, describes in ecstatic terms the happiness that has come to her through him, how she could die of gratitude, of the sense of boundless love"). In the poem this became:

Fühl' ich zu dir so süss mein Herz entbrennen,
Athme ich Wonnen, die mir Gott verleiht.

The musical idea, then, was in Wagner's mind, complete in rhythm and harmony, before the words—which we erroneously assume to have generated the music—were in being.

Wagner began his composition with the third act, the music of which was finished on the 5th March 1847. The first act was then taken in hand and finished on the 8th June; the third was completed on the 2nd August, the prelude to the opera being written on the 28th of that month. The orchestral score occupied him until the end of March 1848. The work was first produced in Weimar, under Liszt, on the 28th August 1850, with the following casting of the principal parts:

Lohengrin	Beck.
Elsa	Aghte.
Ortrud	Fasztlinger.
Telramund	Feodor von Milde.
King Heinrich	Höfer.

Wagner, who had had to fly from Dresden in May 1849 because of his complicity in the insurrection in the Saxon capital, did not hear his work until the 15th May 1861, in Vienna.

13

The prelude to *Lohengrin* was the early Wagner's finest achievement of the kind both in expression and in form. While it is thematically related to some extent to the drama it is neither a mere string of melodies from the score nor an attempt, as in *The Flying Dutchman* and *Tannhäuser* overtures, to tell the story of the opera by the succession and interplay of leading motives. In the *Lohengrin* prelude he works for the first time not on exterior but interior lines, as it were. The sole subject of it is the mystic Grail, the nature and being of it, its descent to the mundane sphere, its gradual revelation of its spiritual glory, then its gradual return to whence it had come. Wagner's own programmatic elucidation of it cannot be bettered:

"Out of the clear blue ether of the sky there seems to condense a wonderful yet at first hardly perceptible vision; and out of this there gradually emerges, ever more and more clearly, an angel host bearing in its midst the sacred Grail. As it approaches earth it pours out exquisite odours, like streams of gold, ravishing the senses of the beholder. The glory of the vision grows and grows until it seems as if the rapture must be shattered and dispersed by the very vehemence of its own expansion. The vision draws nearer, and the climax is reached when at last the Grail is revealed in all its glorious reality, radiating fiery beams and shaking the soul with emotion. The beholder sinks on his knees in adoring self-annihilation. The Grail pours out its light on him like a benediction and consecrates him to its service; then the flames gradually die away, and the angel host soars up again to the ethereal heights in tender joy, having made pure once more the hearts of men by the sacred blessing of the Grail.''

Some quiet reiterations of the chord of A major in upper strings, flutes and oboes having raised us at the outset into the rarefied upper air, the divided violins give out the theme of the Grail:

the falling second shown in bar two being more specifically related in the opera to the swan that is the material symbol of the Grail's commission to Lohengrin to go to the aid of Elsa. The Grail motive is continued for a further four or five bars along the same lines:

As it gradually draws nearer to the world of men it repeats itself on another plane (this time in the key of E major) in the middle

wood wind, with delicate violin embroideries. After a long slow
descent it begins to ascend again in a variant of itself:

the stressed notes in the second and third bars of the quotation
being of particular importance in the texture. Slowly the theme
develops itself in solider harmonic masses and richer colours,
always festooned with the same decorative figures, until, having
touched the lowest point of its windings, it gathers itself up
again for another great ascent, this time approaching the basic A
major by way of D major, with the melody standing out in all
the majesty of trumpets, trombones and tuba:

The actual climax comes at the opening of the fourth full bar of
our quotation, where the kettledrums and cymbals strike in with
arresting effect. This is the point at which we may visualise the
Grail as revealing itself for a moment to the eyes of mortals in the
blinding fulness of its spiritual splendour. Once more, as will be
seen in the latter part of No. 4, it soars aloft into its own rarefied
atmosphere; then, after a long downward sweep of the melody:

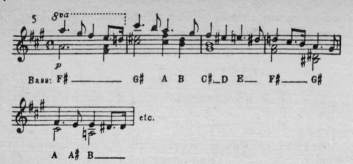

it fades away in the distance in the tenuous violin harmonies of the commencement.

The prelude is perfect in its fusion of musical theme and dramatic meaning, its harmonious design, and its choice of the moment for releasing its maximum of energy. The thunderous chord in No. 4 to which reference has been made above sets free all the forces that have been slowly accumulating inside the music from the first note of the prelude, and what follows is the natural ebb of the preceding flow. There is a law in certain species of musical design—not a law, of course, to which composers consciously conform but a procedure which they follow intuitively— that might be called the law of two-thirds, the time-period that follows the climax being to the time-period of the ascent to the climax numerically as one to two. The peak-point, of course, may be a trifle more or a trifle less on this side or that of the mathematical 2 : 1; a bar or two one way or the other makes no perceptible difference over a total time-stretch of several minutes.[1] In the *Lohengrin* prelude the pivotal point comes with almost mathematical exactitude. The total length of the prelude is 75 bars; the climactic chord comes in bar 54; at the slow pace of the music the time-relation of the two sections is as near as makes no matter 2 : 1.

14

With the rising of the curtain we necessarily sink for a time to a lower musical plane: Wagner now has to explain to us the events

[1] More will be said on this subject of ascent-climax-descent in our analysis of the prelude to *Tristan*.

precedent to the opera that have brought the action to the point at which the drama opens, and this can only be done, working as he still is with the conventional opera apparatus of the period, by means of a pedestrian exposition in quasi-recitative.

The scene is a meadow on the banks of the Scheldt, near Antwerp. Under a judgment oak sits King Heinrich, flanked by Counts and nobles of the Saxon armed levy. Opposite these are Counts and nobles of Brabant, headed by Friedrich von Telramund, by whose side is his wife Ortrud. At a sign from the King's Herald four trumpeters blow a summons, after which the Herald explains to the Brabantines that the German King has come to parley with them on affairs of state. Heinrich tells them that his land and theirs are once more threatened by the Hungarian hordes. By force of arms he had been able to impose on them a nine years' truce, which he has used to strengthen the Saxon defences, building castles, fortifying towns, training men. The truce has expired, and once more the eastern hordes are clamouring for tribute. Now is the time to decide for good the age-old question—which is to rule, East or West? If each Germanic land does its duty now the menace can be met—a sentiment which is greeted by the Saxon group with a clashing of their weapons and a cry of "Arise for the honour of the German land!"

The King goes on to say that he had come to Antwerp to invite the Brabantines to a military concentration at Mainz, but to his sorrow he finds them disorganised and leaderless, one faction at feud with another. So now he calls on Friedrich von Telramund, whom he knows to be a brave and honourable knight, to explain the cause of this disunion. Telramund does so. It appears that when the late Duke of Brabant was dying he had appointed Telramund guardian of his daughter Elsa and his son Gottfried, and Friedrich had tended them with loyal care. But one day he learned that Elsa had gone into the forest with the boy and returned alone, feigning anxiety for news of him, the child, she had said, having strayed from her side and not been seen again. Search for him had been fruitless; and when Telramund questioned Elsa more closely her pallor and trembling betrayed the secret of her crime. Filled with loathing, he had renounced the right given him by her father to claim her hand and had chosen for wife Ortrud, daughter of the prince of Friesland. Advancing a few steps, to the accompaniment of a figure in striding octaves of a type which Wagner will handle much better when he comes to portray his Wotan:

Telramund solemnly accuses Elsa of the murder of her brother and claims for himself the kingdom of Brabant, he being nearest of kin to the late Duke, and Ortrud a descendant of the one-time rulers of Friesland.

15

The bystanders comment on the story in awestruck tones. The King asks how Elsa could have brought herself to the commission of such a crime; and Telramund explains that she is a moonstruck visionary, always lost in dreams, and moreover possessed by a guilty passion for some man or other whom she hopes to take openly for lover once the kingdom has passed into her hands. The King, with a prayer to heaven for guidance, orders her to be brought before him for trial: he constitutes the place a court of justice by hanging his shield on the oak-tree, not to be removed thence until he has pronounced judgment at once stern and merciful. The warriors all draw their swords, the Saxons thrusting theirs into the ground, the Brabantines laying theirs flat on the earth in front of them. Then the Herald summons Elsa to appear.

For a little time after her entry on the scene she remains with her attendant ladies in the background; then she advances slowly and timidly, accompanied by a plaintive phrase in oboe and cor anglais:

which is completed in this fashion:

as the bystanders comment sympathetically on the innocence of her demeanour. The King asks her if she is Elsa of Brabant, and she silently bows her head, still to the strains of No. 7 and No. 8, which continue to accompany her as she signifies, without speaking, in reply to the King's further questions, that she is aware of the accusation brought against her but will make no answer to it. When at last she breaks her long silence it is simply to murmur to herself, as if her thoughts were far away, "My hapless brother!" Gently the King exhorts her to trust him with her story; and she tells them all:

how one day, lost in sorrowful dreams, she had poured out her soul to God in a lament that floated high in the air:

then it had drifted away and she had sunk into a sweet sleep.

The King tries gently to recall her to a sense of her present position, but she does not hear him. Her expression changes from one of dreamy ecstasy to the fanatical exaltation of the visionary, the Grail theme vibrates softly in the upper air, and she tells the further story of her dream that day. She had seen a knight in splendid armour, who seemed purity incarnate, leaning on his sword, a golden horn at his side:

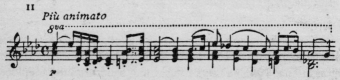

He had come towards her and in courtly wise consoled her; he it is who shall be her defender now. This she sings ecstatically to the theme of the opening of No. 8, which now, however, takes a confident close in place of its former one of melancholy and frustration as she says, "This is the knight I choose: he shall fight for me":

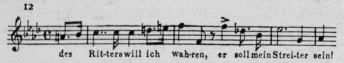

and once more she appears to lose herself in a blissful dream.

The King has been impressed by her mystical self-confidence, but Telramund passionately declares that he is not her dupe: has she not herself proved the truth of his accusation by this admission of a paramour? But he scorns to have his cause decided by any judgment but that of arms. He reminds the King of the gallant service he had rendered him in the war with the Danes: let him now grant him permission to vindicate his honour with his sword. God shall decide, says the King. Drawing his sword and thrusting it into the earth in front of him, to the accompaniment of an imperious figure in the heavy brass:

he puts the formal questions to accuser and accused: "Wilt thou,
Friedrich Count von Telramund, have thy cause tried in mortal
combat before the throne of God? . . . Art thou, Elsa of Brabant,
willing that thy cause shall be decided in combat?" Each returns a
"Yes!", Telramund vehemently, Elsa quietly, without raising her
eyes.

16

Telramund demands the name of her champion. The music of
her vision is heard once more in the orchestra as she repeats firmly
her assurance (No. 11) that the shining knight who had appeared
to her then will fight for her now; and on this champion sent her
from heaven she will bestow her hand and her kingdom.

At the command of the King the Herald advances with four
trumpeters, who take up their stand at the four points of the com-
pass of the central space and sound a summons; after which the
Herald calls on whoever chooses to accept the challenge to fight
on behalf of Elsa of Brabant to come forward. There is no answer.
Elsa's air of tranquil confidence now changes to one of uneasy
expectation, and we get a foretaste of the later Wagner of the *Ring*
in a phrase that projects itself in the dark colour of the bass
clarinet:

Telramund taunts Elsa with her inability to produce her champion,
whereupon she approaches the King timidly with a request that he
shall be summoned again: "perhaps", says the dreamer innocently,
"he dwells so far away that he has not heard."

The summons is repeated by the trumpeters and the Herald,
but again with no response—only a repetition of the uneasy No.
14 in the clarinet. Elsa falls on her knees and prays fervently to

heaven to send her the rescuer it had promised her in her dream. The prayer is answered. As the tempo increases, No. 11, the motive of Lohengrin, is heard in the trumpets, softly, as if coming from afar. The bystanders nearest the river bank catch sight of a figure in a boat, drawn by a swan, in the further reaches of the stream. They draw the attention of the others to this wonder; and the excitement increases as the knight gradually becomes visible to them all and they comment eagerly on his beauty and the splendour of his armour. For a little while Lohengrin has been visible to the audience also; then we lose sight of him at a bend in the river, his slow approach being suggested to us only by the greater and greater excitement of the comments of the chorus, men and women, who have all rushed to the back of the scene for a better view of the unheard-of marvel. In the foreground only the King, Elsa, Friedrich and Ortrud remain: the King, from his raised place, looks down the river: Friedrich and Ortrud are rooted to the spot in amazement: Elsa stands motionless, thrilled by the cries of the bystanders, but not daring to look around. As the excitement piles up to a great climax in the orchestra Elsa's women fall on their knees with a cry of gratitude to heaven for its intervention on behalf of the innocent.

With No. 11 ringing out in the orchestra more commandingly than ever and the chorus hailing the hero sent by God, the boat reaches the river bank in the centre background. In it stands Lohengrin, in gleaming silver armour, helmet on head, shield on his back, a small golden horn hanging by his side, leaning on his sword. Elsa, who had turned round as the chorus sent up a great cry of thankfulness:

gives a startled cry at this coming to reality of her vision. Telramund is too astonished to move; and even Ortrud, whose proud demeanour had shown that her courage had so far not deserted her, is perplexed and dismayed at the sight of the swan. The others uncover their heads in awe.

As Lohengrin makes the first movement to leave the boat a tense silence falls on them all. Softly the violins, in their upper register, give out the theme of the Grail, and in an unaccompanied monologue he addresses the swan:

thanking it for having brought him to his goal, and bidding it return, its task accomplished, to the serene sphere from which he and it had come. The tiny figure shown at A in our musical example No. 1 now takes the definite shape of a Swan motive in oboe and clarinet:

as Lohengrin murmurs his farewell to his companion, on which his gaze lingers sadly and tenderly for a while as the swan turns the boat round and slowly swims away up the stream. The chorus, led by Elsa's women and some of the tenors, murmur admiration of this visitant from an unknown land:

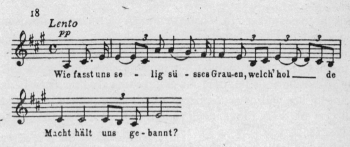

Wagner's marking for the ensemble is "as delicately as possible".

17

Meanwhile Lohengrin has left the bank and advanced slowly and solemnly towards the King, to whom he makes his obeisance, and to whose German cause he wishes success and eternal glory. "It must be heaven that has sent thee here", replies King Heinrich. To the solemn strains of No. 1 and No. 3 the knight announces that he has come to do battle for a maiden accused of a crime: then, turning to Elsa, he asks if she will accept him as her defender. His voice wakens her from the trance into which she had fallen again; now she throws herself ecstatically at his feet, hailing him as her rescuer and offering him herself and all she has to bestow. The Grail music throbs in the air once more as he asks if she will be his wife. She humbly consents. Then comes the crucial motive of the drama: his next question is, if she and her lands are to become his and he is never to leave her, will she make him a solemn promise—never to ask him whence he came, or what his name and race:

(This motive had been foreshadowed in an oath-taking chorus in a work sketched by Wagner in 1837).

Softly, half unconsciously, she gives her word. He repeats the all-important question with still greater urgency, and again, this time with rapturous fervour, she assures him that the trust he is placing in her will never be betrayed. He takes her to his breast with a cry of "Elsa, I love thee!", and the chorus repeat the heartfelt No. 18.

Lohengrin leads Elsa forward and gives her into the care of the King; then, turning to the others, he declares that the princess of

Brabant is free of all guilt, and that Friedrich von Telramund has sworn falsely. The nobles try to avert a conflict, but Telramund will not yield; whatever sorcery may have brought this stranger here, he says boldly, he does not fear his threats, for he himself has sworn truly. So the ring is set for the combat. Three Saxon nobles advance for Lohengrin, three Brabantines for Friedrich; they mark out a circle and define it by thrusting their spears in the ground. The Herald warns everyone against interference in the fight: the freeman who offends will pay for it with the loss of a hand, the serf with his head. Then, advancing to the centre with great solemnity, the King prays to heaven to look down and see that justice is done; and the concluding strain of his prayer:

Des Rei-nen Arm gieb Hel-den-kraft, des
Fal-schen Stär-ke sei er-schlafft:

is taken up by the assembly and developed into an impressive ensemble. Elsa and Lohengrin commend their cause to God, to whom Telramund also appeals that his name may not be disgraced: the imperious Ortrud places her trust in her husband's strong arm.

18

The long chorus over, the six nobles take up their positions by the side of their spears, the other fighting men massing themselves around them. Elsa and her ladies are with the King under the oak-tree. The trumpets blow the battle summons; the King draws his sword from the earth and strikes three blows with it on his suspended shield; Lohengrin and Friedrich enter the lists; and the combat begins. The twenty bars that accompany it in the orchestra have for present-day ears all the naïveté of their epoch. The more practised Wagner of the later years would have somehow or other caught up this little episode in dumb show into the main stream of his music; in 1847 he could do nothing better than put No. 13 through some obvious repetitions and imitations. At the seventeenth bar the Lohengrin theme (No. 11) rises in triumph as the knight of the Grail fells his adversary, and in the twenty-first a downward plunge of the lower strings depicts Telramund's vain attempt to rise and his final collapse with Lohengrin's sword at his throat. The hero grants his enemy his life, however, bidding him devote it to repentance for his crime.

The King takes down his shield from the oak-tree and sheathes his sword; the six orderers of the combat withdraw their spears from the earth, and all press eagerly and joyously forward. Elsa runs to Lohengrin, and with a great cry of gratitude:

launches the jubilant finale; Wagner the musician is back in his true element once more. Elsa surrenders her whole being to her deliverer in the last soaring phrase of her glad cry to him:

Out of these two melodies, and a third of similar contour but in a contrasting key:

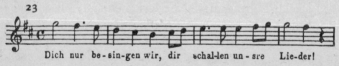

plus the Lohengrin motive proper (No. 11), Wagner builds up an ensemble that reaches its climax in a line thrown out in the highest relief by Elsa against a sequence of ascending chromatic harmonies:

This was a favourite technique of Wagner's throughout his life for creating emotional tension by a prolonged conduct of a falling upper and a rising lower line, converging in closer and closer chromatics. (Our quotation, of course, shows only the skeleton structure of the passage).

Throughout the general jubilation Ortrud and Friedrich, could we hear them through the enveloping thunder of tone, would be found to be expressing their own sentiments about the situation. Telramund, still prostrate on the ground, laments his defeat and the shame on his honour, in which he sees the hand of God. Ortrud, whose gods are those of heathen mythology, asks herself and the universe wonderingly who this hero can be that has vanquished her husband and brought her plans crashing to the ground: but, now as always indomitable, she cannot bring herself to believe that the last blow has been struck and all her hopes destroyed.

At the end of the ensemble the proud No. 11 rings out once more as the younger warriors raise Lohengrin upon his shield and Elsa upon the King's, over which they have spread their mantles, and carry the pair off amid general rejoicing.

19

The second act, as we have seen, was the last of the three to be composed; and it has many touches that show Wagner to have been developing in musical-dramatic power all the while he was engaged on the opera. In the character of Ortrud in particular he has achieved a new kind of characterisation, in a vein that was to be opened out more fully later in the *Ring*. The second act, indeed, may be said to be mainly Ortrud's. She now comes into the forefront of the action: the determining dramatic threads pass into her masterful hands, and we see her shaping, half with purpose, half unwittingly, the ending of the drama she had set in motion before the opera began.

There is a foretaste of the *Ring*—of Alberich and Hagen as instruments of evil—in the orchestral prelude to the second act, which first of all projects across the scene the sinister personality of Ortrud in a long 'cello melody the rises and falls and syncopations of which combine to produce an impression of something evil uncoiling itself in the darkness:

The slow development of this is twice interrupted by the motive of Lohengrin's warning (No. 19) in the cor anglais. Ortrud's mind is festering with Telramund's and her own defeat and hatred primarily of Elsa, secondarily of Lohengrin. The latter, she knows instinctively, she cannot harm directly. But he may be driven away, and Elsa brought to ruin, by sowing the seeds of doubt in her mind: somehow she must be brought to ask her deliverer the question she had promised not to ask on pain of losing him. How to accomplish this end is the subject of her scheming when the curtain rises for the second act.

It is now night. The scene is the citadel of Antwerp: at the back is the Pallas (the knights' quarters), on the right the minster, on the left the kemenate. Ortrud and Telramund, both meanly clad, are sitting on the minster steps, Friedrich sunk in gloomy thought, Ortrud never taking her eyes off the windows of the Pallas, which are brightly lit. From inside there comes for a moment the sound of festal music, with which is linked a reminder of Elsa (No. 8); and a return of No. 25 in the orchestra shows the mind of Ortrud still at work on her evil plan.

At last Friedrich rises suddenly with a cry of "Bestir thyself, companion of my shame! The dawn of day must not find us here." Ortrud does not move. "I cannot go", she says; "I am bound here by a spell. From the sight and sound of our enemies' feasting I would distil a deadly poison that would put an end alike to their exultation and our shame." Then, in an outburst of grief and rage, Telramund reproaches her bitterly for having brought him to the present pass. "Unholy woman! what keeps me bound to thee? Why do I not leave thee and fly somewhere where my conscience may find rest again?" Through her he has lost honour and reputation; his sword is shattered, his escutcheon soiled, his ancient house disgraced. Shame is henceforth his sole portion, wherever he may go; would he had died in the fight! In a paroxysm of despair he flings himself on the ground.

There is another wave of festal music from the Pallas: then Ortrud speaks, still without moving. Why, she asks Friedrich with quiet scorn, has he lost faith in her? At this he breaks out afresh. Was it not she who, with her false witness, had induced him to make the charge against the innocent Elsa? Had she not assured him that from a window of their castle she had seen with her own eyes the maiden drown her brother in the pond? Had she not assured him that Radbod's ancient princely house would rule again in Brabant? Pouring these lies into his ears, had she not persuaded him to renounce Elsa's hand and take *her* to wife? And for his belief in her lies God has smitten him into the dust. Scornfully the pagan woman replies that his "God" is only his name for his own faintheartedness; and when he moves threateningly towards her she tells him that had he confronted the stranger as boldly as he does her, victory would have been his: for in the face of anyone who knew how to meet him the knight would have been as feeble as a child. To Friedrich it appears that the more vulnerable his antagonist the more apparent it is that he had been aided by God. Give her the power, she rejoins, and she will prove to him how weak is this God that fought for his enemy.

20

Filled now with a strange fear of the sinister creature, Telramund would fain learn more. She points to the Pallas, the windows of which are now quite dark, and, with No. 25A stealing in in the cor anglais, she bids him seat himself by her, and she will tell him what her second sight reveals. More and more helpless in her hands, he listens while she unfolds her plan for vengeance. The stranger knight's strength is given him by magic; but it will desert him if he is compelled to disclose who he is and whence he came. "So that", ejaculates Friedrich, "was why he laid that ban on her!" No one, continues Ortrud, can wrest his secret from him but Elsa, so it is through her that they must work. Telramund is not to flee the land but stay, and waken suspicion in Elsa by accusing the knight of having obtained judgment in his favour by magic. If this plan should fail, Ortrud has another. She is versed in black arts; she knows that if one protected by magic loses only the smallest limb the charm fails and his strength is at an end; had Telramund so much as wounded a finger of him in the fight he would have had him at his mercy.

Pride and rage combine to make him credulous: he had been tricked and degraded by fraud, he cries. He will live now to avenge his shame, retrieve his honour, and drag his rival down. But if Ortrud should be again deceiving him let her beware! The opening bars of No. 25 are heard again, this time threateningly in trumpet and trombone, as she assures him that he shall yet taste the sweets of vengeance; and together they call on the powers of darkness to aid them:

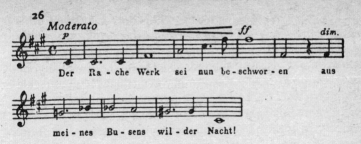

The duet, in which the voices are in octaves throughout, ends with a warning to those lying in happy sleep in the citadel that calamity awaits them:

When the voices have ceased, two reiterations of a sinister phrase in the bass clarinet, followed by a quiet trombone chord, complete the dark picture. But instantly a new mood is established by a placid melody in the wood wind that looks forward to the wedding music at the end of this act. (See No. 38). Elsa, robed in white, appears on the balcony of the kemenate: Telramund and Ortrud, on the opposite side of the stage, maintain their positions on the minster steps. Elsa pours out her happiness in lyrical strains to the breezes of the night:

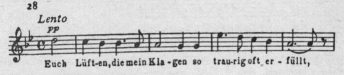

those soft caressing breezes to which she had so often confided her pain, that had brought her rescuing hero to her, and that now

cool her glowing cheek. Between the phrases of her song we hear
the muttering of Ortrud and Friedrich: "she will live to rue the
day", says the former venomously, "when her eyes again en-
counter mine!" Hastily she bids Friedrich withdraw for a while
and leave the dreaming maid to her: the stranger knight shall be
his concern later. So Telramund disappears in the shadows.

The calm atmosphere that has enveloped Elsa's monologue is
suddenly disturbed by a minor harmony in oboe and stopped
horns and a cry of "Elsa!" from Ortrud; and we have an unmis-
takable touch of the later Wagner in the instantaneous suggestion, with this minimum of means, of Lohengrin's warning
(No. 19):

With a shudder at something eerie which she senses in the air Elsa
asks who it is that is calling her name. Has she forgotten the voice,
Ortrud asks her, of the hapless woman whom she has consigned
to utmost misery? In hypocritical, insinuating tones she paints the
quiet happiness of her life in days gone by:

How had she ever injured Elsa? Her life had been one of mourning
for the vanished glory of her ancient line: how could Elsa envy
her the good fortune of having become the wife of the man whom
she had rejected in scorn? Misled by powers of evil she had brought

a false accusation against Elsa; now she is condemned to fearful punishment and racked with remorse. Elsa is happy; after a brief moment of undeserved suffering life smiles on her again: let her turn now from Ortrud and leave her to her fate. From time to time Elsa has interrupted her with a pitying word or two: now she gives a cry of gratitude to God for this chance to bestow blessing on a poor creature kneeling in the dust before her; and she hurries back into the kemenate to open the door to her enemy.

21

Ortrud springs up in a frenzy of exaltation. She cries loudly to her dishonoured gods to avenge themselves and her:

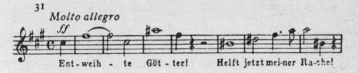

"strengthen me in my fight for you; make an end of the vile pride of this apostate!" She calls on Wodan the strong, on Freia the gracious, to bless her and make her revenge sure.

The fury of the orchestra dies down as Elsa, accompanied by two maids carrying lights, enters by way of the lower door of the kemenate. Abruptly changing her tone, Ortrud throws herself humbly at her feet. Elsa is grieved by the change in her since last she saw her in her pride and pomp. With kindly words and gestures she exhorts her to rise and believe that there is no enmity in her own heart towards her. On the morrow she is to be wedded to her rescuer; she will entreat him to pardon Friedrich for her sake. Let Ortrud, then, reappear on the morrow in fine raiment and go to the minster with her and see her become the honoured bride of her hero. Ortrud thanks her humbly; she will live henceforth as a beggar in the sunlight of Elsa's charity and grace.

Then she begins to lay her snare. In her abasement, she continues, she has lost all her former powers but one, but in virtue of that she may be able to protect Elsa's life and ward misfortune

from her.[1] She warns her against believing too blindly in her
present happiness; and to ward evil from her, let Ortrud read the
future for her. This suggestion is accompanied by the motive
of Ortrud's machinations (No. 25A) in the bassoon, which is
followed by the motive of Lohengrin's warning as she continues
to distil her poison into Elsa's ear. Has she reflected, she asks,
that he who had come to her by magic art may some day by
magic leave her? Elsa turns on her for a moment indignantly;
then, filled with sorrow and compassion, she says, "Thou, poor
one, canst never know love so trustful as mine, the love born of
perfect faith":

To a phrase that will become important later, in the colloquy of
Lohengrin and Elsa in the third act:

[1] This is the text as it appears in the scores and in Wagner's own imprint
of the poem, but an error seems to have crept in somehow. In the manuscript
of the full score the second and fourth lines end not with "gegeben" and
"Leben" ("only one power is *given* to me . . . perchance with it I may guard
thy *life*") but with "geblieben" and "Lieben" ("only one power *remains* to
me . . . perchance with it I may guard thy *love*"). As the eminent Wagnerian
scholar Wolfgang Golther has pointed out, this latter reading makes the
better sense: "it is not Elsa's life that is threatened", he says, "but her love".
He would not take it on himself, however, to change the current wording,
though he tells us that the great Wagnerian singer Anna von Mildenburg
used always to sing "Lieben", not "Leben", at Bayreuth, and that Hans
Richter had assured him that Wagner himself had ordered "Lieben" to be
inserted in the score for the Vienna production of 1875. On the general
difficulty of arriving at a definitive text of the Wagner operas see *supra*,
p. 122[n].

she exhorts Ortrud to come with her and learn the happiness that love and faith alone can bestow. As she repeats these last words, Ortrud mutters to herself, "Ah! this very pride of hers shall teach me how to destroy her faith; I will turn her own weapon against her!"; but the orchestra envelops the brief duet in a tranquil melody of its own:

on which it dwells ardently while Ortrud, with hypocritical reluctance, accompanies Elsa into the kemenate, the two serving maids lighting their way and closing the door after them. When all have disappeared, Friedrich comes out of the shadows with a masterful cry: "Thus enters evil into yonder house! Carry to the end, my wife, the craft thou hast begun; no power have I to hinder thee. With my abasement began this fateful mischief; now let those who cast me down into the dust fall with me. One thing only see I in the mists around me—the destroyer of my honour shall himself be destroyed!"

22

The stage directions at this point are "First gleam of dawn". We have now to imagine, in defiance of the laws of solar time, even of stage time, that several hours have elapsed between the chord that accompanies Telramund's final words and the one that immediately follows it. For in a trice a new day is here, the wedding morn of Lohengrin and Elsa. "Day gradually dawns", we read a little later, and soon, evidently, the whole population is awake. We would have been less conscious of the anachronism

had Wagner removed Friedrich from the scene after his monologue and brought him back later. But he does not: he makes
Friedrich seek, before our eyes, a "place of concealment from the
concourse of people", which he finds behind a buttress of the
minster. In a few minutes Elsa will reappear on the stage; she can
manifestly have had very little time for her talk inside the kemenate
with Ortrud, and none at all for sleep before the wedding; for very
soon we shall see both her and Ortrud in festal raiment. There is
no way of making sense of the situation. The stage directions at
the opening of the second act had been "It is night"; and later
Ortrud and Friedrich had described the occupants of the citadel as
"sunk in soft sleep". Later still, when Ortrud calls out Elsa's
name, the latter says, "How fearfully and mournfully my name
resounds in the night". Later, again, she speaks of her wedding as
"tomorrow". Wagner's confusion is further shown by his giving
contradictory stage directions in the poem and the score: in the
latter "Day gradually dawns" at the commencement of the scene
that immediately follows the exit of Elsa and Ortrud into the
kemenate, while in the poem we are told "It is full daylight"—
which has come up, seemingly, between one bar and the next.
Wagner must have been fully aware of the illogicality of the situation, but presumably was indifferent to it. The difficulty probably
arose with Telramund: he had to be on the stage when the Herald
appears and reads his sentence of banishment, and a plausible
reason for sending him off and bringing him on again later could
not be found; so Wagner keeps him there, lurking behind a
buttress, and blandly telescopes several hours into a stage minute
or two.

The time, then, is now morning. Two trumpeters on the turret
of the citadel blow a reveille:

which is answered in softer tones from a distant tower. The same
procedure is followed with the next phrase:

and its successors; and gradually the orchestra takes up the fanfares and builds them up in great masses while the watchmen descend and open the citadel gates. Servants enter from various quarters, greet each other, and then go quietly about their routine duties, some drawing water from a fountain, others going into the Pallas. Eventually the four royal trumpeters emerge from the Pallas doors; and an arresting effect is made by a sudden unexpected switch for a time from the key of D major to that of C major. The trumpeters blow a stirring summons, in response to which the Brabantine nobles and the personnel of the citadel pour in from various quarters and greet each other excitedly—in an extended double chorus, as the operatic conventions of the 1840's demanded. They speculate as to what new wonders the day may bring forth to cap those of yesterday.

The King's Herald advances from the Pallas, and after a fresh fanfare from the four trumpeters he proclaims the royal decree: for his impious acceptance of the ordeal of trial by battle before God, Friedrich von Telramund is disgraced and banished, and with him all who side with him and harbour him.[1] The chorus break into wild curses of Telramund; but a fanfare calls them to order again and the Herald resumes his proclamation—Lohengrin will be Protector of Brabant: today he will celebrate with them his wedding feast, but on the morrow he will lead them against the eastern enemy.

23

While the chorus are enthusiastically acclaiming all this and clamouring to be led into the field, four nobles, formerly liegemen of Friedrich, detach themselves from the crowd, advance to the front, and express their discontent with the new turn of events: so Brabant is to have a new ruler, who is to lead them against a

---

[1] It had been Wagner's original intention to have the ban—on both Friedrich and Ortrud—proclaimed in the first act.

foe who has not threatened them? But who is there to gainsay him? "I!" says Friedrich, who has approached them unobserved and now reveals himself by uncovering his face. They are astonished at his braving danger and death by still being in Antwerp. He dares do more, he tells them—he will convict the intruder of sorcery. Horrified, they take the raging man aside and conceal him among them by the minster; he is lost, they tell him, if he is recognised by the crowd.

Just then four noble pages appear on the terrace of the Pallas and announce the coming of the princess, Elsa von Brabant: they clear a way through the willing crowd to the minster steps, where they take their stand. On the balcony of the kemenate appear four more pages, the advance guard of the procession of Elsa's ladies, who come out richly robed and make their slow way to the minster, on the steps of which the first comers group themselves. In time Elsa herself appears, the nobles greeting her with bared heads. The magnificent final scene of the act is now launched. The orchestra gives out a solemn strain:

which has a pendant equally majestic:

these are gradually built up into an imposing choral and orchestral ensemble in praise of Elsa. Among the ladies accompanying her is Ortrud, now richly dressed. Apparently it occurred to Wagner at some time or other that her presence there after the ban on Telramund might arouse some wonder in the spectator, for in the Prose Sketch he has a marginal note running thus: "the ladies keep aloof from Ortrud in the procession, which seems to offend her greatly", and in the poem this is expanded into "among the ladies

who follow Elsa and close the procession is Ortrud, also richly
dressed. The ladies nearest her keep at some distance from her,
hardly concealing their displeasure, so that she appears markedly
isolated: her expression is one of sullen anger".

As the chorus of greeting reaches its climax of power and Elsa
places her foot on the second step of the minster, Ortrud breaks
from the ranks, hastens to the front, and faces her truculently.
"Stand back, Elsa!" she cries. "No longer will I endure it that I
must follow thee humbly as a serving maid! Precedence is mine,
here and everywhere; before me thou shouldst bow thyself in due
humility!" What is hers she claims of right, she tells the astounded
onlookers; for what she has suffered she will have revenge. Elsa
is as amazed as the others at this change from the suppliant of last
night to the termagant of the present moment; how, she asks, can
the wife of one whom God himself has condemned now flaunt
her arrogance before her? Ortrud, assuming an air of outraged
dignity, replies in a melodic vein that anticipates to some extent
the Fricka of the *Valkyrie*:

39

Allegro

Wenn falsch Ge-richt mir den Ge-mahl ver-bann-te,

war doch sein Nam' im Lan-de hoch ge-ehrt: etc.

"Though my husband has been condemned by a false judgment,
his name is honoured in this land, his virtues praised, his sword
feared. But *yours*—who here can know him, since his bride herself
cannot call him by name?" Despite the angry protests of the
bystanders she goes steadily on: can Elsa assure them that her hero
is of noble race, tell her whence the river had brought him to her,
when and whither he will go from her again? She does not know;
and to keep her from knowing, the stranger has craftily persuaded
her that to ask these questions would bring disaster on them both.

Elsa replies exaltedly that her lover is so noble that only the
basest of beings could doubt his lofty mission; and she appeals

to the assembly to choose between him and his traducers. Ortrud
plays mockingly upon the weakness of Elsa's case—she will not
ask by what magic the stranger has triumphed because she dares
not, because she is racked by doubt of him. As Elsa's ladies come
forward to support her the door of the Pallas opens and the King
appears, heralded by the fanfares of the trumpeters, and accompanied by Lohengrin and the Saxon Counts and nobles.[1] Elsa falls
on Lohengrin's breast with a cry of "My lord! My rescuer!", and
tells him how she had taken Ortrud in out of compassion, and
now the woman taunts her with excess of faith in him. Lohengrin
cows Ortrud with a look and bids her go; then he bends tenderly
over Elsa and exhorts her, if she must weep, to shed tears of joy.

24

He is leading the way with her to the minster when Friedrich
appears suddenly on the steps. All recoil from him in horror and
loathing. Wildly he tells the King and all of them that they have
been deluded by an enchanter's craft, and demands a hearing. At
the King's command they seize him, and as he struggles frenziedly
with them he accuses the shining knight of having imposed on
King, nobles and people by magic arts. They should have asked
him, before they allowed him to enter the lists, the questions Telramund asks him now—what is the name, what the station of this
stranger brought to them down the river by a wild swan? Has an
honourable knight need of such an escort? "Now let him stand and
answer. If he can, then was I justly cast down: if not, let it fare
with this pretended pure one as evilly as he deserves."

All, including the King, are impressed by Friedrich's vehemence
and his evident conviction, and they look expectantly towards
Lohengrin. Proudly he tells Friedrich that he refuses to answer
the charges and satisfy the doubts of one so degraded. Not even
to the demand of the King and of all the princes of earth for his
name and origin would he accede. What doubt can they have of
him? They saw his deed, which is its own witness of its worth.
To one alone he owes an answer—Elsa. He turns towards her

[1] Thus in the score. In the poem it is "Saxon and Brabantine Counts and
nobles".

confidently; but as the baleful Ortrud motive (No. 25A) steals out in the orchestra, followed by No. 19 (his warning to Elsa), he pauses in dismay when he sees that she is gazing fixedly before her, pale and trembling, a prey to the wildest agitation. What his secret can be baffles them all, they murmur, but—to the accompaniment of No. 25 in the orchestra—in Elsa's face they can read the doubt taking shape in her heart despite her effort to fight it down. In a trance, oblivious of the others, she murmurs, "What he hides would doubtless work him evil were he to reveal it before them all. I, whom he rescued, would be traitor to him were I to ask for it. Did I know his destiny I would faithfully keep the secret; yet in the depth of my heart doubt raises its head." "Let him keep his secret", say the King and the others. "His deed is witness enough to his nobility. We stand by the hero's side with full belief in him, even if his name he will not tell". Lohengrin thanks them warmly, pressing the hands stretched out to him.

While he is thus occupied, standing a little in the background, Friedrich goes up to Elsa, who remains a little apart from the others, lost in thought, not daring to look at Lohengrin. With the sinister No. 25A again uncoiling itself in the bass clarinet he addresses her softly with feigned sympathy: "Give me your trust: I can show you a means by which you may learn the truth. Let me but wound even his finger-tip, and, I swear to you, all will be clear that he is now concealing. So will he be faithful and bound to you for ever. Tonight I shall be nigh; call me, and it will be done in a trice."

Elsa repulses him with horror, and Lohengrin, stepping forward, commandingly bids Ortrud and Friedrich depart and never be seen by him again. Friedrich makes a gesture of rage and despair. Lohengrin raises Elsa, who had sunk at his feet, bewildered and exhausted. "In thy hands, in thy faith", he says, "lies all our happiness. Does doubt still torture thee? Wouldst thou ask me the question?" Torn between shame and exaltation she replies, "My preserver, my saviour, my hero in whom alone I live, my love shall soar above all clouds of doubt!" Taking her by the hand he leads her to the King, the nobles and ladies dividing respectfully to let them pass, and No. 37 is once more built up into a massive choral and orchestral ensemble, with bells ringing and the organ pealing from inside the minster, and trumpet fanfares piercing through it all from the turret of the Pallas and from the balcony. Taking Elsa by the right hand and Lohengrin by the left, the King conducts them to the top of the minster steps, where Lohengrin takes Elsa in his arms. But at the supreme moment she looks back apprehensively and sees Ortrud raising her arm as if in triumph, while trumpets and trombones thunder out the motive of warning, which, however, is swept aside by a final fanfare as the bridal pair enter the minster and the curtain falls.

It is not to be wondered at that Wagner left the composition of the second act to the last, for psychologically and musically it confronted him with the most difficulties. He was quite at home in choral and lyrical episodes, and his Ortrud of the second act was a dramatic creation of a kind new to opera. But he was still ill at ease in what we may call the passages of lower emotional temperature, essential to the carrying on of the action but not always of the stuff that music can take to its heart. He had not yet reached the stage at which he could see his own solution of the age-old operatic problem of making the whole tissue musical—in the first place by so constructing his drama that pedestrian explanation could be reduced to the minimum, in the second place by a continuous symphonic weaving of significant motives in the orchestra. It was no doubt the intuition that this problem would somehow have to be solved in the *Ring* that made him delay the composition of the *Rhinegold* for six years after the completion of *Lohengrin*.

25

In the third act, the first of the three to be set to music, we get a hint of the line along which his development as a musician might have proceeded had not that deep inner change taken place in him that was to result in an entirely new synthesis of the factors of opera. The third act is predominantly lyrical, and the ease and power with which Wagner creates in this field suggest that had he been allowed to remain content with the old formulae he could have endowed them with a new life. This third act shows him at that stage in the development of a great artist when not only does each component of his genius seem to have attained its fullest individual development but all are in smooth equilibrium. It is the stage represented, for example, by Beethoven in his fifth symphony and Goethe in the First Part of his *Faust*. But artists of this type, by the very nature of their complex genius, cannot rest on their oars when this kind of consolidation of their various faculties has been accomplished. Their daemon drives them on to create difficulties of all kinds for themselves, difficulties of conception, of architecture, of craftsmanship; and by the very process of overcoming these difficulties they become masters of a new way of thinking and a new way of working. So it was with Wagner after *Lohengrin*. To have stood still would have been, for him, to go back; but going forwards meant the slow conquest of entirely new territory. Of such conquests, however, only the most powerful minds, with infinite capacity for growth, are capable. *Lohengrin* was finished in January 1848. By 1858 Wagner had written the *Rhinegold*, the *Valkyrie*, two-thirds of *Siegfried*, and the major part of *Tristan*. In no ten years of the life of any other great creator is the distance so enormous between the first peak scaled and the second.

In the third act of *Lohengrin* Wagner abandons himself to the luxury of lyricism. It opens with an animated orchestral introduction descriptive of the wedding festivities. In some respects Wagner was at this time more at his ease technically in what we may call free music than in music that had to go in harness with words. Attention has already been drawn to that four-square regularity of beat in much of his earlier vocal writing at which he himself could smile in later years. It was the inevitable result of his casting his libretti in the ordinary poetic moulds—long lines in regular metre with click-clack end-rhymes; the uniform line-lengths and the goose-step of the verbal accents imposed on him a certain monotony of melodic stress, from which he only emancipated himself later by a drastic shortening of the lines and, in general, an avoidance of the fetters of rhyme. But already in the *Flying Dutchman-Tannhäuser-Lohengrin* period he was feeling his way towards a more flexible rhythm in the orchestra, of which we have a foretaste in the varied accentual footfalls of the brilliant introduction to the third act:

This is followed by an energetic theme in horns, bassoons and 'cellos:

which appears later strengthened by trombones and tuba (in which presentment it is generally vulgarised by conductor and players alike). There is a contrasting section in a quieter vein in wood wind and horns:

after which Nos. 40 and 41 are resumed.

The curtain rises on the bridal chamber. In the middle background stands a richly furnished bed, and on the right a low couch by an open oriel casement. Through two doors in the back come two processions, one of ladies escorting Elsa, the other of the King and the nobles with Lohengrin. During the few bars of transition from the close of the introduction to the stage scene we are to imagine the bridal music drawing nearer and nearer. When the two cortèges reach the centre of the room the King presents Elsa to Lohengrin, and the pair embrace while the chorus sing a simple little song of congratulation:

Noble pages divest Lohengrin of his rich outer vestment and lay it with his sword, on the couch. Eight ladies similarly disrobe Elsa. The King embraces the pair, the pages give the signal for departure, and, to the strains of No. 43, the two processions re-form and go out slowly, their song dying away gradually in the distance.

26

By a sudden enharmonic shift of key, from B flat major to E major, the atmosphere changes to one of tender intimacy as Lohengrin, seating himself on the couch, draws Elsa to him, and, accompanied by the muted strings, begins the long duet. First he sings of his happiness at being alone with her for the first time since they had met, and at her loving confidence in him:

A tender little phrase in the clarinet:

soon becomes the subject of a fresh development:

as Elsa assures him of her own happiness. Little more than this broad outline of the colloquy of the pair is necessary to the listener, for what they have to say in words is said more directly and more ardently in the music, in which theme succeeds theme in spendthrift profusion, the total effect being of a symphony of solo song and duet. Lohengrin launches a new melody as he speaks of their having been destined for each other from the beginning, he to be her rescuer, she to be drawn to him by love:

She had already beheld him in her dreams, she replies, so that his appearance on the river—here No. 11 is breathed softly by flute and clarinet—had been only her dream made reality.

But soon we have a hint of the impending tragedy, the seeds of which had been sown in Elsa's heart by Ortrud. Her name sounds sweet in his mouth, she says: perhaps some day she will be able to murmur his, some day when they are alone together and the world cannot overhear. Lohengrin, however, only draws her to the open window, points to the garden, and tells her that as the flowers give forth their scent unasked, so her beauty and innocence had stolen irresistibly on his senses at the first sight of her:

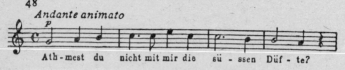

She replies that she longs to be worthy of his love, to serve him even at the cost of suffering. The motive of warning (No. 19) intrudes itself softly into the orchestral tissue as she goes on to surmise that perchance his secret contains in it a threat of evil to him should the world discover it; but if she were allowed to share

it no power on earth would tear it from her. In growing excitement she begs for his confidence, for the thought of his mistrust
weighs heavily on her: "reveal to me thy noble being; tell me
whence thou comest; of my silence be assured."

Gravely he reminds her that when he came to her he had put
his whole trust in her, accepting her word that she was innocent
of the charge against her; then he turns lovingly to her again, and
the orchestra, with a new theme:

launches him once more on a flood of protestations; he had given
up more than she knows to come to her in her need, and in return
he asks for nothing but love and faith. The warning No. 19 is
heard again as he entreats her to put doubt away from her: one
thing alone he can tell her—"I come not from night and woe, but
from a home of light and bliss".

The Ortrud motive threads its way through the texture again
as Elsa recoils from him. He had thought to reassure her, but his
words have only stirred more anxious doubts in her:

He has come, then, for her sake from a land where all was joy.
Will he not be always longing to return? What power has one so
poor as she to hold him? The day will come when he will regret
his sacrifice: wasting away, must she count the days until the one
dawns when she must lose him? In vain he assures her that so long
as she is free from doubt he will not change towards her: to
another insistent reiteration of the Ortrud motive she wails that as
by magic he had come to her, so by magic he may be taken from
her: that fear will ever haunt her. She becomes again the visionary

she was in the first act, but now with a touch of madness in her.
In imagination she hears and sees the swan (No. 17 in flute and
oboe) approaching down the river, and Lohengrin summoning it
to take him away. That vision will ever be before her eyes: Lohengrin alone can rid her of it: she must know his name, what his race,
whence he came; and the orchestra points the climax of her delirium with an ominous upsurge of No. 19.

Lohengrin has tried in vain to check her. Suddenly she is recalled to reality by the sight of Friedrich and his four partisans,
with drawn swords, breaking in through one of the doors at the
back. With a wild cry to Lohengrin to save himself she hands him
the scabbard that is resting against the couch. Swiftly drawing the
sword he strikes Telramund dead; the others let fall their weapons
in terror and kneel before him. To the tumult succeeds a fateful
silence—which Wagner intensifies, as he was so often to do in his
later works, by a throbbing pulse in the kettledrums—and a last
melancholy suggestion of the motive of Ortrud's machinations:

Lohengrin makes one brief, poignant comment on it all—"Alas,
now is our happiness for ever at an end!":

To a sad reminiscence of No. 46 in clarinet (then oboe) and strings
he bends down over Elsa, raises her gently, and places her on the
couch. "Oh God in heaven, have pity on me!" she moans. At a

sign from Lohengrin the four prostrate nobles rise; "Bear this body to the King's judgment seat", he commands them. When they have gone he strikes a bell: two of Elsa's women enter, whom he bids take their mistress away and prepare her for her appearance before the King, to whom he will disclose who and what he is. Then, slowly and sadly, he himself leaves the stage, the orchestra giving out first the motive (the latter half of No. 19) that had accompanied his warning to Elsa at their first meeting, then the warning itself (the first part of No. 19), and finally the solemn Grail theme (No. 1).

27

The curtain having fallen, trumpet calls, sounding from the courtyard, prepare the way for the orchestral introduction to the final scene. When the curtain rises again we see once more the meadow on the banks of the Scheldt, as in the first act; it is dawn, broadening into full daylight as the action proceeds. To the accompaniment of martial music, with recurrent trumpet fanfares, the Brabantine nobles and men-at-arms come on the scene from various directions and take up their positions by their respective banners.[1] When all are assembled the King enters with the Saxon levy, and after a fanfare he thanks them all for their welcome. He is about to lead them against the foreign foe; but where is he whom God had sent to be the guardian and the glory of Brabant? The assembly is startled by the entry of the four Brabantine nobles carrying a bier with a covered body on it. All look round fearfully and questioningly; the men, they say to each other, are Telramund's liegemen, but whose is the corpse they bring? "We come", say the four, "by order of the Protector of Brabant: who he is he himself will make known." Then all eyes turn wonderingly to Elsa, who comes in slowly and falteringly with her ladies, the orchestra giving out the motive of warning and its afterstrain (No. 19), followed by the motive of Ortrud's evil. The King goes to meet her and conducts her to a seat opposite the oak. Why is she so pale and sad? he asks her: is it for grief at parting? She cannot speak; she tries to raise her eyes to him but cannot.

[1] See *supra*, pp. 127-8.

From the background come shouts of "Make way for the hero of Brabant"; and soon Lohengrin enters, fully accoutred as in the first act. The King and the others greet him warmly as their leader in the coming campaign; but to their dismay he declares that he cannot take the field with the heroes who have rallied to the banner at his summons. He comes among them now only as an accuser demanding justice. Uncovering Telramund's body he says, "This man fell upon me in the night; say now, did I right in slaying him?" All absolve him. Then he accuses Elsa, "the woman God gave to me", of having allowed herself to be betrayed by evil counsel into falsity to him. They all had heard her sacred promise never to ask his name: that promise she has broken. Now she shall learn what she desired to know, and that before them all. "Learn then", he says, drawing himself up proudly, "whether I am as noble as any here."

To the accompaniment of the Grail music of the prelude to the opera he tells his story. Far away from here, in a land which they will never see, stands a castle, Monsalvat by name:

Within it is a shining temple, the like of which for splendour the earth cannot show; and within the temple is the holiest of treasures, a cup divinely blessed, brought down from heaven to earth by an angel host and given into the keeping of stainless men. Once in each year a dove descends from heaven to renew the mystic virtue residing in the cup. It is called the Grail; it preserves unsullied the knights who are dedicated to its service. Whomever it summons to that service it endows with supernatural might; evil is powerless before him. Some are called by it to go into distant lands to champion the cause of innocence in distress. Nought can prevail against a knight of the Grail so long as the secret of his origin remains

unrevealed; but if it is disclosed to the profane world he must
return whence he had come. He himself had been sent among them
as an emissary of the Grail: the King of the Grail is his father
Parzival: "his knight am I, and Lohengrin my name"; at which
last words the proud No. 11 rings out in the full orchestra.

28

The King, the women and the men muse upon the mystic story
to the strain of the concluding portion of the prelude (No. 5).
Elsa gives a cry of despair: Lohengrin takes her in his arms and
tenderly, but in profoundest sorrow, reproaches her for having
wrung his secret from him by her betrayal of his trust. She pleads
desperately to be allowed to make reparation, but he assures her
that it is in vain; he has no choice; he must leave her. The King and
the others add their supplications to hers, imploring him at least
to lead them into battle. But this also he has to refuse; if he, the
servant of the Grail, should disobey the Grail, he would only
bring disaster on them. He prophesies, however, success for the
German cause: "no eastern hordes, now or in times to come, shall
lord it over German lands".

Amid the excitement comes a cry from the men at the back—
"The swan! the swan! see, it draws nigh again!" Elsa, waking
from her swoon, stands up and sees, like the others, the swan at
the bend of the river, drawing the empty boat. She gives a wild
cry that agitates Lohengrin: too long, he says, as No. 17 hovers in
the air, has he lingered: the Grail has sent for him. Watched in
suspense by the others he goes up to the bank and bends mournfully over the swan. "My beloved swan", he murmurs, "now for
our last sad journey":

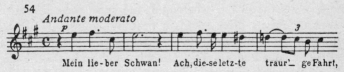

"How gladly would I have spared it thee! Within a year, thy
term of service o'er, the Grail would have freed thee, and I would
see thee in another guise." Then he turns with a cry of bitter re-

gret to Elsa: had he spent but one year with her in happiness the Grail would have restored to her her brother Gottfried, whom she believed to be dead. "Should he return, though I shall then be far away:

Kommt er dann heim, wenn ich ihm fern im Le - ben,

give him this horn, this sword, this ring. The horn will bring him help in time of need, the sword victory in battle; as for the ring, let it remind him of one who saved thee from shame and woe." He bids the fainting Elsa farewell: "wroth is the Grail with me that I have tarried so long"; and he goes quickly to the river bank, accompanied by the lamentations of them all.

Suddenly Ortrud emerges from the crowd and comes to the front with a cry of triumph: "Go home in all thy pride; and to thy foolish one I will tell who it is that draws thy boat. Well do I know the chain about his neck, the chain by which I had made him not child but swan: he is the heir of Brabant." Then, turning exultantly to Elsa, "My thanks that you drove your hero hence. Now the swan takes him home again: had the knight bided here a little longer he would have freed your brother!" The men press round her with curses and threats, but she faces them undismayed: "See now how the gods avenge themselves on you for having turned away from them!"

Lohengrin, who has heard all this, sinks on his knees in silent prayer while the Grail music pulsates in the air above him once more. The white dove of the Grail descends and hovers over the boat: perceiving it, Lohengrin springs up with a look of gratitude and loosens the chain, whereupon the swan sinks beneath the waves and in its place stands a beautiful youth—Gottfried— whom he lifts to the bank, crying, "Behold the Duke of Brabant; he shall be your leader!" To the accompaniment of the chivalrous No. 11 he springs into the boat, and the dove, seizing the chain, draws it down the river. Ortrud, at the sight of Gottfried, has fallen to the ground with a shriek. Gottfried, after making obeisance to the King and receiving the acclamations and homage of the men of Brabant, runs joyously to Elsa. She looks despairingly at Lohengrin, who is now visible in a further part of the river, standing upright in the boat with drooping head, leaning on his shield; and with a cry of "My husband!" she sinks lifeless into Gottfried's arms. As Lohengrin slowly disappears in the distance the curtain falls, the last word of the opera being given, as the first had been, to the music of the mystic Grail.

29

Strange as it may seem to us today, Wagner was urged by several people to change the ending of his opera. Among the friends to whom he read his poem in 1845 was one Hermann Franck, who could not stomach the cruelty, as he thought it, of Elsa's abandonment by Lohengrin. "Serious reflection", Wagner tells us in *My Life*, "aroused in me later grave doubts—which had been expressed to me in thoughtful and tactful fashion by Franck—with regard to the tragic element of the subject. Franck found the punishment of Elsa by Lohengrin's departure rather offensive; he recognised that this highly poetic feature was a characteristic of the legend, but at the same time he doubted whether it met adequately the demands of tragic feeling in relation to dramatic actuality. He would have preferred to see Lohengrin die before our eyes because of Elsa's treachery-through-love. As this did not seem feasible, however, he would have liked to see him spellbound by some powerful motive or other and so prevented from leaving her. Although, of course, I could not agree to all this, I went so far as to ask myself whether I could not avoid the cruel separation and yet retain the essential element of his departure. So I sought for a means by which Elsa could go away with Lohengrin, paying some sort of penance that would mean her withdrawal also from the world." Franck approved of this. Wagner, however, in his perplexity, spoke of his difficulty to Frau von Lüttichau, the wife of the Intendant of the Dresden Opera, who told him bluntly that Franck must be devoid of any sense of poetry if he could not see that Wagner's dénouement was the only right one for the work.

Wagner had a somewhat similar experience five years later in connection with the journalist Adolf Stahr, who, after seeing a performance of the opera under Liszt in Weimar, raised much the same objection to the tragic ending. Wagner was for the moment quite shaken by this apparently widespread view of the matter; and as by that time he had rather lost touch with the characters and the milieu of *Lohengrin* he was weak enough to write to Stahr that in the main he agreed with him. But after some days of mental misery his artistic sense steadied him again, and he sent a laconic message to Liszt, who had been incensed by Stahr's article: "You have the right understanding of *Lohengrin*, Stahr hasn't. I withdraw my agreement with his judgment; I wrote in too much of a hurry."

His own considered view of the moral and dramatic problem of the ending was set forth in a long letter of May 1846 to Franck. Elsa's peculiar offence, he points out, can be atoned for only by separation, not by chastisement of any kind or by death. "Elsa has forfeited Lohengrin: their remaining together is impossible, because the pair have already been severed by her asking him the question." Wagner had given a great deal of thought to the matter from the moment of his first acquaintance with the legend, he tells Franck; and he had rejected every other dénouement as illogical and impossible. To alter it now would mean a total re-casting of the drama, leaving only the mere externalities of the story, the spiritual nucleus of it having gone. He sees it as a fundamental point that although a supernatural being and an earthly one may come into contact with each other it is impossible that their association shall endure, for the lower nature is bound to act according to the law of its own being.

30

But though he cannot adopt Franck's suggestion that the ending shall be changed he has decided, he says, to make Lohengrin's share in the tragic outcome clearer to the spectator. How the knight originally becomes involved in the action he has already shown sufficiently in the first act, more especially in the music, which can convey so much that it is beyond the power of words to express—Lohengrin has come only to carry out the command of the Grail, but at the first sight of Elsa he is filled with love for her. Wagner can change nothing in the passage in the duet in the earlier part of the third act in which Lohengrin assures her that her love will be for him compensation more than enough for the surrender of his heritage of the Grail; and once more he insists that his *music* at this point makes the import of the words doubly clear. But he is prepared to make an alteration later in the act, after Lohengrin has told the assembly the story of his home and origin and the mission entrusted to him by the Grail. In his poem Wagner had made the knight turn to Elsa, after the "Narration", in sad reproach: "O Elsa, what hast thou done to me? When first I saw thee my heart was filled with love for thee and with a sense of a new happiness. The noble power inherent in my origin I was prepared to surrender for love's sake. Why didst thou force my secret from me? Now, alas, I must part from thee." He will now alter this, he says, after the first two or three lines, and will continue thus: "At once I loved thee warmly, and felt my heart turning away from the chaste service of the Grail. Now must I endure endless remorse and pay eternal penance for having longed for thee more than for God. For alas! I see now my transgression— that I thought a woman's love could be of heavenly purity!"

After that, Lohengrin is to tell Elsa, as in the poem, that there can be no changing of her punishment: they must separate, even though his grief is as profound as hers. Then the dialogue is to continue with some new lines: "*Elsa:* Woe is me! could punishment be harder? Parted from thee, nothing remains for me but death! *Lohengrin:* The knight of the Grail must live far removed from here; but thy husband, alas, succumbs to the necessity of parting."

In the end, however, Wagner decided that his original handling of the final scene was the only logical one, and virtually none of the alterations he had outlined in his letter to Franck were carried over into the poem, which agrees with the Prose Sketch in all essentials.

But we have only to study the Sketch to realise how the necessity for compression for stage purposes forced him to omit or condense several features that are vital to our full understanding of the drama. As has been pointed out on an earlier page, he cut out in 1850 a large section, which he had actually set to music, from Lohengrin's "Narration" in the third act, in which the knight had told in detail how the mission to go to the rescue of Elsa came to be laid on him by the Grail. From the stage point of view he was right in sacrificing all this: it would have made the "Narration" inconveniently long. But psychologically the excision was a mistake, for the passage throws a needed light on Lohengrin, his origin, his super-earthly nature and his mission, that is lacking in the opera as we now have it.

The same comment has to be made on the deletion of a passage in an earlier part of the "Narration" which begins thus in the Prose Sketch, after the point at which Lohengrin has told the assembly of the powers of the Grail: "Whoever is dedicated to its service must forswear the love of woman: to the King of the Templars alone is it permitted to take a pure wife, to the end that his exalted line shall be perpetuated unsullied." An emissary of the Grail may descend to the common world of men to relieve oppression or rescue the innocent, but he must never disclose to profane eyes either his origin or the mystery of his supernatural powers. If these secrets should be wrung from him he must return at once to Monsalvat. Lohengrin's dwelling among the Brabantines would have brought untold blessings upon the land —on the sole condition that the Grail's secret remained inviolate; and this fair prospect had been blasted by the feminine indiscretion of Elsa, who had brought about a fatal clash between the higher and the lower elements of the world. Reconciliation of the two is impossible: so for all his love for Elsa he must abandon her and return to the spiritual world from which he had come.

The character of Lohengrin, we see, is a far more complex problem than any singer of the part ever realises. It is not for him to be just a tenor; he must be a psychologist and a student of mediaeval poetry as well. And for the complete key to the character he and we must sometimes go, as so often happens to be the case, to Wagner's first extensive prose draft of the drama, which contains a number of vital pointers which stage exigencies compelled him to omit from his poem.

TRISTAN AND ISOLDE

CHARACTERS

TRISTAN	*Tenor*
KING MARKE	*Bass*
ISOLDE	*Soprano*
KURVENAL	*Baritone*
MELOT	*Tenor*
BRANGAENE	*Soprano*
A SHEPHERD	*Tenor*
A STEERSMAN	*Baritone*
A YOUNG SAILOR[1]	*Tenor*

I

As is the case with many another great legend, the origins of that of Tristan and Isolde are lost in the mists of antiquity. This or that element in it may possibly have its roots in remote historical fact; others are no doubt connected with some primitive form of hero-worship or god-worship; others again are importations, at the first or the fifty-first remove, from romances of the Graeco-Roman past. The moving final motive of the black sail and the white, for instance, is met with in Plutarch's life of the legendary Theseus, and elsewhere in classical literature; it appears that when the ship carrying the annual tribute of youths and maidens for the Cretan Minotaur set out from Attica, "no one had any hope for safety", says Plutarch, "so they used to send out the ship with a black sail, as if it were going to certain doom. But now Theseus so far encouraged [his father] Aegeus, and boasted that he would overcome the Minotaur, that he gave a second sail, a white one, to the steersman, and charged him on his return, if Theseus were safe, to hoist the white one, if not, the black one as a sign of mourning." On the return of the victorious Theseus, however, "both he and the steersman in their delight forgot to hoist the sail which was to be the signal of their safety to Aegeus; and he in his despair flung himself down the cliffs and perished."

[1] The Young Sailor sings, but does not appear in person.

When we first meet with the Tristan story in literary form in the twelfth century it is already ancient; the poets and prose writers who gave it shape at that time were working on the basis of a number of episodes that had long been popular in oral form. The perambulating jongleurs would find everywhere, in the relatively cultured baronial court and among the unsophisticated people, eager listeners to the ever-fascinating tale. Each of them would embroider it according to his fancy, inventing, on occasion, new adventures to kindle fresh interest in those who had heard it already more than once; and the quality of these inventions would vary with the intellectual and moral constitution of the narrator and the level of culture and taste in his audience of the place and the moment. Even in the final literary forms in which the legend has come down to us the noble central motives are profusely encrusted with adventures of a rather crude kind.

2

Scholars today mostly agree that the story originated in the Celtic regions of Wales or south-west England, whence it passed in time to Brittany.[1] The French poets Crestien de Troyes,—whom we shall meet again in connection with the Parsifal legend —and La Chèvre reduced it to writing, but no trace of their work has survived. The oldest extant French or Anglo-Norman versions of the tragic story of Tristan and Isolde are the poems of Béroul and Thomas; both belong to the twelfth century, the former being slightly the older. Neither of them has come down to us complete. Towards the end of that century one Eilhart d'Oberge, a Saxon vassal of Henry the Lion, Duke of Brunswick, made a German version that agrees more with that of Béroul than with that of Thomas; the inference is that he and Béroul based themselves on some common source. Early in the following century the German minnesinger Gottfried von Strassburg combined a little of the Eilhart with the main Thomas form; and it is from his version that Wagner mostly drew his material. Gottfried died before completing his work, which was continued by two of his compatriots,

[1] A Persian origin has been claimed for it, but a consideration of this theory would take us too far afield.

Ulrich von Türheim (about 1240) and Heinrich von Freiberg (about 1300). By an odd coincidence, Gottfried's unfinished narrative breaks off at virtually the exact spot at which the surviving fragments of Thomas's poem begin.

This latter was imitated in prose, in 1226, by a Norwegian writer, a monk of the name of Robert, at the behest of a king of Denmark, Haakon V, who was an ardent admirer of the French romances of chivalry. This manuscript, which figures in the treatment of the subject by modern scholars as "the Saga", has fortunately survived intact and is accessible in print. Another valuable source for the reconstruction of the legend is a poem entitled *Sir Tristrem*, apparently dating from the early years of the fourteenth century, which was discovered in the library of the Faculty of Advocates in Edinburgh and published by Sir Walter Scott in 1804. The only other source that need be mentioned here is a manuscript in the Bodleian Library, dating probably from the end of the twelfth century, of a poem dealing with *The Mad Tristan*—a series of episodes that play a large part in the story, but for which, of course, Wagner had no use.

3

A critical scrutiny and comparison of all the manuscript versions now accessible to us led the great French scholar Joseph Bédier to the conclusion that at the root of all of them lay a lost poem by some man of genius who wrote in the early part of the twelfth century. Bédier's argument is that the Tristan story, in the literary form it took about that time, is not, like certain other epic narratives, the result simply of the more or less fortuitous accretion of a number of independent "lays" treating of the adventures of a hero. Whereas in the case of legends that have grown to great size by the mere aggregation of particles it makes no great difference in which order the episodes are taken, the Tristan story follows a definite and coherent plan. The end is kept in view from the beginning; the nature and the order of the episodes are designed for cumulative effect; the characters and their motives are throughout consistent with themselves and psychologically related to each other; in all the versions which we possess the incidents are largely the same and occur in the same order; and always there is the same over-riding sense of the lovers being in the grip of a fatality to which they were born and against which they and others strive in vain. Bédier draws the conclusion, therefore, that the many ancient versions now accessible to us, English, French, Italian, Russian or Northern, are sub-products of three main works—that of Thomas (about 1160–1170), that of Eilhart (about 1190–1200), and a French prose romance (about 1230). The Saga, the English *Sir Tristrem* and certain other forms derive from Thomas, and Gottfried from Thomas and Eilhart; while the only forms not stemming directly from the main three are that of Béroul (about 1180) and *The Mad Tristan* (about 1170). And the ultimate source of them all is presumed to be the lost poem of the unknown poet.

Bédier conjecturally sets forth the main genealogical table thus:

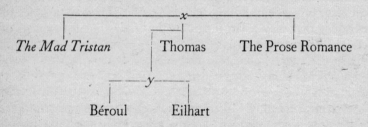

x representing the archetypal work of the unknown prime-poet, and *y* some source or other, ultimately deriving, like the others, from *x*, which was used by Béroul and Eilhart. Manifestly all the episodic Tristan legends current in the early twelfth century were known to the prime-poet, who was perhaps an Anglo-Norman: presumably it was he who welded them into an organic whole some time before the middle of that century. But for him, Bédier opines, we should have no real "story of Tristan and Isolde" but only a number of loosely connected episodes.

There is no necessity for the ordinary reader who is interested in the Tristan saga only as a background to Wagner's opera to embark on the labour of working his painful way through all the mediaeval versions of it. His task has been simplified for him by Joseph Bédier, who, in his book *Le Roman de Tristan et Iseut,* has fused the essentials of all the versions into a single coherent story, told in a charming style that had become second nature to the great scholar through his long absorption in the literature of the Middle Ages. From this one volume the reader can get all the material he needs as a preliminary to the study of Wagner's handling of the legend. The ancient story will be told here mostly along Bédier's synthetic lines,[1] but the reader must bear in mind that the episodes and the names and places differ from each other in an infinity of small points in the various originals.[2]

4

Marc, "King of Cornwall and of England", being hard pressed by his enemies, is aided by Rivalen, King of Loonnois; and in recompense for his services Marc bestows on him the hand of his sister Blanchefleur.[3] The time comes when Rivalen has to return to his own kingdom to defend it against the attacks of his enemy Duke Morgan. He takes Blanchefleur, who is now with child,

[1] It is upon Bédier's book that the Swiss composer Frank Martin has based his very attractive "oratorio profane" Le Vin Herbé.

[2] There is an excellent English prose version of Gottfried's poem by Miss Jessie L. Weston—The Story of Tristan and Iseult, 3rd edn. 2 vols., 1907. Miss Weston omits a few passages of minor importance, and completes Gottfried's unfinished story from Heinrich von Freiberg and Ulrich von Türheim.

[3] At the outset we have a typical example of how the versions differ from each other in minor details. In some of them Rivalen is lord of Ermenie or Parmenie. He comes to Marc's court in the first place in pursuit of glory. He and Blanchefleur love each other in secret, and when she finds herself with child the fact has to be concealed from the King for fear of his resentment; "she conceived in distress the child whose story you are about to hear, who was fated to bring suffering and distress to all, man or woman, who should love him." Rivalen returns to his own land to fight Duke Morgan, and Blanchefleur, unable to bear her grief alone and dreading shame, follows him there. Through all this multiplicity of variants in the sources, however, the main features and psychological motives remain the same; as regards the present matter, for example, Tristan, as his name imports, is in every version a child born to suffering and sorrow beyond those of other mortals. The Fates have marked him down as their victim from the beginning; even his parents have loved under a fateful compulsion, with death as their inevitable portion.

back with him to his castle of Kanoel, and going forth to the war leaves her in charge of his faithful marshal Rohalt. The news comes to Kanoel that Rivalen has been slain; after three days of grieving Blanchefleur gives birth to a son, on whom, because he has come into the world *par tristesse*, she confers the name of Tristan. To save the boy's life after the capture of the castle Rohalt passes the infant off as his own, and after seven years commits him to the charge of a trusty squire named Gorvenal, under whose care he grows up to be a model of manly strength and grace and beauty, skilled not only in arms and hunting but in the seven arts and all other noble accomplishments.

One day the boy is trapped by some Norwegian merchants on their ship and carried off over the seas; but a storm that arises they read as a sign of the displeasure of the gods, whom they placate by setting their captive adrift in a small boat, which carries him to Cornwall. He is taken to the court of King Marc, to whom he soon becomes dear for his comeliness and courtesy—though his cautious account of himself is that he is the son of a merchant in a land beyond the seas. (Some of the old romancers make it clear to us that Marc's great love for him comes from obscure stirrings in the King's heart towards the memory of his sister Blanchefleur). But the time comes when Rohalt arrives in Cornwall, tells Marc that Tristan is his own nephew, and summons the youth back to Loonnois to rid his land of the usurper. This he does; and then, out of the nobility of his heart and the love he bears his uncle, he delegates his lands to Rohalt and returns to Cornwall.

He finds the kingdom in great grief, for a formidable Irish knight has come to claim the tribute due to the King of Ireland,— three hundred noble Cornish youths and three hundred maidens to be taken back with him to serfdom. The emissary is Morholt, whose sister, Queen Iseut, is the wife of the Irish King: he is a man of gigantic stature, invincible in battle. None of the Cornish noblemen dares a trial at arms with him; the young Tristan alone accepts his challenge to single combat. In spite of the entreaties of Marc and the nobles he accompanies Morholt to a nearby island; there he slays the giant, whose body, with a fragment from Tristan's sword embedded in the head, is taken back in mourning by the men of Ireland; "and from that day Iseut the Fair"—the daughter of the Queen—"learned to hate the name of Tristan of Loonnois."

But Morholt's sword had been dipped in poison, and a wound he had dealt Tristan was beyond the skill of healing of anyone in Cornwall. So dreadful was the odour that came from it that none could bear to be at his bedside but those who loved him most, King Marc, Gorvenal, and the faithful knight Dinas de Lidan. He longs for death, yet life and the light of the sun are still dear to his brave young heart; so at his urging they place him in a small boat, without oars or sail, and commit him to the hazard of the sea. After seven days and nights he is cast up on the shore of Ireland. (In Gottfried, Morholt, before the last stage of the combat, tells Tristan that his wound is poisoned, and that no one can heal it but his sister Queen Iseut, who knows the virtue of every herb and the remedy for every ill. Morholt proposes peace between them: Cornwall shall pay the tribute, and he himself will conduct Tristan to Ireland, where the Queen will heal him. Tristan rejects the offer, the fight continues, and Morholt is slain). Those who have rescued him take him to Iseut the Fair: "she alone, skilled in philtres, can save him, but she, alone among women, desired the death of Tristan." When, thanks to her magic arts, he recovers and realises the danger he is in if he is recognised, he saves himself by a ruse: he is a minstrel, he tells her, who had been sailing for Spain, there to learn the lore of the stars; but pirates had boarded the ship, he had been wounded in the fight and had escaped in the tiny boat in which he had been found. All believed him, for not even the Irish warriors who had seen him in Cornwall could recognise him, so cruelly had the venom in his veins changed his appearance. After forty days, being almost wholly cured and restored to his former strength and comeliness, he flies in secret from Ireland, and after escaping many dangers at sea finds himself once more at the court of King Marc.[1]

---

[1] In Gottfried's poem Tristan goes of his own accord to Ireland to seek healing of Iseut. He arrives at the port of Develin (Dublin), whence he is taken to the court. Knowing that, as the slayer of Morholt, he is taking his life in his hands, he tells Iseut that his name is Tantris. This was a touch that would delight the imagination of the Middle Ages, which always admired cunning

5

There his enemies, in particular four "felon barons" who hate him for his favour with the King and do not desire to see him their ruler when Marc shall die, begin to plot his ruin. How has he been able to work wonders beyond the power of ordinary men? they ask. Only by enchantment could he have made his way to Ireland without sail or oars; and now he is once more casting his magic spell upon the King. So they urge Marc to marry some king's daughter who will bear him an heir to his kingdom. Of himself he would never have yielded to them, so great was the love he had for his nephew. But the noble Tristan himself, scornful of the suspicion that he had wormed his way into the heart of the King only for his own profit, swears to him that if he does not do as the barons desire he will leave Cornwall and never return. Wagner makes good psychological use of this motive in his second act.

Thereupon the King, in deep distress of soul, looks about him for a way by which he may appear to yield to the importunities of the barons and yet find a way of escape. One day, as he is musing sadly in his chamber, two swallows who are building their nest fly past, and from the beak of one of them there floats through the open window a long thread of golden hair, finer than any silk, that glistens in the sun. Marc bids the barons assemble, Tristan among them: he will do as they desire and marry, he tells them, but only the woman from whose head the golden hair has come. The barons are baffled: how to find this woman? who can say from what distant land the swallows may have flown? They suspect some crafty ruse on Tristan's part to frustrate them. But he, having examined the golden thread, and knowing whence it could alone have come, turns to Marc with a smile: he himself, he

in the outwitting of an enemy. To us, of course, it is charmingly naive; it is very much as if a modern novelist were to ask us to believe that Mr. Winston Churchill managed to maintain himself for some weeks in the Cabinet councils of the Nazi party by calling himself Chinston Wurchill. Still, there it is in the legend, and an important feature of it; and we have to accept it in the spirit in which it is offered. Wagner himself has to take over the Tristan-Tantris motive in order to account for certain episodes and their psychological results.

says, will find the head from which it grew, even though it should be more difficult to return alive from the lady's land than it had been from the island whither he had gone to fight Morholt.[1]

To Ireland, then, he goes, in the guise of a merchant, taking with him a hundred Cornish men of high degree, their rich apparel being concealed under the bridge of the vessel. Apparently he has not thought out any plan for the vicarious wooing of Iseut; but accident puts him in the right way. The ship anchors on the Irish coast, and for a while he and his companions pose as traders. Then, one morning, Tristan hears that a fearsome dragon is terrorising the countryside. He returns to his ship, arms himself, brings out his horse, and attacks the dragon, which he slays; its tongue he cuts out and places in his tunic. But the beast has poisoned him with its noisome belchings, and, faint after the combat, he makes his way to a pool in the distance, where he falls unconscious.

6

Now the King had promised the hand of his daughter Iseut to whoever should rid him of the dragon; and his seneschal, though an arrant coward, has gone out that day as usual to see if fortune will somehow favour him, for he desires Iseut. Finding the body of the dragon, and near it a dead horse and a shattered shield, he concludes that the slayer of the monster has himself been slain; so

[1] In Gottfried and *Sir Tristrem* it is the nobles who choose the Irish Iseut as bride for Marc, whereupon Tristan, who alone knows her and the King her father, and has already sung her praises to Marc, volunteers to fetch her. Both Gottfried and the author of *Sir Tristrem* mention the story of the swallow, but Gottfried gravely argues that it is improbable that any swallow would have taken the trouble to go all the way from Cornwall to Ireland for material for its nest and return with a single hair. How could it know, asks the implacably logical German poet, that it would find this hair in Ireland, and, if so, on whose head? Why should it make that long journey over the sea when there would be no lack of building material in its own neighbourhood? Gottfried comes to the stern conclusion that those who tell this tale of the golden hair are romancing. Bédier and others think it likely that Thomas, in the lost portion of his poem, had similarly argued against the truth of the episode. To us, however, it is too charming to be rejected on strictly ornithological grounds. That mediaeval swallow evidently had an eye for romance.

he cuts off the dragon's head, bears it to the King, and claims the promised guerdon. The King summons his vassals to meet him in three days, when the seneschal will be required to make good his claim before them all. Iseut, learning that she is to be given to the despised dastard, laments her evil fate; but suspecting some imposture on his part she goes in secret with her maid Brangaene and her squire Perinis to the dragon's haunt, where they find the headless body and a horse; the latter, Iseut observes, is not harnessed or shod in the Irish fashion. They light upon the unconscious Tristan, whom they carry back and conceal in the women's quarters of the castle.

As Iseut is removing his armour she discovers the dragon's tongue. She revives him by virtue of a herb, tells him of the treachery of the seneschal, and asks if he will expose the deceit two days later in combat. He consents. The next day she prepares a bath for him and anoints his body with a potent balm of which her mother alone knows the secret. She finds him comely, and hopes his prowess will match his beauty. Recovering his strength, Tristan opens his eyes, looks at her, and smiles. The reason for this she does not understand. Has she somehow failed in duty to her guest? Has she omitted to cleanse his armour, tarnished by the venom of the dragon? She goes to where his sword and halbert are being kept, and finds them goodly. But when she draws the sword from its sheath she sees a gap in it that reminds her of the splinter taken from Morholt's head. A doubt assails her. She examines the fragment and lays it on the sword: the two fit perfectly. Then she returns in fury to Tristan: "You are the murderer of Morholt", she cries; "now die in your turn"; and she raises the sword to strike him. Tristan knows he is helpless; only his wits can save him now. She has not only the power but the right to take his life, he tells her, for twice he has owed it to her. He was the "minstrel" she had healed in days gone by, after he had slain Morholt in fair fight. It was for her that he had fought the dragon. Let her kill him, then, if that will bring her praise and glory, and in the arms of the seneschal she can think of the wounded guest who had twice risked his life for the conquest of her, and whom she had killed defenceless in his bath. Then he tells her of the swallows and the golden hair left at Tintagel. It was for her he had come a second time to Ireland; and he shows her the hair interwoven with the gold embroidery of his tunic, and still lustrous while that had faded. She looks at the sword and the tunic, and for a long time she is silent: then she kisses him on the lips in token of peace between them.

When the vassals assemble, Tristan appears with his hundred men in their richest apparel. Iseut addresses her father. The seneschal had sworn falsely, she tells him; here is a knight ready to prove in combat that it was he who delivered the land from the scourge: will the King promise to forgive him any ancient wrong he may have done them and grant him mercy and peace? Her father pledges his word. She brings Tristan forward, and at once the Irish knights recognise the slayer of Morholt and clamour for his death. But Iseut reminds her father of his promise; and he kisses Tristan on the mouth in pledge that there is peace between them. Tristan produces the dragon's tongue and defies the seneschal to combat, who dares not accept the challenge. Then Tristan tells the King that twice he has conquered Iseut, once through Morholt, and now through the dragon, and so has the right to take her with him over the sea. But in order that the Irish and the Cornish lands may henceforth live not in hatred but in amity she will be given as wife to King Marc. The hundred Cornish squires vow to serve her in all fealty as their queen. But Iseut is overwhelmed with shame and anguish. This splendid Tristan, having conquered her, now disdains her; perhaps his story of the golden hair was only a falsehood; and now he is delivering her over to another man. But the King, faithful to his oath, places her right hand in that of Tristan, who grasps it as pledge that he takes possession of her in the name of the King his uncle.

7

When Iseut leaves Ireland the Queen her mother gives the maid Brangaene a potent philtre she has brewed by her magic art. None but Brangaene is to know of it, she tells her; on the nuptial night she is to pour it secretly into the cup that will be drained by Marc and his bride. Its virtue is that those who have drunk it will love each other henceforth with all their soul and all their senses, in life and in death.

On the ship Iseut never ceases to brood upon her cruel destiny; and when Tristan approaches her with courteous and respectful speech she repulses him angrily, her heart being full of resentment against him. She hates him for that he had killed Morholt, that he had torn her from home and kindred by stratagem, and above all because he had not claimed her for himself but is carrying her to a strange country to be given to another. Then one day, when the ship lies becalmed in the torturing heat, the pair call for something to slake their thirst. A little serving-maid finds the flask which the Queen had given to Brangaene, and they drink the philtre in the belief that it is wine. "But it is not wine; it is passion, it is bitter joy, and anguish without end, and death for the twain." A strange new emotion courses through their veins. Tristan reproaches himself for unwilled treason to the good King his uncle: he had been free of the taint of desiring his kingdom, yet now he loves the King's bride. Iseut, for her part, had willed hatred to Tristan but can only love him now. They sail on in torment of soul, trying to avoid each other, wretched when apart, more wretched still when they meet, trembling at the sight of the abyss of suffering and danger that has opened before their eyes. And all the while Brangaene, who alone knows what and how the Fates have wrought, watches them in terror. They try to understand and justify themselves and each other; till at last, on the third day, their lips meet. Not until then does Brangaene disclose that they have drunk the draught of love and death. "Then let death come!" cries Tristan; and the lovers become one in soul and in flesh to the end of time.

Our central concern being not the legend in itself but the use made of it by Wagner, we need not set forth in detail the long story of the devices to which the lovers, after their arrival in Cornwall, are compelled to resort to gratify their passion in secret. Many of these devices are very naive, in the mediaeval fashion; others are crude, and some, to modern taste, rather repellent. We can pass on to the tragic end of the story.

The day comes when Tristan, surrounded by spies and enemies and in danger of his life, has to fly to Brittany. For two years he has no news of Iseut: he believes she has forgotten him, and his weary heart fails him. He aids Duke Hoël and his son Kaherdin in their wars, and Hoël, in gratitude, offers him his beautiful daughter Iseut of the White Hands in marriage. "Sire, I will take her", he says; "and for that word he was to die". He weds her; but as his servants are disrobing him there falls from the sleeve of his tunic a ring of green jasper that had been the other Iseut's gift to him; and he sees that once more, unwittingly, he has been for a while false to troth. Iseut of the White Hands remains his wife only in name. In time, tormented by his memories, he goes back once more to the court of King Marc, where, to be near his only love, he disguises and degrades himself and passes himself off as a fool (in the double mediaeval sense of the word).[1] In the end Iseut recognises him; and when dangers accumulate and he has to return to France she swears that she will follow him when he shall call to her.

The legend now repeats itself to some extent, suggesting that two primitive versions of it had at some time or other become fused into one. Yet again Tristan is dealt an incurable wound by a poisoned weapon. Knowing that he is dying, and unable to go to Iseut, he sends Kaherdin to Cornwall to beg her to come to him. Iseut of the White Hands, concealed behind a partition, overhears their talk; hatred of a rival springs up in her soul, and she plans revenge on the lovers. Iseut the Fair obeys Tristan's call. It has been arranged between him and Kaherdin that if he is bringing her back he shall hoist a white sail, if not, a black one. The sick man, unable to stir from his couch, sends Iseut of the White hands to keep watch for the coming of the ship. At last, she tells him, it is in sight of the shore, making for land—under a black sail. Then Tristan turns his face to the wall; he murmurs three times the name of Iseut, and dies. When Iseut the Fair at last finds her way to him she kisses his lips and takes him in her arms, and mouth to mouth, body to body, soul to soul, she joins him in death.

When Marc hears of the pitiful end of the lovers he sails to

[1] This phase of the legend, for which, of course, Wagner had no use, has been treated in dramatic form by Ernst Hardt in his *Tristan der Narr* (3rd edition 1903).

Brittany, has the tombs opened, and carries the two dear bodies back with him to Tintagel. There he buries them, Tristan on this side of the chapel, Iseut on that. But when night fell there sprang from the grave of Tristan a briar that flung its branches across the roof of the chapel and sank them into the tomb of Iseut.[1] Three times the men of the country cut it down, and three times it grew afresh; then Marc forbade that a hand should ever be laid on it again.

8

Certain modern writers, afflicted by Providence with more prim piety than poetic imagination, have turned a coldly censorious eye on the legend of Tristan and Isolde, especially on some of the episodes in the middle part of it. "It will not be worth our while", says one of them, "to follow the details of the rest of the story, which is made up of a series of shameless tricks played by the lovers upon King Marke, whereby they are enabled to enjoy their love together in secret . . . From the time when Isot and her intriguing mother enter on the scene the story is as dull as it is immoral. What sane-minded person can possibly take an interest in a succession of childish tricks played by two lovesick boobies upon a half-witted old man?"[2] This is the type of mind that would ask, after reading *Othello*, what sane-minded person could possibly take an interest in a coloured soldier of violent temper who is such a booby as to conceive a murderous hatred of his wife because she had lost a handkerchief that had belonged to his mother, or in a story like the mediaeval one of Parsifal, where

[1] There are several mediaeval variants of this miracle. The story as told above is the one found in a printed edition of the French prose romance (1514), though not in the surviving manuscripts.

[2] Whatever modern re-telling of the legend the reader may elect to read, it should not be that of Tennyson in the *Idylls of the King* ("The Last Tournament"). The poet went to the worst sources for his material; and Miss Weston is right in saying "it is incomparably the worst version of the story ever given to the world—a gross libel alike on the lovers and on King Mark. For Tennyson's own sake it should be excluded from any future edition of his works: it is little to his credit, either as man or as poet, that in the most famous love-tale of all time he could see nothing but the lowest and most sordid of intrigues."

an infinity of suffering comes upon many people because an un-tutored boy refrains from asking the simple question, "Uncle, what ails thee?"[1]

This sort of moral indignation misses the target badly in a matter of art. It is quite true that we of today do not react to some of the incidents in the Tristan legend as the Middle Ages did. That epoch had its own standards of human excellence, and, living as it did surrounded by dangers, it dwelt with gusto on the ruses by which a favourite hero outwitted his enemies. As Ernest Muret, the editor of the Béroul fragment, has put it, the story is "one of 'adventure', glorifying the two qualities most prized in the Celtic world in which it originated—physical prowess and agility of mind." A society so largely given over to violence and treachery found a healthy human delight in dwelling on the satis-faction of revenge, and a sort of professional admiration of ingenuity in the art of saving one's life by trickery. Every face in the audience must have been wreathed in approving smiles as the jongleur told how cunningly the hunted lovers defeated justice when Iseut was summoned to prove her innocence by undergoing the ordeal of the red-hot iron. Without considerable craft she could hardly have come through that test successfully. But her woman's wit was equal to the occasion. She sends secret word to Tristan, who is in hiding near by, telling him to disguise himself as a poor pilgrim and wait on the further bank of the river beside which the trial is to take place. When the boat has crossed the stream she protests that she cannot land without soiling her robe in the mud. Thereupon the knights call on the shabby pilgrim, who, unlike them, has nothing on him to spoil, to carry the Queen over to the dry land in his arms. He does so. Then Iseut goes with great dignity to the brazier to make her declaration of innocence, raises her right arm towards the relics of the saints, and swears by all that is sacred that never has any man born of woman taken her in his arms except the King and this poor pilgrim. She plunges her bare arm into the brazier, takes hold of the iron bar, walks nine steps with it, throws it down, and crosses her arms on her breast with the palms upward. All see that her lovely flesh is un-scathed. Therefore she has spoken nothing but the truth; and

[1] On this point see the chapter on *Parsifal*.

there goes up from them all a great cry of praise and thankfulness to God.

The modern reader may wonder why offended Heaven did not expose and punish the fraud. Even Gottfried was well aware of this little moral difficulty, and he indulges in some ironical reflections about Providence allowing itself to be outwitted sometimes by the wicked. But the people who originally inserted the story of the ordeal into the Tristan story—it appears, by the way, in various forms in various settings in more than one country—evidently had no qualms about the matter. They and their listeners, as Miss Weston and other scholars have pointed out, "really regarded Tristan and Iseult as irresponsible victims of Fate, and evidently saw no incongruity in their appeals to heaven to demonstrate their innocence."

9

The portrait of Tristan would not have been complete according to mediaeval notions had it not shown him as the superior of his enemies not only in valour but in cunning. Thus Gottfried describes with evident satisfaction the hero's reception by the admiring court when he returns to Cornwall, sound again and safe, after his first audacious visit to Ireland: all laughed heartily when he told how he had gone alone and unarmed into the enemy's country and been healed by the Queen and the daughter of the King: "all agreed that never in their lives had they heard anything so wonderful".

But in the first place the majority of these episodes, in which cunning matches itself against cunning, guile against guile, and the hero and heroine of the tale are of course the most prolific in resource of them all, are merely patches upon the essentially grave and noble fabric of the Tristan story: they probably date from an earlier and half-barbaric period, and had to be retained by the literary romancers of a later day because many of their readers or listeners already knew them and expected them. In the second place, some of the episodes have, for all their naiveté, a curious pathos and beauty of their own. An outstanding example is the tale of how Tristan and Iseut, compelled to flee from the court and live a hunted life in a forest, are discovered by a spy who betrays them to the King. Marc, with vengeance in his heart, comes by night and finds them sleeping in a grotto. He sends the spy away and draws his sword; they are at his mercy. But he sees that while their lips are touching, between their bodies lies a naked sword. A great pity and love for them both, for his beautiful adored Queen and for the nephew who is the dearest of all men to him, take possession of his heart. He will spare them, but he will let them know that he had tracked them down and their lives had been in his hand. He leaves his glove where it will shield the lovely face of Iseut from the unkind light. He takes from her hand an emerald ring he had given her: once it had needed forcing upon her finger to make it fit; now it slips from it, so wasted is she with privation and suffering. In its place he leaves his own royal ring, and with it his sword; that of Tristan he takes away with him. When the lovers awake they realise how near they had been to death, and the greatness of soul and profundity of love of the man who had spared them. There are few incidents in the whole of mediaeval romance more beautiful.

It stands to reason that the legend would never have captured the imagination of the later Middle Ages as it did had it been the mere tale of a couple of lovesick boobies imposing on a half-witted old man. No story was so widely diffused over cultured Europe or evoked so great an imaginative response in the finest minds of the day. Dante, who, though the stern moralist in him would hardly have approved of the pair, as poet could not resist their appeal. In the fifth canto of the *Inferno* they figure among other great lovers of the fabled past pointed out to him by his guide Vergil:

> "*L'altra è colei che s'ancise amorosa,*
>   *e ruppe fede al cener di Sicheo;*
>   *poi è Cleopatràs lussuriosa.*
> *Elena vedi, per cui tanto reo*
>   *tempo si volse, e vedi il grande Achille,*
>   *che con amore al fine combattèo.*
> *Vedi Parìs, Tristano*": *e più di mille*
>   *ombre mostrommi e nominommi a dito,*
>   *ch'amor di nostra vita dipartille.*

(" 'The next is she [Dido] who slew herself for love and broke faith with the ashes of Sychaeus; then wanton Cleopatra. See Helen, for whose sake so many cruel years revolved; and see the great Achilles, who fought at last with love; see Paris, Tristan': and he showed me more than a thousand shades, naming them as he pointed to them, who were parted from our life by love.") The mind of the epoch spent itself affectionately in one medium after another upon this or that episode of the Tristan and Isolde legend, in detached poems, in tapestries, in illuminated manuscripts, in ivories. The mediaeval musicians put some of their best songs into the mouths of the hapless lovers, for Tristan, according to tradition, was a great minstrel, and Iseut too poured out her heart in song. Gottfried speaks of "many lovely melodies" concerning them "that were known far and wide" in his time. He speaks with particular feeling of one noble lay composed by Tristan which, he says, is loved in every land and will not be forgotten as long as the world endures. This song, unfortunately, has been lost; but others have survived, and the words and music of one of them—the "lai de plor" (the song of tears) which, according to the legend, was sung by the wounded Tristan in the little boat that carried him the first time to Ireland—may be found in some of the modern books on the subject.

10

Some of the nineteenth century opponents of Wagner foamed at the mouth over the "glorification of adultery" in this opera of his. Had they read his poem with any understanding they would have realised that the Tristan story, as he tells it, is the most tragically ascetic of tales. But even for the Middle Ages the essential things were not the episodes, the ruses by which the lovers were enabled to gratify their secret passion, but the beauty and pitifulness of their love. The legend became as popular as it did, not because of the piquancy of some of its details but because, in its fundamentals, it had all the qualities that go to make one of those great sagas into which each following age can read itself afresh. There have not been many of them in modern times; they can be counted on the fingers of one hand—the Nibelungenlied,

Tristan and Isolde, Faust, the Cid, Don Juan. In all these the characters and events have the quality of rising from the particular into the universal. They are at once personal and symbolic. Faust is not merely a scholar who strives after knowledge and power: he is the symbol of all striving after those illusions. Don Juan is not merely a licentious young Spanish nobleman: he is the life force for ever condemned to the vain quest of seeking to accomplish itself in the satisfaction of the senses. And Tristan and Isolde were already in mediaeval times not simply a chance pair of lovers but the symbol and the essence of a love so overpowering that it is impossible for the human victims of it to achieve their heart's desire except in death.

From the very beginning the threads of Tristan's life are spun for him with slow inexorable intent by the Fates. He is born of sorrow and for sorrow, as the musician Wagner so finely conveys to us in his third act, where the fevered man's memory runs back to the last time he had heard the mournful strain now piped by the Herdsman—it had filled Kareol with its lament when his father, and again his mother, had perished in the flower of their youth and beauty. It is Fate that in devious ways draws Tristan twice to Ireland and Isolde, Fate that weaves the threads that gradually intertwine Isolde's life with Marke's. And even for the Middle Ages the love-philtre that is the explosive core of the story, the point towards which everything that has happened before inevitably tends and from which everything that happens later inevitably flows, was not solely and simply a magic brew, working by physical means, but a symbol, the instrument through which Love has its imperious way with men and women. Gottfried achieves a finer touch than his French predecessors by not speaking of love in the abstract but incarnating it in Frau Minne, the old Teutonic goddess of Love: it is always Frau Minne who is working her irresistible will upon these two fated human vessels.

The sympathies of the old romancers are all with Tristan and Isolde even as against the good King Marke. Tristan, for them, is in his inmost self always the flower of truth and loyalty and honour; it is precisely because of these great qualities in him that he unwittingly forges the first link in the chain of his own destruction—

his altruistic bringing of Isolde to Cornwall to be the bride of
King Marke, so that he may free himself of the suspicion of any
taint of self-interest in his love for and gratitude to the King his
uncle. (Wagner makes great use of this psychological motive in
his second act). And the final testimony of the Middle Ages to its
belief in the essential innocence of Tristan and Isolde is the ending
of the story, with that exquisite symbolic figure of a tree springing
from the grave of each of them and twining its branches with those
of the other. This, as Wolfgang Golther points out, was the
poetic mediaeval way of indicating that physical love had been
purified into the spiritual by death. The "flower-symbol", he
says, "in the sense it carries in the legend, means that before God's
throne Tristan and Isolde are absolved of all guilt . . . An earnest,
pessimistic spirit breathes through the story from first to last;
whoever turns away from it on moral grounds has simply mis-
conceived its profoundest being and its true worth, which consist
in this—that behind all the glitter of the incidents there lies a conception of the utmost gravity . . . Not every one of the poets was
conscious of it, of course; but the really great masters, and Gottfried most of all, had at least an intuition of it."

Wagner penetrated as no other modern poet or dramatist has
done to this spiritual core of the saga, and thanks largely to the
unique expressive power of music he has been able to raise the
lovers from the plane of the individual to the higher sphere of the
symbolic. His poem is not a mere re-telling of the ancient story of
Tristan and Isolde but in several respects a radical re-creation of it.

II

He had made the acquaintance of the legend in the course of
his study of mediaeval literature in his Dresden period, and we
may be sure that it had often been in his mind since then. He had
read Gottfried in the modern German rendering of Kurtz, a
second edition of which was published in 1847. Kurtz had made
an ending of his own for the unfinished original, and, in a passage
that no doubt struck light and fire into Wagner's imagination,
had said that the story contained all the materials for a tremendous
tragic drama. Wagner was also acquainted with certain by-pro-

ducts of the legend that had been discussed by F. H. von der Hagen in the fourth volume of his *Minnesinger*, a mine of information about the German poems of the twelfth, thirteenth and fourteenth centuries (1838). We first hear of the story taking definite shape within him as an opera in a letter of his of December 1854 to Liszt, at the time when he was engaged on the music of the second act of the *Valkyrie*. He hopes, he says, to finish the *Ring* by 1856 and produce it in 1858. But, he continues, "since never in my whole life have I tasted the real happiness of love I mean to raise a monument to that most beautiful of dreams, in which, from beginning to end, this love shall really sate itself to the full for once. I have in my mind a plan for a *Tristan and Isolde*, the simplest but most full-blooded musical conception; in the 'black flag' that waves at the finish I shall then enshroud myself— to die." From this it would appear that his intention at that time was to introduce the second Iseut—Iseut of the White Hands— and the dramatic culminating motive of the white flag and the black. As the reader knows, he dispenses with these addenda in his poem, though, it is true, he makes his Tristan, during his delirium in the third act, see in imagination Isolde's ship approaching with "the flag at the mast"—as it stands a somewhat irrelevant touch, the significance of which comes home only to the listener who is acquainted with the episode of the second Iseut and the two flags from other sources than the libretto. But it was not only in this respect that the final conception of *Tristan and Isolde* was to differ from that outlined in the letter to Liszt.[1]

The lovers of romantic biographic fiction will have it that Wagner wrote *Tristan and Isolde* because he was in love with Frau Wesendonk. That he loved the fair Mathilde during those Zürich years is beyond question, also that there was a close emotional association in his mind between her and the opera all the time he was writing it. But to suppose that Mathilde "inspired" *Tristan* is to take a very unsophisticated view of the nature and the workings of the artistic imagination. The mind of a great creator is a much more complex piece of machinery than this would suggest; and in Wagner's case there were other and even more potent forces at

[1] He had originally intended to bring in Parsifal in the third act. On this point see *infra*, p. 698.

work within him than the golden hair of the pretty young lady
in the luxurious house on the Green Hill at Enge. He was in a
highly febrile state all through those years. The fact that he was
intensely unhappy cannot be regarded as a prime determining
factor in the conception and execution of *Tristan*, for the side of
the artist that has daily commerce with the outer world and the
side that is concentrated inwards have often the minimum of connection with each other. Wagner was equally unhappy, if not,
indeed, more so, during most of the time when he was writing
The Mastersingers, which is the sunniest of all his works. To
suppose that a great artist is optimistic or pessimistic in his creative
work according to whether things are going well or ill with him
in actual life at the moment is to assume, to borrow a phrase of
John Stuart Mill's, that because there is pepper in the soup there
is pepper in the cook.

What was really happening in the depths of Wagner during
the middle 1850's was that an enormous volume of music, of a
type which the world had not yet known, was pressing imperiously
for another outlet than the heroic *Ring*, upon the composition
of which he was engaged at that time. It was a common experience
with him to find that the very intensity of his concentration on
one subject called up from the deeps another that had long been
slumbering in his subconscious. In the present instance the whirl-
ing nebula of incandescent dust from which the *Ring* music was
being generated spontaneously threw off, at a given place and
time, without much conscious volition on his part, a mental and
musical world entirely different from the other. He himself saw
clearly enough, in later years, what had happened within him
about 1854. He would have smiled then at the theory that *Tristan*
had been "inspired" by Frau Wesendonk, whom, it is instructive
to note, he no longer saw through quite the same eyes of idealising
romance when the score of the work was off his hands and the
volcano that had been raging within him had died down. When
he came to write his memoirs he was able to see more clearly the
hidden inner processes that had brought forth *Tristan*. As usually
happened with him when his musical faculty was working at high
pressure, he says, there had come over him in 1854 an urge to
express himself in poetry. It is a fundamental misconception of

him to suppose that his practice was that of the ordinary opera composer—first of all to decide upon a "subject", make a three-act "libretto" of it, and then sit down and invent music to fit the words and follow the action. The process with him was, in some essentials, the reverse of this; a more or less indefinite and mainly musical complex within him kept calling on him to give it poetic and dramatic actuality, for which words and a stage action would be necessary.[1] His melancholy broodings in the 1850's upon the innate tragedy of the cosmos had been both clarified and intensified by his reading of Schopenhauer at that time. The result of it all, as he himself tells us, was that the attempt to find "an ecstatic expression of the profoundest elements" in this philosophy "generated in me the conception of a *Tristan and Isolde*."

12

He talked the matter over with his young Zürich companion Karl Ritter, who, it appeared, had also become interested in the Tristan theme. Ritter showed him his own plan for a drama on the subject. The experienced eye of the musical dramatist saw at a glance that the young man had gone entirely the wrong way about it. Evidently he had lost himself in the picturesque details and the conventional "love interest" of the tale, whereas what was needed was a concentration on the eternal and tragic core of it, with the employment of no more incident than would be necessary to show this core in conflict with the world of material reality. So after thinking it all out on one of his walks Wagner drew up a scenario of his own in three acts.

Whether that sketch has survived among his papers we do not know; it is possible that he destroyed it when, in 1857, he took up

[1] "I can conceive a subject", he once wrote to a friend, "only when it comes to me in such a form that I myself cannot distinguish between the contribution of the poet and that of the musician in me; and its completion in word and tone is simply the ultimate realisation of something that had originally presented itself to me only in vague outlines. This is the foundation of all my productive, and more particularly my musical-productive, power."

the operatic plan again in good earnest. During those three years a great deal had happened to him, internally and externally. Continual brooding upon philosophical problems and eager readings of Schopenhauer and of Buddhist literature had deepened his feeling that the outer world is a tragic illusion. He had last appeared before the public as a composer with *Tannhäuser* in 1845 and *Lohengrin* in 1850. Since then he had written the *Rhinegold*, the *Valkyrie*, and the greater part of *Siegfried*, works in which he had developed opera to a point hitherto undreamed of. Of all this astounding creative work the public as yet knew nothing. The completion of the colossal *Ring* seemed at the moment to lie in a distant future; and when the scores of the tetralogy were finished there would still be before him the terrifying task of staging the huge work. Meanwhile the problem of merely existing was becoming more and more difficult. So on the mundane side of him he came round to the view of his friends that he ought to write something more practicable, under existing conditions, than the *Ring*, something for which he could hope for immediate payment from the German theatres. He deluded himself with the belief that his *Tristan* would be such a work, for it would call for only five principal singers and a couple of subsidiary characters, virtually no chorus, and the minimum of staging. Little did he dream at that time that his *Tristan* was to turn out to be the most difficult work in any dramatic genre which the world had yet seen.

But perhaps more potent than any of these influences was the fact that although his mind was alive with music, a large part of it was unconsciously seeking an outlet which the *Ring* could not supply. He had been continuously engaged on the poems and the music of the latter since 1848, and no doubt he was beginning to feel a little weary of the company of his more-than-life-size Germanic gods and heroes. In the summer of 1856 we find him telling Liszt that at the moment he would rather write poetry than music, and that he had "two marvellous subjects" which he must work out. One of them was the *Tristan* of which he had already spoken; the other was an Indian theme. This latter work, the title of which was to be *The Victors*, haunted his imagination for another twenty years or so, but never came to fruition, partly because much of the emotional and metaphysical impulse that would have gone to the making of it had been expended on *Tristan*, partly because, in the late 1870's, he found that a good deal of what he would have to say in connection with it was finding its natural expression in *Parsifal*.

In the primitive Teutonic world of the *Ring* he was probably becoming, from sheer repletion, less interested each month. A crisis was reached in June 1857. On the 28th of that month he wrote to Liszt that he had "torn *Siegfried* from his heart and buried it alive under lock and key": "there will I keep it; no one shall see anything of it, for it will be sealed up even from myself." "I have led my young Siegfried into the beautiful forest solitude again; there I have left him under a linden tree, and, with tears from the depth of my heart, said farewell to him: he is better there than anywhere else." (The point in the score to which he was referring is the second scene of the second act: after the hero's words "Dass der mein Vater nicht ist" he had written in his Composition Sketch, "27th June 57. R. W. When shall we see each other again?"). So long as his letter of the 28th June to Liszt was the sole source of our knowledge of this matter it was naturally assumed by the biographers that it was at that point that work upon *Siegfried* was suspended for several years. We know now, however, that he took it up again a fortnight later and completed the second act on the 30th July. No doubt he foresaw that the composition of *Tristan* would mean a long separation from the *Ring,* and he thought it as well to finish the second act of *Siegfried* while the "feel" of the *Ring* milieu was still lively within him.

13

Letters of his to other friends confirm and amplify the evidence of his letter of June 1857 to Liszt. As early as the 19th December 1856, while he was engaged on the *first* act of *Siegfried,* he told the young Princess Marie Wittgenstein (the daughter of Liszt's unofficial wife Princess Carolyne von Sayn-Wittgenstein) that while trying to work "today" at the music of *Siegfried* he had "unawares fallen into the Tristan" subject. "For the moment", he continues, "music without words: several things I would rather treat in music than in verse"—one of the many indications we have that the prime impulse to the writing of his dramas was generally not so much a literary as a musical one. "Today, as I have told you", he goes on to say, "Tristan has come between [myself and Siegfried] in the shape of a melodic thread which, though I fain would have quitted it, kept on spinning itself, so that I could have spent the whole day developing it."

The precise meaning of this will appear in a moment. Meanwhile we must draw attention to a salient characteristic of his artistic psychology. As a rule he was occupied simultaneously with more than one work; even if he were not actually putting B upon paper it was gestating in his subconsciousness while he was formally engaged upon A. His dramatic characters and situations had a life of their own within him that was independent of his surface consciousness and even of his volition, so that while at work on the score of one opera a theme would suddenly spring up within him which had nothing to do with the subject in hand but, as he would soon realise, belonged of rights to some other work that had not been consciously occupying his thoughts at the time. One day in 1876 when he was writing the American Centennial March the idea flashed across him for the ensemble of the Flower Maidens in *Parsifal*; and in 1859, while engaged on the third act of *Tristan*, the joyous melody of the Herdsman took, without his willing it, a turn which, as he soon saw, was more appropriate to his forgotten young hero Siegfried: it became later the "Love's Resolution" motive of the *Ring*.[1] And after telling Marie Wittgenstein, in December 1856, that he could not get on with *Siegfried* because the Tristan subject kept throwing out its own musical roots within him, he informed her in the following August that the reverse had latterly been the case. He had carried, he said, the composition of the second act of *Siegfried* as far as the words "Dass der mein Vater nicht ist", and then closed the score with the intention of saying a long farewell to his hero. A few days later, he continues, he had sat down at his desk to make a sketch for the poem of *Tristan*, "when suddenly I was overmastered by so pitiful a longing for *Siegfried* that I took the score

[1] See *infra*, musical example No. 153 in the analysis of *Siegfried*.

out again and decided to complete at any rate the second act. This has now been done: Fafner is dead, Mime is dead, and Siegfried has followed the flying Forest Bird; and this, my dear child, has turned out very nicely, so that now I know my hero is all right. Yet all this has been a great strain on me, for while I was once more working at *Siegfried* I could get no peace from *Tristan*. I actually worked simultaneously at them both, the *Tristan* taking more and more definite shape, and I being so passionately occupied with it that in the end the double labour was a perfect torment to me."

The truth is that a tremendous psychic upheaval had begun in him as early as 1856, which put him rather out of tune for the time being with the joy-in-life of which his youthful hero Siegfried had been the ardent optimistic expression. He had become introspective, pessimistic, mystical. Three days after his letter of the 19th December 1856 to Marie Wittgenstein he wrote thus to Otto Wesendonk, who was at that time in Paris: "I can no longer get into the mood for my *Siegfried*; my musical sensibility is now reaching out far beyond that, into a realm more consonant with my mood—the realm of melancholy. It is all coming to me, though as yet quite flatly and superficially." He was beginning, in fact, to *feel* the Tristan subject very definitely as music, before it had taken a definite shape within him dramatically.

14

Let us now turn back to the passage in the letter to Marie Wittgenstein in which he says that while working at the music of the first act of *Siegfried* he had "unawares fallen into the Tristan subject" ... "for the moment, music without words", in the form of a "melodic thread" which kept on "spinning itself" almost against his will. We are fortunate in being able to identify that "thread" now.

There has survived in the Wahnfried archives a scrap of music which was evidently intended to accompany an (unpublished) letter of his to Frau Wesendonk of the early part of 1857. It consists of eighteen bars beginning thus:

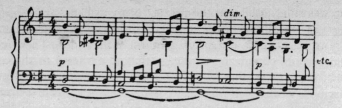

The reader will recognise this as the foreshadowing of one of the most important themes of the second act of *Tristan*. (See musical example No. 41). In the opera it appears in 3/4 time, but in this primitive form it is in 4/4: the harmony on the third beat of the first bar is less chromatic and therefore less poignant than it afterwards became, while after the third bar the strain develops in a manner rather different from the one we know so well in the opera.[1]

Wagner was only copying, however, for Frau Wesendonk's benefit, from a still earlier sketch, which also happens to have been preserved. This is dated by Wagner himself "19 Dec. 56"—i.e. the very day on which he was telling Marie Wittgenstein that a "melodic thread" had been "spinning itself" of its own volition within him. There can be no doubt then, that this is the "thread" to which he was referring.[2] And, again fortunately for us, this earlier sheet contains not only the above-mentioned eighteen bars with a few variants, but the first draft of what was afterwards to become world-famous as the motive of "Longing" or "Desire" in the opera (see No. 1B); and the sheet is headed "Love Scene: Tristan and Isolde". Now it was not until August 1857 that Wagner began the Prose Sketch for his drama—some ten days after he had finished the composition of the second act of *Siegfried*. It is clear, then, that even in December 1856—that is to say, while

[1] A facsimile of the manuscript page will be found in the Bayreuth *Festspielführer* for 1938, p. 160.

[2] The word "thread" (*Faden*) was one often used by Wagner to describe the material from which he did his musical "spinning". It does not mean simply a "theme" in the sense in which other composers employ that word, but, as it were, the musical incarnation of a situation, a character, or a mood, from which all conceivable tonal and psychological mutations would follow later as a matter of course. Thus he told Cosima in 1871 that his heart was not really in such a work as the *Kaisermarsch*, and he was writing it with some difficulty. It "meant" nothing to him: "I must have my big threads", he told her.

he was still working at the *first* act of that opera,—the *music* of *Tristan* was already imposing its will upon him before he had drawn up so much as a formal scenario of the action. There could be no more convincing demonstration of the truth of the statement that if ever there was an opera born of the spirit of music itself it is *Tristan and Isolde*.

Towards the end of April 1857 he drafted a scenario for *Tristan* that served as foundation both for a later detailed Prose Sketch (finished on the 20th August and now available in print), and then for the poem. The latter was completed on the 18th September of that year. The Prose Sketch and the poem do not differ greatly from each other; where they do, the Sketch is useful as showing more clearly what was at the back of Wagner's mind here and there, for the hyper-laconic style in which the poem is written makes it a little difficult sometimes to grasp his full meaning.

15

As usual with him, his first concern had been to rid the immense mass of mediaeval material of everything merely accessory and condense the sprawling action into its essentials. He dispenses, for example, with the four "felon barons", enemies of Tristan, who in the legend play a considerable part in laying traps for him and denouncing him to the King. All he needed in this respect was the single character of the false friend Melot, and even of him we learn more through the mouths of others than in person, for he makes only two very brief appearances in the drama—at the end of the second act, where he brings in King Marke to surprise the lovers, and in the final stage of the third act, where he sings a couple of lines "off" and then enters only to be slain by Kurvenal. To the whole opera Melot contributes no more than twenty bars of music. The King, again, appears only twice, and as a commentator on events rather than a participant in them; his share in the long chain of episodes stretching from Tristan's combat with Morold to the final catastrophe we mostly learn from others. Of ordinary stage incident there is exceedingly little in the opera; it is virtually unnecessary, for the veritable drama is not in what "happens" to Tristan and Isolde in the world of reality but in what evolves within themselves, and this is revealed to us principally by the music.

Wagner's most difficult problem was in connection with the love-philtre. It was impossible for him to employ this in its more materialistic mediaeval sense—to make the inextinguishable "passion" of the lovers for each other the crude physical result of a magic brew; though unfortunately it is still in that naïve sense that the majority of listeners to the opera still conceive it. Even the more refined of the old romancers, as has already been pointed out, seem to have had a poetic intuition of it as a symbol rather than a material agency; that is to say, the lovers were predestined to each other in life and in death, and the draught brewed by Isolde's mother for a purpose of her own was merely the Fates' way of accomplishing their far-seen purpose. But Wagner would have to refine this central motive of *his* drama far beyond this. Manifestly the problem was the most crucial of the many he had to face; and the only valid solution of it was the one finally adopted by him—Tristan and Isolde were to be shown drawn together from the beginning by some compulsion which they themselves did not comprehend; the near approach to the shore of Cornwall, where Isolde would be handed over to the King and Tristan would depart from her sight and Marke's for ever, had strained both of them to breaking-point, so that each of them saw that the only way out of a lifelong torment was through the gates of death; to that end they were to drink gladly of what they imagined to be a poisoned cup; and then, in the belief that death was at hand, the barriers raised between them by Tristan's sense of honour and loyalty to King Marke would go down, and they could confess their love without restraint and without self-reproach. In this reading, the love draught is really a subsidiary rather than a cardinal motive; it does indeed fill their veins with a fire that can never be extinguished, but only because the materials for the fire were there before.

16

The point was, how could Wagner introduce this new psychological motive, which transformed the saga so radically as to make his own version of it virtually a new creation on his part? Obviously it would have to become operative during the first (and only) sojourn of his wounded "Tantris" in Ireland. The moment chosen by Wagner to constitute this nodal point of his drama was that in which Isolde stays her avenging hand just as she is about to slay the man whom she recognises as the hated vanquisher of her affianced Morold; and the medium through which this was to be brought home to the audience was Isolde's Narration to Brangaene in the first act. That Wagner was at first not entirely clear how this was to be done is manifest in the Prose Sketch.

The old poets had told how Tristan, at Isolde's mercy in his bath when she discovered that the splinter taken from Morholt's head fitted exactly into the notch in the sword, had saved his life in the first instance by denying that he was Tristan, and then by a crafty appeal *ad misericordiam*. In the end it is the "sweet womanliness" in her, as Gottfried puts it, that gets the upper hand of her fury; she throws away the sword and weeps bitterly. The Queen, Isolde and Brangaene go out and take counsel together. Brangaene's advice to them is to spare the alien knight, in the first place because they will need him to dispose of the troublesome seneschal who is claiming Isolde's hand, in the second place because this Tristan has evidently been sent to Ireland on some important mission, and it behoves them to find out what it is. When they return he once more begs for grace, and promises them that if his life is spared the young Irish princess shall go back with him to be the proud wife of his uncle the noble and powerful King Marc, and the two countries will henceforth be bound together in friendship. The three women kiss him on the lips in token of amity, Isolde, however, with reluctance, for to her he is still Ireland's enemy and hers. Then he confesses that he had ventured to Ireland the second time for the very purpose of taking back with him Iseut, whose beauty he had praised to Marc. The Irish King is summoned and let into the secret, and he too makes peace with Tristan and with Cornwall.

17

Obviously this very earthly web of mediaeval intrigue and ruse could not be utilised for Wagner's drama, the central psychological point of which was to be that the pair already loved each other before the stage action opens, that Tristan had fought down his love out of loyalty to King Marke, that Isolde was torn between love for the hero Tristan and hatred of him as Ireland's conqueror, and that the pair feel themselves liberated from all worldly constraints only at the moment when, as they believe, they are about to end their souls' intolerable torment by a voluntary death. Wagner could safely follow the old story, as indeed he does in Isolde's Narration, as far as the moment when she refrains from killing Ireland's enemy and hers with his own sword. But why does his Isolde so refrain? "Recognising him as the slayer of the Irish hero", so runs the Prose Sketch in its outline of the Narration, "and recalling her vow of vengeance, she had seized the sword and rushed at Tristan to kill him; then she had felt pity for the wretched sick man". The reader will recall that whereas in the legend this episode occurs during Tristan's *second* visit to Ireland, when he is helpless not through sickness but because, like the doomed Agamemnon, he is in his bath and unarmed, Wagner transfers it to the first visit, the motive of which, in the legend, had been to win healing from the magic medical art of Isolde's mother. This enables him to employ with all the more force the motive of "sweet womanliness", as Gottfried calls it, the sudden surge of pity in Isolde for the grievously sick and helpless man. But of itself that psychological motive, moving as it is, is still insufficient for Wagner's full purpose; it does not explain how, from that moment onward, each had read *love* in the eyes of the other.

The problem of how to bring this new and vital factor home to the listener must have cost Wagner much anxious thought. This is clear from an insert he has made in the Sketch—manifestly an afterthought—after the sentence quoted above, "she had felt pity for the wretched sick man"; before passing on to the next stage of the Narration, in which, very much as in the legend, Isolde communicates to Brangaene her discovery of the identity of Tristan and Tantris, he now inserts in a parenthesis, "Here she makes it clear that it was an awakened passionate inclination towards him that had stayed her hand". But in the Sketch he still does not go on to show just how this is to be "made clear" to the

audience, perhaps because he himself did not know precisely how
at that time. But when he came to write his poem, a few weeks
after the completion of the Sketch, he saw a satisfactory solution
of his problem, though in terms more of music than of verbal
exposition. He makes the wounded man turn upon Isolde a look
that melted her heart, for she read in it the secret of an unspoken
love.

> *Then from his sick-bed*
> *up he gazed—*
> *not on the sword,*
> *not on my hand—*
> *his eyes in mine were looking;*
> *and his woefulness*
> *pierced to my heart;*
> *the sword—fell from my hand.*
> *The wound that Morold dealt him,*
> *with my own hand I healed it,*
> *that home he might betake him*
> *and rid me of the load of that look!*

But even this does not make the psychological point absolutely
clear to us when we read the poem alone for the first time;
illumination comes rather from the music, from the so-called
"Look" motive that wells up in the moving tones of a solo viola:

a motive that has already played a most significant part in the prelude, and is later to be charged with an infinity of meanings in
the opera itself. Wagner never tired of assuring his correspondents
that something that was not quite clear to them in a text of his
would be made perfectly clear by the music. This is a case in
point.

The poem of *Tristan and Isolde* was completed and the manuscript presented to Frau Wesendonk on the 18th September 1857. (A few changes in the text were made by Wagner in later years). The dates of composition of the music are as follows:

COMPOSITION SKETCH[1]

Act I. 1 October—31 December 1857.
Act II. 4 May—1 July 1858.
Act III. 9 April—16 July 1859.

ORCHESTRAL SKETCH

Act I. 5 November 1857—13 January 1858.
Act II. 5 July 1858—9 March 1859.
Act III. 1 May—19 July 1859.

The full orchestral score was finished on the 8th or 9th August 1859.

The first performance of the opera was given in Munich, under Hans von Bülow, on the 10th June 1865, with the following cast:

Tristan:	Ludwig Schnorr von Carolsfeld
Isolde:	Malvina Schnorr von Carolsfeld
Brangaene:	Anna Deinet
Marke:	Zottmayer
Kurvenal:	Mitterwurzer
Melot:	Heinrich

18

Wagner was a *musical* dramatist, a fact which permitted him a technique of exposition entirely different from that of the prose or poetical dramatist. The normal way of the latter is to start at A and go step by regular step to Z. Wagner, relying at least as much on music as on words to tell us who and what his characters are and what they feel at a given moment, and being more con-

---

[1] The "Composition Sketch" of a Wagnerian work was, in general, the first swift outline of the music. The "Orchestral Sketch" was a rather more developed lay-out, with a summary indication of his orchestral intentions. The final stage was the Orchestral Score.

cerned, in the main, with mental states than with incidents,[1] could plan his stage action in ways that would give the freest imaginable play to music. This was especially the case with *Tristan and Isolde*, which is *musical* from centre to periphery—so much so that the bulk of the opera would make an organic musical whole if played through by the orchestra without the voices. If ever there was an opera "born out of the spirit of music", to adapt the title of one of Nietzsche's books, it is this. The words are not so much the generators of the music as the crystallisation of musical moods into the accepted symbols of speech. Wagner himself pointed out how different his procedure had been from that of the ordinary dramatist or poet. The latter would have had to explain, for example, at the outset, at some length, who Tristan was, how he came into the world, what adventures he had already gone through, and so on; and out of all this statement of fact there would emerge, bit by bit, our emotional reaction to the characters, their milieu, and the things that happen to them. But the musician, says Wagner, can strike at once to that emotional core which it takes the poet or the prose romancer so long to reach by the slow way of description; we are given the whole complex of longing and suffering that is the essence of the souls of the two chief characters in the opening bars of the prelude. The music in and by itself shapes their total stage life into a kind of ring, a circle in which there is no apposition of starting-point and finish; the strain of longing is the first that greets our ears in the prelude, and it is the last to resound in them in the opera; and, as with a ring, it is equally appropriate to say that the work begins where it ends as that it ends where it began.

19

The musical texture of *Tristan* is different from that of any other of Wagner's works in that it is almost purely "symphonic"; often

---

[1] In the *Mastersingers*, of course, incident follows incident in quick succession and in the order of actual life; but that is because here the drama comes nearer to the world of ordinary people than in any other work of his maturity.

he abandons himself to the sheer intoxication of "developing" the mood symbolised by a particular motive for pages at a time, the stage situation meanwhile remaining stabilised. Not only is there hardly any action, but action of any kind would mostly be out of place: the movement of the drama is not realistic but psychological, not external but internal, the music passing through all kinds of metamorphoses to which the words serve only to give us the objective clue. For the greater portion of the time the actors hardly need to change their positions on the stage; the consequence is that when something does "happen", in the ordinary theatrical sense of the word, it strikes with tremendous force; it does precisely what Wagner intended it should do—the brief intrusion of reality gives us a blinding sense of how entirely Tristan and Isolde had lived, in the only sense that they would have called living, in a world of non-reality of their own. In the first act, apart from the episode of the coming of Tristan into the presence of Isolde, very little "happens" until the end, when the ship arrives in Cornwall and the King and his courtiers and people come to the shore to meet it; and the stir and excitement of this are suggested in the music rather than shown on the stage. In the second act there are only two disruptions of the inner drama by external reality—the entry of Tristan, and, later in the act, that of Marke and Melot, with the wounding of Tristan. In the third act there is virtually no action until the very end—the arrival first of Isolde, then of Marke and the others.

The real drama, as has been already pointed out, is not external but internal, a state of affairs made possible to the musical dramatist only in virtue of the vast superiority of music to speech and to the pictorial arts in range and subtlety and intensity of emotional expression. Taking advantage of this, Wagner exploits a favourite technique of his; instead of burdening his stage with a multiplicity of characters and "effective" episodes he concentrates the very essence of these into a reference to them by one of the few main actors at some vital point or other. There is no need, for instance, for him to begin by telling us in words that Tristan was foredoomed to sorrow from the moment of his birth: he conveys this to us not at the commencement of his story but near the end, and that by the simplest and most affecting of means, by a few bars in which, moved by the Shepherd's mournful melody, the hero's thoughts go back to the tragic death of his father and mother. Again, Wagner shows us nothing of the Breton and Cornish milieu in which the young Tristan had lived, nothing of the events that had led up to the fateful journey to Ireland, nothing of what happened there. All that is necessary for us to know about these and other things he communicates to us through the mouths of the lovers in the first and second acts, where the story is told not for its own picturesque sake—as it would be by a poet—but because it furnishes the explanation of the situation and the state of mind in which the lovers now find themselves: it is not the incidents themselves that he gives us but the incidents remembered in, and blindingly illuminated by, emotion.

It has to be admitted that the rigour with which he follows this system in *Tristan and Isolde* sometimes makes it difficult for the casual listener in the theatre to follow all the windings of his poetic imagination. It is impossible, indeed, to see the work precisely as the creator of it conceived it without a close study not only of the poem but of the prose Sketch—which accounts for the fact that even today ninety-nine people out of a hundred in the theatre come away with a totally wrong idea of much of it. If they had the smallest understanding of it they would not speak of the second act, as they do, as "the love duet", for all the world as if "love" meant here what it does in the case of Romeo and Juliet, or Faust and Marguerite, or Pinkerton and Madam Butterfly, or a hundred other operatic lovers. Throughout the poem Wagner restricts himself to the barest minimum of words—sometimes no more than two or three to a line of verse,—having no need of speech beyond what is necessary to concretise the emotion that is being poured out by the prime expressive instrument of the work, the music. Occasionally his condensation has been so drastic that, as we shall see when we come to the analysis of the second act, it is only after reading his more detailed exposition of events and motives in the Prose Sketch that the almost too laconic poem conveys its full meaning to us.

20

The selection from *Tristan* known in the concert room as the Prelude and Liebestod—the latter being the closing scene of the opera—makes an admirably rounded whole, musically and psychologically. It is worth noting, by the way, that when Wagner first linked up the Prelude with the finale for concert purposes it was to the former that he gave the explanatory title of "Liebestod"; the finale he described as "Verklärung" (Transfiguration). In a programme note of his own on the concert arrangement he explained the Prelude (in his nomenclature at that time the Liebestod) as a progression from "the first timidest lament of inappeasable longing, the tenderest shudder, to the most terrible outpouring of an avowal of hopeless love", the music "traversing all phases of the vain struggle against the inner ardour, until this, sinking back powerless upon itself, seems to be extinguished in death." The Verklärung he elucidated thus: "Yet what fate divided in life now springs into transfigured life in death: the gates of union are thrown open. Over Tristan's body the dying Isolde receives the blessed fulfilment of ardent longing, eternal union in measureless space, without barriers, without fetters, inseparable."

Until the final scene of the opera was written, the Prelude, of course, would have to stand on its own feet if given in the concert room; and as it has no formal ending, one would have to be provided. A passage in a letter of Wagner's to Bülow of the 12th March 1859 has misled many people into imagining that the ending now in use was Bülow's work. As a matter of fact what Wagner had said to him was, in effect, this: "If you want to give the Prelude at your concert in Prague, well and good. But you will have to supply an ending of your own; don't ask me to make one." No doubt Bülow did the best he could; but the few bars he quotes from his effort in one of his letters to Wagner do not suggest that included in the talents with which Providence had so richly endowed him was the capacity to write Wagner's music for him. Wagner explained later to Frau Wesendonk that his reason for refusing Bülow's request had been that he himself had not seen at that time precisely how the thing was to be done, that perception having come to him only after he had written the last page of the opera, in July 1859. In the following December he sent Mathilde a sheet of music containing his own ending to the Prelude in piano score.[1] He had made it for performance at the concerts he gave in Paris on the 25th January and 1st and 8th February 1860.

His own exposition of the thus re-modelled Prelude in a programme note written for these concerts is interesting. The tale of Tristan and Isolde, he says, is one of "endless yearning, longing, the bliss and the wretchedness of love; world, power, fame, honour, chivalry, loyalty and friendship all blown away like an insubstantial dream; one thing alone left living—longing, longing unquenchable, a yearning, a hunger, a languishing forever renewing itself; one sole redemption—death, surcease, a sleep without awakening." For the composer whose aim it was to express this in music, he continues, there was but one over-riding care, "how to impose restraint on himself, since exhaustion of the subject is impossible". So "in one long succession of linked phases" he "let that insatiable longing swell forth from the first timidest avowal to sweetest protraction, through anxious sighs, through hopes and fears, laments and desires, bliss and torment, to the mightiest forward-pressing, the most powerful effort to find the breach that will open out to the infinitely craving heart the path into the sea of love's endless delight. In vain! The exhausted heart sinks back, to pine away in a longing that can never attain its end, since each attainment brings in its wake only renewed desire, till in final exhaustion the breaking eye catches a glimpse of the attainment of the highest bliss—the bliss of dying, of ceasing to be, of final redemption into that wondrous realm from which we only stray the further the more we struggle to enter it by force. Shall we call it Death? Or is it not the wonder-world of Night, whence, as the story tells, an ivy and a vine sprang of old in inseparable embrace over the graves of Tristan and Isolde?"

This may not be ideally lucid, but Wagner can be forgiven for

---

[1] A facsimile of it will be found in both the German and the English edition of the Wesendonk correspondence. A separate edition of the Prelude, with the new concert ending, was at once published in full score by Breitkopf and Härtel.

that; he was engaged on the impossible task of finding equivalents in the crude medium of words for the infinite intimacies and trackless subtleties of music. But what was in his mind is clear enough for all that: the Prelude, as he had conceived it, traces the vicissitudes of inextinguishable longing, yearning ever renewed after each illusive satisfaction of it and finding real consummation only in death. We shall see in a moment just how he rounded off this mystical conception, so far as the Prelude is concerned, by the concert close he wrote for it in December 1859; meanwhile let us look at the Prelude as it appears in the opera.

21

There is here no attempt, as in the Prelude to the *Mastersingers*, to epitomise the stage action and the characters of the opera. Wagner concentrates on the inmost essentials; the Prelude is the slow musical elaboration of a single bitter-sweet mood. For convenience sake we have to attach labels to the "motives" upon which it is constructed, but the reader must be warned against interpreting these too literally. As a rule the commentators have decided upon a label from a hint given by the words or the situation with which a motive is associated on its first appearance in the opera. But we shall go hopelessly wrong if we allow that particular association to occupy our minds each time we hear the motive; it may undergo all kinds of metamorphoses and take on all shades of meaning as the drama goes on.

It is easy for the casual listener to get a false notion of the opening bars of the Prelude:

The melodic line seems to be a continuous one, running from the opening A in the lower clef to the final B in the higher. But in reality there are two motives here: the first (No. 1A), extending from the opening note to the D sharp of the second full bar, is given out by the 'cellos in the upper register of the instrument, where the tone has a peculiar poignancy; the other (No. 1B) comes out in the penetrating timbre of the oboes, over a wood wind harmony of bassoons, cor anglais, and (in the second bar) clarinets. We shall call No. 1A the Grief or Sorrow motive, though it must be understood at the outset that its expression in the course of the opera is too multiple and too complex for it to be always tied down to the connotation of a single word: it has in it at various times something of longing, of pain, of hopelessness, of resignation, and many things more. No. 1B is called by some analysts the motive of Desire, by others the motive of Magic, for no better reason than the fact that when it is first heard in the opera Isolde is speaking of her mother's craft in the brewing of magic potions. Our own rough-and-ready label for it will be Desire, with which the magic art of Isolde's mother necessarily has a certain external connection. But it must always be borne in mind that, as has been pointed out in the foregoing pages, Wagner never intends to imply that the love of Tristan and Isolde is the *physical consequence* of the philtre, but only that the pair, having drunk what they imagine to be the draught of Death and believing that they have looked upon earth and sea and sky for the last time, feel themselves free to confess, when the potion begins its work within them, the love they have so long felt but have concealed from each other and almost from themselves. Nor will the reader need to be reminded that this motive No. 1B was committed to paper in December 1856, before a word of the scenario of the opera had been written. Consequently there is no warrant whatever for identifying it literally, as we were taught to do at one time, with the "magic" of Isolde and her mother: for Wagner it stood primarily for the predestined yearning of the lovers towards each other.

He himself, in a letter of March 1860 to Frau Wesendonk, has given us a clue to the complex of emotions the motive symbolised for him. He is in Paris, unhappy and sick to the depths of him with a sense of loneliness and alienation from his environment, and looking forward wistfully "towards the land of Nirvana". But Nirvana, it appears, becomes identical in his mind with Tristan, and Tristan and himself with the Buddhist theory of the origin of the world—the troubling of the primal cloudless heavens by a breath that swells and swells and finally condenses into our visible world in all its "inscrutable and impenetrable variety"; and he gives us the key to his meaning by quoting the music of our No. 1B, in a way that shows that he identified it just then with the "breath" out of which the cosmos has condensed. In a word, it is Desire, for ever expanding and retracting, for ever seeking to realise itself and for ever being frustrated.

22

Repetitions of No. 1 at various pitches and in various colours lead to a sforzando which introduces two new motives:

The first of these (A) relates particularly to the Anguish of Tristan; the second (B) is generally described as the Look (or Glance) motive, from the fact that it first appears in the opera at the point in the first act where Isolde tells Brangaene how her resolve to

avenge herself on the slayer of Morold melted away under the
glance that the sick Tristan had turned on her. No. 2 merges
insensibly into a third motive of a similar cast, which the commentators associate with the love-philtre:

A half-passionate, half-mournful development of this is broken at
one point by the reiteration of figures of this type:

which answer each other in different registers and colours. In his
letter of December 1859 concerning the concert close to the Prelude, Wagner tells Frau Wesendonk that she will "recognise ivy
and vine in the music, especially when you hear it in the orchestra,
where strings and wind alternate with each other". He was re-

ferring to the antiphonal figures shown in No. 4. But it would be the height of folly on our part to take all this too literally. The ivy-and-vine legend plays no part whatever in Wagner's drama. It may have pleased him and Frau Wesendonk to associate privately No. 4 (and themselves) with ivy and vine, but nowhere in the opera has the motive any such connotation; and here in the Prelude it depicts simply one more phase of the yearning of the lovers.

A point that should not be overlooked is the bass line (B, C, D sharp) in the fourth and fifth bars of No. 3. It wells up and subsides ominously in the double basses, bassoons and bass clarinet, and symbolises Death (or Fate). It is curious that Bülow, who made the first piano arrangement of the score, should have failed to see that these three notes constitute a definite motive; otherwise he would not have altered Wagner's slurring of them in the arbitrary way he does here and elsewhere.

Wagner now works up to his climax by way of a new motive:

which incorporates in itself more and more insistent reminiscences of No. 1B. The culmination is heralded by a fortissimo enunciation of No. 2B in increasingly complex harmonic forms, and with a terrific fortissimo in the full orchestra the climax is reached and passed. The fortissimo quickly subsides to a piano; the orchestra dwells sadly upon echoes of No. 1, No. 2B and No. 4, and the music gradually ebbs away into a heaving figure in the 'cellos and basses:

that prepares us for the sea setting in which the opera will open.

23

The Prelude is a perfect specimen of musical form at its most consummate, not a schematic mould imposed upon "thematic material" from the outside but a form that has come into being simply as the outcome of the ideas. Once more, as in the Prelude to *Lohengrin*, Wagner unconsciously obeys that natural law of structure that brings in the climax at a point about two-thirds of the time-distance between the beginning and the end. This is not only good art but ordinary experience; while it takes a long time to scale a mountain, the descent may be accomplished in half or a third of the time. Some conductors ruin Wagner's perfect design by pumping an accelerando into the music during the long crescendo that leads up to the climax. Wagner, who, though some conductors will receive the news with incredulity, knew infinitely better what his music was about than they will ever do, has not specified a single change of tempo during the prolonged ascent to the peak-point. He prescribes a slight holding-back after the peak has been reached, which is entirely in keeping with the general law of descent after a toilsome climb. The Prelude—and the same is even more true of the Liebestod—is far more tremendous in its tension when the ascent is not hurried in order to get a conductor's-effect of "increasing passion", a cheap showman's trick upon which Wagner used always to pour out his scorn. The last thing he wanted was that his music should reach the hearer not as he had conceived it but as it appears after it has passed through the distorting and sometimes vulgarising medium of a conductor's mind. As early as 1852 he had written to a friend, "I don't care in the least whether my works are given or not: all I am concerned with is that they shall be performed as I conceived them. Whoever can't and won't do that may leave them alone." Upon tempo he always laid the utmost emphasis: it was his constant complaint during his last years that he did not know a single conductor who could be trusted to find unaided the correct tempi for any of his works.

Let us now glance for a moment at the ending he himself devised for use when the Prelude is to be played in the concert room without the Liebestod. His instinct for form told him that in the first place the terrific climax would have to be dispensed with, since the goal was now different and the descent from the peak-point was going to be accomplished in a new way. With the closing scene of the opera in his mind the ebb of the psychological tide of the Prelude would necessarily have to be brought about in terms of that "Verklärung". So Wagner cuts out the original climax, which had come in the Prelude in bars 83 and 84. In bar 82 the trumpets and trombones had given out No. 2B. He begins his new close at this point: he swiftly dissolves the fortissimo into a diminuendo, cuts out bars 83 and 84, and continues quietly, as in the original, with bars 85 to the first half of 94. Here begins the short "Verklärung". A change in the latter part of bar 94 serves to introduce a motive of ecstasy that had appeared in the opera for the first time in the opening scene of the second act:

(See also No. 31 below). The remainder of the new matter consists almost entirely of wistful broodings upon this theme, until at last it assumes the form in which it plays a dominant part in the closing stages of the Liebestod, with the poignant No. 1B piercing through the texture at the finish, as it does at the end of the opera. (See No. 60). Wagner ends his arrangement, however, not in B major, as in the final bars of the opera, but in A major, thus rounding off the A minor in which the Prelude had begun.

24

A final word on the Prelude may not be out of place: it may help to clarify for the reader the whole problem of Wagner's use of "motives". We are compelled to attach labels to these, for otherwise we could not refer to them in our discussion of a work; but some of these labels have done considerable harm by bringing up in the listener's mind the same too literal connotation each time the motive appears. There are Wagnerian motives, of course, the meaning of which is virtually unchanging; they are definitely associated with a particular character (such as the Beckmesser or the Gutrune motive), or with an object that is at once physical and symbolic, and therefore static, (such as the Spear motive in the *Ring*). But Wagner's conception and employment of motives varied with the nature of the work he had in hand; and when, as in *Tristan*, stage action and external reality count for very little and psychological states for virtually everything, the import of a motive can rarely be pinned down throughout to any particular person, object or episode. The motives are sensitive, plastic musical materials, on a par with those of the symphonist, with which the composer weaves a fabric of thought and emotion of a kind that can exist only in music.

Now the Prelude to *Tristan* was not written, as most introductions to operas are, after the completion of the work, when the composer has the whole of his thematic material before him and can select from it just what seems to him best suited to epitomise the contents of the whole work. The *Tristan* Prelude contains no motive specifically correlated with the second and third acts, for the simple reason, among others, that Wagner had not even begun formal work upon these when the Prelude was written. He commenced the music of the first act on the 1st October 1857; and apparently he began with the Prelude. As his own programme note shows, it is in no way dramatic or pictorial: it expresses the incessant projection and recoil upon itself of a single emotion— that of longing without satisfaction and without end. Even if the opera had never been written the Prelude would still be a perfectly organised piece of mood-music that requires no "explanation" outside itself, a symphonic epitome, as it might be, of an unwritten drama. When Wagner was composing it the separate themes of it had probably no such precise meanings for him as the labels we attach to them are apt to suggest. When the time came for him to embody them in the opera, each of them would necessarily be associated on its first appearance with this, that or the other psychological point of the moment. But it is an error to assume, as the commentators have been inclined to do, that because at this point or that a motive is first heard in connection with certain words or a certain situation, it relates specifically to that sentiment or that situation whenever it occurs later in the opera, or, before that, in the Prelude.

25

Our Nos. 2B, 1B and 4 are cases in point. Because No. 2B first appears in the opera when Isolde tells Brangaene how the sick man looked up at her from his couch and the sword fell from her hand, the analysts have agreed to call it the Look motive, with the result that people innocently read that too definite meaning into it each time it occurs in the Prelude and in the opera. The truth is that it is a musical theme of generalised import, the expression of the love that Tristan and Isolde were fated from their birth to feel for each other; it is only the dramatic exigencies of the text that lead to its first putting in an appearance when Isolde recalls the outer circumstances of their realisation of this fatality. So with No. 1B: there is no necessity, and indeed it is misleading, to tie the meaning of this down to the "Magic" of Isolde's mother merely because it is first given out by the orchestra when Isolde says bitterly, "O futile art of the sorceress, that only balsams can brew!", and is heard again later when Brangaene says to Isolde, "Hast thou thy mother's arts forgot? Think'st thou that she who knows all secrets would have sent me with thee into a strange land without counsel?"—by which she means the philtre that is to ensure Isolde the love of King Marke. The true psychological significance of the potion has already been dwelt upon in the foregoing pages: it is not the prime cause of passion but the symbol of it. To think of the philtre in its material sense on each of the many occasions when the motive recurs later in the opera—for instance, in the prelude to the second act, or in the subtle transformation it undergoes in the introduction to the third act (No. 47)—is to fall into the rankest absurdity.

Again, although Wagner, in his letter to Frau Wesendonk, lets his fancy play upon the ivy and the vine in connection with our No. 4, we must not suppose for a moment that he originally shaped the theme with the intention of setting up any such per-

manent connection in the listener's mind. For him it was simply
another aspect of the predestined passion of the pair. He uses it,
for example, when, after drinking the philtre, they fall at last into
each other's arms:

Here any association of it with ivy and vine would manifestly be
out of place.

26

The Prelude ends, as we have seen, with a suggestion in the
'cellos and basses of the heaving sea—a figure fraught with foreboding.

When the curtain rises, say the stage directions, we see Isolde's
"tent-like apartment on the fore-deck of a ship; it is richly hung
with tapestries, which at first are quite closed in at the back; on
one side a narrow companion ladder leads below. Isolde is on a
couch, her face buried in the cushions. Brangaene, holding open
a curtain, is looking over the side of the ship." From the mast-
head we hear the voice of an invisible young sailor, singing, as
sailors will, a farewell to the girl he has left behind him: "Westward turn my eyes; eastward the ship flies. A homeward wind is
with us now: my Irish child, where waitest thou? Is it thy sighs,
my maiden, wherewith my sails are laden?[1] Waft us, o wind!

[1] *Sind's deiner Seufzer Wehen,*
die mir die Segel blähen?

Wagner's sketches show that these lines were originally preceded by two
which he rejected later:

dem englischen Gast
auf ödem Mast,

("for the English guest on the dreary mast").
The two discarded lines were also excluded from his imprint of the poem.

But alas for thee, my child, my Irish maid, thou wild, winsomest maid!":

The curious little unaccompanied song is invariably taken too slowly. It is some minor tenor or other's only chance during the entire evening to show what he can do; naturally he wants to make the most of it, and the conductor, instead of keeping him on a tight rein, too indulgently gives him his head. Wagner's tempo marking is "moderately slow", i.e. faster than the decidedly slow of the Prelude. The tenor, left to his own devices, is fairly sure to turn it into a spineless, rhythmless adagio.

Isolde hears the song and reads into the "Irish maid" a Cornish jibe at herself, the captive of Tristan, the trophy destined for King Marke. A surge of No. 2B in the orchestra shows that the subject of all her brooding during the voyage—the wrong that has been done her by Tristan—has now come uppermost in her mind; and her anger at the Sailor's words are expressed in a turbulent motive in octaves in the lower strings that will be drawn upon more than once in the course of the act:

Dragged back violently to the world of reality she asks Brangaene distractedly where they are. A phrase from the Sailor's song (No. 9A) now becomes a kind of Sea motive, the symbol of the transit from her home to an alien land. Above this foundation in the orchestra Brangaene, unconscious of the storm that is raging in Isolde's bosom, tells her with a certain satisfaction that the sea is smooth, the ship is sailing swiftly, and by evening they will touch land,[1] where, as the unsuspecting maid believes, a brilliant future awaits her adored mistress. "What land?" asks Isolde absently. "Cornwall's verdant strand", Brangaene replies. "Never!" cries Isolde passionately, revealing for the first time what had been festering in her heart all through the voyage: "not today nor tomorrow!"

Brangaene, alarmed at this outburst, lets the curtain fall and runs anxiously to her side. Isolde breaks out into a violent denunciation of her own "degenerate race, unworthy of its fathers". Where, she asks, is the famed power of her mother over sea and storm, that her child should be delivered up helpless to Ireland's hated Cornish conquerors? As No. 1B sounds in the orchestra she reproaches her mother for brewing nothing now but draughts of healing; she calls on the slumbering winds to obey her will—to whip up the dreaming sea to a fury of greed and make it devour the rich human prey the ship offers it: "Destroy this arrogant ship, engulf its shattered fragments! Take all that lives and breathes on it, ye winds, for your prize!"

At last Brangaene senses that her mistress has been hiding some secret grief from her all this time. She loads her with endearments and begs her to tell her all:

[1] "Blue stripes [of land] have appeared in the west", says Brangaene. It has often been pointed out that the Cornish land towards which she is looking lies not west but east of the ship. The slip of the pen probably came about through Wagner having changed the layout of the Prose Sketch at this point when he came to write the poem. In the former the song of the sailor at the mast-head had run thus: "Towards the west longs the heart; towards the east we sail. Fair the wind, smooth the voyage, calm the sea; blue stripes announce the distant but ever-nearing coast of Cornwall." Here Wagner's geography is correct. A few lines later Brangaene tells Isolde, in the Sketch, that "in the distance blue stripes are coming into view—probably the Cornish coast", which again is correct. There was no necessity, however, for both the seaman and the maid to talk, within a minute or two of each other, of the appearance of the blue stripes. So in the poem Wagner reserved this announcement for Brangaene; but in a careless moment he carried over into her speech the "westward" from the sailor's "westward turn my eyes".

*Without a tear
from father and mother didst part thee,
and scant farewell
to friends and kindred gav'st.
From thy home thou wentest
mute and cold,
pale and speechless;
eat thou would'st not,
neither sleep;
numb and wretched,
wild, o'erwrought:
o what sorrow
thus to see thee,—
thine no more to be,
strangers thou and I!*

and she implores her "sweetest and dearest" to take her to her heart and into her trust. For the accompaniment to all this Wagner plays in various forms with an urgent new figure with which No. 1B is incorporated:

Brangaene's appeal ends in a long-drawn cadence of melting sweetness and tenderness.

Isolde's only reply is a despairing cry of "Air, air, or my heart will burst! Open there! Open wide!" and Brangaene quickly draws asunder the curtains in the middle of the ship, just at the moment when the young Sailor breaks once more into a fragment of his song.

27

Through the opening now made in the curtains we see to the stern of the ship,[1] with the sea stretching out beyond it to the horizon. Round the centre mast sailors are reclining busied with ropes; further back, on the stern-deck, are recumbent groups of knights and squires; a little apart from them stands Tristan with folded arms, sunk in thought, looking out to sea; Kurvenal, his rough, fanatically faithful retainer, lies in a careless attitude at his feet. Isolde's eyes at once settle on Tristan. In an aside, as if communing darkly with herself, she sings softly, to the strain of No. 1B, some words the mystical meaning of which is as yet known only to her—"Chosen [destined] to be mine, lost to me; peerless, proud; brave and craven! Death-devoted head! Death-devoted heart!"

[1] There has been a good deal of unnecessary controversy about the proper setting of the first act of the opera. The stage directions say that "we see right down the ship to the *Steuerbord*." This has been taken in some quarters to mean that we see "to starboard", and it has consequently been argued that the vessel should be shown not end-on to the spectator but slantwise. The Prose Sketch, however, makes it abundantly clear that "Steuerbord" has not its modern nautical meaning here, but simply that of the place where the steering gear is. When Brangaene goes at Isolde's command "along the deck

The melody and harmony of the phrases are those of No. 1B, but
they are given a new and extraordinary significance by the orchestration and the dynamics—a shuddering tremolando in the muted
violins and violas, with a crescendo surge in each phrase. Winding
its way through this texture we hear No. 1A in the poignant quiet
tones of a cor anglais. The passage culminates in a harsh fortissimo
chord in the wood wind at "Todgeweihtes Haupt" ("Death-
devoted head"), ending in a sudden hush and a solemn harmony
in the brass at "Haupt", while at the end of "Todgeweihtes Herz"
("Death-devoted heart") the orchestra subsides again into the
original fateful shudder in the muted strings:

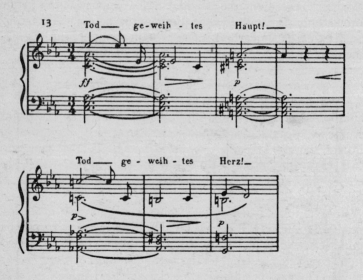

Then Isolde becomes conscious of her surroundings again.
Partially recovering her proud poise, she asks Brangaene, with a

to the *Steuerbord*" it does not mean that she takes a list to starboard but
simply that she goes to the spot where Tristan is standing by the helm. So
again when Isolde, during the dialogue between the maid and Tristan,
"keeps her gaze immovably fixed *nach dem Steuerbord*" it means not that she
keeps her eyes glued to starboard but that she looks steadily at the spot—the
steering place—where Tristan is. "Steuer" is the German for "helm",
"rudder". The verb "steuern" means to "steer".

nervous, uncanny laugh, what she thinks of the menial[1] there, "the hero who averts in shame and fear his eyes from mine". The simple, unsuspecting maid sings the praises of Tristan as the flower of knighthood. "Yet", replies Isolde, "in craven fear he shuns my presence while he carries home the corpse of a bride he has won for his lord." Does Brangaene doubt this? Let her then ask this "free man" if he dares at last approach his lady with the homage due to her—a duty and a courtesy he has neglected all through the voyage, so full of fear is he, this peerless hero. "Oh, well he knows why! To the proud one go: take him his lady's word—let him, as my servitor, at once approach me." "Shall I ask him?" says Brangaene timidly. "No, command him!" is the proud reply: "I, Isolde, bid the stubborn one do my will!"

Obeying her imperious gesture, Brangaene goes humbly past the sailors to where Tristan is standing: Isolde strides back to her couch, where she remains throughout the episode that follows, her eyes never leaving the little group in the stern of the ship. In the orchestra we hear the Sea motive as Brangaene slowly approaches Tristan, who is still motionless, lost in his thoughts. Kurvenal, without rising, plucks at his master's cloak with an ironic "Beware Tristan! A message from Isolde!" Tristan, torn from his dream, makes a convulsive movement, but at once recovers himself and inclines his head courteously as the messenger nears him.

In what immediately follows there is no interplay of musical motives, for it has no psychological bearing on anything that has gone before or anything that will come after; it is just a conversation, conducted quietly to the accompaniment of simple harmonies Tristan throughout is fencing with Brangaene; he is the soul of courtesy to her and to her mistress, but he has no intention of letting himself be diverted from his prudent resolve not to hold converse with Isolde while the voyage lasts. What, he asks the

[1] The usual convenient English translation of the line "Was hältst du von dem Knechte?" is "What think'st thou of the knight there?" But "Knecht" carries the meaning not of "knight" but of "menial": "knight" misses the scorn of Isolde's reference to the man who, instead of boldly declaring himself her lover, behaves only as the respectful servant of his King and the foreign Princess.

maid, is his lady's will? He is at her service; whatever she may command he will obey. If the voyage has irked her, it will soon be over, for before night falls they will reach the land. There, in the green meadows beyond the blue haze of the sea, the King awaits his bride; and to conduct her to him will be Tristan's high privilege and his alone. The more importunate Brangaene becomes the more evasive are his replies, the calmer and more distant his courtesy. The noble and lovely princess can dispose of him in every way but one—for how, if he leaves the helm, can he steer the ship in safety to King Marke's land?

14

Wie lenkt' ich si-cher   deh Kiel   zu Kö-nig Marke's Land?

The maid, in desperation, repeats Isolde's imperious summons; but before Tristan can speak Kurvenal leaps to his feet with a pugnacious "May I make answer?". "What answer would you give?" asks Tristan quietly. "This!" replies Kurvenal. "Let her speak thus to Dame Isolde; it is not for him who won for the Irish maid the crown of Cornwall and the realm of England to do more than conduct her to his royal uncle, for whom she is intended. Tristan the hero is famed throughout the world. Thus speak I; go thou [Brangaene] and repeat it, let a thousand Isoldes rage at it if they will!"

The whole character of Kurvenal as he appears later in the opera—the brave, rough watch-dog, living only in and for his beloved master—is limned in this song of his, the intervals and harmonies of which are as rugged and forthright as himself:

15

Wer Korn - walls Kron'   und Eng - lands
Erb'   an Ir-lauds Maid   ver - macht,

As he goes on to sing before all the crew the story, so hateful in Isolde's ears, of Ireland's abasement and hers, Brangaene turns sadly on her heel. Tristan tries to restrain Kurvenal by a gesture, but he continues at the top of his voice with the savoury tale of how Morold came across the sea to take tribute from Cornwall, how Tristan slew him in single combat on an island, and how the dead man's head was sent back to Ireland as the sole payment that Cornwall would deign to make to the Irish king. "Hail to our Tristan", he concludes, "who pays tribute in a fashion of his own!"; and the knights and sailors repeat with glee the final wounding words of the song:

16

Hei! un-ser Held Tris-tan, wie der Zins zah-len kann!

At last Tristan, with a gesture of annoyance, sends his gruff old henchman below.

28

Brangaene, confused and distressed, has returned to Isolde. She closes the curtains behind her in the vain hope of shutting out from her mistress the sight and sound of the men. Isolde rises with a gesture of rage and despair, while the maid throws herself at her feet with a cry of "Woe, ah, woe is me, that I should have to suffer this!" For a moment Isolde does not speak, but the storm within her is expressed by some furious bars in the orchestra. Mastering herself, she insists on Brangaene telling her all that had passed between her and Tristan. When the maid gives the latter's smooth excuse, "Did I for a moment leave the helm, how could I steer the ship in safety to Cornwall and King Marke?", Isolde repeats the words and the music of the answer (No. 14) with bitter irony: "Yes", she says harshly, "to lay at the King's feet the tribute [herself] he had wrung from Ireland!"—sung to the strain of the corresponding passage in Kurvenal's song. But when Brangaene would repeat the rest of Kurvenal's insulting words

Isolde cuts her short. "That have I heard", she says; "not a word of it escaped me. You heard my shame; hear now, then, how it was wrought." Her final words are accompanied by a furious upward rush in the orchestra:

which, it will be seen, is an expansion of No. 1B; and it is one more proof that we must not read into that motive anything so narrow in its application as the notion of the "magic art" of Isolde's mother: the theme has many a significance beyond that.

Isolde now begins the long monologue that is sometimes sung in the concert room under the title of "Isolde's Narration to Brangaene". It serves a treble purpose: it carries the drama on to its next vital phase, it explains and justifies Isolde's anger over the scene that has just been enacted, and it places the spectator in possession of most of the essential facts anterior to the opera.

The Narration is based mostly on subtle modifications of the opening phrase (No. 1A) of the Prelude, the motive more particularly associated with Tristan and his sorrows. It now assumes the following form:

and is generally referred to as the motive of the Sick Tristan. It weaves for some time a symphonic web of its own in the orchestra as Isolde tells Brangaene how once a frail boat had drifted to the Irish coast, with a man in it calling himself Tantris, sick nigh to death, who had come to consult the far-famed healing art of the

Irish princess (here No. 1B is heard in the wood wind); how, after healing his wounds, she had learned, from the splinter and the notch in his sword, that he was no Tantris but the Tristan who had slain Morold. No. 18 goes through some moving metamorphoses—beginning each time in a gust of fury but always dying away at the end of the phrase—as Isolde describes how a voice within her had called to her to kill this man, who was Ireland's deadliest enemy, and she had stood over him with the sword raised to take vengeance for Morold, when of a sudden he looked up, not at the sword, not at her hand, but into her eyes, and his wretchedness melted her heart and the sword fell from her grasp. As she begins this part of her story the tempest in the orchestra dies down, and we hear No. 18 in a peculiarly poignant form:

The scoring is noteworthy, but one rarely finds the full expressiveness of it realised in performance. The melody is sung by the violas, with the violins beneath them; the tenor part of our quotation is entrusted to the 'cellos, where the curious sob of the dotted note and the following slur, if properly brought out, is extraordinarily moving. At the words "He looked into my eyes" we hear No. 2B in the expressive tones of a solo viola.

Still to the accompaniment of No. 18 Isolde tells how she tended the sick man again, that he might go home healed and rid her of the anguish of that look. And so the conquering Tristan (No. 16) had left her and Ireland, after having sworn a thousand oaths of gratitude and fidelity. "Hear now", she says bitterly, "how a knight keeps his oath!" He whom she had protected as Tantris and allowed to go away unscathed, unrecognised by her kindred, had returned in pomp and pride as Tristan, to solicit the

hand of the Irish princess for Cornwall's old and weary King, his
uncle King Marke. Had Morold lived, who would have dared to
put that insult on Ireland and on her? And it was herself who had
wrought her own shame; "the avenging sword! instead of striking
with it I let it fall from my feeble hand; and now I am thrall to him
who was my vassal!" Through all this we hear frequently the
motive of Isolde's anger (No. 10).

29

After an astonished interjection from Brangaene she renews
her complaint. They had all of them been weak and blind, she
says. Tristan had been a traitor; while she had hidden from her
own kindred all she knew and felt in the troubled silence of her
heart, he had returned to Cornwall and sung her praises to the
court as a splendid morsel for the King, and had himself offered
to go to Ireland and bring her back with him. In this part of the
Narrative two motives are dominant, that of Tristan as conqueror
of Ireland (No. 16), and a triplet figure of this type:

which had been heard in an earlier part of the Narration but
now assumes greater prominence; Wagner makes it express now
rage, now tenderness, now deep suffering. Isolde's outburst
ends with a wild curse on the traitor and a call for vengeance on
his head.

Brangaene runs to her mistress in an access of tenderness,
draws her gently to the couch, and pours out words of comfort,
to a new and tender figure in the orchestra:

But she still cannot unravel the complex of emotion in Isolde's heart. Her simple mind finds what Tristan has done quite natural; how better could he show his loyalty to his King than by bringing him so fair a bride, and how better prove his gratitude to the princess who had saved his life than by conducting her to a splendid throne? But when Isolde finds speech again it is clear that she has hardly been listening to Brangaene. Looking fixedly before her, as if staring into a future visible only to herself, she says in a low, brooding tone, "I, unloved, to have ever before my eyes the noblest man of all! How could I endure that torture?"

Once more the maid misunderstands her; she takes these words to refer to the noble King Marke. The orchestral tissue seems one long caress:

as she asks where in all the world there lives a man who could see Isolde and not love her and gladly die for her? But in the worst case, were the King cold, or turned against her by magic, Brangaene is the custodian of the secret of a stronger magic that will bind him to Isolde by a spell. Lowering her voice confidentially she asks, to the accompaniment of No. 1B in the orchestra, "Know'st thou not thy mother's arts? Thinkst thou that she who knows and weighs all things would have sent me with thee into a strange land without counsel for thee in the hour of need?"

30

Well is Isolde aware of the love-philtre her mother has brewed to ensure her the love of the old King. But she ignores the obvious meaning of Brangaene's words and gives them one of her own. "Truly I know", she says darkly, "my mother's counsel, and her arts I prize. They can accomplish vengeance for betrayal and bring rest to the heart in anguish"—this to the significant motive of "Death-devoted head! Death-devoted heart!" (No. 13). "That casket there—bring it hither to me!" Still misunderstanding her, Brangaene does so: "it holds", she says soothingly as she points to the phials it contains, "what will bring the balm thou need'st to thy soul"; but the orchestra, with the motives No. 4 and No. 5, gives another significance to her words than the one her simple mind intends. "Here they lie as thy mother laid them out, the mighty magical potions—balsam for woe and wounds, for grievous poisons antidotes, and" —as she draws one of the phials from the casket—"here the noblest draught of all."

"Thou err'st", replies Isolde; "I know better the one I need." She seizes another of the phials and holds it up: "*This* draught it is that serves my end! I graved a secret sign upon it"; and beneath the outline of No. 1B in wood wind, horns and tremolandi strings we hear, in the dark colours of the bassoons, trombones and bass tuba, the sinister motive of Death (No. 3, bar 4), beginning softly but quickly swelling to a fortissimo. "The draught of Death!" cries Brangaene, recoiling in horror. Isolde starts from the couch in panic as the sailors are heard shouting roughly to each other to go aloft and take in sail: the moment so long dreaded by her has arrived—the ship is nearing the Cornish land.

The rhythmical cry of the crew:

and a brisk handling of the Sea motive in the orchestra fill the scene with excitement; and the intrusion of the real world upon Isolde's broodings is carried a step further by Kurvenal, who comes boisterously through the curtain roaring a message from his master that the two women are to make themselves ready for the landing. For a moment Isolde recoils aghast; then, recovering her regal self-mastery, she quietly but firmly bids Kurvenal take Tristan her greetings and a message: she will not stand by his side to be conducted to King Marke until, as ancient custom prescribes, he has made atonement to her for a wrong as yet unexpiated. To this the rough old warrior replies merely with a defiant and insolent gesture. Isolde repeats her words, still calmly, but with an added emphasis: she will not prepare herself, she will not stand at Tristan's side, until her forgetfulness and forgiveness have been granted for a dire wrong unatoned; let the knight then come and ask her grace. The quiet resolution of her words is underlined by a steady beat in the orchestral accompaniment.

31

Kurvenal is quelled into obedience, but is still defiant: he will take her message, he blusters, but let her wait and see what kind of answer his master gives! When he has left, Isolde turns quickly to her maid and takes her into a feverish embrace. "Now farewell, Brangaene!" she cries; "greet for me the world; greet for me father and mother!" Brangaene does not understand. "What is it? Would'st thou flee? Whither am I to follow thee?" Once more the sinister motive of Death surges up from the depths of the orchestra as Isolde makes her purpose clear to her. She is not fleeing; she will await Tristan here; Brangaene is to obey her in everything to the letter, and first of all prepare the drink of atonement and peace. All this time the Death motive—our clue to what is really in her mind—has become more and more insistent; at last it finds its culmination in the motive of Desire (No. 1B) as Isolde takes the fateful phial from the casket and hands it to the maid. Wagner's use of the motive at this point is one more proof that for him it does not signify merely a product of the magic art of the Irish Queen, designed to fill the veins of Isolde and King Marke with passion. For Wagner, as for Isolde, Desire is the gateway to Death, and Death the sublimation of Desire.

At long last everything becomes clear to Brangaene. She takes the deadly phial in her hand and throws herself in terror and horror at her mistress's feet. The imperious Isolde subdues her as she had subdued Kurvenal. With bitter irony she flings in Brangaene's face the maid's own words in an earlier scene, giving them now a new application: "Know'st thou not my mother's arts? Think'st thou that she who knows and weighs all things would have sent me with thee into a strange land without counsel for me in the hour of need? Balsam for woe and wounds has the Queen given; for deadly poisons antidotes; and for the deepest woe and greatest grief of all—the draught of Death; let Death now give her thanks!", which the orchestra points with a statement of the "Death-devoted head! Death-devoted heart!" motive.

Hardly knowing what she is saying, Brangaene echoes in stricken tones Isolde's "O deepest woe! O greatest grief!", while the oboe wails over a string tremolo and the basses project the sombre outline of the motive of Death:

She raises herself, frightened and bewildered, as Kurvenal enters with a brusque announcement of "Sir Tristan!". For a moment Isolde's old anger flames out again; then she says calmly and proudly, "Sir Tristan may approach!" Kurvenal withdraws, and the trembling Brangaene retires to the back of the scene. Isolde, mastering herself with a mighty effort, walks slowly and with royal dignity across to the couch, on the head of which she leans, her eyes fixed on the opening in the curtain.

32

In the few moments that elapse before Tristan appears and the characters find speech again the orchestra conveys the tremendous inner tension of the situation in an impressive passage of thirty bars commencing thus:

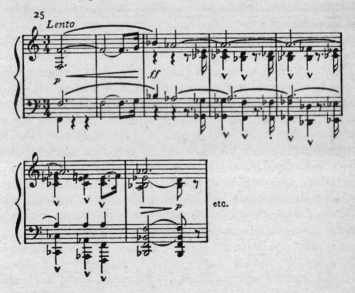

The new motive shown in the opening bars of this quotation has been given different labels by different commentators. Because it is associated later with Tristan's words when he takes the fateful cup from Isolde:

Tristan's honour—
highest troth!
Tristan's anguish—
proudest scorn!

it is called by some the motive of Tristan's honour. Others have
dubbed it the Morold motive, because it recurs when Isolde speaks
of Morold. If one prefers to call it the motive of Isolde's anger one
does so purely as a matter of convenient shorthand. As with so
many of Wagner's motives, it is simple in itself but complex in its
range of psychological reference. On the broad view, it is the expression of Isolde's anger and her thirst for revenge for the slaying of
Morold; but as this anger and this thirst trail other ideas and emotions
along with them from moment to moment, and as there is always
something at the back of her mind that does not reveal itself in
her words—which, indeed, are sometimes designed less to express
her thoughts than to conceal them—the precise nuance of its
meaning is to be sought elsewhere than in the words—in the music.

This is a point that has to be constantly borne in mind in connection with the dramas of Wagner's maturity. As the musician
in him grew to greater power it aimed more and more at making
the drama music's own concern. His aim was to reduce words to a
minimum; and in trying to do this his poems, in and by themselves, sometimes veil his meaning rather than disclose it. This is
particularly the case in *Tristan*; there are many passages which we
have to read again and again, not merely by their own light but by
that thrown on them by some perhaps distant part of the drama, before we can pierce to the real meaning of them, or all the meanings
they can convey. Wagner was perfectly aware of this difficulty,
and his answer to friends who, after reading his text, drew his attention to it was always the same—"Wait until you hear the work
with the music; that will make everything plain to you, in terms,
however, not of words, which are a clumsy tool created by human
reflection, but of feeling; for music, which comes from the foundations, not the surface, of man and things, is capable of a thousand
shades of suggestion that are beyond the capacity of words."[1]

[1] I am of course condensing and paraphrasing a number of his remarks on
this subject at different times.

If we apply his advice to "wait for the music" to the present case our difficulty with regard to finding a label for example No. 25 vanishes: it symbolises not just Morold *qua* Morold, or Tristan, or anyone or anything else with a fixed material outline, but the obsession of fury that has been taking more and more complete control of Isolde's soul from the moment when Tristan had claimed her, in Ireland, as King Marke's bride, to the present moment when, hardly knowing herself whether she loves or hates Tristan more, she is bent on making an end of herself and of him. Within that broad framework of complex passion there is room for an infinitude of nuance of thought and emotion from moment to moment; and that is where music comes into its own. For music can not only express, where feeling is concerned, far more than words; it can, if need be, subtly give the lie to the words that accompany it—as Gluck pointed out to his critics long ago in connection with a famous episode in his *Iphigenia in Tauris*.

33

To resume our survey of the opera.

As yet, while Isolde has told us a good deal about herself, and about others as they appear in her eyes, we have learned next to nothing about Tristan from his own mouth; and even during the remainder of the first act he scarcely lifts a corner of the veil that hides his secret self from us. Yet he is not, as the casual spectator is apt to think, a merely negative character all this while. One critic has told us that in the scene with Isolde that now follows he is "as helpless as a bird in the claws of a cat". It is true that Isolde does most of the talking, in tirade after tirade, Tristan making no attempt to match her in either fluency or vehemence or even to counter her in argument. But if his rôle is largely one of silence, or of an economy of speech that is hardly more than a nuance of silence, that is by no means because he is merely the helpless negative to Isolde's vehement positive. He is silent not because he has nothing to say but because he has far more within him than he can find words for at present.

The key to his reticence will not be given us until the second act. Here, in the first, we hear Isolde's case against him stated in full: his defence we do not hear, because if he were to allow himself the luxury of stating it he would be false to what it is in him that makes him most truly Tristan. Superficially Isolde is justified in her charge of treachery against him: out of pity she had spared his life when it would have been so easy for her to slay the Cornish enemy who had vanquished Morold and humbled her country, and he had repaid her, on his return home, by singing the praises of her beauty to King Marke, and then coming once more to Ireland to carry her back with him as a sort of rich tribute to the royal house of Cornwall. But Tristan had acted as he had done in the name of the loftiest of knightly principles, that of honour. To give Cornwall internal peace he had put away from himself the succession to Marke's crown; he had brought his noble benefactor the fairest jewel among princesses to be his Queen and to bear him an heir, he himself, his mission accomplished, intending to leave Cornwall afterwards for ever.

But to make a parade of his honour now would be to lapse from his own lofty standard of honour; so he says nothing in reply to Isolde's furious upbraidings. He himself, indeed, is as yet not fully aware of the true meaning, the mystical meaning, of the dilemma in which he now finds himself, how it is that in willing the highest good he has wrought the direst harm. The full consciousness of all this only comes to him, and to us, in the second act: the world of Day in which he had been living until now has cheated him into acceptance of its own false values. Worldly fame and even worldly honour, he realises at last, are only the glittering simulacra of things really beautiful and worthy and desirable; the ultimate and only value is Love—not earthly love but a mystical consummation that can be found only in Death. Three times in the course of the drama we shall find him deliberately seeking death as the gateway to a purer happiness than the shows and gauds of earth can ever bring him after having learned to know Isolde— first when he accepts what he believes to be death in the cup she proffers him, then when he lowers his own sword before the thrust of Melot's. At his third attempt, at the end of the drama, he succeeds; when, to the worldly eye, he has attained the summit of his desire in the reunion with Isolde, he tears the bandages from his wounds and dies in her arms. Lovers such as they can never, in their own language in the second act, be wholly one in the garish Light of Day, but only in the ecstatic Night of Death.

34

The motive of Isolde's anger (No. 25) may be said to dominate the scene now to be enacted, though of course a number of other motives with which we are already familiar, and especially the "Death-devoted head" motive and that of the Sick Tristan, play their psychological parts in the orchestral texture. Tristan enters halfway through the orchestral interlude that commences as in No. 25. For a moment he stands respectfully at the entrance to Isolde's apartment. Her agitation increases as he comes slowly towards her, and an upsurge of the Death motive in the orchestra tells us what is the purpose at the back of her mind.

Tristan asks quietly why she has sent for him. Her reply is that he must know that full well, even though the fear of having to obey her will has kept him discourteously aloof from her throughout the voyage. He pleads, in excuse, his respect for her: in his country, he says, knightly custom dictates that he who brings the bride home must remain apart from her. She reminds him of a custom no less binding—that atonement must be made to foes if they are to be turned into friends. He professes not to understand: "Who then is my foe?" he says. "Ask of thy fear!" she retorts; "between us lies blood-guilt." "No", Tristan rejoins; "that feud was ended by the solemn oath of us all, taken in the open field." "Not by me!" replies Isolde; "for I had learned silence." She has had to do with two Tristans, she continues. The earlier one was the sick Tantris whom she had spared when he was in her power, though she knew him to be the slayer of Morold: yet even when checking the sword in its descent she had sworn within herself to have vengeance. "Betrothed he was to me, the noble Irish hero. His weapons had I blessed. For me he fared forth to fight. When he fell, shamed too was I. In my soul's dire anguish I swore an oath—he should be avenged, if not by a man's hand then by mine." At this point we hear a new figure in the violas that plays a prominent part in the texture for a while:

It is impossible to label it definitely; to call it, as some analysts have done, the "motive of psychical excitement" is to say no more than that it gives an extra orchestral emphasis to Isolde's exasperated words, now and later.

Then she begins to be a trifle self-contradictory. Hardly have the words "if not by a man's hand then by mine, a maid's" left her lips than she veers round to another line of attack. "You were in my power, sick and faint", she says; "why did I not strike thee then?" The answer she gives to her own question is a curious one: it reads thus in Mr. Frederick Jameson's translation, which, though not strictly true to the original, we may adopt for convenience sake: "Thy wound I tended that, when hale and strong, then vengeance might strike thee down, by a hand that Isolde should choose."[1] But, she continues, since all men join in paying homage to Tristan, who is there to strike him down?

Tristan, pale and gloomy, replies: "If Morold was so dear to thee, take my sword"—which he draws from its sheath and offers

---

[1] "She states the reason why she did not slay him when he was in her power", says Mr. G. Ainslie Hight, "in language so strange that I can only give a literal translation: 'I nursed the wounded man that, when restored to health, the man who won him from Isolde should smite him in vengeance'. Such is the German; what it means I must confess myself unable to explain, and can only suspect some corruption in the text."

The German runs thus:

> *Ich pflag des Wunden,*
> *dass den Heilgesunden*
> *rächend schlüge der Mann,*
> *der Isolden ihn abgewann.*

My own conjecture is that the accusative "ihn" should be the ablative "ihm", in spite of the fact that "ihn" appears not only in the poem but in the scores, including the manuscript of the orchestral score. I take it that what Isolde means is this: "I tended your wounds in order that when you were sound again you should be struck down in vengeance by a man [some future lover] who had won Isolde from you."

to her,—"grasp it firmly and wield it better than that other time".
Isolde answers that King Marke would have small cause to thank
her were she to slay the best of his knights, who had won him his
crown and his land and is now bringing him his Irish bride. Her
tone is bitter and ironic; but, as is Wagner's way, the orchestra,
in a curiously softened transformation of No. 25:

tells us that her anger with him is not so great as her words would
suggest. "Put up thy sword", she continues; "once I raised it
against thee, when thy measuring gaze was turned on me to judge
if I were a fitting wife for the King. But I let the sword fall from
my hand: now let us twain drink atonement."

35

The dramatic action is mounting to its climax. The orchestra
gives out a solemn statement of the Death motive (No. 3, bars 4
and 5) in conjunction with No. 26, as Isolde makes a sign to
Brangaene to prepare the draught. The horror-stricken maid can
hardly bring herself to obey, but Isolde urges her on with nervous
gestures. The psychological tension of the scene is broken in upon
for a moment by a loud cry from the seamen, "Ho-he-ha-he! All

hands aloft! Take in sail!", to the strain of No. 23; and Brangaene's anguish is painted in the oboe figure (see No. 24) to the
accompaniment of which, in an earlier scene, she had wailed "O
deepest woe! O greatest grief!" when Isolde had commanded her
to prepare not the love elixir but the potion of death.

The shouts of the sailors rouse Tristan from his sombre brooding. "Where are we?" he ejaculates convulsively. "Near the
goal!" replies Isolde; and the subtle double meaning of the word
"goal"—the outer one of reaching the Cornish land and the inner
veiled one of nearing their own last hour—is brought out by the
orchestra with an enunciation of the "Death-devoted head!
Death-devoted heart!" motive in dark wood wind colours.
"Tristan", she continues, "shall I be given atonement? What word
hast thou for me now?" His reply is an antithetical play upon
words:

> *Des Schweigens Herrin*
> *heisst mich schweigen:—*
> *fass' ich, was sie verschwieg,*
> *verschweig' ich, was sie nicht fasst.*

("The mistress of silence commands me silence. What she concealed I can grasp; but what I concealed she cannot grasp.") That
is to say, he had long ago divined the love for him that she had
endeavoured to conceal under a mask of enmity; but the sense of
honour that forbade him to confess his own love for the King's
bride she does not understand, nor can he speak of it.[1]

But Isolde reads, or professes to read, a meaning of her own
into his words. "Thy silence I grasp", she says; "thou wouldst
fain evade the issue between thee and me. Wilt thou not make
atonement?" The cries of the sailors break in harshly once more.
Brangaene, in response to an impatient gesture from her mistress,
brings the cup—not of Death but of Love—to Isolde, who takes
it from her and strides towards Tristan. "We are nigh our goal",
she says again; "in a moment we shall be standing before King

---

[1] The passage was evidently a stumbling-block to some of Wagner's
contemporaries, for we find him patiently explaining it in 1876 to a
correspondent.

Marke"; and to these last words she gives an ironic inflection. Then she plays her last card: "Were it not well that thou couldst say to him: 'My lord and uncle, look upon her! A gentler wife thou couldst not find. I slew her lover and sent her his head. My wound she healed in kindness. My life was in her power, but the gentle maid gave it to me. Her country's dishonour and shame— these too she gave that she might become thy bride. And these gracious thanks for worthy gifts I earned by a sweet draught of atonement, graciously offered me by her in expiation of all my guilt' ".

She says all this quietly, for the time for storming is past; and the deceptive surface-placidity of her words is reflected in the orchestra, which plays in one honeyed modulation after another upon a variant of No. 26:

28

It is only the muttering of the Death motive towards the end of her appeal, as she speaks of the "sweet draught of atonement", that lets us see what is really in her mind.

36

Again there comes from the ship's crew a shout of "Stand by the cable! Let go the anchor!" For a moment the seaman in Tristan is recalled by habit to the real world: "Drop the anchor!" he cries wildly; "put the helm round to the tide! Furl the sails to the wind!" Then he turns to Isolde, takes the cup from her hands, and for the first time in the whole scene finds words for what had been locked in his breast: "Well do I know Ireland's Queen and the magic might of her arts. Once, of old, I took for my weal the balsam she gave me; now I accept from her the cup that will bring me full and final healing this very day.[1] Here is my atonement-oath: I give it thee with thanks; mark thou it well. 'To Tristan's honour—supremest troth! To Tristan's distress—boldest defiance!'[2] Heart's delusion; dream of presage! Sole balsam for endless grief! Kindly cup of oblivion, I drain thee without flinching"; and as he raises the "cup of oblivion" to his lips the orchestra gives out again the significant motive of "Death-devoted head! Death-devoted heart!" He drinks what he imagines to be the fatal draught. Isolde wrests the cup from him with a cry of "Betrayed here too? Mine the half! Traitor, I drink to thee!" The orchestra gives out a passionate statement of the "Look" motive; in what the pair believe to be their last hour their thoughts go back to the moment that had been the decisive point in their lives—when Isolde stayed her hand because of what she read in the helpless man's eyes.

Then follows the episode—generally an awkward one on the stage—that makes heavier demands on the singers as actors than any other situation in Wagner's works, demands which not one Tristan or Isolde in a hundred can meet. The slow operation of the philtre, the clearing away of the mists from their tortured brains, the gradual recognition that the barriers are down at last and the love of each for the other cannot and need not be any

---

[1] The Prose Sketch makes it clearer than the poem does that Tristan is fully aware that there is death in the cup. The Sketch runs thus at this point: "Healing potions she brewed for me, balsam to heal all wounds, even the most mortal",—that is to say, not the physical wound that Morold had once dealt him but the unendurable suffering which his hopeless love for Isolde had brought him. And to the words "blessed be this draught thou proffer'st me" Wagner added later in parentheses, "whatever marvel it may work in me, whether it takes me to hell or to heaven".

[2] Wagner's economy of words has obscured his meaning for most readers of the passage. The German runs thus:

> *Tristans Ehre—*
> *höchster Treu'!*
> *Tristans Elend—*
> *kühnster Trotz!*

"Ehre" (honour) and "Elend" (distress) may be either nominatives or datives. It is in the latter sense that we must take them: Tristan's meaning, in more expanded terms, is this: "In taking this oath and drinking this draught I am supremely faithful to my honour, and I hurl defiance in the face of my misery".

longer concealed, are depicted in reminiscences in the orchestra
of the opening bars of the prelude to the opera, the characters remaining silent. The stage directions run thus: "Seized with
shuddering, excited but motionless, they look fixedly into each
other's eyes, in which the expression of defiance of death soon
gives way to the glow of love. Trembling seizes them; they
clutch convulsively at their breasts and pass their hands over their
foreheads. Then their eyes again seek each the other's; for a
moment they sink in confusion, then fix themselves again on each
other with increasing longing."

At last, to the strains of No. 2 and No. 4, they ejaculate "Tristan!" "Isolde!" "Faithless dear one!" "Most blessed of women!"
They fall into each other's arms. The orchestra lashes itself into a
passion which, it now seems, it has been holding in leash ever since
the first bars of the prelude: No. 4 is marked no longer "slow and
with yearning" but "animato, with a crescendo of passion". The
ship's crew strike in with an excitement of their own as a trumpet
fanfare, ringing out from the land, announces that the ship bearing
the King and his retinue has come in sight.[1] Brangaene, who has
been standing at the side of the ship, her face averted in confusion
and horror, turns round at the brazen clang of the trumpets and
the sailors' jubilant shouts of "Hail, King Marke, hail!" She sees
the world-forgetting lovers locked in an embrace, and rushes
forward, wringing her hands in despair; for she foresees all the
tragic consequences of her substitution of the love-potion for the
draught of death. "Woe! Woe!" she cries; "not death but in-
escapable, endless woe! This well-meant deceit of mine, the work
of my foolish fidelity, now wails to high heaven!"

37

But Tristan and Isolde neither see nor hear Brangaene and the
others; they are lost in their brooding upon their self-delusion in
the past and the dazzling illumination that has suddenly come to
them. Tristan's honour, Isolde's shame, what meaning has all this
now? they ask themselves and each other. How could they have

---

[1] Bülow, in his piano score of the opera, has shirked the problem of in-
corporating the fanfare in the complex harmonic texture. He merely inserts
the stage direction "Trumpets on the stage".

been so blind? There is no room in their hearts at this moment for anything but supreme joy; and the orchestra envelops their ecstatic cries in a rich texture derived from the prelude, with the old yearning, however, now changed into rapture.

But once more the world of crude reality breaks in upon them. The curtains across the centre of the stage are flung wide apart, showing the whole ship thronged with knights and sailors, shouting and making jubilant gestures towards the land, where we now see a cliff crowned with a majestic castle.

Brangaene forces herself between the lovers, who are still blind and deaf to everyone and everything but themselves, and throws the royal mantle round the tranced and passive Isolde. The shouts of the men on the ship, "Hail, King Marke!" are borne upon an exuberant version of the Sea motive (No. 9A) and more fanfares in trumpets and trombones. Kurvenal enters, in high spirits, to tell Tristan that the King is nearing them in a boat, rejoiced at the arrival of his bride. The dazed Tristan can only ejaculate "*Who* is coming? *What* King?" His clouded eyes mechanically follow Kurvenal's pointing finger, while Isolde turns to Brangaene with a bewildered cry of "What call is that? Where am I? Do I live? What was the draught you gave us?" "The draught of love!" is the maid's despairing answer. Then at last the full horror of her earthly destiny dawns on Isolde. She falls on Tristan's breast with a despairing cry of "Tristan! Must I still live, then?", while a great tragic cry is wrung from the knight, "O rapture rich in spite! O bliss dedicated to guile!" By now a bridge has been lowered, people have swarmed on board from the land, and as the curtain falls a tumult of joy on the part of the seafolk, with fanfares ringing out in the brass, indicates that the King and his retinue have arrived. Perhaps the most shattering feature of the whole first act is this stark antithesis of physical joy present and spiritual suffering to come with which the act ends.

38

The second act opens with a long orchestral prelude which originally began at what is now the ninth bar of the score, where we meet with a new motive expressive of Isolde's Impatient Expectation. In the course of this act Wagner had made great use of an important motive known as that of Day, the mystical significance of which word will become clear later: this motive he prefixed later to the original opening of the prelude, which thereby assumed its present form:

29

A being the motive of Day, B that of Isolde's Impatience as she awaits the coming of Tristan. Soon a fresh motive, that of Love's Longing, appears in the upper strings:

30

in combination with a modification of No. 29B in the 'cellos. Then comes a reminiscence of the motive of Desire (No. 1B), which leads into yet another new motive, that of Love's Bliss (derived from No. 1B):

which will be chosen later by Wagner to be the last strain to linger in our ears when the final curtain falls.

At the end of a rich symphonic development of this feverish material the curtain rises, showing us a garden with high trees in front of Isolde's chamber in the castle, with steps leading up to this on one side of the stage. It is a clear, balmy summer night. The door to the castle is open, and at the side of it is fixed a burning torch. From the adjacent forest comes the distant and slowly receding sound of the hunting horns of King Marke and his knights:

Brangaene is looking anxiously back into the chamber, from which Isolde is shortly seen approaching.

For a long time the orchestral texture is made up of a free play upon motives by now familiar to us, in particular combinations of No. 30, No. 31 and No. 1B, with the distant horn fanfares piercing through the complex of sound from time to time. Isolde is fretting for the moment to arrive when she can give Tristan the signal to leave the hunt and come to her; that signal, at once material and symbolic, is to be the extinguishing of the light of the torch.[1] Brangaene warns her mistress again and again that the

[1] Wagner remarked one day to Frau Eliza Wille, after playing to her the music of the second act to which the lovers sing their rhapsody upon Night and Death, that "the ancients used to depict Eros as the genius of Death, with a torch turned downwards in his hand".

horns of the hunters are not so far away as Isolde, in her impatience, is too inclined to imagine, for all *she* can hear is the rustling of the leaves and the gentle laughter of the wind. Brangaene tells her that she is deceived by her desire, hearing only what she would fain hear. The orchestral tissue softens to an exquisite sweetness as Isolde sings of the loveliness of the night and the lover who is straining towards her far away in the velvet silence of it.

<h2 style="text-align:center">39</h2>

Brangaene becomes more urgent: he for whom Isolde is looking so eagerly is being spied upon, she says. "Because thou art self-blinded, deem'st thou that the eye the world turns upon thee is blind? On the ship, when Tristan's trembling hand delivered the pallid bride to Marke, and all gazed in wonder on her, and the good King spoke kindly of the hardships of the voyage, one there was—I heeded him well!—whose crafty, evil eyes never left Tristan, seeking some sign in him that would serve his own ends. Oft have I seen him, since then, lurking and spying and laying subtle snares for thee. Beware, I say, of Melot!" But the love-blinded Isolde will not believe her. "Is not Melot Tristan's trustiest friend? When my dear one must shun me, it is with Melot alone that he bides." Brangaene repeats that she distrusts the man: "Melot's way to King Marke lies through Tristan, and he is sowing evil seed. Those who hastily planned this hunt by night were bent on a nobler quarry than thou, in thy illusion, dost imagine."

No! Isolde insists. Was it not Melot, the trusty friend, who, out of pity for her and Tristan, had devised the stratagem of this hunt to serve them? "Better than thou he cares for me; ways he opens that thou wouldst close. Oh end this my misery of waiting! The signal, Brangaene! Give the signal! Quench the last of the torch's light! Give Night the sign that she may descend upon us and enfold us. For now she has spread her silence over castle and grove, filling the heart with shuddering bliss. Put out the light! Make an end of its frightening glare! Let my loved one come to me!"

In vain does Brangaene continue to plead with her. The distracted maid curses the moment when, out of excess of love and

mistaken fidelity to her mistress, she had substituted the potion of
Love for that of Death. The deed of woe has been hers, and the
guilt of it will be hers for ever. "No", replies Isolde, "not thy work
but Frau Minne's, the mistress of magic, the queen who subdues the
boldest spirit, the shaper of the whole world's destinies. Life and
death are thralls to her, out of joy and sorrow and hate and envy
she weaves love. Presumptuously I took the work of death into
my hands; Frau Minne snatched it from my grasp: me, the Death-
devoted one, she took in pledge, made the work her own." The
orchestra gives out a gracious new motive of Frau Minne as the
source and symbol of Love:

upon which Wagner proceeds to execute a symphonic fantasia, as
he does with the other themes of this scene.

Isolde continues with her rhapsody: "Whatever the turn she
gives it, whatever the end she has appointed for it, whatsoever she
may have in store for me, whithersoever she may choose to lead
me, hers was I, hers alone; now let me show obedience to her." In
vain does Brangaene repeat the warning and implore her to have a
care, this day of all days: "Let the bright beacon, the token of
peril, burn on today, at least today! Extinguish not the torch!"
Isolde only repeats that what she is about to do is simply to
fulfil Frau Minne's will; "Let Night descend, that she may shed
her light." This fixed resolve of Isolde's is the turning point of the
action; and Wagner throws it into the highest relief by a sudden
great broadening-out of the time-values of his melodic and harmonic line, which until now has been one of unceasingly shifting
and intertwining smaller notes:

(The harmonic texture is here shown in skeletonised form). This broadening-out is a simple stroke, but a most effective one: the action seems to pause and take a great breath after the haste and fever that have characterised it until now, and to be gathering strength for its next passionate flight.

40

Isolde snatches the torch from its socket and with a glad laugh throws it to earth, where the flame gradually dies out; and Brangaene, at her bidding, ascends the outside steps leading to the battlements, slowly disappearing from our sight.

The orchestra now takes possession of the field once more for a while as Isolde looks nervously down the avenue, listens intently, and then beckons again and again with a veil, at first at intervals, then more and more continuously as her impatience increases. A sudden gesture of delight indicates that she has seen the beloved in the distance. She hastens to the top of the steps, whence she beckons to him. The orchestra works itself up into a tornado of passion by way of No. 29B and, in combination with this, an excited new figure that is repeated incessantly in one form and another:

Tristan enters, and Isolde rushes to greet him. For a while the ecstasy of the pair can find voice only in breathless ejaculations— "Tristan!" "Isolde!" ... "Art thou mine?" "Once more I hold thee?" ... "Can I believe it?" and so on.[1] At first they cannot

[1] There has been much talk about the "deceit" of King Marke, and commentators, with the mediaeval legend too much in their minds, have assumed previous clandestine meetings of the lovers. There is not the smallest authority in Wagner's text for that assumption. We are nowhere told how long or how short an interval of time has elapsed between act I and act II, nor is there a single line in the poem to indicate even that the wedding has yet taken place. Wagner's mystical drama was not concerned with realistic irrelevancies of that sort. It is inferable, from one passage and another in the text, that this is the first time the lovers have been thus alone with each other since they arrived in Cornwall.

believe in the reality of their happiness. "Tristan mine!", "Isolde mine!", "For ever one!", they cry, to cumulative repetitions of the passionate motive of Love's Bliss (No. 33) in the orchestra. Then the "action"—in the ordinary theatrical sense of that term —of the opera becomes suspended for a considerable time; that is to say, it ceases to be in any degree physical and becomes entirely psychological. The lovers launch into a long mystical meditation and communion upon their past and present and future, which they see in terms of an antithesis of the real world—symbolised as Day—with its deceits, its illusions, its false values, and a mystical other-world symbolised as Night, in which all that is superficial and transitory in the human mind and heart is merged in the eternal, the only true. The extinguishing of the torch has been symbolic rather than realistic; it marks the severance of the last bond that had held the supra-mundane love of Tristan and Isolde in servitude to the cruder world of Day.

What follows now in the opera, until the irruption of realistic Day once more into their ecstatic dream-world when Melot brings King Marke and the others upon the scene, is the most difficult section of the whole work for both the listener in the theatre and the reader of the poem. Not one spectator in a hundred grasps the inner meaning of the lovers' long poetic fantasia upon Night and Day,[1] or, if he happens to have read the text, perceives even the meaning of many of Wagner's lines, for his imagery becomes more and more recondite, his words fewer, and his syntax more and more condensed and elliptical as he indulges himself in the luxury of exploring this mystical world that lies deep below and high above the material one. Yet without a complete understanding of all that the characters are saying it is a pure impossibility to know what the whole opera *Tristan and Isolde* is really "about".

Only an integral reproduction of the text of the remaining hundred pages of the second act could reveal all the psychological subtleties of Wagner's handling of his poetic thesis. That being

[1] Matters in this respect are not improved by the cuts made in the second act in the ordinary theatre performance. Cuts are unavoidable except when the opera is given under "festival" conditions; but they make a sad mess of both Wagner's musical design and his poetic idea.

impossible—and in any case a great many of the lines are almost inconvertible into English or any other language,—the next best thing is for the student of the opera to read a translation of the outline of the scene given by Wagner himself in his Prose Sketch. He will then see that, for the first time, Wagner here discloses one or two psychological "motives" antecedent to the opera which were passed over in silence in the first act, but which are vital to our comprehension of the drama. We now realise, for example, what Tristan meant when he spoke to Isolde, in the first act, of his "honour" having barred him from an admission, even to himself, of his love for Isolde: before his fateful second visit to Ireland he had vowed within himself, in order to save Cornwall from internal strife and not to have it believed that he had played upon his uncle's love for him for his own ambitious ends, to leave the country for ever after having persuaded the King to marry and beget an heir to the throne. Honour, in the world's sense of that word, had forbidden him later either to break that vow or reveal it to Isolde.

Here, then, is a translation of the relevant pages of text and stage directions from Wagner's Prose Sketch.

41

(Tristan rushes in. A long and passionate embrace. Overflow of long-suppressed emotion. Exultant rapture. Praise of Night, which has brought them joy after the agonies of Day ... Impeachment of Day as the bringer of all sorrows for lovers: they outbid each other as to who has suffered most from Day. Tender reproaches).

Is. Day it was when you wooed me for Marke.

Tr. Day it was that blinded me, persuading me that honour was the world's highest treasure, dazzling me with its false beams and making me strive after vanity and emptiness. [In an insert Wagner elucidates this as "Fame".]

Is. What lie did Day tell you to make you betray me?

Tr. The image of you in the pure Night of my heart it seduced me into disclosing in its shameless glitter: loudly I sang your praises before them all,[1] awaking desire and envy. All would have you for their Queen, to the end that they might avenge themselves on me for my fame and good fortune. The noble Marke, who had chosen the orphan to be his son, had promised him the inheritance of his kingdom, vowing that he himself would never marry. For that, and because fortune had been bountiful to me, all envied me. The courtiers urged the King to wed—Isolde were a fitting bride for him, and Tristan should woo her for him, for the ancient blood-feud between the two kingdoms made them all dread the perilous quest for themselves. All believed I would refuse, and then they could make it appear that I was a self-seeker bent on my own advantage alone. So I was goaded into claiming the task as mine and renouncing my heritage in favour of the offspring that would be born to the King. Thus I paid homage to my Day-sun—to honour and fame.

Is. And so you surrendered me to increase your honour and fame?

Tr. Accuse the Day, that blinded me into revelling in arrogance!

Is. How can *I* accuse the Day, I who let it urge me on to death and revenge? It showed you to me only as an evil-doer, my coldest, most treacherous foe. When I would fain see you in another light, as you were in the depth of Night in my heart, always there lingered in me that harsh picture of you as my deadly enemy alone.

Tr. When you proffered me the Draught of Death, then dawned within me sublime Night. My senses swooned; I would fain plunge into Death, there to belong to you for ever.

Is. Yet alas! it was the Draught of Love that bore you away from Night, and bringing you Love brought you also the falsity of Day?

Tr. O rapture! Hail to that Draught! Through the gates of Death it opened out to me the blissful realm of Night, in which till then I had only been groping blindly: now there fell away from me everything that had been deluding me so long.

Is. Yet Day took its revenge. For your trespass we had to pay atonement to him: you had to deliver me over to the King:

[1] i.e. in Cornwall, after his first stay in Ireland.

to the stars of Day you had to yield, leaving me solitary in empty splendour. How did I ever bear that?

Tr. But then we were consecrated to Night: Day could divide but no more blind us. We laugh at its vain glitter: Fame and Honour—mere fleeting motes in the sun—were scattered: their falsehood became manifest in face of the profound secret that Night confided to us, a secret that disclosed to us the deception even of troth and friendship themselves. Day may still hold us fast in his toils, but he deludes us no more: to eyes that have Night-sight he is but desolate darkness. One longing only have I in the Day, the longing for holy Night! Descend upon me, Love's own Night! Take me up into thy bosom! Let me forget that I live, blot out the world from my eyes! When I find myself, how poor am I! When I lost myself wholly, how rich I became! Then my gaze is blinded with rapture. When the world I see no more, then am I myself the world, life uplifted to holiest Love! When the sun no longer lights me, its warmth lies hidden in my heart; then to light me I have the stars of bliss! Heart to heart with you! Mouth to mouth! When sight is shattered I am ruler of the world!—(Mutual heightening of the utmost transport, release from the world, intoxicating presage of death. Never to wake again! Longing for death! Speech fails. Brangaene's watching-song—deepest woe! Dismay at the thought of awaking! Warning. It sinks into Isolde. Anxiety!).

Tr. Let me die. (Sorrowfully tender reproaches from Isolde).

Tr. How could we die? What is there in us that could be slain that were not Love itself? Are we not wholly and solely Love? Can our love ever find an end? Could the day come when the love of Love could die in me? [Then, in a footnote: My body is Death's property: stood he before me, would my love quail? Were I to die, would my love die too? What does not die with me, how could that ever cease to be? And I myself, am I aught but Love, Love without end?] Did I will to die now, would Love also die, seeing that we are naught but Love?

Is. Yet it is we who love, Tristan and Isolde, you and I? Were Tristan to die?

Tr. Then would not merely that pass away that bars me from loving you for ever?

Is. Of Tristan's dying I can think only along with Isolde's death!

Tr. Thus would we have died only to love. Then could no Day divide us any more: wakened no more by its dismaying gleam, for ever would we be hidden in the Night of Love: what rapture were higher than this, which is freedom from all torment? (A still more anxious summons from Brangaene. Tristan becomes aware of it). Who calls to me there to awaken?

Is. Death! Tristan, let me die!

Tr. He summons us to waken: not yet does Day dawn for us, still is eternity ours. (Isolde's growing anxiety for Tristan, allayed by him in a renewed ecstasy).

Tr. Should we flee from the fate that leads us to an eternity in which there will be no awakening? Death joined us together: at his gates we drank Love: dedicated to Death, ever-loving, ever-living, let us clasp each the other, to be separated no more! (Redoubled rapture. New and highest intoxication: an ardent embrace. Day dawns. A cry from Brangaene. Marke, Melot and courtiers enter hurriedly. Before this, a short combat—in the foreground Kurvenal falling back before the assailants). Isolde sinks in terror on to a flowery bank. Tristan, holding his cloak before her with one arm, as though to conceal her, stands immobile, as if turned to stone, his eyes fixed on the newcomers. A long silence.

Tr. (in a choked voice) The dreary Day has dawned![1]

42

With this epitome of the poem firmly fixed in our minds we can devote our attention mainly to the musical working-out of the scene.

[1] The antithesis of the passing falsity of Day and the eternal truth of Night had been a favourite one with the German romantics, and it had found its most elaborate expression in Novalis's *Hymns to Night* (1800). The reader with a knowledge of German who wishes to follow up the subject will find a number of parallels between the *Hymns* and the *Tristan* text set forth in an article by Arthur Prüfer on *Novalis Hymnen an die Nacht in ihren Beziehungen zu Wagners Tristan und Isolde*, in the Wagner-Jahrbuch for 1906, pp. 290–304.

The lovers begin with a lament over their enforced separation: "How long so far apart! How far apart so long![1] So far when near! So near when afar!"—to the strains of No. 33 and No. 30. This latter motive (Love's Longing) is given a darker and wilder significance as Tristan speaks of the warning light that seemed to have been burning for so intolerable a time:

(In the centre voice of this quotation No. 35 is seen weaving its way in and out in the second violins).

It is impossible to set forth in detail the infinitely subtle recurrences and metamorphoses of the motives in this great symphonic structure. When first Isolde, then Tristan, speaks of the lovers' defiance of the hateful, envious Day we hear the first statement of the Day motive (No. 29A) which, as we have seen, was afterwards used by Wagner to introduce the prelude to the second act. As the light of the torch had kept the lovers apart that night, so the lying light of Day, the false standards of the Day in which the outer world lives and moves and has its being, have been the source of all their miseries from the first moment they looked into each other's eyes. It was through craven subservience to these false standards that Tristan had allowed his impulse of honour towards Marke and Cornwall to prompt him to undertake the mission to Ireland, a mission that had ended in self-denial of his love and treachery towards Isolde. She too had been Day's dupe, hating Tristan as Ireland's enemy and hers; until, on the

---

[1] These "longs" are not to be taken literally, as signifying that a considerable time has elapsed between the first act and the second. The separation has been "long" in the sense in which lovers invariably speak of separations, even the shortest.

ship, the moment had come when she would have made an end of it all in death:

> *The light of Day*
> *I fain would flee;*
> *away into Night*
> *fare forth with thee,*
> *where an end to falsehood*
> *my heart foretold;*
> *where the dreaded might*
> *of the lie would vanish;*
> *there would I drink*
> *our love for ever,*
> *us twain, thou one with me,*
> *would I in death entwine!*

It was death, rejoins Tristan, that he had gladly accepted at her hands. Yet the false draught, she reminds him, had practised a deceit on him; instead of the hoped-for Night, Day had dawned for him once more. But Tristan now sings the praises of the draught, of which, on the ship, he had been conscious only of the horror of its deceit of him: the gates of death had been flung open before him, and through them he had passed from Day to "the wonderworld of Night".

Once more Isolde extends the poetic antithesis: the affrighted Day had taken its revenge on him, for Tristan had been compelled to take up his life in the real world again. But he sweeps her reproaches and regrets aside: Day might indeed still hold them in his toils, but no longer had he power to delude them:

> *O now were we*
> *to Night enhallowed!*
> *The envious Day,*
> *with hate o'erbrimming,*
> *could but hold us apart,*
> *but no more blind us with lies!*
> *Its empty pride,*
> *the vaunt of its glare,*
> *derides he whom Night*
> *her own has made!*

> *All its fugitive lightning's*
> *flickering flashes*
> *blind us twain no more.*
> *Who at death's dark Night,*
> *love-led, has gazed,*
> *who at her heart*
> *her secrets has learned,*
> *the lies of daylight,*
> *honour, fame,*
> *profit and power,*
> *how dazzling soe'er,*
> *no more to him are all these*
> *than dust before him driven.*[1]
> *In the daylight's foolish fancies*
> *holds him one single yearning—*
> *the yearning hence*
> *to holy Night,*
> *where unending,*
> *only true,*
> *laughs to him Love's delight.*

The orchestral texture in this section of the score is made up of an endless series of metamorphoses of the relevant motives: Wagner, having no stage traffic to distract him, can abandon himself to the luxury of weaving his musical material into ever new patterns.

[1] In the poem, at this point, are eight lines which will not be found in the score:

> *Selbst um der Treu'*
> *und Freundschaft Wahn*
> *dem treu'sten Freunde*
> *ist's getan,*
> *der in der Liebe*
> *Nacht geschaut,*
> *dem sie ihr tief*
> *Geheimnis vertraut.*

Wagner had set them to music in his Composition Sketch, but he rejected them later.

43

Gradually a change comes over the music. No. 31 (the motive of Love's Happiness) is spun into a thread of long-drawn sweetness:

as Tristan, according to the stage directions, "draws Isolde gently down on to a flowery bank, sinks on his knee before her, and lays his head on her arm." The Day motive, now shorn of its hard urgency, steals out softly in cor anglais and horn, and the scene settles into a kind of rapturous nocturne as the pair call upon Love's Night to descend upon them and bestow on them oblivion of the world. The new theme that dominates the scene had been foreshadowed harmonically a little earlier, at Tristan's words, "Da erdämmerte mild erhab'ner Macht im Busen mir die Nacht" ("Then Night descended on my bosom in mild majestic might"); now it comes out in its full form, with the harmonies in throbbing irregular pulses:[1]

[1] Wagner drew upon this music for his setting of the song *Träume*, the words of which were by Frau Wesendonk. He called it a "Study for *Tristan and Isolde*". Two sketches in one of Wagner's pocket-books reveal the curious fact that at one time he associated the words "O sink' hernieder, Nacht der Liebe" not (as in the present score) with the melody of No. 38 but with that of Love's Peace (No. 39). The first sketch begins thus:

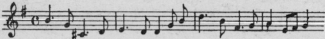

Sink' her - nie - der, Nacht der Lie - be, nimm mich auf in dei - nen Schoss

and the second thus:

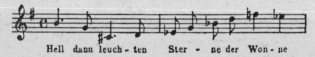

Hell dann leuch - ten Ster - ne der Won - ne

The motive of Day (No. 29A) recurs in a softened and subtle form, and later No. 38 generates a new theme:

This is generally referred to as the motive of Love's Peace, but there is no need to attach any definite label to it. It becomes of special importance at a crucial point in the third act.

"Heart to heart", Tristan and Isolde sing:

and lip to lip;
thou and I
one soul, one breath;
faint with bliss
my eyes are failing,
the world with all
its shows is paling—
world that the Day
lit with its lies;
from blinding illusion
now set free,
I now,
I am the world,
life in rapture stirring,
life of holiest loving—
no more waken,—
swooning,
thus and now to die!

As their world-forgetting ecstasy reaches its climax:

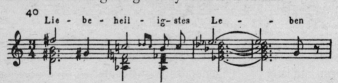

and dissolves in soft harmonies, Wagner introduces one of his most telling strokes—one that is at once musically serviceable and dramatically effective. The lovers have still much to say to each other, but a relief from the intensity of their emotion is as necessary, at some point or other, to them as it is to us. Wagner takes advantage of this momentary muting of their passionate song to introduce a warning voice from that outer world which they had forgotten; and he brings in that voice in felicitous accord with the mediaeval milieu of the story.

Some of the most deeply felt of the Minnesinger poems are what are known as "Warder's Songs".[1] In that age of loveless

---

[1] Or "Watchman's Song", "Dawn Song", "Alba", "Aubade", "Day Song", "Morning Song", etc.

aristocratic *mariages de convenance* the sympathy of the poets and romancers was all with lovers who defied the bonds of the law; and this sympathy found expression in the song of a watching friend in a tower, who, at the approach of dawn, gave the lovers warning that the night was past and they must tear themselves from each other's arms. It was an artistic convention of the period, but one into which the Minnesingers and Troubadours threw themselves with passionate sincerity: sometimes the Watchman's song alone floats down from the tower, sometimes the Lady dialogues with him, reproaching him for his cruelty and bewailing the harshness of separation from her beloved.[1]

This convention is now put to admirable use by Wagner. As Tristan and Isolde sink back upon the bank of flowers the warning voice of the unseen Brangaene peals out from a turret:

> *Lone I watch here*
> *in the night;*
> *ye there, lost*
> *in love's delight,*
> *to my warning*
> *give good heed:*
> *o'er the sleepers*
> *evil broods;*
> *wake, I warn you,*
> *waken now!*
> *Have a care!*
> *Have a care!*
> *Soon the night will pass.*

[1] Some charming English versions of mediaeval "Watchman's Songs" will be found in Jethro Bithell's *The Minnesingers*. The reader will hardly need to be reminded of Swinburne's glowing poem based on an old Provençal *alba* commencing:

> *En un vergier sotz folha d'albespi*
> *tenc la dompna son amic costa si.*

Each of the stanzas ends with the lady's cry of "Oi Deus, oi Deus, de l'alba! Tan vost ve!".

44

The orchestra plays subtly round Brangaene's words with
suggestions of the lovers' own music, particularly Nos. 37, 38 and
39. As her song dies away, No. 39 reappears in its fuller and true
form in the quiet tones of the strings:

and Tristan and Isolde resume their fond dialogue upon Love and
Life and the impotence of Death to part lovers such as they. Of
what, Isolde asks, could Death make an end but the bar to their
eternal union? And they sing in antiphony, "Then should we
together die, one for ever, never waking, never fearing, the very
names of us forgotten, thou and I, with no life but in our love":

Isolde sinks her head on Tristan's breast. Once more the warning voice of Brangaene breaks in upon them: "Have a care! Now

Night gives way to Day!" And once more they turn smilingly to each other, defying Day and his menace and avowing their faith in Night;[1] and their last words before the disaster of the world's Day falls on them are an ecstatic hymn to sweet Night, eternal Night, in which their individual beings shall be lost: "Thou Tristan, I Isolde!" Tristan cries; and she answers antithesis with antithesis—"Thou Isolde, Tristan I!". "How to grasp it?", they cry, to a rapturous expansion of the melody of No. 40:

As they speak of their "tender yearning" and "sweet longing" first the clarinet, then the flute gives out a tender little figure:

that is destined to play an important part later in the final Liebestod. The climax of their ecstasy is reached with No. 31 piling up in wave on wave in the orchestra.

But their final long cry of "Highest joy of love!" ends in a rending dissonance in the orchestra, accompanied by a piercing shriek from Brangaene, who from the turret has seen the coming of the catastrophe she has dreaded. Kurvenal rushes in with drawn sword, shouting "Save thyself, Tristan!" as he looks with horror behind him into the forest, from which Marke, Melot and the

[1] In the poem, between Isolde's "Lass' den Tag dem Tode weichen" and Tristan's "Des Tages Dräuen nun trotzten wir so?", there are fourteen lines which Wagner set to music in his Composition Sketch but omitted from his final score.

courtiers, in hunting attire, now come upon the scene. They are accompanied by a curiously harsh re-statement by the orchestra of the motive of the hunting horns (No. 32) that had figured so largely in the prelude to this second act. At that time Isolde, in her infatuation, had refused to listen to them, to believe they were what they really were; now they have become the most tragic of realities to her.

Brangaëne comes down from the tower and hurries anxiously to her mistress. Isolde, "seized with involuntary shame", as the stage directions have it, "leans on the flowery bank with averted face. Tristan, with a movement that is also involuntary, stretches out his mantle with one arm so as to hide Isolde from them all. In this position he remains for some time motionless, staring blindly at the men, who keep their eyes fixed on him with a variety of expressions. The day begins to dawn." The orchestra gives out mournful variants of No. 43 and No. 44; and, to the accompaniment of the Day motive (No. 29A), Tristan at last breaks the long silence with the despairing words, "The dreary Day for the last time dawns!".

45

The treacherous Melot[1] points in triumph to Tristan and asks King Marke if he has not been as good as his word: "Plain is his guilt; have I saved thy name and honour from shame?" A mournful figure in the bass clarinet:

45 *Andante moderato*

mf espress.

anticipates the old King's sorrowful reply. "Hast thou, in sooth?" he asks Melot; and he points to Tristan:

[1] In the old legends Melot is a cunning dwarf.

See him there,
of all true men the truest;
look on him,
most faithful he in friendship:
'tis his loyal
deed of old
now my heart
with base betrayal wounds!
Tristan traitor,
why dost mock me
with the hope
that my lost honour
by a Melot's word
now can be restored?

Tristan ejaculates convulsively:

Daylight phantoms!
Morning visions!
Lying and vain,
away, begone!

The King, deeply moved, reproaches him with his deception: if
his Tristan can be false, where in all the world is honour left?
Tristan's eyes sink slowly to the ground as Marke continues, with
increasing grief, to paint the situation as it appears to his uncomprehending eyes. A new motive in the bass clarinet:

threads its melancholy way through his long lament, the burden
of which is the futility now of all the loyal service Tristan has
done him in the past. They two had loved each other greatly;

Marke had destined him to succeed to his kingdom, and Tristan had unselfishly sacrificed himself to confer the loveliest of Queens on Cornwall. And now his peerless knight has dealt him this deadly wound where his heart lay most open; and the greatest grief of all to him is not to know where to look for honour now that his Tristan has been false. How has it all come about?

> *Why this shame immense*
> *for which no grief atones?*
> *The secret and unfathomed*
> *cause of all my woe*
> *who will e'er reveal?*

Tristan turns a look of profound compassion on him: "That", he says, "I cannot tell thee: the meaning even of thy question is beyond thy grasping"; but the motives of Grief and Desire (Nos. 1A and 1B) in the poignant timbres of cor anglais and oboe give us the answer to the riddle.

Tristan turns to Isolde, who looks up tenderly at him; and with the orchestra musing softly and sadly on the theme of their dreamed-of escape from the world (No. 39 etc.) he asks her a mystical question which only she among them all can understand: "Where I am going now wilt thou, Isolde, follow? It is to a land unlit by the sun, the dark land from which I took my being, in which my dying mother bore me. The wondrous realm of Night it is that Tristan offers thee now; will Isolde follow him there, loyal and true?" For the second time, then, of his own accord he is about to choose death; and for the second time she is willing to die with him. Once, she reminds him, she had followed him unwillingly into a strange land—when he, untrue to love, had torn her from home and kindred to take her to Cornwall as King Marke's bride. Now he is summoning her to go with him to a "land" of his own, a "land" that spans the whole world:

> *To Tristan's house and home*
> *glad will Isolde go:*
> *the road that, fair and true,*
> *she now must follow,*
> *prithee show!*

He bends over her and kisses her gently on the forehead, while the orchestra turns, as it were, a last wistful glance back on their world-forgetting happiness of an hour ago (No. 37, No. 44).

Melot steps forward furiously with drawn sword. Tristan draws his own sword and faces him. "This was my friend", he says sorrowfully and scornfully. "Once he loved me truly, cared more than any for my fame and honour. 'Twas he who led those on who urged me on to win more fame, more honour, by bringing thee, Isolde, to be the King's bride. But thy glance blinded him too; and from passion he betrayed me to my King, whom I betrayed." He hurls himself on Melot; but as the latter strikes at him Tristan lets his own sword fall, and sinks, wounded, into Kurvenal's arms. Isolde throws herself on his breast. The King holds Melot back; and the curtain falls to some mournful mutations of the main motive of the grief-stricken Marke (No. 45).

46

The orchestral prelude to the third act begins with a melancholy transformation of No. 1B in the strings (in six parts), which spirals out into the upper air, as it were, in a slowly ascending passage in the violins:

The music gives an extraordinary impression of the loneliness, physical and spiritual, of the wounded Tristan as he lies on the rock on the Breton coast to which the faithful Kurvenal has borne him, where he awaits in longing and suffering the coming of Isolde. She alone had been able to heal him that earlier time when, as the sick Tantris, he had been cast up on the Irish shore:

she alone, old Kurvenal has divined, can heal him now, and he
has sent a ship across the sea to bring her.

After an extended development of No. 47 and of a new motive,
which is afterwards associated with the Distress of Tristan:

the curtain rises, showing a castle garden on a rocky height, with
the sea visible here and there as far as the horizon: "the whole
place suggests", say the stage directions, "the absence of a master;
it is ill-tended, in places overgrown, and in ruinous decay." On
one side of the garden is a suggestion of a lofty castle, on the
other side a long fortification-wall broken by a watch-tower. In
the foreground Tristan, seemingly lifeless, lies on a couch in the
shade of a great lime-tree: at his head sits Kurvenal, bending over
him in grief, listening intently, anxiously, to his breathing. From
without comes the sound of a shepherd's pipe:

This long unaccompanied cor anglais melody is one of the
strangest and most poignant ever imagined by man. It accelerates
towards the end in a series of triplet turns:

and at last dies out mournfully in the lowest register of the instrument.

His tune ended, the shepherd shows himself above the parapet.
He hails Kurvenal, asking solicitously if the master is yet awake.
The old retainer shakes his head sadly: were Tristan to awake, he
says, it would only be to leave them for ever, unless there comes
first the only leech who can heal him. Has the shepherd yet caught
sight of a sail on the sea? he asks. No, replies the shepherd; when
he does, the tune he will pipe will be merrier than the one he has
just played! But what is it ails his lord? Kurvenal evades the
question: "That thou could'st not understand: only watch thou,
and if thou seest a ship, pipe lustily and merrily." The shepherd
turns and looks over the sea, shading his eyes with his hand; and
seeing nothing he goes slowly out, playing his sad melody once
more.

But the tune had awakened Tristan. To Kurvenal's astonishment and joy he opens his eyes, turns his head a little, and asks
feebly, "What ancient tune is that that wakens me? Where am I?"
"Safe here in Kareol", the old man answers, to the accompaniment
of a characteristically bluff motive in the orchestra:

"Here in thy father's castle. It was thy own shepherd that woke
thee, piping as he tends thine own flocks on thine own hill. Thou
art among thy faithful people, who served thee before thou
turned'st thy back on all that was thine to go and dwell in Cornwall?" "Am I then in Cornwall?" Tristan asks faintly. "No, here
in Kareol. I bore thee on my broad shoulders to a ship, and from
the ship here to the castle. Thou art at home, in the land of thy
fathers, with the old sun shining on fields and herds; here wilt
thou be healed of thy sickness"; and the old man lays his grizzled
head on his master's breast.

47

Consciousness comes back to Tristan very slowly. He remembers little of what has happened to him—only that he had been in a strange land:

> *The sun I could not see,*
> *nor land, nor people:*
> *but what I saw,*
> *of that I nought can tell thee.*
> *I was*
> *where once I drew my being,*
> *where once again I go:*
> *the vasty realm*
> *of dateless Night.*
> *But one thing*
> *is there our knowing:*
> *godlike, endless*
> *all-forgetting!*
> *How faded then the presage?*
> *Longing and foreboding,*
> *these it was*
> *that once again*
> *to light of day did urge me?*
> *What still is left within me,*
> *life's fever madly raging,*
> *from rapturous dread of death*
> *towards the light now drives me,*
> *that dazzling, false and golden,*
> *round thee, Isolde, shines!*

Tristan says all this like a man only half-emerged from sleep trying to recapture the elusive threads of a dream: but things that are as yet not quite clear to him are made clear enough to us by the orchestral commentary—the motive of Longing, for instance (No. 1B), and the phrase to which he had sung, in the second act, "Life of holiest loving" (No. 40). The motive of Day (No. 29A) is added as Tristan goes on to speak, with growing excitement, of Isolde being still in the realm of garish sunlight, and of his longing to see her again: "I heard the crash of Death's door closing behind me. But now once more it stands ajar, forced open by the sun's beams; and I, with eyes open and clear, must now break forth out of Night, and go to find her with whom alone united Tristan may find surcease of being." This to the accompaniment of a passionate reminiscence of No. 41.

The gloomy transformation of No. 1B with which the third act had opened (No. 47) comes to the forefront again as Tristan speaks of the horrors which he knows await him on his return to the outer world of Day and its attendant deceits. "Cursed be the Day and its lying appearances!" he cries frenziedly. "Must thou ever wake and re-wake my anguish? Must the light for ever burn that even in the night kept me far from her? O Isolde! Sweet one! Fair one! When at last shall be quenched the beacon that keeps me from thee? The torch—when dies it out?" He sinks back exhausted as the muted violins give out the softest and sweetest reminiscence of No. 31:

Kurvenal, stirred to pity by his master's grief, makes a mighty effort to shake off his own dejection. "Once, from fidelity to thee", he says in self-reproach, "I scorned and defied her; but now my hunger for her is as great as thine. Trust thou my word; thou shalt see her again, here, today, if only she yet be living." But Tristan's mind is still in the borderland between sleep and waking, where past and present run confusedly into one. "The torch still burns", he says faintly; "not dark is it yet in the house; Isolde lives and watches; she called me out of the night." If she is living, Kurvenal assures him again, then let him take heart and hope. For he, the rough untutored one, had been wise enough, he says, to see that the wound the traitor Melot had dealt Tristan could be healed only by the physician who had once closed the wound inflicted by Morold. To Cornwall he has sent a trusty messenger for her, and soon Isolde will be here.

48

Beside himself with excitement, Tristan draws Kurvenal to him, embraces him, and sings the most moving paean to friendship ever penned. Always this old Kurvenal of his has been the faithfullest of friends, his master's shield and guard in battle, one with him in sorrow and in joy: "whom I hated, him hated'st thou too; whom I loved, him too thou loved'st; to good King Marke thou wast true when I was true, false when I was false; never thine own but always mine, when I am suffering thou sufferest with me—but the depth of my suffering, that canst thou not fathom! This terrible yearning that sears my soul, this fever of longing that eats out my heart—could I name it, couldst thou but know it, no longer here would'st thou stay; thou would'st be there at the watchtower, straining for a sight of the sail that will bring me Isolde and her love!"

> *It nears! it nears,*
> *so blithe and fast!*
> *It waves, it waves,*
> *the flag at the mast!*
> *The ship! the ship!*
> *it glides by the reef!*
> *seest thou it not?*
> *Kurvenal, seest thou it not?*

The musical texture of these few passionate pages is a remarkable weaving of motives, sometimes so metamorphosed harmonically and dynamically, however, as to strike the ear at first as new. The motive of Longing, for instance (No. 1B) now takes this form:

and, later, still more subtle shapes. Nos. 40 and 48 (the latter the motive of Tristan's Distress, from the prelude to the third act) appear in new forms, with new psychological nuances. The scoring, too, takes on new colours; the orchestra lashes itself into a tempest as Tristan, in growing excitement, tries to make Kurvenal see the ship that is only a figment of his own disordered imagination. The episode ends with a piercing reiteration of a B flat in octaves high up in the violins and violas as Tristan cries in a final frenzy, "Kurvenal, seest thou not?"

He looks up in expectant silence at the old man, who hesitates whether to leave his master or not. But there is no need for him to go to the tower to see if Tristan's vision of the ship is fact or fancy: the poignant wordless answer to the cry is given by the shepherd's pipe, which once more strikes in, from afar, with its mournful melody (No. 50). Kurvenal understands: "Yet is no ship in sight!" he says in deep dejection. Tristan, his fever now dying down, begins also to perceive the bearing on his own life and lot of that old tune, familiar to him from childhood, immemorially associated with his tragic house:

> *This was the meaning, then,*
> *thou song so old, so mournful,*
> *of all thy long lament!*
> > *On breeze of evening*
> > *wailed it once*
> > *when I, a child,*
> *my father's death did grieve for:*
> > *through mists of morn*
> > *it rang yet sadder*
> > *when the son*
> *his mother's fate was told.*
> *When he begat me and died,*
> *When dying she gave me birth,*
> > *the tune so olden*
> > *wept and wailed,*
> > *upon their souls*
> > *its pain it poured.*

It asked me then,
and asks me now,
what fate it was before me
to which my mother bore me?
o what the fate?—
Again the strain
tells me truly:—
for yearning—and dying!

Throughout Tristan's long monologue the mournful melody of
the shepherd keeps weaving its way in and out in one orchestral
voice and another.

Yearning and dying—between these two poles his life has been
one long oscillation: "in death for ever yearning, yet of yearning
never able to die!" And now this ancient tune rings out in appeal
to the distant healer, bidding her come and bring her lover the
peace of death. His mind, now calm and clear again for a brief
spell, runs over the episodes of his life in which Isolde had figured.
When, long ago, he lay in the boat, mortally wounded as he
thought, that ancient strain had sounded in his ears. The wind had
carried him to Ireland; there Isolde had healed him, but only to
deal his heart a worse wound. Later she had given him a poisoned
draught to drink—a draught intended to be of death, but one that
had turned to unquenchable fire within him. And at the thought
of that fire his fever returns. With growing excitement he speaks
of the endless torment of longing to which he is now condemned,
a torment from which death itself cannot free him. Brain and
heart are on fire in the terrible heat of the Day; where will they
ever find a cooling shade? All this has been the work of the potion,
"and I myself it was who brewed it":

from father's grief
and mother's woe,
from all earth's endless
tears of love,
from laughter and weeping,
sweetness and sorrow,
did I distil
the potion's poison!

Thee that I brewed,
thee I created,
on whose delight
I ever feasted—
I curse thee, terrible draught!,
and him who brewed thee first!

49

He sinks back exhausted. Kurvenal, who has vainly been trying to calm him, gives a terrified cry of "My master! Tristan!", and breaks out into a bitter reproach of Love, its illusions and deceptions, for it is that that has brought his Tristan to this sorry pass, Tristan, the flower of knighthood, loving as no man had ever done, loved as no man had ever been; and for the first and only time in the work the old warrior reveals the wealth of tenderness that lies at the heart of his rough nature.

He turns to his master again with a sob, listens to his breathing, and is rejoiced to find he is still alive. The orchestra, with its soft, honeyed reminiscences of themes previously associated with the longing and the rapture of the lovers, tells us where Tristan's thoughts are. He asks Kurvenal faintly if the ship is yet in sight, and the old man assures him fondly that it will come that very day. Thereupon Tristan loses himself in beatific contemplation of an Isolde smiling on the deck, bringing him atonement and the final peace. No. 41 now becomes the basis of a rich four-part harmony in the horns:

over which Tristan dreams his dream of the coming of the gentle, smiling Isolde:

ending with a long-drawn sigh, that is half pain, half ecstasy, on the words, "Ah, Isolde! How fair art thou!"

Then his fever begins to master him again. He bids Kurvenal go to the watch-tower and look for the ship. He struggles to rise from his couch, and while Kurvenal is trying to restrain him the shepherd's pipe is heard preludising in a new way:

and then breaking out unrestrainedly into the joyous melody for which Kurvenal has so long been waiting:[1]

[1] Like its predecessor, the shepherd's new melody is allotted in the score to the cor anglais. But at the foot of the page (307) on which it appears in Wagner's manuscript of the full score the following note has been added— apparently at some later date, for the script is slightly different from that in the score itself, as if another pen and another ink were being used: "The cor anglais should produce the effect here of a very powerful natural instrument such as the Alpine horn: it is therefore advisable to have it reinforced (according to the particular acoustic circumstances) by oboes and clarinets: unless, which would be the best plan, a wooden instrument of the type of the Swiss Alpine horn could be specially made. This, by reason of its simplicity—it would need only to be capable of producing the notes of the natural scale— would be neither difficult nor costly." This note was printed at the foot of the page in the published score. When the Vienna Opera was engaged on its abortive rehearsals of the work in 1861/2 Wagner told the conductor, Esser, that the proposed horn should be of wood, "at least three feet long, almost trumpet-like, but with a rather crooked curve at the end, so that the bell faces sideways"; its tone was to be "that of a medium-sized Alpine horn, fairly powerful, even rough, but in any case of a natural naïveté."

57

The old man runs to the watch-tower, looks out over the sea, and excitedly announces the coming of the ship. "The flag? The flag?", asks Tristan breathlessly. "The flag of joy!" Kurvenal assures him. Excitement is piled on excitement as he describes to the anxious Tristan how the ship is making its way safely through the dangerous reefs, for the steersman is a chosen man, skilled and trusty. The shepherd too has been watching the course of the ship; and when at last he sees she is safe he pipes his merry tune more exultantly than ever before, while Kurvenal, from the tower, and Tristan, on his couch, shout for joy. The ship is safe in port, the old man tells his master; Isolde is springing to shore. At Tristan's imperious command he goes down to bring her to him.

When Tristan is alone the fever mounts in his blood and brain once more. How, he asks, can he stay fettered to his couch on this best of all days? He must rise and be with the others. He manages to stagger to his feet. Against a reiterated G in the violins, the horns, wood wind and lower strings thunder out a variant of No. 39. This motive, which in the second act had expressed the emotion of the lovers at its peak-point of mystical ecstasy, now has a touch of madness in it. It is in 5/4 time, and much of the music that follows is a combination of triple, quadruple and quintuple metres: simple as the device is, it is sufficient, by sheer contrast with all the other rhythms of the work, to convey to us that something has broken in Tristan.[1] "Tristan the hero", he cries, "exulting in his strength, has snatched himself from death":

[1] The device had previously been employed by Handel in the second act of his opera *Orlando* (1733). "The whole last scene of this act", says Burney, "which paints the madness of Orlando, in accompanied recitatives and airs in various measures, is admirable. Handel has endeavoured to describe the hero's perturbation of intellect by fragments of symphony in 5/8, a division of time which can only be borne in such a situation." The formal-minded eighteenth century evidently found it a little difficult to reconcile itself to so "irregular" a metre, even as a token of "perturbation of intellect".

"Once with a bleeding wound I fought with Morold; now, bleeding from another wound, will I today make Isolde my own!" They are mystical words, the inner sense of which is apt to be missed by the casual listener in the theatre: for the third time Tristan is bent on seeking union with Isolde not in life but in death. "Heia, my blood!" he raves as he tears the bandage from his wound; "joyfully flow now!" He springs from his couch and staggers forward. "She who shall close my wound for ever draws near to save! Let the world perish; jubilantly I hasten to her!"

50

As he stumbles towards the centre of the stage a wild cry of "Tristan! Beloved!" is heard from Isolde (without), and, by one of those psychological strokes of which music alone among the arts is capable, the orchestra, by a harmonic mutation of No. 30, brings us a bitterly ironic reminder of that earlier scene, in the second act, in which it had been Isolde who was so impatiently awaiting the coming of Tristan. His mind, too, goes back to that night, but in its delirium it runs sensations of sound and of light into one; by a bold use of poetic imagery Wagner makes him, when Isolde's cry rings out, imagine he is *hearing* the light of the signal torch. "It dies out!" he cries; "to her! to her!" Isolde enters breathlessly. Tristan, in wild excitement, but near the end of his strength, makes his halting way towards her. They meet in the centre of the stage; she clasps him in her arms, and he sinks slowly to the ground, locked in her embrace. The orchestra, playing reminiscently upon motives with which the prelude had opened (No. 1A, 1B, etc.), and the lovers, with their last cries to each other of "Tristan!" "Isolde!", take us back in imagination for a moment to the scene in the first act that had followed immediately upon the draining of the love potion.

Tristan, with a last look up at Isolde, dies in her arms. In vain does she call on him to speak to her. She had come there to die with him; and he has cheated her of that last satisfaction, for which she had waited through so many weary days. Her wretchedness had been equal to his, as the orchestra tells us by accompanying her with the motive of Tristan's Distress (No. 48). Where is his wound, she asks, that she may heal it for a moment and then be blissfully enveloped with him in Night:

> *Not of thy wound,*
> *not of thy wound, my hero, die:*
> *let thee and me*
> *together bid life farewell.*

But it is now too late:

> *O cruel one!*
> *Lay'st thou on me*
> *so dire a scourge?*
> *Grantest no grace*
> *for all my pain?*
> *Still art thou deaf*
> *to all my sorrow?*

And with a last appeal to him to wake, if only for a moment, she sinks down, unconscious, on his body, while the orchestra breathes a soft reminiscence of No. 42, to the strain of which, in the second act, they had called upon Death to make them one for ever.

Kurvenal, who had returned to the stage immediately after Isolde, has all this while been gazing in mute despair at Tristan. From behind the scenes there now comes the sound of raised voices and the clash of weapons. The shepherd rushes in to announce the sighting of a second ship. Kurvenal, roused from his torpor, springs up and looks over the battlements. He utters an imprecation, for on this other ship he has recognised King Marke and Melot. He and the shepherd hasten to the gate, which they try to barricade. The steersman of Isolde's ship, rushing in, warns them that it is useless, for Marke is coming with many men. But Kurvenal is now beside himself with grief and rage; no one, he swears, shall enter while he is alive. Hearing Brangaene calling to her mistress to open the gate, he curses her too as a traitor. Then Melot's voice is heard, warning him not to oppose them. Kurvenal, with an angry laugh, blesses the day that has brought him face to face with Tristan's false friend; and as Melot appears in the gateway with a company of armed men Kurvenal hurls himself on him and strikes him dead.

From behind the scenes first Brangaene's voice, then the King's is heard, telling the furious old man that he does not understand; but Kurvenal's only answer is, "Here death alone holds sway: nought else is there to win: wouldst thou have it, come here to me!" He throws himself on the King and his retainers, who have now appeared in the gateway, while Brangaene, who has climbed over the wall at the side of the stage, hastens to the front to deliver a message of joy to her mistress. She finds her prostrate over the body of Tristan, apparently dead; and while she is solicitously tending Isolde the King calls out, "O lies! O madness! Tristan, where art thou?" Kurvenal, now mortally wounded, staggers up to him: "there lies he", he says, "and there lie I". He sinks down at Tristan's feet, groping blindly in his death agony for his master's hand, and stammering "Tristan! Loved one! Chide me not that the true one follows thee!"

51

The tangled threads of the drama pass for a moment into the hands of the old King. "Dead, alas! all are dead!" he ejaculates mournfully. In a passion of futile grief he reproaches his Tristan for once more having betrayed him, for now it is too late for Marke to give him the message of understanding and love and trust that he had come to Kareol to bring. "Awake! Awake!" he cries; "Awake to the call of my woe! Thou faithless-faithfullest friend!" and he bends over the two bodies with a sob.

Meanwhile Brangaene, by her ministrations, has succeeded in calling Isolde back to the semblance of life. She tells her what had happened in Cornwall—how she had revealed the secret of the substituted potion to the King, who, comprehending all now, had straightway hurried over the sea to yield Isolde up to

Tristan.[1] Marke also addresses her, speaking such consolation as his simple old heart knows:

> *Why this, Isolde,*
> *why this to me?*
> *When clear 'twas revealed*
> *what before I could fathom not,*
> *what bliss to find my friend*
> *was free of all reproach!*
> *With him I loved*
> *then to mate thee,*
> *with swelling sails*
> *I flew on thy track.*
> *But who, bearing*
> *peace with him,*
> *can the torrent of woe o'ertake?*
> *A richer harvest reaped death:*
> *more woe I blindly have wrought!*

But Isolde has already passed to a sphere in which words and thoughts like these have no meaning. Fixing her eyes—the eyes now of a visionary—on Tristan's body, she begins, to the melody of No. 42, her mystical monody of *Verklärung*, of eternal reunion with him. The poetry of the Liebestod is in large part quite untranslatable. She does not see her lover as the bystanders do. For her he is not dead but transfigured, open-eyed, smiling:

> *See ye not*
> *how he beameth*
> *bright and brighter,*
> *lapped in star-shine*
> *high he soars?*
> *See ye not*
> *how his heart*
> *is pulsing brave,*
> *strong and calm*
> *within his breast?*

[1] In Gottfried von Strassburg's poem it is Kurvenal who tells King Marke of the love potion. This dénouement could not be employed by Wagner, who needed Kurvenal in Kareol.

Or is it, she asks the world, she alone who can see all this, she alone who can hear the great melody pulsing in the air about her, sad and sweet, all-revealing, all-reconciling, streaming from Tristan's being into hers? What and whence are these wonder-tones that envelop her?

> *Are they waves*
> *of breezes fashioned?*
> *Are they clouds*
> *of perfume woven?*
> *How they billow,*
> *thunder round me!*
> *Shall I breathe them?*
> *Shall I listen?*
> *Shall I drink them,*
> *plunge beneath them?*
> *In their odour*
> *die entranced?*
> *In the billowing sea,*
> *in the ocean of sound,*
> *in the world-soul's*
> *depths profound,—*
> *to drown now,*
> *go down now—*
> *swoon in night—*
> *last delight!*

It is the mystical union, at last, for which they had longed. The music is dominated, at the finish, by the motive (No. 31) which, in the prelude to the second act, had been the symbol of Isolde's joy at the thought of reunion with Tristan. Now it becomes the symbol of another union, a more cosmic joy, the ecstasy that throbs "in the world-soul's depths profound":

It broadens out into wider and wider waves of tone as Isolde, lost in her inward vision, sinks transfigured upon Tristan's breast. The last word is given to the motive of Longing with which the opera had begun, outlining itself now through the orchestral texture in the poignant tones of oboe and cor anglais:

THE MASTERSINGERS
OF NUREMBERG

CHARACTERS

HANS SACHS, SHOEMAKER		*Bass*
VEIT POGNER, GOLDSMITH		*Bass*
KUNZ VOGELGESANG, FURRIER		*Tenor*
KONRAD NACHTIGALL, TINSMITH		*Bass*
SIXTUS BECKMESSER, TOWN CLERK		*Bass*
FRITZ KOTHNER, BAKER		*Bass*
BALTHASAR ZORN, PEWTERER	MASTERSINGERS	*Tenor*
ULRICH EISSLINGER, GROCER		*Tenor*
AUGUSTIN MOSER, TAILOR		*Tenor*
HERMANN ORTEL, SOAP-BOILER		*Bass*
HANS SCHWARZ, STOCKING-WEAVER		*Bass*
HANS FOLTZ, COPPERSMITH		*Bass*
WALTHER VON STOLZING, A YOUNG FRANCONIAN KNIGHT		*Tenor*
DAVID, SACHS'S APPRENTICE		*Tenor*
EVA, POGNER'S DAUGHTER		*Soprano*
MAGDALENA, EVA'S NURSE		*Soprano*
A NIGHT WATCHMAN		*Bass*

I

The opera-goer without any first-hand knowledge of the German Mastersingers must not take them at Wagner's valuation. He was writing a lusty comedy, not a specialist treatise, and he exercised to the full the comic dramatist's or novelist's right to use only so much of the historical material lying to his hand as suits his purpose, and occasionally to exaggerate the comicalities of it for his own ends. When he conceived the idea of an opera on the subject in 1845 he could have known not much more about the Mastersingers than he had derived from a reading of Gervinus's *History of German National Literature* (1826); and it is evident from his own account that what mostly interested him at that time in connection with them was the opportunities for fun they presented him with. They caught him on the rebound, as it were, from the deeply serious mood induced in him by his absorption in the ethical milieu of the Lohengrin and Parsifal epics; and just then he wanted nothing more from the Marker and the apprentices and the rest of the Nuremberg crew than material for kindly laughter.

But as the years went on, the subject struck deeper and deeper roots into him. The character of Sachs took on a graver tinge; a philosophy, if not of actual pessimism, at any rate of resignation slowly spread its grey veil over the central motive of the action; so that just before the first performance of the work (in Munich in 1868), he could write to King Ludwig in this strain: "It is impossible that you should not have sensed, under the opera's quaint superficies of popular humour, the profound melancholy, the lament, the cry of distress of poetry in chains, and its reincarnation, its new birth, its irresistible magic power achieving mastery over the common and the base." This was a vast expansion and a decided re-tinting of his own first feeling with regard to the work some twenty-three years earlier.

2

His own account of the genesis of the opera, given us in his autobiography, runs thus. During his reading of Gervinus, he says, "I was especially tickled by the title of 'the Marker' and the function he exercised in the Mastersinging. Without knowing very much about Sachs and his poetic contemporaries, I conceived the idea, during one of my walks, of a droll scene in which the cobbler, in the capacity of a popular artisan-poet, makes the Marker sing, and, by the application of his hammer to his last, gives him a lesson by way of punishment for his pedantic misdeeds. For me the whole thing concentrated itself on two points—on the one hand the Marker with his slate covered with chalkmarks, and on the other Hans Sachs holding up the shoes he had managed to finish by 'marking' faults on the soles, each of them indicating that the singer had been 'versungen'.[1] In addition I

---

[1] The technical term in the Mastersingers' Guild for the failure of a candidate at his trial for Mastership: he had "un-sung" or "mis-sung" himself.

worked out swiftly, for the conclusion of my second act, a scene in one of the narrow, crooked alleys of Nuremberg, with the neighbours roused from their beds, plunging into a street brawl. And so my whole Mastersingers comedy suddenly sprang into such vivid life within me that, as it was a particularly merry theme, not likely to over-excite me, I felt justified in disobeying my doctor's orders and putting it on paper." The immediate pull of *Lohengrin* was so strong on him, however, that he soon put the comic opera out of his mind.

The street scene to which he refers was a reminiscence of an experience of his own, as a young man of twenty-three, in Nuremberg itself. While staying there in 1835 with his brother-in-law Wolfram he had made the acquaintance, in a local beer-house, of a master carpenter named Lauermann, a grotesque creature who was the stock butt of the local wags. Wolfram had sportively passed off Wagner on him as the famous singer Lablache, visiting Nuremberg incognito; he had heard, it appeared, of Lauermann's wonderful singing and was anxious to hear him and learn from him. The carpenter was gulled one night into giving an exhibition of his art. After the ludicrous exhibition a shindy broke out outside the tavern, and for a little while it looked, says Wagner, as if the whole town would be engaged in a free-for-all fight. The knocking-out of one of the rioters brought the tumult to an end with a suddenness that seemed magical: "within little more than a minute the roaring crowd of several hundred men was quiet, and my brother-in-law and I were able to stroll home arm-in-arm, laughing and joking, through the deserted moonlit streets." The scene was undoubtedly before his eyes when he sketched the closing scene of his second act.

His first Prose Sketch for *The Mastersingers* is dated "Marien-bad, 16 July 1845": it is very detailed, running to some twelve pages of print in the modern imprint. A Second Sketch, equally rich in detail, was made in Vienna in October 1861. As there was no hope at that time of *Tristan* being produced in Vienna for at least another twelve months, Wagner told Bülow on the 17th December, he felt he ought to set to work at something new and different. He turned in horror from a "passionate" subject of the *Tristan* type, with all that it would involve in the way of knocking his new ideas into the noddle of a tenor. But by good luck, he said, his thoughts had suddenly reverted to "my old plan for a *Mastersingers of Nuremberg*." He found his memories of that plan astonishingly fresh, and his imagination at once began to play upon it. He had already broached the scheme for "a popular comic opera" to his publisher Schott on the 30th October. The "jovial-poetic" hero of it was to be Hans Sachs; it would be full of drollery, light in style, and easily staged; he particularly congratulated himself on the fact that "this time I shall need neither a so-called first tenor nor a great tragic soprano", the difficulty of finding which rare birds had been the main cause of the long delay in producing *Tristan*.

Schott having shown an interest in the scheme, Wagner sent him a copy of his Second Sketch on the 19th November.[1] Once more, in all innocence, he stressed the simplicity and practicality of the new work; "it will not call for an outstanding tenor—and this, as things are just now, is almost everything—nor for a great tragic soprano, which is a good deal. The leading rôle, that of Hans Sachs, will be written in a convenient bass register, so that it can be sung in any theatre by the best of the baritones or even deep basses." It will all be relatively simple and well within the scope of any small opera company, while the larger theatres will find in it ample opportunities, especially in the choruses, for showing what they can do.

In all this, as was not unusual with him, he was deceiving himself. The *Mastersingers* grew far beyond his first intentions as he became absorbed in it. The orchestral score became the biggest ever published until then. The opera turned out anything but "light" for the most part; and it called for a first-rate tenor

---

[1] This copy, though it counts technically as a Third Sketch, is virtually identical with the Second.

Sachs, David and Magdalena are the only characters who bear the same names in the First Sketch as those by which we know them now. Eva was for a time simply "The Daughter" or "The Maiden"; then, later, Emma. Similarly Walther von Stolzing was at first only "The Young Man" (later Konrad), and Beckmesser only "The Marker". At a later stage he became, "Hanslich", or "Veit Hanslich". Pogner began as "Bogler"; while Magdalena became for a while Kathrine. In the first two Sketches the opening scene was set in St. Sebald's Church.

and soprano in addition to the central Sachs. Wagner, in his
first enthusiasm, counted on performing the work in the early
part of 1862; but the score was not completed until October
1867.

3

For the Second Sketch Wagner sought out more material than
had been available to him in 1845. He made a close study of Jakob
Grimm's *Ueber den altdeutschen Meistergesang* (1811), a book
into which he had probably dipped, however, in the 1840's; and
through Peter Cornelius he obtained the loan of Wagenseil's[1]
Nuremberg Chronicle from the Vienna Imperial Library. This
curious old book was for a long time almost the only source of
information about the Nuremberg Mastersingers and their school
rules. The famous Chronicle was not published until 1697, by
which time the art of Mastersong was well in decline in Nuremberg and elsewhere; Wagenseil based himself, however, on manuscripts of an earlier epoch, and his account of the mid-sixteenth
century Masters and their rules is reliable. The bulk of his curious
volume is devoted to a history and description (in Latin) of the
ancient town of Nuremberg: it is only in the last hundred-and-
fifty pages or so that he settles down to set forth (in German) the
"Origins, Practice, Utility and Rules of the Gracious Art of the
Mastersingers".

From Wagenseil Wagner now made copious extracts, which
are today printed in full at the end of his Second Sketch. He
jotted down for his own use the names of twelve "old Nuremberg
Masters": the list agrees with that of the Masters who appear in the
opera, except that there he changes the first name of the historic
Fritz Zorn to Balthasar and dispenses with one Nikolaus Vogel,
making up the intended round dozen, however, by including
Sachs. (He probably left out Nikolaus Vogel for a simple but
artful reason which will be suggested later). He copied out with
comic gusto the rules—the "Tabulatur"—that governed the
Mastersong, the list of the various "faults" for which the Marker
debited a candidate with this or that number of points, the list of

[1] Wagenseil was born in 1633 and died in 1708.

the Mastersinger "Tones", and the quaint definitions of the various types of rhymes. It was on the basis of all this that he constructed David's exposition of the rules of the Mastersong in the first act of the opera, the faults noted by Beckmesser in Walther's singing and by Sachs in Beckmesser's, and Kothner's formal reading of the Tabulatur to the young knight before he embarks on his "Trial".

As we have just seen, the names of the Masters given in his list of dramatis personae are authentic enough; but the spectator of the opera must not take it for granted that the bearers of those names were in real life merely the uncouth figures of fun he sees on the stage. Wagner, for one thing, follows his own fancy in the trades he allots to them. Wagenseil gives only their names; but Adam Puschman (1532–1600)[1] supplies us with the real occupations of some of them. Wagner makes Kothner a baker; actually he was a clasp- or pin-maker. So was Hermann Ortel, who in the opera sinks to a soap-boiler. The historical Ulrich Eisslinger was not, as in the opera, a grocer but a timber merchant, and Friedrich Zorn not a plasterer but a nail-maker. These people were probably not artisans, in the sense in which Wagner employs that term, but well-to-do business men; for Nuremberg was a rich and handsome city, and there was a great demand in it for good building materials, fine metal work, handsome furniture, artistic pottery and so on. Wagner's "tinsmith", "coppersmith", "tailor", "stocking-weaver" etc. are pure fancy; nor is there any historical justification for his making Beckmesser the Town Clerk or for depicting him as a comic and stupid pedant. The melodies of his preserved for posterity by Puschman show him to have been no worse a composer than the majority. (Wagner, following Wagenseil, gives him the forename of Sixtus; according to Puschman it was Sigismondus, abbreviated for ordinary purposes to Six). We possess also authentic specimens of the melodies of Nachtigall, Eisslinger, Kothner, Ortel, Vogelgesang, Zorn, Foltz, a certain Bogner, and, of course, Hans Sachs. Foltz and Nachtigall appear to have had a genuine melodic vein of their own; the former's setting of a poem on the theme of death is a really creditable piece of work.

[1] Puschman was a pupil of Sachs.

4

As has just been pointed out, the Mastersingers were by no means the monsters of bourgeois absurdity which the spectators of Wagner's opera can too easily assume them to have been. They had done much good work throughout the generations, and their rules and faults and definitions were simply the codified results of long experience; it goes without saying, indeed, that no Guild of mere pedantic dunderheads could have earned and kept the respect of intelligent people all over Germany for so long a stretch of time. Their intentions, seen at their best, were a combination of those of, say, the French Academy, the prosodist, the grammarian, the musical Conservatoire, and the adjudicators at a competition festival. A few illustrations will make this clear.

One of the functions of the French Academy is to preserve the purity and uphold the dignity of the French language. The Mastersingers were similarly concerned with the employment of the still rather uncouth German language in its then best forms. They insisted on the use by the candidate of the High German that had become the standard speech of the upper classes and the government offices, and had been put to such fine use by Luther in his translation of the Bible. The dialect of this locality or that was not absolutely barred by the Mastersingers, but it was to be kept within bounds; it must not obtrude itself at points in a poem where it would attract too much and unfavourable attention to itself, and in rhymes it must be used only in conjunction with words from the same dialect, not with words in High German. This was an eminently sensible rule, which must have done a great deal to bring local dialects into conformity with the standard speech of cultivated people, if only by ensuring that the same vowel would have the same sound on all like occasions.

Several of the "faults" enumerated and penalised are quite rightly characterised as such. One of them—referred to in the opera—was "blinde Meinung" (obscure meaning), i.e., saying what one had to say in an irregular or cloudy style. Wagenseil gives as an example "Ich du soll kommen" instead of "Ich und du soll kommen". Browning would thus have been heavily penalised by the Marker for saying:

> *For I am ware it is the seed of act*
> *God holds appraising in His hollow palm,*
> *Not act grown great thence on the world below,*
> *Leafage and branchage, vulgar eyes admire.*

Apart from other small obscurities in this, a "which" should logically come between "branchage" and "vulgar".

It was always a "fault" in the Mastersingers' eyes and ears to play tricks with the language simply to get an easy rhyme or to make the number of syllables in one line correspond to that in another. Shakespeare, for example, would have lost a mark for writing:

> *And winking Marybuds begin*
> *To ope their golden eyes;*
> *With every thing that pretty bin,*
> *My lady sweet, arise;*

where "bin" has artfully been used instead of "is" to make sure of a rhyme to "begin". The Tabulatur specifies a good many sins of this and kindred sorts against the German language, and is appropriately severe on them; and it is particularly censorious of poetry that does not make its meaning clear at once: the "blinde Meinung" of some modern poetry would have kept the Marker's chalk working overtime. The trouble always is that to insist through thick and thin on general rules of this kind is not to meet a particular case: a thing may be beyond question a technical fault, yet be accepted by us because without it the poet could not have said with the same pungency just what he wanted to say at that particular moment and in that particular connection.

5

In this respect the Mastersingers' rules were calculated to do more harm than good in the long run. They would ensure technical propriety at the occasional cost of individuality; the spirit of the poetic idea would sometimes suffer in order that the letter of the language might be safeguarded. But broadly speaking the Masters of the best period, seen in the light of their own time and place, were proceeding in these matters along the right lines;

and it is hardly fair to laugh at them for the exaggerations into
which their principles landed them now and then, and to forget
how just, in principle, their principles really were. To insist too
rigidly on rules, however excellent they may be in theory, is in
practice to start sliding down the slippery slope that lands us in
pedantry and hide-bound formalism. One of the "faults" the
Masters frowned upon was that described as "the soft and hard",
that is to say, rhyming a word in which a consonant is by definition hard with another word in which it is defined as soft; for
example, "Knaben" with "Knappen", "laden" or "Gnaden" with
"Thaten", "Tod" with "Gott", "her" with "Lehr". The purist
may say they were mostly right in this; but the poet will plead for
a trifle more licence in practice. It is the old story—give the man
in office too much power and he will settle down before long into
a bureaucrat who is more of a menace than a help to the plain
citizen.

There was nothing essentially wrong, again, with the Mastersingers' sifting of rhymes into categories, however comical the
names they gave to these categories may sound in the ears of
today. There were, for example, the "blunt" rhyme, the "clink-
ing", the "orphan", the "pause", the "blow" ("stroke", "per-
cussion"). The "orphan" is an ending that does not rhyme with
anything that has preceded it; Wagenseil's example is the hymn
"Allein Gott in der Höh' sei Ehr' ". The first verse of this runs
thus:

> *Allein Gott in der Höh' sei Ehr'*
> *Und Dank für seine Gnade;*
> *Darum, dass nun und nimmermehr*
> *Uns rühren kann kein Schade.*
> *Ein Wohlgefall'n Gott an uns hat;*
> *Nun ist gross Fried ohn' Unterlass,*
> *All Fehd' hat nun ein Ende.*

It will be seen that the final lines do not rhyme; and this procedure
is repeated in the following verses. These, therefore, said the
Masters, are "orphan" rhymes; they have no family ties, no home
to go to.

The "pauses", on the other hand, rhyme only at a distance

from each other and with a break-off from the adjacent words, as
in the following hymn quoted by Wagenseil:

> *Ach,*
> *Was hab' ich, o Herr, begangen!*
> *Meine Sünden sind zu gross,*
> *Meine Glieder liegen bloss!*
> *Herr, nach dir steht mein Verlangen!*
> *Wach,*
> *Du, mein Gott, und hilf nun mir,*
> *Dass ich bleibe stets bei dir;*
> *Lindre du mir meine Schmerzen,*
> *Denn ich bin von ganzem Herzen*
> *Schwach!*

6

All this elaboration of definitions is really, soberly considered,
a credit rather than otherwise to the Mastersingers, for it proves
that their art had reached a stage of such variety of rhymes and
rhythms that the necessity was felt for defining, classifying and
organising them. Their predecessors the Minnesingers had gone
quite as far if not further in the same direction. It is a phase that
always follows, and indeed presupposes, a considerable artistic
development; as soon as the creators have demonstrated the
variety of which practice is capable the theoreticians step in, sort
out the structures and technical devices into categories, and give
each of them a label. The Mastersingers' categories are a legacy
from the Middle Ages, and, indeed, from Graeco-Roman times,
with their passion for verbal hair-splitting, every device of rhetoric
being resolved into its constituent atoms and each atom then
given a name of its own. The trouble was that as the creative
faculty slowly dwindled among the Mastersingers too much
importance came to be attached to labels and rules for their own
sweet sakes. We have to remember that these "rules" that have
come down to us were committed to paper at a time when the
Mastersong had entered upon its decline as a living art. And of
course it was no business of Wagner's to weigh the historical and

other pro's and con's of the matter. All he was concerned with was the opportunities for comedy it presented him with. Wagenseil's solemn enumeration of all the quaintly-named categories had tickled his fancy, and he was determined that other people should share in the fun.

These considerations apply also to the famous "Tones" or "Modes". The names of these amused him immensely; he particularly enjoyed the "Lonely Gormandiser" Tone. And when David reels off the long list of some forty Modes to Walther—the "Hawthorn Bloom Mode", the "Love that Passes" Mode, the "Fresh-gathered Oranges" Mode, the "True Pelican" Mode, and so forth, ending proudly with the "Thread-bright-at-the-end" Mode[1]—we laugh as heartily as the young knight and ejaculate with him, "Heaven help us! There seems no end to the code!"

But it is all quite simple. If we examine any collection of songs, old or new, we see at once that the lines of the poems differ in length, in the number of syllables, in the distribution of the accents, etc., while the melodies differ from each other in respect of the way they begin and end, the extent to which one phrase or more of them is repeated, and where, and so on almost ad infinitum. If we wanted to refer to one of these many variants in such a way that our interlocutor would know instantly which one we meant, we should have to give it a name of its own of some sort, just as horticulturists give fanciful but practicable distinguishing names to the many varieties of the rose. That, in essence, is what the Mastersingers did.

In their further capacities of examiners for a diploma and adjudicators at a competitive musical festival the Masters simply catalogued certain faults that were to be avoided in performance. With these, as with certain other points of their theory and practice, we shall deal as occasion arises in our analysis of Wagner's opera.

[1] As it happens, there was no such Mode as this. In the German it is "die buttglänzende Drahtweise." Nobody has ever been able to say precisely what the "butt" signifies, and after a good deal of discussion it is now generally accepted that it is simply a misprint, in Wagenseil, for "gutt"; for we read elsewhere of a "guttglänzende Drahtweise" ("Well-shining-thread Mode") as the creation of one Jobst Zolner.

7

Wagner had not been the first in the field with some of the elements of the plot of *The Mastersingers*. Sachs had already figured as the hero of a drama, *Hans Sachs*, by a now forgotten dramatist of the name of Johann Ludwig Ferdinand Deinhardstein (1794–1859): the play had been produced in 1827. It is to be presumed that Wagner had read it; but he could have obtained from it very little for his own purposes except the idea of showing the poetic cobbler in love and at variance with his fellow-poets. In Deinhardstein, Sachs is the accepted lover of Kunigunde, the only child of the richest man in Nuremberg, the goldsmith Steffen.[1] Their love has to be kept secret because Kunigunde knows that her father will never consent to her marrying a shoemaker; and she tries her hardest to persuade Sachs to exchange that prosaic profession for one held in more esteem in the best Nuremberg circles. Deinhardstein's Sachs, however, is not at all the humble old cobbler of Wagner's opera: he is young and gallant and well-to-do, evidently a shoemaker in a large way of business. He turns a deaf ear to all Kunigunde's entreaties because he sees nothing to blush for in his line of trade. He has been engaged in it all his life; he has shod half Nuremberg and shod it well. Nor is there any of the humorous diffidence of the Wagnerian Sachs in him; he could easily retire or turn to another trade, he says, but will not do so because he is a fighter, and because he regards a good pair of shoes as no less admirable than the product of any other Nuremberg workshop.

Steffen, unaware of his daughter's clandestine passion, has chosen for her one Eoban Runge, a fop and noodle from Augsburg, who has the distinction of being a senator of his native town. Runge and Sachs soon come into collision, and the former shows himself to be a sneak and a poltroon. But he has assured Steffen (who is proud of being a member of the Mastersingers' Guild), that in Augsburg he enjoys a great reputation as a poet; and this counts with the goldsmith. From Runge Wagner may perhaps have derived a hint or two for his Beckmesser.

[1] Sachs's first wife, whom he married in 1519, was a Kunigunde, but her family name was Kreutzer.

But Kunigunde is not Sachs's only trouble. He is perpetually in conflict with the professed Masters. He has no exaggerated opinion of his own poetry, in which he can afford to indulge himself only one day in the week; but poetry is the life-breath of his soul. The other Masters criticise him harshly for not keeping to the rules. One of them plumes himself on having put the would-be cobbler poet in his place at a recent meeting of the Guild: he had exposed so many faults in Sachs's latest poem that the rafters had rung with the laughter of the Masters, and the poor man, according to him, had left the assembly pale and trembling. A second Master praises the first for his frankness: there is no enduring this Sachs who is "always different from the rest of us", who does not appreciate their poetry and their rules, and does all he can to avoid their company. When he is accused of flouting the rules his answer always is that the vital thing in poetry is not the form but the spirit that animates the form. One of them hesitatingly admits that the man has some talent. "Talent! Talent!" replies another; "we have no use here for talent. Let him stick to the Tabulatur, avoid the *equivoca*, the *relativa*, *blind words*, and all the other offences against the rules". It is observance of these, not talent, that makes the poet: "anyone can have talent, but not everyone has the fineness of ear and the solicitousness that enables us to steer clear of errors. Sachs is not solid enough yet; his imagination gets in his way." Here again Deinhardstein may possibly have provided Wagner with a few hints for the apposition of Sachs and Beckmesser.

In other respects Wagner has virtually no points of contact with his predecessor. In Deinhardstein, the shoemaker, angered by Kunigunde's insistence and the ill-will of the Masters, turns his back at last on his beloved Nuremberg and goes out to seek his fortune elsewhere. He falls in with the Emperor Maximilian and his train, who are out hunting; they have lost their way, and Sachs guides them to the city. Neither man is aware of the identity of the other: the Emperor is travelling as a Count, and as the guide does not give his own name Maximilian does not know that he is the Hans Sachs whose poetry he admires and whom he has long been anxious to meet. The play ends, of course, with the Emperor putting everything right when he reaches the city:

Sachs gets his Kunigunde, Steffen is reconciled to the thought of a shoemaker for his son-in-law now that Sachs is seen to stand high in the favour of the Emperor, and Runge, his machinations exposed, goes back to Augsburg with his tail between his legs.

8

Wagner may have been indebted for a hint here and there to two or three other German plays and novels of the early nineteenth century. Although there must have been stories from time immemorial of the offering of a maiden's hand as prize in a contest of some kind or other, he may quite possibly have been influenced in the shaping of the central motive of his opera by E. T. A. Hoffmann's well-known tale of *Master Martin the Cooper and his Men*. From the same writer's *Signor Formica* he may have taken the idea of Beckmesser coming to grief through his over-eagerness to pass off some one else's work as his own in order to make sure of winning a prize; and it is on the cards that he may have known Deinhardstein's bright little comedy *Salvator Rosa* (1823), which is a dramatised version of the Hoffmann tale. Deinhardstein's *Hans Sachs* was made into an opera for Lortzing by Philipp Reger and Philipp Düringer: the work was produced in 1840, and Wagner certainly made its acquaintance during his Dresden period. All these odds and ends of fact, however, while necessary to complete the historical record, do not make the *Mastersingers* anyone's work but Wagner's. We are reminded of the research that has proved that this phrase and that of the Austrian national hymn is to be found in this or that popular melody of the period, and of a modern German writer's sensible summing up that Haydn can be credited with the composition of nothing of the hymn except the whole of it.

The poem of the *Mastersingers* was written in thirty days and finished on the 25th January 1862. It was printed towards the end of that year. The prelude was completed by the third week of April 1862. Wagner set to work at the music to the opera about the same time, but often during the troubled years that followed he was either interrupted for long periods or temporarily lost heart for it. The final note of the full score was not written until the 24th October 1867. The first performance was given in Munich, under Bülow, on the 21st June 1868, with the following cast:

Hans Sachs	Franz Betz
Pogner	Kaspar Bausewein
Vogelgesang	Karl Heinrich
Nachtigall	Eduard Sigl
Beckmesser	Gustav Hölzel
Kothner	Karl Fischer
Zorn	Weixlstorfer
Eisslinger	Eduard Hoppe
Moser	Pöppl
Ortel	Thoms
Schwartz	Grasser
Foltz	Hayn
Walther von Stolzing	Franz Nachbaur
David	Schlosser
Eva	Mathilde Mallinger
Magdalena	Sophie Dietz
The Night Watchman	Ferdinand Lang

9

The prelude, as Wagner styles it in his score, though he had begun by calling it the overture, opens with the sturdy theme of the Mastersingers in their corporate capacity—a solid bourgeois crew, firm on their feet, very self-conscious and sure of themselves:

In the opera the theme represents more particularly what is best in the Guild, as transmitted by tradition and typified by Pogner and Sachs, its genuine concern for art according to its lights, and above all its love for, and pride in, the splendid ancient city of Nuremberg. The strain runs its dignified course for twenty-six bars, gathering strength as it proceeds, and closing in the key of the dominant. Then flutes and clarinets strike in more softly with the motive of Walther's wooing; the marking is espressivo:

But for the moment Walther and his youthful romantic ardour are only a timid intrusion into the pageantry of Nuremberg and the Mastersingers: they are brushed aside magisterially in a downward swoop of the unison strings, to make way for the brave fanfare—derived from the commencement of an actual Mastersinger melody—that is the badge, as it were, of the ancient and honourable Guild, whose patron saint is King David:

As if exhilarated by this appearance of the Guild banner, the festal procession now gets thoroughly into its stride with a motive which, in the opera, will be more particularly associated with the Guild as the trustees of the arts of poetry and music; the honest breasts of the Nuremberg burghers are swelling with pride:

With a magnificent development of this theme the Masters have had their say for the time being. They pass out of our sight for a while, and first of all there comes into view the young knight from the country, Walther von Stolzing, his boy's heart aching with rómantic yearning:

which almost immediately finds a fuller and more definite outlet in the theme of his passion for Eva: later in the opera we shall hear it in the final section of the Prize Song:

It merges, by a transition so natural that one wonders whether, in Wagner's original conception, the two did not form part of the same lyrical outburst, into a melody drawn from his Trial Song in the first act: it is youth's cry for the beauty and love of earth in the spring:

The music unfolds itself in more and more luxuriant foliations, till the time comes when the knight in his turn must make way for a group of apprentices that suddenly breaks into the scene. As is only fitting, they have no distinct theme of their own, for so far as Nuremberg is concerned they are insects not yet out of the grub stage; they are only potential tinsmiths and pewterers and cobblers and tailors and what not, possibly also, if the Fates are very kind, Mastersingers some day, entitled, they too, to walk with swelling chests behind the banner of King David; and so, being burghers and Masters only *in posse*, not *in esse*, the crisp wood wind theme allotted to them is simply that of their graver

elders diminished to the scale of their age and mentality—No. 1
with a brisker gait and a perkier manner:

Obviously we need never expect much more from them than a
love of chaff and horse-play among themselves and an occasional
guying of their grave seniors.

For a moment now and then we get a glimpse in the strings of
Walther and his Spring Song, but it cannot make any headway
against the gay impertinence of the apprentices, who, after parody-
ing the first of the Mastersinger themes, now subject the second
of them (No. 4) to the same treatment. From this they gabble on
to a new figure in the 'cellos:

which, it will be seen, combines in the lower part with their own
version of No. 4 above it. About this chattering figure we shall
have one or two conjectures to make later.

A lively development of this combination of themes, in which
the apprentices are obviously making merry at the expense of the
Masters—as they must often have done in old Nuremberg—
reaches its climax in a couple of bars in which they seem to be
dancing with glee:

But into their merriment there suddenly strikes the motive of Walther's yearning (No. 5); the marking is molto espressivo. (The piano arrangements for two hands are necessarily an imperfect representation of the orchestral tissue at this point. They can show only the tail-end of No. 5; as a matter of fact it enters in the orchestra, not *after* our No. 10 but during it). This is followed by a blow delivered with the full strength of the orchestra as the Masters sweep the apprentices aside, No. 1 thundering out in the trumpets and trombones. Then Wagner gathers himself up for a last mighty effort. It is the musician, revelling in his craftsmanship, rather than the dramatist or the descriptive writer, that now comes uppermost in him: he has some fine themes on his hands of which he sees the contrapuntal possibilities, and he means to make the most of his opportunity. Three of them, Nos. 1, 3 and 6, he seizes upon and welds into a massive polyphonic whole:

Here we have in the upper part the melody of the final stanza of Walther's Prize Song (No. 6), in the middle part the King David or Banner fanfare (No. 3), and as a foundation, in the double basses, bassoons and booming bass tuba, the main Mastersingers' motive (No. 1). The impudent staccato figure shown in the lower part of No. 9 makes a passing appearance or two, but broadly speaking the tissue from now to the end of the overture is woven out of the dignified motives associated with the Mastersingers and Nuremberg. There is a comic touch at one point, where the bass tuba, with a heavy trill on the low A, seems to be shaking its fat sides with laughter. The climax comes with an imposing statement of No. 3, then No. 4, and finally No. 1. But—a point not always made sufficiently clear in performance—the merry bass of No. 9 plays about to the last, and it is actually this, in conjunction with a trumpet fanfare, that has the last word:

In its operatic form the prelude has no formal ending, but runs straight on into the opening scene.

10

The *Mastersingers* prelude having become a stock piece with conductors and orchestras, it goes without saying that in nine instances out of ten it is inadequately performed. Many of the finer points of the score are not brought out because the quiet significance of them has escaped the executants, who are content to rely upon a general effect of massive sonority. We hardly ever hear, for example, the bass line in bars 59–70 (entrusted to bassoons, double basses and bass tuba) phrased in accordance with Wagner's instructions, which he makes so clear that it is evident he attached some importance to the matter. He has marked the passage thus in the tuba and bassoons:

It is the custom, again, of some conductors to slow down considerably the King David fanfare theme (No. 3) in its final statement 26 bars before the end of the prelude, following this up with a pumped-up accelerando in the last dozen bars. But if Wagner had wanted any of these violent changes of tempo he would have specified them. All he has asked for at the first point mentioned is a more *emphatic* delivery of No. 3: his marking of it is simply "sehr gewichtig", i.e. molto pesante. Neither then nor later does he indicate any change of speed.

Conductors would do well to make themselves thoroughly acquainted with Wagner's long dissertation on the tempo of the overture in his treatise *On Conducting*. He always attached the greatest importance to tempo; it was his constant complaint in his later years that there was not a single conductor in Germany who could be trusted to find the right tempo for a passage without himself standing at his elbow; and the imagination boggles at the thought of what he would have said of some of the Wagner conductors of the present day. He was particularly severe on those of the tribe who, without any experience of opera, performed this or that excerpt from his works in the light of their feeling for concert music only, without any real understanding of the drama from which the excerpts have been taken.

To the opening and main tempo of the *Mastersingers* overture he gave conductors a clue when he said that it must be that of the corresponding passage in the third act of the opera at the point where Kothner comes forward carrying the banner of the Guild. But the last thing he ever desired was a rigid metronomic time-beating throughout a work or an episode; a tempo should always be subtly inflected from moment to moment, without, however, any violence being done to the basic speed; the music should *sing*, in the way a few of the really great singers have made familiar to us. He had intentionally marked the overture, he says, "sehr mässig bewegt"; i.e. molto moderato but at the same time with animation. The music has to be "kept moving", and "moving" means slightly different things in different conjunctures. When specifying the tempo, Wagner says, he had in mind something like the old allegro maestoso, "and no tempo stands more in need of modification from time to time in a long work than this, especially when the thematic contents are the subject of markedly defined episodic treatment". He shows how easily a steady basic 4/4 can be made to lend itself to this subtle flexibility. Beaten in "vigorously animated" crotchets it can express a lively allegro, as in the eight bars of our No. 5; conceived as a "half-period" resulting from "the combination of two 2/4 beats", as in the diminution which our No. 1 undergoes in No. 8, it can give us the feeling of a "brisk scherzando"; conceived as an alla breve (2/2) it may suggest "the older easy-going tempo andante with its two moderately slow beats", in which sense, he continues, he has employed it during the combination of themes shewn in our No.

11; while the upper melody of this, at its first "diminished" appearance "in pure 4/4 beats" (No. 6), can be made to express both tenderness and impulsive passion. For No. 6 a slight easing of the tempo is required; and it was in order to prepare unobtrusively for this that he had marked the preceding bar rallentando. Other little nuances of time and beat are set forth in Wagner's exposition, which should be read and digested by conductors and orchestral players before they attempt the prelude. The overture had gone extremely well, he says, at the first performance under himself in Leipzig; but no sooner did the German Kapellmeisters get hold of it then they made nonsense of it. "Only imagine anything so animated and yet so sensitive and so delicately organised from first to last as the tempo I have indicated for the prelude being suddenly packed into the Procrustes-bed of one of these 'classical' time-beaters! It's a case of 'Get in and lie down: where you are too long I will hack a bit off you; where you are too short I'll stretch you!' and the music strikes up to drown the martyred victim's moans!"

11

The construction of the overture presents us with one or two little puzzles.

It was first performed at Leipzig, under Wagner himself, on the 31st October 1862, at a concert given by him in conjunction with a young protégé of his of that period, Wendelin Weissheimer. As a rule the overture to an opera, like the foreword to a book, is written last; and it was perhaps because Wagner, in his first enthusiasm for his subject, departed from this sound rule that to us of today who know the whole opera so well the "programme" of the overture is not quite as clear as we could wish it to be.

The prelude appears to have been drafted in the early weeks of 1862, when Wagner was living at Biebrich, near Mainz, for Weissheimer tells us in his memoirs that about February or March of that year Wagner showed him "a sheet containing the broad working-out of the initial motive, and, lower down, the second motive in E [our No. 6] and the trumpet passage characterising the Mastersingers [No. 3]. He consequently wrote the prelude before he had composed a note of the text. . . . The astonishing thing about the motive in E was the happy accident that later on the words of Walther's Prize Song fitted this wonderful melody precisely. Certainly when conceiving the prelude he had not the remotest idea of that Prize Song in the third act." What was in Weissheimer's mind was probably that in the main the Prize Song as we now have it runs on quite other lines than those of No. 6, which constitutes only an item in the conclusion of the melody. The curious story of the origin of the present Prize Song will be told in full later; all we are concerned with at present is the undoubted fact that the prelude, which has superficially the appearance of being "constructed out of motives from the opera", was conceived and completed before Wagner had begun the formal musical setting of his text. This is established by a letter of his to Minna of the 21st April 1862, in which he says, "Actually I have done nothing of my opera except the overture [*sic*]; but this has turned out very well, and will probably cut out all my other overtures."

We may correlate this passage with one in his autobiography. His pleasant walks in Biebrich in the early spring of 1862, he says, awoke in him once more the desire for work. (By "work" he means musical composition: the poem of the *Mastersingers* had been completed by the 25th January of that year). "Watching one evening from the balcony of my house a fine sunset, lighting up in glory the splendid view of 'golden Mainz' and the majestically flowing Rhine, the prelude to my *Mastersingers* suddenly sprang up clearly in my mind as I had once before beheld it in a troubled mood, as it were a distant mirage, and I proceeded to draft out the prelude precisely as it appears today in the score, that is to say, setting forth with the utmost definiteness the main motives of the whole drama. Then I went on at once to work at the text, composing the scenes in due sequence." Manifestly, then, even while working at the text of the poem, and probably for some time before that, he had decided upon several of his leading motives. This indeed, was in accordance with his general practice; the musician and the poet in him went hand in hand. When, however, he speaks of having set forth "the *main motives* of the *whole* drama" in the prelude he was obviously generalising very broadly and not entirely in consistency with the facts. The overture contains, for instance, no reference to Sachs, either as poet, as cobbler, or as the wise old man, mellowed by adversity, who has a tender spot in his heart for Eva. The profounder depths of the character did not reveal themselves to Wagner until he had begun to create him musically; and there are good grounds for conjecturing that the theme of "Wahn" (No. 43), which is the very key to the lovable old cobbler's soul, had not so much as entered the composer's consciousness at the time he was writing the overture. Further, there is no reference in the prelude to Beckmesser and what he stands for. Wagner, in fact, had concentrated on what must have seemed to him at that early stage the three seminal elements—Nuremberg and its Masters, the youthful ardour of Walther, and the apprentices and the Folk, who formed the lighter counterpiece to the Mastersingers.

12

But the upshot of it all is a little point that is not quite clear. While there is no reference in the overture to Sachs or Beckmesser, and we hear little more of Walther than is hinted at in the conclusion of the Prize Song and a fragment from the Trial Song, a fair amount of space is allotted to the motive for the 'cellos in our No. 9, which even takes possession, as we have seen in No. 12, of the final bars of the prelude.[1] Does this rather liberal use of it, one ventures to surmise, represent some first intention or other on Wagner's part in 1862 that was not carried into effect later in the opera itself? For this "motive"—if we can call it that—really cannot be regarded as constituting one of those "*main* motives of the *whole* drama" of which Wagner speaks in *My Life*. After the prelude we hear no more of it until near the conclusion of the opera,

[1] That is to say, in its operatic form. For concert purposes Wagner had to supply a few more bars of formal close. In the manuscript of the full score of the opera, at the double bar marking the point at which the curtain rises and the prelude runs without a break into the chorale with which the drama opens, he has scribbled a note "for the engraver" which runs thus: "The two bars added in pencil are valid only for the special edition of the prelude for concert purposes; in this the double bar must be omitted, while in the opera score the two added bars must be left out, and the double bar holds good."

when it makes a brief appearance—for no more than three bars—at the end of our No. 1, at the point where the procession of the Masters reaches the platform. Later it crops up in the comic episode of Beckmesser ascending the mound to compete for the prize, where it points the jeering words of the populace:

> *She will never choose him!*
> *If I were the maiden I'd refuse him!* etc.

After that we do not meet with it again until the final two pages of the score, where it dances about in glee as the people shout their last word of homage to "Nuremberg's darling Sachs". This tiny and scarcely-used figure, in fact, is the one chosen to end the opera, as it had been the one chosen to end the overture.

How are we to account for this somewhat strange procedure on Wagner's part? The only possible conclusion seems to be that originally it was designed to play a much larger part than ultimately fell to its lot, and it was with this intention at the back of his mind that Wagner, writing the prelude in advance of the opera, gave it the prominence he did. The commentators, who have to give a name to everything, refer to it as the "Hilarity" motive, though strictly speaking, as we have seen, it occupies so infinitesimal a part of the opera as hardly to warrant its being regarded as a "motive" at all.

To summarise the argument. The full score of the opera runs to 570 pages. It is not until page 485 that the "Hilarity" figure makes an appearance in the opera itself, and that a very brief one. It recurs on pages 504, 505 and 506; after which we hear no more of it until the final page of the score, where, in conjunction with the trumpet flourish (as in our No. 12), it joyously concludes the opera as it had concluded the prelude. My suggestion is that Wagner had planned this conclusion to the whole work even before writing the prelude, with the intention of letting the Folk have the last word as against the Masters. It was only when he came to write the opera proper that he found there was no valid excuse or opportunity for so employing the motive until within a few minutes of the end. Meanwhile, however, it had taken a place in the overture from which there was now no ejecting it without re-modelling the whole piece; so there it had to stay. Few concert-room listeners to the prelude associate the "motive" with any-thing in the opera itself. Those who have read an analysis of the *Mastersingers* recognise it as the snippet of tune to which the people sing "She will never choose him", and therefore associate it in some dim way with Beckmesser, which could not possibly have been Wagner's intention when writing the prelude; as the Marker makes no appearance there as either a personage or a symbol, a jibe at him is surely pointless.

13

The place and period of the action of the opera are "Nuremberg about the middle of the sixteenth century"; and it is as well to have at the back of our minds some notion of what that Nurem-berg was like. It was a proud and prosperous city of some thirty thousand inhabitants, very beautiful with its innumerable gable roofs, its many handsome patrician houses, its eleven bridges across the river Pegnitz, its exquisite churches, its magnificent castle, its climbing and winding streets, its many fountains, its triple circle of walls with their close on two hundred towers. No other German town, and few in other lands, could compare with it for beauty: "in all Europe", wrote the sixteenth century Italian traveller Aeneas Sylvius (Pope Pius II), "you will find nothing to surpass it in magnificence and wealth of ornament". "When, coming from Lower Franconia, one perceives this glorious city", he says, "its splendour seems truly magnificent . . . The imperial castle proudly dominates it, and the burghers' dwellings seem to have been built for princes. Indeed, the kings of Scotland would be glad to be housed as luxuriously as the ordinary citizens of Nuremberg." At the time when Hans Sachs lived there the town harboured artists and scientists of the calibre of Albrecht Dürer, Holzschuher (the architect of the old Rathhaus), Peter Vischer (the designer of the exquisite shrine in the church of St. Sebald upon which Sachs must often have feasted his eyes), stoneworkers and art-craftsmen of the quality of Adam Krafft, the great human-ist Willibald Pirkheimer, and the explorer Martin Behaim, who constructed the first geographical globe. We may take it for granted that the Mastersingers who were held in esteem in such a town as this were not the purely burlesque figures that Wagner makes of them.[1]

We may fix the time of the action of the opera more precisely at 1560, when Sachs would be sixty-six, for he is shown us as a widower, and his brief widowerhood lasted only about a year from that date. (He was born in 1494 and died in 1576). When the curtain rises we see an oblique section of the interior of St. Catherine's church, a building, by the way, which it is no use the tourist going in search of, for it long ago ceased to exist in its ancient form.[2] The nave is supposed to run crosswise from left to background of the stage, only the last few rows of seats being visible to the spectator. In the foreground is the open space before the choir; this will be closed off later by a black curtain. The service is nearly over. In the last row of seats are Eva and Magdalena; while a short distance from them, at the side, the young Walther von Stolzing is leaning against a pillar, his rapt gaze fixed on Eva, who repeatedly turns towards him with silent gestures: he is conveying his passion in dumb show, while Eva is visibly torn between the impulse to respond in kind, maiden modesty, and respect for the church service.

14

The final bars of the prelude run straight into a noble chorale— the only really first-rate thing in that genre, we are tempted to say, since the great days of German Protestant chorale-writing;[3] it is accompanied by an organ on the stage, and between the lines of the hymn the orchestra breathes softly fragments of the three motives already associated in the prelude with Walther, Nos. 2, 6 and 7: No. 2, however, becomes a flood of passion at the finish, as the congregation rises and makes its way to the door. Eva, followed by Magdalena, slowly comes forward in Walther's

---

[1] A general idea of the city may be had from Dürer's engraving of St. Anthony (1519), the background of which represents Nuremberg.

[2] In point of fact, it was the smaller church of St. Martha that was used for the meetings of the Mastersingers in Sachs's day. St. Catherine's did not come into use for that purpose until 1620.

[3] Wagner had made a close study of German chorales and German folk-songs before writing the opera.

direction. He forces his way towards her through the crowd and implores her to tell him his fate: dare he hope, or must he despair? Is it life for him or death, heaven and sunlight or death and hell? He ends with the point-blank question, is she pledged to wed? Eva, to get a chance to reply lucidly to this torrent of enquiries, sends Magdalena back to retrieve first her kerchief, then its pin; but the over-zealous maid returns each time before Eva can open her mouth. The lovers' opportunity seems to have come at last when Magdalena discovers that she has left her prayer-book in the pew and goes back for it; but unfortunately she is with the pair once more just in time to hear the young knight's last question. She curtseys to him, puts him out of his stride by thanking him for the flattering attention he has shown in accompanying Eva thus far, and asks whether Herr Pogner may expect the honour of a visit from him.

Walther, angry at having been frustrated, replies passionately, "Would I never his house had seen!" Magdalena reproves him: he has only just arrived in Nuremberg, and had not Herr Pogner received him in the friendliest fashion, making him free of his house, his table and his cellar? Surely a little gratitude is due for all this kindness? Eva, to the accompaniment of the motive of Walther's wooing (No. 2), explains that the young man is duly sensible of it all, but the fact is that he wants to know whether she is already affianced. Magdalena is shocked at such unmaidenlike bluntness: suppose someone should overhear them? Eva points to the empty church, but even this does not reassure Magdalena. Before she can hurry Eva away, however, she catches sight of Sachs's apprentice David, with whom she herself is in love, entering from the sacristy and beginning to close the black curtains. Apparently the sight of him gives her a sentimental fellow-feeling for the other pair of lovers, and she so far softens towards the knight as to explain to him that, in a sense, Eva is a bride—"But no one yet has seen the groom!" Eva interjects hastily—though only the song contest on the morrow will reveal who has won her hand. By means of rapid question and answer the knight discovers that when the Masters have chosen the winner of the prize of song the destined bride herself will crown him and give him her hand.

Eva complicates matters a little by declaring enthusiastically and not quite logically that it will be Walther or no one. The scandalised Magdalena points out to her that she had met this young man for the first time in her life yesterday. True, replies Eva, but she had fallen in love with him instantaneously because he is the living image of David, whose characteristic motive—Music No. 14—now appears in the wood wind:

For the moment this is beyond poor Magdalena's comprehension, and Eva has to explain that the David she means is not hers, and not even the sweet singer of Israel who figures with his harp on the escutcheon of the Masters' Guild—the orchestra, by means of No. 3, tells us who that is—but a better David still, the glorious young David with golden hair of Meister Dürer's picture, sword at side, sling in hand, making short work of Goliath. The poetry and the passion of all this are beyond poor prosaic Magdalena; but the mention of David has made her quite emotional on her own account.

David, after disappearing for a moment, has returned with a rule stuck in his belt and a large piece of white chalk, attached to a string, in his hand. Magdalena's first coquettish thought is that he has shut them up in the church to have her all to himself; but he explains, to the accompaniment of No. 14, that he has serious business in hand. He has to prepare the church for a Song Trial at which the Masters will elevate to their own dignity some novice or other whose performance is fortunate enough to please them by its strict observance of the rules. This, Magdalena opines, is a stroke of luck for the knight. He could not have come to a better place or at a better time if he wants to qualify for Eva's hand; made, with luck, a Master today, he can compete for her tomorrow. She will not dream of allowing him to see them home, as he fain would do: she will leave him in charge of David, who will do him the service of coaching him in the rules and procedure of these trials. Walther and Eva bid each other a passionate farewell to the strains of No. 5, he assuring her that she shall see him again that evening, and that if his sword does not suffice to win her he will sing her to his side as a Master among Masters, laying his ardent youth and his poet's heart at her feet, she vowing to return his love in full; and the two voices blend in a brief duet on the theme of No. 6.

Magdalena, rather scandalised and scared by this outburst, hurries Eva away, leaving Walther to the care of David, who has been vastly amused at the suggestion that this young lordling may have the luck to graduate as a Master straight away. Walther, feverish and brooding, has thrown himself into a high chair which two apprentices who entered a little while ago, carrying benches, have just moved from the wall towards the centre of the stage. Sunk in his own thoughts, he hardly notices what now goes on. A number of other apprentices have come in, bringing more benches, which they arrange, according to their lights, for the session of the Masters. The lovelorn David's thoughts are not with them and the inexpert attempts they are making to set the scene; he is thinking how agreeable it would be if he himself were to be made a Master. The apprentices go about their task gaily but clumsily, chaffing David all the time; the cobbler's boy and his rather elderly Magdalena are evidently a standing butt for their wit.

15

As we have just learned from David, a "Trial" is to be held in the church that day. "Is there to be a 'Singen'?" Magdalena had asked him; and his reply had been, "Not today; only a 'Freiung' ". The distinction between a "Freiung" and a "Singschule" was that the former was of a more preliminary and private character. Candidates were heard in the first place and sifted out by the Masters alone, whereas the "Song School" was of a more advanced character and open to the public. The route to Mastership was a long and difficult one. Aspirants and practitioners were gradated very much on the lines of the commercial guilds: there were (a) Scholars (beginners) with no knowledge of the Tabulatur, (*b*) School-friends (those who had a good acquaintance with the rules), (*c*) Singers (who could sing some half-dozen Master-melodies without faults; this implied a knowledge of the various established "Melodies" and "Tones"), (*d*) Poets (who could write a song of their own to fit some recognised "Tone"), and (*e*) Masters (who could turn out not only an original poem but a "Tone" of their own). David, we gather, had got as far as the "School-friend" stage; it is this proud knowledge of his that now enables him to reel off a long list of "Tones" to the dazed Walther.

Of the open Song Schools, we learn from Wagenseil and others, the citizens of Nuremberg were informed by means of four or five tablets, three at least of which were affixed to poles in the market-place, and one outside St. Catherine's Church. These tablets displayed painted emblems of the Guild and the Mastersong, and were accompanied by posters announcing that "at today's Song School sundry lovers of the art present the Mastersingers with certain prizes to be sung for. First of all there will be sung, in the Free Singing, veracious and proven stories tending to Christian edification"; the songs were to consist of a certain specified number of lines. "In the Chief Singing no song will be allowed that does not conform to Holy Scripture, being taken from the Old or the New Testament"; and here again the number of lines for the day was laid down. "The proceedings will open with the singing of a fine New Song after our fashion". "Whoever wishes to listen, let him come to St. Catherine's Church, where a beginning will be made after the noon sermon."

The singer at the Free Singing had to bare his head, keep his hat or cap in his hand, bow to the Masters, and seat himself in the "Song Chair". Great pains were taken to ensure competence and impartiality on the part of the Markers. In Nuremberg four of these—the most eminent members of the Guild—sat in the box. The singer, before he began, had to announce the book and chapter of the Bible from which his words were taken; and the function of the Senior Marker was to follow him from the Bible and note any deviations from the text. A second concentrated on the rules of the Tabulatur, giving the singer bad marks with a chalk on the desk, according to a fixed tariff, for this or that failure to comply with them. A third paid particular attention to the metrics of the versification and jotted down the rhymes; while the fourth kept a sharp eye on the "Tone" or melody of the song. All the Markers were pledged to do their work honestly and without personal prejudice. It was laid down that they could either point out the candidate's faults to him immediately after his trial or, in some cases, later in private, "so that he might not be derided by the others". To this there was a corollary—the singer who had done well must not show contempt for the less fortunate ones. After the session there was an informal convivial gathering of the Masters, to which the prizewinners were invited. Adam Puschman, who had had experience of the Mastersong not only in Nuremberg but in other towns, tells us, among other things, that the two winners of garlands had the privilege of standing at the church door at the next session and collecting cash contributions.

Wagner keeps, for the most part, very close to Wagenseil in his representation of the procedure of the Guild, modifying it a little only when that becomes necessary for his dramatic purpose; he has, for example, only one Marker in action, though he makes it clear, through the mouth of Sachs, that complete impartiality is expected of him:

> *The Marker must be known to be*
> *above the mere suspicion*
> *of friendship or of enmity.*

This, then, in broad outline, is the strange milieu into which the romantic young Franconian knight finds himself suddenly plunged by his passion for a Master's daughter.

16

David has been immensely amused by Walther's parting words to Eva—that if he cannot win her by his sword he will do so as a Master. "That's good!" he chuckles. "A Master straight away! He's got a nerve!" While Walther is brooding darkly in the chair the others get on with the business of preparing the church for the meeting of the Masters. They call on David to help them, but he, like the knight, has his thoughts turned inwards. He is deaf to their gibes at him—the cobbler's apprentice, according to them, makes his poems with awl and thread and writes them down on raw leather; and speaking of leather, they add gleefully, how often *they* have tanned his hide!

Still lost in an ecstatic vision of himself as a Master, David surprises Walther by suddenly calling out, "Now begin!" "Whatever do you mean?" the young man asks. "That's what the Marker says", David explains: "it's the signal for you to start. Don't you know that? Were you never at a Song Trial before?" Not one where the judges were artisans, says the young aristocrat. And so the dialogue continues. "Are you a 'Poet'?" "Would I were!" "Are you a 'Singer'?" "Would I knew!" "But surely you have passed through the 'Scholar' and 'School-friend' stages?" "The terms are new to me." "Yet you would become a Master at one jump?" "Would that be so difficult?" He begs to be told all about it; and David, delighted to oblige, strikes an appropriate attitude and begins:

> *Good Sir! the singer's topmost height*
> *is not attained in one day's flight.*

As for himself, he is lucky enough to enjoy the instruction of Nuremberg's greatest Master, Hans Sachs. For a whole year now the apprentice has been studying cobbling and poetry-making simultaneously:

> *When I have hammered smooth the leather,*
> *vowels and consonants string I together;*
> *when I have waxed my thread right well,*
> *what rhymes with what I quick can tell.*
> > *I ply with zest*
> > *my bradawl fleet,*
> > *and learn about rest,*
> > *and time, and beat,*
> > *with knees round my last,*
> > *the slow, the fast,*

and everything else embodied in the Masters' lore as set forth in Wagenseil—long syllables and short, clear and dark, hard rhymes and soft, orphan rhymes, pauses, corns, flowers, thorns, and all the rest of it; and at the end he asks triumphantly,

All this have I learned with care and smart:
how far now, think you, extends my art?

for he is proud of his accomplishment. Walther is frankly contemptuous: "Perhaps", he suggests, "as far as a pair of right
good shoes?"

But David is not to be thrown out of his stride by a sarcasm
which, properly taken, can be read as a compliment. Is there not,
rightly considered, the closest analogy between a well-made pair
of shoes and a poem constructed according to the rules of art?
For a Mastersong, he says, is constructed, like a shoe, out of
certain well-defined materials. A song is made, as the rules prescribe, of several sections and joins, properly cut and stitched and
seamed and the stanzas well soled and heeled. Then comes the
Aftersong, which must be neither too short nor too long, have a
melody of its own, and not contain a single rhyme that has already
been heard in the stanzas.[1] Yet even this staggering accomplishment does not exhaust the list of qualifications required by a
Master. "God help me!" ejaculates Walther. "Must I become a
cobbler then? Tell me rather how to become an artist-singer."

With a sigh that he himself has not yet scaled that dizzy height
David obliges him:

with a long list—which is almost entirely Wagenseil in Wagnerian
rhymes—of some forty "Tones" that have to be learned, beginning

---

[1] In the Mastersingers' nomenclature the complete song was a "Bar". It
could run to as many sections ("Gesätze") as the creator of it chose. Each
section consisted as a rule of two stanzas ("Stollen") to the same melody, followed by an aftersong ("Abgesang"). The procedure can be followed, along
with Sachs's comments, in Walther's Morning Dream Song in the third act.

with the "soft" and "strong", the "short" and "long" and "over-
long" Tones, and so on, and ending with the "tawny lion's skin"
Tone, the "true pelican" Tone, and the "bright-ended thread"
Tone. Walther now begins to realise what he is up against. "Good
heavens!" he cries, "there seems no end to the code!" But David
has the bit between his teeth now, and there is no stopping him.
He launches out into a long catalogue of the rules laid down
by the Nuremberg Masters for good singing. Words and notes
must be clear; the singer must begin neither too high nor too low
for his particular voice, having regard to the range of the melody;
the breath must be carefully managed so as to last out to the end;
there must be no rumbling, no mumbling; liberties must not be
taken with the coloratura flourishes of the original:

> *For if you go wrong, or alter one jot,*
> *or lose yourself, or get tied in a knot,*
> > *though in nought else they could correct you,*
> > *for this alone they'll reject you!*

and you will be "versungen". As for himself, he sighs,

> *With all my zeal and diligence*
> *I've not attained this eminence;*

and whenever he makes a fault his master Sachs corrects him, he
says feelingly, in the "Kneestrap-whack" Tone; and then, if his
Lena does not bring him consolation, he sings the "Sad-dry-bread-
and-water" strain.

> *So be you warned in time;*
> *give up your dream sublime;*

he concludes; for to become a Master means no less than being
both poet and singer.

17

The apprentices, who have been getting into more and more of
a mess with their job of fixing up the stage, appeal at this point to
David to come and help them out. But there is still no holding the
enthusiast. "What and who *is* a poet?" Walther has asked him.

To be a poet, David replies, you have first to graduate as a singer, knowing all about the Master Tones; then, if you can take one or two of these and fit words and rhymes to them in proper style you are received as a poet.

By this time the apprentices have had enough of it, and they insist on some attention being paid to the practical business in hand. David, however, has to answer one more question before the knight will let him go—What must one do to be named a Master? "The poet", the apprentice answers solemnly,

> *The poet who, no toil despising,*
> *to words and rhymes he himself has found*
> *a melody adds of his own devising,*
> *he will as 'Mastersinger' be crowned,*

and he sings the final line to the proud melody of the King David motive (No. 3). "Then there is nothing else for it", cries Walther, to the ardent strain of No. 2, "but for me to become a Master, creating my own poem and my own Tone!"

Turning at last to the other apprentices, David finds that they have done everything wrong.[1] He quickly tears their work to pieces; and in its place soon appears a Marker's box—a small platform with a little desk and chair, and a large blackboard to which is attached a piece of chalk by a string; the whole is enclosed in curtains, which are first of all drawn at the back and sides, then across the front. The apprentices, to the merry tune of No. 14, congratulate David at each evidence of his skill. He is a knowing young fellow, they ironically assure him, the pride of Nuremberg, who may perhaps enter for a trial himself some day; for everyone knows how he can sing, and as for technique, does he not already know the "Whack" rhyme and the "Hunger" tune inside out, and—suiting the action to the word—has not his master taught him all there is to be known about the "Hearty Kick" melody? "Laugh if you want to," he tells them, "but not today at me." Here is a gallant young knight who means to try his luck. He knows nothing, is neither a Scholar nor a Singer,

[1] The apprentices have been arranging the scene for a full "Song School" instead of for the more elementary "Free Singing", or "Trial", which is the business for that particular day.

thinks being a Poet as easy as A B C, yet fancies he can become a
fully-fledged Master at the first attempt. So let them rig up the box
in good style and put the board where the Marker can get at it
easily, for there's going to be some fun. Then he turns to Walther
and tries to curdle his blood. Aren't you scared? he asks him.
Many a one has the Marker laid low! He will allow you seven
faults, which he will mark on the board with his chalk; but just
one more than that and you can take yourself off, "versungen"
and done for. And so, he concludes piously:

Glück   auf   zum Meis - ter - sing - en!
Mögt   euch   das Kränzlein er - schwing - en!
Heaven save   you from dis - as - ter,
And   make   you soon_   a   Mas - ter!

and joining hands and dancing round the box the other apprentices
sing with him:

Das   Blu - men-kränz-lein aus   Sei - den fein,   wird
The   pre - cious chap-let   of   silk - en flowers, we

das dem Herrn Rit - ter   be - schied - en   sein?
hope,_ Sir   Knight,   may   soon_   be   yours!

(This chaplet was bestowed on the successful candidate at the
end of a trial).

18

The young imps scatter in alarm and make off towards the
back as the vestry door opens and Pogner, a benign and dignified
figure, enters accompanied by the acidulous Beckmesser. They go
to the back of the stage, which by this time has been fully arranged
for the trial. On the right some cushioned benches for the Masters

curve towards the centre. At the end of them, in the middle of the scene, stands the Marker's box, while on the left, facing the benches of the areopagites, is the high ecclesiastical chair—the "Singer's chair". In the background is a long bench, *not* cushioned, for the apprentices. Walther, exasperated by their jibes, has flung himself on the front bench. The apprentices, putting on their most respectful look, are standing at the back—all except David, who has taken up a position by the vestry door.

Pogner and Beckmesser enter to a strain associated with the "Freiung" contest (marked A in the next quotation). The episode that follows is based musically, for the most part, on three tiny figures constructed upon what may be called the fishing-rod principle: they can be employed now as a whole, now in sections. They are here shown, for convenience sake in quotation, as they occur in connected form a little while after the opening of the scene:

Wagner employs any or all of the three figures as the fancy takes him, skilfully weaving them into a symphonic web that makes a continuous musical background in the orchestra to the easy conversation-tone of the characters. Interwoven at times with No. 18 A, B and C are hints of other motives, such as No. 2. The use of this latter may serve to point further the moral so often stressed in our analysis of *Tristan and Isolde*. It has always been convenient, for purposes of exposition, to label No. 2 the motive of Walther's wooing. In the present connection, needless to say, that description does not apply: though it appears in the texture during Pogner's greeting to the knight, there can be no possible reference of it here to "Walther's wooing". That wooing manifestly has to come about in the first place by way of a trial before the Guild; so Wagner sees no incongruity in using the motive as part and parcel of the background to the conversation now in progress.

Pogner and Beckmesser, on their way to the church, have been discussing a matter of great importance to the learned Town Clerk. The rich goldsmith has offered his daughter's hand as chief prize in the song contest on the following day, with the proviso, however, that the maiden herself shall accept the victor willingly. Beckmesser, who is in love with Eva, has a lurking fear that his suit may not be acceptable even if he should win, which he is confident of doing. Pogner tries to reassure him; yet, as Beckmesser logically puts it:

> *Yet why not this concession make me,*
> *for I confess it troubles me;*
> *if Eva be not bound to take me*
> *what good will all my mastery be?*

Pogner, though friendly, is equally logical: "Surely this reflection ought to have occurred to you before; if you are not sure of Eva's approval, why enter for the contest?" Beckmesser sees the point of this, but makes a last attempt to secure his strategical position: will Pogner speak for him with the maiden and tell her what a good, kind, virtuous man he is, and that her father thoroughly approves of him? This Pogner promises cordially to do.

19

Walther now comes forward to greet the goldsmith. The latter is a trifle astonished to find the young knight at a Song School, but Walther glibly explains that he had left his home in the country and come to Nuremberg for love of art: "I forgot to tell you yesterday, but now I must make it known—I want to become a Mastersinger. Accept me, I pray, in your Guild."

Here, however, Wagner seems to have fallen into some confusion. If that had been the knight's purpose in coming to Nuremberg, why, we naturally ask, had he not said so to Pogner when introducing himself at the goldsmith's house on the preceding day? If it had not, then he is fibbing now. The truth appears to be that Wagner was not quite sure how he ought to handle this part of the dramatic action. In the First Prose Sketch (1845) he had outlined it thus: "The young man, son of an impoverished knight, has come to Nuremberg to try to get admission to the Masters' Guild: his reading of the *Heldenbuch*, of the works of Walther von der Vogelweide, etc. has kindled in him a passionate love for the poetic art. He had announced himself to the senior of the Guild and met his daughter; and the two had quickly fallen in love with each other." According to Wagner's first plan, all this was to be made clear to the spectator in the conversation between the lovers in the opening scene in the church. But, as the reader is aware, that conversation runs on rather different lines in the opera. Nothing whatever is said by Walther about his having come to the town to become a Mastersinger: having fallen in love with Eva, it is only after he has learned from Magdalena that the maiden's hand is to go to the victor in a coming contest of song that he decides to become a Master. His later colloquy with David shows that he knows nothing at all about even the commonest terminology of the Guild routine: he does not even know what a Marker is; he is entirely ignorant of the rules of rhymes, Tones, and all the rest of it, and has to ask David to explain just what a Master may be. A young man afire with Minnesinger poetry, who had gone to Nuremberg expressly to gain admission into the Masters' Guild, could not possibly have been so completely uninformed.

In *A Communication to my Friends* (1851) Walther's motive is set forth as in the First Sketch: the young nobleman, inspired by the *Heldenbuch* and the songs of the Minnesingers, "leaves the ruined and impoverished castle of his ancestors to learn the Mastersingers' art at Nuremberg", which, one makes bold to surmise, he would hardly have thought of doing had he not already learned enough about it to inspire him with respect for it. But in the Second Sketch we are told that "Konrad [Walther] had arrived in Nuremberg from his ruined castle only yesterday; *while discussing business with Bogler* [Pogner] *he had seen Emma* [Eva], and the two had immediately fallen in love." There is no hint here of his having been fired by the old poets with the desire to become a Mastersinger; he had left his home and gone to the rich

goldsmith to try to discover some means of re-establishing the
family fortunes. He learns later from Kathrine [Magdalena] "that
Eva is not actually affianced, but has been destined by her father
to be the bride of the winner in the Free-singing to be held on the
morrow in the St. John meadow. *His resolution is quickly taken—
he himself will get admission to the Guild in order to compete for the
prize.*" A few lines further down it appears that, as in the opera,
until David begins his exposition he does not even know the
names of the Masters, let alone the rules of the craft.[1] In a Third
Sketch we are told still more explicitly that what had brought the
young knight to the town and to Pogner was business.

The two dramatic motives, it will be seen, are inconsistent with
each other. If Walther had gone to Nuremberg to see Pogner on
business, the latter can hardly be expected to take seriously the
young man's assurance now that what had really brought him
there was enthusiasm for the Mastersingers' art and the desire to
become a Master himself; while if that had actually been his prime
object it is odd that he should have said nothing to Pogner about
it until now. Why then did Wagner not take more trouble to
reconcile these little discrepancies and make the matter more self-
explanatory to the spectator? The answer seems to be that, as
happened once or twice again both in the *Mastersingers* and the
Ring, he was well aware of the slight confusion but did not regard it as important enough to put himself to a great deal of
trouble to clear it up: the spectator would get the general idea,
and that was all that mattered; the music would carry it all off.

20

For the moment Pogner does not answer Walther's fervent
appeal to be admitted to the Guild; he turns away to give a joyful
welcome to two newcomers, Kunz Vogelgesang and Konrad
Nachtigall, and to tell them the good news—"this knight, whom I

---

[1] In this Second Sketch David, after explaining the functions of the
Marker, tells the knight that the present holder of that office, who bears the
name of "Hanslich", is regarded as the greatest authority on the rules, a
fact which has made him very arrogant. There is no hint of this communication in the opera.

know well, wishes to devote himself to the Master-art." Other Masters drift in, and general greetings and introductions follow. Then Pogner turns warmly to Walther, assuring him of his sympathy and support: "Gladly I helped you to sell your land; now I shall be delighted to see you become one of us."

Beckmesser meanwhile has been standing apart, brooding over his own problem. He will make a last attempt, he soliloquises, to influence Pogner; if that fails he will throw in his grand strategic reserve—he will serenade Eva tonight and discover what impression his art has made on her. But suddenly he catches sight of the handsome young Walther in close colloquy with Pogner, and he scents danger in the air. "Who is this? I mislike the man!"

> *What wants he here with his smiling air?*
> *Holla! Sixtus! of him beware!*

He listens with scorn to Walther's thanks of Pogner and his expression of the hope that he may today win Mastership. "Oho! that's good!" he mutters; "a nice conceit he has of himself!" Pogner, of course, makes it clear to the young man that the rules of the Guild must be complied with; but anyhow he himself will stand as his sponsor at today's preliminary trial. (He has not yet realised that Walther is in love with Eva; he is aware only that he desires to become a Master).

By now all the Masters have arrived, including Sachs; and it becomes the duty of the baker Kothner to call the roll. Producing a list, he does so in appropriately official style. First, as the regulations prescribe, he names himself; then he calls in succession on the others, beginning with the head of the Guild, Pogner. Each Master seats himself after answering to his name. When that of Niklaus Vogel is called out his prentice pops up and says "He's ill!" whereupon the others express sympathy and send best wishes for his recovery. (We may now be permitted to guess at Wagner's reason for omitting Vogel from his list of dramatis personae, though he had copied out, in the Second Sketch, his name along with those of the other eleven mentioned by Wagenseil. He had learned from that old author that the Masters were under strict obligation either to attend the sessions of the Guild or to send a valid excuse for not doing so; and by making Vogel an absentee he both brings in a neat historical touch connected with the rules and enables a charming break to be made in what would have otherwise been the monotony of a continuous calling of eleven names and answering to them). When Sachs's name is called, David jumps up, points to him, and says "He's there!", for which bit of pertness his Master threatens to tan his hide. Beckmesser, for his part, answers to his name with an acid joke at the expense of Sachs, whom he despises both as cobbler and as artist: "always by Sachs", he says, "so that I may learn the rhyme to 'bloom and wax'."[1]

Wagner, with easy contrapuntal art, sets all this conversational give-and-take against a constantly moving but always firmly built background of interwoven motives and fragments of motives. The musician in him was enjoying himself hugely throughout a long scene which to any other composer would have seemed to offer the minimum of opportunities for music.

The roll call having been completed, Kothner asks if they shall proceed next to elect a Marker. This brings the cantankerous Beckmesser to his feet again: suspecting that the baker wishes to supplant him in the office he acidly offers to retire in his favour. But Pogner intervenes. A little thing of that sort, he says, can wait until after he has told them something of importance. To-morrow, he reminds them, is Johannistag—Midsummer day—when the Nurembergers are wont to hold a festival in the meadows outside the town, in the course of which the Masters regale the folk with song, and a grand Song School is held at which prizes are competed for. One thing saddens him, however. Travelling recently through the German lands he had been grieved to find that everywhere, among princes and peasants alike, the burgher

---

[1] *"Immer bei Sachs,*
dass den Reim ich lern' von 'blüh und wachs' ".

The historical Sachs was fond of rhyming about himself in this joking fashion in his poems: for example,

Daraus ihm Glück und Heil erwachs,
Den treuen Rat gibt ihm Hans Sachs.

And everyone knows his autobiographical couplet:

Hans Sachs was a shoe-
maker and a poet too.

is held in low esteem. He is charged with thinking of nothing but trade and gold, whereas they in Nuremberg, at least, have taken art under their protection. As God has made him a man of wealth, he proposes to remove the stigma from his dearly-loved town by giving all his goods and gold to the winner in the Johannistag Song School, with the hand of his daughter Eva into the bargain. The generous offer is applauded enthusiastically by Masters and apprentices. But Pogner has not yet finished: the Masters, it is true, are to choose the prize-winner, but the maiden herself shall be free to take him or not, according to her fancy.

21

Pogner's Address, as it is generally styled, is constructed musically upon (*a*) a rich symphonic development of a motive:

always associated with the joyousness of Midsummer day, and (*b*) the dignified motive of the Guild (No. 4).

The Masters are a trifle damped, as Beckmesser had been, by the final clause of Pogner's offer. As they reasonably point out, it "leaves them in the maiden's hands"; what validity will their award of the prize have if she is to be free to reject the victor? But Pogner has an answer to this: his daughter can indeed throw the man over, but in that case she can take no other lover; the fortunate man must be a Master or no one. Sachs now comes into the forefront of the action. Rising from his seat, he suggests a simple way out of the difficulty. The mind of woman, he says, is like that of the folk, unschooled, but sound in its instincts and intuitions. So why not leave the decision to the folk, who may safely be trusted to choose just as the maiden herself would do?

At once the Masters are up in arms. The proposal is outrageous, they cry; if the folk are to be given the decisive word, what will become of art? Sachs explains patiently. No one is more loyal to the rules of the Guild than he, he says. Still, it would not be a bad idea if just once in the year the Masters were to overhaul their rules, lest they should come to cling too blindly to the letter and lose the spirit. After all, nature is the best guide in everything, as those will tell them who have no technical knowledge of the Tabulatur—a revolutionary sentiment received glumly by the Masters but warmly applauded by the apprentices, who jump up and rub their hands. (Here Wagner is speaking, through Sachs, in the first person: he had always maintained that the opposition to him came mostly from the "Guilds" of critics, professors and so on, and that the ordinary listener, with a mind unclouded by theory and unbefuddled by learning, never had any difficulty in understanding and liking him).

Sachs continues earnestly:

> *Believe me, ye ne'er would rue it,*
> *if on Midsummer's day each year*
> *ye asked no more the people here,*
> *but from your Master-cloud-land broke*
> *and went yourselves towards the folk,*

letting *them* decide by the evidence of their own ears what was good and what bad.

When Pogner had said to the company:

> *A lifeless gift I offer not;*
> *a maiden helps to cast the lot:*
> *the prize the Masters shall declare:*
> *but for the rest 'tis only fair,*
> > *whome'er the Masters choose*
> > *the bride may still refuse,*

he had been accompanied by a quiet passage in the violins:

which is one of the minor puzzles of the *Mastersingers* score. Wagner has marked it scherzando. Why? It bears the same marking when, a trifle later, it passes to the oboe as Pogner says, in reply to Beckmesser's angry objection that if the maiden is to have free choice the Masters might as well be left out of the game:

> *Nay, nay! Why so? Let me explain!*
> *any man who the prize shall gain*
> *the maid may throw him over,*
> *but take no other for lover.*
> *A Mastersinger he must be,*
> *one crowned by you, or nobody.*

Why, we ask again, the "scherzando"? Is Pogner pulling their leg? We do not dispose of the difficulty by saying, as some commentators do, that No. 20 has no actual existence of its own but is merely a flourish, thrown off *en passant* from the motive of the Masters (No. 4, bars 3 ff.). That fails to explain why twice, when Pogner is imposing his curious proviso on his offer, it should be just this figure that the orchestra should use to point his words, and that each time it should be marked scherzando. Has he perhaps seen some reason, after his colloquy with Walther, for guessing that the problem of the coincidence of the Masters' choice with the maiden's choice will solve itself in a way that none of the others suspects? It is curious, again, that No. 20 should be drawn upon once more when Sachs says:

> *then let the folk the judges be;*
> *with the maid, I'm certain, they will agree;*

and later, when he urges that the judgment of the folk should be trusted, the flute and oboe give out No. 20 again, and once more it is marked scherzando. That the figure had, for Wagner, some special inner connection with the verdict of the folk and the choice of Eva seems indicated by the fact that it does not appear in the score again until the last few minutes of the opera, when, as we shall see, it is once more associated with the folk as the final arbiters in matters of poetry and song.

22

Sachs's approval of the popular judgment, of course, is rank heresy in the ears of the Masters. They are up in arms at once.

Kunz Vogelgesang admits that Sachs means well, but that is all there is to be said for him. For Nachtigall, when the mob speaks it is time for a Master to be silent. Kothner sees nothing but the ruin of their art ahead of them if they make it dependent on the likes and dislikes of the people. Beckmesser, cantankerous as usual, says the proposed New Order would be a fine thing for the cobbler-poet, who for the most part can turn out nothing but street songs; and even the big-hearted Pogner thinks his colleague is going a trifle too far and too fast. So he brings them all back to his original proposition: do the Masters accept it or not? The winner, of course, says Kothner thoughtfully, will have to be a bachelor, he being presumably a bachelor himself. But why not a widower? snaps Beckmesser; why not Sachs? The old cobbler disclaims any ambition of that sort, and at the same time gets a shaft through the Town Clerk's armour—the wooer will have to be younger than either of them if little Eva is going to accept him. This reference to his age adds to Beckmesser's ire.

As the discussion looks like becoming acrimonious, Pogner, in virtue of his position as head of the Guild, recalls them to the business of the day. They have come to the church for a trial; and he himself wishes to commend to them a young man who is anxious to become a Master. Walther steps forward and bows to the company, to the accompaniment of the proud motive of himself *in propria persona*:

Beckmesser, scenting trouble, suggests that it is too late now for a trial that day. Some of the others are inclined to caution—an aristocrat presenting himself for Mastership is a novelty, and there is no knowing what a dubious innovation of that sort may lead to. Kothner insists that anyhow the young man must undergo the regulation trial. Pogner agrees with him that the rules must be observed: whereupon Kothner puts to him the prescribed questions about the candidate. First of all, is he a freeman of honourable birth? Pogner will go bond for that: the young man is Sir Walther von Stolzing, a Franconian knight, the last scion of an ancient line, who has come to Nuremberg with the desire to become a burgher. (A burgher, be it observed, not a Mastersinger, as Walther had assured Pogner only a few minutes earlier. Wagner is still careless about reconciling his varying accounts of Walther's motive in the Sketches and in the poem). "This Junker breed is good for nothing!" growls the democratic Beckmesser. But for the others Pogner's word is good enough, while Sachs points out that in the Mastersingers' articles it is laid down that no distinction shall be made between lord and peasant, the only thing that matters being art.

23

From this point onwards the action of the scene follows the historic rules of the Guild. First of all Kothner calls on the candidate to name the Master under whom he has worked. Walther replies in a long lyrical passage commencing thus:

He tells how one winter's day he had been thrilled by the reading of an ancient book that sang of the loveliness of spring; the author was the poet whom he names as his Master, none other than Walther von der Vogelweide. "A right good master!" Sachs interjects. "But long since dead", objects the peevish Beckmesser; "what instruction could *he* give him in our rules?" "And where did you study after that?" is Kothner's next question.

"When the frost had passed away", replies Walther in a second stanza to the melody of the first, "and summer sang its roundelay, in the woods I saw and heard what the old book described: there it was I learned my singing." This is too much for Beckmesser. "Oho! so you got your melodies from the finches and the tit-mice?" Vogelgesang tells him that he must at least admit that so far the young man has turned out two very decent stanzas; and Beckmesser, always apt at small repartee, turns on him with a savage "I suppose you praise him, Master Vogelgesang, because he learned his song from the birds? (Wohl weil vom *Vogel* er lernt' den *Gesang*)".

Kothner now begins to have his doubts. "Should we go on?" he asks them; "I fear the knight has done for himself." It is left to Sachs, as usual, to say the sensible thing: "that we shall soon find out; if his art is good, what does it matter where he learned it?" So Kothner asks the young man if he is prepared to sing them then and there a true Mastersong, in which words and music shall both be his own. (Wagner's sly reference to his own case is obvious here).

For answer, Walther plunges into an aftersong with a new melody, commencing in a new key but finishing in the main one:

Everything he has seen and heard and read, he says, has turned to music within him; and if it is a Mastersong they want he will do his best to satisfy them. The others are puzzled, for all this is new and strange to them; but they decide to let him try his luck. Wagner has woven the whole long episode into a single musical pattern by a ceaseless play of the orchestra upon some of the main elements of Walther's lyrical preamble.

24

The trial proceeds according to the rules of the Guild. Beck-messer, the Marker for the day, goes with a hypocritical show of reluctance into the box: his chalk, he fears, is going to have its work cut out! As in duty bound, he explains to the candidate that he will be allowed seven faults, all of which will be chalked on the board. If he makes more than seven he will be pronounced "versungen". The Marker's ears, he says,

> *are keen;*
> *but as your nerves, if he were seen,*
> *might be depressed,*
> *he leaves you at rest,*
> *and hides him in his lair:*
> *so heaven have you in its care!*

He pokes his head out with a malicious leer, then draws the curtains to. The acid, niggling nature of the man is defined for us from the outset in his characteristic motive:[1]

Kothner makes a sign to the apprentices, who take down from the wall the board containing the "Leges tabulaturae"; they hold it up in front of him and he reads out the rules to Walther. A Master-song must be made according to a plan. Each stanza must consist of two strophes sung to the same melody, and extend to several lines rhyming at the ends: then must come the aftersong, having another melody than that of the strophes: not more than four

[1] It is possible to see in this, as some commentators do, a sort of degradation by Beckmesser of the dignified theme of the knight (No. 21).

syllables in succession must have been used by any other Master in a previous song; and giving back the board to the apprentices, who hang it up again, he bids Walther seat himself in the singer's chair. Wagner makes delightful music out of the reading of the rules; especially piquant are the conventional coloratura flourishes that adorn the ends of the phrases—a feature of the Mastersong—which are imitated with great zest by the orchestra.

"In this chair?" the young romantic asks with a shudder; this is not at all his notion of the freedom due to a poet and musician. But Kothner insists—"That is the rule,"—and the young man takes his seat, remarking aside, "For you, beloved!" "The singer sits!" Kothner calls out loudly to the Marker, and from within the box comes the regulation order, "Now begin!"

Walther's trial song is an inspiration of the moment, evidently, for he fastens on the "Now begin!" as a kind of poetic motive and embroiders upon it. "So cried the Spring through the land", he says:

and the forest heard it and responded, the whole glad earth rejoicing in the liberation of Spring:

The lovely song is filled with the ardour of youth; but apparently it sins grievously against the Nuremberg rules, for the sound of vigorous scratchings on the board comes from the box. Walther is perturbed, but masters himself and proceeds with a description of gloomy old winter cowering and snarling in its lair, listening enviously, bent on turning this song of the gladness of earth into one of sadness: whether Walther intends it or not, his song of wintry petrifaction and Spring renewal is symbolical of the pedantic Masters and himself. Now all on fire, he rises from the chair—a capital crime according to the rules—and launches out into a paean to youth and Spring and love. One feature of the song, the soft murmur of Spring:

has to be specially noticed, for, as we shall see later, it struck deep into the poetic and still young heart of old Sachs.

The curtains are flung violently aside and Beckmesser's head appears. "Have you finished?" he asks harshly. "Why?" says Walther. "Because there's no more room on my board!" and the Marker holds it out, showing every inch of it covered with chalk marks. The Masters break into loud laughter, to the accompaniment of a derisive figure:

in the orchestra.

Walther tries to make them understand that he has another stanza to sing, this time in praise of his lady. But Beckmesser, cutting him short, steps out of the box and invites the Masters to inspect

the board in detail. Never has he listened to such an exhibition of
incompetence, he says—"cloudy meaning", mistakes in quantity
and time, "too short", "too long", "faulty rhyme", the melody a
nonsensical mixture of the "Adventure" mode, the "Blue-knight-
spur" Mode, the "High fir-tree" Mode, the "Proud stripling
Mode", and heaven knows what; all the faults, *mutatis mutandis*,
of incompetence and plagiarism and bad taste which the critics
and professors used to try to fix on Wagner himself. The other
Masters agree with Beckmesser; Kothner's special grievance is
that the singer in his enthusiasm had risen from the chair before
receiving permission to do so.

25

One alone among them keeps his head. Sachs, whose interest
in the song had manifestly increased the more he heard of it, now
comes forward. The serious, even mournful side of the nature of
the shoemaker who is also an artist and a philosopher is expressed
in a little phrase in the orchestra of which we shall hear more later:

But this gives way at once to the motive of Sachs's Benevolence, as
it may be called:

as he gives the company his own view of what they have just
heard. The song, he says, is undoubtedly novel in substance and
form, but he has not found it, as they have done, wild or confused.
True it had not run along the lines laid down by the Masters, but

its course for all that had been steady and sure. And he gives the
Guild some good advice:

> *Before you try to measure*
> *what does not with your rules agree,*
> *forget the laws you treasure,*
> *ask first what its own rules may be!*

Beckmesser's derisive reply to this is the traditional one of the
academic—"To tell the poet that he should sing just as he feels,
regardless of rules, is to throw the doors of art wide open to the
common herd. Sing to the people in the street and the market-
place in this style if you like, but here among *us* nothing is
permitted that runs counter to the rules."

Sachs tells him, in effect, that what *he* needs is a new pair of
ears. Anyhow, since he is so concerned for the sanctity of the
rules, let him remember the one that lays it down that the Marker
must be above all suspicion of friendship or enmity towards a contestant. How does Beckmesser come through that test? Since he
is going a-wooing, would it not be only simple human nature in
him to do what he can to shame his rival before the School?

Does Sachs, perhaps, half-suspect *why* the knight is so anxious
to be accepted as a Master this very day? It may be so. Anyhow
Walther seems to be sensitive to the unspoken nuance of suggestion, for he "flames up", as the stage directions put it. The others
think that Sachs has "gone too far"; Kothner reproves him for
"being personal". Beckmesser, feeling that the best defence is
attack, rounds on Sachs. Let the cobbler stick to his last, he says;
since Sachs took to poetry his shoemaking has deteriorated.
"Just look at this shoe of mine", he cries; "see how loose it is;
hear how it cracks!"

> *This stuff he loves to scrawl,*
> *for me he may keep it all,*
> *his histories, plays, and his farcical muse,*
> *if tomorrow he'll bring me my new pair of shoes;*

and a figure suggestive of the cobbler hammering away at a shoe
is reiterated by the orchestra:

31

Animato

ff

Sachs scratches his head in humorous discomfiture: no one, he says, objects to his scribbling a bit of doggerel on the soles of a donkey-driver's shoes; can't he be permitted, then, to decorate the Town Clerk's in the same harmless way? The trouble is that so far he hasn't been able to think of a couplet worthy of so august a subject. Possibly it may come to him if he hears the remainder of the knight's song; so he suggests that he shall be allowed to continue.

26

The Masters protest that they have had enough of it, but Sachs gives the knight a bit of sensible advice—"Sing on, just to annoy the Marker!" So Walther mounts the chair once more and breaks into the final section of his song, which describes the screech owl and the raven, the magpie and the crow, making the woodland hideous with their raucous voices—for all the world like so many Masters—until a bright and beautiful bird soars up into the blue above him, inviting him to join it in its flight, and filling his heart with joy and his throat with song:

> *towards the light*
> *I take my flight,*
> *from the city dead,*
> *with wings wide spread,*
> *to the hill of my desiring,*
> *to the Vogelweid' so green, so free,*
> *where Master Walther sang to me;*
> *and there my voice I raise*
> *to sing my lady's praise;*

forth it flows,
unheeding croaks of Master-crows,
the song of love's sweet spell!
Farewell, ye Masters, farewell!

But the croaking crows and chattering magpies of the Guild are not so easily silenced. Throughout the big ensemble that terminates the act the Masters keep up a machine-gun fire of disparaging comment as Walther sings. Beckmesser trots from one to another of them, exhibiting the board with its scoring of not a mere seven but more than fifty faults; and this presumptuous young lunatic wants to qualify as a Master! The apprentices, including David, are delighted to join in: they link hands in a ring and dance round the box, singing their merry motive of the Silken Chaplet (No. 17). It is all wrought into one massive choral structure, with the angry Walther going on indomitably, his song soaring above the turmoil. Sachs is barely audible, but what he is saying is that the knight is a true poet and singer who can hold his own against the rabble of Masters.

At last Beckmesser is heard inviting the others to register their final verdict. They raise their hands *en masse* (except Sachs) and declare the knight "versungen und verthan". Walther, with a proud contemptuous gesture, leaves the chair and stalks out. The hullabaloo increases; the apprentices take possession of the Marker's box, and even jostle the august persons of the Masters as they leave. Finally Sachs alone, apart from the apprentices, remains in the church. We hear for a moment No. 26 in the oboe, as if this passage from Walther's song were still humming in the old cobbler's head; but it yields to No. 17 and then to a comically pompous strut of the motive of the Masters (No. 1) in the bassoons. Sachs sums it all up in a gesture of humorous discouragement, turns on his heels, and, as the apprentices make merry with the singer's chair, leaves the stage as the curtain falls.

27

The second act is Wagner's most dexterous achievement in the way of dramatic structure; the action is kept always moving, and piece fits into piece with such perfect neatness that it is only after close analysis of it all that we realise the skilled craftsmanship of the carpentry.

The act opens with a joyous orchestral prelude on the Midsummer day motive (No. 19), now gay with trills and glissandi and bubbling over with high spirits in little turns like these:

As the curtain rises we see a group of apprentices closing the shutters of the houses on one side of an alley and looking forward happily to the morrow's festival:

while David, engaged in the same task on the opposite side, is wishing that the silken chaplet to be awarded in the contest might be his (No. 17).

Along the foreground of the scene runs a street in Nuremberg, from the middle of which branches a narrow alley, winding crookedly towards the back. This presents the spectator with two corner houses—a handsome one (Pogner's) on his right, with steps leading up to it and embrasures with stone seats along its front, and a humbler one (Sachs's) on his left. At the right-hand edge of the stage, close to Pogner's house, is a stately lime tree; at its base are green shrubs, and in front of it a stone bench. The door of Sachs's house is overhung by an elder tree. The entrance to the house is from the front street; a divided door leads straight into the workshop; on the alley side of the house are two windows, one to the workshop, the other to a room beyond. It is a beautiful summer evening, night gradually closing in as the action develops.

The apprentices are teasing David as usual when Magdalena arrives, bringing him a basket of dainties. She asks him eagerly how the knight had fared that afternoon at the Song School; and when she learns that he was "versungen und verthan" she peevishly snatches back the basket and goes into Pogner's house in great dejection. The apprentices, who have seen and heard it all, make merry once more at poor David's expense. In his rage he is about to attack them when Sachs comes up the alley. The boys scurry away: David protests that it wasn't he who began the row, and his master orders him to go in, lock up, bring a light, and put the new shoes on the last. As they enter the workshop and pass on through the inner door Pogner and Eva appear in the alley, returning from their evening walk. David emerges from the inner room, places a light by the shop window, and sets Sachs's work out there.

Pogner has half an idea to look his friend up, but thinks better of it: evidently something is troubling him. He appears to be in some doubt now whether he has acted quite wisely in the matter of the prize; he would like to talk it over with his old friend Sachs, but is not sure that any advice at all would be helpful just now. To tranquil music he bids Eva, who also seems to have something on her mind, sit down with him on the bench under the lime tree. To a new motive in the orchestra, henceforth to be associated with grand and dear old Nuremberg:

34
Moderato molto

p dolce

Bass: F.

he drinks in the soft evening air with satisfaction, tomorrow, he says, promises to be fine. Does not his daughter's heart rejoice, he asks her, at the thought of the festival, when she will crown the one who has proved himself Master? "Dear father, *must* it be a Master?" she asks. "For sure", he replies; "but", speaking more prophetically than he knows, "a Master of your own choice."

Eva, with a sigh, agrees with him as to that. She calls out to Magdalena, who has appeared at the door of the house and is beckoning to her, that she is coming, and then reminds her father that supper is waiting. "But no guest?" he asks with a touch of irritation; and when she replies "Perhaps the knight?" he looks at her wonderingly. Did her father see him that afternoon? she asks. "Yes, but I was not pleased with him." Then it begins to dawn on him what is behind her curiosity with regard to Walther; he taps his forehead and asks himself whether, maybe, he has not been a trifle dull-witted until now.

She makes him precede her into the house, and manages to have a word with Magdalena behind his back. She learns of Walther's failure. Her first impulse in her distress is to go to kindly old Sachs and ask for first-hand news about it all. But the maid restrains her: her father is sure to notice her absence, so it will be wiser to wait until supper is over. Besides, Magdalena has "something to tell her", a "secret message" from "somebody". "Sir Walther?" Eva asks eagerly. "No, Beckmesser!" With a contemptuous shrug of her shoulders at this unimportant piece of news Eva goes into the house, followed by the maid.

28

Street and alley are both empty now. Sachs, in indoor clothes, comes back into his workshop from the inner room. With the Cobbler motive (No. 31) in the orchestra punctuating his remarks he tells David, who is still at the bench, to place the table and the stool at the door of the shop, where Sachs can work in the fresh air, and then "get off to bed; sleep off thy folly, and tomorrow have a little more sense". David goes off to his own room, which is on the alley side. Sachs sits down, takes up his tools, lays them down again, and leans back with his arm resting on the closed lower half of the door.

The orchestra, with softly-breathed reminiscences of No. 26 and No. 27, shows us where his thoughts are: they have gone back to Walther's song before the Guild and the glowing sense of the loveliness of youth and spring it had brought him. He revels for a moment in the scent of the elder tree above his head, and then humorously reproves the poet in him for standing in the way of work. Making an attempt to drive poetry out of his head, he takes up his hammer and sets to work noisily at the shoe—Beckmesser's—on the last. But in vain; No. 26 and other snatches from Walther's melody pass through one transformation after another in the orchestra as he recalls that ardent song of love and youth and the beauty of earth. From the heart that song had come, and to the heart it had gone. The old man plays, as the historical Sachs was so fond of doing, on his own name and the homely wax of his trade that rhymes with it: one may roughly render the final quatrain of his monologue thus:

> *The bird who sang today*
> *I warrant knows the singer's knacks well!*
> *Masters may say him nay,*
> *But this I know, he pleased Hans Sachs well!*

and, like the philosopher he is, he puts poetry out of his mind for the time being and begins working cheerfully at the shoe.

Meanwhile Eva has come into the street. She goes to the shop door and greets him. He is very glad to see her. Over two gracious motives in the orchestra:

that keep weaving the loveliest of symphonic patterns, the pair engage in a long fencing bout. Eva fishes for information about the knight, but dares not ask outright what she desires to know:

wise old Sachs reads her thoughts, but will not let her see that he does so. The new shoes he has made for her, she begins by saying, are very fine, but she hasn't worn them yet. "Tomorrow, of course", he suggests, "as bride?" "No doubt, but who will the bridegroom be? How do you know I shall be a bride?" "Well, everyone knows that." "What everyone knows, no one knows. Is this the best Sachs can do? I thought he knew more." "What ought I to know then?" "Ah, friend Sachs, I see now that pitch is not wax! I credited you with more shrewdness." "My child, I know all there is to be known about pitch and wax. I waxed the silken threads of your shoes to make them dainty; but now I must work in pitch, to harden the thread for a rough man's use. Need I name him? The shoes are for Beckmesser, who hopes that all will acclaim him as singer and wooer tomorrow."

> *Then use the strongest pitch you can:*
> *may he stick, and I escape the man!*

she cries; and the verbal duel continues.

She ought not to be so uppish, he tells her; good single men are scarce. "But why should a widower not succeed?" "My child, he would be too old for thee." "Too old? what counts in this case is art; let him who understands it woo me." "You jest!" "No, it is you who are shuffling. God knows what maid Sachs holds in his heart now, but for years I have thought it was I. You carried me in your arms, but only, I see now, because you had no child of your own." "Once I had wife and children too", he replies gravely; "but they are dead, and you have grown tall and fair." "I thought I should be wife and child to you. But now I see how it is; Master Sachs would not grieve if tomorrow Beckmesser were to carry me off under his very nose." "How can I stop him? It all rests with your father." "Oh, you Masters! Where do you keep your brains? Yours seem to have left you." "Yes, yes, mine's a poor addled head":

> *I've had much care and fret today,*
> *and all my wits have flown away;*

to which the orchestra gives point with No. 29.

This remark of his gives Eva the opening she has been manoeuvring for. "Was it in the School?" "Yes, at a trial that went not well." "Ah, Sachs, had you but told me *that* I should not have wearied you with my chatter. But tell me now, who was at this trial?" "A knight, my child (No. 21), lamentably untaught." "A knight, eh? was he elected?" (No. 28). "No, they were against him to a man."

29

At this point Magdalena slips out of the house and calls softly to Eva, warning her that her father is asking for her. But she only turns the more eagerly to Sachs. "Is it hopeless? Why? Did he sing so badly that he will never be a Master?" "Never, anywhere! for the Master born will always fare worst at Masters' hands." Another urgent call from Magdalena goes unregarded. "But tell me, did he win any friend at all among them?" "Impossible! All felt too small beside him. He has too much pride: let him see the world a little. Why can't he leave us in peace to what we have learned with so much toil and smart? If he wants to kick over the traces let him go somewhere else to do it!" At this, Eva loses her temper. "Aye", she cries, to the accompaniment of the Derision motive (No. 28):

> *Aye! elsewhere then he'll fortune find,*
> *whate'er a nasty jealous man says—*
> *where hearts are generous and kind,*
> *far from all spiteful Master Hanses!*
> *Yes, Lena, yes! I'm coming, dear!*
> *Small consolation is there here!*
> *It smells of pitch, God save us from harm!*
> *Let him burn in it and keep himself warm!*

She leaves him in a rage and goes over to Magdalena. "I thought as much", says Sachs to himself, looking thoughtfully and tenderly after her, while the Care motive (No. 29) wells up once more in the strings. "Now to find a way!" He closes the upper half of the door, so that only a glimmer of light comes through it and he himself is almost invisible.

On the other side of the stage Eva and Magdalena engage in excited talk. Eva tells the maid to go to bed and cease worrying her; but Magdalena insists on giving him the commission she has received from Beckmesser. She is to persuade her mistress to be at her window when it gets dark, to hear him try out the song with which he hopes to win her hand the next day. "This is the last straw!" cries poor Eva. "Oh, if only *he* would come!" she wails; and that motive No. 29 was for Wagner the symbol not only of Sachs's cares but of care in general, Eva's and humanity's, is shewn by his employing it again in some peculiarly poignant forms in the present connection. (Occasionally, indeed, his motives must have had for him psychological connotations that escape us: how, for example, are we to account for the persistent use of the Cobbler motive (No. 31) in the orchestra during the closing passage of this dialogue between the two women?)

Eva has heard footsteps which she takes to be those of Walther. In vain does Magdalena try to induce her to go indoors before her father notices her absence. "Go thou to the window in my stead", she tells Magdalena, still listening in the direction from which she had heard footsteps.[1] The idea of appearing at the window dressed up as her mistress appeals strongly to Magdalena: David, who sleeps on the alley side, is sure to hear the serenade, and it will make him jealous and perhaps bring him to proposal point. She manages to draw Eva towards the door, but just then Walther turns the corner, and Eva runs to meet him with a glad cry. The orchestra whips up the excitement of anticipation very much as it does just before Tristan's entry in the second act of *Tristan and Isolde*.

---

[1] Wagner's handling of the change-of-clothes motive is not entirely lucid, and the variants between the Sketches and the poem show that it constituted something of a problem for him. The difficulty had arisen through the insertion in the opera, at the last moment, of the long conversation between Sachs and Eva, an episode for which there had been no provision in any of the Sketches. The slight confusion which this insertion introduced into his original plan, and the not wholly convincing devices by which he sought to remedy the confusion, are of considerable interest to the student of his dramatic technique. To go over the whole ground critically here, however, would delay us unnecessarily. The reader will find a full discussion of the matter in my *Life of Richard Wagner*, III, 159–163.

30

The impassioned dialogue of the lovers begins to the accompaniment of No. 36, now, however, in a more fiery form. Beside herself with joy, Eva greets the knight as her destined own, her poet and her friend. "Friend indeed", he replies, "but not poet, for as poet they have rejected and derided me, and so I have lost your hand." They go despairingly over the old ground again— she swears she will accept no one but him, but how are they to evade the hard conditions laid down by her father? He had sung his heart out at the trial, he says; but those accursed Masters, those hide-bound pedants and poetasters, had spurned him! Only one thing is left to them—flight together to freedom, into a world where he will be a Master by the grace of God. At the very thought of his enemies he sees red: the orchestra executes a wild fantasia upon the Derision motive (No. 28) as in his imagination he still sees and hears them all about him:

> *Markers beset me,*
> *torment and fret me;*
> *round me they're flocking,*
> *gibing and mocking:*
> *Markers from boxes,*
> *cunning old foxes,*
> *up from the highways,*
> *down all the byways . . .*
> *insult thee and flout thee,*
> *dance about thee,*
> *snuffling and screeching,*
> *thy hand beseeching:*
> *a Master takes thee,*
> *wretched bride he makes thee,*
> *trembling and weeping;*
> *round thee they're creeping!*
> *And I must bear it,*
> *may not pursue them,*
> *may not strike my good sword through them!*

At the height of his delirium the horn of the Night-watchman is heard not far away—a single note that strikes into the tissue of both the music and the action with extraordinary dramatic effect. Walther's first impulse is to draw his sword and cut his way through a danger which he senses but does not comprehend; but Eva lays her hand on him soothingly, and in an instant the music softens to the melody of the Magic of Midsummer eve:

"It was only the Watchman you heard", Eva tells him; "conceal yourself under the lime tree until he passes." Magdalena calls to her to make haste; and as the orchestra gives out quietly the tender Love motive (No. 6) she follows the maid into the house, giving Walther, as she goes, what seems to be an assurance that she will elope with him.

As he conceals himself the Watchman comes slowly down the alley, reaches the street, turns the corner of Pogner's house, and gradually passes out of sight, singing the simple traditional warning to all good citizens to look out for fire and evil-doers:

Hearken to my words, good people;
strikes ten from every steeple;
guard well your fire and eke your light,
that no one may be harmed this night.
Praise the Lord of all!

He sings it on a key-basis of F major, and then startles us by blowing on his horn a booming G flat. (In the old Germany that still survived in Wagner's young days the Night-watchman still went his rounds, waking the citizens up to assure them that it was all right to go on sleeping. Wagner must often have heard the call and the horn blast as a boy. Perhaps the words and the melody were to some extent the same everywhere, for a night-watchman's song of the mid-sixteenth century has come down to us that begins thus:

The similarity between the melody and the words of this—"Hear me now, it has struck four"—and those of Wagner's Night-Watchman is too close to be accidental).

31

A quiet enunciation of the Cobbler motive in the violas tells us that Sachs has been listening and taking notice of it all. He withdraws his lamp and opens his door a little further: "This is getting serious", he remarks; "an elopement on foot? That mustn't be. I must keep my eye on them."

Walther, behind the lime tree, is surprised to see, as he thinks, Magdalena approaching him; but as No. 6 unfolds itself he perceives that it is Eva, who throws herself on his breast. Now, he says, he no longer doubts that he has won the Master-prize! They prepare to make their dash for freedom. It is time now for Sachs to act. He places his lamp behind a glass globe, and as the lovers turn into the alley he opens the shutter again, so that a beam of light shoots steadily across the road. Eva and Walther, thus suddenly made visible, withdraw hastily into hiding, and to add to the tension of the situation the harsh G flat of the Watchman's horn strikes in again from a distance. There are only two routes open to the lovers, the way by the street—which Eva does not know very well—and that through the alley. Walther is sure he has only to appeal to Sachs and all will be well, for the cobbler is his friend; but Eva assures him that he is nothing of the kind: "he had nothing but evil to say of you." "Sachs too?", says Walther; "then out goes his light!"

But before he can go towards the shop to carry out his purpose the sound of a lute being tuned is heard. Beckmesser had crept down the alley in the wake of the Watchman: now he seats himself on a stone bench between the two windows of Sachs's house and looks up enquiringly at Pogner's windows. For a moment it seems to Walther that the coast is clear, for Sachs has withdrawn his light a little, closed the lower half of his door, and placed his work-bench right in the doorway. The lute has given the cobbler a brilliant idea: he sees now how both to check the imprudent plan of the lovers and have some fun of his own with Beckmesser. When Eva tells Walther that a newcomer has appeared in the alley, and that he is none other than the Marker, Walther is for paying off his score against him at once. The anxious Eva holds him back: her father will be roused if there is any commotion in the alley; Beckmesser will merely sing a song and go away, and then the coast will be clear. So the pair withdraw further into the shadow of the bushes by the lime tree.

Beckmesser, not seeing the expected figure at the window, begins strumming his lute impatiently:

unconscious of the trouble that is brewing for him, a hint of which we get from a whisper of the Cobbler motive in the orchestra. Before he can begin his serenade, however, Sachs hammers on his last and trolls a hearty "Jerum! Jerum! Hallo-hallo-he! Oho! Tralalei!":

and then launches into a ditty in popular style:

the burden of which is that when the Lord drove Eve out of Paradise for her fault He took pity on her poor feet and sent an angel after her with instructions to make her a pair of shoes, and one for innocent barefoot Adam into the bargain.

32

Then the rich comedy begins. Sachs, in reply to Beckmesser's protests, explains that he has to work late to finish the pair of shoes in which the Marker is to go singing and wooing on the morrow. There is no stopping the jovial cobbler: a second verse, which Eva and Walther have a suspicion refers to themselves, tells of the responsibility of mother Eve for angels like him getting no rest, for they have to sit up to all hours shoe-making:

> *If you'd been more discreet,*
> *no stones would hurt our feet:*
> *but for that little slip you made*
> *I now must ply my awl and thread;*
> *and since poor Adam fell with you,*
> *I ply my wax and sole my shoe!*
> *But were not I*
> *an angel from on high,*
> *devil make your shoes, I'd cry!*

In the final stanza Sachs asks mother Eve (and through her the descendant and namesake of hers who is in hiding across the road), to feel for the cobbler in his woe; for are not all his works trodden upon and ruined past repairing?

Did not my weary soul
an angel oft console,
and call me up to Paradise,
I'd leave this world which I despise.
But when with him to heaven I go
this world of care I leave below;
          peace fills me through,
          Hans Sachs is shoe-
      maker and a poet too.

As he begins this stanza we hear in wood wind and horns a
countertheme to the melody of No. 42 that symbolises the heart-
ache of the sensitive old poet in Sachs over the evil and misery of
the world; it becomes of prime importance later in the orchestral
prelude to the third act:

43

Beckmesser is in despair: how is he to sing to his beloved—
Magdalena has just appeared at the window in Eva's clothes—
if this noise goes on? Eva, indeed, may even imagine that Sachs's
ribald song is *his* serenade! He and Sachs discuss the situation.
The shoemaker, for his part, pleads that he must get on with his
work: has not the Marker, indeed, already reproached him pub-
licly for giving more time to his poetising than to his cobbling?
Beckmesser tries a combination of diplomacy and flattery: will
not so excellent a judge as Sachs just listen to his song and tell
him what he thinks of it?

Still of my shoes you're thinking solely,
while truly I'd forgot them wholly.
Of cobblers you're the best, I swear;
as critic you're beyond compare.
Your judgment mightily I prize;
this song, then, prithee, criticise,
with which tomorrow, when I chant it,
I'll win the maid, if God but grant it.

Finally, after much argument, they arrive at a compromise. Beckmesser is to get on with his song, Sachs with his work. But if he is to mark, obviously it can't be with chalk: the shoes will never be finished that way. So why shouldn't he combine the functions of cobbler and Marker? Why not score the faults, if any, with his hammer? His professional pride making him feel safe on that score, Beckmesser agrees. He tunes his lute, but in his agitation screws the D string up too high. He corrects it and begins his serenade.

It is impossible to follow Wagner's words faithfully and at the same time throw the stresses on the same wrong syllables as in the German. In another language only the absurdity of the general effect can be conveyed, something in this fashion:

> *I see the dáwning dáylight,*
>
> *that ímparts gréat pleásure;*
>
> *it doth my héart so excíte,*
>
> *promísing soón rápture,*
>
> *I do not think of dýing,*
>
> *ráther of trýing*
>
> *to secúre á young bríde;*

and so on:

Den Tag seh' ich_ er - schei-nen, der mir wohl ge_ fall'n tut:
I   see the dawn-ing day-light that im-parts great pleas-ure.

The whole thing is a burlesque by Wagner of the type of song in which the melodic stresses fall with mechanical regularity on the strong beat of the bar, regardless of whether the accompanying word or syllable calls for accentuation or not.

Sachs's hammer marks three faults in the first four lines of the song, and Beckmesser angrily asks him what is wrong. Would it not be better, says the shoemaker, if instead of:

he had proceeded something like this?

Sachs, in fact, would handle the words, for musical purposes, with the rhythmic freedom with which Hugo Wolf and other moderns have familiarised us, making the vital words coincide with the strong beats. But in that case, Beckmesser asks testily, what becomes of my rhyme of "sich einen" and "erscheinen"? They argue this technical point for a moment, and then the Marker continues as best he can, for the further he goes the more faults the shoemaker marks, till in the end we can hardly hear the song for the hammer-strokes; we perceive, however, that it is liberally larded with the coloratura flourishes of which the Masters were so fond. Matters are not improved by the exasperated Beckmesser losing both his head and his wind, so that he commits more and more offences against good song and good speech as he goes on. In vain does he protest:

> *Now art's the thing;*
>
> *he who can fling*
>
> *his soul into his throat and sing*
>
> *a song both learned and loving*
>
> *will win the maid for his darling,*
>
> *and be by her beloved.*

33

By this time the shoes, thanks to the faults that have been scored on them with the hammer, are quite finished, and Sachs holds them up in glee; but regardless of the shoemaker's reminder that:

> *Good song keeps time*
> *and proper rhyme;*
> *when Town Clerks clean forget it,*
> *upon their soles do I set it,*

Beckmesser, now quite out of breath and shaking his lute furiously at Sachs, keeps rambling on to the tune of No. 44:

> *I know the rules perfectly,*
>
> *I keep excellent time;*
>
> *but to sing incorrectly*
>
> *for once were no great crime,*
>
> *when my heart quakes within me,*
>
> > *trying to win me*
>
> *the fair maiden I woo.*

All this long while the lovers have been watching and listening, half-wondering, half-amused: Walther asks Eva if he can have gone mad, or is it all a dream, for he has the feeling that he is back in the School again, on the singer's chair.

But the end is near. The hullabaloo has wakened David, who looks out and sees, as he imagines, his Magdalena being serenaded by a stranger. He comes out armed with a cudgel. Magdalena signs frantically to him to go away; Beckmesser thinks Eva is signifying her displeasure with his song, and he flings himself into the sorry remnants of it with the energy of despair. David collars him and begins to thrash him. By this time the neighbours also have been aroused, and now they begin to pour into the alley and the street. Seeing two men fighting they automatically take sides, as crowds will do, without understanding or caring anything about the rights and wrongs of the squabble. Guild rivalries and jealousies come into play: the cobblers swear it is the tailors, the tailors the cobblers; the locksmiths, the butchers, the bakers, the weavers, the tanners, the grocers, the joiners, the tin workers, the glue boilers, the wax makers, the flax weavers, soon are all in it, acting on the Irishman's sound precept for behaviour in a free-for-all—"wherever you see a head, hit it".

The women look out of their windows, and seeing their husbands and brothers being assaulted scream blue murder and start emptying cans and buckets of water on the milling crowd. The apprentices, of course, have been in it joyously from the beginning; now the journeymen rush in with clubs and take a hand in the game. Finally the dignified Masters and grave elderly citizens come in and exhort the madmen to stop before they are all murdered. All Nuremberg seems to be jostling and shouting in the streets.

34

Sachs, meanwhile, has extinguished his light and closed his shutters so that, without being visible himself, he can see through a chink the lovers by the lime tree. They have been watching the turmoil with increasing anxiety. Walther draws Eva to him and wraps his cloak round her, and they take cover as best they can in the bushes by the tree. More and more respectable citizens, roused from their sleep, come out in their night attire: Pogner appears at the window where the pseudo-Eva is weeping and wringing her hands, and, under the impression that it is his daughter, drags her back into the room. At last Walther draws his sword, clasps Eva in his left arm, and decides to cut his way through the mêlée; but when they reach the middle of the alley Sachs darts out, scatters the combatants with his strap, seizes Walther by the arm, and pushes the half-fainting Eva up the steps of her father's house, saying "In with you, Mistress Lena!" She is received and taken away by Pogner, who, what with the darkness and the change of costume, believes she is Magdalena. Then Sachs turns his attention to David, who is still, as he has been throughout, hard at work on Beckmesser. The Watchman's horn strikes in once more, and at the sound of it the crowd breaks up and flees in panic: the women disappear from the windows, the house doors are hastily closed. Sachs seizes David, gives him one with his strap and kicks him into the shop; Beckmesser picks himself up and staggers out with the others. All this while Sachs has not relaxed his hold on Walther; now he hustles him into the shop and closes the door.

When the Watchman enters he can scarcely believe his eyes and ears; he finds the place empty and as quiet as the tomb. He sings his ditty again in a quavering voice, this time making it eleven o' the clock; and once more he blows his discordant G flat against an F major harmony as he walks away slowly down the empty alley, which is now bathed in soft moonlight. An immense peace seems to have descended upon the town: the strings give out softly the motive of Midsummer eve Magic (No. 37), which is followed by quiet echoes of a motive that has played a great part in the texture during the cudgelling of Beckmesser and the accompanying riot:

The peace deepens, the last word being given to a tender little thought for Beckmesser, whose attempt at a display of Mastership seems to peter out, like the poor singer himself, in a sort of sore and sorry limp:

The slow-moving Watchman turns the corner and disappears from sight at the exact moment of the falling of the curtain.

35

In the third act Sachs—not the cobbler or even the Master but the wise and humane old poet—comes into his own; even Walther and Eva now become subsidiary characters. Perhaps the most remarkable thing in connection with the opera is the way the character of Sachs developed silently within Wagner in the course of the years. In the First Sketch of 1845 the shoemaker–Master had in him something of the aggressiveness and irritability of the Sachs of Deinhardstein. There Wagner had shown him on terms of hostility, secret or avowed, with the whole Guild. In the trial scene in the first act he had been the "keeper of the rules" for the day, in which capacity he has to read them out to the young aspirant for Mastership: this he does "with a touch of irony", and his behaviour every now and then strikes the other Masters as "suspicious". He "speaks sharply to the young man, so that the latter is a little abashed and anxious", though as Walther's song proceeds Sachs "looks at him sympathetically and at the Marker with irony". When the Masters declare themselves outraged by the song he turns on them, makes merry at their expense, and challenges the Marker to contribute a song of his own which *he* will take pleasure in marking. All through the work, in the First Sketch, there is a touch of personal frustration and bitterness in Sachs; when he hits out, as in the serenade with Beckmesser in the second act, it is to hurt.

Wagner, again, had seen him at first too much in terms of not only the artistic but the social and political and religious milieu of the divided Germany of the sixteenth century. In what is now the famous monologue upon life and art in the third act of the opera Wagner had made him, in 1845, lament that German poetry was coming to a degenerate end: "am I, a cobbler, the only man left who breathes the spirit of the great German past?" This note of personal exasperation disappears from the final work; Sachs now bemoans not his own lack of recognition as a poet but the folly of humanity in general, a humanity, however, which he loves deeply and would fain lead to higher things. Furthermore, when, in the Sketch of 1845, the young man comes into the room in the third act and Sachs questions him about his poetic ideals and looks through some of his poems, his advice to him is couched in terms of the German situation of his own day; "Sachs reflects for a time, then turns to the young man again. 'You are a poet; yet you will not prosper in the present time'. He depicts with melancholy humour the times they live in, the impending disappearance of the last sad remnants of the old art of Mastersong. 'Look at me: I would have found it impossible to carry on had I not been able to occupy my mind with these thoughts. That is why I am a cobbler, and, believe me, this cobbler is the last poet of the old German song-craft.' The young man protests energetically. *Sachs:* 'Believe me, for a long time to come men will not be interested in poetry. They will fight with other weapons than songs—with reason, with philosophy, against obscurantism and superstition,[1] aye, with the sword men will defend these new weapons. In that fight you, who have such beautiful and noble sentiments, ought to take your part; in this way you will achieve more than by the exercise of a gift which no one thinks anything of today. And when centuries have gone by and a new world has come into being perhaps men will turn back and glance at what they once had; then, perhaps, they will return to Hans Sachs, and he will point them still further back, to Walther [von der Vogelweide], and Wolfram, and the *Heldenlieder.' The Young Man:* 'Advise me, then, what to do.' *Sachs, cheerfully:* 'Return to your castle, study the writings of Ulrich von Hutten[2] and the Wittenberger,[3] and then, if it be necessary, defend with the sword what you have learned.' 'Very good, Meister! But now I need a wife!' 'You shall have one. Leave that to me' ".

None of this political and religious motivation is carried over into the Second Sketch, a fact on which we can congratulate ourselves today. Between 1845 and 1861 the character of Sachs had developed within Wagner on other and more broadly humanistic lines; the shoemaker-poet is no longer the specific product of the epoch of Luther and Hutten but a universal type of poetic ardour, understanding of the world of men, and resigned toleration, flecked with humour, of its weaknesses.

[1] The reader will remember that Sachs was a contemporary of Luther.
[2] One of the leaders of the German Reformation.   [3] Luther.

36

Had Wagner written the music of the opera in 1845 he could not have presented us with such a Sachs as the one we see in the orchestral prelude to the third act. The composer has left us, in a letter of 1869 to King Ludwig, the clue to the sequence of moods in the music. As we have seen, in the third stanza of the Cobbling song in the second act Wagner had introduced a countertheme (No. 43) to the main melody: this, he says, is "the bitter lament of the resigned man who shows the world a cheerful, energetic countenance; that cry from hidden depths had been understood by Eva, and so profoundly was her heart pierced by it that she would fain flee away, that she might hear no more of that song which on the surface was so cheerful."

The spectator may reasonably ask how we are to read Eva's thoughts to that extent; is not Wagner expecting us to take for granted, on his bare word, something that we should not have been able to deduce from the stage action itself? The answer is "No, or at all events not entirely": the clue *is* there in the poem, though even the most attentive listener in the theatre is certain to miss it; and for this Wagner himself must be held responsible. After the final words (quoted on page 364) of the Cobbling song —"Hans Sachs was a shoemaker and a poet too"—the full orchestra had given out the main melody (No. 42) fortissimo, with trumpets and trombones in full blast, the countertheme also (No. 43) asserting itself fortissimo in the horns. It is against this tornado of sound that Eva has to say "That song grieves me, I know not why!" There is the minimum chance of her being heard at all at the pitch at which she is singing, and hardly the ghost of a probability of the spectator catching the words. The stage direction in the score is that she is "greatly agitated"; but the audience is hardly likely to perceive this, in the first place because she is tucked away at the side of the darkened stage, and in the second place because at that precise moment Beckmesser looks up at Pogner's house and cries "The window opens!", and Magdalena appears at it in Eva's clothes: naturally the eyes of the audience turn at once in that direction.

While the orchestra is proceeding with No. 42 and Beckmesser is ejaculating "Good God! 'Tis she!" the lovers, in their hiding-place, have the following little dialogue:

Eva: That song grieves me, I know not why. Let us hasten away!
Walther (half-drawing his sword): Aye, now, with my sword!
Eva: No! Forbear!
Walther (withdrawing his hand from his sword): Scarce worth
    the while.
Eva: Yes, patience is best. O friend in need! That I should cause
    thee such trouble!

Naturally, after what has immediately preceded these last words, the casual reader of the poem takes them to be addressed to Walther. But obviously they apply to Sachs: *he* is the friend who, as she now sees, has divined Eva's need and suddenly come to her help; he it is whom she regrets having drawn into the tangled web of her own troubles. Wagner is manifestly carrying further the psychological motive that began with the "greatly agitated" and "That song grieves me, I know not why." But he has presumed too much on the spectator's hearing all these words, and, assuming him to have done so, on his reading into them, in that fleeting fifteen seconds or so, the wealth of meaning they had for the composer.

However, since he has made that meaning clear to us in his analytical note on the prelude to the third act, we can only accept it with gratitude and read it into the scene in the second act the next time we see the opera on the stage. We are reminded of Lord Burleigh's silent shake of the head in Sheridan's *The Critic:*

Sneer: He is very perfect indeed! Now pray what did he mean by
    that?
Puff: You don't take it?
Sneer: No, I don't, upon my soul.
Puff: Why, by that shake of the head he gave you to understand
    that even though they had more justice in their cause, and
    wisdom in their measures—yet, if there was not a greater
    spirit shown on the part of the people, the country would at
    last fall a sacrifice to the hostile ambition of the Spanish
    monarchy.

Sneer: The devil! Did he mean all that by shaking his head?
Puff: Every word of it—if he shook his head as I taught him.
Sneer: Ah! there certainly is a vast deal to be done on the stage by
　　　dumb show and expressions of face; and a judicious author
　　　knows how much he may trust to it.

37

To return to the prelude to the third act. The 'cellos having
given out No. 43, it is taken up in imitation by the violas and then
the violins, and woven into a texture of profoundly sorrowful
meaning. Then the key shifts to G major, and horns and bassoons,
with a passing intensification of the harmonies in trumpets,
trombones and tuba, give out a theme:

which, says Wagner, is "the solemn song with which Sachs greets
Luther and the Reformation; it had won the poet an incomparable
popularity". (We shall meet with it again later). "After the first
strophe", Wagner continues, "the strings take up once more
single fragments of the Cobbling song, as though the man were
turning his gaze from his handiwork heavenwards and losing
himself in tender reveries." (Reiterations of phrases from the
song, gradually soaring up into the higher reaches of the violins).
"Then, with increased sonority, the horns continue the [Luther]
hymn, with which Hans Sachs, on his appearance at the festival,
is greeted by the whole of the Nuremberg folk in a thunderous
unison outburst. Next the first motive of the strings [No. 43]
recurs, in a massive expression of the perturbation of a pro-
foundly-stirred soul: finally, allayed and calmed, it attains the
utmost cheerfulness of a benign and blissful resignation."

Before quitting the prelude let us give a glance at a little chronological difficulty connected with it. In May 1862 (not long after

he had started work on the music of the opera), Wagner wrote to Frau Wesendonk that the idea had just come to him for the orchestral introduction to the third act. The emotional climax of this act, he says, will be the moment when Sachs stands up and is acclaimed by the whole assembly. "The people sing in solemn style the first eight lines of Sachs's poem on Luther: the music for this is already written. Now in the prelude to the third act, where, on the rising of the curtain, we see Sachs brooding in his chair, I am making the bass instruments play a soft, subdued, profoundly melancholy passage that bears the imprint of the deepest resignation". (This is our No. 43). Wagner goes on to describe the further course of the prelude. Now why is there no mention here of this motive appearing earlier as a countertheme to the third stanza of Sachs's cobbling song in the second act? The inference would appear to be that the idea of introducing it there had not yet occurred to Wagner—that so far from the motive having been transferred from the song to the prelude (as we have always supposed to have been the case), Wagner conceived it first of all in connection with the prelude, and only later, perhaps when he was at work on the second act, had the idea of inserting it in the cobbling song. It would be interesting to know what light, if any, Wagner's musical sketches throw on the matter.

38

The curtain rises, showing Sachs's workshop, with a half-open door in the background leading to the street. (It is one of the marvels of stage setting that the humble cobbler's workshop here looks larger than the whole house had done in act two. Sachs, we feel, must have been in an enviably large way of business—and with no one but David to help him!—to keep up an establishment of this size). On the right of the room is the door to an inner chamber. On the left, a window overlooks the alley; it has flowers before it; beside it is Sachs's work-bench. He is seen sitting in a large armchair by the window, absorbed in a big folio volume that rests on his knees: the sun shines brightly on him. It is the morning after the second act.

To the bright little tune of No. 14 David comes jauntily up the

street and peeps in at the door. He is a trifle abashed when he sees
the Master, but is reassured when it looks as if the latter had not
noticed his entry. He carries a basket which he deposits on the
work-bench at the back by the door; he draws from it flowers and
ribbons, lays them out on the table, and, from the very bottom
of the basket, extracts a sausage and a cake. These he is going to
eat when Sachs, who has still not observed him, turns over a page
of the folio noisily. David hurriedly puts the food out of sight and
reports for duty: the shoes, he says, he has taken to Herr Beckmesser's house. He stops his chatter when he becomes aware of
what looks like calculated silence on his master's part, which his
guilty conscience puts down to displeasure over his rowdy behaviour last night.

He approaches Sachs humbly and begs for forgiveness: "can a
prentice always behave as he should?" Can Sachs blame him for
sticking up for his Lena as he did? She is so good to him, looks at
him so tenderly, consoles him when he has had a thrashing,
brings him titbits when he is hungry. But yesterday she had first
of all hurt him by snatching a basket of food out of his eager
hands; and afterwards when he found another man serenading her
he lost his temper, he confesses, and gave the fellow a hiding. But
today Magdalena has explained everything and has sent him nice
flowers and ribbons; and he, for his part, is willing now to pass the
sponge of oblivion over last night's unorthodox proceedings.

39

Perhaps this scene had been rather better handled in some
respects in the Second Sketch than it is in the opera. In the First
Sketch David did not make his entry after the rise of the curtain
and find his master there already, reading; he was in the room with
him from the first, at work on a pair of shoes by the window.
During Sachs's long reverie Magdalena called languishingly,
from outside, "David!"; and he signified his annoyance over her
conduct last night by "reproachful gestures". But when Wagner
came to draft his Second Sketch, fifteen years later, he seems to
have realised that a bit of explanation was called for at the opening
of the third act.

The spectator may be expected to remember that the previous night's darkness had been so complete that not only did Walther believe at first that the woman in Magdalena's clothes who approached him was really Magdalena, not only did Beckmesser believe that the woman in Eva's clothes at the window was really Eva, but Pogner himself had mistaken the figure for his daughter when he dragged her back into the room, and had then gone down to the street door and cried "Ho, Lena! where art thou?" It might strike the spectator as a little odd, then, that David should have seen at once, when he opened his own window, that it was not Eva but his own Magdalena who was being serenaded; and stranger still that he does not recognise Beckmesser even while he is cudgelling him. (This is evident enough from the text of the opera: not only are we nowhere given the smallest hint that the apprentice knows his victim to be the Marker but the few words he addresses to him are such as no prentice in Nuremberg would ever have dared to use to one who was Master, Marker and Town Clerk. "Who's that up there?" David had cried at the first sight of the figure at the window. "Upon my word it's Lena. Good Lord! she has given him an assignation. This is the man she prefers to me!"; and when he falls on the serenader it is with the remark, "To the devil with you, you damned churl . . . I'll break every bone in your body!" And Magdalena screams to him from the window, towards the end of the mêlée, "Listen, David: it's Beckmesser!").

It is evident enough that at some time or another between the Sketches and the final poem Wagner felt himself in a little difficulty as regards all this, and tried to put it right. In the Second Sketch he does a little explaining. When David slinks into the room at the opening of the third act he apologises humbly to his master for his disgraceful conduct the night before; "he confesses", says the Sketch, "that he had 'intentions' with regard to Frau Magdalena", who had been very kind to him in many ways. "Then he had seen a coxcomb serenading her—for in spite of her clothing he had recognised Frau Magdalena. Thereupon he had seen red, and when he further became aware that his rival was the Marker who had behaved so vilely to Sachs the day before [at the Song School], he just had to give him a thrashing. Now he begs forgiveness." That is not a very plausible explanation, all things considered, but at least it is an explanation of sorts. Yet when Wagner came to write his poem he cut out the passage relating to David's recognition of Beckmesser. "When I found", says the apprentice in the poem,

> at nightfall another sneaking round,
> who sang to her, and howled like mad,
> well! such a drubbing he's ne'er had.
> Should I be blamed if others choose to fight?
> Besides, for our love 'twas a godsend quite;
> and Lena has explained the whole affair,
> and today sends me flowers and ribbons to wear.

Here, it will be observed, he says nothing at all about having recognised Beckmesser from the first and chastised him not only for coming courting Lena but for his impudence to Sachs, nor, for that matter, does Beckmesser himself, in the poem, ever drop the least hint, either during the fight or in his colloquy with Sachs in the third act, that he knew his assailant to be the cobbler's apprentice. Yet if we grant that the darkness made this mutual recognition impossible, how are we to account for it not having been too dark for David to recognise Magdalena at the window? The whole thing is yet another instance of Wagner's conceiving an episode in different terms at different stages of his work upon a subject, and failing to smooth out all the discrepancies when he came to give his poem its final form.

40

To resume our account of the scene at the commencement of the third act. Sachs's continued silence terrifies David. It is ended by the shoemaker suddenly closing the folio with a bang that brings David to his knees in front of him. But when he speaks it is with a friendliness that astonishes the apprentice: how came these lovely flowers and ribbons here? he asks. David reminds him that it is Midsummer day, when everyone adorns himself in his best. So last night was "Polterabend"? (the evening of licensed rowdiness), the Master asks abstractedly. Then, pulling himself together, he bids the boy repeat his verses, if he knows them. David, delighted that all is going so well, begins to reel the lines off, but, with his mind still on last night, sings them to the tune of Beckmesser's serenade (No. 44).[1] Sachs calls him sharply to order, and David now sings quite correctly, to a simple melody in folk-style, a little song about the good St. John by Jordan's strand, baptizing all comers, among them the child of a German woman, to whom the Saint gives the name of Johannes:

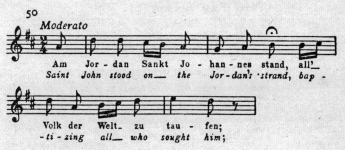

50
Moderato

Am Jor-dan Sankt Jo - han - nes stand, all'
Saint John stood on— the Jor-dan's strand, bap -

Volk der Welt zu tau - fen;
- ti - zing all— who sought him;

When the pair get back to Nuremberg, however, what was Johannes by the Jordan becomes, on the banks of the Pegnitz, plain Hans, which by an odd coincidence, is the name of the master to whom David now cajolingly offers the flowers and the ribbons, the cake and the sausage. He even suggests that Sachs should compete for the hand of the bride that afternoon; if he does, he assures him, Beckmesser won't stand a chance against him. Sachs puts the question aside with an indulgent smile and sends him away, bidding him dress up in his best clothes for the coming festival. David kisses his hand with emotion, and goes out quite overwhelmed by the unexpected mildness of his master; the least he had expected for his riotous behaviour the night before had been a taste of the strap.

[1] In the First Sketch this episode had been handled very differently. There Magdalena calls to him from outside, and to annoy her with an affectation of indifference he starts singing Sachs's Cobbling song of the previous night. "Sachs is at first startled and vexed. But the thought of the popularity he has acquired delights him; he lets David continue and himself sings with him." There is nothing of this in the Second and Third Sketches.

41

Sachs, with the folio still on his knees, takes up again the broken thread of his meditations. The Renunciation motive (No. 43) comes out softly, first in the 'cellos and basses, then in a solo trombone, as he begins his famous "Wahn! Wahn!" monologue.[1] The burden of it is a lament over the folly of men, who will not live in peace together, but brother falls on brother "in aimless, frantic spite":

> *Nought does he know*
> *but grief and woe:*
> *he flies in fear*
> *yet deems he is pursuing;*
> *hears not his own wild cry of pain*
> *when his own heart he rends in twain,*
> *but glories in his anguish.*
> *What name were fit for this?*
> *The ancient madness 'tis*
> *that runs through all our striving,*
> *to folly ever driving!*

His dear old Nuremberg has been free of this madness:

> *Thy peaceful ways pursuing,*
> *serene thou dost abide,*
> *far from the clash of nations,[2]*
> *dear Nuremberg, my pride.*

[1] There is a footnote in the orchestral score at this point: "If there is not a first-rate trombonist who can play the passage tenderly and legato it should be entrusted to a horn player."

"Wahn" means all kinds of things in different connections—according to the dictionaries "erroneous or false opinion", "illusion", "delusion", "hallucination", "error", "monomania", "folly", "madness" etc. Only two monosyllables are available for the English translator of the monologue—"craze" and "mad". "Craze! Craze! Everywhere craze!" conveys the literal meaning of Sachs's opening line very well, but "craze" has a touch of awkwardness about it when sung. "Mad" is perhaps better, if the listener understands it not in the sense of insanity but of folly in act and thought. The Italian version gives us "follia", which carries the right shade of meaning but compels Sachs to sing three syllables where there is only one in the German.

[2] Literally "in the centre of Germany".

But last night the universal madness had broken out there, and why? Because, forsooth, some sprite or other had flitted through men's minds: two lovers had tried to make for freedom and a cobbler in his workshop had happened to give a tug at the strings of folly: a riot had broken out:

> *and madness with madness vieing,*
> *the cudgels soon are flying;*
> *each madman must belabour*
> *his own best friend and neighbour:*
> *God knows how that befell!*
> *Some goblin wove the spell!*
> *Some glow-worm sought his mate in vain;*
> *'twas he who brought this bitter bane!*

Was it the elder's scent? Midsummer eve? But now, God be praised, Midsummer day has dawned; so let Hans Sachs turn, if he can, this evil to good, direct folly to a noble end.

We may be permitted to ask, as a simple matter of dramatic consistency, why Sachs should now be taking the trifling events of the previous night with such tragic seriousness, seeing in them a symbol of the evil that is at the core of the cosmos. The answer seems to be that Wagner had still not purged his mind of the original conception, with all that it implied, of Sachs as a definite historical character, lamenting not only the decline of poetry in his day but the strife of political and religious parties in the Germany of the period of the Reformation. In the First Sketch Wagner had made the subject of Sachs's broodings, when poring over the folio, the bitter thought, "Has an end really come to the divine art of poetry? Am I, a cobbler, really the only man left who breathes the spirit of the great German past?" This motive does not appear in the present poem; we are given no clue at all to Sachs's thoughts in the opening scene. The motive had, in fact, already been discarded in the Second Sketch, where it is made clear to us that what the shoemaker had been brooding over when turning the pages of the old world-chronicle was the ineradicable unfriendliness of man to man.

"Sachs", says the Second Sketch at the point where the monologue is reached, "remains for some time with his arm resting on the closed folio, sunk in reverie. He had been searching the world-chronicle for similar crazy proceedings that might explain for him the nature of the *Wahn* that so often takes possession of mankind and urges it on to the maddest deeds, so that men attack each other without any reason, seek out and shun each other, make war on each other, persecute one another, without a single one of them being any better for it all in the end. He discovers that all the books are at one on this matter; everything in the world is filled through and through with unreason [*Unsinn*]. This time, no doubt, it was because of Midsummer eve: a glow-worm failed to find its little mate; in its alarm it flitted through many a weary human brain; it set sparks crackling there; the world breaks into flame; the heart awakes and throbs and rages; fists are clenched, cudgels are seized, and it takes a rain of blows to put out the world-conflagration! A goblin's fit of insanity!"

Obviously all this grave philosophising, with its talk of a world-conflagration, developed from Wagner's original conception of Sachs and Nuremberg in the setting of the Germany of the sixteenth century, torn by political and religious hatreds: it is straining dramatic probability a little too far to make it appear that the Sachs who, the night before, had played the joyous part he did in the harmless baiting of a comically bad singer, should this morning see it all as a symbol of the universal and eternal human woe.

But what does it matter to us now if Wagner made a slight mistake in dramatic psychology, when the mistake has brought us words of such wise humanism and music of such heart-searching beauty as the "Wahn! Wahn!" monologue?

42

The first section of it, in which Sachs muses on the innate and universal folly of mankind, is based upon that sorrowful motive of Resignation (No. 43) which had first appeared in the second act as a countertheme to the cobbling song, and had served to introduce the prelude to the third act. As the old man thinks with a glow of pride of the general tranquillity of his own beloved town the Nuremberg motive (No. 34) comes to the forefront. Then we hear reminiscences of the music of the ensemble at the end of the second act as Sachs recalls the tumult of the night before, when for a moment the quiet town seemed to be caught up in the general madness of the world. But this temporary fret yields place to the Magic of Midsummer's eve (No. 37), which touches with tender beauty even the echoes of the cudgelling scene that flit through the cobbler's mind as he speaks of the havoc wrought by the "glow-worm" that had flitted from brain to brain in frantic search of its little mate. "That", Sachs muses tenderly, "was Midsummer's eve; but now has dawned Midsummer's day"; and with a great crescendo that is one of the most thrilling moments of the whole score the monologue settles into its final stage. Through an orchestral tissue woven out of the Midsummer day motive (No. 19) in conjunction with that of Nuremberg (No. 34) the old cobbler turns with a mixture of philosophy and humour to the business he has set himself for the day, that of drawing all the tangled threads together and weaving a new pattern of human-kindliness out of them:

> *We'll see now how Hans Sachs intends*
> *turning this madness to his ends,*
> *that good may come of ill;*
> *for if it plagues us still,*
> *e'en here in Nuremberg,*
> *let's make it do such work*
> *as needs a touch of madness in it;*
> *and so let one who's mad begin it!*

How that end is to be achieved will soon be made apparent, by no less an agency than the would-be cunning and folly of the one disturbing element in the picture, Beckmesser.

43

As the last strains of the monologue die away, with the orchestra throwing out the Midsummer day motive in peal after joyous peal, Walther emerges from the inner room. He is warmly greeted by Sachs, who enquires how he has slept. "A little, but soundly", replies the young man, who is obviously in a subdued mood this morning, for he had had a dream so beautiful that he hardly dares recall it, lest it should slip away from him. To the accompaniment of the motive of Sachs's Benevolence (No. 30), which had played so large a part in the dialogue between him and Eva in the second act, the cobbler assures him that it is precisely the poet's function to give expression and form to dreams, which are the best things in us. "Did your dream", he asks, "give you any hint of how you might become a Master?" The knight tells him, however, that after his reception by the Masters the day before he had given up all hope in that direction.

Sachs reproves him gently but earnestly. He himself, he says, has not abandoned hope; had it come to that pass he would not merely not have frustrated the young man's flight but would have kept him company. Walther must not judge the Masters too harshly; they may be narrow in their views, but at bottom they are honest souls who mean well. And was there not a certain amount of justification for their behaviour at the trial yesterday? For the knight's song had been, to say the least, a trifle unusual:

> *Your song the Masters somewhat scared,*
> *and with good cause, for on my word,*
> *if maids hear songs so hot and glowing*
> *what they'd be up to there's no knowing!*

The calm joys of wedded life call for other words, other melodies. "Yes", Walther retorts drily, "so I gathered from last night's affair; the alley resounded with them." "Aye, aye", Sachs chuckles, "and no doubt you heard me beating time to them!" But, he continues more seriously, "put all this out of your head now and think of making a Mastersong." The young man objects that were he to achieve a beautiful poem and melody the Masters would only declare them not a Mastersong. Thereupon the wise old man gives him, to a new motive:

51 Tenderly

Mein Freund, in hol - der Ju - gend-zeit, wenn
My friend, in youth's en-chant-ed days, when

uns von mächt'-gen Trie - ben
warm the blood is flow - ing,

etc.

some wise counsel as to the difference between life and art. The burden of the lesson is that "inspiration" is all very well in its way, but it is not the whole of art. In youth the warm blood makes every man something of a poet: "'tis Spring that sings, not he". The testing time for the artist comes later—in the summer, autumn, and finally winter of life, when work is hard and cares accumulate, and the heart tends, in self-defence, to harden: if *then* a man can fashion a lovely song, he is a real Master.

Walther, now all afire, protests that he is in love with a maid whom he means to woo and win. "Then submit your mood", says his mentor, in effect, "to the discipline of art: learn the Master-rules, by doing which you will not fetter your imagination but give it stronger and surer wings." "But what are these rules?" asks the impatient young poet, "which you praise so highly? "By whom were they made?" Sachs's reply is warm with the wisdom of age and experience:

> *By Masters whom the world had wasted,*
> *who life's embittered draught had tasted:*
> > *with pain and sorrow mated,*
> > *a vision they created*
> > > *of youth's first madness,*
> > > *its love and gladness,*
> *to give their souls the old free wing,*
> *and feel again the joy of Spring.*

"Yet how", asks Walther,

> *Yet how can dreaming age recapture*
> *the vanished Spring and all its rapture?*

Sachs's reply is:

> *It takes a draught whene'er it can:*
> *so let me, a soul-thirsty man,*
> > *teach you the rules as I know them;*
> > *then with new meaning endow them.*

"See", he continues, "here are pen, ink and paper. Dictate your morning dream to me, and I will take it down." But Walther needs yet another lesson in the psychology of the artist, which

Wagner, speaking through Sachs, proceeds to give him. "To think of your rules", the young man had objected, "is to make me forget my dream." Sachs's reply is, in essence, Wordsworth's tracing of poetry to emotion recollected in tranquillity:

Sachs:	*Then call the poet's art to aid;*
	it oft recalls what from memory's strayed.
Walther:	*Then 'twere no dream, but art alone?*
Sachs:	*Good friends are they; the twain are one.*
Walther:	*But how can I your rules obey?*
Sachs:	*Make rules of your own, then sing away!*

It is the artist Wagner speaking *in propria persona*.

44

Standing by the work-bench beside Sachs, who takes the words down as they fall from his lips, the knight launches into what will ultimately become the Prize Song, but at this stage is known to the German commentators as the Interpretation of the Morning Dream:

The first stanza consists of seven lines, rhyming thus, 1 + 6 + 7, 2 + 3, 4 + 5 ("Schein", "Duft", "Luft", "Wonnen", "ersonnen", "ein", "sein")—a good metrical scheme, with the two inner rhymes held in the strong armature of the first and the two last.

That, Sachs tells him approvingly, was a "Stollen" in the nomenclature of the Mastersingers; let him follow it up with another on the same pattern. "Why the same?" Walther asks. A modern teacher of "musical form" would reply: "In the first place to impress your opening, with its main idea, firmly on the mind of the listener, in the second place, by the slightest of divergences from it, to achieve a certain necessary unity-in-variety and pave the way for a transition to a new idea." Sachs says much the same thing in the imagery of his own day, combining homely humour with sound aesthetics: "to let men see that you have chosen a bride like yourself." So the young man, whose first impulse had been to take a new flight straight away, disciplines his inspiration as ordered, keeping it on a level wing until it shall be time to make an effective swerve. His second "Stollen" is constructed on the same metrical pattern as the first, with the rhymes "Raum", "Frucht", "Wucht", "Prangen", "Verlangen", "Saum", "Baum". It tells how in the garden of the young man's dream stood a tree laden with golden fruit; and it ends not in the key of the tonic, as the first "Stollen" had done, but in that of the dominant. This procedure, Sachs tells him, would hardly be approved of by the Masters, but it is quite right in *his* eyes. And now let him make an "Abgesang" ("Afterstrain"). "Why?" Walther enquires. Because, the older poet informs him, pursuing his homely metaphor of the two "Stollen" standing in the relation to each other of bridegroom and bride, it is now necessary to think of the children; just as these are like the parents yet unlike, so the "Abgesang" must resemble the two "Stollen" yet differ from them, carrying on the idea but having a shape and rhymes and tones of its own. In other words, a "development section" is now called for.

So Walther fashions a new stanza, this time of eleven lines, with the rhymes pairing thus, 1 + 5, 2 + 4, 3 + 6, 7 + 8, 9 + 10, with the final line standing apart from the others in unrhymed self-assured isolation.[1] This "Abgesang" is sung to a new melody which we have already met with in the overture and elsewhere as the Love motive (No. 6); now, however, it is in 3/4 time, and the words describe what befell the dreamer beneath the tree—a vision appeared to him of a maid more fair than tongue can tell,

[1] Actually it rhymes ("Lebensbaum") with the final "Baum" of the second "Stollen" and the "Lorbeerbaum" ("laurel tree") of the twenty-fifth (the last) line of the next and concluding strain of the song; but these subtleties, though obviously factors in Wagner's poetic idea and technical design, are not likely to be perceived by the casual listener in the theatre.

who took him to her breast and pointed out to him, with a smile, the object of his heart's desire, the lovely fruit upon the tree of life. The close is in C major, the key of the opening of the song, thus rounding off the curve of the whole.

Sachs, who had begun by giving a lesson in the interpenetration of matter and form, is now receiving one. Though deeply moved by the song, he confesses that while the complete "Bar" is satisfactory he finds the melody "a trifle free": not, he hastens to add, that *he* regards that as a fault, but freedom of this sort makes it a little difficult to retain the melody in the mind, and the ancients of the Guild do not like anything of that kind. It is Wagner himself once more defending himself against the contemporary charge that his "free" melody was not melody at all. However, Sachs continues, the young man must now compose a second "Bar" to make the first one quite clear; "for really your song, well as it is rhymed, leaves me in some doubt as to how much in it is your dream, how much your art."

So Walther sings a second "Bar", symmetrical with the first, i.e. having two "Stollen" and an "Abgesang", all three metricised and rhymed on the plan of their predecessors; and this second "Bar" tells how, when morning gave place first to evening, then to night, two stars appeared and beamed softly on the dreamer, the murmur of a stream stole on his ear, the stars broke into a dance among the leaves and branches, and "not fruit but a starry host hung from the laurel tree". The musical form of this second three-limbed "Bar" is that of the first one, with a tonic close to the first "Stollen", a dominant to the second, and a clinching tonic again to the third.

45

More profoundly moved still by the youthful fire and beauty of it all, Sachs suggests a third "Bar", which would make the poet's interpretation of the dream clear beyond all doubt to him. But Walther brushes the invitation aside: "How could I do that? Enough of words!" (Wagner, of course, like a good dramatist, is keeping the third section of the song up his sleeve for a later occasion, when it will be twice as effective as it would be if put before us now and merely repeated towards the end of the opera).

Sachs is wise enough to see that it would be tactless to press the young poet further just then. He rises and goes up to him; "then let us have word and deed at the proper time", he says. "But don't lose the melody, for it seems to me the very thing for poetry; and if you sing it later before them all, don't forget your morning dream." As Walther does not quite understand this, Sachs explains further. "Your trusty squire followed you here with your bag and baggage, including the clothes you will wear at the marriage feast. Some dove, surely, must have brought him to the nest where his master lay dreaming. So back to your chamber; we will both of us array ourselves in our best, for there is notable work ahead of us." Walther grasps the friendly old man's hand. Sachs leads him quietly to his room, opens the door for him respectfully, and follows him in.

The build of this scene seems so natural, the sequence of episodes and the flow of conversation so easy, that it all has the appearance of a happy improvisation of the moment. Yet manifestly it had cost Wagner a great deal of thought, for in the Sketches it had been handled quite differently. In the First Sketch Walther, entering the room immediately after the departure of David, had been gently reproved by Sachs for his rash attempt at elopement with Eva. The knight confesses his error, but asks what he is to do now. Is he to stand idly by and see his beloved carried off by his enemy Beckmesser? "That mustn't happen", replies Sachs. "But you will have to win her in the contest: leave it to me." How different the kind old cobbler is, says Walther gratefully, from those tiresome Masters who treated him so badly! He had thought to find the love of art in them, but how woefully he had been disappointed! The Sketch continues thus: "*Sachs:* 'What have you written so far?' 'Hero-songs; praises of the great Emperor; look; look!' 'No Minnesongs?' 'Here is my latest.' 'Give it me.' Sachs reads it through attentively. (The orchestra plays the melody). Sachs remains for a time sunk in reflection; then he turns to the young man: 'You are a poet!' "; after which the dialogue continues as on page 371. After Walther's declaration that he "needs a wife", and Sachs's assurance "You shall have one;

leave that to me", the Sketch continues thus: "The Beloved enters to discuss the question of her shoes. Terzett. She begins to overwhelm Sachs with reproaches, but the young man defends him. Sachs consoles them both and hints at a happy outcome: he tells them the part each must play. They thank him and promise obedience. The three go out by different exits"; whereupon Beckmesser enters.

46

In the Second Sketch, after Sachs's monologue, Walther enters and reproaches him for having hindered his flight the night before. Sachs explains that things like that are not done in respectable circles in Nuremberg; while he is on the knight's side he wants to be sure that his love for the maiden is genuine and that it will last. Walther turns away from him impatiently. The old man had noticed that it was daylight before the other had gone to rest, and Walther explains that, being unable to sleep, he had spent the time writing a poem to his beloved. He produces it and hands it to Sachs, and while the latter is silently reading it the orchestra plays the melody softly. (We may take it, from this, that the poem was a short one, or that the cobbler did not read it all; for we cannot imagine his doing so in silence for anything like the time occupied by the present singing of the Morning Dream song). Delighted with the poem, he promises Walther that the "Wahn" started by some kobold or other the preceding night shall today turn to his advantage. "How?" asks Walther. "By diverting the minds of men for a little while from their dull beaten track", says Sachs. "Come into the other room with me; I am going to dress for the festival, and we will have a talk about it all." Both go into the inner room, and while they are out, Beckmesser enters.

Evidently, then, the plan for the present superior handling of the scene did not occur to Wagner until he was actually at work on the opera. But the curious history of the Prize Song does not end here.

In March 1862, shortly after he had begun work at his score, Wagner, in a letter to Mathilde Wesendonk, quoted the opening lines of the Prize Song as it stood in the original poem:

Fern
meiner Jugend gold'nen Toren
ʒog ich einst aus
in Betrachtung ganʒ verloren:
väterlich Haus,
kindliche Wiege,
lebet wohl! ich eil', ich fliege
einer neuen Welt nun ʒu!

"I have fitted these lines", he said, "to a melody already in my head", and he quoted the first few bars of the music:

As the reader will be aware, the music of the present Prize Song runs on entirely different lines from these. Nor have the words of the song, in that first form, the smallest connection, either in metre or in meaning, with those in the opera.

As time went on, the Prize Song, and its forerunner, the Morning Dream Song, and the stage situation in which the latter was to be floated, all took quite other shapes in Wagner's mind. In October 1866 he wrote to King Ludwig, "I am now well into the [music of the] third act, and one of these days I shall have to write the words of Walther's Prize Song [i.e. the Morning Dream Song], the melody of which is already finished." The popular belief that Wagner's way with an opera was first to put together a "book" and then "set it to music" is quite mistaken. Here we have two instances of his writing the music first and finding words for it later—for, as the reader will have observed, the melody of 1862 which he had quoted for the benefit of Frau Wesendonk had been complete in his head before he "began to make lines to fit it". Precisely the same thing happened in 1866 in connection with the present Morning Dream Song. "Melody of the Prize Song, without text", is one of the jottings in his private "Annals". The entry was not made until near the end of the year, but it relates to the previous September, by the 28th of which month the melody was fully sketched and dated. He did not trouble at the time about the words, but went on tranquilly with the composition of his third act: pages 19–22 of his Composition Sketch, we now know, present a curious spectacle—the broken dialogue between Sachs and Walther is complete, words and music, while the Morning Dream melody is written out in full, but without any words. These were not ready until Christmas of that year.

One other curious feature of this scene may be noted here. We have heard (page 389) Sachs telling Walther that his clothes have been brought to the house by his "trusty servant"—"some little dove must have shown him the nest where his master lay dreaming". Why the "little dove" (*Täubchen*)? The explanation is that in the poem of the Morning Dream in its original (and later discarded) form the Beloved had appeared to the knight, in his dream, as a dove. Obviously only Eva knows where Walther had gone after their separation the night before, and only she can have told the servant where he was to be found. A jocular allusion to her as the *Täubchen* on Sachs's part would therefore have been quite in order in the earlier scheme. But there is no dramatic reason why this image of her should occur to him in the present poem, for there is no allusion to her as a *Täubchen* in the Morning Dream as Walther now sings it. Presumably the image had stuck in Wagner's mind, and he carried it over from the old to the new version without giving the matter any thought. The user of the Schott score of the opera misses the point, because Mr. Frederick Jameson has translated the passage "some *bird*, sure, must have shewn the nest wherein his master dreams". *Täubchen*, by the way, carries a double meaning, upon which Sachs is slily playing; colloquially it is a term of affection—"lovey" or "duck".

47

To resume our analysis of the opera.

As soon as Sachs and Walther have left the room Beckmesser comes in, and the delicious scene begins in which he unwittingly sets a trap that will snap decisively on him a few hours later. The devising of that trap cost Wagner a good deal of hard thinking. Beckmesser was to catch sight of the manuscript of what he naturally took to be a song by Sachs, and by some means or other be led to pass it off as his own at the contest, to his utter and final discomfiture. The problem before Wagner was a double one—how to give the utmost plausibility to those means, and how to manage it that our sympathies did not turn against Sachs. Let us first of all see how the action runs in the opera as we now have it.

Beckmesser comes in showily dressed, but obviously in poor shape physically after his experience of the night before. He is accompanied graphically in the orchestra by cunning inter-weavings of the theme of his serenade (No. 44), the Cudgelling motive (No. 27), the Marker motive (No. 24), etc. The music not only depicts his physical twinges but shows us that he is living over again, in imagination, the painful events in the alley. It is all set forth for us in the detailed stage directions for the long episode in dumb show.

He peeps round the door before venturing in. He limps for-ward, but, feeling a sudden twinge, gives a convulsive quiver and rubs his back. At the next step he takes his knee hurts him, and he rubs this. He sits down on the cobbler's stool, but at once starts up in pain. Perspiration breaks out on his brow as he visualises all he went through last night. He staggers about blindly in all directions, trying to escape from an invisible David. At last he steadies himself by holding on to the table; then he goes to the window and looks up at Pogner's house, trying to find consola-tion in the thought of Eva. But this brings up memories of Wal-ther, and in a fit of jealous rage he beats his forehead. Once more he hears the derisive laughter of the women in the alley; he slams the window angrily and turns mechanically to the table, his worried mind occupied with the new song he will have to com-pose for today's contest, the one he had intended for the occasion having come so sadly to pieces.

The manuscript left there by Sachs catches his eye: he picks it up inquisitively, runs a rapid eye over it, and finally bursts out wrathfully, "A wooing song! By Sachs! Ha! now all's as clear as day!" He smells rivalry and treachery in the air: so that is what the artful cobbler had been up to all the time! Now he understands why the old rascal slaughtered his serenade and got him thrashed last night; it was to get a rival out of his way today.

48

As Sachs comes in in holiday attire Beckmesser hastily crams the paper into his pocket. For a little while the two fence with each other; Beckmesser is irritable and rude, the cobbler ironic and polite. The Marker charges him with engineering the shindy of the evening before in order to ruin his chances today: Sachs's jocular reply is that as it was Beckmesser's wedding eve the usual jollification was quite in order. The Marker now loses his temper completely. A new motive appears—that of Beckmesser's Indignation:

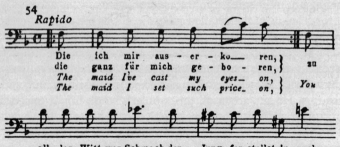

as he traces all his misfortunes to his supposed rival for Eva's hand. It was Sachs who had cunningly persuaded Pogner to put that clause about the maiden's consent into the offer of the prize, hoping she would fall into *his* hands. It was Sachs who with malice aforethought had ruined his song:

> *That's why! That's why!*
> *And blind was I!*
> *He tried to stop my song last night,*
> *he banged and bawled with all his might,*
> *to keep back from the maid*
> *another man's serenade.*

> *Aye, aye! Ho, ho!*
> *Was it not so?*
> *You sat there in your cobbler's den,*
> *and called your friends up, boys and men,*
> *to beat me black and blue,*
> *and clear the course for you!*
> *Oh Lord! Oh Lord!*
> *My back they've scored,*
> *and shamed me 'fore the maid adored;*
> *they did so swipe and switch me*
> *that no tailor, sure, could stitch me!*
> *To treat a man so!*
> *My hide to tan so!*

and so on at great length, in the finest piece of vituperation in all opera.

Taking up the theme of No. 54, Sachs replies quietly that he is mistaken: "believe what you like about me, but at any rate calm your jealous fears. I am no wooer, and not your rival." The furious Marker gives him the lie direct. A dialogue of the swiftest and neatest give-and-take ensues. As proof that he is right, Beckmesser produces the manuscript, with the ink hardly dry on it. Perhaps, he surmises sarcastically, it is just a biblical song? Sachs waves the suggestion aside. Then what?

> *Oh Sachs, for all your virtuous pose,*
> *for craft you'd run the devil close!*

Maybe, the cobbler replies quietly:

> *Maybe, but yet I was never known*
> *to pocket things I did not own:*
> *and so that you may not be called a thief,*
> *no longer 'tis mine—I give you the leaf.*

Beckmesser can hardly believe his ears. But is there not a catch in this generous offer somewhere? What is the use of the gift if Sachs remembers the song?

Beckmesser:	*Perhaps it's all well fixed in your mind?*
Sachs:	*No fear need you have of me, you'll find.*
Beckmesser:	*You give me the leaf?*

Sachs: To save your good name.
Beckmesser: To use as my own?
Sachs: Pray feel no shame.
Beckmesser: To sing if I like?
Sachs: By all means try.
Beckmesser: And if I succeed?
Sachs: None more surprised than I.

Beckmesser is overwhelmed by this generosity. After the hammering he has had, he says, he doesn't feel equal to writing a new song today, and one by Sachs is sure to be first-rate. Let them be friends for life! Then a new suspicion worms itself into his mind, and he exacts a promise from Sachs:

>   Yet one thing swear—
> if the song you should hear anywhere,
> you'll promise to make no remark,
> not claim it as yours, but keep it dark?

Sachs: I swear it: may I punished be
                if e'er I mention the song is by me.

Beckmesser rubs his hands with satisfaction: now he feels perfectly safe. Sachs gives him a final piece of friendly advice—to study the song well before singing it, for it isn't easy, and he may come to grief over both the melody and words. His old belief in himself fully restored, Beckmesser assures him that all Nuremberg admits he hasn't a superior when it comes to tones and modes. And now he must not fritter away any more time here; he must be off to con the song. Buttering his dear friend Sachs with compliments and protestations of undying affection:

55

Vivo

Kanf' eu - re Wer - ke gleich, ma-che zum Mer - ker euch,
I'll buy your po - e - try, you shall our Mark - er be,

poco rit.

doch fein mit Krei - de weich, nicht mit dem Ham-merstreich!
chalk you must keep to, though, ham-mer won't do, you know!

he cavorts to the door, imagines he has forgotten the poem, rushes back anxiously to the table, finds the manuscript is in his hand, embraces Sachs again, and at last limps out. Sachs gazes thoughtfully after him, smiles sardonically, and looks forward with satisfaction to the time when the foolish fellow's sin will find him out. The long scene is an incomparable scherzo, equally symphonic and dramatic.

49

Let us now glance at the slow process by which Wagner arrived at the present dexterous handling of the scene.

In the opera, Walther's song is taken down on paper by Sachs, whereas in the First Sketch the young man had brought with him a copy of his latest poem to show the cobbler. It is this manuscript, left on the table at their exit, that catches Beckmesser's eye when he comes into the now empty room. In the opera he arrives boiling over with rage against Sachs for his behaviour the night before, while to the pains of the cudgelling he had received there is now added the suspicion that the cobbler, judging from the freshly-written poem in his handwriting on the table, intends to enter the lists for Eva's hand. This line of procedure had not at first suggested itself to Wagner; for in the Sketch "the Marker comes in diffidently: he is in great distress, for now he is convinced that last night his chances with the maiden had been ruined. He wants to make sure of Sachs, for he knows how great his influence is with the people."

It was at this point that Wagner's difficulties began. How was Beckmesser to be caught in a trap entirely of his own setting? Was he to be shewn as fully deserving all he got later, or was he to be the victim to some extent of Sachs's craft and malice? Wagner's first idea took the following form: "The Marker catches sight of the song on the work-table, reads it, and finds it will suit him. He is in doubt whether to pocket it or not: when Sachs enters he slips it hastily but involuntarily into his breast. He is embarrassed. He feels that he cannot make use of the song without Sachs's permission; hence the milder tone he now adopts. At last, his conscience getting the upper hand, he confesses the theft and is pre-

sented with the song by Sachs." "Perhaps", Wagner adds in a
parenthesis, "Sachs can make out that he has no idea whose the
song is—it might be the young man's, who by this time is over
the hills and far away. 'It seems to be a magical song! If only the
melody were there with it! Take good care to find the right
tune!'"

But in a parallel column Wagner sketches an alternative procedure, in which the cobbler plays rather maliciously on the
Marker's weaknesses. When Sachs re-enters the room he is
astonished, or professes to be, to find the Marker there. Is there
anything wrong with the new shoes? he asks innocently. Thereupon Beckmesser vents his gall on him for the trick of the night
before. Sachs defends himself humorously. Then the Marker tries
a smoother tone: his wooing song had been ruined, and how is he
to find another? Taken in by Sachs's friendliness he becomes
more and more confidential: he has no doubts as regards his own
powers, but he mistrusts the maiden and the folk, who understand nothing of the art of the Masters. In the end Sachs offers
him a song of his own, which, written in the days of his youth, is
not known to anyone in the town. Beckmesser is at first suspicious
of a trap: suppose, in the event of the song bringing him success
at the contest, the cobbler comes forward and claims it as his?
Sachs reassures him on this point: he is an old greybeard, a
widower for some years: is he likely to be so foolish as to want to
marry again? It ends in Beckmesser, his suspicions allayed, going
off with the young man's song in the belief that it is one by Sachs;
and as he departs, the latter maliciously instructs him how to sing
it.

50

In this version, then, Sachs deliberately deceives Beckmesser.
After riper reflection Wagner must have seen that this would
alienate the audience's sympathies to some extent from the cobbler;
so he went back, in essentials, to the first of his two alternative
plans, dexterously making the Marker fall into a pit of his own
digging, with Sachs assuredly not pushing him in, but as assuredly
doing nothing to hold him back. Thus both characters are rescued

so far as dramatic psychology is concerned. In the opera we do not censure Beckmesser for his hasty pocketing of the song in the first place, and in the second place for his willingness, when it is turned over to him, to palm it off as his own, because he is throughout a figure of farcical fun, against whom, by the conventions of the theatre, the ordinary laws of good behaviour are not so sternly invoked as they are against more serious characters. Sachs, however, must not be allowed to lapse from normal standards of honour; so it has to be not he who hangs Beckmesser but Beckmesser who hangs himself, Sachs merely letting him have the rope he is so keen on getting. From first to last, in the admirable scene as we now have it in the opera, the cobbler does not say a single untrue thing about the song or his own share in it; he is speaking no more and no less than the simple truth when he admits that the handwriting is his, with the ink still fresh, and tells the Marker he can have the document if he wants it.

This is the really artful touch on Wagner's part. Sachs does not present Beckmesser with the *poem*, but with the bit of paper on which it is written: what he says is "Behaltet das Blatt, es sei euch geschenkt" ("Keep the sheet; I make you a present of it"). All he does is to present Beckmesser with a bit of his own property, *the scrap of paper*; if the schemer chooses to make the false inference that because the writing is Sachs's the poem is Sachs's, that is the man's own affair. It is Beckmesser who, in his haste and greed, picks out the card the conjuror wanted him to draw. The English translators, myself included, somewhat obscure the matter when, to avoid the repetition of the word "sheet", they make Beckmesser ask "You give me the song?", to which Sachs replies, in effect, "Yes, so that you won't have theft on your conscience." But what Beckmesser really says to him, in the German, is not "You give me the song?" but "You give me the *leaf*?", which Sachs can do without having anything on *his* conscience. He is not making himself an accomplice in an infringement of literary copyright, but merely presenting Beckmesser with a bit of his own legal property, to wit, a sheet of paper with some words on it in his own handwriting. With the whitest conscience in the world he can assure the Marker that at no time and in no place will he claim the song as his. The cobbler's reputation remains as pure as driven snow; Beckmesser, for his part, leaves the court, as an Irish judge said of a lucky defendant, without a stain on his character beyond those on it when he came in.[1]

51

The scene that follows in the opera is also a later invention of Wagner's. Originally, as we have seen, he had made Eva appear earlier in the action and sing a trio with Walther and Sachs; later he cut out that episode entirely and delayed her participation in the drama until after the departure of Beckmesser. She now enters, from the street, in splendid attire, for she is dressed for the festival; she is pale and sorrowful-looking, however, and she comes towards the old man slowly, accompanied in the orchestra by the gracious motive (No. 35) that had served as background to their colloquy in the second act. Her anxiety is depicted in a new motive:

56

first breathed in the soft tones of the wood wind, which runs symphonically through the dialogue that ensues.

Sachs congratulates her on looking so smart; but her heart, she assures him, is anything but as gay as her dress. Can't he guess where the shoe is pinching her? Their dialogue, like their former

---

[1] In *A Communication to my Friends* (1851) Wagner gave his readers an outline of the story of the new opera he was planning. This is in the main a swift summary of the First Sketch; but manifestly he was still doubtful, after six years, how to manage the episode of Beckmesser and the manuscript, for this is how he now describes it: "The next day the Marker comes disconsolately to Sachs and begs of him a new song with which to woo the bride. The cobbler gives him a poem of the young knight's, pretending not to know how it had come into his possession; he warns him, however, to be careful to find a fitting melody to which to sing it." This "pretence", it will be seen, evades the ethical problem of how Sachs is to plant the poem on Beckmesser without himself incurring the charge of trickery. Evidently Wagner was content just then to leave this knotty problem to solve itself later.

one in the second act, is a fencing bout. Everything she says has another meaning than the literal one: she is fishing for information about the knight, but will not say so openly; while Sachs affects to take everything she says quite literally, though he is perfectly aware of what is unspoken in it. Ostensibly she is complaining about the fit of the new shoes he has made for her; but what is really pinching her is not the shoes but the uncertainty about Walther. The odd thing about these shoes, she says, is their contrariness; when she stops they would go, and when she wants to go they stop. The reference is plainly to her love and the frustrated elopement. Cannot Sachs do something about it? At his bidding she puts a foot on the stool, and he examines the shoe. "It's too wide, you see." "Nonsense, my child; that's pure vanity; the shoe fits close." "Just so; my toes are pinched most shockingly." "Here, on the left?" "No, on the right." "The heel?" "No, the instep." Then, in a flash of petulance, "Ah, Master, do you know better than I where the shoe pinches?"

Just then, to a mighty surge in the orchestra of the motive of the Magic of Midsummer eve (No. 37), Walther, in splendid knightly array, appears at the open inner door. Eva gives a cry, but does not move, her foot remaining on the stool all the while she gazes at him. Walther is also immobilised, spellbound at the unexpected sight of Eva. Sachs has his back to the door; he knows well the cause of Eva's cry, but he does not look round, pretending to be professionally intent on the shoe. He takes it off her foot, saying he will ease it on the last, and goes to the bench with it, still betraying no recognition of the new situation. Eva does not move. At work on the shoe, Sachs grumbles about the hardness of the cobbler's life, always at work, day in, day out, early and late. He has a plan in his mind, he tells her. No more cobbling for him; he will woo her today, hoping to have better luck as singer than as shoemaker. Had not she herself suggested this the previous day? "Well, well," he goes on, as she makes no reply, "I see what your answer is—'Stick to your shoes!' If only I could hear a song while I work! I heard a lovely one today; I wonder if there is a third verse to it?"

Walther, his gaze still riveted on Eva, breaks into the third section of the Dream Song, for which we, like Sachs, have long

been waiting. Metrically and melodically it is made on the pattern
of the two previous ones. The poetic content of it is the completion of the vision seen in his dream—the dancing stars had lighted
on the head of the Beloved, her eyes had become two suns of
beauty, and she had crowned his head with a wreath and filled the
poet's breast with the rapture of paradise.

52

"My child", Sachs had remarked to Eva after the first "Stollen",
"that is a Mastersong!" When it is over he returns with the shoe,
fits it on her foot, and plays once more with the literal and the
veiled meaning of it all: "Let's see if the shoe fits now. I think I've
managed it at last. Stand up and try it. Does it pinch you still?"
Eva bursts into passionate tears, falls on his breast, and clings
sobbing to him. Walther goes up to him and presses his hand, his
heart too full for words. Mastering himself, Sachs tears himself
away as if displeased—leaving Eva resting unconsciously on
Walther's shoulder,—and, as usual with him, finds relief in
homely, half-serious, half-humorous disparagement of his craft.
But here again there is something unexpressed at the back of his
words.[1] What a life is the cobbler's! he grumbles:

> *Were I not a poet too,*
> *henceforth I'd never touch a shoe!*

For a shoemaker is a drudge, a slave at everyone's beck and call,
abused by everyone for his bad workmanship. If he happens to be
a poet as well, he gets no peace: if he is a widower into the bargain,
everyone imagines he is a fool. The maidens would take him, for
better or for worse, when younger men are scarce; but in the end,

> *the smell of pitch they catch,*
> *and call him fool, rascal and wretch.*

For the first time we see right into the kind old heart, realise how

---

[1] His melody is that of his cobbling song in the second act (No. 42), but it
is accompanied in the horns by the melancholy motive (No. 43) of Sachs's
heart-ache. This latter, however, the piano scores cannot show.

profound is his love for Eva, how nobly and unselfishly he has worked for her happiness.

He ends by railing at David for not being there: the fellow thinks of nothing but his Lena and his stomach! And he makes as if to go in search of him, leaving the lovers to each other. But Eva falls into his arms, and, in a great cry that is one of the blinding emotional high lights of the opera, hails him, to his own motive of Resignation (No. 43), as the friend in need for whom she cannot find adequate words of thanks. The orchestra accompanies her with a theme curiously suggestive of *Tristan and Isolde*:

as she pours out her gratitude to him: he had wakened her, she says, when a child; he had watched over her as she grew to womanhood; and now he wakens her to a new free life; through him she is born anew. She deserves a scolding from him: had her choice been free it was he whom she would have chosen for husband: and No. 57 rises to new heights of expression as she says:

> But now my will is dead,
> no more I may rejoice;
> and if today I wed,
> I am bereft of choice;

that were to catch me in a net!
E'en you, my Master, would regret!

No. 57 becomes frankly a quotation from the opening of the
Tristan prelude as Sachs reassures her:

> *My child, of Tristan and Isolde*
> *the grievous tale I know;*
> *Hans Sachs was wise, and would not*
> *through King Marke's torments go.*
> *'Twas time to find the proper groom,*
> *or I at last had met my rightful doom.*

He turns from half-grave to wholly gay as Magdalena enters
through the shop door and David from the inner room, each of
them beflowered and beribboned for the festival; and the motive
of Eva's anxiety (No. 56) becomes all innocent joy as the cobbler
demands the attention of them all. To the strain of the chorale
from the church scene in the first act he summons them to a
christening. It is the custom of the Masters, he reminds them,
when a Mastersong is born, to give it a name by which it shall
always be known. Well, the young knight here has created a
Master-melody, to which he, Hans Sachs, and Eva Pogner are to
stand godfather and godmother, with David and Magdalena as
witnesses. But as by Nuremberg law no apprentice can be a
witness, and as David has sung creditably today, he makes the
boy a journeyman. The delighted David kneels down, and receives the accolade in the form of a smart box on the ear.

Sachs names the new song, in true Mastersinger fashion, "the
Morning Dream's Interpretation", and bids the young godmother say the appropriate thing about the infant. She does so by
launching the great quintet:

58

She sings of the joy this day has brought her, the day when her lover shall prove himself Master and win the highest prize. The more prosaic David and Magdalena are lost in astonishment that the former is an apprentice no longer, and they dream of a day when he too shall be a Master, with Lena as bride. Walther, to the melody of No. 52, sings of the felicity of the discovery that his Morning Dream has come true. Sachs, for his part, once more lets us see into the depths of his kind and philosophical old soul:

> To the maiden dear I'd fain
>   sing my song of sadness;
> but must hide my heart's sweet pain,
>   wear a mask of gladness.

For him the message of the Dream is clear:

> Love and youth that never dies
> bloom but through the poet's prize.

His one thought now is for the lovers whom he had saved from the consequences of their folly the night before and brought within sight of triumph and happiness.

The noble quintet finished, he turns abruptly to practical affairs. Eva he sends off to her father, Magdalena with her; and bidding David see that the shop is properly locked up he takes Walther away with him to the festival.

53

During the change of scene on the stage the orchestra develops the Nuremberg motive (No. 34) at some length. Horn and trumpet fanfares ring out from afar, and the motive of the Mastersingers (No. 4) blends with that of Midsummer day (No. 19). All Nuremberg, we feel, is *en fête*.

When the curtain rises again we see an open meadow outside the town. Across the stage winds the little Pegnitz river, which is bringing boat-loads of men, women and children to the festival, all in their holiday clothes. On one side of the stage is a raised platform with chairs and benches on it; it is decorated with the banners of the Guilds that have already arrived, and as the others come in their banners also are added to the number, so that finally they enclose the platform on three sides. In the foreground and at the sides of the stage the populace is lying about or making merry outside tents and drinking-booths. The prentices, arrayed in their best, adorned with flowers and favours and carrying slender be-ribboned staves, act as heralds and marshals for the procession that now appears; they conduct the members of each Guild in turn to the platform; there the respective banners are planted, after which the burghers and journeymen break up and make for the booths.

At the point when the curtain rises it is the shoemakers who are arriving, singing—to the accompaniment, of course, of the Cobbling motive (No. 31)—to their patron, St. Crispin, who taught the world how to be comfortably shod. The fanfares ring out again (this time on the stage): the town trumpeters and drummers, lute-makers, and journeymen with toy trumpets are all showing what they can do. The Tailors come in with their appropriate banner flying: they tell, with goat-like trills,[1] the heroic tale of how, when Nuremberg was once beleaguered and famine threatened, a tailor appeared sewn up in a goat-skin, who walked boldly out on the battlements with many a skip and caper and put the astonished enemy to flight: "who'd think a tailor could rise to such heights?" In the course of the narration Wagner slyly turns to his own purposes a passage in one of the most popular Italian opera arias of the day, the "Di tanti palpiti" from Rossini's *Tancredi*. The Tailors are followed by the Bakers, who sing the praises of bread as the dispeller of hunger; and these by the Cobblers, who are no less lyrical in praise of leather.

A gaily decorated boat brings to shore a number of young girls in rich peasant finery; the prentices, with a glad cry of "Maidens from Fürth!", run to help them to land, and all break into a rustic dance over a drone bass:

[1] There is a traditional German association of tailors with goats.

the prentices contending with the journeymen for the girls.
David, conscious of the dignity of his new standing as journeyman, views it all with disapproval: let them look out if the Masters
catch them! he says. But in the end he too seizes a pretty girl and
joins the dance; he breaks away from her in fright for a moment
when the prentices tell him that his Lena is coming, but sees that
he has been fooled and throws himself into the dance again more
ardently than ever.

It comes to a sudden end with a cry of "The Mastersingers!"
from the journeymen on the bank who have been looking towards
the town. The apprentices and the folk prepare to receive the
Masters, who come in, in solemn procession, to the dignified
music of the opening of the prelude to the first act: at the sight of
Kothner, who carries the banner on which King David is depicted with his harp, the people cheer and wave their hats.
Pogner leads Eva by the hand: richly dressed, and accompanied
by Magdalena and a bevy of maidens, she is shown to the place of
honour. When the muster on the benches is complete the fanfare
rings out once more, and the prentices come forward ceremoniously and call "Silentium! Not a word! Be ye all as dumb!" Sachs
rises in his place. All raise their hats and caps and press forward,
pointing to him; and with a general cry of "Begin!" the whole
assembly thunders out the song to the words of which the historical Sachs had hailed Luther and the Reformation:

> *Awake! full soon will dawn the day!*
> *I hear within the coppice gray*
> *a rapture-laden nightingale,*
> *his song resounds o'er hill and dale:*
> *the night expires in western skies,*
> *the new day in the east doth rise,*
> *the red dawn floods the fields with light,*
> *and puts the gloomy clouds to flight.*

At the conclusion of the mighty chorus the people, to the music always associated with the Masters, break into jubilant praise of "Nuremberg's darling Sachs".[1]

[1] Sachs's poem falls, after the manner of its epoch, into a regular succession of iambics:

> *Wacht auf, es nahet gen dem Tag,*
>
> *ich hör' singen im grünen Hag, etc.*

Wagner, of course, could not confront the modern ear with what it would regard as a misaccentuation of the second syllable of "singen"; so, as the reader will perceive from the above musical quotation, he shapes his soprano part in such a way as to ensure that the first syllable of the word gets a stronger accent than the second. But in the inner parts he is less careful, and one jibs at the stressing of "-gen" at the expense of the "sin-" in these: the tenor part, for instance, is phrased thus:

No. 61

The critical Sachs of the opera would have given Beckmesser's shoe several reproving hammer-strokes for false accents of this kind.

54

One man alone in the joyous company has care in his heart. The torrent of sound dies away suddenly to a pianissimo as the strings alone give out the motive of Resignation (No. 43). Immobile, sunk in thought, Sachs's gaze all the while has been over the heads of the crowd. Now he turns to them with a kindly glance. Beginning in a voice tremulous with emotion, but growing firmer as he proceeds, he thanks them for the honour their love has prompted them to do him. To the accompaniment of the motive of Benevolence (No. 30), which had originally been heard in the first act, at the point where Sachs pleaded with the Masters for Walther, and had figured again in the colloquy between him and the knight in the earlier part of the third act, he tells them that today he is to be their spokesman. They prize the art of song indeed, he says, and one among them, "a Master rich and high-souled", today shows such love for it that he offers daughter, land and treasure as prize in the coming contest. Let all who wish to try for it be noble and pure of heart, for never has so great a prize been known before, in ancient times or modern. Pogner, deeply moved, presses his hand and thanks him: his old cobbler friend alone knows what a load had been lying on his heart of late.

Then Sachs turns to the Herr Marker, who, all this while, in an agony of apprehension, has been taking the poem from his pocket, furtively trying to memorise it, and wiping the sweat from his brow: do what he will he cannot fix the difficult thing in his mind. "Well, my friend, you're not committed to it", Sachs tells him. "Too late!" replies poor Beckmesser: "my own came smash, thanks to you." Blaming the cobbler for all his troubles, he still entreats his help. He is confident he can beat all comers if only Sachs does not compete. But this new song! No one will understand it; so will Sachs use his popularity with the crowd and tip the beam in his favour?

55

Kothner, coming forward, proclaims the session open: bachelors first, and the older before the younger; so let Herr Beckmesser begin. The prentices, to the accompaniment of their impudent No. 8, conduct the singer to a small mound of turf they have beaten up in front of the platform and covered with flowers. Beckmesser, after many a stumble, manages to scramble to the top of it, the people all the while commenting unkindly on his awkwardness: this, surely, is not the man for the maiden; he may be an ornament to the Town Council, but as wooer he is a comic loon! Once more the prentices call out "Silentium!", and Kothner launches the official "Now begin!" Beckmesser, who has managed at last to find a firm footing on the mound, bows clumsily first to the Masters, then, with a leer that is meant to be ingratiating, at Eva, who averts her eyes from the grotesque spectacle. He tries to collect his thoughts with a prelude on his lute, but the orchestra replies with an ominous thumb-nail sketch of himself as the one-time all-powerful Marker (No. 24).

At last he begins to attempt to sing the song he had so rashly accepted from Sachs. It is an even more ludicrous performance than his serenade in the second act: the knight's poetry becomes utter balderdash in his mouth, though he takes a furtive peep at the manuscript every now and then; for the melody he falls back on tags from his earlier song. The Masters and the folk can hardly believe their ears: has the man gone out of his mind? they ask each other as they repeat some of the more absurd of his lines. He breaks into a cold perspiration, mops his brow, and has another try; but after his first "Abgesang" the crowd burst into loud laughter.

He gives up. Leaving the mound he goes up to Sachs in a fury:

> *Accursed cobbler, this is your snare!*
> *The song is not my own, I swear:*
> *'twas Sachs, to whom you bow the knee,*
> *your precious Sachs, who gave it me.*
> *Has he not shamed me quite enough,*
> *but must palm on me his wretched stuff?*

and he rushes out madly and is lost in the crowd.

Kothner and the others call on Sachs to explain how Beckmesser's song can possibly be his: "a scandal!" says Konrad Nachtigall reprovingly; "an extraordinary thing!" opine Hermann

Ortel and Hans Foltz. Sachs, who has quietly picked up the manuscript Beckmesser has hurled at him before leaving, assures them that the song is not by him; *his* modest muse could never rise to such heights. Let Herr Beckmesser tell them, if he cares to do so, how he came into possession of it. The others are astounded at this assurance that the song is a good one. Sachs explains that it merely wants singing properly, with the right words and the right melody; and he calls on a witness to prove his point, if there be one present who is prepared to do so.

56

Walther steps forward and salutes the Masters and the folk with knightly courtesy; all look at him in silence, but sympathetically.

> *Bear witness this song is not by me;*
> *and sing it so that all may see*
> *my praise of the song*
> *was not a whit too strong,*

Sachs tells him. Walther ascends the mound with firm steps, and Sachs hands the manuscript to Kothner for him and the other Masters to follow from. The knight now converts the Morning Dream song into the Prize Song: the meaning and the shape of it are essentially the same, but after the sixth line it takes a new turn both verbally and musically.

Wagner's original intention had been that the Prize Song should be simply a repetition of its predecessor. His sense of the theatre made it clear to him later that this would result in monotony, if not in actual anticlimax; yet the situation demanded that what is now sung shall correspond literally with what is on the paper, so that the Masters can see for themselves that Sachs was speaking the truth when he said that the words and the melody were alike good, with the present singer as the only possible author of them. A letter from Cosima to King Ludwig in the early part of 1867 shows how Wagner tackled and solved this problem. He had "lately come to the conclusion", Cosima wrote, "that it was absolutely impossible to have the same poem sung twice in the same act. It must be the same yet different, clear and concentrated; moreover, it would have gone against the grain with Walther to repeat before the Masters and the folk the intimate happenings in Sachs's room. This difficult problem, which has kept him uncommonly busy during the last few days, has in my opinion been solved with wonderful success . . . ." The discovery by the Masters that the song is *not* the one on the paper is now side-stepped in the simplest way imaginable. When Walther has reached the sixth line, Kothner, overcome by emotion at the beauty of the song, involuntarily lets the manuscript fall from his hand. No one picks it up; all are too intent on the song and the singer for that. Walther, according to the stage directions, perceives this, and now boldly goes on to re-shape his lay as the inspiration of the moment dictates. The effective little point is almost invariably missed in the theatre because the eyes of the audience are naturally fixed on the tenor: the spectator who does not know all that is involved does not see Kothner let the manuscript fall, or, if he does so, does not grasp the meaning and the implications of it all.[1]

Now and then Masters and people interject a naïve admiring comment on the song:

> *Ah yes! I see it improves a song*
> *to sing it right instead of wrong;*
>
> .　　.　　.　　.　　.　　.　　.
>
> *'Tis strange and daring, that is true;*
> *but rhymed quite well, and vocal too!*

and so on. At the conclusion of it the people unanimously award Walther the prize, and the Masters confirm their judgment: Pogner turns to Sachs with a warm word of thanks for having lifted a load from his heart.

---

[1] In the original edition of the orchestral score the stage directions are merely "at this point Kothner, who has been following from the manuscript with the other Masters, involuntarily lets it drop; he and the others now merely listen, absorbed, to the remainder of the song", and that is how the direction appears also in the earlier piano scores and translations. A succeeding sentence—"Walther perceives this, and, without betraying that he has done so, now continues in freer style" (i.e. with changes in words and melody)—was added by Wagner in a later imprint of the poem.

57

The knight is led to the steps of the platform, where he falls on one knee before Eva, who crowns him with a wreath of laurel and myrtle; then both of them kneel before Pogner, who gives them his blessing. Sachs turns in triumph to the assembly: "Was I not right? Was not my witness well chosen?" The Masters call on Pogner, as the senior of the Guild, to confer Masterhood on the young man; the goldsmith holds out to him the gold chain with three large medals on it, and dubs him Master in the name of King David. But Walther turns away impetuously. He does not want their Masterhood; the only reward he values is one that Eva alone can bestow. In perplexity and embarrassment everyone looks towards Sachs, who advances to Walther, takes him meaningly by the hand, and, to the accompaniment of the various motives associated with the Guild, reads him a little lecture. Let him not disdain the Masters, but honour their art. It is not lineage, wealth, weapons that have served him so well but his art. The Masters have tended their own art lovingly and well, and have kept it noble and German in soul through difficult days. An evil day may dawn, when Germans shall be no more one: then,

> *if foreign kings should rule our land,*
> *no prince his folk will understand,*
> *and foreign mists before us rise*
> *to dupe and blind our German eyes;*
> *the good and true were lost for aye*
> *if German art we should betray.*
> *So heed my words:*
> *honour your German Masters,*
> *if you'd forefend disasters!*
> *Let us but take them to our heart,*
> *though should depart*
> *the might of holy Rome,*
> *no harm will come*
> *to holy German art!*

The whole assembly repeats the final words in chorus. Eva takes the wreath from Walther's brow and places it on Sachs's, who takes the chain from Pogner's hand and hangs it on the knight's neck. In a final tableau Walther and Eva stand one on each side of Sachs, before whom Pogner bows the knee in homage, while all the other Masters hail him as their chief; the people wave hats and kerchiefs, and the prentices dance and clap their hands, to a general cry of "Hail! Sachs! Nuremberg's darling Sachs!"

In the First Sketch (1845) Sachs had merely admonished Walther to honour the Masters and their art; the lines "Though should depart the might of holy Rome" etc. were added in 1861, at a time when the long-suppressed impulse towards German unity was moving at last towards realisation.

It is interesting to learn, from a letter of Cosima's of January 1867 to King Ludwig, that when Wagner was completing his score he planned to end the opera with the Prize Song and its jubilant reception by the assembly: "Sachs's big address, he contended, was not really part and parcel of the matter, but rather a speech of the poet to the people"; so he proposed to omit it. But Cosima protested vehemently against this; and Wagner, she says, "thought it over, though naturally he remained of his own way of thinking." In the end he gave way to her, and worked out the "address" in full between two and three o'clock of the morning of January 28th, after Cosima "had been talking to him the whole day about the conclusion of the work". Perhaps, on the whole, Wagner would have been wiser to have "remained of his own way of thinking about it".

THE NIBELUNG'S RING

It is only within the last few years that it has become possible to trace the evolution of the stupendous *Ring* drama in complete detail, thanks to the publication of several important documents for the first time. Wagner's scenarios, prose sketches, drafts of the poems and fair copies extend over a number of years and occupy in all more than 750 pages of closely-written manuscript.

His studies in the 1840's of the Teutonic and Norse mythologies and sagas having supplied him with an immense amount of possible material, his first task was to reduce it to a manageable bulk and give it some sort of dramatic coherence. This he did in a detailed Prose Sketch which he entitled *The Nibelungen Myth as Scheme for a Drama;* it bears the end-date of the 4th October 1848. The ground plan of this is virtually that of the complete *Ring* as we now know it, from the *Rhinegold* to the *Twilight of the Gods*, though several of the details were modified or completely changed later. A knowledge of all his Sketches, by the way, is essential to our understanding of the tetralogy, as they often reveal something that was at the back of his mind when shaping the drama but could not be transferred to the stage.

The opening sentences of the Sketch of 1848 run thus: "Out of the womb of Night and Death there came into being a race dwelling in Nibelheim (Nebelheim),[1] i.e. in gloomy subterranean clefts and caverns. They are known as the Nibelungs: feverishly, unrestingly they burrow through the bowels of the earth like worms in a dead body: they anneal and smelt and smith hard metals." One of these Nibelungs, Alberich, the Sketch continues, having possessed himself of the "pure and noble Rhine-gold", and being of an intelligence superior to that of his fellows, fashioned from the Gold a Ring which gave him mastery over them all. They became his slaves, compelled to labour unremittingly to amass for him the immense Nibelung Hoard. His brother Reigin (Mime,

---

[1] "Nebelheim" means literally Home or Place of Mist, Fog, Obscurity, and the like.

Eugel) he forces to make for him a Tarnhelm that enables him to assume any shape or be invisible at will. And so, by means of wealth and might and magic, Alberich sets himself to establish his dominion over the world and all it contains. It will be observed that at this stage there is no mention of the later important motive of Alberich having won the Gold and the power to make the Ring by forswearing love.

In the present *Rhinegold*, as the reader will know, the final cosmic catastrophe has its distant roots in Wotan's desire for world mastery. To secure his power against possible insurgents he needs an impregnable fortress: this he persuades two Giants, Fasolt and Fafner, to build for him, promising them in payment Freia, the goddess of youth—a promise which, as he admits later, he hoped he would not be called upon to make good. When the Giants demand their wage he turns to Loge, the crafty god of fire, for help out of his difficulty. Loge tells him of the Hoard amassed by Alberich, and the Giants agree to accept this in lieu of Freia. Wotan, by superior guile, obtains the Hoard, the Ring and the Tarnhelm from Alberich, who lays the curse of death upon everyone into whose possession the Ring shall come. The two Giants, moved by greed of possessions, accept, in place of Freia, the Hoard and all that goes with it. At once the curse operates: Fafner slays his brother, and then changes himself into a huge Dragon so that he may sleep upon and guard the Hoard.

All this had been conceived in quite another fashion in Wagner's First Sketch. There it is *the whole race* of the Giants, rivals of the Nibelungs, who, troubled at the sight of Alberich's growing power and foreseeing their subjugation by him, yet lacking the intelligence to cope with the menace themselves, turn for help to the Gods, a race already "waxing to supremacy", anxious to govern the world in orderly fashion, but feeling themselves impotent against the dreaded crafty Nibelung. The Gods, *en masse*, contract with the Giants—not simply with two of them but with the whole race—for the building of a fortress from which they can govern the world in security; and when it is finished the Giants demand the Hoard as payment. Thus in the original Sketch both the Gods and the Giants already know of the Hoard, whereas in the present *Rhinegold* neither have the Gods any

knowledge of it and of the events that led up to Alberich's acquisition of it until Loge tells them the story,[1] nor do the Giants
know anything of it until they too hear the tale and realise the
danger they will be in if the Hoard remains in the hands of their
terrible Nibelung foe.

2

In the First Sketch of 1848, Wotan, having trapped Alberich
by craft and gained possession of the Hoard and the Ring,[2] is
willing enough to let the dull-witted Giants have it if only he can
keep the Ring, in which, as he knows, is incarnated the power of
which Alberich has been stripped: this power Wotan intends
shall henceforth be his. But the Giants insist on having the Ring
as well as the Hoard, for they too know its immense virtue; and
counselled by the three Norns (Fates), who "warn him of the
downfall of the Gods themselves", Wotan yields it to them.
Alberich, before giving up the Ring, had laid the curse of ruin
upon every future possessor of it. But the Giants are too sluggish
and stupid to make any use of the power inherent in it: it is sufficient for them that there is an end now to the danger of their
falling into servitude to Alberich. They place the whole treasure
in a cave in the Gnitaheide (Neidheide),[3] where they leave it in the
guard of a monstrous Dragon. (There is no hint, as yet, that this
Dragon is one of themselves transformed). Their end—security
for themselves—being thus achieved, the Giants relapse into
torpid impotence, while the race of the Gods rises to a new lustre.
They use their now unchallenged power to bestow order on the
world; they "bind the elements by wise laws and devote themselves to the careful nurture of the human race."

[1] It is true that in the opera, after Loge's account of the rape of the Gold,
Wotan says, "I have heard rumours of the Rhine-gold: runes of riches are
hidden in its golden glow: a Ring would confer power and treasure". But the
ascription to him of even this much knowledge is superfluous, and, indeed,
meaningless: the little speech could be omitted without making any difference
to the action. It seems to have occurred to Wagner only at the last moment,
when he was writing the poem; there is no suggestion of it in either of his
two Sketches for the *Rhinegold*.

[2] Loge does not figure in the Sketch.

[3] The Heath (or Wood) of Envy (or Grudge).

Yet their power, with all the moral benefit to the world that may flow from that power, is morally flawed at the very core. The peace they had given the world had been achieved not by reconciliation but by force and guile. "The purpose of their higher world-order," says the Sketch, "is moral consciousness; but the wrong against which they fight attaches to themselves. From the depths of Nibelheim [where the Nibelungs still groan in bondage, labouring not for themselves but for others] the sense of their own guilt surges up in complaint against them. For the bondage of the Nibelungs is not annulled: merely the lordship has been wrenched from Alberich, and that not for any higher end—the soul, the freedom of the Nibelungs lies buried uselessly under the belly of a sluggish Dragon. Consequently there is justice in Alberich's grievance against the Gods." Yet the latter cannot seize the Hoard and the Ring a second time, in order to render them harmless to the world, without committing yet another wrong. The beneficent deed of liberation can be wrought only by a free Will independent of them. They see in Man a faculty for such a Will; so they strive to implant their own divinity in him and raise him to such a moral height that by his free Will he may win strength enough, independently of the Gods, to cancel out their own prime guilt, even if this means, in the end, their own annulment, in that they will no longer work directly upon the world, being supplanted by the free human consciousness. So they set themselves to bring into being, in the process of time, the human hero who shall redeem them from their primal guilt and fulfil the high moral purpose upon which they have been bent from the beginning.

3

In the present *Ring* it is Wotan who, in pursuit of this aim, takes on human form, contracts a human marriage, and begets Siegmund and his sister Sieglinde, who in the end find each other, recognise in each other the same father, mate in defiance of law, and produce the redeeming hero desired by the God, Siegfried. But Wagner's original plan had run on somewhat different lines. According to the Sketch of 1848, "vigorous human races, fruited by the divine seed, already flourish. In strife and battle they steel their strength; Wotan's Wish-Maidens carry those of them who are slain in fight to Walhall, where the heroes re-live a glorious life of jousts in Wotan's company." It is long, however, before the favoured race of Volsungs produces the hero longed for by the Gods. At last "a barren Volsung union is fertilised by Wotan by means of one of Holda's apples which he gives the spouses to eat; and from this marriage spring the twins Siegmund and Sieglinde (brother and sister). Siegmund takes a wife, Sieglinde weds a man (Hunding). But both unions prove sterile, and to beget a genuine Volsung the brother and sister wed each other. Hunding, Sieglinde's husband, learns of this misdeed, casts off his wife, and assails Siegmund. The Valkyrie Brynhilde shields Siegmund, defying the command of Wotan, who has decreed that he shall fall in expiation of his offence", etc. In this first draft, then, Wotan is not, as in the opera, himself the parent of the two fated Volsungs.

From this point onward the Sketch proceeds, in the main, along the lines of the present *Valkyrie*, *Siegfried* and *Twilight of the Gods*. The final solution of the central moral problem, however, was not the same in 1848 as the one we now know. In the closing scene of the present tetralogy Brynhilde, before hurling the burning brand into Siegfried's funeral pyre, bids the ravens command Loge to "hasten to Walhall, *for the Gods' end dawneth at last*." But in the First Sketch what Brynhilde says is this: "Hear then, ye mighty Gods; your wrong-doing is annulled; thank him, the hero who took your guilt upon him. Into my hands he entrusted the completion of his work: loosed be the thraldom of the Nibelungs, the Ring shall bind them no more. But not Alberich shall receive it; no longer shall he enslave you [i.e. the Nibelungs], but he himself shall be free as you. For to you, wise sisters of the water-deeps, I deliver this Ring. The fire that burns me, let it cleanse the evil trinket; do ye melt and keep harmless the Rhine-gold that once was ravished from you, for the forging of servitude and ill-hap. One only shall rule, All-Father, Glorious One, Thou [Wotan]. This man [Siegfried] I bring to you as pledge of thy eternal might: good welcome give him, as is his desert!"

As will be seen, Wagner had rounded off his first plan for the drama in logical accordance with its opening premises. Both Alberich and the Nibelungs whom he had enslaved are to be set free, for the Ring by which so much evil was wrought has been restored to the primal innocence of the pure waters. The Gods too are free henceforth to rule the world and lead it upward in growth of moral consciousness—which had been their desire and their purpose from the beginning. Wagner's thought was to go through many metamorphoses before the ending of his drama took the form familiar to us today.

4

One or two other differences between the earliest and the final scheme may be noted here. In the former, Siegfried's first act after he has forged the sword is to avenge on Hunding the death of his father. The Rhinedaughters who accost him during the Gibichung hunt are in the First Sketch mermaids with swans' wings. Nothing is said in the Sketch about Alberich having forsworn love in order to possess himself of the Gold. In the final episode the light from the burning pyre shows Brynhilde, once more the armed Valkyrie on her horse, leading Siegfried by the hand to Wotan, to join the other heroes who guard the Gods; whereas in the *Twilight of the Gods* we see no more of Siegfried and Brynhilde after the blazing up of the fire, which gradually engulfs not only the hall of the Gibichungs but Walhall itself and the Gods and heroes in it.

This, then, was the vast dramatic scheme as it first formed itself in the imagination of the thirty-five-year-old Wagner. Obviously in its huge entirety it could not be condensed into an opera for a single evening, which was all he contemplated at that time. But considerably more than half of the Sketch is taken up by the events that followed the introduction of the race of the Gibichungs into the story; and it is evident from the close detail in which Wagner has worked out this section that even while he was outlining the cosmic story as a whole the final part of it was taking definite shape in his mind as a self-sufficing dramatic action. The ground covered by this section is, indeed, that of the present *Twilight of the Gods* from the moment when the curtain rises on the scene between Gunther, Hagen and Gutrune to the end of the opera. For some reason or other Wagner made a fair copy of his First Sketch between the 4th and the 8th October 1848, and then addressed himself to drafting in prose a scenario, which he completed on the 20th, of the opera he now had it definitely in his mind to write. It was to be in three acts and to bear the title of *Siegfried's Death*. This scenario, which runs to seventeen large pages of print, was published for the first time in 1930.

5

As the spectator of the projected opera would necessarily have to be made acquainted with a great deal that had happened before the action opened in the hall of the Gibichungs, this would have to be conveyed to him at one point or another by means of narrative. Thus in the opening scene of the new Sketch Alberich's son Hagen, very much as in the *Twilight of the Gods*, tells Gunther and Gutrune the story of the Hoard and the power inherent in it, of the slaying of the Dragon by Siegfried, and of the Valkyrie Brynhilde on the fire-girt rock. In the later episode of Hagen's Watch by the Rhine, Alberich tells his son of the Nibelungs and their work in the bowels of the earth, of his own achievement of power by the seizure of the Gold and the forging of the Ring, of his compelling his brother Mime to fashion the Tarnhelm for him, of his amassing of the Hoard, of the fear that then took possession of the Giants, of their compact with the Gods, of his own overthrow by craft, of the God's bestowal of the Ring and the Hoard on the Giants at the bidding and the warning of the Norns, of the guarding of Hoard and Ring by a Dragon, and of Siegfried's slaying of the Dragon and of Mime. Much of this, though not all, has been carried over into the corresponding scenes of the *Twilight of the Gods*. In addition, Siegfried, during the hunting scene, tells the story in the Sketch, as he does more or less in the opera, of his upbringing by Mime, of his own forging of the fragments of his father's shattered sword, of his combat with the Dragon and his slaying of Mime, of his taking the Ring and the Tarnhelm from the cave, leaving the rest of the Hoard there, of his journey to Brynhilde's rock and his conquest of the fire, and of his winning of the Valkyrie maid.

This necessity for elucidating certain parts of the stage drama by means of narrative beset Wagner all through the many phases of the construction of the *Ring*. For the most part the dovetailing of action and narrative is skilfully done: Hagen's tale to Gunther and Gutrune, for instance, not merely instructs the spectator but serves to launch the plan for wedding Gutrune to Siegfried and Gunther to Brynhilde, and so brings the hero within the orbit of Hagen, where his ruin is to be slowly accomplished; and in the same way Siegfried's telling of the tale of his own life to the Gibichungs during the hunt, reaching its climax as it does in the revelation that it was he, not Gunther, who had wakened and wedded Brynhilde, who is now Gunther's bride, not merely enlightens the spectator of *Siegfried's Death* as to all this but furnishes the immediate pretext for Hagen's swift slaying of him. At the same time this procedure on Wagner's part, involving as it did much harking back to earlier aspects of his plan, landed him now and then in trifling difficulties of which he does not seem to have been sufficiently aware at the time. Thus in the Prose Sketch of 1848 for *Siegfried's Death* he had made Hagen tell Gunther and Gutrune, in the opening scene, that Siegfried's seizure of the Hoard has made the Nibelungs subject to him. This was carried over in due course not only into the poem of *Siegfried's Death* but into the much later *Twilight of the Gods,* as thus:

Gunther: This Hoard have I often heard of: it holds a treasure most rare?

Hagen: The man who its might can wield, the lord of the world will he be.

Gunther: And Siegfried won it in fight?

Hagen: Slaves are the Nibelungs to him;

which naturally moves us to comment that while, in general terms, possession of the Hoard and the Ring may be said to give Siegfried power over the world—as the Wood Bird had told him would be the case after he had slain Fafner—there has never been the smallest hint in the drama of the Nibelungs having become his slaves, or, indeed, of his having any interest in them. As our investigation proceeds we shall come upon other instances in which Wagner has unwittingly carried over into his final plan some earlier motive that now either shows itself as a loose end or is at variance with its context.

6

The Prose Sketch for *Siegfried's Death* still embodies certain features of the original "Sketch for a Nibelungen Drama" that were to disappear from the plan later. Siegfried's sword is still called Balmung instead of Nothung; and other names retain their original spelling. It is once more intended that Siegfried's first deed after making the sword shall be to kill Hunding. Siegfried's colloquy in the forest is with the Wood Birds in the plural, not with a single bird as in the present *Siegfried*. In the scene—corresponding superficially to that in the first act of the *Twilight of the Gods* in which Waltraute comes to Brynhilde's rock to beg her to give up the Ring—it is Brynhilde's eight former fellow-Valkyries who appear. They have come to ask her the meaning of the dying down of the fire that had so long encircled her rock; and Brynhilde seizes the opportunity to tell them—and through them the audience—the story of her punishment for having shielded Siegmund against Wotan's will and of Siegfried's conquest of the flames and his awakening of her. All this narration had become unnecessary by the time Wagner had arrived at the *Twilight of the Gods*, for it had been fully set forth before the spectator in the *Valkyrie* and *Siegfried*. And in the *Twilight of the Gods*, of course, the meeting with Waltraute has quite another significance than the scene with the eight Valkyries in the Sketch had had. In the latter they are concerned simply with the fate of their erring sister: in the *Twilight of the Gods* Waltraute has come to implore Brynhilde to give back the Ring to the Rhine Daughters and so avert the doom with which the Gods are threatened. In 1848 the present ending of the tetralogy had not occurred to Wagner: *Siegfried's Death* was to end, like the Sketch, with the complete establishment of the Gods' power for good through the redeeming deed of Siegfried.

7

It was on the basis of the scenario of the 20th October 1848 that Wagner went on to write the poem of *Siegfried's Death*. That poem has long been accessible in the Collected Edition of his prose and poetical works, where for some time it confronted researchers with a small puzzle. In his autobiography (published in 1911) Wagner told the world that when he read the poem in 1848 to the actor Eduard Devrient, who was at that time the producer at the Dresden theatre, the latter pointed out to him a little defect in it from the point of view of practical theatrics. Some knowledge on the spectators' part of the earlier relations of Siegfried and Brynhilde would surely be necessary, he said, if they were to grasp the full tragic significance of the conflict that arises between the pair in the middle of the opera. Wagner recognised the justice of this observation. "I had in fact", he says in *My Life*, "begun the poem of *Siegfried's Death* simply with the scenes that now constitute the first act of the *Twilight of the Gods*, merely explaining to the spectator, in a lyric-epical dialogue between the hero's wife in her solitude and the other Valkyries flying past her rock, all that elucidated the early relationship of Siegfried and Brynhilde. To my joy, Devrient's hint on this point at once turned my thought in the direction of the scenes which I worked out later in the prelude to the drama."[1]

Until lately it was difficult to make sense of this, for every reader of the poem of *Siegfried's Death* knew that it commenced *not* with the scene in the hall of the Gibichungs but with the Norns Scene, which is followed by that between Brynhilde and Siegfried. The mystery was only cleared up when, in 1930, the Prose Sketch for *Siegfried's Death* was published for the first time. It then became evident that Wagner's memory was at fault when he described, in *My Life*, that talk of his with Devrient in

---

[1] The reader should always bear in mind that for Wagner the "first act" of the *Twilight of the Gods* begins with the scene in the Gibichung hall; he invariably referred to the long prologue to this—the Norns scene and the scene between Siegfried and Brynhilde—as the "prelude". Unless he is forewarned the reader will be apt to take this latter term in its usual operatic sense of an orchestral prelude or overture. There is nothing of that kind in the *Twilight of the Gods*.

October 1848. It was not the *poem* which he had read to Devrient on that occasion; it was the Prose Sketch, which does begin with the scene between Gunther, Hagen and Gutrune. Perceiving that Devrient was right, he at once drew up a supplementary prose plan for a "prelude", as he entitled it—i.e. a Norns Scene and a Siegfried-Brynhilde scene which between them correspond broadly to the present "prelude" to the *Twilight of the Gods*.

8

This supplementary Sketch was also published for the first time in 1930. It is based, of course, on the first Sketch for the whole drama as originally projected: the Norns prophesy that when the Gold is returned to the Rhine the Nibelungs, Alberich among them, shall be "free"; it is the "Giants" in general who build Walhall for Wotan and receive the Ring in payment; these Giants then beget a Dragon to guard the Ring. The scene that follows between Siegfried and Brynhilde runs on the same general lines as the corresponding later one in the *Twilight of the Gods:* the Valkyrie sends the hero out into the world to win glory, and as the curtain falls his horn is heard sounding merrily as he recedes into the distance. The horn melody, the draft concludes, is to be "taken up by the orchestra and developed in a spirited movement", precisely as it is in the now familiar "Siegfried's Rhine Journey".

The next stage in the evolution of the drama was the casting of the scenario and the supplementary Sketch for the "prelude" into verse. This task occupied Wagner from the 12th to the 28th November 1848. He gave his poem the title of *"Siegfried's Death, a grand heroic opera in three acts"*. In December he made a fair copy of his manuscript, leaving the text virtually as it was, but making some modifications in the stage directions.

In the following January he worked over the poem once again.[1] He made no changes in the third act, but the first now

[1] One reason why until recently there were so many gaps in our knowledge of all the stages traversed by the *Ring* is the fact that the various manuscripts are scattered about in private and public possession. That of the first "Sketch for a Drama" is now at Wahnfried. The first manuscript of the poem of

received the form familiar to us in the *Twilight of the Gods*. In the second act several changes were made: these will be pointed out in our later analysis of the opera. The result of all this recasting was that a third fair copy became necessary. This, which of course represents the *second* actual version of the drama, was made in January or February 1849; and now the "grand heroic" in the title becomes simply "heroic". It is evident that Wagner was now coming up against a difficulty that was to plague him for a long time yet—that of the ending of the work and the summing-up of the moral purport of it in Brynhilde's final words; for on the last page of the beautifully written third copy he made later some significant changes in the text of this episode. The stages by which the close of the vast drama gradually received its present form will be set forth in detail later in our enquiry.

9

In May 1849 Wagner, having become involved in the revolutionary movement in Dresden, had to fly to Switzerland. In the following May he planned to publish the poem of *Siegfried's Death*, and for this purpose he made a fourth fair copy and added a Foreword. At that time he shared the passion of some "reformers" of the period for using the Latin instead of the German script, and for spelling substantives (other than proper names) with a small initial letter instead of the capital customary in Germany. The Leipzig publisher to whom he offered the libretto assured him that if he insisted on these whimsies he would not sell a single copy. The plan for publication therefore came to nothing.

Siegfried's Death is the property of Siegmund von Hausegger, of Munich; the copy made by Wagner in December 1848 is in the Winterthur (Switzerland) Town Library. This manuscript was drastically revised by Wagner at some later date, and a fair copy of the revision was then made by Nietzsche: it was from Nietzsche's copy (now in Bayreuth) that the poem of *Siegfried's Death* was printed by Wagner in 1871 in the second volume of his Collected Works. All the later editions, of course, follow that imprint; consequently the poem of *Siegfried's Death* which is so well known to all Wagner students represents not the first but a revised version.

Wagner's *third* fair copy of the poem—a model of calligraphy—is in the possession of Herr Eduard Sulzer of Zürich. A *fourth* copy, made in 1850, is at Wahnfried.

In the late November and early December of 1852 he worked over his latest manuscript afresh, giving it its final form, in which it corresponds in general to the present *Twilight of the Gods*.

Meanwhile, between 1849 and the summer of 1851, he had written a number of prose works, the chief of them being *Art and Revolution*, *The Art-Work of the Future*, *Opera and Drama*, and *A Communication to My Friends*. The basic purpose of these was to clarify his own mind with regard to the tremendous new artistic impulses, affecting the whole problem of modern opera, of which he was inwardly conscious. His artistic intuitions were driving him irresistibly towards a new type of music drama, but he was not yet quite sure how this could be realised in practice. When he had read his Nibelung poem in 1848 to his friends in Dresden some even of the best-disposed among them shook their heads doubtfully over it. While he himself knew well, as he hinted in a letter of November 1850 to Liszt, that *Siegfried's Death* would have to be *musically* something entirely different from *Lohengrin*, his friends could as a matter of course conceive the musical structure of the new work only in terms of "opera" past and present; and within the traditional framework of that genre *Siegfried's Death* obviously would not fit. It had no set "forms", no sharply differentiated self-contained "numbers"—solos, duets, choruses, and so forth. The lines were curt, rhymeless, often irregular in length, seemingly unrhythmical and formless because of the total absence of the *carrure* of the ordinary poetic line and stanza. A single illustration will make this clear. The poem of *Lohengrin* is cast in square-cut rhyming line-lengths of which the opening of "Lohengrin's Narration" may serve as an example:

> *In fernem Land, unnahbar euren Schritten,*
> *liegt eine Burg, die Monsalvat genannt;*
> *ein lichter Tempel stehet dort in Mitten,*
> *so kostbar, wie auf Erden nichts bekannt:*
> *drinn ein Gefäss von wunderthät'gem Segen*
> *wird dort als höchstes Heiligthum bewacht,*
> *es ward, dass sein der Menschen reinste pflegen,*
> *herab von einer Engelschaar gebracht:*

etc. This was poetry in the accepted sense of the term, in lines of regular feet and rhymes. *Siegfried's Death*, however, discarded, in general, the ordinary end-rhymes in favour of the *Stabreim*— answering assonances of the first consonants or vowels of words or syllables, as in the following example, where the assonances are picked out for our present purpose in italics:

> Was du mir *n*ahmst, *n*ütztest du *n*icht,—
> deinem muthigen *T*rotz ver*t*rautest du nur!
> Nun du, ge*f*riedet, *f*rei es mir gabst,
> *k*ehrt mir mein *W*issen *w*ieder,
> er*k*enn' ich des *R*inges *R*unen;

etc. Stabreim was a very ancient device in German and English poetry. It is found in the former as early as the ninth century, and in the latter there is a fine old poem, known as *The Harmonious Blacksmiths*, dating from the fourteenth century, that has quite a Wagnerian ring in its hammering assonances:

> *Swarte smekyd smethes smateryd wyth smoke*
> *Dryve me to deth wyth den of here* [*their*] *dyntes,*
>
> . . . .
>
> *Thei spyttyn and spraulyn and spellyn many spelles,*

and so on. Wagner's instinct in 1848 was perfectly sound. His young Siegfried, the symbol of a new and ardent life, could not possibly express himself in regularly shaped verse such as that of *Lohengrin*; a mode of speech would have to be found for him as forthright as himself.

Moreover, Wagner's Dresden friends were puzzled by the curt give-and-take of passages of this type:

Gutrune:	*Hielt Brünnhild dich für Gunther?*
Siegfried:	*Ihm glich ich auf ein Haar;*
	Der Tarnhelm wirkte das,
	wie Hagen mich es wies.
Hagen:	*Dir gab ich guten Rath.*
Gutrune:	*So zwangst du das kühne Weib?*
Siegfried.	*Sie wich—Gunther's Kraft;*

etc. They could imagine no other way of setting such lines as these to music except that of "recitative"; and they had dismal forebodings of what would happen to an opera which, as they saw it, would be largely dry recitative. Wagner, of course, had somewhere at the back of his mind a kind of music entirely different from that of *Tannhäuser* or *Lohengrin,* where, in spite of the unbroken continuity of the texture, the framework of the older forms of solo, duet, ensemble and so forth had still been visible. He must already have seen, though subconsciously rather than consciously, that the solution of his new problem—which was how to let the drama run its unbroken course from the rise of the curtain on each act to the lowering of it, without holding up the action every now and then in order to let a purely musical "form" impose itself on it—lay in a new logic of musical spinning, which would allow music and drama to work hand in hand throughout, instead of first one, then the other breaking the unity by insisting on its own rights, the result being a continual oscillation between lyrical expansion and explanatory recitative. This complete fusion of drama and music implied two pre-requisites. In the first place the drama itself would have to be conceived *in terms of music;* in the second place the music would have to be of such a kind that no matter how freely it worked itself out according to its own inner laws the drama would be assisted, not constrained, by it.

10

As regards the first of these points, we can see now what was hidden from Wagner's contemporaries—that the *musician* in him was co-operating with and guiding the *dramatist* in every phase of the poem. Here was not the customary procedure of a non-musical playwright putting together a "libretto" and then handing it over to a composer to be "set to music", the product of their joint labour being afterwards turned over to actors, producers, machinists, designers and all the rest of them to add *their* several little contributions, but of the operation of a complex faculty of which the world had had no experience until then, the operatic creator being at once dramatist, musician, mime, producer, conductor and everything else. It was not even that Wagner, during the creation of an opera, was dramatist *and* composer *and* stage practitioner in successive layers, as it were, the one faculty taking up the job where the other had laid it down. He did not put together the words of *Siegfried's Death* and then "set them to music", and after that "put it on the stage": the three faculties worked simultaneously in him in all the operas of his maturity. This does not mean, of course, that when writing the words he already had in his mind the actual notes that were to accompany them. But the musical *mood* was operative within him all the time, determining or accompanying each of the windings of the drama. We can see the functioning of this double faculty in him in such a seeming trifle as his jotting down in the margin of his *Young Siegfried*[1] the musical rhythms intended to accompany one of Siegfried's speeches to Mime. The words run thus:

> *Aus dem Wald fort*
> *in die Welt ziehn!*
> *nimmer kehr' ich zurück!*
> *Wie ich froh bin,*
> *dass ich frei ward,*
> *nichts mich bindet und zwingt!*
> *Mein Vater bist du nicht,*
> *in der Ferne bin ich heim:*
> *dein Herd ist nicht mein Haus,*
> *meine Decke nicht dein Dach!*
> *Wie der Fisch froh*
> *in der Flut schwimmt,*
> *wie der Fink frei*
> *sich davon schwingt:*
> *flieg' ich von hier,*
> *flute davon,*

etc.

> (*From the wood forth*
> *in the world fare,*
> *never more to return!*
> *Gladness floods me*
> *for my freedom,*

[1] This work was the next stage in the evolution of the *Ring*, to which we shall come shortly.

> *nothing now binds me here.*
> *My father art thou not,*
> *and afar I know my home;*
> *thy hearth is not my house,*
> *nor thy cave my rightful roof.*
>> *As the glad fish*
>> *in the flood swims,*
>> *as the finch free*
>> *in the wind soars:*
>> *I fly from here,*
>> *fleetly I flow,*
>> *like the wind o'er the woods),*

etc.. Opposite "Aus dem Wald fort" Wagner has written in the margin of his manuscript:

$\frac{3}{4}$ ♪ ♪ ♪ | ♩ ♩ ♪ ♪ | ♩ ♩ ♪ | ♪ ♪ ♪ ♪ ♪ | ♩ ♪

opposite "Mein Vater bist du nicht" he has noted this:

♩ | ♩ ♩. ♪ ♪ ♪ ♪ | ♩ ♪ ♪ ♪ ♪ | ♩. ♪ ♪ ♪ | ♩ *etc.*

and opposite "Flieg' ich von hier" this:

$\frac{2}{4}$ ♩ ♪ ♪ | ♩ ♪

Observe now how he has handled the passage later in the score of *Siegfried*.

The boy's impatience at the impotence of the dwarf to forge him the sword he needs has been expressed, from the point denoted by the words:

> *Auf! Eile dich, Mime!*
> *Mühe dich rasch;*
> *kannst du 'was Rechts,*
> *nun zeig' deine Kunst! etc.*

> *(Up! Quick to it, Mime!*
> *Shape me the sword;*
> *cravest thou praise?*
> *then prove me thy craft!)*

in an impetuous 2/4 accompaniment figure:

A

When the dwarf asks him "What wouldst thou today with the sword?" the ardent boy breaks into a new rhythm—that of the first of the marginal notes quoted above:

B

Aus dem Wald fort in die Welt ziehn: nimmer kehr' ich zu - rück.

With the new thought that springs up in him—"My father art thou not"—the rhythm of the lines instantly changes, and with it that of the music, as in the second marginal note:

C

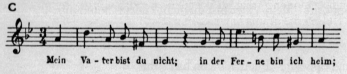

Mein Va - ter bist du nicht; in der Fer - ne bin ich heim;

His torrent of similes finished—"Wie der Fisch froh" etc.—he speaks *in propria persona*, as it were, again. The speech-accents now fall on the verbs that hammer out the idea of flight into the world—"*Flieg'* ich von hier, *flute* davon"—and with the change in verbal rhythm comes a change in the musical rhythm. But it will be seen that at this point the present score and the marginal note do not agree. In the latter a change from 3/4 to 2/4 is prescribed; but in the score Wagner continues with the former 3/4:

D

Flieg' ich von hier, flu - te da - von,

The explanation of this is that on second thoughts he saw that it would be better to make Siegfried sing, instead of the:

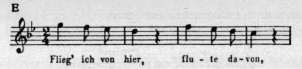

Flieg' ich von hier,   flu - te da-von,

originally intended—which would have meant holding up the torrent by the crotchet rest—the melodic line shown above to the words "Flieg' ich von hier". But though the metre remains, as before, 3/4, the rhythmical effect is different, because there is no longer an uptake word and an uptake note before the heavy beat of the bar, as there had been, for instance, at "Mein Vater bist du nicht". Here the word ("Vater") that gives its impulse to the line comes second. In "Flieg' ich von hier" the propulsive word comes first, and with the musical stress now falling on "flieg'" and "flute" Wagner gives the lines an energy which they would have lost had he clung to his first idea of phrasing them in 2/4 time with a crotchet rest at the end of each second bar. There is abundant evidence that all the while he was writing his poem he was feeling the drama in terms of music.

II

But his contemporaries necessarily saw the matter in reverse, as it were. He was producing during the years around 1850 a vast amount of argumentative prose and no operas; therefore they began to think of him as a composer with whom theory came first and practice second, whereas, in fact, it was the musician and the poet in him that were driving him towards the creation of so new an inner world that for sheer mind's comfort's sake he had to try to take his bearings in it, and this could be done only by reasoning it all out in prose. It would have been better for him, perhaps, in the long run, if he had never published any of these prose works but waited till he had a new opera to speak for itself to the public. But that was not Wagner's way; he always had an excess of mental energy that had to find other outlets than that of purely creative art. Without these outlets his path as a creator would probably have been cumbered for a while with an immense amount of unassimilable material; by means of his prose speculations he shovelled all this on one side and could then forget it and surrender himself to pure creation. He himself was well aware of this peculiarity of his being. In November 1850, when embarking on the immense *Opera and Drama*, he wrote thus to Liszt: "Between the musical working-out of my *Lohengrin* and that of my *Siegfried*[1] there lies, for me, a turbulent yet, I am confident, prolific world. I had a whole life to clear away behind me, to bring into the forefront of consciousness what was in me only in a sort of twilight, to master my reflection by means of its own self—by getting to the very core of it—in order thereafter to immerse myself again, with clear and joyous consciousness, in the exquisite unconsciousness of artistic creation." After he has finished *Opera and Drama*, he goes on to say, "then, in the spring, joyful and clarified, I will take up my *Siegfried*, and not drop it until I have completed it", i.e. in music.

He was thoroughly aware that works of the type he now had in his mind would mean a break, sooner or later, with the existing German theatre. "I will write no more operas", he told a friend in 1851. "As I do not wish to invent an arbitrary title for my works, I call them dramas, a term which at least will indicate clearly the standpoint from which the thing I am offering should be accepted." Experience soon taught him that whatever else he might do he could not impose a new nomenclature on the world; and so he had to refer to his works, as everyone else did, as operas. With the traditional operatic world and its forms, however, he had finished for good after *Lohengrin*. And as he was living, in the late 1840's and the early 1850's, in a world of political and social upheaval, he easily managed to persuade himself that somehow or other his own new kind of creation was part and parcel of these changes. For the acceptance of his new and regenerating art he looked forward to a new structure of society, and so he became a revolutionist. But he could never make up his mind which of the two, chicken or egg, would have to come first, whether his own creative work would help to build up a new society or such a society would have to come into being before his work could find acceptance. And so, from posterity's point of view, he wasted a vast amount of his time and his intellectual energy on not only

[1] i.e. *Siegfried's Death*.

artistic but political and social and economic theorising. But we
need to remember that his powerful mind was all of a piece; without the gymnastic afforded it by all this ardent and sometimes
futile speculation it would have been less athletic; his art would
not have had behind it the tremendous driving force that now
excites our wonder and compels our admiration.

12

It was his guardian angel that wisely held him back from setting
formally to work at the music of *Siegfried's Death* as soon as he
had completed the dramatic plan for this, though he must, of
course, have been always brooding upon it and doing a certain
amount of musical sketching for it. In 1933 there was published
for the first time a Sketch,[1] running to some 150 bars, for the
music of the Norns Scene with which the opera was to open. It is
dated "12 August 1850", and is very interesting in respect both
of what was carried over from it into the present *Ring* and what
was changed or discarded.

The first thing we observe is that already Wagner's instinct
had decided on the key of E flat minor and a 6/4 motion for the
opening of his drama. But in this sketch the Norns plunge *in
medias res*, without the orchestral preamble that is a feature of the
corresponding scene in the *Twilight of the Gods*:

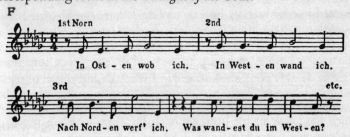

(The words are: "1*st Norn:* In the east I wove. 2*nd N.* In the west
I wound. 3*rd N.* To the north I cast [the rope]. What woundest
thou in the west? 2*nd N.* What wov'st thou in the east?". The
reader will hardly need to be reminded that for the *Twilight of the*

[1] In the possession of M. Louis Barthou.

Gods another and more detailed text was written for this scene).
It will be seen that the melody foreshadows the one associated in
the present *Ring* not with the Norns but with the Valkyries:[1]
moreover it loses its vitality in the fourth bar and never regains
it, drifting off into an undistinguished quasi-recitative. But it has
already become evident that even when engaged on his poem
Wagner had a *musical* texture and a *musical* form at the back of
his mind. If the reader will glance at the poem of *Siegfried's
Death*—of which an English version will be found in volume
VIII of Ashton Ellis's translation of Wagner's prose works—he
will see that in the five lines quoted above—"functional" lines we
may perhaps call them, for they define the nature and function of
the Norns as the weavers of destiny—the Norns have begun to
outline the story of Alberich's theft of the Gold and the events
that followed in its train. Three times in the course of their narrative they break off to repeat their "functional" lines. At the conclusion of each section of the story (except, of course, the last),
Wagner has written between the staves "3 Takte"; i.e. there are
to be three bars of orchestral development at each of these points;
and each time the Norns begin their ritual winding of the rope
again from east to west and so on they do so to the melody quoted
above (or a suggestion of it). The form of the episode is therefore
a musical one, a kind of rondo.

At a later stage of this musical sketch we find, at the point
where the scene merges into the colloquy between Siegfried and
Brynhilde, a descending figure in the orchestra:

G

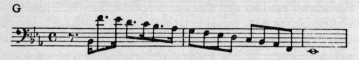

which has no definable function here, but from which, as we can
now see, was subsequently evolved the Treaty motive associated
in the present *Ring* with Wotan. (See Example No. 13 below).
We first meet with this motive in the *Rhinegold*, the music of
which was written between November 1853 and January 1854.
The "reminiscence" hunters have for long assured us that this

---

[1] See Example No. 74 in our later analysis of the opera.

Treaty motive was one of the themes Wagner "borrowed" from Liszt, in whose piano sonata something resembling it appears. The musical Sketch we are now considering disposes of that assumption once for all. The first statement of the motive in the *Rhinegold* agrees with the Sketch of 1850 in (*a*) general outline, (*b*) the change from dotted to non-dotted quavers, (*c*) the coming to rest on a long note at the end of the descent. But Liszt's sonata was not written until 1852/3, and not published until 1854.

13

We have every reason to be thankful that Wagner did not set to work at the systematic composition of *Siegfried's Death* in 1850. The musician in him was manifestly unripe for it just then; and it may have been because his instinct warned him of this that he did not work out in full whatever musical sketches he may have made at that time. But there was another and a stronger reason for the long delay. On the 3rd May 1851 he had written to a correspondent, "I am now setting to work at the musical working-out of my *Siegfried* [i.e. *Siegfried's Death*]". But only a week later we find him writing to another friend in quite a different vein. "All through last winter I was plagued by an idea which lately has taken possession of me to such an extent that I must bring it to fruition. Did I not once write you with regard to a lively subject? It was that of the youth who sets out to 'learn what fear is' and is so stupid that he never manages to learn. Imagine how startled I was when I realised that this youth is no other than—the young Siegfried, who wins the Hoard and awakes Brynhilde! The plan is now ready. I am gathering my strength together to write next month the poem of *The Young Siegfried*. I will set to work at the music in July", after which, he continues, he will address himself (in 1852) to the composition of the music of *Siegfried's Death*.

The popular story of the youth too stupid to learn what fear is had long been a favourite with him: already in the Dresden days he had told his friend Kietz that he would write no more "grand operas", but only "fairy tales, such as that of the boy who does not know what fear is." And now in 1851, by one of those tricks of the subconscious so familiar to us in the case of poets, this old folk-tale had become fused in his imagination with that of his hero Siegfried. He was very pleased with his discovery. For one thing, in the new opera (*Young Siegfried*) he could set visibly before the spectator a good many details of the pre-history of the Ring and the struggle for world power which could have been told in *Siegfried's Death* only in narrative form, through the mouth of this character or that. In the second place, a *Young Siegfried*, with its atmosphere of gladsome youth, would serve, he thought, as a welcome foil to the tragic *Siegfried's Death*.

He at once drew up, in some twenty-three lines in pencil, the ground plan of the new three-act opera, to which some supplementary paragraphs were added at some later date. We owe the chance preservation of this precious scrap of material to the fact that the large sheet of paper on which it was written was utilised by him in later years as a wrapper for the first draft of the new poem. The plan now sketched conforms in general to that of the present *Siegfried*—Act I: the scene between Siegfried and Mime, the dwarf's talk with the Wanderer, and the forging of the sword by Siegfried; Act II: the action in the forest (Alberich, Fafner and Wotan), the dialogue between Siegfried and Mime, the death of Fafner, the altercation between Mime and Alberich, the acquisition of the Ring by Siegfried, the birds'[1] warning, the slaying of Mime, and the news brought by the birds of the Valkyrie Brynhilde on the rock; Act III: Wotan and the Wala, Wotan and Siegfried, Siegfried and the awakening of Brynhilde.

14

Broadly speaking, what Wagner was now doing was to elaborate into a three-act opera a single paragraph of the first Prose Sketch of October 1848, which had told how, after the slaying of Siegmund by Hunding, Sieglinde had given birth to a son in the forest, how the boy had been brought up and taught smithing by Mime, and so forth along the lines in general of the first act of the present *Siegfried*. There are some small differences, however, between that earlier paragraph and the draft of May 1851, and between both of these and the opera. For example, Wagner's

[1] Here and in a later more extended sketch the birds are still in the plural.

first idea was to have Mime go on with his labours at the forge during his conversation with the Wanderer! In the Sketch of 1848 Siegfried had forged the sword "under the direction of Mime"; in that of 1851 the boy impatiently smashes up the dwarf's sorry attempt and proceeds to make the weapon himself. In 1851 Siegfried no longer seeks out and slays Hunding as he had done in the first Sketch. In 1848 the wood birds—whose song the boy understands after tasting the Dragon's blood—had warned him to beware of Mime, who plans to do him evil in order to get the Hoard, whereupon Siegfried kills him at once. In the Sketch of 1851 this episode begins to take the more extended shape with which we are familiar today: "the taste of the blood gives also the power to pierce to the true sense of the false words. Mime's dissembling is understood throughout by Siegfried in the sense in which Mime means it. (The birds reveal this also to him)".

At the bottom of the page containing the short swift draft of May 1851 are three jottings which were evidently made later. The first of these, relating to Act I, runs thus: "the Wanderer and Mime. Explanation of the relations between Giants, Dwarfs and Gods. Suggestions of Siegfried's mission, and frustration of Mime's design." Clearly it had occurred to Wagner that here was the opportunity to acquaint the spectator with that primal conflict of Gods, Giants and Dwarfs in which the whole vast dramatic action had had its roots: he now saw his way to do this by means of a series of questions and answers between the Wanderer and Mime. The second jotting is as follows: "Wotan and the Wala. Guilt of the Gods, and their necessary downfall. Siegfried's mission. Self-annihilation of the Gods." Here, it will be perceived, the original ending of the drama had already taken an entirely new turn in Wagner's mind. In the First Sketch of 1848, it will be recalled, Brynhilde, after restoring the Ring to the Rhine and declaring Alberich and the Nibelungs to be free again, had proclaimed that "One only shall rule, All-Father, Glorious One, Thou. This man [Siegfried] I bring to you as pledge of thy eternal might: good welcome give him, as is his desert!" But now, in 1851, the final consummation of the drama is to be not the eternal establishment of the power of the Gods but their annihilation by their own willing of that end.

15

What had brought about this fundamental alteration in Wagner's ethical design? We cannot trace in detail all the mysterious spiritual changes in him that had led to this surprising result; but it has been argued, with a certain plausibility, that by the early 1850's his optimism with regard to the coming of a new and better European social order—one in which the Gods, so to speak, would at last rule the world wisely and well—had given way to a pessimism that saw no way out of the contemporary evil and misery, and that the final blow to his optimism had been dealt by Louis Napoléon's coup d'état of the 2nd December 1851. That unexpected event certainly shook him to his foundations. In 1851 he had been convinced that the trend of opinion in France was towards a new social democracy which would change the face of things for the better; and he shared the general confidence that the French elections in December would be the beginning of an upheaval that would inaugurate an epoch of social and political freedom and happiness not only for France but for Europe. When the news came of Louis Napoléon's seizure of power it was at first, he tells us in *My Life*, something so "absolutely incredible" that he could hardly believe it: "it seemed to me", he says, "that the world was really coming to an end. When the success of the coup d'état was confirmed, and it appeared that what no one had thought possible had actually happened and had all the appearance of enduring, I turned my back on this incomprehensible world as a riddle not worth the attempt to solve. As a joking reminder of our earlier hopes for the year 1852 I suggested, in my correspondence with Uhlig, that we should treat it as nonexistent and go on dating our letters December 1851[1]—in consequence of which this month of December seemed to last an inordinate time." And he goes on to speak of the profound depression into which the new state of things had thrown him, its

---

[1] As a matter of fact in only one of his letters to Uhlig—that of the 22nd January 1852, which he dated "53rd December 1851"—did he carry out this plan. His account of the matter in the later years when he was writing his autobiography, however, is quite accurate as regards his general state of mind in 1851/2.

dire effect on his health, and his despair for the future of European culture.

This theory that the change from an optimistic to a pessimistic ending of the *Ring* drama came about through Wagner's political disillusionment at the hands of Louis Napoléon in December 1851 was plausible enough at one time. But the recent publication of his sketches has negated it. We have seen, on page 439, that the passage in the *Young Siegfried* Prose Sketch of May 1851 running thus, "Wotan and the Wala. Guilt of the Gods, and their necessary downfall. Siegfried's mission. Self-annihilation of the Gods", is a jotting on the lower part of the sheet. Both the ink and the script of this jotting suggest that it was made later than the Sketch itself.[1] How much later, whether days or weeks or months, we do not know. But the actual date is immaterial, for in the main body of the Sketch, in the outline of the third act of *Young Siegfried*, we find this: "Wotan and the Wala: end of the Gods. Wotan's resolution: the Wala sinks into the earth"; and Wagner's letters of that date place it beyond doubt that this plan was committed to paper some time between the 3rd and the 10th May 1851. His decision to change the 1848 ending of his Nibelungen drama had therefore been made long before Louis Napoléon's coup d'état had plunged him into pessimism about the actual world in which his lot as an artist was cast.

16

In the first swift Sketch of the 3rd/10th May 1851 for a *Young Siegfried* there is a sentence which, as it stands, is rather puzzling. In the scene in the second act in which Fafner, Alberich and Mime figure we have this: "Siegfried goes into the cave.—Mime. Alberich.—Siegfried [reappears] with the Ring: all scatter." Why "all"? we cannot help asking, for only Mime and Alberich are there besides himself. A glance at the facsimile of the manuscript clears up the mystery. The draft for Act II had originally run thus: "Neidwald. Alberich *comes up out of the earth with Nibelungs: they have to follow him. Reproaches. Appeasement.*—Siegfried and

---

[1] A facsimile of the page is given by Otto Strobel in his book *Richard Wagner, Skizzen und Entwürfe zur Ring-Dichtung* (1930).

Mime.—S. alone.—Morning. Fafner appears: his dying speech. Bird-song. S. goes into the cave.—Mime. *The Nibelungs seize him: anarchy: promises.* Alberich. *Derision.* Siegfried [emerges] with the Ring: all scatter", etc. It was Wagner's intention, then, in the early days of May 1851, to introduce the Nibelungs—still subject to Alberich—in this scene, and have them seize Mime at their Master's bidding: the dwarf makes them promises if they will release him, and Alberich derides his brother. In a further jotting Wagner elaborated the action in this way: Alberich summons the Nibelungs, who reproach him bitterly as the originator of their slavery. He pacifies them, tells them that Mime is bent on getting the Ring, and counsels them to frustrate him, whereupon they all scurry into the earth or into fissures in the rocks and lie in wait. After Siegfried has slain Fafner and gone into the cave, Mime runs in and is seized by the Nibelungs. He promises to liberate them if the Ring falls to him; but Alberich derides him as a deceiver. "Siegfried comes out with the Ring, which he places on his finger. Mime decides to kill him and goes to one side. The Nibelungs declare themselves to be Siegfried's bondsmen: he commands them to go", etc.

A further jotting goes into yet closer detail. Alberich, we learn, is bent on acquiring the Ring again because he knows that if Mime obtains it he, Alberich, will be eternally subject to his brother Nibelung, whereas he himself will know how to deal with the simple boy Siegfried, who is ignorant of the Ring's power. "When Mime enters, the Nibelungs fall upon him: he wants to go into the cave, and makes all kinds of promises in order to get free. Alberich mocks him: the two quarrel. Siegfried comes out with the Ring: all scatter before their new lord. Mime remains concealed.—Bird-song.—Mime comes forward."

From the point of view of a contemporary spectator of *Young Siegfried*—who, we must bear in mind, would have nothing like our present knowledge of the preceding events and psychological and moral motives of the drama,—there was a good deal to be said for Wagner's projected elaboration of this scene. In the end, however, he decided not to introduce the Nibelungs, perhaps because it would have meant employing an ensemble for which he would have no use anywhere else in the opera. It is possible also that already he had a vague suspicion that just as *Young Siegfried* had become necessary to elucidate some features of *Siegfried's Death*, so it might be necessary for him some day to explain *Young Siegfried* in turn by means of a preliminary opera. But whatever his reasons may have been, he scrapped the episodes in which the Nibelungs were to have taken part, and concentrated the action at this point into the superb scene of mutual recrimination between Alberich and Mime which we have in the present *Siegfried*. When putting his pen through so much of the Sketch of 1851 as he had decided to dispense with, however, he forgot to score out the now meaningless words "all scatter".

17

On the 12th May 1851 he wrote to Bülow, "I have greatly expanded my plan. *Siegfried's Death* is at present unproduceable, and, for the public, ununderstandable; so I am going to preface it with a *Young Siegfried*." Between the 24th May and the 1st June, accordingly, working at fever heat, he drafted a full Prose Sketch for the new opera which runs to twenty-seven pages of print. This Sketch was so detailed, and so much of it was already couched in actual dialogue, that giving it poetic form was fairly easy for him: this task occupied him only from the 3rd to the 24th June. On the 29th he wrote to Liszt apologising for being too exhausted to make him a copy of the poem, as he would have liked to do. Cannot they meet soon, he asks, when he will read the work to his friend? This, he says in a significant passage, will really be the better plan, for he could read it to Liszt in such a way that his intentions would become clearer than the mere written word can make them. He was an incomparable reader of his own dramas; more than one witness has testified that, with his extraordinary range of vocal inflection, the scope and plasticity of his poses and gestures, and the intensity of his feeling, he gave the characters and the action a life which the best of his singers was never able to achieve in the theatre, even with the assistance of the music.

We have arrived, then, at the point when, in May 1851, Wagner felt that he could say all he had to say on the Nibelungen subject in two operas, *Young Siegfried* and *Siegfried's Death*. Had he stopped there, instead of going on to add first a *Valkyrie* and then a *Rhinegold*, would the world have gained or lost? We should have been the poorer, of course, by a large amount of magnificent music. But from the purely dramatic point of view it is possible that we might have gained slightly: for *Young Siegfried* and *Siegfried's Death*, as originally planned, constitute in combination an almost perfect whole.

What had been Wagner's original purpose in 1848? Not a stage packed with so much picturesque incident as we have in the present *Ring*, but a concentrated presentation of one great central dramatic motive, that of the stupendous moral implications and consequences of a single act of well-meant wrong-doing on the part of the Gods. Unless the present-day spectator of the *Ring* has learned to see beyond the actual characters and episodes set before him on the stage he has failed to understand the work at all as it was planned and as it really is. There has been much censure of Wotan for his alleged airy breach of agreement with the Giants; he has been playfully described as the ancient equivalent of a fraudulent building contractor who gets a house built for himself and then tries to bilk the labourers of their wages. That is good enough as a joke, but if it is taken seriously it shows a lamentable failure to grasp the most elementary facts of the matter, as set forth in the First Sketch of 1848 for a Nibelungen drama. We have to rid our minds, in the first place, of all the modern connotations of the word "Gods". For the ancient Teutons, as for the Greeks, the Gods were not all-powerful beings. They were subject to time and change and fate —"necessity"—like ordinary mortals, and like the world itself they were doomed to "go down" some day. ("Twilight of the Gods" is the most convenient but not the most literal English rendering of this concept: what has been foredoomed to happen is a going-under of the Gods, a passing-away of them in the course of the cycle of ages, just as human and other life on the earth will some day go under or pass away).

Wagner's root-conception was of a world divided between three prime other-than-human forces, each striving for mastery over the others—a race of Giants, incapable of rising above the lowest materialism but too indolent and too stupid to aspire to world-mastery, desirous only of being left to live their own brute lives in safety; a spirit of acquisition and of domination symbolised by Alberich, whose superior cunning brings him untold wealth, leading to the subjection of the Nibelungs as the first step towards mastery of the world; and a loftier spirit, represented by the Gods, that would fain rescue the world from the two evils that threaten it,—on the one hand power incessantly bent on more power for its own base ends (Alberich and Mime), on the other hand a sloth that cares for nothing beyond the lowest satisfaction of the desire to go on living in comfort (the Giants). But these Teutonic Gods lack of themselves not merely the power but a cosmic right to power over the others; they too are subject to law and are prisoners of fate. It is the problem of how to break out of that prison, not for their own sakes but for the world's sake, that constitutes the basic moral problem of the *Ring*.

18

We have seen Wagner's first approach to that problem in 1848; it is a better approach, in some ways, than that of the tetralogy as we now have it. In the latter, Wotan, desirous of world-power, has the Giants build for him a fortress that will give him security; he promises them, in return, Freia, the goddess of youth and gladness and beauty. He has no intention of fulfilling that rash promise, but hopes that when the time comes for payment he will be able to find some means, less disastrous to the race of the Gods, of discharging his debt to the earthy-minded Giants. Loge tells him and the others of the rape of the Rhine-gold and the power it and the Ring have conferred on Alberich, whereupon the brute cupidity of Fafner and Fasolt impels them to ask for this Hoard in lieu of Freia. Wotan deprives Alberich of his Gold, his Ring, his Tarnhelm and his power, by means of guile and force. The Hoard passes into the possession of Fafner and Fasolt; in their base greed they fight for the treasure, Fasolt is slain, and Fafner, changing himself into a Dragon, intends to sleep for endless time upon it. So long as he is alive no one else is strong enough to possess himself of it. But Alberich, though checked, is still dangerous. He lives obsessed by one purpose only, to regain the

Hoard and Ring and make himself master of the world. This is the desire also of his brother Mime; and if either of them succeeds there is an end to the human freedom and the growth in moral stature for which Wotan had been striving. To kill the mighty Dragon is a task too great for either of the Nibelungs unaided; but none the less the danger exists for each of them that some day, somehow, the power for world-evil after which they both lust will pass into the hands of one or the other. The moral grandeur of Wagner's conception of the drama resides in the fact that Wotan, God though he is, is caught in a net of his own careless weaving: he cannot get power for good into his own hands now without using force, that is to say, by adding another crime against morality to his original one of robbing Alberich by force and craft. This problem he ultimately solves by the creation of a hero, Siegfried, who will win the Hoard unaided and unprompted by the Gods, and, by his death, make it possible for the Gold to be given back to the pure waters from which it was stolen, and the power for evil inherent in it to be broken for ever.

That is the impressive sequence of conceptions underlying the present *Ring*. The first conception of all, however, that of 1848, was in some respects better. There the beginning of the drama had not the quasi-personal form it assumed later by the narrowing down of the opening action to Wotan on the one side and Fasolt and Fafner on the other. This *personalising* of the broad moral conflict was a necessity dictated by the transference of the world-sweep of the action of the saga to the restricted space of the stage. The original cosmic idea was more impressive but less realisable in terms of the theatre: originally it had been not merely Fasolt and Fafner who were concerned in the struggle for world domination but the whole race of Giants. They and Wotan already knew, before the drama opens, of Alberich's seizure of the Gold and the use he had made of it: it was therefore a simple necessity for the Giants to have him deprived of that power, and only by the intervention of the Gods could that be made possible for them. But all this was in essence symbolic, which precisely constituted the grandeur of it; and symbols are not easy to realise on the stage.

There had been several points in *Siegfried's Death* which Wagner rightly felt would have to be elucidated for the spectator by means of a preliminary opera. Therefore a good deal of his space in *Young Siegfried* was taken up with explanation rather than action—at this point or that we in the theatre would have to learn from the mouth of one or other of the characters the episodes antecedent to the present action that had made this turn of events not merely possible but inevitable. Neither Wotan, Mime, the Nibelungs nor the Giants had appeared in *Siegfried's Death*. Alberich had figured there, his function being to explain to Hagen, and through him to the spectator, how he had robbed the Rhine of the Gold, how he had in turn been robbed of it to satisfy the Giants, Wotan having unwillingly surrendered it to them on the warning counsel of the Norns; how a Dragon now slept upon the Hoard; how Mime had schemed to acquire the Ring; how Siegfried had slain him and the Dragon and won him the Hoard and the Ring; and how he, Alberich, had begotten his son Hagen to wrest the Ring from this simple boy who does not know the virtue that resides in it. (In the corresponding scene of the *Twilight of the Gods* Alberich does not go into so much detail; it is unnecessary for him to do so, for it had all been set visibly before the spectator in the *Rhinegold*, the *Valkyrie* and *Siegfried*). But there still remained much to be elucidated, and to this task Wagner addressed himself in *Young Siegfried*. It marked the beginning, for him, of a new type of musical-dramatic construction which he was to employ most effectively later in *Tristan*, the *Mastersingers* and *Parsifal*; at a certain point in the action one or other of the characters would explain what had happened before the commencement of the opera, the narrative being made an organic part of the action, however, and raised to the emotional temperature of that, by means of Wagner's new art of the symphonic development of forward-reaching and backward-glancing "motives" in the orchestra.

The first thing he did in *Young Siegfried* was to explain in the opening scene, through Mime, how Siegfried had come into the world with the fragments of his father's sword as his legacy.

Then came the skilful telling, in the colloquy between Mime and the Wanderer, of the story of the long-antecedent strife of Gods and Giants and Nibelungs for the Hoard and the Ring. Two other vital matters called for elucidation. First of all, how did Wotan come into the action which henceforth was to centre in Siegfried and Brynhilde? Wagner conveyed this information in the dialogue in the third act between the Wanderer and the Wala (Erda): there we learn that Brynhilde is the daughter of the pair, that she had disobeyed the God and been put to sleep on the fire-girt rock and that Wotan had afterwards gone among men and bred the race of Volsungs from which had sprung a hero who should unconsciously take the guilt of the Gods on him. The troubled God asks the seeress what will be the end of it all. She tells him: the Gods must pass away, for their guilt lies heavy on them; they will be supplanted by something better than themselves. "Crazed are the Gods", says the Wala in the Sketch of 1851, "turned in their foolishness against themselves. They avenge guilt, yet are themselves all guilty. What they have profaned they still call holy: faith they break, yet faith they guard! What, you ask me, must the Gods now will? They must will what they will not: the end of the Gods, their passing away, I foresee."

20

But the moral problem at the very core of the drama needed even further exposition than this; and Wagner supplied that elucidation to perfection, in *Young Siegfried*, in the great scene of Alberich and the Wanderer outside Fafner's lair in the second act. The dialogue is a series of forensic pleadings in which the God comes off second-best, for Alberich has an effective counter to every one of his pleadings. The long colloquy may be paraphrased and summarised thus:

The Wanderer: I come to see, not to intervene. You are free, Nibelung, to act as you choose.

Alberich (with a bitter laugh): Free, you say? Behold the shameless insolence of the master race! When you wrested my power from me did you leave me free? I am in a slave's bonds; and he who bound me now mocks me! Ye great and wise ones stole my power from me. You and yours came to me like thieves: first you stole from me my Tarnhelm, then you fettered me and dragged me to the upper earth. I offered you, for my freedom, the whole Hoard the Nibelungs had amassed for me; but nothing less would content you than my veriest own, my Ring. Was I free then to do as I would?

The Wanderer: You were as free as you deserved to be. You call the Ring your veriest own because you made it. But from whom, fool, did you ravish the Gold? Was *that* your own? Ask the Rhine-Daughters! Yours is the earlier and older guilt: blame that if now you are unfree.

Alberich: Shameless twister of the right! You reproach *me* with the guilt that served *your* ends so well? What *I* robbed from the Rhine, did *you* give it back to the Rhine-Daughters? No: you used it to pay the dull-witted Giants for building you the fortress from which you could rule the world in security. And now you reproach me for the deed that won you your power. How gladly would you yourself have ravished the Gold from the Rhine had you known how to smith it! But your craft did not extend that far at that time; now that you are older and wiser and know more you chastise the guilt that serves you, but you yourself sin when it is to your advantage to do so!

The Wanderer: Pure and guiltless were we all until the Gold was smithed; but the race of the Giants murdered each other for the Hoard, till only one remains.

Alberich: But all that served your ends. So long as the Giants were slaying each other the Gods lived in bliss. But now that Fafner's end is near, who will inherit from him? That is the question that eternally gnaws at you. You have begotten and cherished a race of human heroes: will they, like the Giants, destroy each other for the Ring, or will it come back to the Nibelung again? Let it once come into my hands and I will lead the depths to storm the heights. I will make better use of it than the stupid Giants could do. And then, thou holy shielder of heroes, tremble, for I shall be master of the world!

The Wanderer: The Gods do not covet the Ring. What they gave away they do not take back; but one who does not know its power, and wins it by his own deed, *he* will deal with it in his own fashion.

Alberich: Your sophistry does not deceive me! The heroes to whom you trust are beings of your own blood. You have raised a youth whom you are cunning enough to leave free to do the deed you dare not do yourself.

And so on.

Hardly anything of this magnificent give-and-take was carried over by Wagner later into the equivalent scene in *Siegfried;* there was no vital necessity for it there, for the spectator would already have learned it all, most of it at first hand, from the two preceding operas of the *Ring*. But now we have to piece it together bit by bit for ourselves, whereas in *Young Siegfried* it is given us in concentrated form at the precise moment when it is most essential that we shall know and understand the dilemma of the Gods, who cannot work the good they fain would work for the world because their moral authority has been cankered from the outset by that first piece of necessary wrong-doing.

One or two other points of difference between *Young Siegfried* and the present *Siegfried* may here be noted for completeness sake.

In the former, Siegfried *twice* terrifies Mime, and at the same time demonstrates his own fearlessness, by bringing into the cave a wild animal he has captured—in the first instance a wolf, in the second a bear. It probably occurred to Wagner later that the rather extensive *Ring* menagerie might with advantage be thinned out a little; so he reduced the two episodes to one, dispensing with the wolf. In *Young Siegfried* it is no longer, as in the First Sketch of 1848, the forest birds in consort who direct Siegfried to Brynhilde's rock after the slaying of Fafner, but a single nightingale, which becomes, however, in the final *Siegfried*, a "wood bird" of no classifiable ornithological species. And in 1851, as in 1848, it is still the Giants *en masse* who had coveted and obtained the Ring, Fafner being the last survivor of the strife that had broken out among them afterwards for the possession of it.

21

In the Sketch of 1851, and in the poem of *Young Siegfried* based on this, we see Wagner coming up against one or two difficulties that cost him a good deal of trouble from time to time, and which he never overcame completely. The first of these was the handling of the "Fearing" motive.

We have seen him telling Uhlig, in May 1851, of a surprising discovery he had made—that his "Young Siegfried who wins the Hoard and awakes Brynhilde" has become identified in his imagination with the boy in the old folk tale who "sets out to 'learn what fear is' and is so stupid that he never manages to learn". What exactly does this mean? The more obvious explanation would be that about this time the old tale, of which he had always been fond, sprang up in Wagner's memory and grafted itself on the Volsung legend of Sigurd. It seems equally probable, however, that the reverse process may have taken place within him, that the fearing motive *per se* had already occurred to him in connection with the first act of his *Young Siegfried* and had afterwards linked itself up subconsciously with the tale of the youth who was anxious to learn what fear is but never could.

This was only one of the many difficult problems of new motivation and construction that confronted him when he began to elaborate *Young Siegfried* for the stage. In the poem of *Siegfried's Death* we had been told nothing more about the hero than was contained in Hagen's narration to Gunther and Gutrune in the first act: "From Wotan sprang Wälse and from him a twin-pair, Siegmund and Sieglinde; the truest of Wälsungs they begat. His father's blood-sister gave him birth in the depths of a forest . . ." There is no mention here of his upbringing by Mime, who comes, however, into Alberich's later narration to Hagen: "Mime the false one brought up the hero in hopes to win through him the Hoard. A wise fool he! His trust in the Wälsung cost him his life!" All this, and more, had now to be set visibly before the spectator in the first act of the new drama, *Young Siegfried*; and at the outset it confronted Wagner with some difficulties.

In the opening scene he makes it clear to us that after Siegmund's death the dwarf had found Sieglinde in the forest, where she died giving birth to a son. She had told Mime her own name, but ostensibly he does not know that of the child's father; all he knows, he insists, is that with her last breath the woman had told him that the father had died in combat, and had asked that the boy should be called Siegfried, "for with that name he would grow great and strong". She had with her the pieces of a broken sword, relics of her husband's last fight; and these Mime had preserved. (Wagner fell into some confusion later with regard to these fragments. In *Young Siegfried* Mime tells the boy they had been given to him by the dying Sieglinde; but in the later dialogue with the Wanderer, after the latter has put to Mime the question he cannot answer—"Who will forge the sword anew?"—the dwarf cries out distractedly, "Accursed steel! would I ne'er had stolen it!" When Wagner came to write the present *Siegfried* he failed to remove this contradiction; he still made Mime tell Siegfried that the fragments had been given him by Sieglinde, yet still retained, in the scene with the Wanderer, the lines about his "stealing" them).

As the child grew up, his strength and courage had bred in Mime the hope that he might be trained to accomplish the deed for which the dwarf himself was too feeble. So he had brought the boy up in ignorance of everything but his foster-father and his cave and the nearby forest, and had tried to make him love him as his benefactor, to regard him as his father and mother in one. In this he had failed, the healthy natural instinct of the child making him loathe the evil dwarf and feel more companionship with the beasts of the forest. The dominant impulse of the boy had been to break away from the repulsive Mime and go out to learn something of the world, for which purpose he had kept on demanding that a sword should be made for him out of the fragments of his father's. Hence Mime's perpetual problem; he can neither forge the sword himself, cunning smith as he is, nor think of anyone who can, for the high-spirited boy has disdained to learn the hated old Nibelung's craft. Moreover, if by any chance the sword should be made, the first thing the boy would do would be to depart with it, which would put an end to the dwarf's dream of acquiring the treasure, the Tarnhelm and the Ring, and the world power inherent in them. At all costs, then, the boy must be kept in the cave until events somehow shape themselves in a way propitious to Mime's purpose.

22

For the solution of this problem Wagner fastened on the psychological motive of fearing. When *Young Siegfried* opens, Siegfried has once more been pestering the dwarf to provide him with the sword he desires. "If I did", asks Mime, "what would you do then?" "I have told you again and again", replies Siegfried; "I would go out into the world to learn fearing, since I will never learn it here with you." Now Mime had tried to instil fear of the unknown outer world into the boy in order to keep him to himself for his own ends. When Siegfried goes off into the wood in a temper he leaves Mime in sore perplexity, says the Sketch of 1851, "lest he will lose him before the boy has brought him the reward for all he has suffered on his account . . . Now he wants to depart; it is high time, therefore, to lead him to Fafner; the boy's foolish curiosity to learn fearing he must make use of to egg him on to Fafner."

Wagner's doubts as to how to handle the situation are shown by a supplementary note he had made in the Sketch at this point. "Merely this motive—Siegfried feels himself now quite free of Mime; he will leave him and go into the world; so now he asks him once more for the sword. Mime, in order to retain him in the forest, tries to instil fear of the world in him. He paints a picture of one terror after another beyond the forest, and asks, 'Don't you feel fear'? Argument about fearing. Mime is called upon to explain it. He describes fear. Siegfried cannot learn it, and will go away at once to do so. (Mime suddenly resolves to teach him it himself. Fafner? Later)". That is to say, Wagner must first have had the idea of bringing the action to its decisive point then and there; he would have Mime describe fear in detail to the boy. Later it occurred to him to make the dwarf give the boy the lesson himself, by means of Fafner; and then, still later, came the idea of postponing that lesson for a while—which is the meaning of the query in brackets, "Later?"

In the end he decided to make it "later". Having got thus far in the Sketch he now introduces the Wanderer, who plays his famous game of questions-and-answers with the dwarf. The God's final question, "Who will forge the fragments of the sword?", Mime, to his dismay and terror, cannot answer. The Wanderer does so for him: "Know then, doomed dwarf, that only Siegfried himself can forge the sword. As far as I am concerned you can keep your forfeited head; I have no use for it. But from now onwards have a care; indulge in no foolish chatter, for it may go badly with you if you do". And with a laugh he leaves him.

Siegfried now enters with the bear he has fearlessly subdued, which terrifies the dwarf. When he recovers from his fright, however, he thinks he sees the solution of his problem, for at last he knows the answer to the question that had always baffled him —who will forge the sword anew? "Mime pulls himself together", says Wagner in a marginal jotting: "he will make it appear that he has been doing something better than trying to make a sword himself [as the boy had ordered him to do before leaving him],— he has been pondering how to teach Siegfried fearing. He unfolds to him the plan with regard to Fafner. Siegfried accepts it." And Wagner makes the dramatic and psychological point still clearer for us by a gleeful aside which he puts into the Nibelung's mouth: "Oh clever Wanderer, see how dull-witted this bright sprig of humanity is; he himself puts into my hand the craft by means of which I will make him serve me!" He turns to Siegfried and offers to take him on the morrow to the dragon's lair, where his desire to learn what fear is shall be gratified. Siegfried, afire at the delight-ful prospect, once more demands the sword. "It is not yet ready", says Mime; "but I can tell you that you will learn fearing only with the sword you yourself have forged." Thereupon the boy brushes him aside and makes the sword himself, greatly to the delight of Mime, who, brewing a stupefying potion in a corner, gloats over the stupidity of Gods and heroes, who are all playing into his hands, and foresees his own winning of the Ring and with it world might. This brings the first act to a close.

23

This lay-out of the action was changed radically later. In the present *Siegfried* Mime's lurid description of fear is postponed to a later stage. In the poem of 1851 Mime had tried to teach Siegfried fearing *before* his colloquy with the Wanderer, his object being to prevent the impetuous boy leaving him. He argues, soundly enough, that without fear, and the caution it induces, existence is impossible in the great outer world. "Without it you will be lost; you will meet with your father's fate. He whose senses are not sharpened by fear goes about blindfolded. Danger lurks for you in all you do not see and do not hear. Just as steel has no cutting edge until it has been through the fire, so the man who has not been sharpened by fear is blind and deaf in the world; the waters will engulf him. So heed the old man's counsel, foolish boy; remain in the forest." Siegfried storms out in a passion, warning Mime of what is in store for him if the sword is not ready on his return. Mime broods sadly on the bitterness of his lot, and the Wanderer enters.

But in the present poem of *Siegfried* all this is altered. The Wanderer now does not tell Mime outright that it is Siegfried who alone can forge the sword; his parting words are these: "Hear this now, discomfited dwarf, Fafner's bold vanquisher! *Only he who has never known what fear is*[1] shall forge Nothung anew. Have a care for thy wise head from now on; I leave it to fall to him who has never learned fearing." This new turn of the phrasing led as a matter of course to further changes. In *Young Siegfried* it had been Mime himself who, having learned definitely from the Wanderer that it is Siegfried who will forge the fragments, eggs the boy on to attempt that feat. In the later *Siegfried* however, the more ambiguous message of the Wanderer leaves Mime in great perplexity. When Siegfried returns and demands the sword the agitated dwarf can only express his despair in broken mumblings. "The sword? The sword? How could I forge it? (Half to himself): 'Only he who has never known fear can forge Nothung anew'. Too wise was I for such a work! . . . Where can I find good counsel? My wise head I wagered: I lost, and my head is to fall to 'him who has never learned fear'." He sees now that his policy with the boy has been the wrong one from the beginning; instead of teaching him fearing he had schemed to win his sole affection. That plan having failed, there is nothing for it

[1] Italics mine.

now but to teach him fear. He slowly reassembles his scattered wits and tries another line. "For your sake", he tells the boy, "I have been thinking hard, trying to discover how I could be of greatest help to you. For your sake I have discovered what fearing is, that I might pass my knowledge on to you"; and he launches upon the long description of the terrors of the forest—the spectral lights, the roaring winds, and so forth—with which the spectator of *Siegfried* is so familiar. The boy merely laughs at him. Then Mime promises to take him to a terrible dragon who will teach him fearing. Siegfried begins his forging of the sword, and Mime, aside, exults in his coming triumph over Alberich and the others— Siegfried having disposed of the dragon for him, he in turn will make an end of the ignorant boy with the potion he is now brewing, and make himself possessor of Tarnhelm, Hoard and Ring.[1]

24

Let us now take up again the chronological threads of the evolution of the *Ring* drama.

We have seen Wagner, in May 1851, happily convinced that with the writing of the poem of *Young Siegfried* he had reached the end of his labours in connection with the stage lay-out of his big Nibelungen drama. He was soon to discover that however hard he might try to persuade himself that, apart from the setting of the two texts to music, he had now finished with the subject, it decidedly had not finished with him. In July he could assure Liszt that he was going to settle down to the musical part of his task "next month", when, he hoped, his health would have taken a turn for the better. After making a copy of the poem of *Young Siegfried* for his own future use he presented the manuscript to his friend Frau Julie Ritter. In the copy he was keeping for himself he made a few alterations, which Uhlig transferred to Frau Ritter's copy. (This latter is now in the possession of Herr Fritz von Hausegger). Yet another copy—which later became the

---

[1] The ramifications of this "fearing" motive and of the difficulties Wagner had with it are endless. It is impossible to pursue the subject further here: for further light on it I can only refer the reader to my *Life of Wagner*, Vol. II, Chapter XVII.

property of King Ludwig—he made about the same time for Liszt. But by now his restless imagination had evidently got to work afresh on the whole subject; for in September we find him telling Uhlig in one breath that he is about to set to work on the music—which, he says, will give him little trouble, for the musical phrases are fitting themselves to the words almost without conscious effort on his part,[1]—and in the next that although he has finished the fair copy intended for Liszt it is doubtful whether he will send it to him just yet.

Why that hesitation? We have the explanation of it in a letter of his to Liszt of the 20th November: his intensive work at the Nibelungen subject during the last few months, it appears, has made him doubt whether a simple reading of the poem of *Young Siegfried* will make it all as clear to his friend as he could wish. More than a month before this, in fact, the conviction had taken root in him that he could give the spectator an adequate idea of the whole scope of the myth only by prefacing *Young Siegfried* and *Siegfried's Death* with two further operas,—or, in his own nomenclature, an opera (*The Valkyrie*) and a "big prelude" (*The Rhinegold*). He had broached this new scheme of his in letters to Uhlig of the 10th October and 3rd and 12th November. In the last of these, and again in the letter of the 20th November to Liszt, he brings out into the open, for himself and for others, what must have been fermenting for a long time in the depths of his subconscious mind. He had begun in 1848, he says, with a plan for a vast drama on the myth of the Nibelungen Hoard. Still thinking at that time in practical terms of the contemporary theatre, he had condensed the enormous material as best he could into a single opera—*Siegfried's Death*—embodying "one chief catastrophe" of the myth, i.e. the doom that at long last overtakes Siegfried and the Gods through the rape of the gold from the Rhine and the curse laid upon it by Alberich, certain antecedent matters that could not be included in the stage action being "indicated", as Wagner expresses it, to the audience at this point or that in narrative. Then he had realised that there was too much narrative—too much "epic", as he put it—in his drama; and to remedy that

---

[1] "I already have the opening in my mind; also various plastic motives, such as that of Fafner", he says.

he had written *Young Siegfried,* in which some of these precedent matters were not merely told to the spectator but set visibly before him on the stage. And now, on further reflection, he has decided on two more preliminary operas, partly in order to get the whole myth on to the stage in plastic dramatic form, partly because the more he has brooded upon the subject the more fascinated he has become by the possibilities it opens out to his imagination as poet-musician.

25

Though he could hardly have realised it to the full just then, this resolution was the decisive turning-point not only of the *Ring* and of his art in general but of his whole outer life. A work on the huge scale he now had in mind would be a pure impossibility in the German or any other theatre of that epoch. He was well aware of this, and accepted it, and all its staggering implications, with characteristic courage. As he put it to Liszt, the big tetralogy he now had in view could be produced only at some "festival" or other: "how and in what circumstances such a production can become possible is something I am not going to worry about at present", he said blithely, "for the first thing for me to do is to work out my big plan, and this, if I am to give due consideration to my health, will take me at least three years." The Fates mercifully hid it from him that the last note of the tetralogy would not be written until near the end of 1874 and the whole work not performed until 1876, and then in a theatre of his own which he had somehow managed to bring into being at murderous cost to his happiness and his health: "every stone in that building", he said to Cosima bitterly one day as they were returning from the Bayreuth theatre after the first festival of 1876, "is red with my blood and yours."

The practical man of the theatre in him had become critical of the turn that *Young Siegfried* had taken towards epic rather than drama. *Siegfried's Death* had been, as the present *Götterdämmerung* is, full of dramatic movement; it was only occasionally that one of the characters launched into a narration of earlier events, and even these passages fitted quite logically into the dramatic fabric; far from holding up the action of the moment they helped it along and gave it greater point. But once Wagner had decided to set some of the events antecedent to *Siegfried's Death* on the stage in *Young Siegfried*, the amount of material presented him by the various myths became an embarassment to him. The actual stage action would permit of only so much; once more, as had been the case with *Siegfried's Death*, there remained whole stretches of the long story that would have to be communicated to the audience by means of narrative. In *Young Siegfried*, as Wagner must soon have recognised, there was comparatively little action after the first act, and even there a good deal of space had been taken up with acquainting the audience, by means of the series of questions and answers between Mime and the Wanderer, with the happenings that had led up to the scene now being shown on the stage. In the second act the action had been halted at this point or that for the enlightenment of the spectator by means first of all of the wrangle between the Wanderer and Alberich, then by a long survey of antecedent events in the colloquy between the Wala and the Wanderer. In the third act much space had been taken up by Brynhilde's acquainting the audience, *via* Siegfried, with the full story of the origin of the Volsungs, of Siegmund and Hunding, and of the death of Siegmund and the birth of Siegfried.

26

As has been pointed out already, Wagner had a double motive for deciding to replace these and other narrative episodes by a stage presentation of precedent events: the dramatic action would gain by the elimination or reduction of certain too "epic" elements, and the new dramas would provide him with a fascinating wealth of material for poetic characterisation and musical expression. Having resolved upon prefacing *Young Siegfried* with a *Rhinegold* and a *Valkyrie* he could now tighten up the action of *Young Siegfried* by taking out of the text of it a good deal of mere explanation. He began by shortening the scene of the exchange of recriminations between the Wanderer and Alberich, and then that between the Wanderer and the Wala. But the biggest cut of all was in the final scene on Brynhilde's rock between the Valkyrie and Siegfried. Some hundred and twenty lines of Brynhilde's narration—which, in a musical setting, would certainly have immobilised the stage action for a dangerously long time—were taken out at one slice and recast, to our eternal gain, as the three acts of the *Valkyrie*.

Having decided to complete his already double-barrelled scheme by writing two preliminary dramas, Wagner first of all drafted, apparently between the 3rd and the 10th November 1851, a short scenario for the *Rhinegold*. (For a while he could not make up his mind whether to give the new work that title or *The Rape of the Rhinegold*. It is obvious, by the way, that his first idea had been to make it an opera in three acts).[1] A few days later he made a tentative Prose Sketch for the first two acts of the *Valkyrie*. Why he did not draft the third act then we do not know; it may possibly have been because in the main the details of it were already too clear to him for him to need to put them on paper, and he was more immediately anxious to get to grips with the *Rhinegold*.

This preliminary Sketch bore the provisional title of "Siegmund and Sieglinde: the Chastisement of the Valkyrie". There are a few small differences between the plan for these two acts and that of the present *Valkyrie*. In the latter, the Volsung sword has been embedded by Wotan in the tree of Hunding's hut before the action opens; whereas in the Sketch, Wotan arrives in the hut while Hunding, Siegmund and Sieglinde are seated at the "guest meal". The stranger drives the sword into the ash-tree and departs: Siegmund withdraws it, whereupon Sieglinde surmises that he must be, like herself, a Volsung. (Here Wagner was proceeding on the lines of the Volsunga Saga). The second act was planned to begin with Fricka upbraiding Wotan for his condonation of the illicit love of the twin pair; judging from a marginal note in the Sketch it was only later that he decided to preface this episode

---

[1] The oddest feature of this first *Rhinegold* sketch is that Wagner proposed to begin the opera with "Wotan bathing", and in that condition learning from the three Rhinemaidens the peculiar virtue of the Gold. Then Alberich was to appear, woo the Maidens in vain, see the glowing Gold, and learn that it could be won only by one who forswears love.

with the present one, in which Wotan instructs Brynhilde to shield Siegmund in the coming fight. When Fricka, in the Sketch, asserts herself as the protectress of marriage vows, Wotan reminds her ironically that one of her sex, Grimhilde, had given herself to Alberich for gold: "he inveighs against Grimhilde and women". This little exchange of marital courtesies Wagner eliminated later, and it is not until we come to the *Twilight of the Gods* that we learn of the begetting of Hagen by Alberich upon Gunther's mother, the Gibichung Queen Grimhilde.

Wagner's bad health held him up for a time with his *Rhinegold* plan, though in a note book he drafted various little expansions of his first swift scenario. But as the days went by he realised, as he had often done before and was often to do in the future, that the best cure for his bodily malaise was not rest but creative work; and so, as the winter of 1851/2 drew to its close, we find him once more immersed in his great subject. In the spring of 1852, besides making a few jottings by way of elaboration of his first *Valkyrie* outline he committed to paper within no more than eight days— from the 23rd to the 31st March—a long Prose Sketch, occupying today more than sixteen large pages of print, for the *Rhinegold*.

27

This had been preceded by a fair amount of tentative sketching of certain details. A jotting on the theft of the Rhinegold had run thus: "Wotan knows nothing as yet of the power of the Gold. Fasolt and Fafner demand it as the price of the release of Freia (the Rhinedaughters have already said that the Giants too had hungered after it),[1] but they [Fasolt and Fafner] do not know of Alberich's rape of it. Wotan and Loge go first of all [i.e. after the Giants have demanded the Hoard in lieu of Freia] to the Rhinedaughters; here they learn what has happened, and their help is asked for the recovery of the Gold. Then they [the Gods] go to the Nibelungs . . ." Wagner is evidently puzzled, as yet, how to launch the work. In this jotting, though Wotan knows nothing of the virtues of the Gold, Fasolt and Fafner do; indeed, they

[1] This, of course, does not appear in the present poem.

have at some time or other wished to gain possession of it[1]—
which is a last rather blurred echo in Wagner's mind from the
First Sketch of 1848, where the action begins with the robbery of
the Gold by Alberich, a robbery of which the Giants are aware
and the consequences of which they dread. Now, in 1852, Wagner
shows them ignorant of the fact that Alberich has acquired the
Gold, though they themselves have lusted after it in the past. Yet
while the Giants had known all about the Rhinegold the Gods
are still ignorant of it, or at any rate of the power inherent in it.
In the end Wagner wisely deprived both Gods and Giants of pre-
knowledge of the Gold and the Ring, and cut out his projected
first scene of a colloquy between the Giants and the Gods and the
visit of Loge to the Rhinedaughters, while a second jotting shows
him to have already hit upon the right layout for his second
scene—Wotan and Fricka, the castle completed and payment
demanded, the return of Loge with the news of Alberich's rape of
the Gold, the distress of the Gods over the loss of Freia, the
Giants' demand of the Gold, and the journey of Wotan and Loge
to Nibelheim.

28

Further note-book jottings of the Spring of 1852 show him
gradually beating the first act of the *Valkyrie* into its present
shape, though he still clings to the idea of introducing Wotan in
the scene in Hunding's hut and having him leave the sword in
the ash-tree as a "guest-gift". Wagner even makes Wotan go to
sleep there, "after a short address of urgent warning to Siegmund,
who, however, in the impatience of his passion [for Sieglinde]
pays no attention to him. When Wotan appears to be asleep (in a

[1] Two passages in the present *Siegfried* show Wagner unconsciously
reverting to the abandoned plan of 1848. Mime jeers at Alberich in this
fashion: "Where now is that Ring of thine? Thou coward, the Giants
wrested it from thee"; whereas it was not the Giants but Wotan and Loge
who had robbed him. Again, in reply to Mime's second question, the
Wanderer says: "On the broad earth dwells the race of the Giants. Fasolt and
Fafner, their princes, envied the Nibelung's power: the mighty Hoard they
won for their own, and with it took the Ring." This is consistent with the
original plan of 1848 but quite inconsistent with the present *Rhinegold*.

recess in the background), Sieglinde enters." Wagner's stage sense made him discard all this later, though apparently it appealed to him for a considerable time, as is shown by a jotting in the margin of his first rapid Sketch (of November 1851) for the first two acts of the *Valkyrie*. Opposite the passage relating to the wrangle between Wotan and Fricka over the love of Siegmund and Sieglinde, he has crammed into the margin this suggestion for an effective retort by the God: "Wert thou[1] witness of their love? What knowest thou, who saw'st and heard'st them not?" The handwriting of this jotting seems to indicate that it was not contemporary with the Sketch itself; perhaps it was added when Wagner, in the spring of 1852, made the further sketches with which we have just been dealing.[2]

The beautifully written manuscript of the full *Rhinegold* Sketch, which followed next, runs to some seventeen pages of print, and must have been the outcome of much concentrated thinking during the winter of 1851 and the spring of 1852, so complete is it in detail, and so correspondent to the present poem. The variants from the latter are few. Two vital features alone of the ultimate poem are lacking in the Sketch: there is no reference to Freia's apples as the source of the wellbeing of the Gods, and in the stage directions for the transition from the scene on the sunlit heights to that in Nibelheim there is no mention of the clangour of Nibelung anvils. On the other hand, Erda, when she rises to warn Wotan to give up the Ring, speaks in more detail than in the present poem. In the latter, all she says about the future at the point in question is:

> *All that exists endeth!*
> *A day of gloom*
> *dawns for your godhood:*
> *I charge thee, give up the Ring!*

In the Sketch she is much more explicit: "Hear the counsel of the Norns that I bring thee! Ill will it fare with you Gods if you are false to treaties, and yet more ill if you, Wotan, keep the Ring.

---

[1] "As I was" is implied.
[2] A facsimile of the manuscript at this point will be found in Dr. Otto Strobel's *Richard Wagner: Skizzen und Entwürfe zur Ring-Dichtung*, p. 206.

Slowly to their ending the Gods will go, but swift your downfall
if you do not give up the Ring." More she refuses to say, in spite
of the God's anguished entreaty; and there can be no doubt that
Wagner was right in leaving the matter, for the time being, veiled
in a certain mystery. So with the later episode in which Wotan
greets the resplendent Walhall and bids the Gods enter with him.
In the Sketch he says, "Thee, majestic pile, I won for myself, paying the price with the accursed Gold. Now let the curse run its
course; I cannot avert it, but within thy mighty walls I will gather
round myself noble companions to uphold the world joyously
with me. Let Dwarfs and Giants band themselves against me in
envy and greed; there will I bring a new race into being." And a
little later, when Fricka asks him the import of the name Walhall,
he replies, in the Sketch, "When those are born whom I shall
summon thither, then will the meaning of the name be clear to
thee." In the present poem, however, Wagner wisely leaves the
future enveloped in mystery; into Wotan's mouth he puts the
studiously enigmatic words:

> *What strength 'gainst my fears*
> *my spirit has found,*
> *when vict'ry is mine,*
> *maketh my meaning clear.*

In all such contingencies as this, Wagner could rely on his music
for a potency of suggestion beyond the scope of words.

29

By this time he had manifestly decided to cast the *Rhinegold*
into one-act form; and we may be sure that even when he was
drafting the Sketch he was seeing and hearing everything in
terms of music. In a marginal note we see him hesitating for a
moment over the names of the three Rhine Maidens, and finally
keeping Flosshilde and Wellgunde but rejecting "Bronnlinde"—
which perhaps came too near to "Brynhilde"—in favour of
Woglinde. In the text of the opening scene of the Sketch he had
merely specified that the swimming Maidens should sing "a
joyous melody of the waves, without words". Then, in a later

marginal note, he decided, after much scratching out, upon the
half-words, half-nature-sounds of "Weia! Waga! Woge du Welle!
Walle zur Woge! Waga! laweia! Wallala weia la wei!", which
agrees as nearly as makes no matter with the song in the present
opera.

For the rest, we see from the Sketch how far Wagner had
travelled by now from the original scheme of 1848. There the
drama had begun on a cosmic plane, with three primal forces—
Gods, Giants and Nibelungs—locked in a combat upon which
the future of the world depended. The Nibelungs aspire cease-
lessly to power; the Giants seek only the safety of dull inaction;
the Gods, seeing further and more nobly than the others, work
for the making of a world in which everything shall tend towards
ultimate righteousness. But in the full *Rhinegold* Sketch and the
opera as we now have it the motivation of the Gods is something
quite different. They have lost almost all their collectivity and
with it their cosmic grandeur. In their collective place we now
have the single God Wotan, half human in his qualities and
motives. Like Alberich, he is possessed by the lust for world
power. In pursuit of his aim he is none too scrupulous; for the
building of the fortress that is to ensure his safety against all
enemies he enters into a compact with the Giants which he never
had any intention of carrying out, bartering Freia against their
labour, and trusting, when the hour of settlement should come,
to the crafty and cynical Loge to find for him a way of evading
his obligation. Nor is his wife Fricka any less free of ordinary
human weaknesses. When she reproaches him for the levity with
which he had placed Freia and them all in such peril he counters
with the reminder that she herself had counselled him to build the
castle. She, in her turn, rounds on him in purely human terms:
Wotan is too fond of "ranging and changing" in the egoistic
pursuit of love; and it was to bind him more closely to his own
hearth that she had favoured the building of the fortress on which
he had manifestly set his heart—only to find later that he had duped
her into acquiescence, his immovable purpose all along having
been to achieve through it domination of the world. And Fricka
herself, when she hears from Loge of the treasure the Nibelung
has accumulated by means of the *Ring*, is all for robbing him of it

to turn it into trinkets for feminine adornment; gladly she seconds the proposal that Wotan and Loge shall descend to Nibelheim and despoil the too fortunate gnome.

This personalising of the force of the Gods in the single character of Wotan, and the humanising of him and Fricka, certainly presents Wagner with endless opportunities for musical expression; but it can hardly be denied that it deprives, for a while, the general scheme of the *Ring* drama of some of the ethical loftiness of the original plan. Wagner will reach his first far-foreseen ethical heights before the vast drama is over, but by a rather different route from the one he had first intended.

30

The full-scale Prose Sketch for the *Valkyrie*, made between the 17th and the 26th May 1852, runs to twenty pages of print. It is mostly in the first act that it differs occasionally from the present poem. It shows us Wagner still bent on introducing Wotan in person in the opening scene and striking the sword into the ash-tree in the presence of Siegmund, Sieglinde and Hunding. But in a couple of marginal jottings we see him hitting on the right course of procedure—Sieglinde is to tell Siegmund of a mysterious stranger who had once come into the hut and struck the sword into the tree. This new conception necessitated, of course, a re-handling of the scene in which the two Volsungs declare their love for each other. But it did more than that. Obviously the climactic point of the first act should be that in which Siegmund proves his Volsung blood by doing what none of the other heroes who had passed through the hut from time to time had been able to do—drawing the sword from the tree. In the Sketch this highly dramatic moment had come comparatively early in the act, just before Hunding retires to the inner chamber to sleep. The later plan enabled Wagner to postpone Siegmund's acquisition of the sword to the point at which it is most dramatically effective—the very end of the act, when Siegmund and Sieglinde rush out into the forest and to freedom together.

The end of the second act presents us with one of those curious instances in which Wagner, when he came to write his opera poem, modified the plan of the Sketch without taking sufficient care to eliminate all traces of the change. The reader who knows the *Valkyrie* will remember that at the end of the second act, after the death of Siegmund, the angry Wotan turns to Hunding with the words:

> *Get hence, slave!*
> *kneel before Fricka:*
> *tell her that Wotan's spear*
> *avenged what wrought her shame.—*
> *Go! Go!*

and strikes him dead with a contemptuous wave of his hand. More than one puzzled spectator has probably asked himself how a dead Hunding could go and kneel before a living Fricka. But if we turn to the Sketch we find at this point: "Wotan (bitterly): Go hence, and tell Fricka, on whom you called for help, that you have been avenged by my spear"; and the God strides away in fury to seek out Brynhilde and punish her, leaving Hunding still in the land of the living. This links up, of course, with Wagner's original intention that Siegfried's first act after the forging of the sword should be to track down his father's slayer and kill him.[1]

In the final *Valkyrie* Sketch, as in that for the *Rhinegold*, we see once again how changed Wagner's conception of Wotan now is from what it had been in 1848. More and more human elements have gathered about Wotan in the process of concentrating "the Gods" in his person. In his dialogue with Fricka in the second act

---

[1] Discrepancies and loose ends are almost inevitable in the case of a vast design upon which a poet has worked for many years: changes are made at this point or that without the necessary adjustments being made at another. It was so with the *Aeneid*. The third Book is now in the form of a narrative told by Aeneas to Dido. But originally this tale of the voyage from Troy had been told not by Aeneas but by the poet himself, and the design of the Book —as, indeed, of the *Aeneid* as a whole—was altered later. The result is that it is sometimes difficult to square the course of events in the later Books with that suggested in the third. There are evidences, says Mr. W. F. Jackson Knight, "that Vergil wrote the Third *Aeneid* early, perhaps while he still designed a more historical poem than he eventually wrote, and that he did not finally adjust the book, either by revising it or by rewriting it, to the scheme which he finally chose". (*Roman Vergil*, pp. 71–2).

we find him charged by her, as he is again in the present poem, with a number of marital infidelities; as the poem has it:

> *Thy own true wife*
> *thou oft hast betrayed;*
> *never a deep*
> *and never a height*
> *but there wandered*
> *thy wantoning glance;*
> *all the joy of change thou wouldst win thee,*
> *and griev'd'st my heart with thy scorn.*
> *Sad at heart*
> *I saw thee forsake me,*
> *fly to the fray*
> *with the savage maidens*
> *whom thou in lawless*
> *love didst beget;*

and so on. Is this drastic humanisation of the God a final gain or loss to the drama? It is hard to say: it gives Wagner an opportunity to bring him nearer to us in his music, showing us the depths of tenderness there are in Wotan's heart for his beloved daughter, his second self, Brynhilde, and for the tragically fated Volsung race whom he had begotten in the hope that in some way of its own it would accomplish his frustrated will and redeem the world from the wrong he had brought into it; but at the same time no one who has studied the original scheme for the *Ring* can help feeling that something of its first grandeur and the high ethical impulse that brought it into the great company of the Greek dramatists has gone out of it.

31

Working with such passionate concentration that his health suffered for it, Wagner completed the long *Valkyrie* poem between the 1st June and 1st July 1852. In most essentials it agrees with the present poem, though he made some changes later in the handling of the scene between Wotan and Fricka in the second act.[1] His damaged health made progress on the *Rhinegold* poem rather slower than he had hoped, but the task was completed between the 15th September and the 3rd November 1852. It was during this time that he decided at last on the title for the huge drama: rejecting "Der Reif des Nibelungen"[2] and "Das Gold des Nibelungen" he finally settled, apparently in October, on "*Der Ring des Nibelungen*, a stage-festival-play to be produced on three days and a fore-evening". But his labours were still not at an end. The texts of *Young Siegfried* and *Siegfried's Death* had now to be altered in various ways to avoid repetitions of, or clashes with, the course of the action as set forth in the *Rhinegold* and *Valkyrie*. Two episodes in *Siegfried's Death* had to be re-written—the opening scene of the Norns and the scene of the visit of the Valkyries (now cut down to one of their number, Waltraute) to Brynhilde's rock. The colloquy of Alberich and Hagen in the second act of *Siegfried's Death* had to be radically recast, and, of course, a new ending to that drama had by now become necessary. It was not until the 15th December 1852 that he could write at the bottom of the last page of his manuscript "End of the stage-festival-play".

32

So much for the general chronological record. We have now to retrace our steps a little and glance at the artist Wagner in the process of completing his vast plan by the writing of two dramas to precede *Young Siegfried* and *Siegfried's Death*.

[1] When printing the *Valkyrie* poem in 1872 in the sixth volume of his Collected Works he added, at the foot of the relevant pages, the text as he had framed it in 1852, "before I had embarked on the musical setting". Even in 1852, indeed, he had re-written several passages when making a fair copy of the poem as it then was. Dr. Strobel gives us a facsimile of the page of the manuscript containing the words of Siegmund and Sieglinde at the close of the first act, showing the many alterations in the wording. It is rather puzzling at first to find this revised page dated by Wagner "11 May"—a time when he was engaged not on the poem but on the Sketch. As Dr. Strobel points out, however, "11 May" is obviously a slip of the pen for "11 June".

[2] "Reif" has the same meaning as "Ring".

This enlargement of his original scheme landed him in difficulties of various kinds which he could not have foreseen. *Siegfried's Death* had been laid out on broad lines, the protagonists being to a great extent generalised, the Gods, the Giants and the Nibelungs confronting each other as ethical types, in the way they had done in the first Prose Sketch of 1848. Wotan had not appeared in person at all in *Siegfried's Death*. Of the personalities who play so large a part in the present *Ring* only Siegfried, Brynhilde, Gunther, Gutrune, Hagen and Alberich had figured in that first work. *Young Siegfried* had added Mime, the Dragon, the Wala (Erda), and the Wanderer. With the addition of the *Rhinegold* and the *Valkyrie* to the plan a number of new characters had to be created—Wotan in his primal form as chief of the Gods, Loge and the minor Gods, Fasolt and Fafner, Fricka, Siegmund, Sieglinde and Hunding—and appropriate dramatic settings had to be devised for all of them; moreover, all that these new characters did and said had to be brought into logical relation with the final stages of the drama.

Wagner had now to make up his mind once for all as to certain factors which so far he had found it necessary only to treat in generalised fashion or refer to *en passant*. Here the myths could give him little help, for they are silent on several vital points and vague or contradictory on others. What, for instance, was the Gold that generated the Hoard? In different legends it comes into being and disappears again in different ways: sometimes it is associated primarily with the waters, sometimes with a mountain or a cave. Precisely how a hoard came in the course of time to be the *Nibelung* Hoard we do not know; nor do we know exactly who the Nibelungs were. We are no clearer as to the building of Walhall. In one myth a certain master-builder offers to build the Gods a fortress that will secure them against the Giants, naming as his price the Goddess Freia. Loge, the most crafty of the Gods, persuades them to accept the offer, with the proviso that the castle shall be finished by the first day of summer, a feat which appears impossible. The master-builder, however, has a horse, Swadilfari, which performs miracles in the way of conveying the necessary stones. Only three days remain before the coming of summer, and the fortress is complete except for the entrance. The artful Loge saves the situation by turning himself into a mare, which entices the horse into the forest; the builder loses a day and a night in catching it, and so over-runs the time-clause in the contract. The Gods now discover that he is an enemy of theirs—a Giant,—and Thor disposes of him by a blow on the head with his hammer. The legends, in forms as naïve as these, could not be of much use to Wagner.

While for certain episodes of the *Rhinegold* and the *Valkyrie* he drew upon the Volsunga Saga, they were not presented to him there in a form that he could use for his drama. The Saga tells, for instance, of a man called Otter, so named because he was skilled at lying on the river bank and catching fish. One day, after having caught a fine salmon, he is slain by a stone thrown at him by Loge, who happened to be passing with Wotan and another God. Otter's father, Hreidmar, demands in atonement for the killing of his son that the Gods, who have brought him the skin of the otter, shall fill and cover it with gold. The ever-resourceful Loge goes to the sea-goddess Ran, takes her net, and captures in a waterfall a pike which is in reality the dwarf Andvari, whom he deprives of all his gold, including a ring. Andvari lays a curse upon the treasure: it shall bring ruin on every future possessor of it. The Gods go to Hreidmar and proceed to cover the otter-skin with the gold; but Hreidmar cries out that he can still see a hair of the otter's muzzle, and Wotan is compelled to part with the ring to cover the chink. Andvari's curse soon begins to operate; another son of Hreidmar—Fafner—murders his father to gain the treasure, and changes himself into a *Wurm* so that he may lie brooding upon it for ever. Once more we see that such an account as this of the origin of the gold and of the curse upon it, and of Fafner's changing himself into a dragon to guard it, could not furnish Wagner with more than a hint or two for the management of his drama.

33

It would take us too far afield, and fulfil no really useful purpose, to trace the various elements of Wagner's *Ring* to their sources in the myths. He has been reproached for not having kept more closely to these. The reproach has no justification. There is nothing sacrosanct about the legends themselves. They do not form a single organic work of art in which any single mediaeval writer could claim a proprietary right. They are simply a collection, or an amalgam, of stories of varying antiquity, with a touch here and there of the historical, as when the terrible figure of the Hun Attila, "the scourge of God", who destroyed the Burgundians in the mid-fifth century, enters on the scene under this name or that.

The three main sources for our knowledge of the story of the Volsungs and that of the Nibelungen Hoard are the Volsunga Saga, the Thidrek Saga, and the Nibelungenlied. Wagner took from each of them only what he needed for his own vast plan, and, as he was to do later with the Tristan and Parzival legends, condensed the material here, modified it there, and imposed his own ethical scheme upon it all. And out of it all he has made the most stupendous of dramas since the *Oresteia*.

In February 1853 he printed a private edition of the four poems, and he told his friends he hoped to set to work at the music in the coming spring. By July 1857 he had completed only the composition of the *Rhinegold*, the *Valkyrie* and the second act of *Siegfried;* then he laid the work aside to write *Tristan,* and, later, the *Mastersingers*. In April 1863 he brought out a public edition of the *Ring* poem, with a long preface setting forth his plan and hopes for a "festival" performance in some new theatre or other built specially for that purpose.[1] From his fellow-Germans *en masse*, he said, he did not expect much in the way of helping him to realise his ideal of music-drama; but he cherished the hope that some German Prince or other might come to his rescue. "Will this Prince be found?" he concluded. That preface was read and taken to heart by the ardent young Crown Prince Ludwig of Bavaria, then in his eighteenth year. He made a silent vow that if ever it should be in his power to do so he would place the re-

---

[1] This imprint necessarily differed at many points from that of 1853, as Wagner incorporated in it the verbal alterations that had occurred to him, or been forced upon him, when writing his music. In the 1863 edition the titles of *Young Siegfried* and *Siegfried's Death* are definitely abandoned for *Siegfried* and *The Twilight of the Gods*.

sources of the Munich Court Theatre at Wagner's disposal; and when he ascended the throne in March 1864 he sent for the composer, assured him an existence free from ordinary material cares, and urged him to complete as soon as might be the great work which he had had to lay aside for so long.

34

The composition of the *Rhinegold* had occupied Wagner from the 5th September 1853 to the 14th January 1854, the full score being completed on the 28th May. The *Valkyrie* was composed between the 28th June and the 27th December 1854, and the orchestral score finished by the end of March 1856. The first two acts of *Siegfried* took him from the 22nd September 1856 to the 30th July 1857, the third act from the 1st March to the 14th June 1869. The full score was completed on the 5th February 1871. The dates of composition of the *Twilight of the Gods* were: act one, the 2nd October 1869 to the 5th June 1870, act two, the 24th June to the 19th November 1871, act three, the 4th January to the 10th April 1872. The full score was finished on the 21st November 1874.

The *Rhinegold* was first performed in Munich, on the 22nd September 1869, with the following cast: Wotan:—August Kindermann; Fricka:—Sophie Stehle; Alberich:—Karl Fischer; Mime:—Schlosser; Loge:—Heinrich Vogl; Donner:—Heinrich; Froh:—Nachbaur; Fasolt:—Petzer; Fafner:—Bausewein; Erda:—Fräulein Seehofer. The *Valkyrie* followed on the 26th June 1870, the principal rôles being cast as follows: Siegmund:—Vogl; Sieglinde:—Therese Vogl; Brynhilde:—Sophie Stehle; Wotan:—Kindermann; Fricka:—Anna Kaufmann; Hunding:—Bausewein. Both operas were conducted by Franz Wüllner.

The first public performances of the *Ring* in its entirety took place in Bayreuth, under Hans Richter, on the 13th, 14th, 16th and 17th August 1876, with the following casts:

Singer	Rhinegold	Valkyrie	Siegfried	Götterdämmerung
Betz	Wotan	Wotan	Wanderer	
Gura	Donner			Gunther
Unger	Froh		Siegfried	Siegfried
Vogl	Loge			
Hill	Alberich		Alberich	Alberich
Schlosser	Mime		Mime	
Eilers	Fasolt			
Reichenberg	Fafner		Fafner	
Sadler-Grün	Fricka	Fricka		3rd Norn
Marie Haupt	Freia	Gerhilde	Wood-Bird	
Jaïde	Erda	Waltraute	Erda	Waltraute
Lilli Lehmann	Woglinde	Helmwige		Woglinde
Marie Lehmann	Wellgunde	Ortlinde		Wellgunde
Marie Lammert	Flosshilde	Rossweisse		Flosshilde
Niemann		Siegmund		
Niering		Hunding		
Scheffzsky		Sieglinde		2nd Norn
Materna		Brynhilde	Brynhilde	Brynhilde
Antonie Amann		Siegrune		
Reicher-Kindermann		Grimgerde		
Johanna Wagner		Schwertleite		1st Norn
Siehr				Hagen
Weckerlin				Gutrune

THE RHINEGOLD

I

The first sound we hear is a long-held E flat deep down in the
double-basses, a primordial element, as it were, out of which the
world of water represented by the Rhine will come into being by
slow differentiation. At the fifth bar the next decisive note of the
natural scale, the dominant, B flat, is added in the bassoons, and in
the seventeenth bar the horns, in an ascending arpeggio, further
add the third, G natural. The triad of E flat major is now fully defined, and out of that primal substance:

Wagner proceeds to shape the 136 bars of the prelude proper. In
the 49th bar the addition of intermediate notes of the scale gives
us a motive more specifically that of the Rhine itself:

though in the later course of the drama it will gather to itself other
associations. In the episode of Siegfried's Rhine Journey in the
Twilight of the Gods, for instance, it unquestionably refers to the
river, while as accompaniment, later in the *Rhinegold,* to Erda's
warning to Wotan, where she speaks of "the three daughters
born to me ere the world was made", and of her knowing all
things that were and shall be, the motive is manifestly associated
in Wagner's mind with the primal element to which reference has
just been made. It is one more illustration of the inadequacy of
any one verbal label to cover all the significances which this or
that motive originally had in Wagner's mind, or all the symbolisa-

tions that clustered about it as he sank himself more deeply into his subject.

The motion of the music gradually gains strength, and No. 2 floats now upon a series of arpeggio figures:

suggestive of waves. While the tempo of the music remains always technically the same the sense of inner motion keeps on increasing, until the waters seem to be in full flood; and at this point the curtain rises.

Through a greenish twilight, that is darker below, lighter above, we see the bottom of the Rhine. In the lower depths the waters shew more as a thin, humid mist, while in the upper part of the scene they are waves flowing in a mighty tide from right to left. Through the gloom of the lower mist craggy points of rock are visible jutting out everywhere, while in the enveloping darkness great fissures are suggested. As the flood of tone surges up in the orchestra to the highest point it has yet attained, one of the Rhinemaidens, Woglinde, comes into sight, swimming in a graceful circle round a rock that rises from the centre of the scene, the slender peak of it being visible in the clearer upper waters.

The E flat harmony that has run through the whole of the orchestral prelude so far suddenly shifts over, at the 137th bar, to the plane of A flat as Woglinde sings a greeting to the waters:

Wei - a! Wa - ga! Wo - ge, du Wel - le, wal - le zur Wie - ge!
Wei - a! Wa - ga! Wander, ye wa - ters, lap me and lull me!

She is answered by the voice of her sister Wellgunde from above, then by that of Flosshilde; and the trio pursue each other in innocent merriment, though Flosshilde chides the others for losing sight in their play of what should be the object of their constant care—the sleeping Gold which it is their duty to guard.

2

While they are laughing and sporting the Nibelung Alberich has emerged from a dark chasm and clambered up to one of the rocks; himself hardly visible as yet in the darkness, he watches the gambols of the Rhinemaidens with growing pleasure. He hails the sisters in a raucous voice; he comes from Nibelheim, he says, and would gladly share in their sport. The Rhinemaidens dive deeper, see the uncouth creature who is addressing them, recoil from him in disgust, and dart upward again to swim in circles round the central rock: it was against some such foe as this, they remind each other, that their father warned them. The amorous Alberich begs them to descend again, that he may clasp the slender form of one of them in his arms. The grotesque spectacle of this repulsive gnome in love moves them to laughter, and they begin to tease him, swimming within clasping distance and then swiftly darting out of his reach, while he clambers awkwardly after now one, now another of them, slipping on the slimy crags and gasping and sneezing as he gropes his way through the mist. At last he loses his temper and tells the "cold and bony fish" who are laughing at him to "take eels for their lovers", since he is too ugly in their eyes for love.

Hitherto his attentions have been paid mostly to Wellgunde and Woglinde; now Flosshilde pretends to take pity on him, and in an enchanting lyrical interlude, in which the insinuating beauty of her song draws a corresponding sweetness of response even from the uncouth gnome, she promises him better fortune with her than he has had with her sisters. She maliciously simulates the passion and cajoleries and gallantries of genuine love:

> Oh thy sharp-pointed glance
> and thy stiff scrubby beard,
> for ever to see and to hold!
> Might those bristles, thy curls,
> so wiry and wild,
> float round thy Flosshilde for ever!
> And thy form like a toad,
> and the croak of thy voice,

Oh might I, mute and amazed,
nought else hear and behold!

For a moment she takes him in her arms, then breaks away
cruelly from him and swims towards her sisters, and at a safe distance the three burst into heartless laughter at his expense.
Goaded to fury, he swears he will capture one of them: he clambers with terrifying agility over the rocks, trying to seize now one
of the Maidens, now another; but always they elude and deride
him. At last he pauses, speechless, breathless, foaming with rage,
and shakes a menacing fist at them:

But his attention is suddenly drawn away from them by a glow
that spreads gradually over the upper waters, finally concentrating itself in a dazzling gleam on the high point of the central
peak. It is the sleeping Gold awakening, and through a gentle
undulation of the strings we hear, in a horn, the motive of the
Rhinegold:

The Rhinemaidens hail the Gold joyously, and as the shimmer
increases and No. 6 peals out again in a trumpet they break into
a rapturous trio:

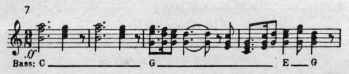

as they swim gracefully round the rock. The orchestra seems to bathe the scene in a bright golden light.

3

The wondering Alberich asks the sisters the meaning of it all. They tell him what this golden glory is that floods the deeps with its radiance, and invite him to join them in their revels round it. He replies scornfully that if the Gold serves merely for childish games like theirs it has no attraction for him.   But he would not talk like this, they assure him, if he knew the wonder that resides in the Gold: could anyone win it for his own and fashion a Ring from it he could make himself master of the world; and the wood wind give out softly the all-important motive of the Ring:

Because of the virtue that is in the Gold, Flosshilde reminds her sisters reprovingly, their father has warned them to guard it watchfully lest some robber seize upon it. But Wellgunde and Woglinde in their turn remind her of what it is that secures the Gold against falling into hands that may use it to work evil: only one who had forsworn love could forge a Ring from it; and the motive of Renunciation of Love is heard for the first time as they sing:

He who the power
of love forswears,
from all delights
of love forbears,
alone can master the magic
that makes a Ring from the Gold:

Nur wer der Min - ne Macht ver - sagt, nur wer der
He who the power of love for - swears, from all de-
Bass: G_____ C_____ F_ G_____

Lie - be Lust ver - jagt,
-lights of love for - bears,
_Ab_____ G

Secure they may be from care, then, "for all that liveth loveth,
and no one in all creation will forswear delight of love". And
least of all, Woglinde adds, this languishing, lusting imp here,
visibly racked with love; and they ironically invite him to join
them in their laughter, for the glory of the Gold has laid a touch
of beauty even on his hideous form.

Soft enunciations of No. 6, followed by No. 9 in the darkest
colours of the brass, show us what is passing through the gnome's
brutish mind; with his eyes fixed on the Gold he says to himself:

> *The world's wealth*
> *can I win for my own then through thee?*
> *If love be denied me,*
> *delights by my cunning I'll seize!*
> *Mock as ye will!*
> *The Niblung neareth your toy!*

The Rhinemaidens scatter before him in terror as, with a supreme
effort, he springs over to the centre rock and clambers to the
summit of it. With a demoniacal laugh he stretches out his hand
towards the Gold and cries:

> *Then frolic in darkness,*
> *brood of the waves!*
> *Your light lo, I put out,*
> *I wrench from the rock the Gold,*
> *forge me the Ring of revenge;*
> *for hear me, ye floods:*
> *Love now curse I for ever!*

While the terrified Rhinemaidens fly from him he tears the Gold from the rock and plunges with it into the depths, where he disappears from sight.

With the rape of the Gold the whole scene is suddenly plunged into darkness. The waters seem to sink into the depths below, and from the lowest deep of all Alberich's mocking laughter is heard. To a dark swirl of orchestral sound the rocks disappear in a billowing flood of black water that seems to sink and sink unendingly. The motive of Renunciation of Love strikes across it all like a sinister shadow, to be succeeded by the Ring motive in a new and broader form:

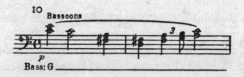

By this time the waves have gradually changed to clouds, and these to a fine mist, which slowly disperses as an increasingly bright light pierces through it from behind; and as the mist finally drifts away we see an open space on a mountain height.

4

Day is dawning. At one side of the scene are Wotan and his wife Fricka, both asleep on a flowery bank. As the light grows stronger there becomes visible, on the top of the cliff in the background, a majestic castle with glittering battlements; between this and the foreground where Wotan and Fricka recline we are to suppose the broad Rhine to flow.

From the orchestra the noble Walhall motive wells up in soft harmonies in trombones and tuba, with an occasional trumpet fanfare pealing out:

The conclusion of the motive:

is in the same rich colours. An immense peace seems to brood over the scene.

Wotan is dreaming blissfully of the splendid castle that has been built for him, a stronghold from which he sees himself, in imagination, ruling the world in unassailable might and to his own eternal glory; through the tissue of his dream, however, the theme of the Ring (No. 10) winds softly in the 'cellos. Fricka shares none of her spouse's illusions about the matter: she rouses him from what she calls his "deceptive dream" and exhorts him to take thought for the realities of the situation as it is bound to shape itself soon for him and herself and the other Gods. But for the moment reality has no meaning for the ecstatic, power-drunk dreamer. Raising himself slightly he catches sight of the majestic stronghold across the river, which he apostrophises: "'Tis completed, the everlasting work! There on the mountain top stands the citadel of the Gods with its stately soaring walls. In dreams I conceived it; my will called it into being; strong and fair it stands, fortress proud and peerless!"; and the trumpet hails it also with a final solemn gesture of its own.

But Fricka tells him that what makes his heart glow with pride of possession fills hers with dread. The fortress is indeed there, but the price has yet to be paid. The grave motive of Wotan's Treaty with the Giants, that has been engraved in runes on the God's spear:

Cellos & Basses in 8ves

is heard in 'cellos and basses as she reminds him of his compact: Freia, the Goddess of youth and beauty and health and charm, had been promised to the Giants in payment. The infatuated Wotan waves her cares aside. Let her not fret over the price to be paid, he tells her; that is his affair—though manifestly he had hardly given it a serious thought, trusting to Loge, the nimble-witted and none too scrupulous God of fire, to solve his problem for him when the hour of reckoning should come. Fricka overwhelms him with reproaches for his levity: without ever consulting her and the other Gods he had callously bartered her sister Freia for the gratification of his lust for power.

Wotan ripostes that Fricka herself had been in favour of the building of the castle, and she explains why—heavy at heart over her spouse's infidelities she had thought to bind him to hearth and home by means of this splendid toy on which his heart had been set; and her sorrow finds expression in the gracious motive of Love's Enchantment:

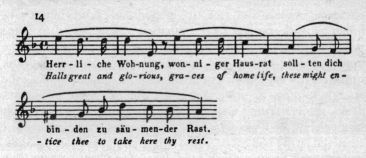

Herr - li - che Woh-nung, won - ni - ger Haus-rat soll - ten dich
Halls great and glo-rious, gra-ces of home life, these might en-

bin - den zu säu - men-der Rast.
- tice thee to take here thy rest.

But now, she continues, she sees that she has been mistaken; Wotan's one thought had been and is for power. With a smile, echoing ironically the gracious line of No. 14, he admits his double-dealing. "Ranging and changing" is his delight, as it is that of all who love, and he cannot desist from it; but if henceforth he is to be confined to his home, at least it shall be one from which he can subject the whole world to his rule. Again she reproaches him for his heartlessness in sacrificing love—here the orchestra breathes softly the melody of No. 9—for "the tawdry toy of empire and power". The consummate casuist replies that to win her own love

in days gone by he had forfeited an eye, so that her present reproof is unjust. In any case, it is because he prizes woman and
woman's love so much that he will not resign Freia to the Giants;
never, indeed, had that been his intention, he assures her.

5

A quickening of the tempo and a succession of urgent figures in
the orchestra suggest hurried action behind the scenes. Fricka,
looking off the stage, bids Wotan save Freia now, "for, defenceless and in grief, hither she hastens for help". Freia enters, as
if in flight, to a motive that will always be associated with her
later:

(The segment of this marked A has been a source of much trouble
to the analysts. They have dubbed it the motive of Flight, because
it occurs now and later in some sort of connection with that idea.
But we meet with it also in Wagner in quite other connections;
and the truth seems to be that it was a musical *tic* into which he
was inclined to fall on various occasions, sometimes, as here, with
a specific purpose, sometimes without any).

In distracted tones Freia calls on Wotan and Fricka to save her,
for Fasolt is hard on her heels for the payment promised to the
Giants. "Let him threaten", says Wotan tranquilly; "saw'st thou
not Loge?" Fricka scornfully upbraids him for putting his trust in
that trickster; he has already done the Gods much harm, yet always Wotan is caught in his snares. Still tranquilly sure of himself, the God replies that his only need for and his only use of
Loge are in cases like the present one, where wisdom fails and
craft and guile alone will succeed; when Loge had counselled him
to make his compact with Fasolt and Fafner he had promised to
find him a way to cheat them out of Freia; and Wotan still has
faith in the cunning rogue.

Freia calls desperately on her brothers Donner and Froh to come to her aid now that even Wotan has abandoned her. "They who wove this net of treachery about thee", Fricka tells her sombrely, "have all forsaken thee now!" At this tense point in the action Fasolt and Fafner enter, men of rough aspect and gigantic stature; their heavy tread and lumbering gait are depicted in their characteristic motive:

Quietly and patiently, for he feels he has right on his side, Fasolt, who is throughout of a milder nature than his brother, uncouth yet not essentially evil, brutish but not brutal, states their case to Wotan. With endless toil, heavy stone they have piled on heavy stone, and now the fortress stands there, resplendent in the light of day: "pass thou in, and pay our wage!" What that wage is Wotan knows—"Freia the fair one, Holda the free one;[1] the bargain is that she goes home with us twain." Wotan contemptuously rejects the demand: "Crazed must ye be to talk of that bond! Other payment ask: Freia is not for sale!" Through all this conversation, of course, run the motives of the Treaty (No. 13) and Freia (No. 15).

[1] Holda is another name for the Goddess of youth in the mythologies. Wagner here plays antithetically upon the two names and adjectives— "Freia, die Holde, Holda, die Freie."

6

Fasolt is for a moment speechless with amazement; then he asks the God if the solemn runes of treaty engraved on his spear are nothing more than a sport to him. The more realistic Fafner turns to his brother with a sneer: "My trusty brother, see'st thou not, fool, his deceit?" He sings the words to a phrase that is simultaneously outlined by the orchestra in this fashion:

This is obviously a broadened version of a motive associated later with Loge (No. 23 below). That Wagner should employ it as he does here is one of several indications that when he was writing the *Rhinegold* he was not yet fully master of his new method of constructing his musical fabric out of leading motives; he was sometimes inclined to introduce them without reasons that we can now regard as valid. It is true that Wotan had relied on the guile of Loge to get him out of his difficulty on the day of reckoning; but as Fafner knows nothing of all this there seems to be no justification for the Loge motive to be anticipated here in connection with the Giant's remark to his brother. Wagner is obviously speaking to us here not as dramatist but *in propria persona,* telling us in the audience something *he* knows and feels we ought to know.

Fasolt solemnly warns Wotan of the consequences of a breach of faith on his part. "What thou art", he reminds him, "art thou only in virtue of treaties by which thy power is defined. We in our turn are bound to thee in peace. Cursed be all thy wisdom, perish all peace between us, if, no more open, honest and free, thou breakest the troth thou hast plighted." The Treaty motive (No. 13) here takes a slightly different form in Fasolt's mouth, and Wagner makes the 'cellos and basses imitate the vocal line at a time-interval of a minim:

It is not over-fanciful to assume that he intended to imply by this thematic dualism that the treaty was a bilateral one, for in order to force the accompanying orchestral part on our attention Wagner has marked it "staccato but with decision".

These, Fasolt concludes, are the words of a simple-minded Giant; "do thou, wise one, mind our words!" But Wotan waves the admonition airily aside:

> How sly to take in earnest
> what but in sport was agreed on!
> The beauteous Goddess,
> sweet and bright,
> what need ye louts with her grace?

Fasolt turns on him in anger. Is Wotan mocking them? he asks. "Ye who by beauty reign" (here the violas give out a soft reminiscence of the motive of Love's Enchantment), "ye, the regal, radiant race, yearn like fools for a fortress of stone, bartering for it woman's grace and charm. We dullards sweat with toil-hardened hands to win us a woman who, winsome and sweet, shall smile on our homestead; and now ye would break your own bond!" As Fasolt speaks of the charm of woman Wagner indulges himself in a stroke worthy of Mozart, who loved his characters so much and was so completely one with each of them at the moment he was describing him that he could not touch the humblest and awkwardest of them without a caress: Wagner here lays the gentlest of hands on the uncouth Giant who has a strain of tenderness in him:

But the brutal Fafner strikes in with his usual realism. Why argue with these Gods? he asks his brother contemptuously. What, after all, is Freia to Fasolt and himself, except as a means of putting pressure on the Gods? For it is they who need her most. In her garden grow golden apples:

> Gold - ne Äp - fel wachsen in ih - rem Gar - ten
> Gold - en ap - ples bloom with - in her gar - den

which she alone knows how to tend. They bestow on her kindred everlasting youth; without them—and here No. 20 takes on a darker tinge in bassoons and horns:

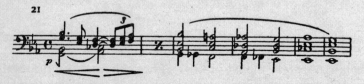

the Gods will grow old and weak and waste away. Therefore let the Giants wrest Freia ruthlessly from this arrogant, faithless race.

7

Fear begins to take possession of Wotan. "Why tarries Loge so long?" he asks in an anxious aside. To the Giants he says, "Demand another wage!"; but Fasolt refuses, and he and Fafner make to seize Freia, who runs, crying for help, to her brothers Donner and Froh, who have now entered hastily. Froh throws a protecting arm round her, and Donner, the god of thunder, stands in the way of the Giants, brandishing his hammer and threatening to pay them in a coin for which they had not bargained. Freia wails "Woe's me! Woe's me! Wotan forsakes me!". Wotan, now thoroughly sobered, stretches out his spear between the disputants and bids Donner stay his hand. Force will not avail, he tells him; the treaty is engraved in runes on his spear-shaft, and he is bound by it. As he turns away in anger and disgust and with a secret fear in his heart he sees Loge approaching, coming up from the valley at the back. He is heralded by various motives associated with him at one time or another as the God of Craft:

and the God of Fire:

Wotan reproaches him for his delay in bringing news of the errand with which he had been entrusted—to find some means by which the fatal compact with the Giants could be evaded. Loge raises his hands in cynical protest: what compact had *he* ever entered into? It was Wotan who had pledged his word. For Loge himself is hardly one of the Gods, so different is he from the others. Donner and Froh, he says, dream of hearth and home, Wotan of the stronghold sure which he has now obtained (here the stately Walhall motive surges up in full in the orchestra), thanks to Fasolt and Fafner having carried out their part of the compact. As for himself, he lives in another element and is subject to none of the limitations of the other Gods; a restless, elusive spirit of fire, he sweeps homeless through the world, wandering wherever his fancy leads him.

Wotan reproves his flippancy. If he has been deceiving him all this time, he says, let him beware, for Wotan is his only protector among the Gods, who like not the vagrant and his shifty philosophy. Well he knows that when the Giants named Freia as the price of their labour Wotan would never have consented but for a promise by Loge that he would find a means to evade that article of the bond. To the constant accompaniment of the volatile motives associated with him Loge protests that all he had sworn was that he would ponder upon the problem:

> *But that I'd find thee*
> *some sure way forth*
> *where no way lies,*
> *could I such promise lay on me?*

The other Gods are revolted by his heartless cynicism: Fricka turns to Wotan with an angry reproach that he should ever have placed faith in this treacherous knave: Froh tells the God of Fire that he should be called "not Loge but Lüge" ("lies"): Donner, with a threatening gesture, swears he will put out his light: on all which Loge's sole comment is a contemptuous

> *Their disgrace to cover*
> *the gross fools curse me!*

Wotan steps between them as peacemaker. Let them not affront his friend Loge, he says diplomatically. "Ye know not his wiles; the slower he is to give his counsel the craftier it always is." But at a peremptory command from Fasolt and Fafner for payment of their wage he calls on Loge to explain where and why he has lingered so long. The elusive one launches into the long scena known as "Loge's Narration", a gracious lyrical inset in an action that has latterly been carried on mainly on the lines of dramatic dialogue. Mockingly he reminds them that it is always his lot to get scant praise for what he does for them. The Freia motive (No. 15) takes on a particular grace and sweetness:

as he tells how unceasingly he had searched through the world for a ransom for her that would be likely to satisfy the Giants. But all had been in vain: nowhere in the wide world, in water, earth or air, had he found anything that man valued more than woman's love; for nothing would anyone renounce it. But at last he had heard of one who had cast it aside in scorn, and that for gold. The sorrowing children of the Rhine had told him how the Nibelung Alberich, having sought their favours in vain, had abjured love and robbed them of the Gold with a curse; and they had implored Loge to carry the tale of their loss to Wotan and beg him to punish the thief and return the Gold to the waters from which it had been ravished.

8

It is at this point that Wagner begins to develop real mastery of the new system of leading motives with which he had endowed opera. So far he has employed his motives in more or less literal reproductions of them in their primary form—which was, indeed, to be expected, for as yet everything connected with the drama is in its primary stage of simple exposition, and his first task had been to define the melodic and harmonic and rhythmic shapes by which characters and things were to be identified. But now, when the action begins to be more subtilised, corresponding subtilisations of his thematic material are called for; and we see Wagner taking the first steps towards that psychological variation of the leading motives of the *Ring* that was to find its consummation, twenty years later, in the *Twilight of the Gods*. We see him beginning with the motive of the Rhinemaidens' song (No. 7). When Loge tells how "the lustrous children of the Rhine poured out their lament to me" the opening chords of No. 7 undergo this harmonic transformation:

while at the words "From the glittering toy thus torn from the deep the Maidens are ever moaning" another harmonic change gives the motive, which in the beginning had been so symbolical of primal innocence and joy, a still profounder poignancy:

A little later in the Narration the smooth thirds of the Ring motive (No. 8) take on a darker tinge and a sharper edge:

Loge ends his story with a complacent and ironic assurance that he has now kept his promise to the Rhinemaidens to tell the story of their grief to the Gods. Wotan turns on him angrily: "Myself thou seest in need; what help have I to give to others?" But the story has struck deep into Fasolt and Fafner. "This Gold I begrudge the Nibelung", the former mutters; "much wrong he ever has wrought us, but always the dwarf has slipped away from our hold." "Some new mischief he will brew for us", replies Fafner, "if through the Gold he wins power." He asks Loge what is the greatness inherent in the Gold that the Nibelung lays such store by the possession of it. To the accompaniment of the Rhinemaidens' melody in its first innocent form, Loge tells him that when sleeping in the waters it is merely a toy, serving the laughing children of the deep for sport, but should it be rounded to a Ring it will confer measureless might on its possessor and give him dominion over the world.

"Rumours of this I already have heard", says Wotan reflectively, fitting the news into the pattern of his own thoughts. Fricka takes her own feminine view of it: would the golden toy, she asks Loge softly, serve as well for the adornment of women? More than that, replies the crafty God; she who possessed the golden trinkets which now the Nibelungs, slaves to its power, are making, could ensure her husband's faithfulness to her. She turns to Wotan, and, to the gracious strain of the Freia motive, says cajolingly, "Oh would that this Gold my consort could win!"

Unwittingly she has given utterance to Wotan's own secret thought. The Rhinegold motive (No. 6) peals out softly in the trumpet, then in quiet horn tones, as he says, half to himself, "To win the power contained in this Ring seems to me wise!" He asks Loge how the circlet can be made. Only by a magic rune, he is told; no one knows that rune, and none can learn it save by forswearing love. Wotan turns away in ill humour at this, and Loge remarks ironically, "That is not to thy liking! And indeed thou art too late. Alberich did not delay. Fearlessly he won him the magic spell, and already he has made the Ring."

9

The Gods are aghast. "Slaves shall we all be to the dwarf", says Donner, "if the Ring be not wrested from him." "The Ring I must have!" Wotan cries; while Froh is sure that now it is made it can be won easily without any of them forswearing love. Easily enough, replies Loge harshly: "by theft! What a thief stole," he explains to Wotan, "steal thou from the thief. Could aught be simpler? But Alberich guards himself with weapons of craft; shrewd and wary wilt thou have to be to overreach him and return the lustrous Gold to the Maidens whose cry for it goes up to thee." "Return it to the Maidens?" Wotan repeats incredulously; while Fricka sees no need to consider "that brood of the waves, who, to my grief, have lured many a man to their lair by their wiles." Silence falls upon the Gods; each of them, for reasons of his own, is ready to be an accomplice in the wresting of Gold and Ring and power from Alberich; but Wotan still shrinks from achieving that end by wrong-doing.

Their puzzled brooding is broken in upon roughly by the Giants. Fafner now lusts after the Gold not only because of the menace that Alberich's possession of it constitutes for them, but for its own sake. But to his brother he does not disclose all that is in his mind. He plays on what he knows to be Fasolt's weakness: the glittering Gold, he tells him, will serve them even better than Freia, for it too will bestow eternal youth on whoever makes the magic of it his own. Fasolt, as the upsurge of the motive (No. 20) of Freia's apples in the orchestra indicates, finds it hard to give up the gracious Goddess on whom his rough heart has been set; and his demeanour shows that he is yielding to Fafner against his will. They lumber together towards Wotan, accompanied by the characteristic No. 16, and Fafner tells him the decision they have come to. They will not insist on Freia: an easier quittance of the debt will content them—"for us rough Giants the Nibelung's red Gold will do".

Wotan protests feebly: "Are ye mad? How can I give you what is not my own?" "With toil and moil", rejoins Fafner, "we built thee thy fortress. To subdue Alberich has always been beyond the power of us dull ones; but for you Gods it will be easy to master him by superior strength and guile." This is not to Wotan's liking: is he to conquer the Nibelung, he asks them all, half indignantly, half despairingly, only to satisfy the demands of this shameless pair? He sees now the net of his own careless duplicity beginning to close in on him. Freia he had never intended to give up, trusting to Loge's craft to find him a way out of his compact. His motive in making it had been to acquire a fortress from which he could hold sway over the world, bending both Giants and Nibelungs to his will. Another way of achieving that end has just been disclosed to him by Loge—the seizure of the Gold from Alberich, who will certainly use it to make himself master of the world; and no sooner has this way to the achievement of Wotan's purpose been pointed out to him than the Giants present him with his original dilemma in another form; he must give up either Freia or the Gold.

Fasolt breaks the tension by roughly drawing Freia to his side and bidding her come with them until the ransom is paid. Till nightfall, say the Giants, they will hold her as pledge; if, when they return, the Gold is not there for them, Freia will be forfeit. Screaming for help she is dragged away, and to graphic descriptive music in the orchestra Loge describes to the others how the rough pair stride away over stock and stone through the valley and across the Rhine by a ford, with the fair Goddess slung across their shoulders.

10

A change comes over the scene; a pale mist spreads over the stage, becoming gradually denser. The Gods look old and wan: in the orchestra the motives associated with Freia take on more sombre tints. At first only the cynical, detached Loge can find words for what is in the thoughts of all of them: they seem sick and withered, he tells them, the bloom has fled from their faces, dimmed is the light of their eyes; Froh's high courage has left him; Donner's arm is too feeble to hold up his great hammer; and Fricka—is she not grieving for Wotan, now grown old and grey in a trice? He sees it all: nothing of Freia's golden apples have they eaten today, the apples that renew their youth and strength; and now the Goddess herself is ravished from them, and without her the branches of the tree will droop and the decaying fruit fall to the ground. Loge does not spare them in their misery. He himself, he tells them, suffers nothing of all this; Fricka, who likes him not, has ever been sparing of the delicate fruit to him, nor does he miss it as they do, for by nature he is at best only half a God. But for the others the hour of doom has sounded, and the Giants know it and are calculating on it: "lacking the apples, old and grey, haggard, hoary, withered, the scorn of all the world, the race of the Gods is passing away."

Fricka's voice is raised in weary lament:

Her reproach rouses Wotan. Starting up as a resolution suddenly shapes itself in his mind he bids Loge come with him to Nibelheim, where they will seize the Gold. Loge plays cruelly with him once more: he is going, then, after all, in answer to the prayer of the Rhinemaidens, to whom he intends to return the Gold? Wotan furiously bids him hold his peace. The Rhinemaidens do not concern him; all that matters is the ransoming of Freia. Loge suavely consents to go with him: "shall we descend to Nibelheim straight and steep through the Rhine?" "Not through the Rhine!" replies Wotan. "Not through the Rhine?" Loge echoes ironically, for he knows the God's reasons for not wishing to meet the Maidens now: "then swing we ourselves through the sulphur cleft there yonder; slip down it with me!" He disappears in a fissure at the side of the stage, from which a sulphurous vapour immediately rises. Wotan follows him, telling the others to wait there until evening, when he will return with Freia's ransom.

11

The long descriptive orchestral piece that accompanies the change of scene depicts the course of the two Gods to Nibelheim, and is necessarily constructed at first out of such motives as that of Loge and that of Alberich's Renunciation of Love (No. 9), the latter now in ominous dark brass colours. Then we hear what is generally described as a reminiscence of a figure:

which, in the opening scene of the opera, had expressed the gnome's anger and despair over his repulse by the Rhinemaidens. In the form it now takes:

it becomes a motive, usually labelled that of Servitude, which is put to important uses later. There is no necessity, however, to assume any hard-and-fast connection, on Wagner's part, between No. 30 and No. 31. A semitonal descent of this kind—naturally expressive of a wail or moan—appears in his works in all kinds of associations.

A figure that immediately follows No. 31 is usually described by the analysts as a development of the so-called Flight motive (No. 15A), though just why this concept should be drawn upon here is not explained. We are on surer ground when we hear the Rhinegold motive (No. 6) in the bass trumpet, and then a hammering figure:

which we have already heard in Loge's Narration, at the point where he had told the other Gods of "the toiling dwarfs, slaves to the power of the Ring, who are smithing the Gold for Alberich". As with so many of Wagner's motives, this can be labelled in more than one way: primarily, as its rhythm implies, it describes the frenzied hammering of the enslaved dwarfs, and so constitutes what may be called a Smithing motive *per se*; and later in the *Ring*, as in the scene in *Siegfried* in which the hero forges his father's sword anew, Wagner employs it in this generalised sense. But in so far as the hammering is done in the *Rhinegold* by the Nibelungs the figure can with equal legitimacy be taken as *their* characteristic motive. It is an admirably malleable piece of musical material; it easily passes from the primarily rhythmical to the harmonic, and as easily combines with other motives, as in the following example at the point we have now reached:

where, in the lower part, the lament of the enslaved Nibelungs is heard piercing through the rhythm of their hammering.

We can coldly dissect this orchestral interlude for purposes of anatomical demonstration, but it is an organic musical structure, developing according to its own laws at the same time that it tells in graphic form the story of the Gods' journey. After Wotan and Loge have plunged into the fissure and disappeared from our sight a sulphurous vapour spreads rapidly over the stage in dense clouds. These ascend for a while, ultimately revealing a dark, solid rocky chasm which appears to be moving continuously upward, creating in the spectator the illusion that the stage is sinking deeper and deeper. Wotan and Loge, still unseen by us, are evidently nearing Nibelheim: a dark red glow becomes visible at various points in the distance, and on all sides we hear the clang of smithing: at the point denoted by our No. 33 the purely musical texture is reinforced by the smithing rhythm hammered out on eighteen anvils behind the scenes. The din increases, rises to a climax, and gradually dies away; and at last our eyes distinguish a great subterranean cavern that opens out on all sides into narrow shafts.

12

To graphic orchestral figures Alberich now appears, dragging his shrieking brother Mime out of one of the clefts in the rock. Mime, most skilful of smiths among the Nibelungs, has been trying a little sharp practice. Alberich has the Ring, which gives him the power to force his fellow-gnomes to tear the Gold out of the bowels of the earth for him. But what if Mime, whose cunning he knows well, should decoy him into some trap or other, or rob him of the Ring when he is asleep? To guard against this, Alberich has ordered him to make him a helmet which, he hopes, will enable him to be everywhere and at all times among his slaves, himself unseen, keeping them to their work, and secure against surprise when he sleeps. He knows, or strongly suspects, that Mime's craft has been equal to the task, but that he is concealing the Tarnhelm, hoping to use it himself to overcome his stronger brother. So now Alberich is urging the dwarf, with threats and blows, to give it up to him. Between his shrieks for mercy Mime makes stumbling excuses: the work is indeed finished, he admits, but he has been holding it back to see if it can be improved upon in any way. In his fright he lets the little piece of delicate metal work fall from his hand. Alberich pounces on it and examines it closely: it is the Tarnhelm, the characteristic motive of which, charged with mystery, is given out softly by the muted horns:

It is quoted here in its full form. Only the first half of it is breathed by the orchestra as Alberich takes the work in his hand and studies it critically: the second section, from A onwards (where we see the so-called motive of Servitude in the upper part), appears a little later, when he places the object on his head and tests its powers by murmuring a spell: "Night and darkness— nowhere seen!" At once, to Mime's astonishment, Alberich disappears, only a cloud of vapour appearing where he had been standing. "Where art thou? I see thee not!" says Mime. "Then feel me, idle rogue!" replies Alberich; and we see the dwarf writhing under the blows from an invisible scourge.

Sure of himself now, Alberich, still invisible, imperiously apostrophises the Nibelung hordes: let them all kneel to him as their master, for now everywhere, at all times, himself unseen, he will be among them, keeping them to their work; slaves will they be to him for ever. The column of vapour that is Alberich disappears towards the back of the stage, and we hear his roaring and cursing receding into the distance; howls and shrieks come from the lower depths and die away from point to point as he makes his way further through the earth; and the hammering Nibelung rhythm in fortissimo combination with the Servitude motive (as in No. 33) tells us that the cowed slaves are being driven with a scourge to their work.

Mime has sunk to the ground in pain and terror; there, groaning and wailing, he is found by Wotan and Loge, who now enter on the scene from one of the clefts. Loge sets the whimpering dwarf on his feet again, and he tells them his sad story—how his brother Alberich had forged a Ring from the ravished Rhinegold and subdued the whole race of Nibelungs, who had once been so innocently happy working for themselves and making trinkets and toys for their womenfolk. Now this brutal brother of his has made vassals of them all: by virtue of the Ring he senses where gold lies, and for him they have to trace and track it, and dig and melt it, and cast it into bars and heap it in mounds. Mime he had compelled to make for him a magic helm, knowing the properties of which he, Mime, had intended to keep it for himself, to escape from servitude, and, perhaps, seize the Ring and so have Alberich in his power. But alas, though his craft was equal to making the object he did not know the spell that alone could animate it; and so it is now Alberich's, who had scourged him cruelly and vanished from his sight: "such thanks for my toil, poor fool, I won!" The opening words of Mime's narrative are accompanied by a figure in thirds in the bassoons:

which will be used later by Wagner (in *Siegfried*) to depict the dwarf once more brooding upon the problems that confront him. It is generally referred to as the motive of Reflection.

The newcomers laugh at the lament of the grotesque little figure. This perplexes him, and he looks at them more attentively. Who are they? he asks. Friends, they assure him, who have come to set the Nibelungs free. But just then Alberich is heard approaching, and Mime runs hither and thither in helpless terror: "have a care", he tells them, "for Alberich nears." "Here will we await him", says Wotan tranquilly. He seats himself on a stone; Loge leans by his side. To the dual strains of No. 33 Alberich enters, now in his own shape again, with the Tarnhelm hung on his girdle, driving before him, with a whip, a multitude of Nibelungs who run up from the cave below: they are laden with gold and silver work of all kinds, which, under the compulsion of the whip, they pile up in a huge mound. Suddenly Alberich catches sight of Wotan and Loge and halts suspiciously. With his scourge he drives Mime into the mass of the other Nibelungs, bidding them all get on with their tasks. He draws the Ring from his finger, kisses it and stretches it out threateningly towards them as the orchestra gives out the Ring motive followed by that of Servitude:

Loitering yet?
Linger ye still?
Tremble in terror,
down-trodden host!
Quick to obey
the Ring's great lord!

The gnomes, Mime among them, scatter in all directions, howling and shrieking, into the shafts.

13

Alberich scans the intruders warily and asks who they are and what they are doing here. Wotan tells him that they have come to see for themselves the wonders that have reached their ears of the great achievements of Alberich. To an angry outburst from the gnome, Loge replies that he should treat his guests with more courtesy. Who is it but he, Loge, who brings light and comforting warmth to the imp as he crouches in his sunless cave? Where would he be with his forging did not Loge light his fires? "I am thy kinsman and was thy friend: not lavish art thou with thy thanks." Alberich, however, is not to be duped by cajoleries. Loge was always false, he rejoins; once, it is true, he was his friend, but now he consorts with the light-elves[1] who dwell above: is he false to them too? But Alberich has no fear of him or them: do they see the Hoard that his host of toilers has heaped up for him over there? And "that's only for today, a paltry measure. Day by day it shall increase my glory:" and the sinister motive of the Hoard wells up in the depths of the orchestra in bassoon and bass clarinet:

---

[1] Lichtalben, the Gods: Alberich himself is a Schwarzalb, a black-elf.

But what use is all this wealth to him, Wotan asks, here in joy-less Nibelheim, where his treasure can buy him nothing? The treasure itself is something, Alberich replies; but it is more than its mere self—by means of it he will bend the whole world to his will. The beings who dwell in the upper air live, laugh and love, lapped in gentlest zephyrs (here the orchestra gives out the motive (No. 15) associated with Freia and her gracious charm); but he will wrench all this happiness from their grasp and make the Gods themselves his vassals. He himself has forsworn love, and at his bidding everything that has life shall forswear it too; by gold overpowered, for gold alone shall they yet hunger. There on the radiant mountain heights (here the Walhall motive rises in serene majesty in the orchestra) dwell the Gods in bliss, despising the black-elves below. But let them beware:

> *For first ye men*
> *shall bow to my might,*
> *then your winsome women,*
> *who my wooing despise,*
> *shall sate the lust of the dwarf,*
> *though love they deny . . .*
> *Beware of the night-nurtured host*
> *when the Nibelung Hoard shall uprise*
> *from silent deeps to the day!*

He is an impressive figure, the incarnation of envy and hatred and evil will, a force which Gods and men will have to reckon with.

He laughs savagely in Wotan's face. The outraged God vents his disgust on him, but Loge, stepping between them, counsels him to control his anger. Then he turns to Alberich with his usual smooth assurance. Who could fail to feel wonder, he asks, when faced by Alberich's wonderful work? If his craft can perform all he claims for it, what limit is there to his future power? Sun, moon and stars will all have to bow down before it. Yet, he deferentially hints, there may be just one thing it were wise to take into his cal-culations—the Nibelung host who are heaping up this treasure for him may possibly become envious of him and it; and by the slightest of harmonic turns to the Nibelung motive Wagner suggests the danger that may be lurking for Alberich in the dark places of Nibelheim:

When he had held up the Ring to the gnomes, continues Loge, they had cowered before him. But what if a thief were to steal on him in his sleep and rob him of the Ring? What counter has he to that?

14

Alberich's vanity makes him fall into the trap. Loge flatters himself he is the cunning one, he says, but in his conceit he deems others witless. He, Alberich, had been clever enough to foresee the danger his kind friend has pointed out to him, and had provided against it. He has made the skilful Mime fashion for him the helm that is now hanging from his girdle, which enables him to change his shape or be invisible at will:

> *No one sees me,*
> *though he may seek;*
> *yet everywhere am I,*
> *though veiled from the view.*
> *So, free from care,*
> *I live secure, safe from thy craft,*
> *thou good, kind-hearted friend!*

Of all the many marvels he has met with on earth, replies Loge, this is the greatest. If Alberich speaks the truth, eternal might is indeed his. But who could believe in such a wonder except on the evidence of his own eyes? The vain gnome is willing and eager to prove it. What shape would Loge like him to assume? Loge has no choice, provided only the deed confirms the word. Alberich places the Tarnhelm on his head, murmurs a spell—"Dragon dread, turn thee and wind thee"—to the strain of No. 34, and instantly disappears: in his stead is a huge serpent writhing on the ground and stretching out its gaping jaws towards each of the Gods in turn:

Loge pretends to be paralysed with terror; "Spare the life of poor Loge!" he cries. Wotan breaks into hearty laughter and compliments the gnome with an ironic "Good, Alberich! How wondrous quick the dwarf changed to a dragon!" The serpent vanishes and Alberich reappears in his own form, saying complacently "Hoho! ye wise ones! do ye believe me now?"

In a quaking voice Loge assures him that scepticism is no longer possible. Alberich has indeed changed himself into a big snake; but can he also accomplish the correspondingly small? That, surely, would be even more serviceable, for in case of danger he could slip away more easily. "As you will", says the vainglorious Alberich; "how small?" "Tiny enough", Loge replies, "to creep into the sort of crevice a toad makes for in its flight." "Pah! nought simpler!". The spell is murmured once more—"Crooked toad, grovel and crawl"; and in the gnome's place appears a toad. At a quick word from Loge, Wotan puts his foot on it; Loge takes it by the head and seizes the Tarnhelm, whereupon Alberich instantly becomes visible again in his own form, writhing helplessly under Wotan's foot and crying curses on him. Loge binds him hand and foot with a rope; despite his struggles he is dragged to the shaft by which the Gods had entered, and the three of them disappear, the orchestra breaking out into a jubilant fantasia on the Walhall motive, that of Loge (No. 22), and that of the Ring (No. 8). The triumph of the Gods seems complete.

15

The scenery now changes as before, but in the reverse order, as though Wotan and Loge were ascending. The motive of the Renunciation of Love is heard in quiet trombone tones: then, as the Gods may be supposed to be making their way past the forges, the Nibelung rhythm is heard once more hammering out on the anvils, but gradually sounding further and further away. For a moment the Freia motive rings out, as if announcing the triumphant return of the Gods from their mission, but, it is to be observed, in darker harmonies, hinting that there may be another side to the picture than the one on which the Gods' complacent gaze is just then fastened. The tone-painting continues with the motives of (*a*) the Giants, (*b*) Walhall, (*c*) Servitude, (*d*) Loge, (*e*) Freia's youthful charm, (*f*) the Rhinemaidens, and finally Servitude in the form (No. 30) in which, at the beginning of the previous scene, it had symbolised the subjection of the Nibelungs to Alberich. Now he himself is at the bottom of Fortune's wheel.

When at last the stage setting defines itself again we see the mountain height once more, still shrouded in the pale mist that had descended on it after the departure of the Giants with Freia. Wotan and Loge emerge from the shaft, dragging with them the bound Alberich. Loge loads him with sarcasms. "There, kinsman, take thou thy seat. Look, my worthy, there lies the world thou longedst to have for thy own: what corner wilt thou give me for my stall?" He dances round him in glee, snapping his fingers at him. Alberich curses him for a rogue and a robber and demands to be set free. His freedom he shall have, rejoins Loge, when he has paid ransom. The dwarf turns furiously on himself for his folly: "O thou dolt, thou credulous fool! to trust blindly this treacherous thief!"; and he vows revenge on his captors.

Wotan tells him what his ransom is to be—nothing less than his Hoard. Harsh as the terms are, Alberich, in an aside, comforts himself with the thought that if only he can save the Ring he can re-create the treasure, and the lesson will not have been too dearly bought if it teaches him to be wiser in future. He will summon the Gold for them, he says, if they will untie his hand. Loge sets his right hand free. The gnome puts the Ring to his lips and murmurs a secret command: a soft mysterious breathing of the Ring motive in the orchestra is succeeded by the motive of Servitude in the dominating form it has assumed in No. 36: there is a moment of fateful silence, then we hear the various motives associated with the Nibelungs as slaves of Alberich. These sounds grow louder as the Nibelungs approach and at last pour on to the scene, running out from the clefts and bringing with them the Gold and treasures of all kinds that constitute the Hoard, which they pile up on the stage. Alberich, impressive even in defeat, writhes at the thought that his vassals should see him thus shamed, in bonds. Imperiously he orders them to be quick with their work and keep their eyes off him:

> Then hence with you, rabble,
> haste to your tasks!
> Back to your burrows!
> Woe if idlers I find,
> for I follow hard at your heels!

He kisses his Ring and holds it out commandingly. "As if he had struck them a blow", say the stage directions, "the Nibelungs rush in terror to the cleft, into which they gradually disappear below." This is one of the most tremendous episodes in the score, with the orchestra thundering out No. 36 in the loudest tones of trumpets and trombones.

16

The turmoil having died away, Alberich demands that he be released and allowed to take with him the Tarnhelm that Loge has thrown on the Hoard. The God contemptuously replies that this is part of the ransom. Alberich curses him, but then reflects that "he who made the one can make me another: still mine is the might that Mime obeys." Loge asks Wotan if he shall release their captive. But Wotan now demands also the Ring that gleams on the dwarf's finger. "My life take, but not the Ring!" cries Alberich in desperation. For life, he says, means nothing to him without it: hand and head, eye and ear, are not his more truly than this Ring. Sternly and bitingly Wotan asks him how he came to possess it. How did he get the Gold from which it is made? Was it not by theft from the Rhinemaidens? To Alberich all is now clear: the Gods are using him for a purpose of their own, and one no better essentially than his. "Do you, vile thief", he cries, "cast in my teeth a crime so welcome to you? You yourself would have robbed the Rhine of the Gold had you known how to forge the Ring from it":

> How well, thou knave,
> it worked for thy purpose,
> that I, the Niblung,
> smarting with shame
> and with anger maddened,
> the terrible magic did win
> whose work now gladdens thy gaze!
> This curse-laden
> and monstrous deed
> of one wild with grief,
> wasted with woe,
> must now serve as toy
> for thy eyes to delight in,
> my curse prove a blessing to thee?
> Heed thyself,
> high-handed God!
> If I did sin,
> I sinned but against myself:
> but against all that was,
> is, and shall be,
> wilt thou, Wotan, sin,
> if basely thou seizest my Ring!

Wagner, it will be seen, is holding the moral scales fairly between the two. For the first time, the central ethical problem of the great drama comes clearly into sight.

But it is too late now for Wotan, caught as he is in a net of his own weaving, to choose the right; he is irrevocably committed to a course of wrong-doing the consequences of which to himself and all of them he cannot foresee; and it is finely significant that Wagner leaves the fitting-in of this cornerstone of the great moral structure not to Loge—who has hitherto carried on most of the dialogue with Alberich—but to the more responsible Wotan. Ruthlessly he flings himself on the dwarf and tears the Ring from his finger; and while Alberich, with a horrible shriek, bewails his ruin, the God, possessed with but one thought—that of the acquisition of the power he has long desired—places the Ring on his own finger and contemplates it. "'Tis mine now", he muses, "the spell of might that makes me lord of the world!" Curtly and contemptuously he gives Loge permission now to release the impotent gnome. Loge unties his bonds and tells him to "slip away home", for he is free.

Raising himself from the ground, Alberich echoes the God's last words with a wild laugh. "Am I then free? Really free? Then hearken now to my freedom's first salute!" He begins the tremendous monologue in which he lays a curse upon his lost Ring and upon everyone into whose hands it shall come:

> As it gave me
> measureless might,
> let each who holds it
> die, slain by its spell!

To no one on earth shall its radiance bring joy: care shall consume each wretched possessor of it, and envy gnaw at the heart of him who owns it not. No gain shall it bring to anyone, but murder shall follow it wherever it goes: the Ring's lord shall be the Ring's slave, till once more it shall return to Alberich's hands:

> So, stirred
> by the direst need,
> the Nibelung blesseth his Ring:
> and now 'tis thine,
> look to it well!
> But my curse canst thou not flee!

The monologue is dominated by two new motives of great importance in the later unfolding of the *Ring* drama, that of the Annihilation prophesied by Alberich:

and that of the Curse on the Ring:

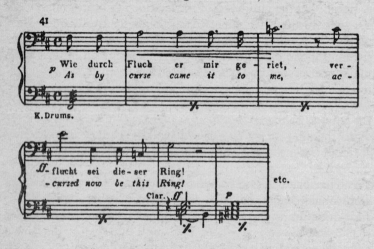

With a demoniacal laugh Alberich disappears into the cleft.

17

"The art of composition", said Wagner once, "is the art of transition". We have one of many examples of his own gift in this respect in the scene that follows Alberich's exit. The furious repetitions of the Servitude motive in the orchestra die down gradually into a succession of falling arpeggios that finally poise themselves on a few quiet, broad harmonies. "Didst thou hear his fond farewell?" asks the cynical Loge. "Let him enjoy his own slaver", Wotan replies quietly, lost in dreams as he contemplates the Ring on his finger. As the light slowly increases a series of tranquil harmonies ascending slowly in the orchestra depicts his satisfaction. But underneath them we hear pulsing insistently the rhythm of the motive of the Giants; and Loge, looking off stage, descries them in the distance, returning with Freia.

But for the present there is no cloud on the bland peace of the scene and the music. The mists disperse still further as Fricka, Froh and Donner enter. Fricka runs to Wotan and asks him anxiously for news of his mission. His answer is to point to the Hoard: "By force and guile our end we gained: there lies Freia's ransom"; but the muttering of the fateful Annihilation motive in the orchestra tells us something he himself, in his self-centred blindness, has not realised yet—that the Fates are brooding over the too complacent God, only waiting their opportunity to strike him down. Froh draws in a breath of ecstatic relief: how lovely is the smile of the earth, he says, how balmy the breeze; what would the Gods be without Freia and the "painless perpetual youth" she bestows on them?

As the light grows clearer still the Gods are seen recovering their old freshness of aspect; the castle, however, remains invisible in the mist that spreads over the Rhine and the heights beyond. (Wagner, like the good stage-craftsman he is, is reserving the sight of resplendent Walhall for a great dramatic stroke in the final moments of the opera). Fasolt and Fafner enter, bringing with them Freia, who runs to Fricka with a cry of joy. But Fasolt steps between them. Not yet, he reminds them, is she theirs; grieving he has brought her back to them; let the Gods now pay the price agreed on for her. Fasolt heaves a sigh: to part with Freia saddens his heart, but if he must lose her, at least let the treasure be heaped so high as to hide her from his sight. To this Wotan consents. The two Giants place Freia in the centre of the stage, and thrust their staves in the ground on either side of her so as to measure her height and breadth. Wotan, sick with a sense of failure and degradation, bids them get on with their work. Assisted by Loge and Froh—the latter as anxious as Wotan to put an end to Freia's shame and theirs—the Giants heap up the treasure between the two poles, Fafner, in his greed for gold, roughly pressing the pile more tightly together and searching for crevices.

Wotan turns away in profound dejection: "Deep in my breast burns this disgrace!" he mutters. Fricka pours reproaches on him for his ambitious folly. "More! yet more!" cries Fafner. Donner rounds on him furiously, threatening him with his hammer; Wotan tries to pacify him, and Loge assures the Giants that the Hoard has given out. But Fafner, peering more closely, catches a glimpse of Freia's golden hair and demands that the Tarnhelm be thrown in to hide it. Wotan, more than ever weary of it all, tells Loge to add it to the pile. Fasolt, still grieving over the loss of Freia, peers more closely at the heap, and, as the orchestra gives out the gracious melody of No. 19, discovers a crevice through which he can still see her eye shining on him: "while its soft beauty doth charm me", he cries, "from the woman I cannot part." Loge protests that the Hoard is quite exhausted; but Fafner points to the golden Ring on Wotan's finger and demands that it shall go to stop the crevice. Loge assures him that Wotan intends to return it to the Rhinemaidens from whom the Gold was ravished; but Wotan swears vehemently that the prize he has won so hardly he will not part with. "But what of my promise to the Rhinedaughters?" asks the crafty, insincere Loge. "Thy promise binds me not;" rejoins Wotan: "the Ring I claim as my own. Boldly ask what ye will", he says to Fafner; "all else I'll give to you; but for all the world will I not surrender the Ring."

18

Fasolt's angry reply to this is to pull Freia out from behind the pile. "We end, then, where we began", he cries; "Freia is forfeit to us for ever!" He makes to leave the scene, but is held back by Fafner. Freia, Fricka, Donner and Froh appeal to Wotan to relent, but he is immovable: he is too deep now in the pit of his own digging to extricate himself by his own efforts. "Leave me in peace", he says moodily; "the Ring I will not yield!" And he turns away from them all in blind, futile anger. The knot of the drama cannot be untied now, but only cut; and that is done by the intervention of a world force greater even than the chief of the Gods himself.

By this time the stage has become quite dark again, and from the rocky cleft at the side there now breaks forth a bluish light, in which Erda suddenly becomes visible, rising from below the ground to half her height. She is the earth Goddess, the mother of the Norns who weave the threads of the world's destiny. Wagner symbolises her primal and eternal quality by a hardly perceptible but curiously significant mutation of the motive of primordial matter with which the opera had begun. (See examples No. 1 and No. 2). The theme is now in the minor, in the grave colours, first of all, of bassoon and tuba, and in a slow tempo:

The Gods stand awed and mute at the sight of this apparition. Erda stretches out her hand commandingly to Wotan and bids him relinquish the Ring and so evade the curse that lies on it; nothing but disaster will it bring him. "Who is the woman who brings me this warning?" he mutters. She tells him: "Whatever was, know I, whatever is, whatever shall be, I can see. The eternal world's Urwala,[1] Erda, 'tis who warns thee." By the most natural of transitions No. 42 resolves itself back again into No. 2:

as she tells him of the three daughters born to her before the earth was made; all that her eyes see is told to him nightly by the Norns.

---

[1] It is as the Wala that Wotan invokes her in the first scene of the third act of *Siegfried*, "the eternal woman possessed of all the world's wisdom". Wagner seems to have taken over this concept from two of the Edda poems, the *Vegtamskvida* and *Balder's Doom*. More will be said on this point when we come to the *Siegfried* scene.

She has come to him now because he is in dire danger (here No. 40 projects its sinister shadow in the orchestra). "Hear me! Hear me!" she urges, to the falling figure seen in the bass part of No. 33 and the first bar of No. 36; "all that exists must come to an end. A day of gloom dawns for the Gods: again I charge thee, give up the Ring!" At this point a new motive appears, that of the Twilight of the Gods:

which concept Wagner symbolises by a simple reversal of No. 43. "Grave and mysterious are thy words", says Wotan thoughtfully; "tarry a while and tell me more that I would know." But already the bluish light has begun to fade, and Erda slowly disappears, with no further message for the tortured God than this: "I have warned thee; thou hast learned enough; brood now in care and fear." Wotan makes a desperate move to follow her into the cleft and ask her the meaning of this enigma: if henceforth he is to live in anxious fear, he cries, she must at least tell him all. But Froh and Fricka hold him back.

19

The God halts and stares thoughtfully before him, then turns resolutely to the Giants; they shall have their Gold, he tells them. We see him brooding profoundly on Erda's last words as No. 42 wells up in sombre orchestral colours. Then, rousing himself from his abstraction, he brandishes his spear as if he had taken a bold resolution, the trombones thundering out the commanding No. 13. Freia shall return to them, he says, bringing them their youth once more: the Giants can take the Ring and go. He throws it on the Hoard; Freia runs to the Gods, and the orchestra becomes all gladness and light as they load her with caresses. That Wagner, as a composer, was still to some extent the Wagner of *Tannhäuser* and *Lohengrin* is shown by the following phrase expressive of rejoicing:

Meanwhile Fafner has spread out an enormous sack, into which he begins to pack the Hoard. At once the Giants begin to quarrel over it. Fasolt demands measure for measure; Fafner reminds him that:

> More on the maid than the Gold
> thy lovesick eyes were set;
> I scarce could bring thee,
> fool, to exchange her;
> hadst thou won Freia,
> no share to me hadst thou given:
> now with the Hoard
> rightly retain I
> the greater half for myself.

The sordid wrangle goes on. Fasolt appeals to the Gods for justice, but Wotan contemptuously turns his back on him. "Resign the treasure", Loge counsels Fasolt, "but make thyself sure of the Ring". The Annihilation motive (No. 40) mutters ominously in the depths of the orchestra, but Fasolt knows nothing of Alberich's curse. He throws himself on his brother, insisting on the Ring as compensation for Freia. They struggle for it, each seizing it in turn. At last Fafner fells Fasolt to the ground with a blow from his staff and wrenches the Ring from the dying Giant's hand: "Now glut thee with Freia's glance", he tells him grimly, "for the Ring seest thou no more!" He puts it on his finger and goes on quietly with his packing of the Hoard: the Gods stand around in horror-struck silence, and the curse motive (No. 41) rends the air in the trombones. Alberich's curse has struck already, Wotan remarks in awed tones.

Loge, to the sinister throbbing of No. 40 in violas and bassoons, congratulates him on a good fortune with which nothing on earth can compare: great had been his luck when he won the Ring from

Alberich, but greater still now he has lost it, for those who won
it fight to the death for it. But one thought only is in Wotan's
brooding mind. Live a slave to fear and care he cannot: how to
end them no one knows but Erda, so to her he must descend.
While the clarinets give out a reminiscence of the caressing No.
14 Fricka approaches him cajolingly: why does he not enter the
noble fortress that awaits his coming? she asks him. "With evil
wage I bought me that!" he answers sombrely.

The air is cleared by Donner, who, oppressed like the rest of
them by the sweltering mists that envelop them, ascends a high
rock that overhangs the valley, swings his hammer, and bids them
disperse. Through swirling clouds of vapour a mighty horn call
tears its way:

He - da!   He - da! He-do!   Zu mir, du Ge-düft!
To me, all ye mists!

A vivid storm-picture ends in a convulsion, as it seems, of all
nature as Donner crashes the hammer down on the rock and a
blinding flash of lightning bursts from the clouds, followed by a
violent thunderclap. For a moment Donner and Froh—the latter
has run to his brother's side at his call—are invisible to the others.
Then, almost in a moment, the clouds disperse; and when the pair
become visible again we see, gleaming in the sunlight, a great
rainbow bridge which they have thrown across the valley for the
transit of the Gods to Walhall. During this storm episode Fafner
has completed his packing up of the whole Hoard, and departed
with the great sack on his back.

With the Rainbow motive:

rising up from the depths of the orchestra in a great span, Froh
points out to the others the way over the rainbow arch to the

fortress where they can live henceforth, free of the terror that has descended upon them since the murderous strife over the Ring and Erda's solemn warning. The noble Walhall theme (No. 11) peals out in full splendour as the Gods gaze at the wonderful sight in speechless astonishment: then, in a great lyrical harangue, Wotan greets the castle which that morning, lordless as it was then, had beckoned to him. From morn to eve, consumed with care, he had worked to make it his own; and now, as night is about to fall, he will enter its mighty walls to find shelter from his own troubled thoughts.

20

Suddenly a great idea possesses him. Snatching up a sword that had formed part of the treasure and had been left behind by Fafner, he hails the fortress, the trumpet giving out the last new motive of the *Rhinegold* score, that of the Sword:

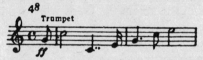

(In the stage directions in the score no provision had been made for this culminating point of the action; presumably Wagner's intention had been that Wotan should simply hail the castle with a gesture. But at the Bayreuth rehearsals of 1876 this course must have struck him as inadequate; and it was then that he hit upon the device with which we are now familiar). He turns slowly to Fricka, bidding her follow him into Walhall, there to dwell with him. What is the meaning of the name? she asks. His answer is enigmatic, because he himself is not yet sure what course he must pursue to win back the Ring or frustrate the evil use of it:

> *What strength 'gainst my fears*
> *my spirit has found,*
> *when vict'ry is mine,*
> *maketh the meaning clear:*

but the ultimate meaning of it will be revealed to us in the later stages of the drama. Taking Fricka by the hand, with all the others, except Loge, following him, he goes slowly towards the rainbow bridge.

But the last word is not to be with him, nor is the last thought left in our minds to be that of Walhall and its supposed security. First of all Loge turns the cold light of reason on it all. "They are hastening to their end", he muses, "though they deem themselves strong and enduring." As for himself he is ashamed to share any more in their activities: he would prefer to transform himself once more into a wayward flickering fire:

> *to burn and waste them*
> *who once held me bound,*
> *rather than blindly*
> *end with the blind,*
> *e'en were they of Gods the most godlike.*

He will think it over, he concludes; and putting on a careless manner he is about to rejoin the Gods when from the depths of the valley comes the haunting song of the invisible Rhinemaidens. In the first scene of the opera they had greeted the Gold with cries of innocent joy. Now they look back sadly to the days when it was theirs and pure: "Give us the Gold", they cry: "Oh give us its glory again!"

The sound reaches Wotan's ear as he is about to set foot on the bridge. Turning round, he asks who are these whose plaint ascends to him. It is the Rhinechildren, Loge tells him, lamenting over the stolen Gold. "Accursed nixies!" says Wotan: "stay them from pestering me!" Loge, calling down into the water, gives them the message in his own ironical form:

> *Why wail ye to us?*
> *Hear what Wotan doth will!*
> *Gleams no more*
> *on you maidens the Gold;*
> *in the Gods' recovered glory*
> *bask ye henceforth in bliss!*

The Gods laugh at his humour and begin to pass over the bridge.

The Rhinemaidens break into a more poignant lament, ending with:

Tender and true
'tis but in the waters:
false and base
are those who revel above!

But the only response is the Walhall motive, growing more brilliant and more imposing bar by bar in the orchestra; and accompanied by a final *fff* restatement of the Rainbow motive the Gods cross the bridge and the curtain falls.

It has been truly said that this final scene has a parallel in the conclusion of the *Agamemnon* of Aeschylus. The murder of Agamemnon has been accomplished; Aegisthus and Clytemnestra confront the Chorus, angrily sure of themselves now and of the future, and the last word is given to the hard and ruthless Queen: "Heed them not; let the pack growl as it will; thou and I will rule the palace." But the Chorus has already hinted presciently at what may happen some day if Orestes should return with vengeance in his soul. In the *Rhinegold* Wotan and the Gods enter Walhall confident that henceforth they will be secure; but the doom foreseen by the cynical Loge will for all that fall on them in the end.

THE VALKYRIE

I

The composition of the *Rhinegold* had thoroughly subdued Wagner's hand to the new kind of material he had come to work in. The result was that in the *Valkyrie* the musician in him opened out in all directions: he abandoned himself luxuriously to the sheer joy of music-making, both enlarging the scale of his design for each episode and delighting in fine filigree work from bar to bar; at the same time he has acquired a completer command of what is really the whole art of musical-dramatic composition of this kind—making his leading motives serve simultaneously a psychological and a musical purpose, in a more effective way than had been possible for him until now.

We have seen, at the end of the *Rhinegold*, a sobered, thoughtful Wotan retiring into Walhall, there to discover, if he can, some way of escape from the doom with which the curse on the Ring threatens the Gods. Wagner does not tell us directly, as yet, what has happened during the years that have elapsed between the last scene of the *Rhinegold* and the beginning of the *Valkyrie*; we learn that gradually as the action unfolds itself. Briefly, Wotan has realised that if an end is to be put to the evil that has stemmed inexorably, and will continue to stem, from the theft of the Gold from the Rhine, the concentration of its power in the Ring, and the curse that the frustrated Alberich has laid on this, the Ring must be returned to the primal innocence of the waters whence it had been ravished. As Wotan cannot deprive Fafner of it by force—for that would be to repeat the wrong he himself had committed by taking it from Alberich—the only hope for salvation for Gods and men resides in someone who, all unknowing, shall take on him the burden and the guilt of the Gods, winning the Ring for himself without their prompting yet remaining wholly ignorant of the power for evil that inheres in it; until, in some way or other which perhaps Wotan himself does not see clearly as yet, it will pass into the possession of the Rhinemaidens again. Wotan's first step towards the achievement of his aim has consequently been to create a race of heroes one of whom, by his own strength and virtue alone, will do what the Gods themselves are barred from doing. So Wotan has gone among men and allied himself with a mortal woman, a Volsung, by whom he has had twin children, Siegmund and Sieglinde. The former, he hopes, may be the instrument destined to accomplish the Gods' desire.

The opera opens with a great storm picture, in which we hear or see by turns the persistent bass of the storm wind:

the crash of thunder, the lightning rending the clouds, and the furious swirling of the rain. The motive of Donner as the God of thunder (No. 46) peals out in the angriest tones of the heavy brass, and in the way in which Wagner combines this with the bass of No. 49 and the scurrying figures suggestive of wind and rain we see him already, before the new work is more than a few minutes old, on his way to that expressive contrapuntal handling of his thematic material that will become a more and more pronounced feature of the *Ring* scores.

As the storm shows signs of dying down in the 'cellos and basses the curtain rises on the interior of the forest dwelling of a Neiding warrior, Hunding. The room is built round the trunk of a mighty ash-tree which occupies the centre of it. In the foreground, to the right, is the hearth, behind which is a store-room. The great entrance door to the dwelling is at the back of the stage. On the left, steps lead up to an inner chamber. In the foreground, to the left, stands a table, behind which is a broad bench let into the wall, with some wooden seats in front of it.

2

The storm subsides to the last distant growlings of No. 49, which now flows quite naturally into:

—the characteristic motive of Siegmund, who stumbles into the room through the great door giving on the forest. For a moment he stands immobile with his hand on the latch, looking warily round him: his appearance and his garb both suggest flight and suffering: his distress is particularly portrayed in the figure shown in the third bar of No. 50. As will be seen, it takes the form of those falling seconds which Wagner, in common with other composers, uses so frequently to express pain of body or soul that it is quite unwarrantable to pin them down rigidly to anyone or anything particular in the drama. Perceiving that for the moment, at any rate, he is safe from his pursuers, Siegmund closes the door behind him, staggers towards the hearth, and throws himself on a rug of bear-skin, saying wearily, "Whose hearth this may be, here must I rest me." He sinks back exhausted and remains motionless.

To the accompaniment of a final muttering of the storm Sieglinde enters from the inner chamber, imagining the new-comer to be her husband Hunding returned from the forest. Her mien is sombre; but her look changes to one of surprise when she sees a stranger stretched out on the hearth. Who can this weary one be, she asks herself, the orchestra giving out softly the motive shown in the bass of No. 50. As she bends over him to discover if he is still breathing, a wave of tenderness and pity sweeps over her:

and in Wagner's combination of this with the Siegmund motive we once more see him using thematic counterpoint for the fusion of a musical and a psychological purpose.

It is left to the orchestra to express all the tenderness the sight of the weary man has awakened in Sieglinde as she goes out with a drinking-horn and fills it with cool spring water, which she hands to him. He takes a deep draught of it and returns the horn to her with a glance of silent gratitude. He fixes his gaze on her, feeling dimly that there is a bond of sympathy between them that comes from something more than a simple kindness bestowed and accepted; and an expressive 'cello solo carries No. 50 to a new conclusion:

52
Lento

that indicates the dawning of something like love between them. The two limbs of this motive, marked A and B, will become the material for a great symphonic development in the duet that concludes the first act.

Who is his benefactor? Siegmund asks her. Sadly she replies, "This house and this wife call Hunding master; take thine ease as his guest; tarry till he return." Surely her husband would not deny guest-right to a wounded and weaponless man, says Siegmund. Yet wounded as he is, he is still hale; and as for his weapons, if they had served him as well against his enemies as his arm and his spirit had been willing to do there would have been a different story now to tell. But shield and spear had been shattered in the fight, and the enemy pack had hunted him hard through the tempest. But all that is over now: his weariness has gone, and after the dark night that had fallen on his eyelids there has come the sunlight of the presence and the kindness of this woman. The whole of the orchestral tissue during this episode and what immediately follows is woven out of the tiny motives Nos. 50, 51 and 52; Wagner's new craftsmanship enables him to weave and reweave them to any extent he desires, and always the mutations of the music go hand in hand with the changing thoughts and emotions of the actors.

3

Going to the store-room, Sieglinde returns with a horn filled with mead, which she offers to Siegmund. He refuses to taste it, however, until her lips have touched it; then he takes a long draught of it, his gaze all the while fixed on her with growing warmth, while the orchestra muses softly upon No. 52B: something stronger than sympathy and gratitude is beginning to stir in both of them. But the unexpected tenderness that has come suddenly into his life of constant warfare brings Siegmund only pain; and by the tiniest of touches—by introducing a stabbing minor ninth into the harmony—Wagner gives a poignant turn to the original mood of No. 52A:

as Siegmund lowers his gaze gloomily to the ground. "Thou hast solaced an unhappy one", he says in a trembling voice; "sorrow would he ward from thee!"

Declaring himself rested now he starts up and goes to the door, but at a word from her he halts; ill fate, he warns her, pursues him wherever he goes, and he would not bring unhappiness on her and her house by staying. He raises the latch, but at an impulsive cry

from her of "Abide thou here! No ill fate canst thou bring where
ill fate has made its home!" he looks searchingly into her face, and,
reading what he does there as she lowers her eyes confusedly and
sadly, he returns to her. The sorrow-laden motive of the Volsungs'
Woe:

wells up in the orchestra, followed by that of Sieglinde's pity
(No. 51) and that of Siegmund (No. 50). " 'Woeful' ", he says,
is my own name for myself; Hunding here I will await." He leans
against the hearth, looking intently at her with calm sympathy.
She turns her gaze on him again, and during a long silence, during
which the orchestra muses softly on the motives associated with
the pair, they look into each other's eyes with an expression of
deepest emotion.

Suddenly an ominous figure in the horns:

announces the nearing of Hunding, who is heard outside, leading
his horse to the stable. Sieglinde, recalled with a start to reality,
goes to the door and opens it; and Hunding enters, armed with
shield and spear, the orchestra thundering out his motive, which
is as dark and dour as the man himself:

Catching sight of a stranger, Hunding turns to Sieglinde with a
look of stern enquiry. She explains that she had found the man on
their hearth, faint and weary, and had tended him as guest.
Siegmund has been looking hard at Hunding all this while: "Rest
and drink the woman has given me", he says; "wilt thou chide her
therefor?" "Sacred is my hearth", replies Hunding, "sacred hold
thou my house"; and doffing his armour and handing it to Sieglinde he bids her set out the meal. She hangs the arms on the
branches of the ash-tree, then brings food and drink from the
store-room and prepares the table for supper. While doing so she
involuntarily turns her eyes on Siegmund again, the orchestra
giving out softly but with intensity Nos. 51 and 52A.

Intercepting the glance, Hunding scans Siegmund's features
keenly, and then, with some surprise, compares them with those
of Sieglinde. "How like the two are", he says in an aside, "and in
his eye too there gleams all the guile of the serpent." Concealing
his astonishment, however, he turns once more with an assumption of unconcern to Siegmund, who, in reply to his enquiry, tells
him that he had made his way thither through field and forest,
bramble and brake, driven by storm and direst need: his way he
had lost, nor does he know where he now is. Motioning to him
to take his place at the table, his host tells him that he is under the
roof of Hunding, whose kinsmen hold sway over all the lands
around. And now, what is the name of this guest of his? The bass
clarinet gives out the darkened outline of No. 54, to which the
wood wind reply softly with No. 51 and No. 52B as Sieglinde's
eyes turn in tender sympathy to Siegmund, who is apparently
reluctant to answer. Perhaps he would not deny the woman here,
his wife? says Hunding, whose eyes have never left the pair: "see
how eagerly she asks." Sieglinde, at once embarrassed and interested, asks the question on her own account, and Siegmund begins
his story, which is prefaced by the motive of the Volsungs' Woe
(No. 54) in the 'cellos.

4

Neither "Peaceful" (Friedmund) nor "Joyful" (Frohwalt) can
he call himself, Siegmund says, but rather "Woeful" (Wehwalt).

His father was named Wolfe, and he himself had a twin sister; but mother and sister he had lost so young that he had hardly known either of them. Wolfe was strong and warlike, and of enemies he had many. One day father and boy had returned from their hunting to find the wolf's nest empty: the hall was in ashes, the great oak-tree only a stump; the mother lay dead, the sister had vanished without leaving a trace; and it was the brood of the Neidings that had wrought this ruin and woe. (Here the orchestra gives out the Hunding motive). After that, father and son had lived year in year out the life of the hunted, but always they were formidable in fight. "A Wölfing it is", Siegmund concludes, "who tells thee this. As Wölfing is he well known."

Wolfe and Wölfing he has never known, says Hunding, but of the warrior pair he has heard much talk. Urged on by Sieglinde, Siegmund continues his story. One day the Neidings had made a furious onslaught on them. Well the pair had fought, and the foe had been scattered in flight. But the boy had been separated from his father, and nowhere could he come upon his traces: "only a wolf-skin found I deep in the forest; my father never more did I find"; and the orchestra, with the softest of reminiscences of the Wotan-Walhall motive from the *Rhinegold* (No. 11), tells us who this Wolfe had been. Then Siegmund had left the forest behind him and fared among men and women; but where'er he went, whatever he did, no friends, no trust, could he find:

> *Ill fate lay on me.*
> *Whate'er to me seemed right,*
> *others reckoned it ill;*
> *what I held to be foul,*
> *others counted as fair.*
>> *In feuds I fell*
>> *wherever I dwelt,*
>> *wrath ever*
>> *'gainst me I roused;*
>> *sought I for gladness,*
>> *found I but grief;*
> *and so must I "Woeful" call me;*
> *for woe still walks in my wake.*

From Sieglinde comes a look of warm understanding, accompanied by a tender breathing of No. 52B in the orchestra: the grim Hunding merely comments that manifestly the Norns who wove this man's fate had small love for him. At Sieglinde's request Siegmund goes on to tell them how it had come about that he is now hunted and weaponless. A maid in distress had cried to him for help against her brutal kinsmen who wished to give her in a loveless marriage. He had fought and killed her brothers, and then the maiden's wrath against them had turned to grief: she had clasped the bodies in her arms and bathed them in bitter tears. A wailing figure that is repeated several times in the orchestra depicts her grief:

The slain men's kindred had gathered from all quarters and fallen on Siegmund and the maid: for as long as he could he had defended her with shield and spear, until at last these were hewn from his hands. The maiden died on her brothers' bodies; he himself, weaponless, had been forced to flee. "Now knowest thou, questioning wife", he concludes, turning a look that is at once sorrowful and ardent on Sieglinde, "why I may not name me 'Joyful' ". Here the orchestra gives out for the first time the important motive of the Volsungs, the tragic race doomed to suffering:

He rises and walks to the hearth. Sieglinde, pale and deeply
moved, does not raise her sad eyes from the ground. Hunding
rises, suppressing his black anger with difficulty. A turbulent
breed he knows, he tells Siegmund, hated by all and by him because it holds nothing sacred that others revere. He himself had
lately been called upon to take toll for kinsmen's blood that had
been shed: he had been too late, but now, when he returns, he
finds his flying foeman's traces leading to his own hearth. For this
day and the night Siegmund shall have guest-sanctuary, but in
the morning he will have to defend himself in combat: "no
longer truce I allow; for murder toll will I take." Sieglinde steps
anxiously between the two men, but Hunding roughly orders her
to leave them; she is to prepare his night-draught and wait for
him within.

To a new mutation of her Pity motive (No. 51) in the clarinet
(afterwards in the cor anglais):

59

she stands for a while irresolute, then goes with faltering steps
towards the store-room; there she pauses again, with half-averted
face, as if turning something over in her mind. During the long
silence that follows, the orchestra plays softly but significantly
with the motives already associated with herself and Siegmund.
A purpose seems suddenly to have taken shape within her: with
quiet resolution she opens the cupboard, fills a drinking horn, and
shakes into it some spices from a box. She looks at Siegmund,
whose eyes have never turned away from her. Perceiving that
Hunding is watching them intently she goes with the drinking-
horn to the inner chamber; but on the steps leading up to it she
once more turns round to Siegmund, looks yearningly at him,

and then, by the fixity of her gaze at a particular spot in the ash-
tree, makes him too look in that direction; and as he does so the
Sword motive from the *Rhinegold* (No. 48) peals out, quietly but
markedly, first in the bass trumpet, then in the oboe. Hunding,
roused from his dark brooding, starts up and makes a violent
gesture to her to leave them; and with a last look at Siegmund she
goes into the inner chamber. The harsh No. 56 shatters the silence
as Hunding takes his weapons down from the tree: with a last
ominous word to Siegmund to prepare himself for the combat to
the death on the morrow he goes into the chamber, and the bolt is
heard shooting from within. Siegmund is left to his own melancholy brooding.

5

By now the room has become quite dark, only a faint glow
from the fire enabling us to see him sink despairingly on to the
couch by the fire. The Hunding motive, reduced now to not much
more than an ominous insistent rhythm, hammers its unrelenting
way through what follows, as if it were a thought that allows
Siegmund no peace of mind. No. 48 projects itself, still quietly, in
the bass trumpet as he begins his long monologue. His father, he
recalls bitterly, had promised him that in his direst need he should
find a sword; yet now he is weaponless in an enemy's house, a
mere hostage awaiting vengeance. A winsome woman has gladdened his eyes, but she is held in thrall by the very man who now
mocks his impotence to defend himself. In his frenzy he gives a
great cry to the father who seems to have abandoned him:

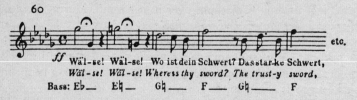

"Wälse! Wälse! where is now the trusty sword that shall serve
me in my need, when the rage that is boiling in my breast shall
break forth and consume me?" The trumpet, projecting the Sword

motive in a bolder line and a brighter colour than before, gives
him the answer as a flicker from the fire on the hearth suddenly
lights up the spot in the ash-tree trunk that had been indicated by
Sieglinde's parting glance, where the hilt of a sword is now faintly
visible. Siegmund does not perceive it as yet; he is intent on the
gleam from the hearth, which he sees, in fancy, as the last look of
Sieglinde still lingering in the room to gladden his heart:

> *Darkening shadows*
> *sank on mine eyes;*
> *but her lustrous look*
> *fell on me then:*
> *summer and sunlight it brought.*

Wagner now opens the floodgates of his lyrical inspiration,
but organically inwrought with the new musical material we hear
the Sword motive taking new and gracious shapes:

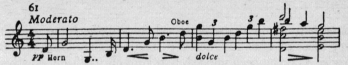

The radiance has departed, sings Siegmund:

> *Yet once more, ere 'twas lost,*
> *fell its light on me here;*
> *e'en the ancient ash-tree's stem*
> *shone forth with a golden glow:*
> > *the flush is fading,*
> > *the light is low;*
> > *darker the shadows*
> > *fall on my eyelids:*
> *deep in my heart there glimmers now*
> *but a faint, dying glow.*

The orchestra sinks to a double pianissimo through which only
the fateful throbbing of the Hunding rhythm is heard in the
kettledrums. The hearth-fire is by now completely extinguished;
the stage is wholly dark.

Sieglinde, robed in white, enters and advances lightly and rapidly to the hearth. Hurriedly she bids Siegmund listen to what she has to say to him. Hunding lies in a deep sleep, for she had mingled a drug with his draught. Siegmund is to fly in the night. But first she will show him a sword of might: would that he could make it his! Could he do so she would call him the noblest of heroes, for only the strongest may win it; and a new motive, that of Victory, is heard in the wind, in combination with the theme of the Sword:

She tells him how the weapon had come there. At her wedding Hunding's kinsmen had filled the hall, drinking to him and to the maiden who had been shamefully sold to him for wife. As she sat there in silent sorrow a stranger strode in; and the Walhall motive (No. 11), welling up in the soft dark tones of horns, bassoons and trombones, tells us who it was—an old man robed in grey, says Sieglinde, whose great hat hung so low that it hid one of his eyes, though in the other gleamed a menace that struck terror in all on whom it lighted. She alone had felt not fear but a sweet yearning and pain, "sadness and solace in one". Then the Sword motive comes to the forefront as she tells how the stranger, glancing at her and glowering at the others, had swung a great sword and struck it up to the hilt in the ash-tree's trunk, saying that it should be his who could withdraw it. All tried, but it baffled the strength of everyone; and there, in silence, it still remains. "Then I", continues Sieglinde to the soft accompaniment of No. 11, "knew who this stranger was who was thus greeting me in my grief; I know, too, who is he for whom the weapon doth wait."

The Sword motive rings out imperially in the trumpet, and then, accompanied by the Victory call (No. 62), Sieglinde sings:

of her hope that this day she may find the friend come from afar to bring her comfort after all her sufferings and all the ignominies that had been put upon her:

> whate'er I've borne
> in my bitterest woe,
> whate'er I have suffered
> in shame and disgrace,
> sweetest of vengeance
> soon should I know then!
> Retrieved then were
> whate'er I had lost,
> again I would win
> all I have wept for,
> found I this holiest friend,
> and folded the hero to me!

Siegmund takes her in his arms and replies with an intensity of emotion equal to her own. He is the friend, he tells her, who shall win both weapon and wife. His own sufferings among men have matched hers; but:

> joy of vengeance
> gladdens our hearts now!
> So laugh I
> in highest delight,
> holding thee, noblest and dearest,
> feeling the beat of thy heart.

6

At this point the great door flies open, for no better reason, one is inclined to think at first, than a desire on Wagner's part to

create a striking stage effect. We soon realise, however, that the
flinging open of the door, revealing a beautiful Spring night with the
full moon flooding the pair with its radiance, is symbolic rather
than realistic. At the flying open of the door Sieglinde had started
back in alarm and torn herself away from Siegmund: "Who has
passed? Who has entered here?" she cries. He draws her to him
again with tender compulsion and leads her to the couch, where
they sit down together. "No one passed", he assures her, "but one
has come: see now how Spring smiles in the hall." Soft orchestral
throbbings fill the air, and Siegmund launches his Spring Song:

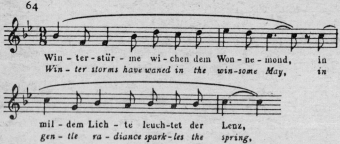

It tells how the storms of winter have waned to the winsome May:
Spring has come, to nature as to them, and makes his laughing
way through the land, with birds singing and flowers coming to
life again after their long frost-bound sleep. To his sister Spring
flies, and she leaps with a laugh to greet him, "for Love did lure
the Spring". Siegmund and Sieglinde too have found each other
and are made one now; Love and Spring have met in them and
kissed each other.[1]

[1] Both words and music of the Spring Song went through many changes
before reaching their present form. Wagner's original draft for the melody
was in C major, in 3/4 time:

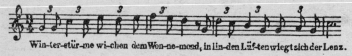

The obvious faults of this melody were corrected later, and as Wagner
developed the song along its purely musical lines he made several alterations
in the words to make them fit in with the melody.

Wagner luxuriates in the opportunity to give the musician in him full freedom of wing. No. 52B takes on a new sweetness and loveliness as Siegmund sings of his own coming to Sieglinde being like that of Spring, drawn by love, to the earth. She answers him, "Thou art the Spring that long I had sighed for through winter's ice-bound days"—to an expansive version of No. 52A, followed by 52B. Friendless and alien, she says, was all around her until he came. She had recognised him for her own the moment she had set eyes on him: what had lain hidden in darkness in her starved and thwarted soul then became clear as light and sang in her ear. A motive of Bliss:

seems an anticipation of *Tristan* as they sing, in modulation after modulation of it, of their joy in each other. The strain ends with a rapturous cadence:

that prolongs its dying fall through voices and orchestra. The rapture of the pair finds expression in modifications of No. 65 that bring us still nearer the *Tristan* idiom:

while their common inheritance, now joyously recognised by
them both, is symbolised by elaborations of the Wotan-Walhall
motive. They understand now why their hearts had been filled
with sympathy and tenderness at the first sight of each other; and
luxuriant reminiscences of No. 52 pack the orchestra. Sieglinde
knows now that he, like herself, is a Volsung, Wälse's child, and
names him "Siegmund". He accepts the name, springs towards
the ash-tree, and seizes the hilt of the Sword: this was indeed the
weapon his father had promised should be his in the hour of need!
The orchestral tissue is throughout an organically woven web of
motives, each of them carrying its own clear meaning—with,
however, one exception. When Siegmund sings:

> *Holiest love's*
> *most mighty need,*
> *passionate longing's*
> *feverish need,*
> *brightly burns in my breast,*
> *drives to deeds and death,*

it is to the strain of No. 9, the motive to which, at its first appearance in the *Rhinegold*, the commentators have all attached the
label of "Renunciation of Love", because it is to this melody that
Alberich avows the renunciation that had won him the Gold.
Manifestly there can be no "renunciation" of love implied in the
episode in the *Valkyrie* at which we have now arrived; rather is it
an assertion of love. Here is yet another warning of the dangers
attending the labelling of a Wagnerian motive, however convenient it may be for us to do so, according to the words or the

situation in connection with which it makes its first appearance in the opera. For the composer, the range of psychological reference of a motive was far wider, and the terms of reference far subtler, than our ready-made tickets can provide for: the musical idea came from a psychical complex within him that may take on an infinity of nuances in the course of the drama. It becomes clear to us now that when No. 9 first appears in the *Rhinegold* it should be taken as signifying not so much Alberich's renunciation of love as the Love itself, universal, omnipotent, which the gnome, in his lust for power, has decided to renounce.

With his hand on the hilt of the sword Siegmund names the weapon Nothung (that which shall serve him in his need):

then, with a mighty effort, he plucks it from the tree and shows it to the astonished and ecstatic Sieglinde, the orchestra giving out No. 48 with the full power of the brass. He has won her, he tells her, he, Siegmund the Volsung, and this is his bride-gift to her. Together they will flee from the foeman's house to the laughing house of Spring, where Love shall hold her and Nothung ward her. She answers him in words of equal passion, and as the orchestra executes an excited fantasia on a combination of the Sword motive and that of Love (No. 52B):

the two fall into each other's arms, and the curtain falls to a final cry from Siegmund:

> *Bride and sister*
> *be to thy brother;*
> *so flourish the Volsungs for aye!*

7

The second act opens with an orchestral prelude of immense energy, woven for the most part out of motives with which we are now familiar. First of all the Sword motive, in a new rhythmic form, rings out in the trumpet:

It is followed by a modification of what we must continue to call the Flight motive from the *Rhinegold* (No. 15A):

for no better reason than that it was first heard in connection with the flight of Freia from the Giants. Precisely what significance it had in Wagner's mind at the present juncture it is difficult to say. A little later it takes a broader form:

Later still No. 65A, in the shape it had assumed in No. 67, reminds us of the love of Siegmund and Sieglinde:

Even in the condensation of this last example for purposes of quotation we can see the motive combined contrapuntally with that of Flight: the whole tissue of the prelude, indeed, is symphonic, the short motives cohering into an organic whole. The general purport of it cannot be expressed in terms of a set "programme"; what we are conscious of is an atmosphere of tremendous excitement, in which the past drama of the Volsung pair is moving towards a new and greater tension.

In that drama a fresh figure, that of the Valkyrie[1] Brynhilde—the daughter of Wotan and Erda, and his favourite among his nine Valkyrie daughters—is to play a prominent part. We find her first characterised in the prelude by a figure that will always be typical not only of herself but of the Valkyries in general:

[1] The "Wal-" of "Walküre" comes from an old German word signifying battlefield, and the remainder of the word from an old verb "küren" (to choose: cf. the present German verb "erküren", p.p. "erkoren", to choose, elect). The duty of the Valkyries was to carry the valiant slain to Walhall, there to form a bodyguard of heroes for Wotan. "Wal" (modern German "Wahl") itself really means "choice", "election"; it survives curiously in such words as "Walstatt" and "Walplatz", signifying a field of battle. It was during and after battle that heroes were "chosen" to people Walhall.

The reader, by the way, must beware of associating some of the names in the *Ring* with modern German words similar in form but different in meaning. The "mund" of "Siegmund", for instance, has nothing to do with the modern "Mund" (mouth): it comes from an old root meaning guardian or protector, which survives today in such words as "Vormund" (guardian, trustee), "Vormundschaft" (trusteeship), and "Vormundschaftsgericht" (Court of Chancery): "Siegmund" is the guardian of victory ("Sieg"). The "Hund" of "Hunding", again, derives not from "Hund" (dog) but from "Hüne" (a giant), which may be related to "Hunne" (a Hun).

The names of Brynhilde and her eight sisters—Gerhilde, Ortlinde, Waltraute, Schwertleite, Helmwige, Siegrune, Grimgerde and Rossweisse—are all composites; Schwertleite, for instance, signifies "sword wielder", Siegrune "the one who knows the runes of victory". The word "Walküre", by the way, is accented by Wagner on the first syllable.

74

(Rarely, and least of all in the concert piece known as "The Ride of the Valkyries", do we hear the theme played as Wagner conceived it. By scamping the short note of each bar the brass almost invariably convert the melody into:

75

Further, Wagner always insisted on sharp definition being given to the first note of each bar, not to the fourth, as is the way with our orchestras).

8

As No. 74 grows more and more jubilant the curtain rises, showing a wild mountain pass, with a gorge in the background rising to a high ridge of rocks. Wotan and Brynhilde enter, she fully armed, the God also in war array, carrying his spear. In energetic tones he bids the Valkyrie harness her horse, for soon there will be work for her to do: there will be a combat between Hunding and Siegmund, in which she is to aid the Volsung; as for Hunding, he may go where he belongs, for in Walhall the God needs him not. Elated at the news, Brynhilde, giving glad repeated cries of "Hojotoho! Heihaha!":

76

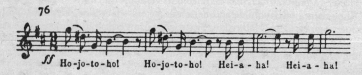

springs up the rocks, accompanied by orchestral figures that convey a remarkable impression of the wild energy of the Valkyries. Pausing on a high peak she looks down into the gorge at the back, and gaily warns Wotan to look to himself, for a storm will soon burst on him—the furious Fricka is coming in her ram-drawn chariot, scourging the terrified beasts in her wrath, eager for the fray with her spouse. Though she herself, says Brynhilde, revels in the strife of heroes, in a combat of this kind she has no part to play; she will leave her father to face the storm alone as best he can; and with another volley of joyous "Hojotohos!" she disappears behind the mountain height at the side of the stage.

Fricka appears in the gorge, dismounts from her car, and, accompanied by a motive expressive of Wrath:

strides impetuously towards Wotan, who turns to face her with a resigned aside: "The old disputes, the old annoys! Yet firmly I must stand and meet them!" Fricka pauses in front of him and begins her harangue with quiet dignity.[1] She has sought him out in the wilds of which he is so fond, she tells him, because she must exact a promise from him. Hunding has brought his plaint to her as the protectress of marriage and cried out for vengeance; and she has sworn to punish the pair who have betrayed him. Wotan asks quietly what wrong they have done, these two who in Spring

[1] In the first form of the poem the dialogue between Wotan and Fricka ran along somewhat different lines from Fricka's words (in the present poem) "Wie thörig und taub du dich stellst" down to her "So ist es denn aus mit den ewigen Göttern". When printing the final text of the *Ring* poem, in 1872, in the 5th and 6th volumes of his *Collected Works*, Wagner gave also, at the foot of the relative pages, the text as it originally was between these two points.

had bowed to the magic power of Love: "not lord over love am I". If anything is unholy it is the oath that binds lives together without love; and as for himself he cannot intervene, for his heart is always with the brave, whom he ever spurs on to strife. That he has small regard for wedlock she knows, Fricka rejoins; but does he go so far as to condone the union of sister and brother?[1] When was that known before? "Thou knowest it now", is Wotan's reply; "that these twain are lovers thou seest for thyself. So hear my frank counsel—give them thy grace and bless Siegmund and Sieglinde's bond."

Fricka flames into anger at this. The honour and glory of the Gods, she says, has been a small thing to him since he begat these turbulent Volsungs; and now the eternal laws of right and wrong are to be flouted for their benefit. She reproaches him with his infidelities to herself:

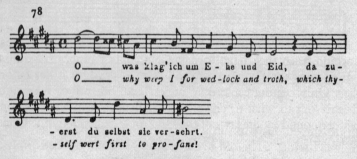

78

O———— was klag'ich um E - he und Eid, da zu-
O———— why weep I for wed-lock and troth, which thy-

- erst du selbst sie ver-sehrt.
- self wert first to pro-fane!

> *Thy own true wife*
> *thou hast oft betrayed;*
> *never a deep*
> *and never a height*
> *but there wandered*
> *thy wantoning glance;*

[1] The concept of a sister-bride has its roots deep in some of the old sagas; it goes back to primitive notions of bisexual deities as principles of nature. Wagner was compelled, willy-nilly, to adopt the idea of the blood-unity of Siegmund and Sieglinde for his drama, though it hardly bears transplantation from the world of the sagas to that of the modern stage. It has always been something of a stumbling-block for some listeners to the *Ring*. The more lunatic among Wagner's critics of the 1870's went so far as to accuse him of "glorifying incest".

> *all the joy of change thou wouldst win thee,*
> *and grieved'st my heart with thy scorn.*

She had been forsaken while he flew to the fray with the lawless Valkyries of his own begetting, whom he had even given as handmaidens to his consort; and later he had left her to dwell in the forest as Wälse:

> *from common mortal*
> *this twin-pair begetting,*
> *at the feet of these wolf-whelps*
> *throwest thou, base one, thy wife!*
> *Then finish thy work!*
> *Fill up the cup!*
> *Let them trample on the betrayed one!*

9

Her eloquence is lost on Wotan. "Ne'er didst thou learn what I would teach thee", the hard-pressed sophist replies tranquilly; "ne'er canst thou comprehend till clear as daylight it lies before thee. Only custom canst thou understand; but my own thought reaches out to what ne'er yet has befallen. A man we need, one neither bound by the laws of the Gods nor sheltered by the Gods; he alone is

> *meet for the deed*
> *which, though the need of the Godhead,*
> *a God of himself may not do."*

She rejects the notion that a hero can do what the Gods themselves cannot. "For who breathed this fire into men? Who gave them the light of their eyes? Without thy shield, what are they? Without thy spur, to what would they aspire? But this new trick thou shalt not work on me! This thy Volsung thou shalt not have from me: in him I find but thee, for only through thee does he dare."

"In deepest sorrow himself did he mould", replies Wotan; "to my protection he owes nothing." But in the anguish of his love for Siegmund he has now made a false move, and Fricka is quick to seize her advantage. "Then leave him now to his own devices", she answers; "shield him not today; take back the sword thou didst bestow." Siegmund had won it himself in his need, says Wotan vehemently. From now onwards the direction of the argument passes more and more into the hands of Fricka; she speaks with mounting passion, while "Wotan's whole demeanour", as the stage directions have it, "from this point onwards expresses a profound and ever-increasing uneasiness and dejection." He listens for a while in silence, only a motive of Dejection in bassoon and bass clarinet:

revealing the completeness of his bafflement and the depth of his despair. "Who was it who planned that need for him", Fricka insists, "and the sword that should serve him in it? Didst *thou* not strike the sword into the tree trunk? Didst *thou* not lead him where he would find it? Didst *thou* not promise it to him?" Touched to the quick, Wotan springs up with an angry gesture, but dares not speak. Perceiving his discomfiture, Fricka grows still more confident and aggressive. With bondsmen, she says scornfully, she disdains to battle; from the free man the felon gets only scourging. Against the power of Wotan she would wage war if need were, but this Siegmund shall be punished only as a slave. Shall such a slave command Wotan's spouse, making her a shame and a scoff before all?

"Wotan", Wagner's stage directions run, "makes another passionate gesture, then sinks down, realising his impotence"; the orchestra underlines the gesture with a vehement statement of No. 77. Fricka presses her advantage home, and Wotan, with the 'cellos and basses muttering the motive of Dejection (No. 79), asks gloomily "What desir'st thou?" "Shield not the Volsung!" is the sharp reply. "His way let him go", says Wotan in a choked voice. But this is not enough for Fricka: she demands that he shall look her straight in the eyes and promise that neither will he aid Siegmund nor—thus shattering the God's last secret hope

—allow the Valkyrie to do so. Wotan makes a final passionate effort to ride the storm. "I cannot forsake him", he cries; "he found my sword." "Then withdraw its magic", replies the pitiless Fricka; "let the blade break; let him be helpless against his foe!"

10

Just then Brynhilde's joyous "Hojotoho!" peals from the adjacent heights, and she herself comes into sight. Perceiving Fricka she suddenly breaks off, slowly and silently leads her horse down the rocky path, and leaves it in a cave. The increasingly sombre orchestral mutations of her call depict her growing realisation of the gravity of the situation:

She stands silent as Fricka majestically orders Wotan to bid the Valkyrie vindicate the honour of the Gods by withholding her aid from Siegmund. Wotan, now utterly defeated, throws himself on a rocky seat in the profoundest dejection, muttering, "Take my oath!" Fricka strides towards Brynhilde and pauses for a moment before her; "War-father doth wait for thee", she tells her calmly; "let him instruct thee how the lot is to fall"; and the Curse motive (No. 41) raises its head ominously in the quiet tones of the trombones. According to Wagner's directions, she enters her chariot and drives swiftly away. But this rather inconvenient piece of realism is generally dispensed with in performance: Fricka walks slowly away from the pair, giving the player of the part a superb opportunity to show us how charged with meaning a mere slow walk can be, provided she has the dignity of mien and gait to enable her to seize the opportunity—which few Wagnerian singers have. Two or three realisations of the difficult episode linger in the older opera-goer's memory.

After Fricka's departure the tense silence is broken by Brynhilde, who goes anxiously to the suffering Wotan and asks him the meaning of it all. The God's head sinks heavily on to his breast: "In my own fetters fast am I held!" he ejaculates mournfully; "I, the least free of all that liveth!" His brooding ends in a terrible cry of "O shame! O distress! Gods' extremity! Wrath and Grief without end! The saddest am I of all living!"[1] The terrified Brynhilde throws away helmet, shield and spear and sinks down at his feet, laying her head and hand lovingly on his breast and knee and imploring him to confide in her, the truest of his children. The motive of Siegmund and Sieglinde's love (No. 52), threading its melancholy way through the silence in the veiled tones of the bass clarinet, reveals to us what is passing through Wotan's tortured mind. For a moment he communes softly with himself: if he were to tell her all, so runs his thought, would he not loosen the inmost hold of his will? Brynhilde reassures him; speaking to her, she says, he will be speaking to Wotan's own will, for what is she but that? When he does so it is indeed, he muses, to himself, for to all others but himself and her his thought must remain for ever secret. It is a point that needs to be remembered by those who find the Narration that follows over-long and repetitive: the God is not so much speaking to another as brooding within his secret self upon the dilemma in which he now finds

[1] In his first swift Sketch of November 1851 for the *Valkyrie*, Wagner's plan for the scene immediately following the exit of Fricka had run thus: "Wotan's profound grief that he must ever find himself in opposition to himself; there must be beings freer than the unhappy Gods are. He longs for the land of Forgetfulness". (Then comes the scene between Wotan and Brynhilde). This plan was not carried out either in the more detailed Sketch of the 17th May 1852 or in the poem, in both of which it is replaced by Wotan's ejaculation, "In my own fetters fast am I—the least free of all living". Apparently the long Narration to Brynhilde only took its present shape in Wagner's mind some time between the above two dates, for in the first Sketch we have merely this: "Brynhilde [after the departure of Fricka] cajoles and tries to console him. Wotan, without willing it, discloses his secret object with regard to the Volsungs, his offspring. Brynhilde understands him completely: she offers to protect Siegmund. Wotan is angry with her, and, mastering himself by a supreme effort, wrathfully commands Siegmund's death. He goes away in a passion. Brynhilde perceives Siegmund and Sieglinde in flight", etc. In the later Sketch these half-dozen lines are expanded to seventy-six, which give us the dialogue between Wotan and the Valkyrie as we have it now.

himself, and retracing in his imagination the stages by which he has brought himself to his present sorry pass.

II

He begins in a hollow, stifled voice, looking steadfastly all the while into Brynhilde's eyes. It is not the impersonal Wotan of Wagner's first cosmic conception of 1848, but the more human Wotan of a later date, who makes his way, as it were, across the screen that gradually unrolls itself before our eyes, the Wotan whose lust for power had led him to the first false step on a path the end of which would be the downfall of the Gods. One passage alone in the monologue is sufficient to show the difference between the two conceptions. As the reader will recall, in the "Sketch for a drama on the Nibelungen myth" (1848) Wotan, standing aloof from both the Giants and the Nibelungs, had engaged the former to build him a fortress "from which he could govern the world in peace and order"; for the Gods had planned a world subject to good laws, and had devoted themselves to the bringing into being of a worthy human race: "the object of their lofty ordering of the world is moral consciousness". Wotan had gradually become involved in a network of evil, though his intentions from the first had been good. In his present Narration to Brynhilde, however, he depicts himself as morally flawed from the beginning, aiming only at power and stopping at nothing to achieve it:

> all whom by our laws
> we had held in bondage,
> the mortals whose spirits
> proud we had curbed,
> whom by guileful agreements'
> craft and deception
> we bound in a blind
> and servile obedience,
> these ye were to spur
> to storm and to combat,
> their desires goading
> to grimmest war,

> *that hosts of hardy heroes*
> *should gather in Walhall's halls.*

He now begins his quiet retrospect at the very beginning:

> *When youthful love's*
> *delight from me fled,*
> *my soul grew athirst for power:*
> *by wildest wishes*
> *blindly impelled,*
> *I won myself the world.*
> *Fraud and deception*
> *unwitting wrought I,*
> *binding by treaties*
> *what threatened harm:*
> *craftily lured on by Loge,*
> *who flick'ring fled away.*

He goes on to tell how "the baffled Nibelung Alberich" had forsworn love and so won the Rhine's pure Gold, and with it measureless might; how he himself had wrested the Ring from him by craft, paying for Walhall with it instead of restoring it to the Rhine; how the wise Erda had counselled him to give up the Ring, warning him of the fate of the Gods if he retained it, but had refused to tell him more; how, in the chill of his fear, he had followed her into the womb of the earth, mastered her in love, and "learned much from her counsel"; how she had borne him his beloved Brynhilde, his second self, whom he had nurtured with eight sister Valkyries; how they had brought him the spirits of heroes who had fallen in battle, to be a guard for him against his foes. Forever lurking in the shadows is Alberich, racked by rage and envy; Wotan does not fear an assault on Walhall by him and his "night-begotten forces", but should the Ring come into the gnome's hands again he would rouse all creation against the Gods. Against Fafner, who now sleeps upon the Ring, Wotan himself is powerless:

> *But I bargained with him,*
> *and may not attack him;*

powerless 'gainst him
would prove all my might:—
these are the fetters
that confine me:
I, who by treaties am lord,
to my treaties now am a slave;

and the weary motive of the Need of the Gods drags its slow length along through the 'cellos:

It will be seen that halfway through the second bar this continues with the Dejection motive (No. 79), while at the end of that bar the Sword motive is heard in the bass trumpet.

To one alone can he look for salvation—to a hero strange to him, free of his will, in no wise helped by the Godhead, one who will fight even against Wotan, as God, yet accomplish what the God himself must not do. For this purpose he had reared Siegmund, giving him the Sword that should do the deed longed for by the Gods. But Fricka had pierced through his deceit and overwhelmed him with shame: to her he must yield. Flee as he will from Alberich's curse, everywhere it pursues him; and his heart's beloved, his Siegmund, he must now abandon and betray.

In his despair he invokes the ruin of the Gods; let all their glittering, shameful pomp pass away. All is in vain: for one thing only he now longs—an end to it all. Then he reflects that it is for that ending that Alberich works unrestingly. Erda had warned him that when "the night-born foe of love" should beget a son the doom of the Gods would be nigh; and of late the rumour had reached his ears that Alberich had bought with gold the love of a woman in whose womb now lies "the fruit of hate, grim envy's son". This wonder, he wails, befell

> *to him, the loveless,*
> *yet of my love so boundless*
> *the free one was born not to me.*

In bitter wrath he gives the Nibelung's son his blessing; let him sate himself on the prize that is to fall into his hands. For himself, he can struggle no more: Brynhilde, in the combat between Siegmund and Hunding, is to fight for Fricka and for wedlock's vows:

> *what she doth choose*
> *is also my choice:*
> *of what avail were my own will,*
> *since the free one I cannot fashion?*
> *to Fricka's vassal*
> *give thou thine aid!*

Brynhilde strives in vain to persuade him to alter this decision of despair, even vowing that she will never fight against the hero whom Wotan loves. But he turns on her in devastating fury. Who is she, "the submissive blind slave of my will", to flout his commands? Let her provoke him to wrath and his lightning will blast her; his breast is filled with "a rage that could lay woeful and waste the world that once delighted my heart". He warns her, then, not to rouse his anger: "Siegmund is to die; this be the Valkyrie's work!" He rushes away, blind-mad with the fury of frustration and despair, and disappears among the rocks, leaving Brynhilde terrified and bewildered.

12

The tremendous monologue, that seems long only to those who merely feel that Wotan is telling them something they know already and have no inward eye and ear for the drama that is being played out in the God's tortured soul and for the new emotional life given to it in his tragic retrospect of it, is necessarily built up, for the most part, on reference after reference to the motives associated with each person, each episode of the story told. But they are not merely pasted in at the appropriate spots; they have a psychological life of their own, and take on new musical forms and colours now in congruence with Wotan's changing emotions. At the point, for instance, where he foresees the doom that will fall on the Gods when a son is born to Alberich, the Walhall motive undergoes this sombre mutation:

82

Musing affectionately on the distress of "War-father", Brynhilde, sad at heart, takes up her weapons, dons them again, and sighs for the Volsung hero whom she must abandon to his fate. Slowly she makes her way to the back of the stage, to the melancholy strain of No. 81. As she reaches the mountain summit the Flight motive comes out hurriedly once more in the orchestra: Brynhilde has caught sight of Siegmund and Sieglinde approaching through the gorge. She watches their movements for a moment, then disappears into the cave in which she had left her horse.

The Volsung pair enter. Sieglinde, flying in blind terror from the pursuing Hunding, would press on, exhausted as she is, but Siegmund tries gently to restrain her. At last he succeeds in bringing her to the stone seat, where she throws her arms passionately round his neck, remains thus a moment, and then breaks away from him again in panic, wildly urging him to leave the woman who has brought this woe on herself and him. To the first rapture of love has succeeded horror and self-loathing: "scorn I bring on my brother, shame to the friend who freed me". For any shame she may feel, Siegmund replies, Hunding shall pay with his life "when Nothung at his heart shall gnaw". The horncalls of the pursuers are heard, pounding out the sinister Hunding rhythm; the kinsmen and the bloodhounds are on her track, she cries distractedly, and some rending dissonances in trumpets and horns graphically depict her frenzy. Then, in sheer exhaustion, she melts again and throws herself on his breast, but once more starts up in terror as the ominous calls boom out again. In imagination she sees the hounds tearing at Siegmund's flesh, their fangs fastened in him, the Sword in splinters, the ash-tree splitting and crashing; and with a last cry of "Brother! my brother! Siegmund!" she sinks fainting into his arms. While the orchestra gives out poignant reminiscences of their love music in the first act (No. 52) he bends over her anxiously, finds that she is still breathing, presses a long kiss on her brow, and seats himself on the rock with her head resting on his lap, in which position both remain during the scene that follows.

13

After a long, expressive silence Brynhilde comes out of the cave, leading her horse by the bridle, strides slowly and solemnly towards them, and pauses to contemplate the man whose fate lies in her unwilling hands. The brass gives out quietly the solemn motive of Death:

The chords marked A, with their curiously impressive crescendo and diminuendo, are more particularly associated in the sequel with the Annunciation of Death which it is the duty of the Valkyrie to bring to the hero at Wotan's command. As she stands gazing earnestly at him, holding shield and spear in one hand while the other rests on the neck of her horse, the orchestra gives out the quietest of reminiscences of the Walhall motive—that Walhall in which the Volsung will soon join the ranks of Wotan's brave and faithful ones. When at last she addresses Siegmund by name it is to an arresting modulation in the wood wind. She bids him look at her; she has come, she tells him, to summon him hence. With the orchestra playing incessantly on No. 83 and the Walhall motive she answers the questions he puts to her:

> *Death-fated men*
> *alone behold me;*
> *who sees my face*
> *must forth from the light of life.*
> *On the war-field alone*
> *I come to heroes;*
> *him whom I greet*
> *I choose him for my own.*

Question and answer succeed each other until the whole story is told: she is going to take him to Walhall, to join the hallowed band of fallen heroes about Wotan; there he will find his father Wälse, and smiling Wish-maidens who will hand him the festive cup; but Sieglinde he will see no more. At these last words of hers he bends gently over Sieglinde, kisses her softly on the brow, then turns tranquilly to the Valkyrie again:

> *Then greet for me Walhall,*
> *greet for me Wotan,*
> *greet for me Wälse*
> *and all the heroes;*
> *greet too the gracious*
> *wish-maidens:—*
> *to them I'll follow thee not!*

Gravely she reminds him, to an impressive modification of No. 83:

84

that having seen the Valkyrie's withering glance he must now fare forth with her: all his courage will be of no avail, for death always prevails, and it is death that she is bringing him. To what hero must he fall? Siegmund asks. "Hunding's hand deals the blow", is the reply. He smiles scornfully at her: it is Hunding who will die, and Hunding whom, if she lusts for strife and death, she can take with her to Walhall. Gently and solemnly she once more bids him hearken to her: it is he who must die today: the Sword on which he counts will fail him, for he who gave it now withdraws the spell from it.

Siegmund bends tenderly over Sieglinde again in an outburst of grief at his father Wälse's betrayal of him:

> *O shame on him*
> *who bestowed the sword,*
> *to make me my foeman's scorn!*
> *If I must fall then,*
> *I go not to Walhall:*
> *Hella[1] take me to her!*
>
> . . . .
>
> *Yet if on my anguish*
> *thine eyes would feast,*
> *then gloat upon my grief now;*
> *let my pain comfort*
> *thy pitiless heart:*
> *but of Walhall's paltry raptures*
> *prithee speak not to me!*

14

This is the turning-point in the action. Brynhilde, deeply moved by this devotion, begs him to give Sieglinde into her protection:

> *thy wife trust to me*
> *for the babe's dear sake,*
> *the pure pledge of her passion for thee.*

[1] The Goddess of the underworld.

His reply is that no one shall protect her but himself, and if he must die he will slay her first. As he draws his sword to kill her, Brynhilde's sympathy overmasters her. In a passionate outburst, to the accompaniment of a striking orchestral foreshadowing of the idiom of *Tristan*, she declares that Sieglinde shall live, nor shall Siegmund be parted from her. She will thwart the death-doom; he shall triumph in the fight. As the ominous horn-calls peal out in the distance again she tells him to take up his sword and strike without fear, for the steel and the Valkyrie's help will both prove true. She rushes away with her horse and disappears in the gorge on the right, Siegmund looking after her with joy and relief, while the orchestra pours out an excited and exultant flood of tone.

The stage darkens, heavy thunderclouds descending upon the background and gradually enveloping the rocks, the gorge and the hills. Siegmund broods tenderly over the sleeping Sieglinde: "so slumber still", he says, "until the fight be o'er and peace doth end thy pain"; while the orchestra breathes softly some of the themes associated with the pair in the first act, such as No. 52 and No. 64 (the Spring Song). But the sounds of the pursuers have meantime been drawing nearer and nearer, until at last a cow-horn (behind the scenes), blaring out the rhythm of No. 56, rouses Siegmund from his dreams. He starts up resolutely with drawn sword, hastens to the background, and at the mountain top disappears in the dark thunderclouds, from which a flash of lightning breaks. The cow-horn sounds again, more insistently than before.

Sieglinde begins to move restlessly in her dreams. The violas give out a short melody:

which the sufferers from "Wagnerphobia" assure us Wagner borrowed from Liszt. Memories of her childhood, her wedding, and the destruction of the Volsung home rise in her: "Would that our father were home!" she mutters: "with the boy he still roams in the woods. Mother! Mother! I tremble with fear: how harsh and

hateful seem all these strangers! Misty vapours darken the air;
fiery tongues are flaming towards us; the house is burning.
Brother! Siegmund! Siegmund!" A crash of thunder and a vivid
lightning-flash awake her; she leaps up and gazes round her with
increasing terror as the storm lashes the scene and Hunding's
horn-call sounds again, this time quite close. His hoarse voice is
heard from the pass at the back, calling on Wehwalt to stand and
face him. He is answered by the voice of Siegmund, who, further
away in the gorge, asks this enemy of his where he is hiding. Not
weaponless is he now, he cries, for from the ash-tree's great stem
he had plucked the Sword he now wields, a Sword that will make
a mockery of Fricka's protection of his foe.

15

In another lightning-flash the two men become visible, locked
in combat. Sieglinde gives a despairing cry of "Stay your hands,
ye madmen! Slay me first!" and runs towards the pass; but
another flash that breaks out over the two men makes her reel
back as if blinded. Through the mounting excitement in the
orchestra the Valkyrie motive (No. 74), accompanied by the
Sword motive in the trumpet, tears its way in the trombones as
Brynhilde suddenly becomes visible, hovering above Siegmund
and guarding him with her shield. But just as he is aiming a blow
at Hunding a red glow appears in the clouds to the left, and by the
light of it we see Wotan standing over Hunding and holding out
his spear in front of Siegmund. At his angry "Recoil from my
spear! Splintered be the Sword!" Brynhilde shrinks back in
terror: Siegmund's sword snaps on the God's spear, and Hunding
buries his own weapon in the unarmed man's breast. Wotan, as
the Treaty motive (No. 13) striding downwards in the bass
instruments of the orchestra reminds us, has remembered and is
keeping his pledged word, upon which his moral power is based.

Through the vague light that now takes possession of the stage
we dimly see Brynhilde running to Sieglinde, who, hearing
Siegmund's death sigh, has fallen to the ground as if lifeless, while
the orchestra throws together in stark apposition the opening of
the Volsung motive (No. 58A) and the fateful form of the

Annunciation of Death motive shown in No. 84. She lifts Sieglinde on to her horse, which is standing near the gorge at the side, and disappears with her. When the clouds that envelop the stage divide, Hunding is seen driving his spear into the breast of the dead Siegmund, and Wotan standing by his side on a rock,[1] leaning on his spear and gazing with infinite sadness at the hero's body. He has done what Fricka had exacted of him, as the Treaty motive making its slow way down in 'cellos and basses again reminds us, and is now free once more to feel and act for himself. "Get hence, slave!" he says with bitter scorn. "Kneel before Fricka: tell her that Wotan's spear has avenged what wrought her shame. Go! Go!", and at a contemptuous wave of his hand Hunding falls dead.[2] Wagner has marked the whole passage double piano and piano; but some singers make the mistake of hurling the "Go! Go!" at Hunding's head in a vehement forte. They have missed the psychological nuance of the situation: at that moment Wotan is too sunk in grief at his own betrayal of Siegmund to do any storming. The tempest breaks a little later: he remembers Brynhilde's flouting of his will, and in an access of rage cries woe upon her: "harshly will I punish her crime, if my steed be as swift as her flight!" He disappears in thunder and lightning in pursuit of her, a brief orchestral postlude depicting the fury of his purpose.

16

From the Prose Sketch we learn that the wild landscape in which the opening scene of the third act is set is the customary rendezvous of the Valkyries "when they return from their various expeditions in order to ride back to Walhall".

Wagner takes advantage of the picturesque opportunities presented by this conception to write a large-scale piece of

[1] In the Prose Sketch of 1852 Wagner says that at this point Wotan appears to Hunding "as Wälse". This little touch was of course not carried over into the poem. The reader will recall that in the Sketch Wotan had appeared as Wälse in the first act, "in the form of an oldish man with grey hair and beard and only one eye, with a round hat and a grey cloak".

[2] As has been pointed out earlier, Wagner has carelessly carried over into the poem here a feature that was valid only for the Sketch.

descriptive music. The thematic bases of it are naturally the
Valkyries' motive (No. 74), the characteristic "Hojotoho!"
(No. 76), and a pictorial figure, suggestive of the mad course of
the Valkyries through the air:

that had been already hinted at in the orchestra at Brynhilde's first
appearance in act two. (What was probably the full theme of the
Valkyries in its earliest form has come down to us on a fragment
of music paper presented by Wagner on the 23rd July 1851 to a
young Swiss enthusiast, Robert Radecke, whose acquaintance
he had just made. There the words and the melody run thus:

The reader who knows his *Ring* will not need to be told that these
words do not appear anywhere in the *Valkyrie* poem. They come
from the *Siegfried's Death* of 1848, in which, it will be remembered,
there was a scene (not carried over into the present *Twilight of the
Gods*) in which the Valkyries visited Brynhilde's rock *en masse* to
condole with her on her punishment by Wotan; and the words of
No. 87 are the first two of the four lines they sing as they ride away
again into the storm. It would be interesting to know how many
more of the musical motives of the present tetralogy were conceived for use in *Siegfried's Death*).

These three motives, together with such realistic effects as the
thunderous gallop and the panting and whinnying of the horses,

are all that Wagner requires to build up the huge structure of the exciting first scene of the third act.

The stage shows us the summit of a rocky mountain, with a pine-wood on the right, and on the left the entrance to a cave; the background is occupied by rocks of various heights that form the verge of a precipice. When the curtain rises, Gerhilde, Ortlinde, Waltraute and Schwertleite are already assembled on the rocky point above the cave. They hail each other, and are answered by a Valkyrie on horseback in the air, who, as a lightning-flash rends the clouds, becomes visible in the distance with a slain warrior hanging across her saddle. One by one the sisters arrive and are greeted joyously by those already on the scene. They indulge in savage merriment; the horses with the bodies have been left in the adjacent wood, and the lifetime enmity of the dead heroes now communicates itself to the animals, who, we gather, have to be separated to keep them from attacking each other.

17

The eight Valkyries are on the point of riding off together to Walhall when they observe that one of them, Brynhilde, is missing:

> *Till she comes hither,*
> *here must we bide:*
> *War-father grimmest*
> *greeting would give,*
> *saw he not her in our midst.*

At last they catch sight of her in the distance, spurring her panting horse Grane towards the rock. There is something with her on her saddle, but this, to their astonishment, proves to be a woman. At last she enters on foot from the wood, leading and supporting Sieglinde, and breathlessly appealing for aid in her need: for the first time, she tells them, she is not the pursuer but the pursued, for War-father hunts her close. They do not understand; but Ortlinde and Waltraute, looking from the summit of the mountain, see a thundercloud approaching from the north, and in it

War-father driving his steed furiously towards them. He is accompanied all the time by the pounding of the motive of the Need of the Gods (No. 81); it is destiny, more than personal anger, that is urging him on relentlessly to punish his rebellious child.

Brynhilde hurriedly makes clear to the others what has happened: the fainting woman with her is Sieglinde, Siegmund's sister and bride; Brynhilde had disobeyed War-father's command to desert Siegmund in his fight with Hunding, and now retribution is about to fall on Sieglinde:

> *Woe to the woman*
> *if he find her here;*
> *to all of the Volsungs*
> *ruin he threatens!*
> *Who'll lend me the swiftest*
> *horse in my need,*
> *to bear the woman away?*

The horrified Valkyries refuse to lend her a horse, for fear of Wotan. Sieglinde breaks in on her piteous appeals for help; she repulses the protecting arm that Brynhilde would throw round her, reproaches her for saving her life when Siegmund had died, and implores her to strike her sword through her heart. But Brynhilde exhorts her to cling to life for the sake of the child that Siegmund has left with her as a pledge of his love; "a Volsung thou bearest to him!" Sieglinde starts violently, then turns in exaltation to Brynhilde: "Rescue me, brave one", she cries; "rescue my babe! Shelter me, o maids, with your shields!"

The clouds pile up at the back, the thunder rolls nearer, and the terrified Valkyries distractedly urge Brynhilde to fly with the woman, for help her themselves they dare not. Sieglinde falls on her knees to Brynhilde, who raises her as a resolution suddenly takes shape within her; she bids her fly to safety, while she herself will stay and face Wotan. But where is Sieglinde to go? The Valkyries tell her of a wood that stretches away to the eastward, where Fafner, changed into a dragon, lies in a cavern guarding the Ring. It is no place for a suffering woman, they say; but Brynhilde remembers that Wotan dreads the spot and shuns it. As the

God draws nearer she tells Sieglinde hurriedly to fly to the wood, be brave and defiant there, enduring hunger and thirst, thorns and rough ways, for in her womb she bears "the world's most wonderful hero". She gives her the fragments of Siegmund's sword which she has carried under her armour, and exhorts her to preserve them for the child, whose name is to be "Siegfried, who shall rejoice in victory"; and the vigorous motive that is to be identified with the future hero of the *Ring* is heard in the horns:

Sieglinde responds with a great cry of thankfulness, to a melody:

which will be used in the closing bars of the *Twilight of the Gods* to symbolise Redemption by Love. For Siegmund's sake, she says, she will save the child; then she bids Brynhilde farewell and hastens away to the wood.

18

The storm has increased in violence, and the approach of Wotan is heralded by a fiery glow that breaks out in the background, to the right. His voice, magnified by a speaking trumpet, is heard through the thunder, bidding Brynhilde stay and face him. For a while she had stood watching Sieglinde's flight; now she returns, full of anxiety, to the centre of the stage. In response to a last desperate appeal to her sisters to shield her from the wrath of the God they draw themselves up in a body on the rocky peak, concealing her in their midst. In mounting excitement they describe the coming of War-father, breathing revenge. At last he enters from the little wood and strides furiously towards them, asking where is Brynhilde, and threatening them with his anger if they conceal her from him. In a brief ensemble in which their agitated cries ascend in wave on wave they try to appease his wrath, but in vain. He upbraids them for their womanish weakness; was it from him, he asks, they got this craven spirit, from him, who had reared them to be hard and ruthless, to fare with joy to the combat:

> *and ye wild ones now weep and whine*
> *when my wrath doth a traitor chastise?*

He tells them, to the accompaniment of the tragic motive of the Need of the Gods (No. 81), what Brynhilde's crime has been:

> *No one but she*
> *knew all the depths of my musing;*
> *no one but she*
> *saw to the spring of my spirit!*
> *'Twas she shaped*
> *into deed what I had but wished:—*
> *and now our holiest*
> *band hath she broke,*
> *the faithless one*
> *my own will hath defied,*
> *my sacred command*
> *openly scorned,*
> *'gainst myself the weapon she turned*
> *that my will alone made hers!*

He summons her to come forth and meet her accuser and receive the scourging she has earned.

The music softens suddenly as Brynhilde emerges from the midst of the Valkyries, comes down humbly but with firm steps from the rock, and pauses a short distance from the God: "Here stand I, father", she says quietly; "pronounce thou my punishment." Her sentence she herself has shaped, he tells her passionately. His will alone had brought her into being, and against his will she had worked; her sole duty had been to carry out his commands, yet she had dared to command against him; his Wishmaid she had been, yet against his will she had dared to wish; Shield-maid she had been to him, yet against him she had raised her shield; Lot-chooser she was, yet a lot against him she had chosen; Hero-stirrer he had created her to be, yet against him she had stirred up heroes. "What once thou wert, I have told thee; what now thou art, that say to thyself: Wish-maid and Valkyrie thou art no more."

We catch a glimpse of the heartbreak at the core of his anger as he goes on to pronounce sentence on her. The motive representative of her as the Announcer of Death (No. 85) receives a great lyrical expansion:

as he tells her, in lines of much poetic beauty, that no more will he send her out to find him heroes and bring them to him in Walhall; no more, at the Gods' festal banquet, will his best-loved one fill his drinking-horn; no more his dear child's mouth will he kiss; the company of the Gods will own her no longer; she will be an outcast from them, "for broken now is our bond, and thou for ever art banned from my sight"; and the theme of Wotan as the guardian of treaties (No. 13), tearing its way downwards in trombones and tuba, gives us the clue to the compulsion under which he is now acting as he does.

"All thou hast given, then, thou takest away?" asks Brynhilde sadly. No, he replies; one who shall come shall take it all, for here on this rock shall she await the fate he has decreed for her:

> defenceless in sleep
> bound shalt thou lie:
> that man shall master the maid
> who shall find her and wake her from sleep.

The Valkyries break into a wail of protest; coming down from the rock they group themselves round Brynhilde, half-kneeling before Wotan and imploring him to relent. Angrily he repeats his decision: their faithless sister shall be found and mastered by a husband:

> by the hearth to sit and spin,
> to all mockers a sport and shame.

His anger mounts as Brynhilde sinks to the ground with a cry and the Valkyries recoil from her. Harshly he bids them leave her to her fate, unless they wish to share her punishment with her. They separate with wild cries and run into the adjoining wood, from which there soon comes a great clamour (No. 86 in frenzied waves). Black clouds gather about the cliffs; and by a lightning-flash the Valkyries are seen, with loose bridles, crowded together and riding away, to the strains of No. 74.

19

Gradually the tempest dies down, the clouds disperse, and the calm of twilight, merging gradually into night, descends upon the scene. Wotan and Brynhilde are now alone, she lying in utter abasement at his feet. A long and solemn silence is broken first of all by the melody of No. 90 in the veiled melancholy tones of the bass clarinet, then by a new motive, beginning in the same instrument and continuing in the 'cellos and basses and then in the cor anglais, symbolical of the Volsung Love that lies deep down in Wotan's hurt and angry heart:

The final limb of the long melody:

will rank later as an independent motive. (Both No. 91 and No. 92 derive from No. 79, which at its first appearance in the scene between Wotan and Fricka has been styled the motive of Dejection. Once more we realise the absurdity of trying to fasten a Wagnerian motive down to a fixed verbal formula. The phrase is psychologically complex in the way that only music can be; it voices the grief of Wotan, evoked at one time by the call on him to abandon Siegmund and surrender his dream of a rescuing Volsung hero, at another time his sorrow both at the shattering of his hopes in that respect and at the necessity of eternal separation from Brynhilde. So again with the figure of No. 84, which reappears, in the course of the present scene, in the 'cellos at one point: it has nothing to do now, as it formerly had, with the Annunciation of Death, but recurs spontaneously to Wagner as the most fitting expression of Brynhilde's grief at her banishment from Wotan and Walhalla).

During the sad dialogue that follows, Nos. 91 and 92 keep winding their melancholy way through the orchestral texture in one instrument after another, but mostly in the poignant timbres of oboe or cor anglais. The Valkyrie timidly asks if her deed was in truth so shameful as to merit such a scourging, such abasement:

Look in my eyes then:
silence thy rage,
master thy wrath,
make clearer to me
the hidden guilt,
that thou set'st thy face like a stone,
and dost turn from thy favourite child.

"Ask of thy deed itself", the God replies gloomily; "thy guilt it
will show thee." She urges that she had but carried out his order
to fight for the Volsung; it was true that he had revoked it, but,
she pleads, only after Fricka had imposed her will on him and
made him false to his purpose. In her mutinous pride, he rejoins,
she had presumed to substitute her own wisdom for his. Gradually
gaining confidence, she tells him how she had pierced beneath his
words to what lay in his heart; her love had seen what he had
striven to hide even from himself—that he desired the victory of
Siegmund; and when she had looked into the hero's eyes and
seen the distress of his soul at the thought of parting from
Sieglinde she had been filled with pity and love for him, and felt
that for her to disobey the God's command would be the highest
form of obedience to his secret will. Wagner's imagination strikes
out a new figure of grief (not a motive):

93

upon which he allows himself the luxury of playing for a considerable time as Brynhilde describes the emotions that had
possessed her in her dialogue with Siegmund. When she tells how
she had disobeyed Wotan's decree because she had recognised
that the love that filled her own heart was one with the love of
Wotan for the Volsungs, No. 92 suddenly becomes luminously
transfigured:

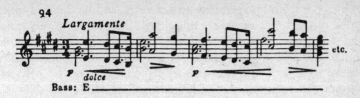

And when the God says "So didst thou do what myself would fain have done, yet what ne'er could be, by fate doubly forbid", we find Wagner unexpectedly taking up again the figure shown in No. 85, where it had accompanied Sieglinde's words "Would that our father were home! With the boy still he roams in the woods!" It now assumes the following form:

being combined, as will be seen, with No. 94. Precisely what psychological significance Nos. 85 and 95 had for Wagner it is impossible to say.

20

Wotan opens out his whole heart now to this beloved child of his. He tells her of his own distress all this long while; he had sought to bury his sorrow for ever under the ruins of the world he so loved; she, not knowing, not understanding, had listened only to the voice of love:

> while I, gall of the Gods'
> bitterest anguish must drink.

For a time the music is of a melting tenderness: then Wotan resumes more drily. She must follow her heart's own folly now to the end: from him she had turned away, and he can no longer work through her or take counsel with her. Her reply is quiet and simple. Unfit was she for him, for to her foolish mind one thing only had seemed good—to love whatever he loved. Yet she asks him not to forget that in dishonouring her he will dishonour the immortal part of himself, soiling himself in shaming her.

Still hard and unrelenting, he tells her that as she has chosen love, now she must follow as her master the man who shall compel her love. Then let it be, she begs him, no common, worthless man who shall take possession of her. The more bitterly he refuses, the more ardently and intimately she pleads. She reminds him of the Volsung race he had bred, which she had preserved from destruction by saving Sieglinde and her child, together with the Sword the God had shaped for Siegmund. At this last reminder of his hopes and his frustration his anger rises again. He will hear no more, he says; she must submit to her fate; he cannot choose for her:

> as from me thou didst turn,
> I turn from thee;
> I may not know
> what now thou dost wish:
> thy chastisement
> must I see fulfilled.

Her punishment is to lie bound and weaponless in deep slumber and become the wife of the man who shall find and waken her. The orchestra gives out softly the mysterious, lulling motive of Magic Sleep:

She falls on her knees before him and breaks out in passionate protest: if she is to be bound in fetters of sleep, let him surround the rock with such terrors that only the freest and greatest of heroes will brave them. Foreshadowings in the minor:

of what will develop later into the motive of Brynhilde's Slumber play continuously about her words. Wotan refuses her request: "Too much thou cravest, too great this grace!" She repeats it more urgently: let him slay her with his spear, let him destroy her utterly, but not inflict woeful shame on her. Then, in wild exaltation, she asks him to surround the rock with a fire that will consume any craven who dares approach it. Fire motives from the *Rhinegold* (Nos. 22 and 24) combine with the Valkyrie motive (No. 74) to give point to her appeal.

At last Wotan's heart melts. To a mighty surge of orchestral tone, in which we hear the Slumber motive now defining itself in its true form:

he raises Brynhilde to her feet, gazes, profoundly moved, into her eyes, and begins his great farewell to her:

If he must really part from her:

Muss ich dich mei - den, und darf nicht
Must I then leave thee, my lov - ing

min - nig mein Gruss dich - mehr grüss - en,
greet - ing no more may I give thee,

if no more she shall hand him the mead-cup at the banquets of the
Gods, he will at least engirdle her rock with "such a bridal fire
as ne'er yet has burned for a bride", a fire that will strike fear into
the heart of all but the boldest:

> *For one alone winneth the bride,*
> *one freer than I, the God!*

The flames seem already to leap out from the orchestra: and as he
speaks of the one who alone shall win her the Siegfried motive
(No. 88) raises its head prophetically.

While the orchestra luxuriates in developments of No. 98 he
folds her in a loving embrace, and suddenly all becomes tenderness again as the Slumber motive takes on a new form and now
runs a long symphonic course:

as the God savours for the last time the honey of this vast love of
his:

> *Thine eyes, so lustrous and pure,*
> *that, smiling, oft I caressed,*
> *when my fond kiss*
> *thy courage won thee,*
> *when heroes' laud*
> *from thy honied lips*
> *in childish lispings flowed forth:*

these unclouded, glorious eyes,
that oft have lightened my gloom,
when hopeless longing
my heart had wasted,
when worldly pleasures
I wished to win me,
by fear fettered and maddened.

Till there comes the motive of the Last Greeting:

Zum letz - ten Mal   letz' es mich heut' mit des
Their gleam once more   glad - dens me now, as my

Le - be - woh - les   letz - tem Kuss!
lips . meet thine in   love's last kiss!

Their gleam once more
gladdens me now,
as my lips meet thine
in love's last kiss!
On hero more bless éd
haply they'll beam:
on me, care-ridden God,
now must thou close them for ever.
For so turns
the God from thee now,
so kisses thy godhead away!

"He imprints a long kiss on her eyes", say the stage directions, "and she sinks back in his arms with closed eyes, unconsciousness gently stealing over her". For some time not a word is spoken, the orchestra saying all that is in the heart of each of them in a quiet meditation on Nos. 96 and 98. "He leads her tenderly to a low mossy bank underneath a broad-branched fir-tree, and there lays her down. He contemplates her, then closes her helmet. His eyes rest for a time on the form of the sleeping maiden, whom

he now covers completely with the great steel shield of the
Valkyrie. He moves slowly away, then turns round once more
with a sorrowful look. He goes with solemn decision to the centre
of the stage and turns his Spear-point towards a large rock."
He strikes it three times with his Spear and summons Loge to
appear and encircle the fell with his fire, which at once, to the
characteristic Loge motives, flames out on all sides. With a final
command:

> *He who my spear-point's*
> *sharpness feareth*
> *ne'er breaks through this fierce-flaming fire!*

he stretches out his Spear, as if imposing a spell: then he turns
and departs, twice looking back sorrowfully at his child. The last
word is left to the orchestra, first of all intoning the Siegfried
motive (No. 88), then playing with the lambent Fire motives.
At one point No. 98 is combined contrapuntally with No. 102 in
this fashion:

(The decorative inner parts are omitted from the quotation). The
Slumber motive is heard again, followed by the fateful No. 83A,
and as the fire music fades away in the orchestra the curtain falls.

SIEGFRIED

I

Of all the characters who had figured in the first drama of the *Ring* only one, Alberich, was destined to play a part in the last. In the new world in which *Siegfried* is set, Wotan appears not *in propria persona* but only as the Wanderer. Mime survives for a while from the *Rhinegold*; so also does Fafner, but in his changed form as Dragon. Alberich remains what he was at the beginning and will be to the end. Brynhilde is taken over from the *Valkyrie*, but psychologically transformed, though the transformation is not as complete as it will become in the *Twilight of the Gods*. Erda, as before, is less a character than a nature-symbol. Siegfried, on whose unconscious shoulders now falls the burden Wotan had laid down, is entirely new.

The prelude to *Siegfried* is psychological; it reveals what is passing, not only at the moment when the new work opens but always, in the mind of Mime,[1] who has never ceased to brood on the problem of the Ring—how to gain possession of it and make himself master of the world. In the Nibelheim scene of the

---

[1] Mime should not be the feeble, pitiful, sympathy-cadging figure that is made of him in most of the performances we see. He is a thing of evil, and, in his debased way, of power for evil. Wagner's conception of him is to be seen in a passage in the stage directions of *Young Siegfried* that was not reproduced in the present opera. "He is small and bent, somewhat deformed and hobbling. His head is abnormally large, his face a dark ashen colour and wrinkled, his eyes small and piercing, with red rims, his grey beard long and scrubby, his head bald and covered with a red cap. He wears a dark grey smock with a broad belt about his loins: feet bare, with thick coarse soles underneath. *There must be nothing approaching caricature in all this:* his aspect, when he is quiet, must simply be eerie; it is only in moments of extreme excitement that he becomes *outwardly* ludicrous, but never too uncouth. His voice is husky and harsh; but this again ought of itself never to provoke the listener to laughter." (Italics mine).

Nor must Alberich be the purely grotesque figure we generally see on the stage: for all his ugliness there must be a certain grandeur about him. "He resembles", says Wagner in *Young Siegfried*, "Mime in every respect [i.e. in that they are brothers]; only his appearance and his expression invariably make a more serious and indeed nobler effect."

Rhinegold we saw him musing mournfully on his subjection to Alberich, on the cause of it, the possibility of escape from it, to a curious little figure in thirds in the bassoons. It is with this motive of Reflection (No. 35), still in the bassoons, that Wagner begins the prelude to *Siegfried*:

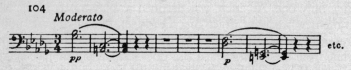

The dwarf's thoughts are fixed, as always, on the Hoard (see No. 37):

as he goes on with his smithing to the familiar motive from the *Rhinegold*:

to which, as will be seen, is conjoined the motive of the Servitude of the Nibelungs (No. 33). This latter swells to a great moan as Mime reflects on his unhappy lot and his impotence to remedy it. Then his thoughts turn to the all-important Ring (No. 8 in the wood wind). If only he could possess himself of that! But how? Only a stronger arm than his, and a weapon better than any he has ever succeeded in making, will ever subdue the monstrous Dragon; and the bass trumpet, giving out the Sword motive (No. 48) softly, hints at what that weapon shall be.

As he plunges afresh into his work with the frenzy of despair the curtain rises, showing a rocky cavern with two natural entrances from the forest, one in the background (right), the other, a broader one, also at the back but sideways. On the left, against the wall, the rocks of the cave shape themselves into a great smith's forge, the chimney of which, also natural, goes up through the roof; only the bellows are artificial. Near by are a big anvil and other smith's implements. At the anvil sits Mime, tapping away with a small hammer at a sword in the making. He is manifestly uneasy and out of spirits. At last he gives it up. All is in vain, he complains; the youth whom he harbours in his cave has once again commanded him to make him a sword, but the best that Mime has hitherto been able to make, though fit for any giant, has been shattered by the malapert boy at a single stroke, as though it were a toy for a child! Peevishly he throws the sword down on the anvil, puts his arms akimbo, and, to the accompaniment of No. 104, stares moodily at the ground. "I know no sword", he says, "that the boy could not break, except one forged from the fragments of Nothung. But all my skill does not suffice for the welding of that; and even could I achieve it it would bring me nothing but shame." The old torturing thought of his impotence fills his mind as the Dragon motive heaves like a brute mass in the depths of the orchestra in the tuba:

There in the dark forest lurks Fafner, his huge bulk stretched across the Hoard. Only Siegfried could slay him, and he only with the so-desired sword: "and I cannot weld it", Mime wails shrilly, "this sword!" Once more he sets to work in hopeless dejection at the steel on the anvil:

> *I tinker and hammer it*
> *at the boy's behest;*
> *one blow and he'll break it to bits,*
> *and scoff and scold at the smith!*

and again he lets the hammer fall from his poor puny hand.

2

As he does so a merry "Hoiho!" is heard from without, and
the young Siegfried, accompanied by a motive that will henceforth characterise him to the end:

enters impetuously from the wood. He is wearing a rough
forester's dress; a silver horn hangs on a chain from his neck; he
is leading a great bear by a bast-rope and setting it with wanton
boyish humour at the frightened Mime. The dwarf drops the
sword in terror and cowers behind the forge, the boy pursuing
him with gay laughter: he has brought the bear, he explains, to
ask in person for the sword. He releases the brute, gives him a
stroke on the back with the rope, and sends him lumbering off
into the wood, whereupon Mime, trembling all over, comes out
from behind the forge: he never objects, he tells the boy, to his
killing bears, but to bring them alive into the cave is going a little
too far.

Sitting down to recover from his laughter, Siegfried explains
that he had gone out into the wood hoping to find some companion more to his liking than the dwarf; he had sounded his
horn (No. 108), and out of the bush had come a bear and growled
at him; and, for lack of something better, Siegfried had accepted
him as at any rate an improvement on the dwarf; so he had bridled
him and brought him to ask about the sword. His usual self
again now, Mime takes the sword from the anvil and hands
it to the boy, singing its praises as sharp enough even for him.
But sharpness and brightness are nothing, Siegfried tells him,
if the steel be not hard and true. Passing his hand over it he
rejects it as merely a useless toy, not a sword but "a pitiful
pin"; and smiting it on the anvil he breaks it into splinters.

Then, to a lively new motive, characteristic of his youthful impetuosity:

which accompanies him all through his harangue, he vents his rage on the terrified Mime. What does the wretched boaster and bungler mean by fobbing him off with a piece of trash of this sort? He is always prating of battles and giants and great deeds and weapons of might; yet when Siegfried essays the swords he has made for him they break in twain at his first grip on them. Were not the pitiful old imp, he continues, too vile for his hate he would break him in pieces, him and his sword. "Then would my torment have an end!"; and he throws himself in a raging temper on a stone seat.

Mime has prudently kept out of his way during this tempest, which goes on raging in the orchestra (No. 109) after Siegfried has ceased railing. He tries the line of suave cajolery. Why is the boy so petulant? he asks him. How is it that he, Mime, can never please him, try as he will? To a new motive, a rhythmical modification of No. 32:

he appeals to his sense of gratitude: "thou shouldst be obedient to Mime, who always thinks but of thee". The sulking boy turns to the wall, presenting his back to the dwarf, who stands for a moment perplexed. Then he goes to the pots on the hearth and coaxingly shows Siegfried the meat and the broth he has prepared for him out of pure affection. Without turning round, the boy knocks meat and bowl out of his hands: "meat did I roast for myself", he says; "and slake thy own thirst with thy swill!" Still to the accompaniment of No. 110, Mime reproaches him in high-pitched querulous tones. So this is the sorry wage he gets for all his love and devotion! In a whining voice:

he reminds the boy how he had brought him up, a whimpering little brat, given him warm clothes and food and drink and a soft bed which he used to smooth with his own hands, and many a toy, including a ringing horn—and all for pure love of him. He had worked for him, thought for him, quickened his wits with wise counsel, given him the golden key to knowledge. He stays at home and toils and moils while the boy wanders at will in the woods; the poor old dwarf withers and wastes for the lad, and all he gets for his work and worry is torment and hatred: and overcome by his own pathos he breaks down and sobs.

But when Siegfried at last turns round and fixes his eyes searchingly on Mime's face the dwarf evades his look. To the accompaniment now of No. 109, now of No. 110, Siegfried, beginning steadily and quietly but soon working himself into a passion again, gives him his frank opinion of him. "Much indeed hast thou taught me, much from thee have I learned; but what thou didst most desire to teach me, that have I tried in vain to learn—how to endure the sight of thee! Thou givest me food and drink, and I feed on loathing alone; my pillow thou makest, but no sleep can I get; when thou wouldst teach me wisdom I remain deaf and dull. I have only to glance at thee, and everything thou dost becomes evil in my eyes". His temper rises as he goes on:

> when thou dost stand,
> shuffle and scrape,
> crouching and slinking,

with thine eyelids blinking,
by the neck I long
to take the nodder,
an end to make
of the misshaped fumbler!
So learned I, Mime, to love thee.

Let the dwarf, if he is as wise as he claims to be, solve this puzzle for him if he can—why is every beast he meets in the forest, and the trees, and the birds, and the fish in the brook, all dearer to him than Mime? Why, indeed, once having left him, does he ever return?

3

Mime is confident he can answer this. As a new motive of great beauty, that of Love, which brings for the first time a note of profound feeling into the score, wells up in the 'cellos:

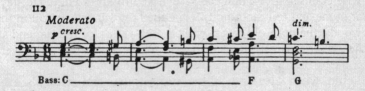

he carefully explains—still keeping at a safe distance, however— that it is only the boy's wilful tongue, not his heart, that makes him talk like this. "Always the young yearn for the parents' nest, and the name of this longing is love. Thus thou dost love thy Mime, and cannot help loving him; for what the parent bird is to the fledgling, nourished in the nest ere he can fly, such to his boy, his bantling, is the sage and unselfish old Mime." Again to the accompaniment of the tender No. 112, Siegfried asks him to explain something more. "When the birds sing for happiness in the Spring, each of them calls enticingly to the other; and thou thyself hast told me that they were husband and wife. They caressed each other, and built them a nest, and brooded there over their little ones until these could spread their wings:

So it is too with the deer in the woods, and even the wild wolves and foxes: the father brings the food to the nest, the mother suckles the young. And thus I learned what love is, and from the mother I never took the cubs. Where then is *thy* wife, Mime, that I may call her mother?"

Ignoring a peevish interjection from the Nibelung, the boy goes on, in a derisive imitation of the words and the tune of the latter's first recital of the kindnesses he had shown him: "The whimpering babe thou broughtest up, fed it and gave it warm clothes. But what wind had wafted the whelp to thee? Didst thou make me, perchance, without a mother?" Mime, greatly embarrassed, assures him that he is his father and mother in one. Siegfried gives him the lie direct. For he has observed that the young of a brood are like the old; he has seen his own face in a brook, and he is no more like Mime than a shining fish is like a toad, and no fish ever had toad for its father. With the orchestra returning to the impetuous figure shown in No. 109 he asks again if the dwarf can tell him why, having fled from him into the forest as he so often does, he ever returns to him; and he answers his question himself—he returns solely to learn from him who his father and mother were, and this he will know if he has to tear it out of him by force, as he has had to wring the knowledge of everything else out of him, even speech.

He seizes him by the throat. Mime, half-choked, at last regains his liberty; and after another lament over the boy's ingratitude he begins to tell him what he knows. Though, it is true, he is neither father nor mother to him, it is to Mime that Siegfried owes everything: "but a fool was I to count on thy thanks!" he wails. The orchestra gives out softly the motive of the Volsung Woe (No. 54); and to modifications of that and other motives associated in the *Valkyrie* with Siegmund and Sieglinde, such as:

he tells how long ago he had found a woman weeping in a desolate wood, how he had brought her to his cave, where he gave her warm shelter, how she had given birth to a child—Siegfried— and died. "So died, then", says Siegfried slowly and sadly, "my mother of me?" Mime starts off again with his hypocritical "A whimpering babe brought I thee up"; but Siegfried cuts him short and demands to be told more. Why, he asks, is he called Siegfried? It was his mother's wish, Mime replies, that he should bear that name, "for as Siegfried shouldst thou be fair and strong". The mother's name he never knew, he says; but under a new threat from the boy he reveals that it was Sieglinde. But the father's name the dwarf had never learned; all he knew of him was that he had died in combat. Once more his attempt to go on in the old whining canting vein is cut short by Siegfried: what proof, he asks, has he that Mime is telling him the truth?

After some pondering, the Nibelung produces the two frag-ments of a broken sword, while the Sword motive (No. 48) comes out quietly in the orchestra, over a bass formed from the Nibelung smithing motive (No. 32). These, says the dwarf, were all the pitiful pay he got for his kindness to the woman—a shattered sword which, she told him, the boy's father had borne in the last of his fights, in which he was killed. At once the boy leaps to the right conclusion: it is out of these fragments that the smith shall forge him the sword he desires—his own rightful weapon; and a phrase that begins as the Sword motive but con-tinues as No. 108 symbolises the bond between the old and the new possessor of the Sword:

To insistent repetitions of the eager No. 109 he bids Mime set to work without delay:

> *Trick me no longer;*
> *no more of thy toys;*
> *in these fragments alone*
> *put I my faith!*
> *Find I a fault,*
> *forge thou it feebly,*
> *bungling and botching*
> *the sturdy steel,*
> *thou hound, thy hide will I baste,*
> *I'll burnish thee brighter than steel!*

He will have the sword this very day, and with it he will leave the wood and go into the world, never to return:

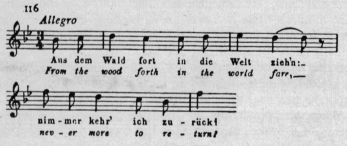

He is filled with a great joy. Nothing binds him any longer to Mime and his cave. "My father art thou not; thy hearth is not my house, nor thy cave my rightful roof". He will be free, like the fish in the stream, the bird on the wind; and the hated little Nibelung he will see no more. He rushes impetuously into the forest, executing a joyous fantasia on the theme of No. 116, and leaving Mime in the utmost confusion and terror.

4

For the dwarf is now a prey to a new anxiety. He has always known that only through Siegfried can he hope to accomplish his scheme for subduing Fafner and winning for himself Ring and

Hoard; and now the headstrong boy is bent on leaving him. He goes back to the forge and seats himself by the anvil. "He storms away", he says dejectedly, "and I sit here, with a new care added to the old one! What way out is there for me? How hold this wildling to me and lead him to Fafner's lair? How forge me those baffling splinters—for no forge-fire can melt them, no dwarf's hammer conquer their hardness"; and he ends with a wail of "The Nibelung's hate, need and toil ne'er can knit Nothung anew, make me the sword as it was!'

As he collapses in despair by the anvil, Wotan enters slowly from the forest by the door at the back of the cave. He is now the Wanderer, wearing a long mantle of dark blue and a large hat that comes low down over the eye that is lacking. With a sudden dramatic change the orchestra slows down to a tempo befitting the gravity of the God, whose characteristic motive, as Wanderer, is intoned solemnly by the brass:

It has a broad pendant that is like the unhurrying tread of a God:

and a majestic ending:

He greets the cowering Nibelung courteously, asking the customary grace of house and hearth for a weary wayfarer. In reply to Mime's timorous enquiries he says he is known to the world as Wanderer, always receiving guest-greeting from good men, learning from them and speaking wisdom to them; for few are wise enough—the shaft is directed covertly at Mime—to know the true nature of their own need, and out of his own store of wisdom he has often been able to help them. All this while he has been steadily approaching Mime, and now he has come right down to the hearth. The dwarf protests that he is wise enough for his own purposes and needs no counsel from strangers, and tells the intruder to go on his way. But the Wanderer calmly seats himself by the hearth and proposes a combat of wits: he stakes his head on his ability to answer whatever question the Nibelung may ask him.

5

The Reflection motive (No. 104) is murmured by the bassoons as Mime ponders within himself how to get rid of this intrusive spy, as he regards him. In the end, confident of his own cunning, he decides to accept the challenge—his hearth against the other's head. He will ask him three questions. This Wanderer boasts of having gone far and wide over the earth's back. Very well; can the wise one tell him what race it is that dwells in the caverns of the earth? To the accompaniment of the familiar motives at the appropriate points (Nos. 32, 8, 33, 105 etc.), the Wanderer replies that it is the Nibelungs, whose home is Nibelheim. Slaves they were to Alberich, who had won power over them and amassed great treasure by a magic Ring. The same procedure then follows, with the same reference to characteristic motives. Mime, after further reflection, asks what race it is that dwells on the surface of the earth. It is the Giants, is the answer, whose home is Riesenheim. Two of them, Fasolt and Fafner, envying the Nibelung's power, made Ring and Hoard their own: then strife broke out between the brothers, Fasolt was slain, and Fafner, transformed into a Dragon, now guards the treasure. And now, what is the dwarf's third question?

Mime, rather baffled by this omniscience, reflects more deeply than ever, and at last asks, "What is the race that dwells on cloud-covered heights?" To a stately enunciation of the Walhall motive the Wanderer replies that it is the Gods. Walhall is their home; the highest of them is Licht-Alberich, Wotan.[1] From the stem of the world-ash-tree he had made himself a Spear, and by virtue of the runes he had carved on it he governs the world: the Giants he curbed, the Nibelungs kneel before him; "ever they bow and obey him, the Ring's most mighty lord!" As if by accident he lets his Spear touch the ground; there is a light rumble of thunder, and Mime shrinks back in terror. "Now tell me, thou wise dwarf, have I true answers given? My head can I have and hold?"

Timidly and ingratiatingly Mime assures him that his head is safe and exhorts him to go on his way; but the Wanderer, to the accompaniment of the stately No. 118, tranquilly reminds him that by the rules of wagering it is now the dwarf's turn to back his own wisdom with his own head. Mime is scared, but pulling his wits together and gaining confidence as he proceeds he prepares to put his first question. A motive that will always characterise him later in his moments of satisfaction with his own slippery craft:

---

[1] Alberich himself, as has been pointed out earlier, is Schwarz-Alberich (Black Alberich). The antithesis is that of the power that works in the light and the power rooted in darkness.

accompanies him as he mock-modestly disparages his own poor knowledge. It is a long time, he says, since he left his mother and his homeland, and his mother-wits are a little moidered. But he will do his best; perhaps his luck will be in and the poor dwarf will save his head.

What is the race, asks the Wanderer, the orchestra giving out the Volsung motive (No. 58), that Wotan wreaked his wrath on, though he loved it more than all others in the world. Little does he know, replies Mime, of heroes in general; but this question at least he can answer fully—it is the race of the Volsungs, which Wotan begat and cherished, though he chastised it too. To Wälse were born Siegmund and Sieglinde, a wild twin pair, and the offspring of their love was Siegfried, of all the Volsungs the strongest. "Now tell me, Wanderer, if so far I have saved my head?" The Wanderer compliments him genially on his knowingness, and poses the second question: Who is the wise Nibelung who harbours Siegfried, to fight Fafner for him and win him the Hoard; and by what sword will Fafner die? This, Mime feels, is almost absurdly easy. He rubs his hands in glee as he answers, to the accompaniment of No. 120, "Nothung is the name of the sword: in an ash-tree's stem it was struck by Wotan, and Siegmund alone could draw it forth. He wielded it in his last fight, but it was shattered on Wotan's spear; and now the fragments are in the possession of a cunning smith, who knows that only with this Wotan-sword can a brave but witless boy, Siegfried, slay the Dragon." The slippery No. 120 comes out boldly in the orchestra as he asks again, highly pleased with himself, "Has the dwarf saved his head?"

Wotan breaks into a peal of laughter. Nowhere on earth, he assures him, is the like of Mime for wisdom to be found. But since he is so wise as to mould this stripling hero to his own ends, perhaps he is wise enough also to answer this third question: By whose hand shall the mighty pieces of the Volsung sword be made afresh into Nothung?

6

Mime starts up in the wildest terror, and with the boisterous No. 108 seeming to mock him all the time in the orchestra he screams, "The pieces! The Sword! Woe's me, I know not! What shall I do? Where shall I turn? Accursed steel! Would I ne'er had stolen it. Nought has it brought me but care and fear! It is too hard for me, hammer and rivet and solder it as I will! The craftiest of smiths here comes to shame!" In a paroxysm of despair he throws his tools about as if demented, crying, "Who'll shape me the Sword that baffles my skill? Who can achieve this marvel?"

Tranquilly, accompanied by the dignified No. 117, the Wanderer rises from the hearth. "Three questions of thine I suffered, three I answered. But as for thee, vain is thy knowledge: what it most behoved thee to know, because it would have served thy need, that thou knewest not." While the Nibelung motive (No. 32) chatters distractedly in the upper part of the orchestra and the Treaty motive (No. 13) goes thundering down against it in the trombones, the Wanderer speaks his final words. "I have won the wise one's head: now, bold destroyer of Fafner, listen to what I have to tell thee. He who knows not what fear is alone shall forge Nothung anew! Thy wise old head ward well from today. I want it not: I leave it to him who has never learned to fear!" He turns away with a smile and disappears into the forest.

Mime has sunk on to his stool, as if crushed. The Wanderer's words are an enigma as well as a threat; for if Siegfried has any fear in him he will never be able to overcome Fafner, while if, unfearing, he should achieve that deed, then, according to this mysterious Wanderer who appears to know all secrets, the dwarf's own head will be forfeit to him.[1] There now follows a piece of orchestral painting of extraordinary power. As Mime stares in desperation at the sunlit forest it seems to him to be alive with menacing lights, flickering and flashing, glittering and swirling,

[1] This question of "fearing" is the knottiest psychological and dramatic problem with which Wagner has confronted us in the *Ring*. He himself never succeeded in steering a quite logical course between the various possible handlings of the motive that occurred to him from time to time. A full discussion of the complicated matter, however, is impossible here: I can only refer the reader who wishes to track it out in all its windings to my *Life of Wagner*, Vol. II, pages 307–18, where I have gone into it at tedious length. In the present analysis we can only keep to Wagner's libretto.

quivering and darting. Loge (Nos. 22 and 23) is filling it with flame, and from the depths of the orchestra comes a roar as of monsters opening their maws to seize on their prey. With a shriek of "Fafner! Fafner!" Mime collapses in terror behind the great anvil.

7

As he does so the Sword motive (this time in the minor) rings out in the trumpet; then the atmosphere suddenly changes, the motive of Siegfried's cry for freedom (No. 116) begins its lively chatter again, and the boy's voice is heard from the wood, hailing Mime with a shout of "Ho there! thou idler!" When he enters the cave he is surprised to find it apparently empty. Gaily he searches for the dwarf, whose voice is at last heard from behind the anvil, asking feebly if the boy is alone. Siegfried humorously suggests that perhaps he is sharpening the sword. The word plunges Mime into confusion once more. How can he forge it? he asks; and half to himself he repeats the Wanderer's closing words—"He who knows not what fear is alone shall forge Nothung anew". Hardly conscious of the boy's presence, he continues to muse aloud on his own baffling problem: his wise old head he had wagered and lost—forfeit to him "who never fear has learned". He sees now the mistake he had made in his bringing-up of Siegfried:

> *Him would I fly*
> *who fear has known!*
> *But that truly ne' er taught I the stripling;*
> *I fool-like forgot*
> *the one thing good.*
> *Love for the dwarf*
> *was his lesson;*
> *but alas, no luck had I!*
> *How now put this fear in his heart?*

Recovering something of his composure, he assures Siegfried that his thoughts had been wholly turned on him during his absence, and the things of weight he might perhaps teach him:

What fear is learned I for thee,
that I, thou dunce, might teach thee.

He begins the lesson. The thoughtless boy means to go out into the world without having learned fear; but without that knowledge the sharpest of swords will not protect him. Approaching the wondering and impatient Siegfried and speaking more and more confidently as he regains his self-possession, he assures him that he had only been keeping a promise of his to the child's mother in preserving him from the guile of the world until he had learned fear.

"What is this fearing?" Siegfried asks; "is it a craft? If so, why have I not been taught it?" The orchestra becomes a pictorial instrument again as Mime asks him if, when night falls on the forest, he has never seen and heard horrors crowding round him, so that he quaked with fright and it seemed as if his throbbing heart would burst. "Feltest thou never that, then fear is far from thy soul". Mime himself quakes with terror as his imagination plays upon the picture he is conjuring up. But Siegfried merely remarks reflectively, "That must be the strangest of feelings, all this shivering and shuddering, glowing and trembling, burning and fainting, and for these delights do I long. But always my heart beats soundly in my breast. Can you, Mime, teach me?"

Mime's great moment has now come. He will teach the boy fearing, he says, if he will accompany him to Neidhöhle, at the east of the wood, where there is a dragon (here No. 107 heaves up its cumbrous bulk in the depths of the orchestra), who slays and devours men; it is "not far from the world", he assures Siegfried, for he knows that to leave the wood for the world is the heart's desire of the boy. To this Fafner he will go gladly, says Siegfried, so let Mime make him at once the sword he needs. To the rhythm of No. 109 he urges the dwarf to set to work. But Mime wails once more that, alas, the task is beyond his strength, though within the power of one who has never known fear. At this, Siegfried brushes the puling little gnome aside and strides to the hearth, saying that he himself will forge afresh his father's blade.

To a vigorous transformation of the Siegfried horn motive (No. 108):

he begins by pitching Mime's tools about. The dwarf tells him
that had he been more willing in the past to learn the smith's
craft he would find his labour lighter now; but the boy replies
that when the master does not know there is not much chance of
the apprentice learning from him. He makes a face at Mime and
tells him to take himself off and not meddle, lest he fall in the fire.
By now he has piled a great heap of charcoal on the hearth: he
blows up the fire, fixes the fragments of the sword in the vice, and
files them vigorously. Mime watches him, from time to time
offering a piece of advice that is contemptuously rejected, and
wondering more and more at the success of Siegfried's unorthodox methods: "My wisdom fails, that see I clearly; the fool is
favoured by folly alone! See how he works! The steel is in shreds,
yet cool is he yet. Old am I, as old as the cave and the wood; yet
aught like this never before have I seen!"

8

As he realises the likelihood of the boy succeeding, as the
Wanderer seemed to have hinted he would, fear steals again into
Mime's heart:

> *where now to hide*
> *my hapless head?*
> *To the valiant boy will it fall,*
> *learns he from Fafner not fear!*
> *But woe is me still!*
> *If Siegfried learns fear,*
> *how then shall the dragon be slain?*
> *Can he win the dwarf the Ring?*
> *Oh fate accurst!*
> *I'm fettered fast:*
> *where shall I counsel find*
> *how to master this fearless boy?*

By this time Siegfried has filed the fragments away and put them in a crucible, which he places on the forge fire. He turns to Mime and asks what name the sword once had. "Nothung", is the reply; " 'twas thy mother told me its name". The characteristic interval (the raised fifth) that has differentiated No. 121 from No. 108 now serves to shape the Nothung motive, which is first of all foreshadowed thus:

before assuming its final form as Siegfried invokes the weapon:

He blows up a roaring fire with the bellows:

as he goes on with his lusty song to the Sword:

125
Animato

Zu Spreu nun schuf ich die schar - fe
To shreds I've shat - tered thy shi - ning

Pracht, im Tie - gel brat' ich die Späh - ne!
steel, now flames the fire round thy frag - ments!

It continues to an orchestral accompaniment that seems to belch
fire as the labouring bellows rise and fall. "Hoho! Hohei!"
Siegfried sings; "bellows blow, brighten the blaze!" Once he had
felled a tree in the forest and burned the good grey ash to charcoal, that now flares and sparkles and fuses the shreds of the steel:

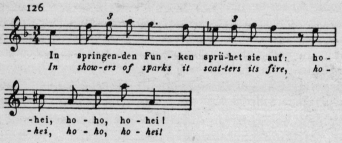

126

In springen-den Fun - ken sprü-het sie auf: ho -
In show-ers of sparks it scat-ters its fire, ho -

-hei, ho - ho, ho - hei!
-hei, ho - ho, ho - hei!

All the while Mime is watching him closely and thinking
aloud: "He'll forge him the sword and fell grim Fafner, that see
I clearly now. Hoard and Ring will fall to him; but how shall I
make him mine?" He has hatched out a plan. He will brew a broth
which he will give to the boy when he is faint after the combat
with the Dragon; in it he will put herbs that will send him into a
sound sleep; and then he, Mime, will kill him with Nothung
itself, and Ring and Hoard will be his. He rubs his hands, delighted with his own cleverness: "Hei, wisest Wanderer, deem'st
thou me dull now? What think'st thou of my subtle wit? Have
I found the way to peace?"

Meanwhile Siegfried continues with his work and his song.
He pours the glowing contents of the crucible into a mould,

which he plunges into the trough, where the steaming steel hisses under the shock of the cold water. Exultantly he thrusts it into the fire and tugs again at the bellows, singing his joyous greeting to "Nothung, the masterful sword, that will soon make hot blood flow", and his good spirits find expression in an exuberant motive of Joy in Victory in the orchestra:

127
Animato

During his work he has kept an interested eye on Mime, who, beside himself with delight at his own cleverness, has been shaking herbs and spices into a cooking-pot which, standing on the opposite side of the hearth, he now puts on the fire. What is the booby doing there with his sauces? asks Siegfried. Hypocritically the dwarf congratulates him on his skill as a smith: the master is learning now from the man, who puts him to shame. Henceforth it is Siegfried who shall do the smithing, while Mime will boil the eggs for his soup. But the boy's healthy instinct bids him beware: he will take care that he eats or drinks nothing of Mime's cooking.

9

He takes the mould from the fire, breaks it, lays the glowing steel on the anvil, and after a derisive comment on the dwarf's incompetence in his craft he launches into the second phase of the forging song. A vigorous new motive pounds out in the orchestra:

128
Pesante

as he rains blow after blow on the steel with his hammer and exults in the new life that he can feel springing up in the fragments of his father's sword: he has tamed its stubborn pride, he cries. Unobservant of Mime, who has been pouring the contents of the pot into a flask and gloating in anticipation over his own triumph, the boy hammers away at the sword, until at last he takes it from the anvil, brandishes it, and plunges it into the water-trough, laughing boisterously at its hissing there.

While he is fitting it into a haft, Mime, to the accompaniment of No. 32, works himself into an ecstasy over the coming success of his plan. He has a vision of a glorified Mime bestriding a subject world. Once he had been slave to Alberich; but soon the Gold will be his, and then the poor despised dwarf will be master of the Nibelungs, with the whole world prostrate at his feet, Gods and heroes cringing before him:

> *Mime, the daring,*
> *Mime is king now,*
> *prince of the Niblungs,*
> *ruler of all!*
> *Hei, Mime, what brought thee this luck?*
> *Who counted that this would come?*

He leaps about and laughs delightedly:

By this time Siegfried has riveted the handle with his last blow. He brandishes the sword, greeting it with a final great cry of "Nothung!", the phrase beginning, as it has always done until now, with a suggestion of the coming of the minor, but changing unexpectedly into the major towards the end, with electrifying effect:

(Wagner's 2/4 notation may perhaps conceal the actual rhythm of this from the reader; the effect on the ear is):

Dead the Sword had lain in splinters, Siegfried sings, but now he has brought it to life again, glorious and proud:

> Show thou the dastards
> how thou canst shine!
> Cut through the false heart,
> strike at the knave!
> See, Mime, thou smith:
> so severs Siegfried's sword!

He aims a mighty blow with it at the anvil, which splits from top to bottom, while the orchestra rushes on with an exuberant combination of No. 115 and No. 108. The curtain descends with Mime, who has been dancing on his stool in rapture, falling off it in terror as Siegfried exultantly holds the Sword aloft.

10

The prelude to the second act prepares us for a different atmosphere from the one that Siegfried has filled with the gladness of his youth in the first act.

Under shuddering tremolandi in the lower strings we hear the motive of Fafner in his reincarnation as Dragon; it will be seen that the fall of a full fourth that characterised the Giants in the *Rhinegold* (see No. 16) has now become an augmented fourth, giving the motive an added cumbersomeness:

The tuba, which plays a large part in the prelude, then gives out the motive (No. 107) which had represented Fafner as he figured in the imagination of Mime in the prelude to the first act; and it links up with No. 132 in this fashion:

Through the subterranean gloom of the orchestral picture the Ring motive pierces occasionally: then the Curse motive (No. 41) makes a sinister gesture in the trombones. It is followed by No. 40—the motive of Annihilation which had accompanied, in the *Rhinegold*, Alberich's warning of the doom that should for ever cling to the Ring of which he had been robbed; and this by the Servitude motive, that of the Ring once more, and finally No. 132 again.

On the rising of the curtain we see a little knoll in the forest, which descends in the background to the entrance to a cave—Fafner's Neidhöhle. To the left, through the trees, a fissured cliff is visible. It is night, the gloom being thickest in the background, where at first nothing is clearly distinguishable by the eye. Crouched by the cliff is Alberich, brooding darkly, to the accompaniment of No. 40. We learn from his monologue that he is at his unresting watch with straining eye and ear upon the cave, in which his hope of world-mastership is buried. Sooner or later, he is convinced, the fateful day will dawn: will it be today? he asks. As a combination of the Valkyries' motive (No. 74) and that of the Need of the Gods (No. 81) is heard in the orchestra he becomes aware of a stormwind blowing towards him through the forest, and the approach of a bluish light. Is the Dragon-slayer coming, the one who shall rid him of Fafner? But the wind dies down and the light fades away, and darkness and a sinister quiet descend upon the scene again. Out of the shadow, however, he sees someone approaching him; and by the light of the moon, suddenly breaking through the clouds, he recognises the Wanderer. For a moment he recoils in terror; then he breaks out in wrathful reproaches. What does this treacherous trickster want here? he asks. Is he bent on more evil? Let him go his way, work new woe elsewhere, and leave him in peace. Alberich's vehemence contrasts with the composure of the Wanderer, who tells him quietly that on this occasion he comes not to do but to witness ("Zu schauen kam ich, nicht zu schaffen").

As has been pointed out on a previous page, the dramatist in Wagner always makes him range himself, for the time being, on the side of whatever character happens to be speaking, get inside the skin of the character and see the matter of the moment from his point of view. He now puts into Alberich's mouth an unanswerable indictment of the God. He is not so dull now, says the Nibelung, as on that day of his sorrow when Wotan ravished the Ring from him by guile and force and gave it to the Giants to redeem his debt to them, a debt engraved in solemn runes on the shaft of his Spear. Now the God is caught in his own net; another crime like his first, and the Spear that is the source and the symbol of his power will crumble into dust.

The Wanderer's rejoinder has truth in it and yet is sophistical:

> *Not by treaties writ upon it*
> *bound art thou,*
> *base one, to me:*
> *it mastered thee by its own strength:*
> *for strength then ward I it well.*

In half-a-dozen words Alberich pierces through the sophistry to the facts:

> *In pride of power*
> *how boldly thou threat'nest,*
> *yet dark is thy heart with dismay.*

For the Wanderer knows that the Nibelung's curse will bring death to whoever holds the treasure; and the God's consuming fear is that it will come back again into Alberich's hands:

> *That gnaws thee with care unending!*
> *For let it but come*
> *again to my hand,*

not like the foolish Giants
I'll use the Ring's great might:
then tremble, thou holy
guardian of heroes!
Walhall's towers
I storm with Hella's hosts:
the world then will be mine!

The Wanderer replies calmly that all this troubles him not, for the Ring's destined master will deal with it in a way of his own. To this the Nibelung has an effective answer: this hero whom Wotan hopes will gain possession of the Ring has been born of a race that the God himself has bred for his own ends, for that sole purpose. The Wanderer breaks off the argument: "Curse me not", he says, "but wrangle with Mime, who is bringing with him a stripling who will slay Fafner. Nought knows the boy of me: it is the Nibelung who is goading him on for his own ends. Be on thy guard: the boy knows nothing of the Ring, but Mime will tell him all. As for myself, I have no longer any part in the matter. Him whom I love I will leave to work unaided, to stand or fall as he may. He is his own lord: heroes alone avail me." Here a new motive appears:

134
Moderato

that will in future characterise certain aspects of Siegfried.

II

The news that the God will not intervene rejoices Albérich, for with both his despised brother and the unsophisticated boy he is confident he can cope. His direct questions, put eagerly to the Wanderer—"Then with Mime I fight alone for the Ring? Will it fall into my hands again?"—are composedly waved aside: all the Wanderer will tell him is that a hero is drawing near to rescue the Hoard. Two Nibelungs lust for the Gold; Fafner will fall, and then the Ring will be his who can seize it. Would Albérich

know more, let him enquire of Fafner himself. The orchestral
texture during the whole scene is as a matter of course woven out
of motives already familiar to us.

"If thou warn'st him of death", continues the Wanderer,
"haply he'll give thee the toy: myself will wake him for thee."
He mounts the knoll in front of the cave and calls out, "Fafner!
Dragon! Awake!", to the great astonishment of Alberich, who
now almost believes, yet hardly dares do so, that the Ring and
the Hoard will soon come to him again. Accompanied by the
lumbering No. 132 Fafner's deep voice is heard booming through
a speaking-trumpet from the dark recesses of the cave. "Who
wakes me from sleep?" it asks. "Here is a friend", the Wanderer
replies ironically, "with a warning for thee; thy life he will grant
thee if only thou wilt yield him the Hoard thou guardest." "What
would he?" says the voice from the cave. "Waken, Fafner, and
listen", says Alberich urgently; "a hero comes to measure his
strength with thine." "I hunger for him", is the reply. The
Wanderer and Alberich, the one ironically, the other eagerly,
exhort the Dragon to take the prudent course. The stripling is
brave, says the former, and sharp is his sword: the golden Ring
alone the boy covets, adds Alberich, and if Fafner will yield it to
him he will stay the fight, and the Hoard shall remain the Dragon's
own, for him to sleep upon in peace. "What I have I hold",
growls Fafner; and then, with a great yawn, "Let me slumber!"

His joke played out to the end he had foreseen, the Wanderer
turns with a hearty laugh to Alberich: 'Well, Alberich", he says,
"that stroke failed!" Then he approaches him confidentially with
some good advice. "All things are as needs they must be", he says,
to the accompaniment of the motive which, in the *Rhinegold*, had
first of all (in the prelude) symbolised primeval nature (No. 4),
and later had accompanied Erda's solemn words to Wotan when
she counselled him to give up the Ring—"Whatever was, know
I; whatever is, whatever shall be see I too" (No. 43):

> all things go as needs they must:
> no whit may they be altered.
> And now do I leave thee;
> look to thyself:

contend with Mime, thy brother;
for truly thou knowest him better.
But stranger things
full soon shalt thou learn!

and the new motive (No. 134) associated with the free Siegfried, followed by that of the Sword, hints at what that knowledge will be.

The Wanderer disappears into the forest, the same wind blowing and the same light flickering that had accompanied his coming. Alberich gazes after him, ill at ease. "There rides he away", he says, "leaving me to care and scorn. But laugh as ye will, ye light-spirited, lust-covetous race of the Gods! Your downfall yet shall I see; for while the Gold gleams in the sunlight the wise one will keep his watch—and Alberich will win at the last!" He slips into the cleft at the side of the stage, which for a little while remains empty, with only the Dragon motive, heaving in the depths of the orchestra, disturbing the silence.

12

Slowly day dawns, and Siegfried and Mime enter, the former wearing the Sword in a girdle of bast-rope. Mime, reconnoitring warily, at last recognises the cave, which now lies in a deep shadow, while the knoll is becoming gradually lighter. "Now we have reached it", says Mime; "we go no further"; and for some reason or other known only to Wagner the Slumber motive (No. 98) is played upon by the orchestra for a few bars. Siegfried seats himself under a great lime-tree and looks round him. So he has come at last, he says, to the place where, if anywhere, he will learn what fear is; and he bids Mime leave him. Seating himself opposite the boy, so that he may keep his eyes constantly on the cave, the dwarf assures him that if he does not learn fear here and now, no other place, no other time, will teach it him. For there in that cavern lies a grim and grisly Dragon, with vast and horrible jaws that could kill him with one snap: poisoned slaver drips from his mouth, and one drop of it will rot bones and body of him: if the great tail should coil round him, his bones would be crunched like glass.

Siegfried is undisturbed by this catalogue of horrors. Still reclining tranquilly under the tree, he tells Mime that if the monster's jaws are so terrible it will be well to close up his gullet; the poisoned slaver he will evade with a leap; the circling tail he will watch. But has the brute a heart, he asks, and is it where the heart is in men and beasts? Assured by Mime of this, the boy raises himself quickly to a sitting posture. "Nothung straight to his heart I will drive", he says; and he laughs at Mime as an old bungler who can babble of nothing more fear-inspiring than this. The dwarf's next move is to appeal hypocritically to the boy's better feelings: when he sees the Dragon, he tells him, his senses will swoon, his heart will beat madly in his breast, the forest will spin round him—and then, he hopes, he will "thank him who has led thee here, and think on Mime's great love". Siegfried's gorge rises at this as of old: when, he asks, with his usual frank vigour of speech, will he be rid of this slinking, blinking creature who professes to love him but for whom his whole being can feel nothing but loathing and hate?

Mime decides to leave him: he will lay him down by the spring, he says; Siegfried is to wait here until the sun is at its height, for at that time the monster always crawls from his cave to water at the stream. Siegfried amuses himself with the pleasing idea that at the spring the Dragon may come upon Mime and devour him; and he advises him, for his own life's sake, to take at once to his heels as fast as he can and trouble him no more. Once more the dwarf hypocritically urges the boy to call on him should he need counsel, and once more he is roughly repulsed. In the end Siegfried drives him off with a furious gesture, and as Mime slinks away he shows us, in an aside, what is at the back of his treacherous mind:

> *Fafner and Siegfried,*
> *Siegfried and Fafner,*
> *would each the other might slay!*

As the gnome disappears in the forest Siegfried stretches himself out comfortably under the lime-tree, and the lovely episode known as the Forest Murmurs begins. A great pastoral peace descends upon the scene as the woodland becomes slowly astir with morning life:

Siegfried falls into a reverie. How fair the forest is, he muses, how it seems to laugh with delight now the loathsome old dwarf has gone, never more, he hopes, to offend his eyes! To have learned that Mime was not his father had filled his heart with joy. But how did his true father look in life—for surely if Mime had a son it would resemble him:

> *grizzled and gray,*
> *cramped and crooked,*
> *hump-backed and halting,*
> *with draggled ears drooping,*
> *bleary eyes blinking?*
> *Out with the imp!*
> *No more his face I'd see!*

The silence seems to become more intense; only the gentle murmur of the forest is heard as the boy goes on with his brooding. Could he but learn what that mother of his was like whom he never saw! Surely her eyes were soft and shining and tender like those of the roe-deer, but even more beautiful? She had borne her son in sorrow: must all mothers, then, die that their young may live? Would his eyes could be gladdened by the sight of this mortal mother of his, he sighs, as the 'cellos give out a tender reminiscence of No. 112, which merges into the soft strain (No. 25) to which Loge, in the *Rhinegold,* had told the Gods of the universal power of love.

13

As the boy leans back, lost in dreams, and the forest murmurs grow louder, his attention is attracted by the song of an awakened bird in the branches above him:

and:

and:

and:

As he listens, he muses on what the bird's message to him may be: is it trying to tell him something of his mother? The fretful old dwarf had told him that there was a meaning in the song of birds, could men but understand it. But how to find the way? What if he were to follow the bird's notes on a reed—"If I cannot grasp his words, let me try to pierce to his meaning through his melody". Running joyously to the neighbouring spring:

where there is a clump of reeds, he cuts one with his sword and hastily shapes it into a sort of pipe. He listens once again to the song, then makes an attempt to imitate it; but his clumsy reed either blows false or gives no sound at all. For a moment he is boyishly peevish at his failure; then he smiles and acknowledges the little songster his superior. Perhaps a slender reed is not the fitting instrument for such a dullard as he: why not essay one on which he already has a certain rough skill, and see if it brings him a better companion than the usual wolf or bear?

He puts his silver horn to his lips and blows a vigorous long-sustained call on it that sets the woodland ringing (No. 108, which branches out into the Siegfried motive No. 88 and then into that of the Sword). As the blithe tune rises to its climax something stirs in the background: he has awakened Fafner, who now lurches through the underwood about his cave and drags his monstrous bulk up to the higher ground, on which he rests the front part of his body, the orchestra accompanying him graphically all the time. As he comes to rest he gives out something like a yawn, which makes Siegfried turn round in astonishment and fix his gaze on him with boyish delight. "Oho!" he says jocularly, "at last my song has brought me something! A sweeter comrade could I find than this?"

The Dragon addresses him, his voice being magnified through a speaking-trumpet: who is it, he asks, that has roused him? "One who would learn what fear is", the boy replies; "haply from thee he'll learn it? If not, soon wilt thou be food for my sword." "Drink I came for, and now food I find", bellows Fafner, opening his jaws and showing his teeth. So the dialogue continues, Siegfried goading him with taunts and threats, Fafner growing angrier each moment. At last he roars defiance at the "boastful boy" and bids him come on. He drags his clumsy body further up the knoll, spouting venom from his nostrils and lashing at him with his tail. Angered by a wound he has received he rears up the front part of his body, meaning to throw his whole weight on the boy; he thus lays his breast open, and Siegfried, quickly sensing the place of the heart, plunges his sword into it up to the hilt.

Fafner, groaning with pain, raises himself still higher for a moment and then sinks to the ground. Withdrawing his sword, Siegfried leaps to one side. In a weaker voice Fafner, to the accompaniment of his own motive and that of Annihilation (No. 40), asks the stripling who has pierced him who he is, and who had egged him on to this murderous deed, for his own childish mind would assuredly never have planned it. The answer, for us, is given by the upsurge of the Curse motive in the trombone. But the boy knows nothing, not even who he is; all he can say is that the monster himself had provoked him to combat. Who it is he has slain, says Fafner, he himself will tell him; and he proceeds with the story of the brother Giants—here the augmented fourth of the Dragon motive becomes once more the perfect fourth of the Giants—who long ago won the cursed Gold from the Gods; Fafner had murdered his brother and changed himself into a Dragon the better to guard the Hoard; and now he, the last of his race, has fallen by the hand of a boy:

> *Heed thyself well,*
> *blossoming hero;*
> *he who drove thee blind to this deed*
> *doth plot now for thee also death!*
> *Mark the ending!*
> *Heed my word!*

and again the sinister Curse motive turns our thoughts to both the past and the future. "Wise are thy dying words", replies the boy; "but tell me now, wild one, whence I came: Siegfried I am called". The Dragon merely repeats the name with a sigh, and dies; from him the boy can learn nothing more of what he desires to know.

14

"The dead", he says to himself, "can give no tidings, so be thou, my living sword, my leader." Fafner, in his death agony, had rolled to one side. As the boy draws the sword out of his breast he smears his hand with blood: it burns him, and involuntarily he puts his fingers in his mouth to suck the blood from them. As he does so the song of the birds once more attracts his attention. They seem to be speaking to him, he says; and he realises that by some spell in the Dragon's blood their song has become intelligible to him. One of them is saying, "Now has the Nibelung Hoard been won by Siegfried: it lies awaiting him there

in the cave. Could he win him the Tarnhelm too, it would serve
him for wonderful deeds; but could he find the Ring it would
make him lord of the world!" Thanking the bird, and resolving
to follow its counsel, he descends into the cavern and is lost to our
view.

The tranquil forest murmurs are suddenly broken in upon by
hurried angular figures of this type in clarinet and bassoon:

as Mime slinks in; looking round timidly to make sure that Fafner
is dead he goes warily towards the cave. But simultaneously
Alberich emerges from the cleft on the other side of the stage,
rushes at his brother and bars his way. There follows an episode
of consummate musical and dramatic characterisation in which
the precious pair volley questions and recriminations at each other.
Each sees what the other is after and disputes his claim to the
treasure. "What I have earned with bitter bane", screams Mime,
"shall not escape me!" "Who was it robbed the Rhine of its Gold
and wrought the spell in the Ring?" cries Alberich. "Who made
the helm that served so well to hide you in your work?" rejoins
Mime. "'Twas I, not a bungler such as thou, who conceived the
Ring that endowed you with the craft to make the helm." "And
where is your Ring now? You let it go to the Giants, and what
you lost I now have won for myself". "Not yours is the Hoard,
but his who won it first." "'Twas I who brought up the boy and
with toil untold made him fit for my work." The more forceful
Alberich ends the angry argument with:

> *For the stripling's care*
> *now the beggarly*
> *niggardly knave*
> *coolly claims*

forsooth, a king he must be!
To scurviest hound
rather the Ring
should go than to thee:
never, thou marrowless
dolt, shall its might be thine!

Mime, baffled and cowed, scratches his head and hypocritically suggests a compromise. "Let Alberich be lord of the Ring, but let him call me still his brother. I'll take the Tarnhelm, the pleasant toy: thus shall we both be paid, the booty fairly shared." With a scornful laugh Alberich assures him that he will never let the Tarnhelm pass into Mime's hands, for him to work his cunning will on him in his sleep. "Nothing then is to be mine?" screams Mime, almost inarticulate with rage; "bare must I go, bled to the bone? Not the smallest share of it all come to me?" "Not the smallest; not even a nail-head, knave, shall be thine." "Then no share shall be thine; I will summon Siegfried, whose deadly sword shall avenge me, brother mine!"

15

At that moment Siegfried comes out of the cave. Mime sees, to his astonishment, that the boy has taken nothing of the treasure, only, like a child captivated by a toy, the Tarnhelm. Alberich curses him when he sees he has the Ring too, and Mime adds to his mortification by giving him the malicious advice, "Get him to give it thee, brother, and soon it will be mine!" Mime runs into the forest: Alberich, muttering "Yet back to its lord it soon will come", slips into the cleft on the other side of the stage. Various motives associated with the Ring, the Rhinegold and the Rhinemaidens steal out quietly in the orchestra as Siegfried, coming forward slowly to the knoll, gazes meditatively at the Tarnhelm and the Ring: he has taken these two from the heap, he says, because that was the counsel given him by the wood bird, but how they may serve him he does not know. To him they are merely baubles, witnesses to his victory over Fafner; yet this has not brought him the one thing he desired—to learn what fear is.

He puts the Ring on his finger and thrusts the Tarnhelm into
his girdle. For awhile there is dead silence, only the forest
throbbing and whispering as before. Then suddenly the wood
bird's voice peals out once more. Siegfried has won him the helm
and the Ring, it says; let him not trust Mime, the treacherous
dwarf, not be deceived by his lies; he has tasted the Dragon's
blood, and through what Mime will say to him next he will be
able to pierce to the dwarf's real meaning. A gesture of Siegfried's
shows that he has understood the bird; and standing quite
motionless, leaning on his sword, observant and self-assured, he
faces Mime, who now slinks in from the forest, saying to himself,
"He is brooding on what the booty may be worth. Can he have
met the Wanderer and been told a crafty tale? I must be doubly
sly. I will spread the cunningest snare for him; with friendliest
falsest words I will befool the perverse boy."

The scene that follows is another of Wagner's masterpieces of
characterisation. Mime comes forward cringing and scraping,
welcoming Siegfried with wheedling gestures:

and putting all the honey he can into his creaking voice. He does
not know, however, that Siegfried, thanks to his tasting the blood
and to the warning of the wood bird, not merely hears his
hypocritical words but reads his mind and realises his treacherous
purpose. The wood bird's constant collaboration with Siegfried
is indicated by the occasional recurrence in the orchestra of No.
138. Necessarily what we in the audience hear is not the words
actually spoken by the dwarf but the unspoken thought at the
back of his mind.

He begins by welcoming Siegfried with effusive deference,
complimenting him on his heroic victory over Fafner. "But",
replies Siegfried, "he did not teach me fearing; and in truth his

death grieves me when I see eviller rascals ranging through the world unpunished. He who egged me on to fight, I hate him more than my foe". So the dialogue goes on, Mime loading him with flatteries and endearments, and astonished that he gets only stern unfriendly words in reply. He tells Siegfried blandly, affectionately, that now he has done the deed desired by the dwarf he will soon close his eyes in endless sleep, and Mime will rob the credulous young fool of all he has won. With each rebuff his tenderness increases, the malignant words become more oily. "Hear me, my treasure! Thee and all thy kind ever I hated. I bore with thee not because I loved thee but because I needed thee to slay the Dragon and win me the Gold." In a cajoling phrase:

143

Sieg-fried, mein Sohn, das siehst du wohl selbst, dein
Sieg-fried, my son, thou seest for thy-self, thy

Le - ben musst du mir las - sen.
life,— my dear one, thou los - est.

he assures him that if he does not yield the booty he will die. He grows peevish at what he takes to be Siegfried's stupid misunderstanding of his words. Taking greater and greater pains to be comprehensible and convincing he shows him the flask containing the broth he has lovingly prepared for the hero's refreshment after the combat: "Drink but one drop, and mine is thy sword, and with it the Tarnhelm and the Hoard." Offering him the draught again, he falls back into the tone of his old whining recital (No. 111) of his unselfish care of him when a child: in those days the boy, petulant and froward as he was, took refreshing drinks from him without demur. "What herb is in it?" asks Siegfried quietly. Merrily Mime assures him that if he tastes it he will soon lie stiff and stark in sleep, and then "with the Sword thou hast made so sharp I'll hack off thy head, and win me rest and the Ring": and he chuckles with delight at the prospect.

"So thou wouldst slay me in my sleep?" says Siegfried. At this,

Mime gets vexed and furious: "Not at all! I said not that! Nought will I do but hack off thy head!":

He continues in the most honeyed tones he can assume, while the orchestra gives out the lovely strain of No. 113: "Were not my heart so full of hate for thee, did not thy past jibes and the shame of my labour for thee goad me on to vengeance, I would delay no longer to sweep thee from my path!" He pours the liquor into a drinking-horn and offers it coaxingly to Siegfried: "Now, my Volsung, thou wolf's son! Drink and choke thee to death; it is the last draught thou wilt drain!", and he breaks into a hysterical laugh.

16

Siegfried, who has maintained a dignified quiet until now, is suddenly filled with a violent loathing for the treacherous gnome: with a swift blow from his sword he lays him dead. The wood wind give out a telling reminiscence of the Reflection motive (No. 104)—a last ironical comment on the futility of all Mime's scheming,[1] and Alberich's mocking laughter is heard from the cleft. As Siegfried picks up the body and carries it to the entrance to the cave the trombones intone the Curse motive: as always, it carries our thoughts not only back but forward—the Curse on the Ring has claimed yet another victim, but he will not be the last; Siegfried now has the Ring.

Heaving the body into the cave, Siegfried, with a great loathing in his heart, tells the wretched gnome to sate himself now on what he has so long desired: "with endless guile thou soughtest the Gold; now thou art lord of the lustrous thing. And a goodly guardian I will leave thee, so that thou mayst have no fear of

---

[1] The reader will no doubt have observed that the motive of Mime's false cajolement (the first two bars of No. 142) is simply another aspect of No. 104.

thieves." With a great effort he pushes the Dragon's huge body to the cave, so that it blocks up the entrance completely: "There lie thou too, Dragon grim! guard thou alike thy glittering Gold and the foe that was so fain to make it his; so find ye both your rest at last!"

He gazes thoughtfully into the cave for a while, then turns slowly to the front of the scene, as if tired. He passes a weary hand over his brow; the sun is now high in the heavens, his blood is afire, and he longs for shelter and shade. He stretches himself out under the lime-tree and evokes again the wood bird which he sees in the branches above him, twittering and chattering with its brothers and sisters, all delighting in love. In his own heart, too, is a great longing for love:

> *But I—am so alone,*
> *have nor brother nor sister:*
> *and my mother died,*
> *my father fell:*
> *ne'er saw they their son.*
> *The one comrade I had*
> *was a hateful old dwarf:*
> *nought to love*
> *did e'er allure us:*
> *craftiest toils*
> *he laid to entrap me,*
> *until I was forced to slay him!*

A new motive, expressive of the boy's ardent desire for love, is heard in the orchestra:

"Find me a faithful friend", he says to the bird, "give me clear counsel. Oft for a friend have I called, yet none ever came to me. Thou, my dear one, perhaps canst help me, for truth thou hast spoken to me until now."

The bird's voice rings out with the melody of No. 138 and No. 139. Siegfried has slain the evil dwarf, it says, and now there awaits him the most glorious of brides. She lies asleep on a fire-girt rock; let him waken her, and Brynhilde he will win for wife. To a great orchestral upsurge of No. 145, which will dominate most of the remainder of the scene, Siegfried springs impetuously to his feet, his heart aflame with love. "Forth I fly, then, full of rejoicing, forth from the wood to the fell. But tell me, dear song-ster, shall I break through the fire and awaken the bride?" The Slumber motive comes out softly in the orchestra as the bird assures him that the deed will be accomplished by one alone— one who has never known fear. "That is I, the foolish boy", he cries in delight. "Today I strove in vain to learn fearing from a Dragon: my heart is afire to learn it from Brynhilde. Where lies the way to the fell?"

The bird hovers for a while teasingly above him, then takes a straight course to the background and is lost to sight. Siegfried follows it, and with the orchestra executing a joyous fantasia on Nos. 145 and 139 the curtain falls.

17

Wotan has set in motion, out of sheer necessity, a chain of events over which he has no ultimate control; and in the first part of the third act we see him, still as the Wanderer, anxiously trying to discover what the future has in store for himself, the Gods, the Ring and Siegfried. One alone, he feels, can raise at any rate a corner of the veil of the mystery that enshrouds and tortures him —Erda; and it is to her that, after leaving Alberich, he has hastened.

His unrest of soul is depicted in the prelude to the third act, which begins with a contrapuntal combination of the motive of the Need of the Gods (No. 81, which is virtually identical with that of Erda, No. 42) and that of the Valkyries; these are followed by the Treaty motive (No. 13), that of Erda, that of the Twilight of the Gods (No. 44), and the moaning figure expressive of grief in general but more specifically associated at times with the idea of Servitude. All these are woven into one compact fabric.

At last the vehement music dies down into a broad statement of the Magic Sleep motive (No. 96) and a hint of the motive of Fate (No. 83); and when the curtain rises we see the Wanderer arriving at a wild spot at the foot of a rocky mountain. It is night: a stormwind is raging, accompanied by flashes of lightning and peals of thunder. The Wanderer strides resolutely towards a vault-like opening in a rock in the foreground, pauses there, leaning on his Spear, and summons Erda (the Wala) to waken from her immemorial sleep in the depths of darkness. The Sleep motive is breathed by the wood wind in soft mysterious tones as she responds to the call: the cavern begins to glow with a bluish light, in which she is seen rising slowly from the depths, covered with hoar-frost, her hair and garments emitting a shimmering light. Who is he, she asks, whose magic power has broken her dream and driven sleep from her? To a constant orchestral interplay of the various appropriate motives he tells who he is and why he has sought her out. Superficially regarded, the long episode merely takes us afresh over ground familiar to us. But, as is the case with all these "narrations" and quasi-narrations of Wagner, it takes us over it in a new way. We do not see the events of old happening under our eyes as before, but as they now shape themselves in retrospect in the mind of this character or that, coloured by his present mood. To achieve this psychological transformation is the business even more of the musician than of the dramatist; and thanks to Wagner's music it is really a new Wotan and a new Erda who play out the following scene before our eyes.

The Wanderer begins by telling her how he had roamed the world in quest of wisdom, seeking it from the wisest of women, the Wala, who knows all that stirs and breathes on earth, in the waters or in the air. "My sleep", she says, in slow grave tones, "is dreaming, my dreaming brooding, my brooding weaving of wisdom. But while I sleep the Norns are ever awake, sitting and spinning what Erda knows: for wisdom, then, seek out the Norns." The Wanderer becomes more urgent: the Norns, he says, weave what they must according to the inexorable law of the world, without power to make or to mar. It is not theirs but Erda's wisdom he needs, counsel "how to hold back a rolling wheel". Again she evades him: in her own mind, she tells him, the

deeds of men move as in a mist since she had bowed to a conqueror's will. To Wotan she had borne a Wish-maiden: brave is
she and wise; let the God not awaken Erda but go for wisdom to
Brynhilde, Erda's and Wotan's child.

Brynhilde had flouted her father's will, replies the God, and
for that had been chastised: deep she lies in sleep on the fell, no
more to awaken until a hero comes and wins her for wife. Erda
broods for a while on this: "Dazed am I since I awoke; strange
and confused seems the world to me. So the Valkyrie, the Wala's
child, does penance of sleep while her all-knowing mother slept?

> *Doth then pride's teacher*
> *punish pride?*
> *Is the deed's enkindler*
> *wroth with the deed?*
> *He who wardeth right,*
> *he, the truth's upholder,*
> *tramples on right,*
> *reigns by untruth?*
> *Let the dreamer depart!*
> *Sleep again seal my wisdom!"*

But the anxious God still will not let her go. Once, he tells her,
she had buried care's bitter barb in his venturous heart, warned
him of woe to come, filled him with fear of a shameful ending:
"tell me now how the God may conquer his care". He becomes
more and more urgent, and at last discloses what it is he now wills.
The thought of the Gods' downfall grieves him no more now he
himself wills it so. Of old he had resolved on it in anguish and
despair; now he faces it freely and gladly; and the orchestra gives
out a new motive:

which is generally referred to as the World Inheritance motive,
because it is associated later with the coming of the new and
better world symbolised by Brynhilde and Siegfried.

Once in his rage and loathing, says the Wanderer, he had flung the world to the Nibelung as his prey; now he leaves his heritage to the winsome young Volsung. "He, though chosen by me, knows nought of me; free of my counsel he has won him the Nibelung's Ring. Over him Alberich's curse has no power, for he is warm and joyous, free from envy, knowing not fear. Brynhilde, the child of thy wisdom, will awake to his call and do a deed that will redeem the world. Slumber thou on, then; close thine eyes, and in dreams witness my ending. To the ever-young the God yields in joy. Away then, Erda, mother of fear! Primal sorrow, away! Away to endless sleep!" During these last words of his she has already closed her eyes; now she slowly descends and disappears, thick darkness spreading once more over the entrance to the cavern. The storm has wholly ceased; the moon comes out, and by its faint light we see Wotan striding towards the cavern; he leans with his back against it, his face turned towards the stage, awaiting a final turn of events which he dares not control and has now no desire to control, yet to which he must somehow yield not assentingly but under compulsion.

18

Siegfried enters, led by the bird, which flutters towards the foreground singing its heart-free little melody. Siegfried, resolved to follow the course it has indicated to him, makes towards the background, but is halted by a voice asking him whither he is going. The boy turns round, sees the Wanderer, and replies that he is seeking, by the counsel of a wood-bird, a flame-bound rock where sleeps a maid who must awaken to him. Wood-birds sometimes chatter without sense, says the stranger: who taught him to read the meaning of the bird's singing? Thereupon Siegfried tells him how he had been brought by a treacherous dwarf named Mime to Neidhöhle, where he had slain a Dragon that had threatened his life, tasted its blood, and so learned to read the song of birds; his own sword he had wielded in the fight, forged by himself out of splinters that had baffled the skill of Mime the smith himself. "Who made the sword from which the fragments came?" asks the stranger. That the boy does not know

—only that unless the sword were new-made the splinters had been useless.

At this naive reply the Wanderer breaks out into a good-humoured laugh. This makes the boy look more closely at him; he asks why he laughs, and why he delays him there, plaguing him with questions. If the stranger knows the way to the rock let him show it; if not, a truce to his talk! The Wanderer reproves him for his petulance; he is old, he says, and youth should honour age. This is too much for Siegfried's patience: all his life, he bursts out, his path had been barred by an ancient whom at last he had had to sweep away; let the stranger have a care lest he share Mime's fate. Then, looking closer at him, he asks why his face is over-hung by a great hat. "That is Wanderer's way", he is told, "when against the wind he goes". And one eye is lacking, the boy con-tinues; no doubt it was struck out by someone whose path he had tried to bar: let him now take himself off, or he may lose the other. The Wanderer replies gravely:

> *I see, my son,*
> *where nought thou know'st*
> *yet well thou know'st how to help thee.*
> *With the one eye*
> *that for long I have lost*
> *thou lookest thyself on the other*
> *that still is left me for sight.*

The subtlety of this is lost on Siegfried: he laughs irreverently and demands to be shown the way to the fell.

Gravely and quietly and lovingly the Wanderer reproves the impetuous boy. "Didst thou but know me, child, thy scoff thou wouldst have spared me. Love I bore to thy race of old, yet in my wrath I scourged it sorely. Thou whom I love, wake not wrath in me now, to the ruin of thee and of me!" Siegfried impatiently orders him to step aside and let him pass to the fell; the bird had shown him the way, though now it had fled from his sight. It fled, says the Wanderer with a touch of anger, to save its life: it saw here the lord of the ravens; woe to it if these fall on it! The way it had pointed out the boy must not take. "It was by my might that the maid was cast into slumber: he who can wake and win her makes me mightless for ever." He points to a glow now visible on the heights, and bids the "foolhardy boy" go back if he would not be consumed by fire.

Siegfried having declared that the fire has no terrors for him, and that he means to go straight to Brynhilde, the Wanderer makes his last effort to assert himself. "At least my Spear shall bar thy path", he says, holding it out. "The haft of it is hallowed; it was on this that the Sword thou bearest was shattered once; now again be it broken on my Spear". Siegfried draws his sword. "So at last I have found my father's foe?" he cries. "Vengeance lies in my grasp! I shatter thy Spear with my Sword." With one blow he hews it in two; there is a peal of thunder, and a flash of lightning darts from the Spear towards the rocky heights, where the former dull glow now becomes bright flame. The fragments of the Spear have fallen at the Wanderer's feet: he quietly picks them up, recedes, and saying "Advance! I can no more withhold thee!" he disappears in complete darkness.

The drama of the Nibelung's Ring will see Wotan no more. Siegfried's sword-stroke was the symbol of the annulment of his power over events: what has happened he had willed, for the accomplishment of the Gods' purpose, the ultimate righting of a primal wrong. The wheel, to adopt his simile in his colloquy with Erda, has been set rolling by Fate, and by the compulsion of Fate it must now roll to the appointed end. All the God could do, his power to shape the external drama any further having ceased, was to play out his own internal drama. This he had done by barring Siegfried's path with the Spear on which were engraved the runes that bound the world by law: the Spear has been shattered, the writ of that primal order no longer runs. With Siegfried and Brynhilde a new moral world-order will come into being, even though they both perish in creating it. Siegfried himself will remain all-unknowing to the last; but to Brynhilde will come, as Erda seemed to have hinted, the all-wisdom that redeems.

19

When the Wanderer has gone, Siegfried's attention is attracted by the growing brightness of the fire-clouds; and with the bird's

song ringing in his ears once more he realises that here, on the
fell, is his goal—his promised comrade and bride. He places his
horn to his lips, and his vigorous call (No. 108A) tears again and
again through the excited orchestral tissue surrounding it. Fire is
in the orchestra as well as on the fell when he disappears from our
sight, making his way towards the rock. The blaze rises to a
climax and then dies down slowly as the Sleep motives go through
one transformation after another. Then the fire-clouds dissolve
into a finer and finer mist, through which the rosy light of dawn
pierces gradually; and when the mist finally disperses we see once
more the setting of the closing scene of the *Valkyrie*. Overhead
the sky is bright blue; but over the edge of the rocky height there
still hangs a veil of reddish morning mist, suggesting the fire that
rages without ceasing at the foot of the fell. In the foreground,
under the great tree, Brynhilde is sleeping in her armour, with her
helmet on her head and her long shield covering her.

The orchestra dies down to almost complete quietude—the
Slumber motive yielding place to the melody (No. 25) to which,
in the *Rhinegold*, Loge had sung of the universal enchantment of
love—as Siegfried becomes visible on the summit of the cliff at
the back. He pauses and surveys the scene in wonder, then
advances a little as he sees first a horse, then a sleeping figure in
armour. Raising the shield, he is rejoiced to find what he imagines
will be a noble companion for him. The helmet seems to be pressing on the recumbent warrior's head; the boy raises it, whereupon
a great mass of hair falls down. Startled but pleased, he bends
over the sleeper to loosen his breastplate, which he does by cutting
through the rings on either side. Seeing a woman's drapery he
starts back in alarm, crying "That is no man!" No. 145 and a new
motive, that of Love's Confusion:

become the dominant strands in the orchestral fabric as his whole
being seems to burst into flame at this new and strange experience;
and in his perturbation he invokes the mother whom he has never

seen, but who incarnates for him all the love for which he has
longed. Can this, at last, be fearing? he asks himself. At last he
masters himself sufficiently to waken the lovely sleeper, which he
does with a long kiss.

Brynhilde opens her eyes, rises slowly to a sitting position, and
raises her arms in silent greeting to the earth and the sky she sees
once more, the orchestra painting the return of life to her in
phrases that seem to ascend in spirals to the ether and finally
break into a motive of her Greeting to the World:

Solemnly she hails the light she now sees with joy again after her
long sleep. But who is the hero who has wakened her? she asks.
The orchestra gives out the brave Siegfried motive (No. 108) as
he tells her it was he, Siegfried, who fought his way through the
flames and loosened her helm and roused her from sleep. The
Valkyrie's mind goes back to her parting cry to Sieglinde, when
she bade her preserve the fragments of Siegmund's sword for the
boy who should be born to her in the forest—"His name from
me let him take; Siegfried, joyful in victory". She breaks into a
rapturous cry at the thought that this Siegfried is her deliverer,
and the pair of them bless the mother who gave him birth:

To this exultant outburst succeeds a new motive, that of the
Rapture of Love:

as Brynhilde sings a paean to Siegfried, the awakener to life, the
most blessed of heroes, whom she had loved and fostered before
ever he was formed. His mother, she tells him, is dead, but in
Brynhilde he now has one who is both herself and him, her wisdom to be his. She had been inspired to flout the decree of Wotan
because she had read the inmost secret of the God's heart; and
now she sees that her disobedience had come from the obscure
prompting of her love for this hero as yet unborn.

20

They lose themselves in blissful contemplation of what each
has won through the other. Then sadness steals over Brynhilde
as she recalls what she has lost in ceasing to be a Valkyrie and
becoming a mortal woman; and when he embraces her she flies
from him in terror:

> *No God's touch have I known!*
> *Before the maiden*
> *low bent the heroes;*
> *holy came she from Walhall!—*
> *Woe's me! Woe's me!*
> *Woe for the shame,*
> *the pain and disgrace!*
> *For he who wakes me*
> *deals me this wound!*
> *He has broken birny and helm:*
> *Brynhilde am I no more!*

For a while she will not be comforted. She doubts her own
wisdom; round her is a darkness peopled with shapes that terrify
her; and she covers her eyes with her hands. Gently he removes
them and exhorts her to rise from the darkness and see the radiant
day that is dawning for them both. "It is the day of my shame,"
she laments: "O Siegfried! Siegfried! look on my dread!"

Then her look softens, as if, according to the stage directions,
"a sweet thought had arisen in her mind". "Ever was I, ever am
I", she says, "ever in rapture of longing, yet ever to make thee

blest!" To these words she takes up, in the minor, a gracious
melody that had just been given out by the strings:

It is a theme familiar to concert-goers as the main subject of the
Siegfried Idyll; and it is to the second chief theme of that work:

that she continues with a greeting of Siegfried as "highest hero,
wealth of the world, life of the life of things, laughter and joy".[1]
She begs him to leave her in peace:

> *Come to me not*
> *with thy madness of longing,*
> *master me not*
> *with thy ruinous might;*
> *thy loved one oh do not destroy!*

Has he ever beheld his own face, she asks him, in the crystal brook,

[1] No. 151 has been dubbed by some commentators the motive of Peace,
and No. 152 that of the World Hoard. Both labels are meaningless. It was
formerly believed that both these motives were originally conceived for the
present episode in *Siegfried* and taken from there later to constitute the basis
of the orchestral *Idyll*. We know now, however, that they were first of all
imported into the opera, and then taken later into the *Idyll*, from a string
quartet which Wagner had sketched in 1864. At this point in the opera, and
again for a moment in the *Twilight of the Gods*, Wagner abandoned his
objective attitude towards his drama and allowed his Siegfried-Brynhilde
music to become a record of his own and Cosima's personal emotions. Why
he did so was a domestic secret to which, at that time, only he and she had the
clue, though it is possible for us now to reconstruct, from one scrap of
biographical evidence and another, the situation as it was in Triebschen in
the summer of 1869. The subject is far too complex to be dealt with here: I
can only refer the reader to four articles of mine in the *Sunday Times* of
February 1946 for a summary of the evidence.

and seen how the fair image was shattered when the waters were disturbed? Even so will his image be destroyed for her by the disturbing mastery of his love. To passionate enunciations of No. 147 and No. 146 (the World Inheritance motive) he beats her protests down. What though the swirling waters deface his image: into them he will plunge, quenching his fire in them, stilling his longing in the flood.

He takes her in his arms, and her own ardent spirit goes out to meet his. When her blood surges like a sea of fire towards him does he not feel fear? she asks. No, he replies: his old courage has come back to him; the fear that his heart could never learn, the fear that she herself could hardly teach him, has fled from Siegfried for ever. She breaks out into joyous laughter, becoming, to the accompaniment of No. 74, almost the wild Valkyrie once more:

> *Thou foolish marvel*
> *of mightiest deeds!*
> *Laughing must I love thee,*
> *laughing bear my blindness,*
> *laughing leap to destruction,*
> *laughing go down to death!*

A last new motive, that of Love's Resolution:

is given out in the horn[1] and combined contrapuntally with No. 149 as the pair blend their voices in a final ecstasy of life and love. Brynhilde bids a glad farewell to the splendours of Walhall and the glory and pomp of the Gods. Let the eternals end in bliss; let the Norns sever their rope of runes; let the night of destruction fall; over her shines Siegfried's star:

---

[1] The evidence suggests that this theme also was taken by Wagner from a chamber music work of about 1864.

He is for ever,
is for aye,
my wealth and world,
my one and all:
light of all loving,
laughing death!

In virtually the same words Siegfried sings of the new day that
has dawned for him with her; and as she throws herself into his
arms the curtain falls to exultant reiterations of No. 150, No.
108B and No. 146.

THE TWILIGHT OF
THE GODS

I

In the *Twilight of the Gods* we arrive, in reverse, at Wagner's
original design for a Nibelungen drama as it was in the *Siegfried's
Death* of 1848.

The new work opens, as the old one had done, with a scene
for the three Norns, the weavers of destiny. After two harsh
chords in the wind instruments the arpeggio-like theme that has
taken so many forms in the earlier operas of the *Ring*, expressing
now, as in No. 2, primal nature and the Rhine, now, as in No. 42,
Erda, appears once more in the strings. Repetition of this sequence
is followed by the solemn Annunciation of Death motive (No.
83B) in the brass, and this again by a new motive symbolical of
the weaving of the Norns:

After some twenty bars of this kind the curtain rises, showing the
same rock setting as that at the end of the *Valkyrie*. It is night,
but fire gleams in the valley at the back. On the right, in the foreground, is a great pine-tree. Three tall women in long, sombre
draperies are seen: the first reclines under the tree, the second is
stretched out on a rock in front of the cave, the third sits in the
centre background, on a rock beneath a peak. The gloomy silence
is broken by the voice of the first Norn, asking "What light
shineth there?" "Dawns the day already?" asks the second; and
the third says "Loge's host licks the fell with tongues of fire: why
spin and sing we not?" The first—the eldest of the three—unwinds a golden rope and fastens one end of it to a branch of the
tree; later in the scene she throws it to the second Norn, who
winds it round the projecting rock at the entrance to the cave;
later still the third Norn catches it and throws the end back to the

second; and this procedure is repeated in the course of their colloquy.

The first Norn tells how long ago, sitting by a spring that whispered wisdom at the foot of the great world-ash-tree, she had sung of holiest things. A God, Wotan, came to drink at the spring, leaving an eye as tribute[1]; from the tree he broke a great branch and fashioned from it a mighty Spear. But the wound cankered the heart of the tree, which became dry and leafless; the water, too, sank in the spring. So the songs she sang were of dark meaning; and now she weaves no more by the world-ash-tree but fastens the rope to the pine.

The second Norn tells how Wotan engraved runes of treaties on the shaft of his Spear, and by them ruled the world. A hero bold had shattered the Spear. Then Wotan had summoned Walhall's heroes to hew the ash-tree stem and branches in pieces. The tree fell; the spring became for ever dry; and only round the jagged rock can she now bind the rope.

The third tells how Giants built the great fortress in which Wotan sits in state with his hallowed heroes: round it rises a mighty wall of riven boughs that were once the world-ash-tree. When that wood takes fire Walhall will go down in flames:

> the doom of the Gods then dawneth;
> down in dusk do they go.

The first Norn takes up the tale again. Is yonder gleam that of the dawn or of fire? she asks. Clouds deceive her eyes now; but dim within her is the memory of a time when Loge ran swift and free, a ravening flame. But Wotan subdued him, says the second Norn. Loge had gnawed at the runes on the Spear-shaft to gain his freedom; but by the power of the Spear-point the God had bound him to flame round Brynhilde's rock. Then, continues the third Norn, Wotan had pierced Loge's breast with the splinters of the broken shaft; fire had flamed from that blow, and this the God had hurled at the pile of the world-ash-tree's boughs encircling Walhall.

[1] It has often been pointed out that in the second scene of the *Rhinegold* Wotan had told Fricka that when wooing her he had forfeited one eye as pledge of his love. Wagner is following different legends in the two instances.

And after that? The Norns do not know; they can see nothing in the waning night about them. The first of them can feel no more the strands of the rope, which is broken, the warp entangled. The second says it is being cut through by the jagged edge of the rock:

> *from grief and greed*
> *rises the Nibelung's Ring:*
> *a vengeful curse*
> *gnaws at the sundering threads.*
> *Know'st thou what comes from this?*

Too slack is the rope, says the third Norn: if she is to throw it to the north it must be more tightly strained. She pulls strongly at the rope, which breaks in the middle. The three start up in terror, go to the centre of the stage, take hold of the pieces of the broken rope, and bind their bodies together with them, saying:

> *The end this of our wisdom!*
> *The world hears us*
> *wise ones no more.*
> *Descend! To Erda! Descend!*

They disappear. The old order is nearing its end, thanks to the chain of events set in motion first by Alberich, then by Wotan. What will the new order be?

This prelude is a continuous symphonic weaving of various motives already associated with the characters, events, objects or forces referred to by the Norns, with the motive of weaving (No. 154) running through the whole tissue and consolidating it, though of course a motive is often transformed in some subtle harmonic way or other in concordance with a change in its terms of reference, as when the Loge Fire motive assumes this form:

and later this:

As the rope of destiny breaks, the Curse motive rings out in the bass trumpet, and the Norns' last words ("The end this of our wisdom", etc.) are accompanied by the motive of Renunciation (No. 9), that of the Curse, that of Magic Sleep, and finally the fate-laden Annunciation of Death (No. 83B).[1]

2

After the disappearance of the Norns a long melodic line uncoils itself slowly in the 'cellos, broken by the Siegfried motive (No. 108) in a broader form befitting the new Siegfried:

and by a new motive characterising a new Brynhilde:

The red glow of the dawn increases, while down in the valley the fire grows fainter. No. 158 ascends in mountainous waves in one reiteration after another; at the mighty climax of its development No. 157 rings out with the full force of the brass, and Brynhilde and Siegfried enter, he fully armed, she leading her horse by the

[1] Wagner was agreeable to the prelude being played at concerts as a purely orchestral piece.

bridle; and the joyous fanfare that had formerly characterised the simple boy (No. 108) receives a rhythmical transformation that shows him as the man he has now become:

To the caressing strain of No. 158 and a new motive, that of Heroic Love:

Brynhilde addresses the hero whom she is now sending forth to fresh deeds of glory. The runes the Gods had taught her she has given to him, she says, while she herself has been bereft of maidenhood by the man who is now her master; weak in wisdom is she now, though strong in love; and she implores him not to forget the poor heart that has given him all it had to give. One thing alone he knows, he replies,—that Brynhilde lives—and this he will always remember. He will leave with her, as token of his love, the Ring. In return she gives him her horse Grane; no more will he carry her on winged feet through the air, but Siegfried he will follow wherever he may lead; thus even in absence each will be present to the other. The long duet ends with their both taking up the Siegfried motive of Freedom (No. 134) in an extended form:

Siegfried leads the horse down the rock, Brynhilde accompany-

ing him, and the orchestral episode known in the concert room as
Siegfried's Rhine Journey begins. It opens with a lively version
of No. 157, followed by No. 161. By the time No. 168 appears
Siegfried has disappeared from our sight; but his further course
can be followed in the orchestra, and, for a while, with the aid of
Brynhilde's gestures. No. 108, intoned by a horn behind the
scenes, indicates that he has reached the valley. Brynhilde
descends the rock, catches sight of him once more, and makes
rapturous signs to him. A vigorous mutation of No. 153:

162

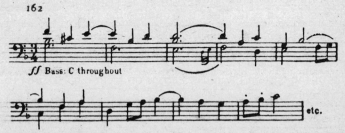

peals out, at which point he is lost to Brynhilde's view and the
curtain falls. A joyous contrapuntal combination of Nos. 108 and
No. 23 (Loge) in a new form suggests that he and Grane are
making their way through the wall of fire round the fell. Then a
mighty surge of No. 2 combined with No. 3, followed by the
song of the Rhinemaidens (No. 7), shows us that he has reached
and is passing down the Rhine. Gradually a shadow steals across
the exuberant music: the Ring motive appears, followed by that
of Renunciation (No. 9), then No. 36 (the groans of the enslaved
Nibelungs and Alberich's imperious orders to them), till at last
the tone and temper of the music change completely as a first hint
of the milieu and the atmosphere of the next scene is given out:

163

The management of the long picture is one of the best examples of Wagner's art of transformation by means of music from one pictorial or psychological plane to another.

3

At this point the tragedy of the *Twilight of the Gods* begins. When the curtain rises we see the great hall of the Gibichungs' stronghold on the Rhine; it is open at the back, where we have a view of the shore running down to the river, with rocky heights enclosing it. On a throne sits Gunther, the King of the Gibichungs, with his sister Gutrune at his side: before them is a table with drinking vessels, and in front of this sits the grim, dour Hagen. He is Gunther's half-brother, the son of Alberich. At the rising of the curtain the music carries on from our No. 163 to a motive representative of Hagen:

the continuation of which:

will afterwards refer more particularly to the Gibichung race.

Gunther addresses Hagen, asking him how his name and that of the Gibichungs now stand on the Rhine. Gunther's fame fills him with envy, Hagen replies; but his glory had been foretold by her who had borne them both, Queen Grimhilde. Gunther in turn envies this half-brother of his for his superior wisdom.

Hagen goes on to say that great as is the Gibichung renown he is not yet content with it, for there are things Gunther might have done but has not yet set himself to do: he has no wife, and Gutrune is still unwedded. Hagen knows of a wife for his brother, the noblest in the world: she dwells on a rock engirdled with fire, through which only a stronger and braver than Gunther could force his way—Siegfried, the son of Siegmund and Sieglinde, who had earned imperishable fame by slaying the Dragon that brooded upon the Nibelung Gold. What is this Nibelung Hoard of which he has often heard? asks Gunther. "The man who could wield its might", Hagen replies, "could make himself lord of the world: Siegfried has won it, and now the Nibelungs are thralls to him.[1] None but he can penetrate the fire."

Gunther rises angrily from his seat and strides agitatedly about the hall. Why raise this discord and doubt? he asks; why spur him on to long for something he cannot accomplish? Hagen, without ever moving from his place at the table, stops him with a mysterious sign as the wood wind gives out softly a suggestion of the Tarnhelm motive:

166

---

[1] Wagner took this line over unthinkingly from *Siegfried's Death*. It has no point in the present *Ring*, where nothing is said of any connection of Siegfried with the Nibelungs.

What if Siegfried could be induced by magic arts to bring the bride to them, he asks; would she not then be Gunther's? And would not the hero do it at the King's request—if he himself loved their sister? The orchestra gives out the motive of Enticement:

as the gentle Gutrune asks what charm she could have for a hero who would have the world's noblest women at his feet. "Remember the drink in the chest, and trust to me who brought it there", answers Hagen; "the hero whom thou desirest shall be afire with love for thee. Let Siegfried but taste of that magic draught, and it will fade from his memory that he has ever seen any woman but thee"; and the orchestra projects the subtle, insidious motive of Magic Deceit:

to which is appended (bar 3) the falling figure always associated with Hagen.

4

"Would that Siegfried I might see!" sighs Gutrune: but Gunther praises the mother who bore so wise a son as Hagen. But how to find the hero? Just then, from a distance, but loudly, comes a horn call, and the orchestra takes up the joyous motive of the young Siegfried (No. 108). The hero is roaming the earth, questing for fresh deeds of renown, Hagen tells the others, and no doubt in time he will come to Gibich's hall on the Rhine. The horn call sounds again, a little nearer. Hagen goes to the shore, and to an accompaniment that embodies both his characteristic interval and a phrase that will form part of the chorus of Gibichung vassals in the second act:

169

he tells them that on the river he sees a boat with a man and a horse; with the strongest and easiest of strokes the man drives the boat against the stream; nobody can it be but Siegfried himself.

Hagen hails him through his hollowed hands, welcoming him to the hall of the son of Gibich, and soon the hero fastens the boat to the land and springs ashore with his horse; and as Hagen greets him with feigned cordiality the Curse motive rings out with terrific power in the orchestra, followed by the motive of Enticement (No. 167). Gunther announces himself as the Gibichung King, and Siegfried, in the approved fashion of the sagas, offers him his choice of combat or amity. Gunther gives him warm welcome as friend. Looking fixedly at Hagen, Siegfried asks how he came to address him by name; and to a fresh enunciation of the Curse motive the sinister Hagen explains that he knew him by his strength. The Curse motive flows without a break into that of the hero Siegfried (No. 108B), in a way that illustrates, on a small scale, Wagner's technique, in the *Ring*, of thematic interlocking: as so many of the motives are variants of the simplest suggestions of tonic and dominant they can join up to or combine with each other in the most natural way:

170

Throughout the *Twilight of the Gods* the orchestral tissue is composed of a constant succession, combination and interplay of motives, in a way that makes detailed specification of them an impossibility.

Siegfried commends Grane to the care of Hagen, who leads him away. Gutrune, at a gesture from her half-brother, has already retired into her inner chamber, as yet unobserved by Siegfried. In courteous fashion Gunther, to the accompaniment of a new motive, that of Friendship:

makes Siegfried free of the hall of his fathers. The hero has nothing to offer in return but his sword; but Hagen, who has now returned, says it is rumoured that he is master of the Nibelung Hoard. "That poor treasure I so despised", replies Siegfried, "that I left it lying there with a Dragon to guard it, taking away only this"—he points to a piece of mail-work hanging from his belt—"the worth of which I do not know." "The Tarnhelm it is", Hagen tells him, "the cunningest Nibelung work; with this on thy head thou canst change thy shape as thou wilt, or fly in a trice to lands afar. Nought else hast thou of the Hoard?" "Only a Ring", says Siegfried, "and that is held by a noble woman." "Brynhilde!" mutters Hagen.

5

Just then Gutrune re-enters, accompanied by her sweet and gracious motive:

There is no evil in her, nor even strength; she is merely a gentle creature caught in Hagen's web and used by him for his own evil purpose. As the daughter of Gibich's house she welcomes the newcomer and offers him a drinking-horn. He takes it from her courteously, and with the motive of Enticement (No. 167) and that of Love's Greeting to the World (No. 148) interlocking in the orchestra, he drinks to Brynhilde. In the softest of tones and colours the orchestra breathes the mysterious motive of Magic Deceit, which is followed by that of Gutrune. While she lowers her eyes before him in shame and confusion Siegfried declares himself aflame with love for her. Her name, he learns from Gunther, is Gutrune; "and good", he says, "are the runes I read in her eyes." Overwhelmed by the passion of his speech she humbly bows her head, and with a gesture indicating her feeling that she is unworthy of so great a hero she leaves the hall with faltering steps: he follows her with his eyes as if bewitched, while Gunther and Hagen keep their gaze steadily fixed on him.

Has Gunther a wife? he asks. Not yet, replies the Gibichung King, nor is the woman on whom his heart is set to be lightly won, for her home is on a rock protected by a fire through which he could never break: her name is Brynhilde. Siegfried's demeanour all this while shows him trying to capture some definite outline in the mist of things forgotten, but even the word Brynhilde does not restore his memory. At the mention of the fire he turns gaily to Gunther and offers to bring him Brynhilde if he may have Gutrune for wife, for by the magic craft of the Tarnhelm he will change himself into the semblance of the Gibichung. On this they swear blood-brotherhood in saga fashion. Hagen fills a drinking-horn with wine and holds it out to Siegfried and Gunther, each of whom cuts an arm with his sword and lets the blood run into the horn, on which he then places two fingers. Siegfried begins the oath:

Gunther answering him with "Brothers' love in bravest blend
bloom from our blood in the cup!":

> *Troth I drink to my friend!*
> *Glad and free*
> *let bloom from our bond*
> *blood-brotherhood here!*

They continue:

> *Breaks a brother the bond,*
> *false if friend be to friend,*
> *what in drops today*
> *we two have drunken,*
> *in streams unceasing shall flow,*
> *so shall traitor atone!*

But the Hagen motive in the orchestra gives a sinister turn to the
oath, and at the supreme moment of the pledge the ominous
Curse motive is heard once more. When each of them has drunk
from the horn the orchestra clinches the oath with a decisive
octave drop, followed by the Treaty motive in the brass, with, as
will be seen (in the third bar) tuba and trombone ejaculating
"Hagen!":

Siegfried, after drinking, has held out the horn to Hagen, who,
however, still standing behind the pair, instead of draining it hews
it in two with his sword. Siegfried, looking hard at him, asks why
he had taken no part in the oath. His blood would poison the
draught, the grim one replies, for it flows not pure and noble like
theirs; so sluggish and cold is it that nothing would redden his
cheeks; hence he holds himself aloof from bonds of fire. Gunther

bids Siegfried give no heed to the gloomy man, and the hero dons his shield and summons the Gibichung to follow him to his boat: in it he will leave him for a night, and in the morning the bride shall be his. So the pair set out down the Rhine, Hagen being left to guard the hall during Gunther's absence. Gutrune returns for a moment, to learn that the pair have gone in quest of Brynhilde; and she goes back to her chamber with an innocently happy cry of "Siegfried—mine!"

Then comes the great interlude of Hagen's Watch. Holding shield and spear he sits down with his back against a post at the entrance to the hall, and his sombre monologue begins, against an orchestral background that incorporates his own characteristic falling diminished fifth with the rhythm of the Annihilation motive previously associated with Alberich (No. 40). The unseen presence of his Nibelung father seems to brood over the scene in an harmonically darkened version of the Motive (No. 36) of the power given to Alberich by the Ring over the Nibelung host:

175

Molto moderato

Gibich's son, Hagen muses, will bring back with him, thanks to Siegfried, the bride of brides; but he will bring also a prize for Hagen—the Ring; and with that Hagen will bring down in ruin all these beings, better than himself, whom, because of the Alberich blood in him, he hates:

Ye sons of freedom,
lusty companions,
laugh as ye sail on your way!
base though ye deem him,
ye both shall serve
the Niblung's son!

6

During the sombre orchestral interlude that follows the monologue the curtain in front of the hall is drawn, hiding the stage from the spectator. The psychological purport of the music is still Hagen's dark plotting; but gradually, by means of one of those slow transitions of which Wagner had the secret, the mood changes, the colour lightens, till finally the clarinet gives out the happy Brynhilde motive shown in No. 158, across which, however, there soon creeps the shadow of the Curse. This kind of apposition is maintained in what follows: Brynhilde is about to look out once more upon the world (No. 148), but, we realise, not with the same prospect of happiness as at the end of *Siegfried*, for beneath these tranquil strains there throbs persistently the broken rhythm of the Annihilation motive (No. 40).

When the curtain is drawn aside again we see the rocky heights once more, with Brynhilde sitting at the entrance to the cave, silently and thoughtfully contemplating Siegfried's Ring. "Overcome by happy memories", say the stage directions in the score, "she covers it with kisses."[1] Twice the orchestra breathes tenderly the motive (No. 152) to which, in the final scene of *Siegfried*, she had greeted the hero as the "wealth of the world, life of the life of things"; but thrice the mysterious motive of Magic Deceit (No. 168) hints at the evil that will soon ensnare her as it had already ensnared Siegfried. She has just heard, for the first time since Wotan laid her in slumber, a sound now almost forgotten but as the breath of her nostrils to her of old, that of a Valkyrie galloping through the air: who can it be, she asks, that is coming to visit the solitary one? She is hailed from afar by Waltraute, who, after leaving her horse in the nearby wood, enters and is greeted joyously by Brynhilde, who at first does not perceive that her sister is agitated and anxious. Brynhilde's first ecstatic thought is

[1] Nothing of all this was in the original poem: Wagner, when he came to write the music, saw fit, as he had done in the final duet of *Siegfried*, to incorporate in it certain emotional experiences of his own and Cosima's. Hence his employment here of No. 152, which, as we have seen, came into the *Siegfried* score from the string quartet of 1864 and was used again in the *Siegfried Idyll*. It is only here that Wagner employs No. 152 in connection with the Ring.

that she comes from War-father with a message that his heart has turned in forgiveness and love again to his child—though her punishment she does not regret, since it had brought her the love of the noblest of heroes; and she breaks into a cry of delight and embraces her sister Valkyrie, whom she imagines to have come to share her happiness.

Waltraute's agitation soon makes her look for another explanation. Has Wotan, after all, not pardoned her? she asks: has Waltraute come to her racked with fear of his wrath? Were that all, the Valkyrie replies, her anguish would soon be at an end; and she tells in detail what had brought her in haste to the rock. Since he had lost Brynhilde, Wotan had sent out his Maidens no more to the battlefield: for a while even his warriors had seen him no more, for he had ranged restlessly through the world as Wanderer. At last he had come back to Walhall, holding in his hand the splinters of his Spear, shattered by the Sword of a hero. Silently he had sent the warriors to hew the world-ash-tree in pieces. (Here the Walhall motive, in a graver form, links up with the motive of the Need of the Gods (No. 81) in a new aspect in the bass):

To this majestic accompaniment Waltraute tells how Wotan had ordered a towering wall to be built with these pieces round

Walhall. Then he had called all the Gods and heroes to council: tortured with fear they had stood in ring beyond ring round him while he sat silent on his throne, still holding the fragments of the Spear in his hand, of Holda's apples eating no more. Awestruck and spellbound the Gods saw him send out his messengers the ravens:

> *when to the hall*
> *with tidings good they return,*
> *then shall Wotan his grief forget,*
> *smiling his fate will he face.*

The trembling Valkyries had clung to his knees, but he turned a blind eye to their imploring:

> *upon his breast*
> *weeping I flung me;*
> *then soft grew his look;*
> *he remembered, Brynhilde, thee!*

and the motive formerly associated with Wotan's Dejection (No. 79) now merges, in an extended form:

into one of the most melting passages in all music as the weary God muses on his parting from Brynhilde, when he had pressed his last kiss on her lips:

With closed eyes, Waltraute continues, he sighed, and whispered, as if sunk in dreams:

> *if e'er the river maidens*
> *win back the Ring from Brynhilde again,*
> *from the Curse's load*
> *released were God and world!*

Then Waltraute, stealing softly from among the silent heroes, had mounted her horse and hastened to her sister, to implore her to put an end to the grief of the Gods.

7

Brynhilde replies tranquilly that all this has no meaning for her now, for it is long since she left the great hall in the cloudy heavens. But what is it that Waltraute would have her do? "Give back the Ring to the Rhinemaidens", says Waltraute vehemently: "from it comes all the world's woe; fling the accursed thing back into the waters, and end Walhall's grief for ever!" But Brynhilde is immovable: the Ring was given her by Siegfried as pledge of his love, and she prizes it more than all the raptures of Walhall, all the fame of the Gods; and she loses herself in happy memories of her awakening on the fell. She refuses to grant the Valkyrie's prayer:

> *Then home to the holy*
> *council of Gods;*
> *and of my Ring*
> *this rede bear thou for me:*
> *while life doth last I will love,*
> *from love they never will win me;*
>   *fall first in ruins*
> *Walhall's splendour and pride!*

With a great cry of "Woe's me! Woe to thee, sister! Woe to Walhall!" Waltraute leaves her, in a tempest that suddenly sweeps over the wood.

Brynhilde follows her sister's course in thought. By now evening has fallen, and down in the valley she sees the fire rising furiously to the very heights of the mountain. It must be Siegfried returning to her, she says; and she springs up in delight as the

familiar horn call resounds from below. Suddenly he becomes
visible on a high rock: the flames leap out fiercely at him, but
recede as he slowly advances. He is in Gunther's form, with the
Tarnhelm concealing the upper part of his face, leaving only the
eyes free. Brynhilde recoils in terror before this sinister apparition,
with a cry of "Betrayed! Who forced my fire?"

A sombre enunciation of the Tarnhelm motive is followed by
a long silence, broken at last by a murmuring of the motive of
Magic Deceit (No. 168) and a fateful suggestion of the Gibichung
motive (No. 165). After another spell of silence, Siegfried, in a
feigned voice deeper than his own, answers her question: a wooer
has come, one whom her fire could not affright: he wins her for
his wife, a hero who, if nought but force will serve, by force will
tame her: let her follow him now where he leads. What is this
shape of dread? she asks again in terror—a mortal? an eagle that
has swooped on her to rend her? one of Hella's night-born host?
"A Gibichung", is the reply; "Gunther is my name, and thou
must follow me." No 177 becomes definitely a motive of her own
calamity:

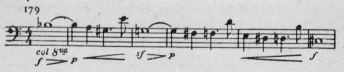

as she breaks into a wild lament: this, then, is Wotan's vengeful
way of punishing her? Now, she thinks, she divines the God's
pitiless purpose. In a frenzy of despair she holds out the Ring, to
which she trusts to guard her. "Husband's right gives it to Gunther", Siegfried tells her, and he will have it by force.

They struggle together for a while, and at last he seizes her by
the hand and tears the Ring from her finger. As she sinks brokenly
into his arms her unconscious look meets his; and the orchestra
gives out a pathetic reminiscence of No. 152, followed by the
motive of the Tarnhelm and that of Magic Deceit as he lets her
fainting body sink on to the stone bench at the entrance to the
cave, tells her that now she is Gunther's bride, and bids her show
him the way to her cave. The sinister rhythm of the Annihilation
motive (No. 40) pulsates in the orchestra as he drives her before

him into the cave with an imperious gesture. Then comes an astonishing musical-psychological stroke, of a kind of which only music among the arts is capable. Three times we hear the decisive octave drop of the motive of the Troth sworn with Gunther, followed by three bars of a contrapuntal combination of the Sword motive in the upper part, the Treaty motive in the middle part, and that of Hagen in the lowest:

Siegfried draws his sword and says, in his natural voice:

> *Now, Nothung, witness thou*
> *that pure my wooing was;*
> *that troth I keep with my brother,*
> *bar me from Gunther's bride.*

There is a bitterly ironic upsurge of the happy Brynhilde motive (No. 158), succeeded by a final triumphal statement of the Troth motive (the octave drop) and a sinister reminder of Hagen in the depths of the orchestra, and as Siegfried follows Brynhilde into the cave the curtain falls.

8

The tremendous second act, which is in some ways Wagner's supreme achievement in music drama, shows us not only Siegfried and Brynhilde but Gunther and Gutrune becoming inescapably entangled in Hagen's net. The drama is tense, the action swift and compact; and the musical fabric consists for the most part of incessant interweavings of the motives now familiar to us.

An orchestral introduction depicts the sombre brooding of
Alberich and Hagen on the problem that obsesses them: prominent
in it are the sinister rhythmic throb of the Annihilation motive,
the Hagen motive, and an harmonic intensification of what we
have sometimes called, for convenience' sake, the motive of
Servitude (Nos. 33 and 36), but which is freely used by Wagner
to express now this aspect of woe, now that:

This harmonic subtilisation of earlier motives is a leading feature
of the opera from now onwards; as the tragedy deepens, the
darker become the meanings with which the themes are seen to be
charged.

    When the curtain rises we see an open space on the shore in
front of the hall of the Gibichungs. The open entrance to the hall
is now on our right; on the left stretches a bank of the Rhine.
Running across the background towards the right of the stage is a
series of rocky heights, on which stand three altar-stones, one for
Wotan, one for Fricka, and one for Donner. It is night: Hagen is
still where we left him when Siegfried and Gunther set out on their
journey down the Rhine—apparently asleep, leaning against one
of the posts of the hall, with his arm round his spear and his shield
by his side. As the moon suddenly pierces through the clouds we
catch sight of Alberich, crouching before Hagen and leaning his
arms on the latter's knees. He asks his son softly if he is sleeping
and unable to hear him whom rest and sleep have long forsaken.
Hagen, who throughout the scene remains motionless and
speaks as if in sleep, though his eyes are open, replies that he
hears him well: what message has the Nibelung for him? Is he as
bold, Alberich asks him, as the mother who bore him? "Stout
heart my mother gave me", is the reply, "yet may her son not

thank her that she was caught by thy craft: old too soon am I, pale
and wan: I hate the happy! Joy I know not." "Hate the happy!"
says Alberich eagerly; "so wilt thou love thy joyless, woe-
weighted father as thou shouldst. Be crafty, strong and bold.
Those whom we fight with the forces of darkness are stricken to
the heart by our hate; for the ruthless robber Wotan has been
vanquished by one whom he begat, and now he sits in dread,
awaiting his downfall." It is not that he fears Wotan, continues
Alberich, for the God is doomed to go down with the rest. It is
his lost power that Alberich covets, and down to ruin he will go if
he and Hagen are true to themselves and each other, linked by a
common rage and hate; and a new motive, that of Murder, is
heard in the orchestra:

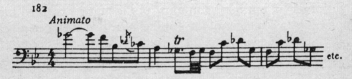

The Ring has passed into the hands of a fearless stripling over
whom Alberich has no power, for he does not know the worth of
it and makes no use of its might; he is warm with life and lives
only for love. One aim alone, says the Nibelung, he and Hagen
should have—the ruin of the God. The Ring has been given by
the boy in love to a woman; if on her prompting it should return
to the Rhinemaidens, all the Nibelung's wiles will be in vain for
ever. Alberich himself had lacked the strength to slay the Dragon;
but he had begotten a grim son and bred hatred and the passion
for vengeance in him. "Win me the Ring, in Wotan's and
Volsung's despite! Swear it to me, Hagen, my son!"

"The Ring I will win thee", Hagen replies; "rest thou and wait!"
Alberich is gradually lost in the shadows as the morning twilight
slowly steals in, but out of the darkness comes the reiterated
hoarse appeal, "Swear to me, Hagen, my son! Be true to me! Be
true!" "To myself I swear", says Hagen; "be silent and have no
care!" Alberich disappears completely; Hagen, still without
moving, looks with fixed eyes towards the Rhine, over which the
light of dawn is now spreading:

The phrase shows Wagner once more practising his art of almost imperceptible transition. (The fragment marked B is a foreshadowing of a motive that will afterwards be associated with the barbaric merriment of Hagen and the Gibichung vassals).

9

The Rhine becomes more and more clearly visible in the red light of dawn, but the warm glow of the music is flecked for a moment by a reminder of the Tarnhelm motive as Hagen gives a slight start. Suddenly, to the accompaniment of his horn call, Siegfried emerges from a bush near the shore: he is now in his own form, but the Tarnhelm is still on his head. Taking it off and hanging it at his girdle he gives Hagen a cheery greeting. Hagen rises to hear the news that Gunther and Brynhilde are following down the river. The hero calls gaily to Gutrune, who comes out from the hall: they shall hear, he says, how he subdued Brynhilde and is now come to claim Gutrune for wife. She hails him joyously in the name of Freia, to the accompaniment of a modification of her own motive (No. 172), to which is now added (at A) a theme that will later be associated with the Gibichung greeting to herself and Siegfried:

Gunther, she learns, had passed unscathed through the fire, which Siegfried had braved for him, singing, as he clove the flames, for love of Gutrune: the Tarnhelm had disguised him, as Hagen had said it would, and it was to Gunther that the Valkyrie thought she had yielded. To her new lord she had submitted all the bridal

night till the dawn; but, he assures Gutrune, between Siegfried
and Brynhilde had been his sword, "as between east and west is
north; so near was Brynhilde to him, so far": and once more we
hear the combination of motives shown in No. 179. In the morning
mist, he continues, she had accompanied him to the valley; when
near the strand, swift as thought Gunther stood there in his stead.
The Tarnhelm had carried Siegfried in a trice to the hall, and
Gunther and his bride were following in the boat. Gutrune hails
him with a glad cry of "Siegfried! Mightiest of men! I faint for
fear of thee!"

Hagen, looking down from the height in the foreground, sees
a sail in the distance on the river. "Give the bride a joyous greeting", cries the happy Gutrune, to the strain of No. 184A, "that
glad and blithe she bide among us"; and she bids Hagen call the
men of Gibich to the hall for the wedding. She herself, taking
Siegfried with her by the hand, goes out to summon the women
to share her own happiness with her.

Ascending a rock in the background, Hagen blows on his
hoarse cow-horn a boisterous, uncouth melody:

as he calls to the Gibichung vassals to assemble with their weapons
—"goodly weapons, strong weapons, sharp for strife, for Need
is here"; and the orchestra comments on these last words with the
motive of the Doom of the Gods (No. 44) plunging downward in
great waves. Cow-horns behind the scenes answer his rough call,
and a wild crew of armed vassals rushes in from all quarters and
gathers on the shore in front of the hall. There follows the first
chorus to be heard in the whole *Ring,* an affair of wild ejaculations to the accompaniment first of all of the motive of the vassals:

They ask why they have been summoned: Hagen tells them that Gunther is returning to them, bringing with him a wife. But no vassals will she have in her train: she comes alone: the King had been shielded from harm by the hero Siegfried, the slayer of the Dragon. What need then has the King of them? they ask: what work have they to do? They are told to slaughter great steers on Wotan's altar, with a boar for Froh, a lusty goat for Donner, and "sheep in plenty for Fricka, that she may smile on the marriage"—and Hagen breaks into an ironic melodic phrase with rough shakes in it. After the sacrifices they must fill the horns deep with mead and wine and drink with their women, carousing till they fall like logs.

They have listened to his rough jocularity with growing merriment; now they burst into ringing laughter, and to strains built up of No. 183A, the Wedding motive already associated with Gutrune (No. 172), and the pendant to this shown in No. 184A, they sing a barbaric paean to this grim Hagen of theirs, who has now become a bridal herald! For all his savage jocularity, Hagen's demeanour all the while has been grave: now he comes down among the vassals and bids them cease their laughter and prepare to receive Gunther and his bride: let them serve their lady loyally, and if she be wronged let their vengeance be swift.

10

The boat with Gunther and Brynhilde comes into sight and gradually reaches the shore: taking her ceremoniously by the hand he presents her to the vassals, who, clashing their weapons together, acclaim them in a massive chorus founded on the Gibichung theme (No. 165):

187

Molto moderato

Brynhilde stands with lowered eyes as Gunther presents her as his wife, who shall be the crowning glory of the Gibichung name. A

hint of what is passing in her mind is given us by a recurrence in
the bassoons of No. 179, which we now begin to associate with
Brynhilde's desire for vengeance on Siegfried. But she does not
speak or raise her eyes even when Siegfried and Gutrune, accompanied by the latter's women, come in from the hall: the happy
Gutrune is now accompanied by a still sweeter form of her
characteristic theme:

Gunther greets them: "two happy bridals", he says "we celebrate
together—Brynhilde and Gunther, Gutrune and Siegfried".

At this last word Brynhilde starts out of her torpor and perceives Siegfried. Her eyes remain rivetted on him in amazement
while No. 179 raises its ominous head in the orchestra, joined
with a suggestion of the Hagen motive and that of Death (No. 83).
She trembles violently; Gunther releases her hand, perplexed, like
the vassals, by her behaviour. Siegfried asks calmly what it is that
troubles her: she can only ejaculate incredulously "Siegfried—
here? Gutrune?" "Gunther's gentle sister", says Siegfried, "won
by me, as thou by him." She gives him the lie, then staggers and
appears about to fall. Siegfried, who is nearest to her, supports
her in his arms; she looks up at him and says feebly, "Siegfried
knows me not!" He calls to Gunther to come to his bride,
and as she does so she sees the Ring on Siegfried's finger and
breaks into a wild cry as something of the truth begins to dawn
on her.

Hagen, recognising that the decisive moment has arrived,
turns to the vassals, bidding them hearken to this woman's words.
Mastering herself with difficulty Brynhilde says:

> *On thy hand there*
> *I beheld a Ring;*
> *not thine to wear it:*
> *he who won it* —
>
>   (pointing to Gunther)
>
> *standeth there!*
> *How came then to thee*
> *the Ring from his hand?*

Siegfried, quietly contemplating the Ring, assures her that it did not come to him from Gunther. Then Brynhilde turns to the latter: "Thou who didst win from me the Ring with which I wedded thee, teach this man thy right: demand back the pledge!" The embarrassed Gibichung disclaims all knowledge of the Ring, and is finally reduced to bewildered silence. Then all becomes clear to Brynhilde: in a passionate outburst she denounces Siegfried— who is still lost in musing on the Ring—as a "treacherous thief" who stole it from her. All eyes are turned enquiringly on him. No woman gave him the Ring, he says; he won it by his sword at Neidhöhle, where he had slain the Dragon who guarded it.

Hagen steps between them: if this is indeed Brynhilde's Ring, he says, the one that Gunther wrested from her, then it is his by right, and Siegfried took it by craft; and for that the traitor should atone. With frenzied cries of "Betrayed! Shamefully betrayed! Deceit, vile beyond all vengeance!" Brynhilde calls on the Gods above to say if all this was part of their decree—to inflict on her a shame past bearing. If so, then:

> *teach me a vengeance*
> *too dire to be told!*
> *Stir me to wrath*
> *that may never be stilled!*
> *Break in pieces*
> *the heart of Brynhilde,*
> *may but this traitor*
> *taste bitter death!*

Gunther tries in vain to calm her: she calls on them all to witness that she is Siegfried's wife. The unknowing Siegfried in his turn accuses her of falsehood. He had sworn blood-brotherhood with Gunther, and he had been true to his bond, for his good sword Nothung had lain between himself and Gunther's wife. By now Brynhilde has reached breaking-point: no longer mistress of herself, possessed by only one idea, that of vengance, she swears that it is Siegfried who is lying—that on the bridal night the sword had lain in its sheath on the wall while its owner forced her love.

II

This is the explosive spark of the drama. Gunther reproaches Siegfried with having betrayed him: Gutrune implores him to swear that Brynhilde is not speaking truth: the vassals demand that he shall confirm his word with an oath. He accepts the challenge: on whose weapon shall he swear? "On mine", replies Hagen. The vassals form a ring round the pair, and Hagen holds out his spear, on the point of which Siegfried lays two fingers of his right hand, the orchestra thundering out No. 179. Solemnly he swears that he has spoken the truth:

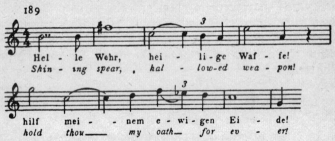

189

Hel - le Wehr, hei - li - ge Waf - fe!
Shin - ing spear, hal - low-ed wea - pon!

hilf mei - nem e - wi - gen Ei - de!
hold thou___ my oath___ for ev - er!

when his hour comes to die, may it be this very spear that deals him his death-stroke if in anything he had betrayed his brother Gunther. Forcing her way through the vassals, the maddened Brynhilde tears his hand away from the spear, seizing the point of it with her own. To the melody of No. 189 she swears an oath like Siegfried's: may the spear-point deal this man death, for he had been false to Gunther and now he has sworn falsehood. The excited vassals call on Donner to break this knot with his thunder. Siegfried, turning to Gunther, bids him take this wild mountain maid—in whose breast some demon or other has instilled his evil craft, so that she now slanders and shames the man who had won her for wife—and lead her back to peace of mind with time and rest. He himself, he thinks, must have played his part ill on the fell, the Tarnhelm having perhaps hidden only half of his face: "but woman's spite is soon at an end, and ere long she will thank thee for having won her through me". The vassals and the women he tells to come to the wedding feast with him and be gay. Light-heartedly he throws his arm round Gutrune and takes her with him into the hall, whither they follow him, carried away by his gaiety.

Only Brynhilde, Gunther and Hagen remain on the stage while the orchestra pours out motive after motive in comment on the situation. The silence is at last broken by Brynhilde, who, speaking more to herself than to the others, asks sombrely what may be the meaning of this mystery. What wizard has stirred up this storm by his craft? Her wisdom fails her: she had parted with all her runes to Siegfried, and now he gaily casts her, sorrowing in her shame, to his friend. "Who now will bring me the sword wherewith I may sever my bonds?" She turns a dull look on Hagen as he approaches her and says, "Trust in me; vengeance I'll wreak on him who betrayed thee!" "On whom?" she asks vacantly. "On Siegfried, the traitor to thee!" She smiles bitterly as she replies:

> One single flash
> of the eye of the hero,
> one glance such as gleamed through the helm,
> shedding glory on me,
> and in fear
> thy hand would falter!

Truth or falsehood, oaths or spears, what will all these avail against the strongest of heroes? Hard indeed will it be to slay Siegfried in combat, Hagen admits; let Brynhilde's wisdom, then, tell him how the hero may fall to his spear. Accompanied by one of the most expressive strains in the whole *Ring,* which Wagner, however, has no occasion to employ later as a regular motive:

Brynhilde laments that every art she knew she had bestowed on him to guard him in battle; and the orchestra gives out sad reminders of the bliss associated with No. 150. But, she recalls, there is one place in which he is vulnerable; knowing he would never turn his back on a foe she had set no spell there. "And there striketh my spear!" says Hagen grimly.

12

Turning quickly to Gunther he urges him to rouse himself to action. For only reply the Gibichung King passionately bewails the deceit that had been practised on him, and calls on his stronger and more crafty brother to help him. Brynhilde taunts him with weakness and cowardice: Hagen insists that

> *no help from brain,*
> *no help from hand,*
> *nought helps but Siegfried's death!*

Gunther recoils in horror: "Blood-brotherhood I swore with him", he cries to the accompaniment of No. 173 in the hoarse tones of the horns. The others goad him on relentlessly to the deed from which he shrinks, and at last Hagen plays the decisive card. Brynhilde's insistence that Siegfried's death alone will glut her vengeance or blot out the guilt of the Gibichung pair who had plotted against her does not move the weak but honourable man; but Hagen wins him over by hinting softly to him that when Siegfried falls the Ring will be his, and with it power beyond his dreams. (The reader will recall that at Gunther's first appearance in the opera he had put to Hagen the question that was evidently always uppermost in his thoughts—"How stands it with my fame? Is the name of Gibich glorious on the Rhine?"; and it was to win the greater fame hinted at by Hagen that he had consented then to the plot for duping Siegfried and beguiling Brynhilde). Sighing deeply, he agrees at last to Siegfried's murder, though he feels he will not be able to face his gentle sister again with her husband's blood on his hands.

At the mention of Gutrune Brynhilde breaks out angrily once more:

> *from depths of despair*
> *it dawns on me now:*
> *Gutrune is the spell*
> *that won my hero from my side.*
> *Woe be to her!*

The cynical Hagen has an answer for Gunther: if Siegfried's death will grieve their sister, she need not be told of the plot; on the morrow they will go hunting, and when they return to the hall their story to her will be that the hero has been slain by a boar. "So shall it be", they decide in a final great trio, in which Brynhilde and Gunther invoke the aid of Wotan, as "oath-witness and ward of vows", in the accomplishment of their vengeance on the traitor, while Hagen exultantly invokes his father Alberich: "So let him die, this hero fair; mine shall be the Hoard and the Ring. Alberich, my father, fallen prince! Warder of darkness! Nibelung lord! Soon shalt thou summon the Nibelung host again to bow down before thee, the Ring's master and theirs!"

As Gunther and Brynhilde turn vehemently to the hall they are greeted by a bridal procession, with boys and maidens waving flower-staves and Siegfried borne by the men on a shield and Gutrune by the women on a chair. Siegfried and the vassals blow a wedding summons on their horns. Vassals and maids are seen on the heights in the background, making their way with sacrificial beasts to the altar stones of the Gods, which they deck with flowers. The innocent Gutrune beckons with a friendly smile to Brynhilde, who at first stares at her blankly and then makes as if to step back; but at a sign from Hagen Gunther seizes her, whereupon he himself is raised by the men on a shield; and to a combination of motives in the orchestra, in which that of Gutrune predominates, only to be ousted at the end by that of Hagen, the procession moves towards the heights, and the curtain falls.

13

To the tension of the tremendous second act succeeds a gracious woodland idyll.

In the orchestral prelude to the third act we hear first of all, from behind the scenes, the horn call of Siegfried, which is answered by the cow-horns of the hunting Gibichungs in the further distance. Next there is a hint of the gently flowing Rhine (No. 2) and a suggestion of the song of the Rhinemaidens (No. 7), with once more a reminder that Siegfried is not far away. Then the orchestra settles down to the elaboration of two new motives to be associated with the Rhinemaidens:

and:

The curtain rises on a wild, wooded, rocky valley by the Rhine, which flows past a steep cliff in the background. Woglinde, Wellgunde and Flosshilde rise to the surface of the water and swim around as if circling in a dance, singing, to the strains of Nos. 190 and 191, a song the sweetness of which is tinged with sadness: no longer, they say, does the Rhine's lustre match that of the sunlight playing on the waves, as it did in the days when the glittering Gold was safe in their keeping. They pause and listen to another horn call in the distance, and their hearts revive a little: will the hero come soon who shall restore the Gold to the waters?

Once more Siegfried's call peals out. "The hero nighs", they say; and they dive swiftly to take counsel with each other.

Siegfried appears on the cliff, fully armed, wondering how he came to lose the track of his fellow-hunters and of the game. The Rhinedaughters rise to the surface again and greet him, tease him over his mishap, and exhort him to tell them all. If it was they, he answers good-humouredly, who had lured to their lair the shaggy brute he was pursuing he wishes them joy of their lover. They laugh loudly. What will he give them, they ask, if they yield him his quarry? Hands so empty as his are today will grant them anything, he replies. They ask for the golden Ring that gleams on his finger, but this he refuses: to win it he had slain a Dragon grim, and shall he now part with it for a paltry bear-skin? Besides, he adds gaily:

> *if my goods in the water I fling,*
> *I fear me my wife will scold.*

They banter him on his miserliness and his fear of his wife. "She beats thee, then, perchance?" says Wellgunde. "The hero feels the weight of her hand!" adds Woglinde. Let them deride him to their hearts' content, says Siegfried, but the Ring shall never be theirs. Still laughing at him—"So fair! so strong! So meet for love! Alas, that he's so niggard!"—they dive below the waters again.

Stung by their gibes he descends from the cliff, calls to them to come back, and offers to give them the Ring, which he draws from his finger and holds aloft. When they reappear they are changed beings, grave and solemn. Let him keep the Ring, they say, until he has learned what ill-fate clings to it: fain enough will he be then to be freed by them from the curse on it. Replacing the Ring on his finger he quietly asks them to tell him what they know.

Three times they address him warningly by his name:

Then they tell him the history of the Ring and the doom of death that lies, through the Curse, upon all who acquire it. As he slew the Dragon, so he himself shall be slain that very day unless he gives it back to the waters that alone can wash out the Curse. He replies that as he was not tricked by their fawning, so now he is not frightened by their threats. To a repetition of No. 193 they warn him once more: there is no escape from the Curse, which is woven by the Norns into the rope of time and fate. With the Sword that had once shattered a Spear, Siegfried answers, he will cut through even that rope, for fear he has never learned. In the Ring, he knows, lies all the world's wealth: he would give it for the grace and joy of love, but not under the threat of his life; this he values no more than the clod of earth which he picks up and throws behind him.

Swimming in wide circles close to the shore the Rhinemaidens excitedly urge each other to leave this madman, who, deeming himself strong and wise, is bound and blind. Oaths, they say, he had plighted and heeded them not; runes he sees and reads them not; a glorious gift [Brynhilde] had been his, and in his ignorance he had spurned it; but the Ring that will deal him death he will not surrender! This very day a woman proud will inherit his treasure and work their will better than they themselves can do; let him go now to her. They swim away to the background, singing their "Weialala, leia" to the strain of No. 191 and No. 192. As they disappear from his sight he philosophises on them after his fashion: women's ways, on land and sea, he has learned; the man who is deaf to their fawning they seek to frighten with threats, and if he smiles at these they give him the sharp edge of their tongue. And yet he had liked these three, and had not Gutrune his troth he would have sought the love of one of them.

14

As the music of the Rhinedaughters dies away in the distance horns are heard, and Siegfried, starting out of the reverie into which he has fallen, answers them with his own horn call. The off-stage voices of the vassals hail him, and soon Hagen and Gunther enter, followed gradually by the vassals: here, says Hagen, they will rest and make a meal. The game is piled in a heap, wine-skins and drinking-horns are produced, and all lie down. Hagen asks Siegfried how it had fared with his hunting since they had lost sight of him, and laughingly he tells them that his luck had been out: no wood-game had he brought down, and only three young water-fowl had he seen who had sung to him from the Rhine a warning that that day he would be slain. Gunther starts at this and looks darkly at Hagen, and the sinister outline of the Covenant of Vengeance motive unwinds its dark coils in the depths of the orchestra:

"A grievous chase that would be", says the grim Hagen, with a double meaning that only Gunther understands, "for the lurking beast he hunts to slay the hapless hunter!" Siegfried says he is thirsty, and as Hagen hands him a drinking-horn he has filled for him he asks him if there is any truth in the tale that he understands the song of birds. It is long since he listened to their chatter, Siegfried replies, and he offers the drinking-horn to Gunther, who looks thoughtfully and sadly into it and mutters gloomily:

> *the draught is dull and blanched:*
> *thy blood alone is there!*

while once more the orchestra gives out a mutation of the ominous No. 194. Siegfried's generous heart overflows with tenderness for this unhappy blood-brother of his; and while Gunther can only ejaculate mournfully, "Thou over-joyous hero!" he pours the wine from Gunther's horn into his own, and asks Hagen if perchance the King is still grieving over the hurt dealt him by Brynhilde. Step by artful step Hagen brings Siegfried to sing them, for the heartening of Gunther, tales of his boyhood and its wonders; and sitting upright while the others recline around him he begins his story.

To the appropriate motives at each stage he tells of his being brought up and taught by Mime for the dwarf's own ends, how he had forged the sword Nothung and slain the Dragon, learned from the taste of its blood how to understand the song of the birds, taken from the cave the Tarnhelm and the Ring, and killed the treacherous Mime. As Siegfried pauses for a while Hagen fills another horn with wine, into which he drops the juice of a herb; then he hands it to Siegfried, saying that the spiced draught will revive his memories of things forgotten. The hero looks thoughtfully into the horn, drinks slowly, and takes up his story again. He tells how the wood bird had sung to him of the bride awaiting him on the fell; and Gunther listens with growing astonishment as he goes on to tell how he had broken through the fire and found the sleeping Brynhilde, wakened her with a kiss, and been folded in her arms. Gunther, enlightened at last, springs up in horror. Two ravens, Wotan's messengers of death, fly up out of a bush, circle over Siegfried, and then take their course to the Rhine. "Canst thou read me those ravens' runes?" Hagen asks Siegfried; and as the hero rises to his feet and gazes after them, thus facing away from Hagen, the latter drives his spear into his back, saying, "Vengeance they cry to me!"

Gunther strikes Hagen—too late—on the arm. With a last mighty effort Siegfried swings his shield aloft with both hands to crush his murderer; but his strength fails him, the shield drops behind him, and he himself falls on it with a crash, while the orchestra throws its full weight into a motive that will shortly become the binding element of Siegfried's Funeral March (No. 195). The horrified Gunther and some of the vassals ask, "Hagen, what deed is this?" "Vengeance for a false oath!" he replies. He turns away and goes out alone, slowly striding away in the twilight that had begun to fall at the appearance of the ravens. The vassals, filled with sympathy, stand round the dying man: Gunther, griefstricken, bends down over him.

Supported in a sitting position by two of the vassals, Siegfried opens his eyes. His memory now fully restored, he hails "Brynhilde, holiest bride!" to the strains that had accompanied her

awakening in the final scene of *Siegfried* (No. 148). He remembers
every episode of that slow ecstatic wakening, and the orchestra
recreates them all for us with reminiscences of Nos. 149 and 150.
But the Death motive (No. 83) throws its shadow over his
darkening mind: he sinks back, dead. By now night has fallen. At
a silent command from Gunther the sorrowing vassals raise the
body and carry it in solemn procession over the rocky height,
Gunther walking by its side.

15

There follows the impressive Funeral March, during which the
mourning train slowly passes out of sight, the moon breaking
through the clouds and for a moment illuminating it as it reaches
the summit of the height; then mists come up from the Rhine and
gradually wrap the scene in complete darkness. The March begins
with the solemn theme of the mourning cortège:

and then passes in slow review a number of motives associated
with the hero—that of the Volsung race (No. 58), those of
Sieglinde's compassion and love for Siegmund (Nos. 51 and 52),
that of the Sword (No. 48), that of Siegfried (No. 88), that of
the horn call that had symbolised him in the lustiness of his youth
(No. 108, now in broad heroic form), and that of Brynhilde as we
saw her at the opening of the *Twilight of the Gods* (No. 158)—all
woven into one great threnody, through which No. 195 runs at
this point or that like a dark connecting thread.

As the last echo of No. 108 dies away and the minor second
familiar to us since its first definite appearance in No. 33 wails out
once more, the curtain rises again, revealing the hall of the
Gibichungs as in the first act. It is night, with the moonlight reflected in the Rhine. To a melancholy re-statement of her motive
Gutrune appears, coming out from her chamber into the hall.
Dreams of evil, in which she had heard the neighing of Siegfried's

horse and the laughter of Brynhilde, had driven sleep from her; now she believes she hears Siegfried's horn, and she listens intently. She has seen a woman go silently towards the Rhine: was it Brynhilde? "I dread this Brynhilde", she says to herself. She goes to the inner room on the right, looks into it timidly, and calls to Brynhilde; but the room is empty. "Were my Siegfried but here!" she sighs. She turns to go to her own room again, but hearing Hagen's voice without she stands petrified with fear.

As the orchestra gives out again the figures shewn in No. 194 Hagen is heard outside, hailing the sleeping household with his hoarse "Hoiho!" and bidding it waken and come with torches, for he brings home a fine booty. Entering the hall he greets Gutrune with boisterous jocularity: "Up, Gutrune, to greet thy Siegfried! The hero strong has come home again." "I heard not his horn", says Gutrune in terror. The savage Hagen replies:

> *his bloodless mouth*
> *will blow it no more;*
> *to hunt or to fight*
> *no more will he fare,*
> *nor woo winsome women to love him.*

A crowd of men and women with lights and firebrands enters confusedly, together with a procession bearing the body of Siegfried on a bier: Gunther is among them. The body is set down on a hastily raised mound in the centre of the hall; and Hagen tells the distracted crowd that Siegfried has been slain by a wild boar. Amid the general agitation Gutrune falls on the body with a shriek, and Gunther tries to comfort her. Recovering herself she repulses him violently, crying out that he has treacherously murdered her husband. "Not I, but Hagen", he tells her; "he was the accursed boar who dealt the hero his death"; and he pours out reproaches on him.

Hagen steps forward defiantly. Yes, it was he, he tells them all, who sent Siegfried to his doom with the very spear on which he had sworn a false oath: hunter's right is now his, and for his spoil he claims the Ring. A quarrel ensues between him and Gunther: claiming "the Nibelung dower for the Nibelung's son", Hagen rushes at his brother and strikes him dead with his sword. Then he grasps at Siegfried's hand, which raises itself threateningly. Gutrune and the women shriek with horror: the vassals draw back, appalled.[1]

16

The clamour subsides to a pianissimo as the motive (No. 44) of that Doom of the Gods that had been foretold by Erda in the *Rhinegold* makes its way downwards in the orchestra and Brynhilde comes forward from the background, slowly and solemnly. The remainder of the great drama now passes entirely into her hands. Sternly, to the accompaniment of Nos. 2 and 44—the antithetical ascent and descent of which seem to hold together and epitomise the two great opposing principles of the *Ring*, the birth of things and the end of things—she bids them all cease their wailing of woe, for the woman they had all betrayed had come for the vengeance due to her—a different vengeance, however, from the one she had had in her heart in the second act, for now illumination has come to her. She hears them crying, she tells them, like children for their mother when sweet milk has been spilled; but not a sound of lament has she heard befitting the noblest of heroes. Gutrune, raising herself from the ground, cries out on her passionately:

> *Brynhilde! Black with envy!*
> *Thou broughtest this bane on us all:*
> *thy tongue did goad the men against him:*
> *woe the day when here thou cam'st!*

Calmly Brynhilde waves her aside: *she* was not Siegfried's true wife, only his light-o'-love: "his troth he had plighted to me ere

[1] This was the greatest difficulty of all that confronted Wagner in the construction of his drama: as Siegfried is now dead, what is to stop Hagen from taking the Ring? Wagner probably took a hint for the solution of his problem from a passage in the *Deutsche Mythologie* of the brothers Grimm, which tells of a figure of one Thorgeror höhgabrûor, which had rings of gold round its arm, before which the people knelt: when anyone tried to snatch a ring from the arm and the goddess was not disposed to let him have it, the figure bent its hand upward. The man would then bring a lot of money, lay it at the figure's feet, fall on his knees and shed tears, then rise and grasp again at the ring, which the figure would now allow him to take.

ever thy face he saw". The poor gentle Gutrune, who has unconsciously helped to weave the net in which she and all of them had been caught by Hagen, turns with curses on him:

> *Ah, sorrow!*
> *The truth I see now!*
> *Brynhild' was his true love*
> *whom through the draught he forgot!*

In grief and shame she turns away from Siegfried and bends over Gunther's body; from now to near the end of the opera she remains motionless. Hagen, standing defiantly apart from the others, leaning on his spear and shield, is sunk in sombre brooding.

Disregarding alike the lamentations of Gutrune and the truculence of Hagen, Brynhilde stands alone in the centre of the stage whiie the orchestra begins a pæan to the dead hero, into which, as will be seen, is inwrought a reference to the majesty of the Gods:

Lost in sorrowful memories she gazes for a moment at the body of Siegfried, then turns in solemn exaltation to the vassals and the women. They are to pile up mighty logs by the river side for a pyre for the hero and kindle a fire to consume him; her horse Grane they are to bring to her that he may share her reunion with his master. They build up the pyre in front of the hall, close to the Rhine, and the women are to strew it with flowers.

A great sweetness transfigures Brynhilde's face as she sings the last praises of the hero she had lost. He was like glorious sunshine, she says: he betrayed, yet he was true: his wife he beguiled, but between them lay his sword. How came the truest of men to play the traitor? She herself gives the answer: the Gods it was, and Wotan foremost among them, who had brought on him and her this woe. "Turn now your eyes on my grievous distress", she adjures them, "and on your own eternal guilt!" The wish of Wotan's heart he had laid on Siegfried, to escape the Curse that was consuming him; and all-unwitting the hero had done the God's will, "that wise a woman might grow". Now her eyes see clear to the heart of it all. The ravens rustle about her; she sends them to Walhall with the tidings Wotan fears yet hopes for; and with a great pity in her great heart she murmurs "Rest thou, rest thou, O God!"

17

At a sign from her the vassals lift the body on to the pyre, to the strains of No. 196. She takes the Ring from Siegfried's finger and gazes at it meditatively. Her heritage has come to her again, she says: the terrible Ring, the accursed Gold, had come to her once, and now from her they shall go. Apostrophising the Rhinedaughters, she promises them the Ring again that had been stolen from them:

> what ye desire
> I give you now:
> win from my ashes
> all ye have wept for!
> The fire that burns me with him
> cleanses the Ring from its curse!
> Ye in the flood
> wash it away,
> and ever the gleaming
> Gold keep pure,
> that once ye lost to your bane!

She puts the Ring on her own finger, turns to the pyre, and takes a firebrand from one of the men. "Fly home, ye ravens", she cries: "take to Wotan the tale of what ye have heard here on the Rhine. But go first to Brynhilde's rock, where Loge flames: bid him haste

to Walhall, for the end of the Gods is nigh. So—cast I the brand
on Walhall's glittering towers!"

She hurls the firebrand into the pile, which breaks into bright
flames, while two ravens fly up from the rock by the shore and
disappear in the background. Brynhilde turns to greet her horse,
which two of the younger men have now led forward. Quickly un-
bridling him, she addresses him in loving, intimate words. Does he
know whither they two are faring? she asks him, as the motive of
Redemption by Love, (No. 89) steals in softly in the orchestra:

(The Siegfried motive combines with it in the second and third
bars). Motive succeeds motive as she tells Grane that there, in the
heart of the fire, lies his master and her lord, Siegfried the hero;
does he not chafe to join him? No. 197 grows into a richer and
richer tissue as she sings of her own rapture as already she feels
the flames leaping about her heart:

> *Siegfried enfolding,*
> *held fast in his arms,*
> *in love unending*
> *made one with mine own!*
> *Heiajaho! Grane!*
> *Go we to greet him!*
> *Siegfried! Siegfried! See!*
> *Brynhilde greets thee in bliss!*

Mounting the horse, she urges him with a single leap into the
burning pile, round which Loge's fire is now raging fiercely.

The horrified vassals and women recoil to the foreground of
the stage, the whole space of which now seems filled with fire.
But suddenly the glow dies down, leaving only a cloud of smoke
which drifts off slowly towards the background, where it over-

hangs the horizon like a dark cloud-bank; at the same time the Rhine swells mightily, rolling in a flood over the fire; and where the flames had been we now see the three Rhinemaidens swimming. Hagen, who all this while has been watching Brynhilde with growing anxiety, is filled with terror at the sight of them: hastily ridding himself of spear, shield and helmet he plunges madly into the flood in pursuit of the Ring; Woglinde and Wellgunde throw their arms around his neck and drag him into the depths as they swim away, while Flosshilde, leading her sisters, holds the recovered Ring exultantly aloft.

Their gracious song is heard in the orchestra, followed by a broad statement of the Walhall motive as a red glow breaks through the cloud-bank, while in the now calmer waters of the Rhine, which has gradually fallen to its normal level, the Rhinemaidens are seen swimming in joyous circles, sporting with the Ring; and now their song blends contrapuntally with No. 197 as the men and women gaze, from the ruins of the fallen hall, at a fire-glow that slowly spreads over the sky. The Walhall motive combines in great masses of tone with that of the majesty of the Gods (No. 196) as the interior of Walhall comes into view, as Waltraute had described it to Brynhilde in the first act, with Wotan sitting mute and grave among the Gods and heroes with his shattered Spear in his hand, all of them waiting in resignation for the end that had been foretold. Flames seize upon Walhall and hide the Gods from our sight as the motive of the Downfall of the Gods (No. 44) comes crashing down in the orchestra. Then comes one of Wagner's most magical strokes: after all this racking turmoil the last word is given to the great theme of Redemption by Love (No. 197), which seems to spread consoling wings over not merely the present scene but the whole stupendous drama:

198 *Sostenuto*

We have seen, in our preliminary study of Wagner's Prose Sketches and poems, the changes the original plan for the ending of the *Ring* drama underwent; from a dénouement in which Siegfried's death and the redeeming deed of Brynhilde's self-sacrifice had effected the firm establishment of the beneficent rule of the Gods, he gradually arrived at an ending in which the Gods pass away in the flames that consume Walhall—"the Gods' great ending dawneth at last".

His conception of the inner meaning of his drama had undergone a drastic change as early as the Spring of 1851, when he put the following final words into Brynhilde's mouth: "Powerless depart, ye whose guilt is forgone. From your guilt sprang the joyfullest of heroes, whose free deed has redeemed it: spared are ye the anxious conflict for your ending power: pass away in bliss before the human hero whom ye begat. I proclaim to you blessed death-redemption from your anxious fear."

But the actual verbal conclusion of the tetralogy and the previous motivation of it remained a perpetual problem for him. One evidence of his confusion is plainly visible in the present *Rhinegold* poem, where Erda warns Wotan to yield the Ring, because if he keeps it:

> *Nought but ruin*
> *and disaster*
> *will it bring to thee!*

.   .   .   .   .

> *A day of gloom*
> *dawns for your godhood;*
> *I charge thee, give up the Ring!*

This implies, surely, that *if* Wotan surrenders it he will avert the doom; yet in the end he and all the Gods of the old order go down in doom in spite of the renunciation! Wagner's friend August Röckel, to whom he had sent a copy of the imprint of 1853, struck at once to the heart of the matter with the commonsense query, "Why, seeing that the Gold is returned to the Rhine, is it necessary for the Gods to perish?" Wagner's involved reply suggests that he himself could not logically justify that dénouement in words but hoped that it would all explain itself to the listener through the medium of his *feeling*—through the intervention of the music.

In 1856 he made a sketch (published for the first time in 1933) for yet another ending; and shortly afterwards we find him telling a correspondent that he had decided not to bring out a public edition of the poem until after he had set it all to music: "not unanticipated changes in the concluding parts are impending", for "it has become clear to me that the poem has travelled far beyond its original schematic tendency, as still retained in the present ending . . . Of course the result remains essentially the same; only the explanation put into the mouth of the all-knowing Brynhilde becomes something different, wider-reaching, more decisive . . ."

He cast this new "explanation" into verse but never set it to music. In the 1872 definitive edition of the poem, however, he printed it all in a footnote to the present text for the scene, with a curious commentary. "Before the musical working-out of the poem the following lines were given to Brynhilde" at the point where she turns towards the background and takes a torch from one of the bystanders. Wagner quotes thirty lines of verse, the last ten of which run thus in Alfred Forman's translation:

> *Not goods, nor gold,*
> *nor greatness of Gods;*
> *not house, nor land;*
> *nor lordly life;*
> *not burdensome bargains'*
> *treacherous bands,*
> *nor wont with the lying*
> *weight of its law;*
> *happy, in luck or need,*
> *holds you nothing but love.*

Then Wagner continues thus: "In these lines the poet had tried to express the musical effect of the drama anticipatorily, in a sententious sense; but in the course of the long interruptions that held him up in the composition of his music he was impelled towards another version of the final words of farewell that corresponded still better to this idea: these lines ran as follows" . . . and he goes on to quote a further twenty lines of explanation by Brynhilde, ending thus: "Know ye how I won to the blessed end of all things eternal? Deepest distress of grieving love opened my eyes; I saw the world end." To them he appended the following remark: "The musician had in the end, in the act of composition, to sacrifice these lines, as the sense of them is fully expressed by the agency of the *musical* drama."

Wagner's words are difficult to translate, but in the light of all we now know of the matter his general meaning is clear: he relied on his music, as he had said to Röckel, to convey to the *feeling* of the listener what the poet in him had found it almost impossible to express in words. His dilemma is the most curious phenomenon of its kind in the whole history of art. As we have seen, it is unnecessary to drag in the political events of the early 1850's to account for his veering round, about that time, from an "optimistic" to a "pessimistic" interpretation of the fundamental meaning of his *Ring* drama. The cause of it all was internal, and, strange to say, *musical*. The poet in him was pulling him one way, the musician another. The man of feeling in him, as distinct from the man of intellect, was being quietly, subconsciously, but irresistibly drawn towards a dénouement in which the world should go down in outer ruin yet somehow be taken up into the arms of a redeeming love. This he could convey, and has conveyed magnificently, in his music to the closing scene; but how to express it in words was a problem that always baffled and finally defeated him.[1]

[1] For a more detailed statement of the vicissitudes of his thought during those many years, together with quotations of the relevant texts, I must refer the reader to my *Life of Wagner*, Vol. II, chapter 17.

PARSIFAL

PRINCIPAL CHARACTERS

AMFORTAS	*Baritone*
TITUREL	*Bass*
GURNEMANZ	*Bass*
PARSIFAL	*Tenor*
KLINGSOR	*Bass*
KUNDRY	*Soprano*

Wagner's description of the Scene of the Action:

In the territory and the castle of the Knights of the Grail, Monsalvat. The scenery is in the style of the northern mountain ranges of Gothic Spain. Klingsor's magic castle is on the southern slope of this range, fronting Arabic Spain.

I

If at any performance of *Parsifal* we were to ask the first man we ran into during an interval what the Grail was, he would almost certainly reply in much the same words as those of Wagner when, in 1865, he was giving King Ludwig II of Bavaria the ground plan of the opera he hoped some day to write: "The Grail is the crystal Cup from which the Redeemer and His disciples drank at the Last Supper; Joseph of Arimathea caught in it the blood that flowed from the spear-wound in His side when He was on the Cross. For a long time it was mysteriously withdrawn from the sinful world and preserved as the holiest of relics. Then, at a time when the world was harsh and hostile and the faithful were hard pressed by the unbelieving and were in great distress, there sprang up in certain divinely inspired heroes, filled with holy love-longing, the desire to seek out this strengthening relic of which tradition spoke, in which the blood of the Saviour (*sangue réale*, whence San Greal, Sanct Gral, the Holy Grail) had been preserved and was divinely potent for a humanity in dire need of salvation. The relic was supernaturally revealed to Titurel and his faithful band and given over into their keeping. He gathered about him a holy company of knights for the service of the Grail, and in a wild inaccessible forest in the mountains he built the castle of Monsalvat, which no man could discover unless he had proved himself worthy to have care of the Grail." And so on, with certain other details which we shall consider in due time.

If our interlocutor were a scholar versed in mediæval literature, however, he would tell us a great deal more than this, and something very different from it here and there. He would outline for us first of all the story of Parsifal and the Grail as it is told by the old German poet, Wolfram von Eschenbach, from whom Wagner primarily derived his inspiration; and we would then discover that there was nothing whatever in that story associating the Grail with the traditional Cup of the Last Supper, or with the blood of the Saviour on the Cross, or with Joseph of Arimathea, or, indeed, any conception even of the Grail as a chalice.

But this would not be all. Our first mentor, in reply to our request for information about the spear that plays so large a part in the opera, would tell us that it was the weapon with which the Roman soldier Longinus had pierced the side of the Saviour on the Cross. But the scholar would assure us that not only had Wolfram no such notion as this of the spear that figures in his story of Parsifal and the Grail, but a sacred spear was not even a feature of Wagner's original plan for an opera on the Parsifal subject. He had been brooding on the theme at least as early as 1857, but it is clear from his letters of that period to Mathilde Wesendonk that as yet he had no notion of introducing what may be called, for convenience' sake, the Longinus motive; Wagner's Amfortas has indeed been grievously wounded by a spear, but it is not yet, for Wagner, *that* spear. Even when he sat down to write the above-mentioned Sketch for King Ludwig in 1865 he appears to have had no thought of making the spear identical with that of Calvary. In his account of the tragic adventure of Amfortas in Klingsor's garden he merely says that, "turning to flee, he [Amfortas] received the spear-wound in his side from which he now suffers and for which no healing can be found". A little later in the Sketch, at the point in the first act where Amfortas is bewailing his sin and its consequences for not only himself but the brethren of the Grail,

Wagner says that once more the wound begins to bleed, "the selfsame wound received by the Redeemer on the Cross and through which He poured out His blood in love and compassion for wretched sinful man". Even in this, however, there is still no hint of any conception on Wagner's part of the wound having been inflicted on Amfortas by the very spear that had pierced the Saviour. In the opera poem as we now have it the words which Wagner puts into Amfortas's mouth at this point are these:

> *In maddest tumult, by sin defiled,*
> *my blood back on itself*
> *doth turn and rage within me;*
> *to the world where sin is lord*
> *in frenzied fear is it surging:*
> *again it forces the door,*
> *in torrents it poureth forth,*
> *here through the spear-wound, alike to His,*
> *and dealt me by the selfsame deadly spear*
> *that once the Redeemer pierced with pain,*
> *and, tears of blood outpouring,*
> *the Holy One wept for the shame of man,*
> *in pity's godlike yearning.*

This agrees with the corresponding passage in the Sketch of 1865 in every respect[1] but one: there is nothing in the Sketch answering to the line in the poem "and dealt me by the selfsame spear".

2

Is it likely we ask ourselves, that Wagner would have omitted so vital a motive from his very detailed epitome of 1865 of the first act had it been present in his mind at that time? It was

---

[1] Even down to verbal parallelisms: for instance, the "sprengt die Wunde von Neuem und ergiesst sich in die Welt der Sünde" of the Sketch links up with the "in die Welt der Sündensucht mit wilder Scheu sich ergiessen" of the poem; and the "durch dieselbe Wunde, wie sie einst der Erlöser am Kreuze empfing" of the former with the "hier durch die Wunde, der seinem gleich . . . der dort dem Erlöser die Wunde stach" of the latter.

probably on the 29th August that he put the plan for the second act on paper. He outlined the final episode of that act thus: "Klingsor appears on the tower of his castle. Armed men rush in. Parsifal recognises the spear with which Amfortas had been wounded and wrests it from the Knight [Klingsor]. 'With this sign I exorcise you all! As the wound once dealt by this spearpoint closes, so let everything here pass away, and its splendour crash in ruins'. He swings the spear: the castle collapses with a frightful crash: the garden withers to a desert." But between "the spear with which Amfortas had been wounded" and "wrests it from the knight" there is added (in parentheses in the printed version), "it is the spear with which Longinus had once wounded the Redeemer in the side, and of which, as a very valuable means to magic, Klingsor had possessed himself". Apparently, then, Wagner had had no intention, until he inserted that parenthesis, of identifying the spear that had once wounded Amfortas, the spear now launched by Klingsor at Parsifal and seized by the boy in mid-air, with the very Spear that had been thrust in the Saviour's side.

And that even yet he had no clear perception of the bearing this new interpretation would have on his future drama is shown by a little phrase near the end of the Sketch. When Parsifal, returned from his wanderings, encounters Gurnemanz and is reproached by him for bearing arms on Good Friday, he stands silent for a moment: "then he opens his helmet, removes it from his head, strikes the spear into the ground, lays down his shield and his sword before it, sinks to his knees, and prays earnestly with his eyes fixed fervently on the bleeding spearpoint". Why "bleeding"? we naturally ask ourselves. In Wolfram von Eschenbach, as we shall see shortly, the spear that is carried into the hall of the Grail has indeed a trickle of blood running down the shaft, but in Wolfram neither is the Grail the Cup of the Last Supper and the Cross, nor is there the smallest identification of the spear with that of the Crucifixion. Clearly by the time Wagner had arrived at the final stage of his Sketch of 1865 he had had an intuition that he must combine Wolfram's account of the ceremonial in the hall of the Grail with the story, stemming from another source, of the spear of the legendary Longinus. The possible significance of the "bleeding" lance was beginning to dawn upon him, and so possessed is he with it that he now describes the spear as "bleeding" when Parsifal thrusts it into the ground, though there has been no suggestion of any such property in it in his preceding references to it in the scene in Klingsor's garden. In his final poem—written years later—the spear does not bleed at any point of the drama; Wagner, indeed, conscious later that there would be no sense in characterising it in that way, omits the "bleeding" of the passage just quoted from the Sketch from the stage directions for the Good Friday scene with Gurnemanz in the opera: Parsifal now simply "thrusts the spear into the ground before him" and "kneels before it in silent prayer". Nor in the crucial moment in the final scene, in which Parsifal heals Amfortas with a touch of the spear, is there any suggestion, either in the text or in the stage directions, that it is "bleeding".

Wagner's difficulty apparently came from his having felt that the bleeding lance of the scene in the hall of the Grail in Wolfram's poem (to which we shall come shortly) must necessarily have some sort of connection with the lance of the Longinus legend, whereas there is no connection at all between the two. His perplexity over the matter is shown by a jotting of the 2nd September 1865 in his diary:

"How am I to deal with the bleeding lance? The poem [i.e. Wolfram's] says that the lance was carried [into the hall] at the same time as the Grail, and that there was a drop of blood on the point of it. Moreover, Amfortas's wound has been dealt by this lance-point. But how does this hang together? There is great confusion here: the lance is a relic that accompanies the vessel in which is preserved the blood drawn by the lance-point from the Saviour's side.[1] The two are complementary. Therefore, one of two alternatives:

"The lance was given into the charge of the brotherhood at the same time as the Grail, and in times of great distress was borne in combat by the guardian of the Grail. Amfortas, in order to overcome the magic of Klingsor, which is so ruinous to the brother-

[1] The "confusion", however, was Wagner's own; it came from his reading into the Wolfram epic something that was never in the poet's mind.

hood, has taken it from the altar and gone out with it to fight the arch-enemy. When he succumbed to seduction, and shield and spear fell from his hands, the holy weapon was used against him, and he was wounded by it as he turned to flee. (Perhaps Klingsor, because he wants to have Amfortas in his power alive, orders him to be wounded by the lance, as he knows that this wounds but does not kill—Why?). Consequently the healing and redemption of Amfortas are possible only when the lance is rescued from unholy hands and placed with the Grail again.—Or:

"When the Grail was given to the knights the lance also was promised them; but it must first be won in hard fights. Were it once lodged with the Grail the knights could no more be assailed by temptation. Klingsor has found the lance, and preserves it partly because of its great magical virtue—for it is capable of wounding even the holiest if there is a trace of a failing in him—partly to deprive the Grail brotherhood of it, as the possession of it would make them invincible. Amfortas has sallied forth to take the lance from Klingsor; succumbing to the seduction of love he is wounded by it when Klingsor hurls it at him.—The outcome remains the same: it must come back into the possession of the knights.—Klingsor hurls the spear at Parsifal, who grasps it; he has heard of it and knows its magic, its significance."

As we know, the first of these alternatives was the one ultimately adopted by Wagner.

But this was only one of the many difficulties he had to overcome before he could shape Wolfram's poem into the opera as we now have it. Let us follow him step by step over the years of the creation of *Parsifal*; and first of all we must survey the story as he found it in the old poets.

3

We must begin our investigation of the story of Parsifal and the Grail with a poem by a French author, Crestien de Troyes, entitled *Li Contes del Graal*, which was written about 1180. (It is impossible to say to what extent Crestien constructed his poem out of legends or written sources already current: scholars are not agreed on this point). In one episode of the poem the young knight Perceval[1] arrives at a castle in which is an old king who, by reason of sickness, cannot rise from his couch. Four hundred knights are with him in the hall. The boy has previously been schooled in courtesy by a certain old knight named Gornemans, who has warned him against asking unnecessary questions: accordingly, though lost in wonder, he remains silent when a strange scene is enacted before his eyes. A squire passes through the hall in front of the couch, from one side-room to another, bearing a lance down the shaft of which runs a trickle of blood.[2] Two other squires follow with lighted candles and take the same course as the first; after them comes a maiden carrying a "graal" of pure gold, set with precious stones, which emits a dazzling light. Supper is served, and at each course the graal is borne across the room. Curious as he is about it all, Perceval refrains from asking the meaning of what he sees, but resolves to do so on the morrow.

When he rises the next morning, however, he finds his horse and armour placed ready for him but no sign of life in the castle. He rides away in sore perplexity. Soon he meets with a lady who learns from him that he has been in the castle and seen the lance and the graal but has asked no question concerning them. For this she upbraids him: had he thought to do so, she tells him, the sick king would have been healed and misfortune averted from the land. Later he encounters another woman, hideous of aspect and riding on a grotesque yellow mule—the "Loathly Damsel" of some versions of the tale: she too reproaches him violently for his failure to ask the question, as a consequence of which the sick king will continue to suffer, wars will break out, many knights will be slain, and the land will be laid waste; and the guilt for it all will be on Perceval's head.

[1] The spelling of proper names in the following pages—Parzival, Perceval, Parsifal; Cundrie, Kundry; Klingsor, Clinschor; Anfortas, Amfortas; Gornemans, Gurnemanz; Graal, Grail, etc.—conforms in general to that of the mediaeval work under discussion at the moment. Wagner himself hesitated for many years between "Parzival", "Percival" and "Parsifal", and only decided on this last in 1877.

[2] There is also a mysterious sword which plays a considerable part in the story. We need not concern ourselves with this, however, as that particular motive was not utilised by Wagner.

The boy, oppressed with a vague wonder, goes on his way in deepest sorrow, vowing never to rest until he has solved this fateful mystery of graal and lance. After years of wandering he finds himself in the company of some penitents who chide him for bearing arms on that day of all days: does he not know, they ask him, that it is Good Friday morning? They direct him to a hermit who turns out to be his uncle on his mother's side: the sick king, it appears, is also his uncle, and his grandfather—the father of the hermit and the king—has sustained life for the last twenty years by virtue solely of the Host contained in the graal. Perceval learns also that he lies under the sin of having unwittingly caused his loving mother's death; it was for that reason that it had not been given to him to ask concerning the spear and the graal. The hermit shrives him, and the twain partake of the eucharist. Crestien's tale ends, so far as the adventures of the hero concern us here, at this point; he died leaving his work unfinished.

4

Passing over, as irrelevant to our enquiry, two or three later re-tellings of part of Crestien's story, with several new inventions, we arrive at the actual main source of Wagner's drama, the masterpiece of German mediaeval poetry, the *Parzival* of Wolfram von Eschenbach, written in the early years of the thirteenth century. Crestien had told his readers that he derived his story from a certain book belonging to Count Philip of Flanders. Of this book nothing is now known. Wolfram, in his turn, seems anxious not to come under the suspicion that he derives from Crestien. He names as his source one "Kyot the Provençal", who, according to him, has alone told "the true story"; Crestien had told it wrongly, for which Kyot "would have been wrathful with him". Of this Kyot, however, we know nothing. (Attempts were made at one time to identify him with the poet Guiot de Provins, but this theory has been abandoned). In the main Wolfram agrees with Crestien so far as the latter's tale of Perceval and the graal extends; but whether he derived his incidents and took over his motives from his French predecessor, or both of them built upon a common foundation that has now disappeared, is a problem

which presumably will never be solved. It is not until the final
stage of his poem (Book XVI) that Wolfram describes how
Parzival found the Grail again and asked the question he ought to
have asked in Book v. Perhaps Crestien too had been reserving
this telling climax for the end of his poem.

As Wagner derived his first impulse to write an opera on the
Parsifal theme from Wolfram, we must now examine in some
detail the latter's treatment of the story. A very large literature has
developed during the last hundred years around the legend of
Parsifal and the Grail, which bristles with problems that still defy
solution. Here, however, we must confine ourselves to the features
of it that bear on the genesis and evolution of the Wagnerian
work.[1]

5

Wolfram's hero is from the beginning the "pure fool" with
whom Wagner has familiarised the world. A brave and essentially
good man "becoming slowly wise" is how the poet describes his
Parzival in his opening pages; this links up with Wagner's well-
known:

> *made wise through pity,*
> *the blameless fool,*
> *wait for him,*
> *my chosen is he.*

Parzival's father, Gahmuret of Anjou, has been slain in one of his
knightly adventures, leaving a widow, Queen Herzeloyde (Heart's
Sorrow), to whom is born, fourteen days after Gahmuret's death,
a comely boy. That the son may not meet with the father's fate the
grieving mother withdraws with him and a few of her people into
a wood, where she brings him up in ignorance of the mad world
in which men fight and slay each other—ignorant, indeed, of his
own name. The child makes for himself a bow and arrow with

---

[1] Wolfram's great poem is written in mediaeval German. It has been
admirably rendered into modern German verse, with a few omissions, by
Wilhelm Hertz. Those who know no German can acquaint themselves with
it in the English verse translation of Miss Jessie L. Weston (1894), which
gives an excellent idea of the original, though its long hexameter lines lack
the directness and concision of Wolfram's pithy couplets.

which he brings down birds in the wood, only to break his heart afterwards with grief for the tiny beings that had sung to him so sweetly. Bigger game he kills with his javelot, for he is strong and daring beyond his years. One day he comes upon a splendid company of knights riding through the wood, whom in his innocence he takes for gods. He learns from their leader what knighthood is, and is bidden, if he wishes to know more, to betake himself to the court of King Arthur. All his desire now is for a horse and armour and adventures; but his mother, anxious to save him for herself and preserve him from his father's fate, sends him forth into the world in a "fool's garb" of sackcloth, with a fool's cap and coarse boots of untanned leather, and mounted on the sorriest of steeds. Her hope is that, humbled and disillusioned by contact with the rough realities of the world, he will be glad to return to her.

But the boy will not be denied. Grotesquely garbed as he is he sets out in blind quest of Arthur's court, in the unconscious cruelty of his ignorance leaving his mother to die of grief. He meets with a maiden—his cousin Sigune, as it turns out—sorrowing over the body of her slain lover. She tells him much he had not known—that his name is Parzival, and that one day he shall be what his father was, King of Norgals and Waleis. The simple boy, whose beauty and frankness win him the hearts of all except the wicked, finds at last the company of the Round Table, and, having killed the Red Knight Ither in single combat, takes his horse and armour and sets out in quest of adventures. One day he meets with a certain Gornemans, lord of Graharz, who instructs him in knightly honour and courtesy: one of his precepts—which becomes of the greatest significance in the sequel, both in Wolfram and in Wagner—is to "ask few questions but give well-considered answers". Thus schooled, Parzival, in his wanderings near and far, does many knightly deeds and marries the Lady Condwiramurs, the queen of a city hard pressed by its enemies.

6

It is in his fifth and sixth Books that Wolfram describes that first strange experience of Parzival's in the castle of the Grail that was later to constitute the core of Wagner's opera. One evening the boy comes to a lake where some men are fishing from a boat; of one of them, who is richly dressed,[1] he asks where he may obtain lodging for the night. The "earnest, sorrowful man", as the old poet describes the Fisher, assures him that within thirty miles of them there is no habitation but one: Parzival is to ride on to where the rock ends, turn to the right, ascend the hill, and, having arrived at the castle, bid them lower the drawbridge and let him enter. "If you do not lose your way", says the Fisher, "I myself will be your host there tonight, and you can thank me then. But have a care! There are many wrong roads and you might easily go astray, and for that I should be sorry." Already we have a hint, though of the slightest, that much, for himself and others, depends on Parzival finding that castle and its lord.

Arrived at the moat he tells the warden of the drawbridge that he has been sent there by the Fisher as his guest. He is courteously received and royally tended; his armour is taken away, and the Queen of the castle, Repanse de Schoye, clothes him with her own mantle of fine Arabian silk. He is ushered into a great hall, lit by the tapers of a hundred chandeliers: a hundred couches, each with a carpet before it, are set out; on each of them is room for four men. The lord of the castle—the Fisher—is carried in on a couch and laid before the centre one of three great fireplaces: "he and joy had long been parted; a painful dying was his life"; his sick body cries out for great fires and many furs.

Suddenly a cry of anguish breaks from the assembled knights as a squire comes running into the hall, holding aloft a spear from the point of which blood runs down the shaft and into his sleeve: at the sight of it all break into tears and lamentations. The squire traverses each of the four walls before returning to, and disappearing through, the door by which he had entered; whereupon the wailing ceases.

Maidens enter who place ivory trestles before the lord of the castle, while others bring in a precious stone of lustrous red jacinth, cut long and broad and thin so that it may be used as a table: this they lay on the trestles. Next come two damsels bearing two bright and sharp silver knives on napkins, which they place

[1] The "Rich Fisher" of some of the legends, the "Maimed King" of others.

on the jacinth table. The maidens are followed by the Queen, clothed in a robe of the finest Arabian tissue, and carrying, on a cloth of emerald silk, "the glory of Paradise, the root, stem and shoot of salvation, a thing called the Grail, a treasury of marvels beyond number"; it is borne by the Queen herself because in virtue of its noble nature only the pure of heart are worthy to tend it. She bows and sets the Grail before the lord of the castle. Then a hundred tables, covered with a cloth of white linen, are brought in, and one of them is set in front of each four of the knights. Parzival, seated by the silent, melancholy lord, washes his hands, like him, in water. Bread, in white napkins, is laid before the Grail by a hundred serving squires and set before the knights. The nature of the Grail was such that whatever food a man desired, cold or warm, new or old, it would yield him in abundance. "For I tell you the story", says the poet to the reader, "as I have received it"; and a little later, "If anyone thinks this too wonderful and unexampled, let him not blame the tale." (This suggests that Wolfram himself had no definite conception of the meaning of the "Grail")."Blessings streamed from it, a rain of earthly felicity; it was equal almost to what we are told of heaven". And as with food, so with drink: with whatever a man desired the Grail filled his cup: all were the guests of the Grail.

7

Parzival watches it all in great astonishment, but out of courtesy he will not ask the meaning of it: "within himself he thought, 'The good Gornemans enjoined me to refrain from asking many questions. I will wait courteously until they tell me everything unasked, as Gornemans did'". While he is thus communing with himself a squire approaches him with a splendid sword, the gift of the lord of the castle. (This sword seems to be an element that has filtered into the Parzival story from another saga, dealing with the obligation of the hero to revenge a murder. Neither Crestien nor Wolfram appears to understand precisely what he should do with it). "Alas", Wolfram comments, "that he did not ask the question then! For his own sake that was a pity, for the sword was a hint to him to speak. Grieved am I also for his host, for the question would have rid him of his unnamed torment."

The meal comes to an end: the Queen approaches the Grail and bows low to the lord and his guest: then all pass out by the door by which they had entered. As they go, Parzival has a glimpse into the room beyond; there, on a couch, lies the most beautiful old man he had ever seen, whiter than hoar-frost. "Who he was", says the poet, "you shall learn later; at the right time, too, I will tell you who and what were the lord, the castle and the land."

Parzival retires to rest, tended with great courtesy. He sleeps uneasily, beset by troubled dreams. When he wakes next morning he finds no squires or pages to do him service, though on the carpet lie his armour, his own sword, and the one given him by the lord of the castle: he dons his mail unaided and goes to the outer door, where he finds his horse, his shield and his spear awaiting him. Perturbed and a little angry at what he takes to be discourteous treatment of a guest he goes through room after room, but nowhere is there a sign of life. He returns to the court-yard, where he sees that the grass has been trodden down and the dewdrops scattered. Mounting his horse he makes for the great outer gates: they stand wide open, and beyond them, stretching away into the fields, he sees the tracks of many horses. He spurs his own steed across the drawbridge, which is raised by an unseen hand almost before he has cleared it, and he hears the voice of the warder saying, "Away with you, and may the sun never shine on you! A goose you are! Could you not have opened your mouth? Would that you had not been so sparing of your speech but had asked your host a question! A great prize have you forfeited!" Parzival asks the meaning of these bitter words but receives no answer; the gates close with a crash behind him. Assuming that the knights have ridden forth to fight in some cause of their lord's he decides to follow them, which he does until the tracks grow fainter and at last he loses the ever-narrowing trail.

He rides on until he comes to a woman lamenting over a dead knight who lies clasped in her arms, and he offers her his knightly service. It is Crestien's Sigune once more. Where did he lodge last night? she asks him. In a lordly castle, he replies. "Only one castle is there in this wood", she says. "In it does every wish find its fulfilment. But whoso seeks for it can never find it: he who is to discover it must come upon it unawares. Its name is Munsalvaesche,[1] and Terresalvaesche is the land in which it lies. The old King Titurel bequeathed his realm to his son Frimutel, a brave knight who died in combat, slain in the cause of love. He left four children: three are rich but full of sorrow; the fourth, Trevrizent by name, has chosen poverty for his portion and does penance for past sin. His brother Anfortas[2] is now lord of Munsalvaesche; he is a stricken man who can neither walk nor ride nor stand nor lie, but only recline. If indeed you came to that castle where all is sorrow, then surely must its lord have been healed of the pain he has borne so long ... Did you see the Grail and its joyless lord? Give me the tidings I fain would hear. If his woes are at an end, then of good omen was your journey, for you shall be praised and served by all things living, and every wish of yours shall be fulfilled if you have asked the question you should have done."

Parzival confesses sorrowfully that he had asked no question. "Alas!" cries Sigune, "that ever I set eyes on you, that were too faint of heart to ask the question. You beheld all the wonders of the Grail, and the silver knives, and the bleeding spear. Why came you to me here? You are dishonoured and accursed; the venomous tooth of the wolf is yours, gall has poisoned troth and love in you. Were you not touched with pity for him? You asked not what ailed the sore-afflicted man? You live, but you are dead to blessing." "Be not angry with me", Parzival replies humbly; "I will atone." But she drives him from her, cursing him for a blot on the fair name of knighthood.

8

So Parzival, sick of soul for that he has somehow failed in kindliness and pity, and with the thought of his beloved Condwiramurs always tugging at his heart, passes on to a series of fresh adventures at the court of King Arthur and elsewhere. At the court a new shame is put upon the ignorant boy. There rides

---

[1] Not Monsalvat (the mountain of salvation), it will be observed. Salvaesche means wild: (French *sauvage*, Italian *selvaggio*, Spanish *salvaje*).

[2] Wolfram spells the name in this fashion and accents it on the first syllable.

in one day a hideous woman, the sorceress Cundrie, who curses him and denounces him as a disgrace to knighthood. He is more loathsome than even she, she cries, for his heart is false: he had been to Munsalvaesche, he had seen the suffering King, the Grail, the silver knives, the bleeding lance, and had failed in the duty laid on him. "Ah, Munsalvaesche!", she cries as she rides away on her ugly mule, "home of grief, woe to thee, for no man comes to thee with pity and with help". And Parzival stands mute under her revilings, suffering he knows not why. He had always been brave and loyal and generous; there was no will to evil in his simple young heart; yet somehow in his ignorance he has done a monstrous, unforgivable wrong.

With his further adventures as a knight, and with those of Gawain, who now plays for a while the more prominent part in the poet's tale, we are not concerned here. It is upon Gawain that, by a new turn in the story, is laid, for a time, the task of going in search of the Grail. But the one predestined to find it is not Gawain but Parzival, who comes into the foreground once more in Wolfram's ninth Book.

After years of wandering through many lands and over the seas he has come to a forest where once again he encounters Sigune, still mourning her dead lover; her own life, it appears, is sustained by the Grail, provision from which is brought to her each week by Cundrie. She recognises him as the Parzival who had gone long ago in search of the Grail, and asks how it had fared with him in his quest. Mournfully he confesses that neither Munsalvaesche nor the Grail has he yet found, and he asks counsel of her in his distress of soul. She bids him follow the track of Cundrie's mule. But the forest is wild and soon he loses his way: once more he has missed the Grail and the opportunity to ask the question from which, he tells himself, he would not shrink a second time. At last he comes upon an old grey knight who chides him gently for bearing arms on that holiest of days, Good Friday, when all creation should be at once mourning and rejoicing. Parzival again rides on. He has been at bitter strife with God all the years since first he saw Munsalvaesche, for God seems to have deserted him and been his enemy. But what if God after all can help him in his torturing need? He lets the reins fall loosely on his horse's neck. The animal takes him straight to the Fontaine la Salvaesche; and there, from the lips of a good old hermit, Trevrizent the pure, he learns the story of the Grail.

No one can ever find it, says Trevrizent, save the Grail's own chosen. It is kept at Munsalvaesche, guarded by knights, who are nourished and kept for ever young by a certain pure and precious stone. Its name is *lapis exilis*[1]; it is the stone that brings the phoenix to life again from its own ashes, and preserves a sick man from death for a week after he has gazed on it; "its other name is the Grail". Each Good Friday its powers are renewed by a white dove which descends upon it from heaven, bearing in its beak a wafer; and thus the stone yields daily to the brotherhood all the meats and fruits they need for their sustenance. The elect of the Grail are chosen when children by the Grail itself, for the name of anyone destined for its service, man or maid, appears in mystic letters on the stone; these letters remain until they have been read, and then fade away. Long ago, when Lucifer contended with God, many of the angels took no side in the strife, for which offence they were cast out of heaven and sent down to earth to tend the stone which they have guarded ever since: "this, Sir, is how it standeth with the Grail".

Hearing this, Parzival thinks that God should choose him to be one of the shining brotherhood, for he has been a knight honourable and brave. But Trevrizent reproves him: "You must beware of pride and insolence of will; your youth may mislead you, for always pride has its fall". And with tears in his eyes the old man tells Parzival the story of King Anfortas, whose undoing had been wrought by pride, for he had pursued an unchaste love. That is not the way of the Grail, says Trevrizent, which demands of its servants not pride but humility and purity of spirit. As for Munsalvaesche and the Grail, none know where they are to be found but those called to their service. "One alone came there unsummoned—a young fool who went away again with the burden of sin on him, for he saw his host's anguish and spoke no word of pity". "I will reproach no man", continues Trevrizent:

---

[1] Or iaspis, lapsit; exilix, erillis; etc., in this manuscript or that. It looks as if the mediaeval scribes had no definite idea of the meaning of the word they were copying.

"yet for that sin, that he asked not the question of the host on whom God's hand lay so heavy, he must pay dear."

9

As they talk, he and Parzival learn more of each other. Titurel, the boy learns, had bequeathed his holy heritage to his son Frimutel, whom Parzival resembles in looks. Herzeloyde was Trevrizent's sister; Trevrizent is the son of Frimutel, and the Queen Repanse de Schoye is sister to Trevrizent and to Anfortas, the present lord of the Grail. He, in the pride and ardour of his youth, had fought many a fight in the service of love, "for *Amor* was his battle-cry". But one day, having ridden out alone on an adventure, he fell a victim to love and was pierced in the groin by the envenomed spear of a heathen who had come over the sea from his own land—"in Ethnisé, where the Tigris flows out of Paradise",—burning to win, if he might, possession of the Grail: "his name was graven on the spear". He was slain, and Anfortas rode home, sick and weary, to his lamenting people. The physician, groping in the wound, found in it the spear-head and part of the shaft, and drew them out. Then Trevrizent, in horror, put away his weapons and forswore henceforth bread and wine and the flesh of animals.

Trevrizent tells Parzival more about the Grail and the trouble of the brethren by reason of Anfortas's fall. The Grail, it appears, chooses for its service young children of noble birth, maidens as well as boys. It will send in secret, if prayed to do so, one of its knights to rule over a lordless land; but the men of that land must pledge themselves to unquestioning allegiance to him.[1] The maidens of the Grail can be openly sent out to wedlock in other lands: Herzeloyde had been such a one. Whoever has been dedicated to the Grail must forswear the love of women; only the King and those sent to foreign lands are allowed a wife, and they must not seek love outside the marriage bond.

To heal the wound of Anfortas every remedy has been sought and tried—the mystic waters of the four streams of Paradise (Fison, Geon, Tigris and Euphrates); the golden bough which the

[1] The legend of Lohengrin is foreshadowed here.

Cumæan Sibyl promised should protect Aeneas against the perils of Hades; the blood of the pelican's breast on which she nourishes her young; the heart of the unicorn and the potent carbuncle that lies beneath its horn; the magic herb that springs from the ground bedewed by a dying dragon's blood. All had been in vain. The knights had prayed for help, and seen it written on the Grail that one should come who would ask the King the question that would lift the burden of suffering from him, the deliverer who should then reign in his stead. But he would have to come unbidden and ask the question without prompting, and that on his first night in the castle. One knight indeed had come, says Trevrizent, but he had failed to ask, and thereby lost his chance of being blessed and plunged the King back into his intolerable woe. Always when Saturn has run his course Anfortas's sufferings increase: the frost enters the wound, and there is no remedy but to cure one maddening pain by another, by thrusting the burning spear into the wound; its heat draws out the frost and turns it to crystals of ice, which can be cut away from the spear only by two sharp silver knives. At the change of the moon the King is carried to the lake called Brumbane, where the pure air cleanses the wound: there he fishes, and so the story goes that he is a Fisherman.

Hearing all this, Parzival discloses that he was the peccant knight who had arrived at the castle and failed in what was expected of him. Trevrizent gives him wise and loving counsel, but urges him to cleanse his soul and atone for the wrongs he had done. For twice the unschooled boy had unwittingly wrought evil: in the thoughtless lustihood of youth he had left his loving mother and broken her heart, and, in his first passion to become a knight, he had slain the Red Knight Ither and possessed himself of his armour. God has not forgotten these misdeeds, and will requite him for them. But the peak of his offending against heaven had been his failure in the castle of the Grail. For his coming, Trevrizent now tells him, had filled them all with hope: it was because they saw in him the healer of Anfortas and the chosen successor to the kingdom of the Grail that the Queen had covered him with her own mantle and the King had given him a sword. The fair old man of whom Parzival had caught sight through the open door was his mother's grandsire, Titurel, the first custodian of the Grail, now old and bedridden, but kept alive by the sight of the Grail. And so, after fifteen days, Parzival rides away from Trevrizent, with the counsel in his ears to be steadfast and true and leave his sins in the old hermit's keeping, who will render account for them in the sight of God.

10

This was the strange story which Wolfram had refrained from telling earlier, leaving it to reach us at this stage through the mouth of Trevrizent. And now his poem takes a curious turn: Parzival becomes for a while a subsidiary character, only to come back in the end, however, as the true hero of the long tale. And much of what now follows is of prime importance to us because of the part it plays in Wagner's drama.

The action shifts to another land of marvels—Terre Merveille, which is not only as wonderful in its own different way as Terre Munsalvaesche but curiously connected with it.

A certain Cidegast, the lover of the queen Orgeluse (who, in Wolfram's poem, is one of the greatest figures in mediaeval literature), having been slain by a rival suitor for the lady's hand, King Gramovlanz, Orgeluse's one passion henceforth is to avenge his death. To this end she had accepted in days gone by the services of Anfortas, who had failed, however, in the combat with Gramovlanz and received a grievous wound. Thereupon Orgeluse, still thirsting for vengeance, had concluded a pact with one Clinschor, a mighty magician, the lord of the enchanted Terre Merveille and its castle, the Schastel Merveille. He had once loved the wife of King Ibert of Sicily, who found them together and by a stroke of his knife unmanned the knight. Thereafter, in a mad hatred of humanity, Clinschor had devoted himself to the study of magic. High up on a mountain he had created a palace and a garden the like of which the earth did not contain. There he held in thrall the knights and ladies who fell into his power, the victims of his malignant hate of all mankind. Orgeluse bribes him with the gift of a pavilion, full of costly merchandise, which she had received from Anfortas, to whom it had been presented by the Indian queen Secundille. Along with it she had sent two messengers to the lord of the Grail. (At this point it becomes tolerably clear that Wolfram was drawing for his material upon more than one oral or written source, and making an attempt to combine certain characters and milieux either in a way of his own or in some way sanctioned by usage. Cundrie, for instance, brings remedies and salves for the healing of Gawain's wounds, just as, in the other story, she brings them for Anfortas).

It was Cundrie who, making one of her mysterious appearances at the court of King Arthur, had persuaded Gawain and other knights to go to the rescue of four queens and four hundred maidens who had been made captive by Clinschor; and it is with the adventures of Gawain that a great deal of Wolfram's space is taken up at this point. It is to Gawain that Orgeluse finally trusts for the avenging of the death of Cidegast. She had indeed met the mysterious Red Knight (Parzival), and after he had over-thrown her men in combat she offered him her hand and her kingdom. But he had passed on his way with a touch of anger and scorn: two desires alone possessed him, to be joined again to his Condwiramurs and to find the Grail. In the end, however, it is Parzival, not Gawain, who overcomes Gramovlanz in combat and so works the will of Orgeluse.

We next find Parzival, in the course of his wanderings, en-countering his half-brother Fierefiz, the son of Gahmuret by a dusky queen of the east, and in face half-black, half-white. After he and Parzival have fought to the equal honour of each of them they discover their blood-relationship; and the pair ride on to King Arthur's court, whither, one day, a changed Cundrie comes. She falls at the feet of the Parzival whom she had once so cruelly derided and cursed, and begs his forgiveness; she tells him that the inscription on the Grail has been read and that he is the destined new lord of the Grail; he has only to ask the question and Anfortas will be made free of his pain; Condwiramurs and one of Parzival's twin sons, Loherangrin, have also been chosen to be of the company of the Grail. So Parzival, Cundrie and Fierefiz set out together for Munsalvaesche. They are well received by the knights. The weary Anfortas implores Parzival to deny him the sight of the Grail for seven nights and eight days and so bring his burdensome life to an end. But Parzival weeps and prays for him, rises to his feet, and asks the simple question, "Uncle, what aileth thee?"; and instantly Anfortas becomes well and young again. Parzival is made King in his stead; and soon he has the joy of being re-united to his Condwiramurs after so many years. Loherangrin he keeps with him; the later story of the boy is enshrined in the anonymous epic of *Lohengrin*. The other son, Kardeiz, is sent to rule over his father's earthly kingdom of Brobarz.

II

The story as told by Crestien and Wolfram differs in many fundamental respects from that of Wagner's *Parsifal*. For neither of the old writers does the Grail mean what it did for Wagner and does for most people today. Crestien, indeed, does not even speak of "*the* Grail"; it is "*a* graal" that the maiden carries into the hall. There is no hint of it containing the blood of the Saviour, and it is plainly, for Crestien, not a cup but a dish. That, indeed, seems to be the true primal meaning of the word itself. All the popular derivations of it are fanciful, whether from the Latin "gradalis", signifying a dish in which the various foods were arranged in rows (gradatim), or from "Sang réal" (royal blood). It comes from an old Latin word "garalis", meaning a dish (old French "graal" or "gréal", Provençal "grazal"). In the will of a certain Count Eberhard (A.D. 873) a bequest is made of several "garales", including "two of silver with two spoons each" ("garales argenteos cum binis cochleariis duos"); and under the rules and regulations of the courts of the Kings of Jerusalem "all dishes and graals" from which the food was served on feast days were placed in the custody of the seneschal.

For Wolfram, as we have seen, the Grail is not even a dish but some kind of talismanic stone. The denizens of Munsalvaesche, Trevrizent tells Parsifal, are miraculously fed by "a stone of pure and sublime nature, called *lapis exillix*. It is this stone that enables the phoenix to rise renewed from its ashes. Be a man ever so sick, a sight of the stone preserves his life and his colour for the space of a whole week. A man might look at it for two hundred years and show no sign of age except a greying of his hair. The other name of the stone is the Grail." Such a stone would presumably be meteoric; and to precious stones in general the ancient and the mediaeval world attributed magic powers. Wolfram is very vague as to the provenance of the stone that is the Grail, but he christianises it to the extent of making it have its powers renewed each Good Friday by a dove that descends from heaven, bearing a sacramental wafer in its beak: this it lays on the stone, which thereafter yields the brotherhood everything it desires in the way of food and drink "in paradisiac profusion". Thus it is no longer the merely talismanic qualities of the stone itself but the sacred Host deposited on it that endows it with its supernatural powers.

It is tolerably clear that neither Crestien nor Wolfram was working upon any clear-cut conception of the nature and origin of the Grail. The complete christianisation of it had gradually come about as the result of the infiltration into the basic Perceval-Grail story of another legend, that of the transmission, through Joseph of Arimathea, of the sacred Blood in a dish or cup: one form of the story even presents us with two holy relics— "li saintisme graals", meaning the dish with the Blood, and "li saintisme vaissaus", the dish from which Christ and His disciples ate at the Last Supper. What is certain is that for Wolfram a "graal" is not a dish or a cup. He probably took over the word, without understanding it, from the French version he had before him; as a German scholar has put it, he imagined "graal" to be a proper name, and so did not translate it into German but changed Crestien's "a graal" into "The Grail".

Of the bleeding lance neither Crestien nor Wolfram gives us any explanation: but certainly for neither of them was it the legendary spear of "Longinus". Manifestly it had great significance in Crestien's eyes, but he died before reaching the point in his poem at which, presumably, he would have told us more about it, as Wolfram has done at a later stage of *his* story, when he makes the bleeding lance of the scene in the hall of the Grail the same poisoned weapon that had dealt Anfortas his wound. (In the old Celtic legends, from which a good deal of the Perceval-Grail story sprang, a bleeding lance was the traditional symbol of the desire of the Celts for revenge upon the Saxon invaders who had driven them from their homes. Crestien seems to have been aware of this aspect of it).

12

The story of Perceval and the quest for the Grail has come
down to us in various forms in poetry and prose: it seems to have
excited the liveliest interest in Western Europe and Britain for a
half-century or so between 1170 and 1220, and then to have faded
out as suddenly and inexplicably as it had come in. As we have it
now it must represent the gradual interfusion and proliferation of
several legends. Crestien and Wolfram, it seems evident, worked
upon a common source or sources, though either they inserted
features of their own in it or the versions that lay before them
already differed from each other in some respects. Crestien's
unfinished poem was continued by three writers, Wauchier (or
Gautier) de Denain, Manessier, and Gerbert de Montreuil. Each
of these seems to have drawn upon sources anterior to Crestien
and in some ways different from his. Wauchier's romance perhaps presents us with the story in its earliest form. In his version
the hero of the Quest for the Grail is Gawain, and the Grail is not
a "holy" but merely a "rich" object which in some mysterious
fashion provides food. Wauchier knows also of a bleeding lance
which is that of Longinus. Gawain asks the King of the castle
what the lance is, and by so doing makes the rivers flow and
brings verdure back to the wasted land again. But he does not
enquire also about the Grail; by his failing to do so the land is not
wholly restored to life, and so the people of it mingle curses with
their blessings of him.

The legend, or complex of legends, seems to have been in a
state of constant inner flux and of amalgamation with others. The
widespread primitive folk-tale of a brave, simple boy coming
slowly to strength and wisdom becomes gradually inwrought
with the conception of a Grail, which mysterious object is now
one thing, now another, until finally it and the lance become
ecclesiasticised as the Dish (or Cup) and the spear of Longinus.
Perceval gradually supplants Gawain in the legends as the quester
for the Grail, and is in turn supplanted by Lancelot, who is later
replaced by Galahad: it is in this last form that the story comes to
us in Malory's *Morte d'Arthur* (first printed in 1485) and in
Tennyson's *Idylls of the King*.

But so far as the brave and simple hero and his quest of the Grail is concerned the best telling of the tale, and, indeed, the finest flower of northern mediaeval literature, is undoubtedly Wolfram's *Parzival*. For Wolfram's genius has fused the romantic and the ethical into one in a way beyond the powers of any of his contemporaries. He alone sees Parzival steadily and whole as a character developing in humanity under the stress of bitter circumstance—the "brave man becoming slowly wise". Here alone in all the Perceval-Grail stories of the Middle Ages was something upon which a modern dramatist and musician could build, though necessarily with a good deal of sifting and modification of the material. Here and there a modern specialist in mediaeval literature has seen fit to censure Wagner for not having kept more closely to Wolfram; but in doing so they lose sight of the difference between epic and drama and between mediaeval and modern ethical concepts. Another core than that of the legend has of necessity to be found for a Parsifal drama or opera of today; had Wagner docilely followed Wolfram he would have had to make the dénouement turn upon the restoration of the King to health and the saving of the wasted land by Parsifal's simple asking of a question, which would have been too naive a climax for the modern mind.[1] Wagner, for his purposes, had to lift the whole action out of the sphere of folk-story into that of ethics; the simple old tale of a misfortune befalling the rash Anfortas had to be made a symbol of sin in general and its atonement by one made wise and understanding by pity not merely for an individual but for all men.

Wagner's letters of 1859—the period of his first struggle with the huge and confused material of the legends—show him to have had rather a poor opinion of Wolfram and of the mediaeval poets in general—which merely means that they saw matters in terms of their own age instead of in those of ours. Wagner could neither

---

[1] Mr. H. O. Taylor, in his searching study of the mediaeval mind, has pointed out that Wolfram was quite logical, from the standpoint of his epoch, in his implied ethical sequence: "failure to ask the question was a symbol of [Parsifal's] lack of wisdom . . . So the sequence becomes ethical: from error, calamity; from calamity, grief; and from grief, wisdom". (*The Mediaeval Mind*, I, 601, 602).

do anything himself with the "question" motive nor understand
what it signified in the legends. "That business of the 'question' ",
he wrote to Frau Wesendonk, "is quite absurd and meaningless.
Here, therefore, I should just have to invent everything for
myself." His problem was *what* to invent that would take the
vital place of the "question" motive in Wolfram. It was not until
nearly twenty years later that he found the solution of his problem. From Cosima's diary we learn that on the 25th January 1877
he said to her, "I am starting on [the poem of] *Parsifal*, and I
shall not lay it aside until it is finished." Three days later he could
tell her that he had got over what had been his greatest difficulty:
the nodal point of his drama would be not the asking of the
question but the recovery of the Spear.

It was necessary, too, for Wagner to fuse Wolfram's account
of the Grail with the later developments that associated it with the
Chalice and the Sacred Blood; Wolfram's Grail—a talismanic
stone with magic-working properties—would have stirred no
emotion in the modern spectator, besides being too weak to bear
the great ethical superstructure Wagner had it in his mind to
raise. In general, Wagner's solution of the problems of the handling
of the varied material presented to him by the mediaeval legend
was to tighten it up everywhere and provide it with one or two
central episodes from which the action and its ethical motives
could consistently develop. It was a stroke of genius on his part
to bring the world of Monsalvat and that of Klingsor into both
connection and apposition, to make the magician of evil wound
the custodian of the Grail with the very weapon that had pierced
the Redeemer's side on the Cross, thus inflicting on Amfortas an
agony for which there could never be any healing save by virtue
of the sacred Spear itself. By adopting this development Wagner
was able to make the essence of Parsifal's long and weary trial
not so much the quest for the Grail as that for the Spear; it was the
loss of this, through Amfortas's sin against the purity of the Grail,
that had brought disaster on the brotherhood, and only the
recovery of it, and the second finding of the hall of the Grail,
could bring healing to the King and restore to Monsalvat its lost
spiritual power.

He had further to compress the meandering action at several

points, to eliminate many superfluous characters, to amalgamate others, and to make Kundry not only a more definite personality but a more significant one. As usual, he concentrated on essentials. The numberless picturesque details in which Wolfram, writing an epic, could safely indulge had to be eliminated—for instance, the poet's expansive and richly wrought picture of the procedure in the hall of the Grail had to be condensed into a single impressive ritual act. Wolfram's long preliminary story of Parsifal's origin, of the death of his father Gahmuret and his mother Herzeloyde, and of his upbringing in ignorance of the world, had to be simultaneously communicated to the spectator and made part of the psychology of the drama by means of Kundry's narrative in the second act.

Of the numerous figures that crowd upon each other in Wolfram's vast tapestry Wagner needed, for his purpose, only four for the main action—Parsifal, Amfortas, Kundry, Klingsor—with a fifth, Gurnemanz, in the second line, to bring the others into connection with each other at vital points of the drama and to make clear sundry things in this that could not be shown on the stage. Gurnemanz himself is an amalgam of Wolfram's Gornemans and his Trevrizent. Klingsor is not simply the traditional magician of mediaeval romance but the incarnation of evil, the force in implacable warfare with the ethical world symbolised by the Grail. Kundry becomes infinitely more than the Loathly Damsel of the mediaeval legends. Her complex nature is difficult to analyse in words—it is defined for us mostly in her music; but we can see how enormously Wagner increased the significance of the character by making her at once the instrument of Klingsor, the servant of the Grail, and a spirit in revolt against the evil which Klingsor compels her to work at times.

13

The basic Gawain-Perceval legends seem to have been Celtic in origin; but from the moment when the Grail came to be associated with the Last Supper the stories tended to become overlaid with an ecclesiastical symbolism which at first formed no part of them. As for the Grail element itself, the truth of the

matter seems to be with the modern scholars who trace it back to
some such ancient fertility rite—the primitive meaning of which,
however, had by Wolfram's time been forgotten—as is set forth
for us in the pages of Frazer's *Golden Bough* and similar works.
Primitive man, like backward tribes today, practised at certain
times of the year a ritual designed to encourage the powers of
nature to make the earth and rivers and seas fertile for his needs.
In the course of time the ritual would take on a dramatic form,
the winter decline of earth and the Spring reawakening being
symbolised in the persons of gods or heroes such as Attis, Adonis,
Tammuz or Mithra, who, like the vegetation, died and after an
interval came to life again. The Mithraic cult in particular, which
was the favourite one of the far-travelled Roman legionaries, had
an extensive vogue in Western Europe and the islands during the
early centuries when Christianity was establishing itself; and a
good case has been made out for seeing in the sick king who is
afterwards healed, and in the aversion of evil from the land by
virtue of that healing, a last vague relic of one of the pagan
fertility cults. This view would help to account, again, for the
title of "the Fisher King" or "the Rich Fisherman", borne in the
Grail legends by the king who is mortally sick from a wound in
the groin: for the fish was one of the most widely-spread symbols
of fertility in the ancient world. But the whole subject, on not
only the literary side but that of comparative religion, is packed
with problems which will perhaps never be mastered, extensive as
the literature dealing with them already is. And with all this we
have on the present occasion nothing to do: all that concerns us
is the nature of the poetic material from which Wagner derived
his subject, and the processes within him that gradually developed
it into the form it assumes in *Parsifal*.[1]

[1] About 1930 a German orientalist, Dr. Fridrich von Suhtscheck, made out
a strong case for a Persian origin and Persian setting of the Parsifal legend.
He contended that "Grail" came from two Persian roots, *gohar* or *ghr*,
meaning pearl, and *al*, meaning brilliant colour, the Grail, therefore, signifying the pearl of pearls. Kyot he identified with Giut, an Armenian who
rendered a Parsifal story into French about the middle of the twelfth century.
His argument is profoundly interesting, but a full statement of it would take
us too far afield.

14

In July 1845 Wagner, having completed the music of *Tann-häuser*, took a holiday and "cure" in Bohemia, taking with him for his reading, as he tells us in *My Life*, "the poems of Wolfram von Eschenbach in the [modern German] versions of Simrock and San-Marte,[1] as well as the anonymous epic of *Lohengrin* with the long introduction by Görres. With the book under my arm I hid myself in the neighbouring woods, and, seated by a brook, feasted myself on Titurel and Parzival in Wolfram's strange yet intimately appealing poem." His imagination was kindled, and he felt a burning desire to cast the rich but diffuse poetic matter into musical-dramatic form. But he had been warned by his doctor against over-excitement during his cure in Marienbad, and so, though with great difficulty, he damped down his passion for the Parzival subject and concentrated on the story of Lohengrin, which had been occupying his thoughts more or less since the Paris days of 1841–2. After that, as a kind of sanitary reaction against the excitement of working out the scheme of his *Lohengrin*, he sketched a text on the subject of Hans Sachs and the Mastersingers of Nuremberg.

He would have been surprised had he been told at that time that a *Parsifal* would be the last of his works for the stage, that it would not be until thirty-seven years after that ardent first reading of Wolfram in the woods at Marienbad that the opera would see the light of day, and that it would show the world a Richard Wagner more remote in every way from the one who had just completed *Tannhäuser* than the Beethoven of the last quartets is from the Beethoven of the Second Symphony. The Parzival subject had to go through a long period of silent gestation within him before he could feel that he was really ripe for it. It was not merely that as dramatic craftsman he did not quite see as yet how to condense Wolfram's long epic into the three-hours' traffic of the operatic stage; and his artistic instinct must have warned him to wait until he was much more developed as poet and musician and man before trying to find the right expression for the strange new world of which the old poet had given him a

[1] San-Marte was the pseudonym of one Albert Schutz.

glimpse. But though we hear nothing more from him about
Parzival for several years it is evident that the subject was often
in his thoughts, working out its own destiny in the silent and
slow but sure way that was habitual with him.

We next hear of it towards the end of 1854, in what seems to us
today, however, the strangest connection with the story of
Tristan and Isolde. He drew up a broad plan for an opera in
three acts on the latter subject; and in the third act, he says, "I
introduced an episode which I did not work out later—Parzival,
in his quest for the Grail, coming to the sick-bed of Tristan: for
Tristan, ill from his wound and unable to die, had become
identified in my mind with Amfortas in the Grail legend."[1] Hans
von Wolzogen, drawing upon his recollection of conversations
with Wagner, gave us further information on this point in 1886.
"Parzival, questing for the Grail, was to come in the course of his
pilgrimage to Kareol, and there find Tristan lying on his death-
bed, love-racked and despairing. Thus the longing one was
brought face to face with the renouncing one, the self-curser with
the man atoning for his own guilt, the one suffering unto death
from love with the one bringing redemption through pity. Here
death, there new life. And it was intended that a melody associated
with the wandering Parzival should sound in the ears of the mortally wounded Tristan, as it were the mysteriously faint receding
answer to his life-destroying question about the 'Why?' of life.
Out of this melody, it may be said, grew the stage-festival-drama
[*Parsifal*]." The melody referred to is apparently the one written
out by Wagner for Mathilde Wesendonk about April 1858; it
runs thus:

[1] It has to be remembered that at some time or other the Perceval saga and
that of Tristan had tended to coalesce, as was the way with many of these
mediaeval stories. "In the final stage of the evolution of the Arthurian cycle",
says Miss Jessie L. Weston, "when its tentacles, stretching far and wide, had
laid hold of the originally quite independent *Tristan* theme, and drawn it
within the meshes of the Arthurian net, the Galahad Quest became enlarged
in order to permit of the participation not only of Tristan himself but also
of other knights who had become more or less closely connected with him."
Wagner must have been aware of this coalescence, but his sense of fitness
soon made him turn away from it.

("Where shall I find thee, holy Grail, for which my yearning
heart is searching?").

15

A note-book of 1854–5 that has survived contains Wagner's
sketch for the episode in question as originally planned for *Tristan
and Isolde*. It runs thus: "Act III. Tristan on his sick-bed in the
garden of the castle. At the side of the stage a battlement. Awaking
from sleep he calls to his squire, whom he believes to be on the
battlement, though he cannot see him. The squire is not there,
but in response to Tristan's call he comes at last. Reproaches.
Excuses—a pilgrim has arrived and has been entertained. Once
and now. Tristan's impatience. The squire can still see nothing
[of the expected ship bringing Isolde]. Tristan's reflections.
Doubts. A melody from the distance, dying away. What can it
be? The squire tells him about the pilgrim—Parzival. Profound
impression. Love and torment. My mother died in giving me
birth; now I live, dying because I was born. Why this? Parzival's
refrain—repeated by the shepherd. The whole world nothing but
unsatisfied longing. What can ever allay it? Parzival's refrain
again."

As the reader knows, this plan for introducing the questing
Parzival into the last act of *Tristan* was never carried out:

Wagner's dramatic sense must soon have convinced him that it would constitute an unmotived, alien element there. And the melody he had put into the mouth of Parzival is obviously not in the vein of the *Parsifal* we now know; Wagner's muse had to pass through a long period of deepening and purification before it was ripe for taking imaginative control of the strange world of Parzival and the Grail.[1]

We next find his thoughts turning in the direction of Wolfram again in the April of 1857. According to his story in *My Life*[2] he awoke in the "Asyl"—the little house on the Wesendonk estate at Zürich that had been placed at his disposal—on a marvellously beautiful Good Friday morning; the garden was freshly green, the birds were singing, and over the whole world brooded a divine peace. He was suddenly reminded, he says, of Wolfram's poem—"with which I had never occupied myself since that stay of mine in Marienbad when I had conceived the *Mastersingers* and *Lohengrin*." [This would seem at first sight to conflict with the fact that in 1854-5 he had planned an entry of Parzival in the third act of *Tristan*. But there is no real contradiction. He had perhaps been concerned with Parzival at that time only as a possible figure in an episode of the *Tristan* drama]. "Now its ideal contents took irresistible possession of me, and out of my thoughts about Good Friday I swiftly conceived an entire drama in three acts, of which I put a hasty sketch on paper." His memory was a little at fault as regards the date, for Good Friday in 1857 fell on the 10th April, and Wagner did not take up his residence in the Asyl until the 29th: no doubt he had visited the garden on the 10th, felt the emotions he describes and been reminded of the Good Friday episode in Wolfram's poem, and

---

[1] We do not know when the melody quoted above was written. One would be inclined *a priori* to date it from long before 1854, perhaps even from the days of the first impact of the Parzival subject on him in the summer of 1845. *The Rhinegold* and the *Valkyrie* had been written between November 1853 and the end of 1854, while 1856 and 1857 saw the completion of the first two acts of *Siegfried* and the first act of *Tristan*. Even by 1854 he had developed so enormously as a musician that it is difficult to believe that for this Parzival theme he had reverted to the *Tannhäuser-Lohengrin* musical idiom of six to ten years earlier.

[2] This section of the autobiography was dictated about 1870.

then, in later years, assumed the date of this experience to have been Good Friday.

If that sketch of 1857 survives it has not yet been given to the world, so we can only speculate as to its nature. It goes without saying that there must already have been a good deal of conscious or subconscious sifting of the Wolfram material on Wagner's part, for a stage drama on purely Wolframian lines was from the beginning an impossibility. We may be sure also that the conception of the Grail as the Chalice containing the Redeemer's blood was already essential to his drama; for although, as we have seen, there is not the smallest suggestion of either Cup or Sacred Blood in Wolfram's poem, the sources consulted by Wagner in 1845 had familiarised him with other mediaeval handlings of the Grail story in which the legend of Joseph of Arimathea and the Holy Blood plays a vital part.[1] The germ-cell from which Wagner's plan for a three-act drama evolved in 1857 must have been the Good Friday scene, which, indeed, is the emotional focal point of the present *Parsifal*, as Senta's Ballad is that of *The Flying Dutchman*. But apart from a few more or less plausible conjectures of this kind we can throw no light at present on the draft of that year.

16

In the late 1850's Wagner's whole thinking about life and the cosmos took a mystical-metaphysical turn, the result partly of his study of Schopenhauer, partly of his contact with Buddhistic literature, partly of his own tortured broodings upon the nature of the world and the destiny of man and beast, partly of the flood of new emotion set coursing in him by the sorrowful Tristan subject. The centre of his ethic now was pity for everything doomed to carry the burden of existence; and it was from this centre outwards that he had already come to survey the Parzival subject afresh.

[1] We first meet with it in a prose narrative, *Joseph of Arimathea*, by one Robert de Boron, which tells of the adventures and the magic properties of the Dish from which Jesus and His disciples ate at the Last Supper, and which later received the Blood that welled from His wounds on the Cross.

The biographical record now shifts to the autumn of 1858, when Wagner began for Frau Wesendonk's benefit that "Venice Diary" that is of the first importance for our understanding of him at that time. "Nothing touches me seriously", he wrote, "save in so far as it awakes in me fellow-feeling, that is, fellow-suffering. This compassion I recognise as the strongest feature of my moral being, and presumably it is also the fountain-head of my art." Even more with animals than with man, he says, does he feel kinship through suffering, for man by his philosophy can raise himself to a resignation that transcends his pain, whereas the mute unreasoning animal can only suffer without comprehending why. "And so if there is any purpose in all this suffering it can only be the awakening of pity in man, who thus takes up the animal's failed existence into himself, and, by perceiving the error of all existence, becomes the redeemer of the world. This interpretation will become clearer to you some day from the third act of *Parzival*, which takes place on Good Friday morning." Manifestly, then, the Parzival drama had already defined itself within him as the drama of compassion.

17

The dates of composition of *Parsifal* are as follows:

Poem. Act	I	finished 29 March 1877.
	Act II	finished 13 April 1877.
	Act III	finished 19 April 1877.
Music. Begun		August 1877.
	Prelude	Sketch finished 26 September 1877.
	Act I	Composition Sketch finished 31 January 1878.
	Act II	Composition Sketch finished 13 October 1878.
	Act III	Composition Sketch finished 26 April 1879.
Orchestral Score.		
	Act I	Begun 23 August 1879 but soon abandoned; resumed 23 November 1880. Finished 25 April 1881.
	Act II	Begun 6 June 1881. Finished 19 October 1881.
	Act III	Begun 5 November 1881. Finished 13 January 1882.

The final page of the manuscript of the orchestral score, however, is dated 25 December 1881. The explanation of the discrepancy is that Wagner had promised Cosima that the work should be complete for presentation to her on Christmas Day, which was also her birthday. Finding himself unable to keep this promise to the letter he scored the final page on the 25th December, inserted the date at the end, and filled in the few pages thus left blank between then and the 13th January 1882.

The work was produced for the first time at the Bayreuth Festival of 1882. Sixteen performances of it were given, running from the 22nd July to the 29th August. Partly to avoid undue strain on the singers, partly to insure against illness or the caprices of the artistic temperament, Wagner employed a double cast. That for the opening performance consisted of (1) Winkelmann (Parsifal), (2) Scaria (Gurnemanz), (3) Hill (Klingsor), (4) Reich-mann (Amfortas), (5) Amelia Materna (Kundry). The alternative cast was (1) Gudehus (and Jäger), (2) Siehr, (3) Fuchs, (5) Marianne Brandt (and Therese Malten). Reichmann sang Amfortas in all sixteen performances. Hermann Levi conducted.

On the afternoon of the 12th November 1880 Wagner, who was in Munich at the time, conducted two performances of the *Parsifal* prelude by the orchestra of the Court Theatre for the private hearing of King Ludwig. To assist the King's comprehension he gave him the following description of it:

"Love—Faith—Hope?

First theme: *Love*.
'Take ye my body, take my blood, in token of our love!' (repeated by angel voices gradually dying away). 'Take ye my blood, take my body, that you may hold me in your remembrance!'
(Again repeated and dying away).

Second theme: *Faith:*
Promise of redemption through Faith. Firmly and stoutly Faith declares itself, exalted, unshakeable even in suffering. —The promise is repeated and answered by Faith from the remote heights—hovering downwards, as it were on the

pinions of the white dove—taking more and more complete possession of the breast, the heart of man, filling all nature with the mightiest force, then looking aloft again to heaven's vault in sweet tranquillity.—

But once more, from out the awe of solitude, there throbs the lament of loving pity: fear, dismay, the holy sweat of Olivet, the divine death-throes of Golgotha,—the body pales, the blood wells forth and glows with heavenly blessing in the Chalice, pouring out the grace of redemption on all that lives and suffers. We are made ready for Amfortas, the sinning keeper of the holy relic, who, racked with repentance, quails before the divine chastisement which the sight of the glowing Grail brings with it; will the gnawing anguish of his soul find redemption?—Once more we hear the promise; and—we *hope*!"

18

This, however, is a doctrinal elucidation of the prelude rather than a musical analysis of it. Anything of the latter kind would have been useless to the King, whereas he had always been intensely interested in the emotional and philosophical motives of the poem, which Wagner now drew into one focus for him.

The long prelude[1] begins with an extended theme that is an entity in itself:

[1] As already stated, it was completed by the 26th September 1877, on which date Wagner played it to Cosima; therefore not only some of the central musical motives of the opera but the psychological connotations and inter-actions of them must have been fully formed in his mind some time before he began regular work at the opera itself.

yet embodies three leading motives that can be used in the course
of the work either in conjunction or separately: that marked B is
always associated with suffering, particularly that of Amfortas,
while C pertains more especially to the Spear. As so often happens
in connection with Wagner, it is difficult to attach to our No. 1 a
single label that will characterise it in every one of its appearances.
It is generally referred to by the commentators as the Love Feast
motive, because it forms the basis of the song that accompanies
the serving of the Bread and Wine in the Hall of the Grail. It must
always be borne in mind, however, that during the opera each of
the three limbs of No. 1 has a life and a function of its own,
calling, for purposes of analysis, for an individual title.

The seemingly indeterminate rhythm of the unaccompanied
melody as a whole, arising from its syncopations, caused much
head-shaking among some of the musical critics who heard it for
the first time in 1882; they were unable to read a shape into a
phrase in which the stresses occurred so irregularly, with such
small concern for the sacred laws of four-four. But Wagner knew
quite well what he was about: the seeming vagueness of the
rhythm and the enunciation of the melody without supporting
and key-defining chords gives us a feeling of being plunged
straight into a world remote from that of everyday reality.

At the end of our quotation No. 1 the orchestra (flutes, clarinets,
etc.) builds up in arpeggios a succession of chords that con-
clusively establish the key as that of A flat major. Wagner is in no
hurry: he has a great deal of mystical emotion to evoke from No.
1 before he relinquishes it for his next main theme, the entry of
which he deliberately delays. First of all he repeats the motive
with arpeggio harmonies an octave higher in the violins, trumpet
and oboe, the soft yet urgent trumpet tone giving it a peculiar
poignancy; and once more the close is in A flat. Then he shifts the
plane of No. 1 to the key of C minor, but follows the same de-
liberate procedure as before—(a) a quiet unaccompanied statement of the melody in strings and wood wind, followed by (b) a
slow building up of the harmony of C minor, (c) a repetition of
the theme an octave higher in violins, oboe and trumpet, which
involves taking the trumpet up to the extreme height of its com-
pass:

and so intensifies the sense of poignancy, (d) a long dwelling on the C minor harmony that has now been reached.

The brass then give out a new motive, that of the Grail, in compact soft harmonies:

It is repeated immediately an octave higher, pianissimo, in the wood wind. There are still innocents abroad who gleefully inform the world that they have discovered this theme in Mendelssohn's Reformation Symphony, so that this is one more instance of Wagner's shameless "stealing" from other composers. The fact is that the theme is the ancient "Dresden Amen", which Mendelssohn had used in 1830, and Wagner used half-a-century later, because it had for them and for thousands of their hearers a special appropriateness to the solemn matter in hand. Wagner must have heard the "Amen" times without number during his kapellmeistership in Dresden.

So far the markings in general have been piano and pianissimo. Now, for the first time, the orchestra rises to a forte as the horns and trumpets give out the resolute motive of Faith, with the trombones coming in later to clinch the cadential harmonies:

The *ff* dies down again to *pp*. A soft repetition of the Grail motive steals in in the strings, followed by a quiet repeat of the Faith theme in a higher register but gradually descending into the depths again. Then comes a dramatic high-light. No. 4 is given out once more fortissimo. When he was writing the prelude Wagner told Cosima that "the modulation into D major" in this section "symbolised for him the spreading of the tender revelation throughout the whole world". But this time Wagner guards against any possible impression of monotony by a majestic extension and rhythmical alteration of the theme:

which afterwards reverts to its original steady 6/4 and dies away into silence.

This concludes the first section of the prelude, which so far has been mainly devoted to establishing the general atmosphere associated with the Grail and stressing the motive of Faith. Now Amfortas and his sufferings become the centre of interest. No. 1 is taken up again and developed, with particular insistence on the agonised No. 1B and a poignant harmonisation at one point of the motive of the Spear (No. 1C):

This is repeated three times at successively higher pitches; then it merges into a figure which is much used later in the opera in connection with the agony of Amfortas:

(See, for instance, No. 26 below). Out of the opening notes of this phrase Wagner distils for a moment the last drops of human anguish:

after which the music slowly soars aloft and poises itself for a while on a prolonged indecisive harmony as the curtain rises.

19

Nietzsche's ill-bred vituperation of *Parsifal* in public in *Der Fall Wagner* will probably be familiar to the reader. Less well known is a passage in one of his private letters to a musical friend in which he confesses to have been shaken to his depths by the prelude. He had not been present at the production of the opera in Bayreuth in 1882; but he heard the prelude at a concert in Monte-Carlo in January 1887, and wrote thus concerning it to a musical friend: "Putting aside all irrelevant questions (to what end such music *can* or *should* serve?), and speaking from a purely aesthetic point of view, has Wagner ever written anything *better*? The supreme psychological perception and precision as regards what had to be said, expressed, *communicated* here, the extreme of concision and directness of form, every nuance of feeling conveyed epigrammatically; a clarity of musical description that reminds us of a shield of consummate workmanship; and finally an extraordinary sublimity of feeling, something experienced in the very depths of music, that does Wagner the highest honour; a synthesis of conditions which to many people—even 'higher' minds—will seem incompatible, of strict coherence, of 'loftiness' in the most startling sense of the word, of a cognisance and a penetration of vision that cuts through the soul as if with a knife, of sympathy with what is seen and shewn forth. We get something comparable to it in Dante, but nowhere else. Has any painter ever depicted so sorrowful a look of love as Wagner has done in the final accents of his prelude?"

And to his sister he wrote a little later: "I cannot think of [the prelude] without feeling violently shaken, so elevated was I by it, so deeply moved." Then follows a passage which those would do well to ponder who rail at *Parsifal*, as Nietzsche did in *Der Fall Wagner*, because it is a "Christian" work, Wagner here, according to Nietzsche—the Wagner who had been a freethinker—having "fallen sobbing at the foot of the Cross". "It is as if someone were speaking to me again after many years", says the philosopher, "about the problems that disturb me—naturally not supplying the answer *I* would give, but the Christian answer, which, after all, has been the answer of stronger souls than the last two centuries of our era have produced. When listening to this music one lays Protestantism aside as a misunderstanding—moreover, I will not deny it, *other really good* music, which I have at other times heard and loved, seems, as against this, a misunderstanding."

The artist in Nietzsche was wiser than the philosopher. The beauty and profundity of the *Parsifal* prelude made him conscious, at any rate for the time being, that in a work of art it is only the art that matters, not the body of knowledge or system of thought with which it happens to be conjoined. The fact that we do not believe in ghosts does not make us shut our ears to *Hamlet*; the fact that the gods of the Greeks are not ours does not make us abuse the Greek dramatists for falling at the feet of Zeus, as we might put it after Nietzsche's fashion. A work of art like *Parsifal* is to be accepted in virtue of the appeal it makes to the artist in us, whether we are Christian or Jew or freethinker. This or that theological or philosophical "answer to the problems that disturb us" —to hark back to Nietzsche's words—is valid for one of us and invalid for his neighbour, but art has no concern with these things; and to fulminate against *Parsifal* for the Christianity of its subject is, even to the freethinker who happens to be also an artist, as absurd as it would be to turn our backs on the *Divina Commedia* because we have no belief in the mediaeval theological system that was accepted as the final truth by Dante. Art of itself has nothing to do with "truths" of the material world that are true for one man, one sect, but false for another. Nietzsche's classical studies should have taught him that more than one ancient critic had pointed out that the "truth" of art and the "truth" of life are entirely different things. Poetic truth, said Aristotle, "should not be confused with truth historical, logical or moral"; and Philodemus of Gadara, writing in Rome in the first century B.C., laid it down that in poetry anything and everything can be "true", "including themes fabulous and even false, monsters or legendary spirits, provided they are artistically represented, in concrete and vivid fashion."

20

The long-drawn-out chord of the seventh that marked the end of the prelude is still poised, unresolved, in the upper air when the curtain rises, showing a forest, solemn and shady but not gloomy, in the domain of the Grail. On the left a road ascends to the castle: at the back, at a lower level, is a lake. In a glade in the foreground Gurnemanz, an elderly but vigorous man, and two young squires are sleeping under a tree. Day is breaking, and from the left, behind the scenes, comes, as if from the castle, the morning reveille of the trombones (the opening notes of No. 1). At Gurnemanz's call the squires leap to their feet; then the three sink to their knees and, to the soft accompaniment (muted strings) of No. 4 and No. 3, silently offer up the morning prayer.

This done, the old man bids the others look to the bath, for it is the hour when the sick King is wont to bathe in the lake, and his litter is even now approaching. A motive symbolising the sickness and weariness of Amfortas is first heard in the strings at this point:

It will appear later in a variety of forms.

Two knights from the castle enter. How fares the King today? Gurnemanz eagerly asks them. Has the wild herb that Gawain[1] lately found brought him any relief? No, they reply; the old irremediable pain racks him more grievously than ever. The faithful, anxious Gurnemanz sinks his head sadly: fools are they all, he says, for ordinary human solace seeking, when one thing only, one man only, can bring the King relief: and in the orchestra we hear a first suggestion of the enigmatic motive of the Pure Fool— the core of the mystery of redemption through simple pity. For greater convenience of reference it is quoted here in the fuller form it assumes later in the act:

[1] This Gawain must not be associated with the famous Gawain who, in some of the legends, shares the quest of the Grail with Parsifal. In the opera "Gawain" is merely the name of one of the knights of the brotherhood of Monsalvat; he is not included among the *dramatis personae,* nor is he even mentioned by name after the present scene.

10
Durch Mit - leid wissend, der rei - ne Tor,
Made wise through pi - ty, the blame-less fool,

har - re sein', den ich er - kor.
wait for him, my own is he.

"Who then is the one? Name him for us!" says the second knight; but Gurnemanz, who alone among them knows the secret of how the King had received his wound, fends him off with an evasive "See ye to the bath!"

No sooner has he said this than the orchestra breaks into a succession of hurrying figures, announcing the approach of "the wild woman", as the squires call her, sweeping across the moss on her "devil's mare". The motive of her frenzied ride runs thus:

11
Allegro

etc.

Notice the stabbing accentuation of some of the notes, with its suggestion of breathless panting—a vital feature of the theme that is rarely brought out properly in performance.

The excited comment of the squires as they watch the approaching figure is cut short by a tearing dissonance in the orchestra as Kundry makes her entrance on the stage:

"She rushes in hurriedly, almost reeling", say the stage directions. "Her garment is wild and looped up high; she wears a girdle of snake-skins the long ends of which hang down: her hair is black and falls in loose locks: her complexion is a deep reddish-brown: her eyes are black and piercing, sometimes flashing wildly, but more often fixed in a stare like that of the dead." Wagner regarded Kundry as the greatest of his female creations; she is certainly the most original and the most enigmatic, and the part is the most difficult of all the Wagnerian characters to play.

She stumbles forward to Gurnemanz and thrusts a small crystal vial into his hand, muttering "Here! Take thou! It is a balsam brought from further hence than thy thought can fly. Should this fail, Arabia holds no other simple for his relief. Ask no further! I am weary!" and she throws herself exhausted on the ground.

21

Gurnemanz turns his attention from her as a train of knights and squires comes upon the stage—to the accompaniment of the weary, dragging No. 9—bearing and escorting the litter in which the sick King reclines. Gurnemanz's heart goes out to him in a surge of love and pity. "Alas!" he cries:

> *What grief beyond enduring!*
> *The proudest flower of manhood faded,*

the master of the conquering race
to his own sickness bound a slave!

The "conquering race" is of course the Grail brotherhood of
knights, leagued to do battle against the heathen; and as Gurnemanz speaks the words the orchestra gives out a theme which will
be recognised as a variant of that of Faith (No. 4):

At A, it will be observed, to the words "to his own sickness
bound a slave", the music melts into the melancholy motive of
Amfortas's Suffering that is embedded in the opening theme of the
prelude (No. 1B).

The King, a little refreshed by the anticipation of his bath in the
lake, would rest awhile. His night of pain, he says to the accompaniment of No. 9, is over: "earth's light is sweet again": and the
orchestra, with the pastoral oboe as soloist, paints a gracious
little vignette of the beauty and solace of uncorrupted nature:

The phrase will appear again, in essentials, in the ecstatic meadow
music of the Good Friday scene in the third act. (See No. 51).

Amfortas calls wearily for Gawain, but is informed that the knight, his search for a healing herb having failed, has set out in quest of another. "Unbidden!" says Amfortas: "the Grail will make him atone for having thus flouted its command"—that is to say, for having looked for the King's healing to any other than the mysterious one chosen by itself: woe to Gawain if he should happen to fall into Klingsor's toils! As for himself, says Amfortas, he can but wait for the promised one, the blameless fool: would that as Death he could greet him! Gurnemanz implores him to essay the balsam brought by "the woman wild" from Araby. The King turns with a gentle word of thanks to the rough repulsive figure crouching on the ground; but Kundry, to a flash of the feverish No. 12 in the orchestra, disclaims the thanks and bids him pass on to the bath. Amfortas gives the signal: the squires raise the litter, and, to the quiet strains of No. 9 and No. 14, the procession moves slowly into the deep background, followed by the grieving eyes of the faithful old Gurnemanz.

22

When the King has disappeared the squires[1] turn savagely on the prostrate Kundry, "lying there like a wounded beast". "Are not even the wild beasts holy in the Grail's domain?" she asks. Doubtless, they reply; but does that tolerance apply to her? Will not "the witch's magic balm" bring bane to the King? Gurnemanz gently intervenes. What harm has she ever done to them? he asks: is it not she who carries messages to the knights in distant lands fighting against the heathen?

> She needs you not—afar she bides:
> naught common has she with you;
> yet need ye her help when danger threats,
> afire with zeal she flies through the air,
> and never word of thanks will ask.
> Meseemeth, is this harmful,
> for naught but your weal it worketh.

[1] Some of the squires of the King's retinue have remained behind after the departure of the litter.

"She hates us though", the squires insist: "her wild eyes flash rancour on us: she is a heathen, a sorceress." "Yea, under a curse she haply lies", Gurnemanz answers quietly:

> *Here lives she now—*
> *perchance her soul*
> *for sins of old is penance paying,*
> *for which in vain she sought forgiveness.*
> *Seeketh she now to make atonement*
> *among our brotherhood by lowly service,*
> *good doth she do, as ye all know;*
> *serving us—herself she aids.*

When Gurnemanz speaks of her perchance paying penance for some sin of old, the orchestra, with a soft suggestion of No. 1A in the bass clarinet, followed by No. 12, gives us a hint that that sin was connected with the brotherhood of the Grail.

"It is some unforgiven guilt of hers, then", ask the squires, "that brings on us this bitter dole?" Step by step Gurnemanz tells them what he knows of the mystery surrounding her. He himself has known her long, but Titurel, the father of Amfortas, longer: for he had found her, one day when the castle was building, asleep in a thicket, frozen, lifeless; and the orchestra, projecting in dark wood wind colours the motive of Klingsor's magic:

tells us what even Gurnemanz himself does not know—that Kundry is bound to the service of the sorcerer Klingsor. It had been benumbed in a thicket that Gurnemanz himself had found her, he tells the squires, on the day when ill-hap fell on the brotherhood through "that evil one beyond the mountains". "Where wert thou, wild one", he turns and asks her, "the day when our King lost the Spear? Why was then thy help withheld?" "I ne'er give help", she mutters; but once more the orchestra, by a reiteration of No. 15, tells us something which the old man himself has never fathomed.

If she be so faithful to them all, and so strong and bold, says a third squire, then let her be sent to find the lost Spear. Alas, Gurnemanz replies, that is another matter; the way to the Spear no one knows. And he breaks into a poignant lament as he recalls that drear day when he saw the sacred weapon held aloft in the unhallowed hand of Klingsor. With the Spear to strengthen Amfortas, how had it come about that he could not lay the evil magician low? Gurnemanz knows only that hard by the castle walls the King had been enticed away by a woman of terrible enchantment: the old man had found him lying in her arms, the Spear fallen from his hand. Amfortas had given a cry like that of death: Gurnemanz had rushed to him, but only to see Klingsor mocking him with obscene laughter and brandishing the holy Spear in triumph. The old knight had brought Amfortas back to safety; but in his side was burning a wound so grievous that it will never close again. The orchestral texture throughout this episode is a complex of motives, including that of Klingsor's magic and those pertaining to the Spear and the anguish of Amfortas. All through *Parsifal*, indeed, Wagner's art of the psychological inter-weaving of motives is at its finest.

The squires who had accompanied the King to the lake now return.[1] The bath and the balsam brought by Kundry had soothed his pain, they say; and we hear in the orchestra the heart-easing No. 14, which, however, merges instantly, by one of those subtle transitions of which Wagner is a master, into the music associated with the King's sufferings as Gurnemanz reiterates mournfully, "This wound it is that ne'er will close again".

23

Wagner's favourite technique of dramatic explanation is a sound one, the product of the musician as well as of the dramatist

---

[1] These are the two original squires. For some reason or other Wagner had made them leave the stage with the King's litter, while some of those who had accompanied its entry remain, and, according to the stage instructions, "pass to and fro". With the return of the original two there are four in all during the present scene. Wagner's procedure was dictated by the necessity of having that number for the four-part harmony of the Pure Fool motive later.

in him. He himself had pointed out long ago, in connection with Tristan, how infinitely richer the musical dramatist's resources are than those of the ordinary playwright or novelist. The latter has to begin with a statement of facts and incidents, material data which he gradually builds up into a complex from which the psychological or emotional essence of the action emerges in due course. The musician has no need to approach the heart of his subject from a remote distance in this slow way: he can pierce at once to the core of *feeling*, leaving the material details to be made manifest later. In the case of *Tristan*, for example, as Wagner says, the artist in prose or verse would have to begin by telling us at great length who and what Tristan and Isolde were, where they lived, what adventures they went through, and how these adventures led them gradually to their dolorous end. But the musician can strike at once, as Wagner does in the first bars of the prelude, into the emotional heart of the story, leaving the factual details to emerge of themselves later.

This is how he proceeds in *Parsifal*. He does not begin, as Wolfram von Eschenbach and the others had had to do, with the ancestry and birth and boyhood of Parsifal, showing how he came to be what he was in himself, how, adventure by adventure, he was drawn into the orbit of the Grail, and so on. Wagner first of all condenses the main emotional motives of the drama in his prelude. In this he does not attempt to tell the full story in the customary overture or symphonic poem form; as the reader will have observed, the prelude contains no reference at all to Parsifal or Klingsor or Kundry. It is sufficient for Wagner's purpose to show us the mystical beauty and solemnity and holiness of the domain of the Grail, the sombre fleck made on all this by the fault and the anguish of Amfortas, and to hint at the end at a possible lifting of the clouds. Then, when the stage action opens, he begins not with a point-by-point exposition of the fundamental incidents of the story—the history of the Grail, the personality of Klingsor, the connection between him and Kundry, the seduction of Amfortas, the rape of the Spear, and so forth—but with the present spiritual consequences of all this. After that, having attuned us by his music to the inner import of all these happenings, he addresses himself to placing us in possession of the facts antedating the emotions—very much as, in the first scene of *Tristan,* he had first of all shewn us the scorn and anger of Isolde and the sombre reserve of Tristan, and then, by means of Isolde's "Narration" to Brangaene, unravelled for us the precedent facts that had led up to the strained phase of the action at which the opera had begun.

24

The device he now adopts, in *Parsifal,* to acquaint the audience with everything that had led up to the emotional tension of the opening scene is again a "Narration". It is not a hoary operatic device dragged in willy-nilly, as in *Il Trovatore,* to tell the audience what it needs to know under the pretext of one character telling another on the stage. It is psychologically justified. The squires are young, new to the castle, to the nature of the Grail and the Spear, ignorant of how these came of old to Monsalvat, ignorant of the nature of the magician on the other side of the mountains, of why he desired to win possession of the Spear, how he came to do so, and the dire consequences of the loss of it to the King and the brotherhood. Only when this has been made clear to all is the action ripe for the entry of the hero who is pre-destined to change the course of events.

How came Gurnemanz to know of Klingsor? the squires ask the old man. They group themselves at his feet under the great tree, and he tells them the whole story. Klingsor had been well known to the pious hero Titurel, who long ago had defended the realm of faith when it was assailed by its enemies. Then had come to him a wonder. One night the Saviour's messengers descended from heaven, bearing with them the sacred cup from which He had drunk at the Last Supper and into which His blood had flowed on the Cross, and the soldier's spear that had pierced His side. The orchestral tissue now becomes a continual linking and inter-weaving of motives, with some of which we are already familiar. At the mention of the bringing of the Cup and the Lance by the angelic messengers to Titurel we hear what at first sight appears to be a new motive:

but is seen, on examination, to be, as No. 13 is, yet another meta-morphosis of No. 4 (the Faith motive). It becomes of great importance in the closing moments of the opera. At Gurnemanz's words:

> *Wherein His blood upon the Cross did flow,*
> *therewith the soldier's spear, that dealt the blow,*

we hear the agonised No. 8 in a new form:

Obviously, therefore, No. 8 is to be taken as pertaining less specifically to Amfortas than to the agony of the Redeemer on the Cross, which becomes the torture of Amfortas himself after he has been wounded by the self-same Spear.

To house the sacred relics, Gurnemanz continues, Titurel had built a fane wherein he gathered a company of the pure in heart, whose mission it should be to purify the world through the wonder-working power of the Grail. Hence Klingsor, whose sinister motive is now heard in clarinets and bassoons:

was excluded from the brotherhood. "Alone dwelt Klingsor in yon distant valley, where all the land is rank with heathendom. Never knew I what sin he had there committed; yet now atone would he—ay, holy make him. No strength had he to slay the raging lusts within him; desperate, he turned against himself his hand. And then the Grail he fain would grasp, but scornfully its guardian drove him forth." But Klingsor's vain mutilation of himself had brought him knowledge of a dark magic (No. 15 in the orchestra, followed by No. 12, indicating Kundry as the instrument of his evil designs). He had turned the desert into "magic gardens, with women rich in all beguilements": whereupon we hear a foreshadowing:

of the motive of the Flower Maidens, which is quoted here in the more definite form it assumes in the second act. "There doth he lurk to lure the Grail's pure warders to shameful joys and soul's defilement. Whom once he snares"—and No. 12 again hints at Kundry as the instrument of Klingsor's magic—"no more is saved: full many hath he now enslaved."

When Titurel, old and weary, gave his guardianship of the Grail into the hands of his son, Amfortas turned with holy zeal to rid the earth of this plague. The rest, says Gurnemanz, his hearers already know: the Spear fell into the hands of Klingsor, who thus has won power over the brethren, and hopes ere long to possess himself of the Grail itself. All the while that Gurnemanz has been speaking Kundry has been silent; but she frequently turns towards him, as the stage directions have it, "in angry and passionate disquiet".

One thing, the old man continues, must before all be done—the

Spear must be won back again. The maimed Amfortas had prostrated himself in prayer before the deserted sanctuary, imploring a sign from heaven. Thereupon the Grail had flooded him with its radiance, and a voice had given him a mystic token: "Made wise through pity, the Blameless Fool—wait for him, my chosen one"; and the squires repeat the words softly and wistfully in four-part harmony (No. 10).

25

There is a long contemplative pause after the mysterious words, and then a wild outburst in the orchestra, and cries of "Woe!" from knights and squires behind the scenes, from the direction of the lake. First of all we hear (No. 20A) the opening notes of the bold motive henceforth employed to characterise Parsifal: for convenience of further reference it is quoted here:

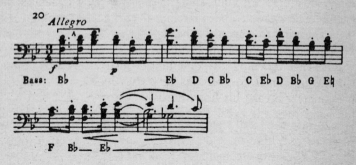

in the full form it assumes a little later. It is instantly succeeded by an agitated passage:

which outlines a motive that will shortly define itself as that of the swan:

which Wagner takes over from his *Lohengrin*. A wounded wild swan flies brokenly across the scene, to the accompaniment of cries of horror from them all: it sinks heavily to the ground, and one of the knights draws an arrow from its breast. The King, says another, had hailed the bird, flying round the lake, as a happy omen; but a wanton shaft had sped through the air and pierced it. Parsifal, a rough boyish figure, is dragged in, carrying his bow and arrows, and he admits it was he who had brought down the swan. The knights and squires clamour for his punishment. Gurnemanz addresses him in sad reproach: he would do murder, then, here in the holy woodland where all is peace, where the dumb creatures are tame and trustful and regard man as their friend? The swan had been circling over the lake looking for his mate, meaning to consecrate the bath for the King; and this brutal boy had no thought but to slay him.

The first dawning of something which afterwards, though slowly, he comes to know as pity rises in Parsifal's heart; he passionately breaks his bow, hurls his arrows away, and passes his hand over his eyes. Does he feel the burden of his guilt? Gurnemanz asks him. What mad impulse had driven him to this deed? "I knew not it was wrong", says the boy humbly. "Whence art thou come?" "That know I not." "Who is thy father?" "That know I not." "Who sent thee here?" "That know I not." "What is thy name?" "Once I had many, but none of them can I now recall"; and the orchestra breathes softly the tender motive that will later characterise his sorrowing mother Herzeleide (Heart-in-sorrow):

"So dull a one ne'er have I found", says Gurnemanz despairingly, "save Kundry here." We are brought face to face, indeed, but in an intensified emotional form, with the all-unknowing boy of the early stages of Wolfram's poem.

But a faint light seems to be breaking upon Gurnemanz. He bids the squires leave him and tend the King, and they go off, bearing with them reverently the dead swan on a bier they have made out of fresh branches from the glade. Only the old man, Parsifal and Kundry remain behind. Gurnemanz turns to the boy again. Something, surely, he must know, he says. "I know of my mother", Parsifal replies: "Herzeleide is her name; my home was in trackless meadows. My bow I made myself, to scare the savage eagles from the forest." "Yet thou seem'st of noble birth", says Gurnemanz; "why taught thee not thy mother the use of worthier weapons?" To this the unschooled boy cannot reply; but Kundry, hoarsely breaking her long silence, answers for him. His father Gamuret, she says, was slain in battle; and lest the same fate should come upon him also his mother had brought him up in seclusion, strange to arms, a simple fool—and no less fool she! Parsifal's memories of his childhood revive, and he breaks into eager speech. He remembers now that once, on the fringe of the wood, men in glittering raiment had swept by him, mounted on splendid animals: fain would he have been like them, but they passed on their way with laughter. This story of his is accompanied in the orchestra by a new version of No. 11: evidently for Wagner the motive did not relate specifically to Kundry's ride but, as it were, to riding in general.

The boy had run after the knights but soon lost sight of them. He had wandered long and far, over hill and dale, night following day; and against robbers and giants and wild beasts he had had no defence but his bow. "Ay!" interjects Kundry, "all feared the valorous boy!" "Who fears me?" asks the astonished Parsifal. "The wicked", she replies. "Were those who threatened me wicked? Who then is good?" he asks. Gurnemanz laughs for a moment at his simplicity; then, becoming serious again, he answers the latter part of Parsifal's question: "Thy mother, from whom thou fleddest, and who for thee now doth pine and grieve." "She grieves no more", says Kundry. "She is dead: as I rode by I saw

her dying, and to thee, fool, she sent a greeting." "It is false!"
cries Parsifal; and he springs at Kundry in a passion and seizes
her by the throat. Gurnemanz restrains him, and once more
reproaches him for his violence. The boy stands for a while as if
turned to stone: then a paroxysm of trembling seizes him, and he
seems about to faint; whereupon Kundry hastens to a spring in the
wood, brings water in a horn, sprinkles him with it, and gives it
him to drink.

Gurnemanz praises her kindness: this is the Grail's own grace,
he says, that turns evil aside from one who meets it with good.
"Good I do never", she mutters, to a motive that has already been
used to symbolise her service:

which is followed by that of Klingsor's magic (No. 15); and when
Gurnemanz turns kindly to Parsifal again she drags herself, unnoticed by them both, towards a thicket. Oh that she might
slumber and never waken! she groans; and yet she hardly dares
to sleep, for horrors and terrors hag-ride her. At last she is overcome by weariness; she lets her arms sink to her side, bows her
head, staggers convulsively behind the thicket, and is lost to
view.

26

Just then the train of knights and squires becomes visible in the
background, bearing the King in his litter back from the lake to
the castle. Something in what Parsifal has said, and, even more,
something in his unconscious bearing has struck deep into
Gurnemanz and raised a faint hope there: he resolves to take the
boy to the holy meal that is to be partaken of in the castle; "for
art thou pure", he tells him, "the Grail will give thee food and
drink." "Who is the Grail?" the ignorant boy asks in wonder.
Gurnemanz evades the question:

I may not say; but art thou to its service bidden,
not long the knowledge shall be hidden.
And lo! methinks I know thee now indeed:
no way doth to its kingdom lead;
no human foot the pathway treadeth
save him whom itself it leadeth.

"I hardly stir", says the astonished Parsifal, "and yet I move apace." This Gurnemanz explains to him: "Thou seest, my son, here time is one with space."

In this world of mystery and magic, indeed, there is no dividing line between the physical and the metaphysical. For some minutes Gurnemanz and Parsifal remain stationary at the front of the stage, while a curtain that has descended, which depicts various aspects of rock and woodland, moves slowly from left to right, thus creating, in the mind of the imaginative spectator, the illusion that the two figures are moving from right to left.[1] "The wood disappears", run Wagner's stage directions; "a gate opens in the rock, through which the pair pass and are lost to sight; later they become visible once more, apparently ascending a path." Accompanying the change is the magnificent Transformation Music. First of all we hear the solemn motive, which has been already anticipated a few times, of the bells pealing out from the castle:

---

[1] I have pointed out elsewhere that Ludwig Börne, in a letter of 1831 from Paris, described at some length a dramatic-panoramic history of Napoléon 1 which he had just seen at the Odéon Theatre: in the episode of the escape from Elba, while the man-o'-war carrying the Emperor remained stationary, the coastal scenery kept changing, "so that", as Börne put it, "the spectator gets the impression that the ship itself is in motion." It is possible that this device was popular in Paris in the 1830's, and that Wagner may have seen it in operation during his residence there between 1839 and 1842.

This is interwoven with the Grail motive and the Faith motive (Nos. 3 and 4), and with the agonised motive of Amfortas's repentance (No. 6) in the heightened form it generally assumes from now onwards; it is quoted here in the last and most tremendous of its three enunciations during the Transformation Music:

where it is given out fortissimo by the full orchestra.

As the theme rises to its climax and dies away again there pierces through the tissue a commanding statement of the Love Feast motive (the opening bars of No. 1), volleyed from the still invisible castle by six trombones behind the scenes:

and then a second time, with the addition of six trumpets; at the same time the solemn chime of the bells comes nearer (No. 25). This tonal picture of the journey from the glade to the castle is one of unrivalled splendour.

27

The curtain having risen again, we see that Gurnemanz and Parsifal have by now come to a vast hall, which is surmounted by a great vaulted cupola through which alone the light enters. From the heights we hear the tolling of the bells, becoming ever louder and louder. "Now," says Gurnemanz to Parsifal, "give good heed, and let me see, if thou art a fool and pure, what wisdom may come to thee." From this point until the end of the act the boy stands immobile at the side-front of the stage, with his back to the audience, lost in wonder at the marvellous pageant that unfolds itself before his eyes.

What he sees first is the great pillared hall, with two doors opening into it from the back. To the pealing of the bells the knights of the Grail enter through the door on the right and proceed in grave procession to their places at two long covered tables, which run in parallel lines from back to front of the stage, leaving the middle of the hall open; on the tables are nothing but cups. Two groups of squires pass quickly across the stage to the back of the scene while the still moving knights sing in unison an invocation to the eucharistic meal of which they are about to partake; and as they seat themselves at the tables a choir—invisible in the mid-height of the dome—of boys' voices gives out the anguished No. 26 to the words:

> *A world sunk in sinning*
> *His pangs redeemed,*
> *its innocence restoring;*
> *now to Him, our Saviour,*
> *my soul in gladness its offering*
> *of blood is pouring;*
> *upon the Cross He gave His breath,—*
> *now lives He in us by His death;*

followed by a call to drink the wine and eat the bread. During this chorus Amfortas has been carried in on a litter by the knights; before them go four squires bearing a shrine enveloped in a purple-red cover. The King is taken to the centre background and placed on a raised couch beneath a canopy; in front of the couch stands an oblong marble table, on which the squires deposit the shrine.

When all are seated, and the singing has ceased, there comes a long, impressive silence: then, from a vaulted niche in the extreme background, behind Amfortas's couch, we hear the blanched voice of the aged Titurel, coming as if from a tomb. Shall he look

upon the Grail again and be quickened, he asks, or must he die?
To the strains of No. 26 Amfortas begs his father to take over his
office again from his own unworthy hands: "live thou, and let me
perish". "Too old and feeble am I", Titurel replies, "to serve the
Redeemer: do thou serve, and in serving atone for thy guilt.
Uncover the Grail!" But before the squires can do so Amfortas
rises on his couch, and in a long monologue pours out all the pain
and bitterness of his unworthy soul—"Grievous the birthright to
me descended; I, the only sinner among the brethren, to minister
the holy relic and pray its blessing on these pure ones!"

He bids them leave the Grail still uncovered. Once again he re-
lives in imagination his fall from grace; he feels his own blood stir
in rapture and pain in mystic communion with the blood in the
Cup; once more he feels the torture of his wound, with its likeness
to that of the Saviour on the Cross, for the same Spear had
pierced them both; and it was he, the Grail's appointed, who had
brought this disaster on himself and the brotherhood. With an
impassioned cry for mercy and forgiveness and for purification
by death he sinks back on his couch, as if unconscious. The
orchestral texture throughout his monologue consists of the finest
interweaving of many of the motives familiar to us by now;
sometimes they are subtly modified, as when the serene Grail
motive (No. 3) undergoes a harmonic and (in the accompaniment)
a rhythmic change:

As the King falls back exhausted the boys' voices from the mid-height intone softly the mysterious motive of the Pure Fool (No. 10), which is followed by that of the Grail as Amfortas raises himself slowly and with difficulty from his couch. The squires unveil the golden shrine and take from it the Grail, which the stage directions describe as "an antique crystal cup"; this they uncover, and then place it in front of Amfortas. He bows devoutly before it in silent prayer as the altos and tenors, from the height of the cupola, sing quietly, to the melody of No. 1, the words with which Wagner began his analysis of the prelude for King Ludwig:

> *Take my body and eat,*
> *take and drink my blood;*
> *this be our love's remembrance;*

to which the boys' voices add:

> *Take and drink my blood,*
> *take my body and eat,*
> *the while of me ye think.*

As in the prelude, between the two enunciations of the theme, and again after the second of them, the trumpet, in soft, solemn tones, throws out the motive in high relief against a background of shimmering arpeggios.

28

During all this the hall has grown completely dark; but as the melody rises to its greatest height (as in No. 2) a dazzling shaft of light falls from above upon the Cup, making it glow with an ever-deepening purple that casts a gentle radiance on the scene. Amfortas, his face transfigured, raises the Grail aloft and waves it gently from side to side in consecration of the bread and wine: the knights, who have sunk upon their knees as twilight descended upon the hall, raise their eyes in devotion to the Chalice. Titurel breaks into a cry of rapture. Amfortas sets the Grail down again, and the squires replace it in the shrine, which they cover with the cloth once more. As the purple glow fades, darkness gives way to twilight in the hall, and this in turn to full daylight.

Now comes the serving of the eucharist. The four squires who have borne the Grail, having closed the shrine, take from the altar table the two wine flagons and the baskets of bread that Amfortas has consecrated. The knights, including Gurnemanz, seat themselves at the tables; the old man, however, has kept a place empty next to his. He signs to Parsifal to come forward and take part in the meal; but the uncomprehending boy remains motionless, lost in amazement. The serving of the communion is accompanied by some higher boys' voices from above:

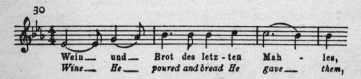

Wein— und— Brot des letz-ten Mah - les,
Wine— He— poured and bread He gave— them,

and then by lower boys' voices reinforced by a few high tenors. Finally the knights themselves take up the strain in a modified form, and the long episode ends with the Grail motive rising slowly from the depths to the supreme height of the dome and dying away as the knights rise from the tables, pace slowly towards each other, and embrace.

Amfortas has taken no part in the meal, of which he feels he is unworthy by reason of his sin against the Grail and his loss of the Spear. His momentary exaltation has ebbed from him: he bows his head in utter weariness, and as he presses his hand to his side and the squires tend him solicitously we realise that his wound has broken out afresh. They place him in the litter and bear him and the shrine out of the hall, followed by the knights in solemn procession. During all this the orchestra pours out motive after motive associated with the Grail and the brotherhood and the anguish of Amfortas. The last of the knights and squires having departed, Gurnemanz turns, half in ill-temper, half with a last faint stirring of hope, to Parsifal, whom he has been watching for some time. Only once has the spellbound boy made the smallest movement since he entered the hall: at the climax of the grievous

cry of Amfortas when he confessed his sin and cried out for the
mercy and pity of heaven:

> *Have mercy! Have mercy!*
> *Thou God of pity! Oh, have mercy!*
> *Take back my birthright,*
> *so Thou but heal me,*
> *that holy I die now,*
> *pure for thy presence!*

the boy had pressed his own hand convulsively to his heart and
held it there for some time: he is at the beginning of the fulfilment of his destiny—through pity he will come to understand
the sorrow of earth and grow slowly wise. But nothing yet is
clear to him; all he knows is that the cry of the suffering King,
of whose story he knows nothing, has unlocked something
in his own breast that makes him one with suffering creatures
everywhere.

Even when he and Gurnemanz are left alone in the empty hall
he stands petrified, mute. The disappointed old man goes up to
him in ill humour and shakes him roughly by the arm. "Why
standest thou here still?" he asks him. "Know'st thou what thou
saw'st?" Parsifal shakes his head and again clutches convulsively
at his heart, but cannot speak. Gurnemanz's patience is now at an
end, his last hope destroyed. "Thou art but a fool, then", he says
irritably:

> *Hie thee hence, get thee gone from us!*
> *Take this from Gurnemanz:*
> *leave thou our swans for the future alone,*
> *and seek thyself, gander, a goose!*

He opens a small side door, pushes the boy out roughly, closes the
door on him angrily, and follows the knights. But the last word is
not with him. His furious gesture is followed by a suggestion to us
of something he himself does not know: the orchestra hints
stumblingly at the fact that this ignorant boy is after all the one
chosen by the Grail:

(See No. 10). A single alto voice, piercing the fateful stillness
from the height of the dome, clinches the point by murmuring
"Made wise through pity, the Blameless Fool"; other voices rise
on the air with a murmur of "Blessed in Faith" that dies away into
the distance, the Grail bells give a last soft peal, and the curtain
falls.

29

In the second act we see illumination coming slowly to Parsifal.
The other characters whom we have so far met disappear from
our sight, with the exception of Kundry; and though Klingsor
makes two appearances, it is upon Kundry and Parsifal that the
main burden of the act rests. For Kundry is, in a sense, the hinge
of the drama, linked as she is on one side of her complex being
with the sorcerer, on the other side with the company of the
Grail. She stands between the two opposing worlds of good and
evil, with something of each of them in her; and it is through her,
though without her intending it, that Parsifal will learn the secret
of the fall of Amfortas and the meaning of the pang that had shot
through his own heart as he watched the agony of the King.

Before the curtain rises, a wild orchestral prelude, of the colour and the demonic power of which no piano arrangement can give any idea, sets before us Klingsor and all he stands for. First of all we hear the sinister motive of the magician himself (No. 18); then the Grail as the object of Klingsor's hatred:

(The upper part of this quotation shows a harmonic distortion of the Grail theme, the lower part the Klingsor motive). This runs into contrapuntal combinations of No. 18 and, first of all, the motive of Amfortas's agony, then that of Kundry as the instrument of the sorcerer (No. 12).

At the rising of the curtain we see the inner keep of a tower of Klingsor's castle, with steps at the side that lead down to the edge of the battlements. From the projecting wall the stage runs downwards towards the back. The tower is stocked with magical implements and necromantic apparatus. Through the darkness that envelops the scene we catch sight of Klingsor, seated on the projecting wall, gazing into a metal mirror that shows him all that is going on in his domain. He is brooding mischief: a hint of the Pure Fool motive in the orchestra, followed by that of Kundry (No. 12) and that of Magic (No. 15), gives point to his opening words:

> The time is come.
> My magic tower the Fool now lureth;
> with childish shouting lo! he draweth nigh.
> In deadly slumber fast the witch lies bound.
> The spell that binds her I will loose.
> Up then! To work!

He descends a little towards the centre and kindles incense, which fills part of the background with a bluish vapour. As No. 15

writhes its way through the orchestral texture he seats himself
once more before his magical apparatus and calls with mysterious
gestures into the depths below: "Arise! To me! Thy master
summons thee, nameless one, first of witches, Rose of Hell!
Herodias wert thou, and what besides? Gundryggia there,
Kundry here! Come hither, Kundry!"

In the bluish light in the background we see the wild creature's
figure gradually defining itself. She seems to be waking slowly
out of a sleep in obedience to the magic summons:

The orchestra has sunk to a boding pianissimo: then suddenly
there comes a startling fortissimo ejaculation of the discordant
No. 12, and Kundry awakes with a blood-curdling shriek—
awakes at the bidding of her master to another of the tasks she
hates: then her wail subsides into a low moan of terror. Where
has she been of late? he asks her: with the brotherhood on the
other side of the mountain, where she is regarded as no better than
a brute beast? Why has she fled from her master after she had
accomplished his design upon their King? She struggles numbly
to find speech again and to shake off her torpor and the sense of
madness that comes with the torturing recall of the past. Yes, she
replies, she has been occupied in service among the knights. He
scoffs at her repentance: as for the Grail brotherhood, to them she
need not look to win freedom, for he can seduce them all to him,
as he had done Amfortas, by bidding the fitting price—they will
succumb to Kundry, and in their weakness he will deal them a
wound with the Spear he has ravished from their King.

But today, he says, there is one in the field against him whom he
feels to be the most dangerous of all, "strong as fools alone are
strong". She struggles impotently against the compulsion of his

will. He reminds her that he, Klingsor, alone is proof against her female wiles: she breaks into mocking laughter over his enforced chastity, and he broods darkly and savagely upon it, for his self-mutilation has after all been unavailing—still the old fierce lusts rage within him, and he can neither gratify them nor quell them. Because of his failure he is consumed with hatred for the knights of the Grail; and he gloats over the destruction he had brought on their King, who of old had spurned him and driven him forth from the holy company. Soon, he is sure, the Grail itself will be his. But Kundry bemoans her servitude to him, and most of all her victory over the weak Amfortas. Could she but sleep for ever, she wails, and work no more evil! and we hear in the quiet strings the subtlest and saddest chromatic musing upon the theme of Amfortas's anguish:

She protests passionately when Klingsor tells her of the new task he has for her, the seduction of the fair stripling who is drawing near; and she breaks into hysterical laughter, followed by a convulsive cry of woe, as the magician describes what he can see from his tower. He sounds his horn, and to the accompaniment of feverishly hurrying figures of the type of No. 11 he tells—not without a certain unholy glee, for he hates his own servitors as malignantly as he does the Grail brotherhood—of the havoc that is being wrought among them by this new assailant of theirs.

The identity of the newcomer is established for us by some subtle transformations of the Pure Fool motive in the orchestra; and the theme of Parsifal himself (No. 20) comes out powerfully.

30

Klingsor makes it clear to us that the intruder is a mere boy, now surveying with a childlike wonder the garden the defenders of which he is routing. The magician has other ways of dealing with him, however, than by the sword. He knows that the stripling's strength is in his primal purity: if that should go, all will go, and accordingly he sends Kundry to work upon him in his and her accustomed fashion. Gradually the bluish light that had spread over the background is extinguished, and Kundry has vanished in the darkness. The tower disappears, and Klingsor with it; and instantly the magic garden comes into sight, occupying the whole stage. "Tropical vegetation, luxuriant flowers", say the stage directions. "At the back the scene is closed by the battlements of the ramparts, which are flanked by projecting portions of the castle (in a rich Arabian style) with terraces." Wagner thus follows the legends that place the Grail setting in Arabic Spain, with Monsalvat on one side of a mountain and the domain of Klingsor on the other.

On the ramparts stands Parsifal, gazing down in amazement at the garden beneath him. Beautiful maidens run in from all sides, clad in light soft-coloured veils that have been hastily gathered about them, as if they had been startled out of sleep. They have heard cries and the clash of arms, and have rushed in to see what was afoot. They are divided and subdivided musically into two groups, each with three leaders and a semi-chorus, a disposition which makes it possible for them to dialogue excitedly as they enter.[1] They have seen their lovers struck down by the comely boy who now stands on the ramparts, in his hand a sword, red

[1] The Flower Maidens' choruses can never have been sung in any opera house as magnificently as they were at the first production of the work in Bayreuth in 1882, when, as Wagner wrote to King Ludwig, he had for the leading sopranos of his chorus distinguished artists who had sung parts like Elsa, Isolde, Eva, Brynhilde, Sieglinde and so on in the leading German theatres.

with blood, which he had wrested from one of Klingsor's knights, Ferris. To the Maidens' question of why he had smitten their lovers the boy gives the naive answer, "Need I had to smite them, for my passage to you they would fain have barred."

As he comes nearer they lose their first fear of him and entreat him to join them in their games. Some of them slip away behind the hedges and return entirely decked in flowers; and their example is soon followed by the rest. In childlike glee they group themselves round him and sing their subtly seductive melody (No. 19), accompanying it with caresses and promises of the delights of an earthly Paradise if he will be theirs. They even bicker among themselves for the possession of the charming boy. But he is too ignorant to understand: half-angrily he repulses them and is about to flee, when—one of the most arresting dramatic moments of the opera—the voice of Kundry strikes through the turmoil with his name:

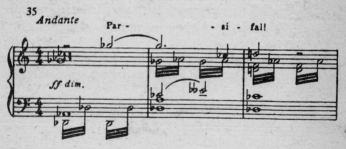

He pauses in perplexity: "Parsifal"? he says; "so named me in a dream once my mother." At the sound of Kundry's voice the Maidens have recoiled in terror, and at her bidding they disappear one by one from the scene, with a parting jibe at the unsophisticated boy—"Farewell, thou proud one, thou Fool!"

31

Parsifal stands as if in a dream. Looking round timidly to the quarter from which the voice had come he sees a young and entrancingly beautiful woman—Kundry completely and unrecognisably transformed: she is robed in a light, veil-like, fantastic garment of Arabian style, and reclines on a couch of flowers. "Parsifal!" she greets him again: "Fal-parsi, Pure Fool!"[1] By this name, she says, before ever he was born, his father Gamuret, dying in a foreign land, had greeted him; and to tell him this has Kundry waited here, and what, except the desire to know it, had drawn him thither? She is not a flower of the garden, as the wondering boy imagines, but one who has come from afar, after seeing and learning many things, to tell him what he should know. She begins in low sweet tones her long narration of his childhood:

The orchestra develops symphonically this motive and that of Herzeleide (No. 23) with many metamorphoses of them as she tells the tender story made familiar to us by Wolfram—how the widowed Heart-in-sorrow had tended the babe of her sorrow, how, in fear of losing the boy as she had lost his father, she had brought him up in the forest in secret and in safety, "afar from arms, from man in madness slaying man", always racked with

[1] Wagner took over from Görres, a German writer of the early nineteenth century, the theory that the name "Parsifal" came from two Arabian words, "Fal" and "Parsi", meaning Pure Fool. The derivation has not found favour with modern scholars.

foreboding when he strayed from her care, raining kisses on him when he returned, till at last there came a day when he wandered away and did not return, and after long days and nights of anxious waiting:

> *too full was her heart of pain;*
> *for death's release she prayed:*
> *her anguish broke her heart,*
> *and—Heart-in-sorrow died.*

Then, for the first time, the boy has an inkling of wrong done by him all unknowing, pain inflicted without understanding and without intent. As Kundry speaks of his mother's death he sinks at her feet, crushed with grief, cursing himself for his childish folly:

> *Mother! Sweetest, dearest Mother!*
> *Thy son, thy son must be thy murderer?*
> *Oh fool! Blind and credulous fool!*
> *Where wandred'st thou, her love forgetting,—*
> *Dearest, fondest of mothers!*

But had he never known this grief, Kundry insinuates, never could love have brought him its solace. But he is inconsolable:

> *My Mother, my Mother—I could forget her!*

he moans:

> *Ha! What more have I, blind one, forgot?*
> *What have I e'er remembered yet?*
> *'Tis only folly dwells in me!*

By knowledge, Kundry tells him, sense returns to the Fool. It is for him now to learn the rapture of love that once burned in Gamuret for Heart-in-sorrow:

> *For she, the woman loved who bore thee,*
> *can death and folly far remove:*
> *she sends thee now a mother's blessing,*
> *greets thy lips—*
> *with this first kiss of love!*

and she bows her head over him and joins her lips to his in a long kiss.

32

But there is evil, the root of the whole world's sad evil, in the kiss, as the slow ascent and fall of the dark motive of Magic (No. 15) in the orchestra warns us. We have arrived at the ethical crux of the drama, a crux that is Wagner's own, not that of any of his predecessors. It is not by surrender to the senses that the brave, simple Fool can become "slowly wise", but only through the lesson of suffering with and pity for others. A shaft of blinding light shoots through Parsifal. A great and terrible change has come over him; he presses his hand against his heart as if to still a rending pain, for now he senses the secret of the agony of Amfortas from his wound. The motive of Suffering (No. 26) goes through transformation after transformation in the orchestra as he pours out his wild lament, for now he is one by sympathetic intuition with the King and what he had once stood for. He understands everything: it is not merely that the guardian of the Grail, sworn to purity, had succumbed to the lure of the senses but that the sanctuary of the Saviour itself, and all it stands for in a world of evil, has been polluted and now calls to him for cleansing:

> *And I—the fool, the coward,*
> *to deeds of boyish wildness hither fled!*
> *Redeemer! Saviour! Lord of grace!—*
> *How for my sin can I atone?*

and he throws himself despairingly on his knees.

His outburst has filled Kundry with wonder and passion; timidly she approaches the boy who has suddenly become a man, and bids him shake himself free of this madness and accept the grace that *she* can bring him. But now he sees her as in essence she is, sensual seduction incarnate, the plague and ruin of noble life; and the primal Kundry motive (No. 12) takes on a new and more insinuating form:

as, still in her arms yet far withdrawn from her within himself, he transfers in his awakened imagination each in turn of her cajolements and caresses to Amfortas:

> *Aye! Thus she called him! This was the voice,*
> *and this her glance—truly I know it now—*
> *what torment its smiling menace brought him!*
> *The lips too—aye—so thrilled they him;*
> *so bent this neck above him—*
> *so boldly rose her head;*
> *so fluttered her locks as in laughter,*
> *so twined she this arm round his neck;*
> *so fawningly smiled she on him;*
> *in league with every direst torment,*
> *his soul's salvation*
> *with that one kiss he lost!—*
> *Ha!—this same kiss!*

and he thrusts her from him violently and rises to his feet.

And now the enigmatic woman feels, or imagines she does, a new kind of passion for him. Since he can thus experience compassion for another, let him now be *her* deliverer, for whom she has been waiting since the day, long ago, when she had reviled and mocked the Saviour of the world, and he gave her—one look!—the deliverer she has ever since been seeking, feeling his eye to be near her in her moments of deepest spiritual need, though always she had laughed her accursed laugh as yet another sinner sank to ruin on her bosom:

> *He I desired in death's deep anguish,*
> *he whom I knew, so weak, derided,*

> *let me upon his breast lie weeping,*
> *be but one hour with thee united,*
> *and though by God and man cast forth,*
> *in thee be cleansed of sin and redeemed!*

But Parsifal replies that were he to yield to her, he who has been destined for her salvation, he would be false to his mission. She must repent of her old desires; for the solace that can end her grief must flow from another source than those desires, and will not flow until that fountain of longing dries up within her. Not this fount of desire was it that his intuition had divined in the suffering hearts of the brotherhood:

> *But who with soul unclouded knows*
> *the fount whence true salvation flows?*
> *Oh mis'ry—that all hope destroys!*
> *   Oh, error's night appalling:*
> *in quest to find salvation's joys*
> *to lusts of hell a victim falling!*

Then she exults that it is she who, by her kiss, has unlocked this wisdom in him, shewn him the world's own heart. In her arms let him learn what it is to be a god, the deliverer of the world; let her perish, unhealed, damned to all eternity, so she but hold him in her embrace. But once more he repulses her: redemption will be hers, he says, only by her shewing him the way that will lead him back to Amfortas. At this she breaks out in fury against him. Never shall he find that way; as for the fallen King, the weak sinner whom she had tempted and derided, let him go to ruin, brought down as he had been by the loss of his own Spear. "Who dared then to wound him with the Holy Lance?" asks Parsifal. It was he, Kundry replies, who once had chastised her laughter, by the power of whose curse she now has strength to call up the Spear against Parsifal himself if he still bestows his compassion on the one who had lost it by his sin. And once more she tries to take him into her embrace.

When he again repulses her she recovers herself by a violent effort, and with a cry of rage breaks from him and calls towards the background, invoking the aid of Klingsor and his warders:

"thou whom I know, take thou this boy for thine own". As for Amfortas, Parsifal shall never find him:

> For fleddest thou from here, and found'st
> all the ways of the world,
> the one that thou seek'st,
> that path thy foot shall find never:
> each track, each pathway
> that leads thee from Kundry,
> thus—I curse beneath thy feet.

By now Klingsor has appeared on the castle walls, to end the matter by means of the only weapon meet for this Fool—the holy Spear that had brought low the King the boy now would serve. He hurls the Spear at Parsifal, over whose head, however, it remains suspended in air. The boy seizes it and holds it aloft. "And with this sign", he cries, "I rout thy magic":

> as the wound shall be closéd
> by the Spear that dealt it,
> in rack and ruin
> thy lying pomp shall it lay!

With the Spear he makes the sign of the Cross: at once the castle collapses as if in an earthquake, the garden withers, the earth is strewn with faded flowers. Kundry sinks to the ground with a cry. Parsifal turns to her again as he is making his way across the ruined wall: "thou know'st", he says gravely, "where thou may'st find me when thou wilt!" Kundry raises herself a little and gazes after him, and the curtain falls to a few bars in the orchestra that begin passionately and end with the conveyance, by their colour, of a sense of utter bleakness and desolation, material and spiritual:

With the loss of the Spear and the transformation that has taken place in Kundry, Klingsor's power is at an end: but for Parsifal the long and dolorous quest for Amfortas and the Grail is now to begin.

33

The third act opens with a grave orchestral prelude the subtle chromaticisms of which are a foretaste of a harmony, throughout the act, the like of which had not been known in music until then, even in the work of such a master of chromatic nuance as Wagner: in some places it marks an advance upon *Tristan* in this field as great as that of *Tristan*—which is the great dividing line between the older harmony and the new—had been upon the *Rhinegold* and the *Valkyrie*.

The prelude covers, in its own purely musical way, the weary years that have elapsed between Parsifal's regaining of the Spear, the origin, the properties and the appointed function of which he now knows, and his arrival once more, all unaware of it, in the domain of the Grail, which Kundry had told him jeeringly he, the youthful Fool, would never find again. (According to the legend it is of the essence of the Grail that he who seeks for it can never find it: he must be led to it by the Grail itself at the Grail's own time). Parsifal has wandered far in these years, been engaged in many battles and beset by difficulties and racked by self-doubts of all kinds; but always with the one great purpose of pity burning within him, some day to light upon the castle of the Grail again and heal Amfortas with a touch of the Spear that had dealt him his wound.

When now we meet with him once more he is no longer

the ignorant boy of the first act but a thoughtful man, sobered by suffering and made wise by compassion. We see him on the last stage of what has been a pilgrimage of endless frustration; in the opening bars of the prelude he, and the community of the Grail with him—for it too has suffered from his inability to find it again—are shewn bowed down beneath a load of desolation:

while a motive of Straying, as we may most conveniently call it:

suggests his confused and stumbling course all these years through a world that has failed to grant him the one thing his heart desired —to find his way back again and heal Amfortas with the Spear. Then comes a subtle modification of the motive of the Pure Fool:

followed by others in which the original simple harmonies of that motive (see No. 10) are made still more poignant, as in this example:

Interwrought with these reminiscences of the Pure Fool of the first act is a figure (shewn in No. 41A) to be associated later with the tortured winter sleep and awakening of Kundry. Now and then we hear also (No. 1C) the theme of the Spear that is at once the instrument and the symbol of the destiny that has been laid upon Parsifal.

The prelude, however, must not be regarded as a mere stringing together of motives in quasi-narrative or pictorial form. It is through-and-through psychological, spiritual: it has a meaning that is none the less definite because it cannot be expressed by us in words. Wagner himself, we learn from a jotting in Cosima's

diary, said when he was writing it that his task—and it had been
a difficult one—was to get down to the "fundamentals" of musical
expression.

34

When the curtain rises at the conclusion of the prelude we see
a pleasant open landscape in the domain of the Grail, with gently
mounting flower-strewn meadows in the background. The foreground represents the edge of a forest which stretches out on the
right to rising rocky ground. In the front, on the side of the wood,
is a spring, and opposite this, a little further back, a humble
hermit's hut, leaning against a mass of rock. It is the early morning
of a beautiful Spring day.

To the soft accompaniment of No. 39 Gurnemanz, now a very
old man, garbed simply in the tunic of the knights of the Grail,
comes out of the hut and listens in the direction from which he has
heard groans that had struck him as too piteous for those of any
beast, especially on this holiest of mornings. As he speaks these
latter words we hear the first foreshadowing of a motive which
later, in various forms, plays a large part in this scene; it is that of
Atonement:

No. 15 (Klingsor's Magic) and No. 18 (the sorcerer himself) in
the orchestra tell us that Kundry, still subject to him, is somewhere
near: her groaning is that of one tortured by evil dreams in profound sleep. Gurnemanz discovers her when he strides towards a
thorn thicket at the side of the stage and draws aside the dense
underwood. "Up, Kundry! Up!" he calls to her; "awake, for
winter is fled and Spring is here!"

The wailing No. 41A is dwelt upon in the orchestra as Gurnemanz chafes the hands and temples of Kundry, whom he has drawn, stiff and numb, from the thicket and borne to a grassy mound near by. At last she opens her eyes, and greets her return to a life she does not desire with a frenzied cry as the orchestra crashes in with the wild dissonance that had accompanied her first entry in act one (No. 12). She is clothed, as when we saw her first, in the rough garment of a penitent; but she is paler now, and the old animal wildness of look has left her. She stares long and uncomprehendingly at Gurnemanz, and as consciousness slowly returns to her she rises, arranges her clothing and her hair, and at once betakes herself humbly to the duties of a serving-maid: the only word she can utter in reply to Gurnemanz's questionings is a hoarse "Service! Service!"

The old man shakes his head sadly: light will be her toil, he tells her, for it is long since the knights of the Grail have sent any message to other lands. The brotherhood has fallen from its ancient high estate: each man lives now on herbs and roots which he has learned from the beasts of the forest to find for himself, the nourishment of the Grail being denied them. But Gurnemanz is struck by the change in Kundry, which, as the orchestra gives out some of the music associated with the Grail and the Spear, he puts down to the benign influence of the Holy Morn: it is not alone her body but her soul also, he feels, that has been awakened from sleep; and the strings breathe softly the tranquil melody of the Flowery Meadow:

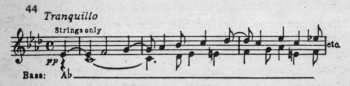

which will later come fully into its own in the Good Friday music.

Kundry, who has gone into the hut, returns with a pitcher, which she goes to fill at the spring. While waiting for it to fill she sees someone approaching from the wood, and turns to point him out to Gurnemanz. The Parsifal motive (No. 10) is intoned in the solemn colours of horns, trumpets and trombones:

It is heavy now with the load of Parsifal's long and fruitless quest.

35

He enters from the wood, a sombre figure in black armour with closed helm, holding the Spear in his hand. He strides forward slowly and wearily, with bowed head, as if in a dream, and seats himself on the little grassy mound. Gurnemanz hails him as a guest, to whom he offers his services; but Parsifal only shakes his head without speaking. The old man gently chides him: the newcomer's vow, he says, may constrain him to silence, but he must be told that now he is in a hallowed place, in which no man must go with shield, spear, and closed visor, and least of all on this day. Does he not know what holy day it is? Parsifal shakes his head. Then from what heathen land has he come, Gurnemanz asks, that he does not know that this is Good Friday? He bids the knight lay down his weapons, that are an offence in the sight of the Lord who shed His holy blood for the atonement of sin.

To the accompaniment of solemn music Parsifal humbly obeys. Still without speaking, he thrusts the Spear into the ground before him, lays sword and shield beside it, opens his helm, removes it from his head and places it with the weapons: then he kneels before the upright Spear in silent prayer. Gurnemanz gazes at him in wonderment and beckons to Kundry; and as the orchestra gives out the full motive of the Spear (No. 6), followed by that of the Love Feast (No. 1), he says to her, "Surely this is the Fool whom in my anger I drove away?" Looking fixedly at Parsifal she inclines her head but does not speak. Gurnemanz has now recognised the Spear also, and in deep emotion he praises the Holy Day for what it has brought him.

His prayer ended, Parsifal rises slowly to his feet, looks tranquilly around him, recognises Gurnemanz, and gently holds out his hand to him: " 'tis well", he says, "that again I have found thee!" Whence and how has he come, the old man asks. "Through error and through suffering lay my pathway", Parsifal replies, to the accompaniment of No. 40; "from their illusion free I sure may deem me, now that this woodland's murmur I have heard once more and give the kind old man a second greeting. Or am I in error still? For all about me seems changed." One alone has he been seeking all this weary while, "him whose dire lament in foolish wonder once I heard, and for whose healing, I deem, I bring now what may serve. But ah! a curse lay on me ne'er to find him. In blindest error through trackless wilds have I come hither: woes without number, battles and conflicts, drove me from the pathway, even when, methought, I knew it. Then dark despair descended on me to keep the treasure unsullied. The sacred relic ever guarding, from every weapon wounds did I win; for it I might not bear with me in battle. Unprofaned at my side I bore it, and now I bring it to its home: lo, there it gleameth bright and pure,—the Grail's own hallowed Spear!"

"Oh bounteous grace! Oh wonder! Holiest, highest wonder!" cries Gurnemanz in transport, as the wood wind breaks into the motives associated in the first act with the agony of Amfortas (No. 17), followed by that of the Spear and that of Faith (in the form the latter takes in No. 16). Parsifal is back again in the Grail's domain, he assures him. Long have they waited for him. They have been in sore need of him, for since the day when he had come among them and left them again the anguish of the King had increased: from the torment of his wound he had craved release in death, and to achieve that end he had refused, despite the entreaties of the brotherhood, to perform his holy office: the Grail had lain hidden in its shrine, the King hoping that deprived of the sight of it he might die. No longer do they eat the divine bread: common food supports them now, and their strength has departed. No longer come messages calling them to holy war in the world outside; weak and sad and leaderless they drag out their painful existence. Gurnemanz himself has come to this forest to await death in solitude and silence, while Titurel, denied too long the renewal that the Grail was wont to bring him, "is dead, a man, like all men"; and the quiet strings clinch the sad story with a solemn enunciation of the desolate No. 39.

36

Parsifal breaks out into passionate self-reproach. And 'tis he, he cries, who has wrought all this woe! What curse has been laid on him from birth, what load of sin must he carry, that no repentance, no atonement could lighten his blinded eyes, since he, the appointed deliverer, arriving here at last after having been caught in so many toils, finds himself in the end defeated! He seems about to fall, powerless: Gurnemanz supports him and lowers him to a sitting posture on the mound, while Kundry hastens to him with a cruse of water with which she sprinkles him. At this point the motive of Devotion is breathed softly by the wood wind:

It had first been heard in the second act, at the point where Kundry, at the commencement of her Narration, had told Parsifal that she had waited there for him to tell him of the death of his father and his mother; and it had reappeared later in that scene when, after being repulsed by him, she had cried, "Cruel one! If e'er thy heart could feel another's sorrow, then let it suffer with mine now! Art thou Redeemer, what bars thee now, harsh one, from making me one with thee in salvation?" Still later it had accompanied her despairing appeal to him—"He whom I longed for in death's deep anguish, he whom I knew and laughed at as a Fool, let me upon his breast fall weeping, be but one hour with thee united, and though by God and man cast forth, in thee be cleansed of sin and redeemed." His reply then had been, "Eternally would'st thou with me be damned if but one hour, unmindful of my mission, into thine arms I gave me." For first of all she must repent:[1] it is not through the flesh but only through the wisdom that comes slowly by understanding and pity that he can bring her salvation. The Devotion motive had been hinted at again, almost imperceptibly, at the moment when, in the third act, Gurnemanz had found Kundry in the thorn thicket. And now, at the point we have just reached, it becomes of prime significance. It is always enigmatic, both in itself and in its various comings upon the scene; but then Kundry herself is all enigma. Yet, as so often happens in Wagner, the music, if we surrender ourselves to that, has a logic of its own that cannot be rendered into words. It is clear, however, at the point at which we have now arrived, that the redemption for which she had longed at Parsifal's hands is nigh, but on his own spiritual terms and those of the Grail and the Spear.

[1] Wagner's stage directions for her entry in the third act are "Kundry is in the rough garments of a penitent, as in the first act". He must have forgotten that on her appearance in the first act she had worn "a wild garment, looped-up high", with "a snake-skin girdle with long ends": "her hair is black and hangs in loose locks: her complexion is a deep reddish-brown: her eyes are black and piercing, sometimes flashing wildly, more often fixed and staring like the eyes of the dead": all which agrees with the description of her in the Prose Sketch. The Kundry of the third act is another being altogether, both in temperament and in appearance. I suspect a last-minute change in Wagner's plan at this point, which he failed to bring into full relation with his general scheme. For in the opera Gurnemanz, after the rising of the curtain, finds her in the thicket, where she has been lying all unknown to him until he heard her groaning, whereas in the Sketch he had found her long before the action of the third act opened, and she had "given him meek and constant service"; until one day, while the old man was praying in front of his hut and she was fetching water for him from the spring, they see Parsifal approaching from the wood.

Gurnemanz is wiser than she. He gently repulses her when she would sprinkle Parsifal; for that lustration, he tells her, only the water of the holy spring itself will serve. A new motive, that of Benediction:

to which are linked further developments of No. 43:

is given out softly by the orchestra as Gurnemanz tells her that this day a wondrous work shall be done among them by the knight: "for holy office is he chosen; if he be pure of stain, then the dust of his long wanderings the sacred stream will wash away."

They lead Parsifal gently to the edge of the spring, where Kundry undoes the greaves of his armour and Gurnemanz removes his breastplate. They will go to the castle, he says, where the funeral rites of Titurel are to be celebrated and the Grail once more unveiled. At the mention of the dead Titurel we hear in the orchestra a suggestion:

of the solemn theme of the Funeral Procession, which will later dominate the episode of Parsifal's re-entry into the castle.

37

But first he must be prepared for the new high office that is to be his, in succession to the fallen Amfortas. Gurnemanz takes in his hand some water from the spring and sprinkles Parsifal's head: let it wash away all guilt and grief from him! Kundry humbly and silently bathes his feet, then draws a golden phial from her bosom and pours part of its contents over his feet, which she dries with her hastily unbound hair. But he takes the phial from her and hands it to the old man: "let the friend of Titurel anoint me", he says, "for today he shall greet me as King". Gurnemanz empties the phial over his head, upon which he lays his hand in blessing, passing it through Parsifal's hair. "All-pitying sufferer!" he says, to a new and sweet mutation of the Pure Fool motive (No. 10), "all-wise deliverer! As the redeemed one's sufferings thou hast suffered, now lift thou the last load from his head!" and the motive of Parsifal himself (No. 20) rings out majestically in the solemn tones of trumpets and trombones.

Parsifal takes, unobserved, some water from the spring and sprinkles the head of the kneeling Kundry, saying gently, to the accompaniment of No. 47, "My first office I perform: baptised be thou, and believe in the Redeemer." The penitent lowers her head and seems to weep passionately.

He turns his ecstatic gaze on the forest and meadow, which are now glowing in the morning light. The oboe gives out the tranquil theme of the Flowery Meadow in its full form:

and the great musical picture begins to unfold itself that is known in the concert room as the Good Friday music. Never, says Parsifal, has the meadow seemed to him so fair as today, never has he seen it put forth such beauty of flower or breathe such fragrance: all is sweetness and loving-kindness. That, Gurnemanz tells him, is Good Friday's magic, the grateful earth not weeping for the Saviour's suffering but rejoicing at its own rebirth through it:

> His wasted body on the Cross it sees not:
> and so aloft it looks to man redeemed,
> set free from sin and all its load of terror,
> by God's love-sacrifice made clean and pure:
> today each blade, each flower that blooms in meadow
> knows well no foot of man will tread it down,
> but e'en as God unmurm'ring died for him,
> in love and pity the Cross endured—
> so man in tender, holy mood
> treads soft the earth today.
> Thus grateful all creation sings,
> all that doth bloom and fade again,
> well knowing nature's pardon won,
> stainless and pure earth's heart today.

Still lost in the quiet ecstasy that is in nature's heart and in his own, Parsifal gently kisses the forehead of Kundry, who has slowly raised her head again and is gazing at him with a look of calm and earnest entreaty. This music of a dream-world of:

summers of the snakeless meadow, unlaborious earth and oarless sea,

spins itself out tranquilly, unhurriedly, loath, as it were, to lose the savour of a single drop of its own sweetness.

At last there steals upon the now almost silent air a peal of distant bells. It is midday, Gurnemanz reminds Parsifal: the hour has come for the new King of the Grail to take possession of his heritage. The motive of Parsifal (No. 20) is significantly combined with that of the obsequies of Titurel (No. 50) as Gurnemanz brings his own Grail-knight's mantle out of the hut and throws it over the shoulders of Parsifal, who takes up the Spear, and, with Kundry, follows the old man towards the castle.

38

The situation and the stage mechanism of the Transformation Scene in the first act are now reversed; the scenery changes gradually in character, as it had done then, but this time from right to left, and the three figures disappear from our view as the woodland changes to rock. The transitional music here is mainly woven out of the motive (No. 50) of the funeral procession:

Wagner distils the last essence of chromatic subtilisation out of this dominating figure[1] and a successor:

[1] On the probable origin of this theme see the final section of the present chapter.

through the texture of which pierces the clang of the castle bells coming nearer and nearer.

At last the walls of rock open, revealing the hall of the Grail, as in the first act, but now, significantly, without the communion tables, for the brotherhood of the Grail has been brought to the last pass of frustration and dejection. The hall is only faintly lit. From opposite sides come two processions of knights, one bearing the coffin of Titurel, the other Amfortas in his litter, preceded by the covered shrine of the Grail. To music through which the figure shewn in the lower part of No. 52 runs like a basso ostinato the two files of knights dialogue as they pass each other:

"I. We bring the Grail in its shrine: whom bear ye in yon coffin?

II. A hero, Titurel, and with him the holy power that of old God gave into his keeping.

I. What hand laid him low whom God protected?

II. He sank beneath the load of age when the Grail he could look upon no more.

I. Who stayed him from the sight of the Grail?

II. He whom ye carry there, the relic's sinful guardian.

I. We bear him here today once more that—for the last time, alas!—he may perform his high office."

"The last time! the last time!" both groups repeat in anguish; "be mindful once more of thy office, but once more!":

Amfortas raises himself wearily on his couch, and, to the accompaniment of the motive of Desolation (No. 39), breaks into a lament for the suffering he has brought on them all through his sin. A general cry of woe goes up as Titurel's coffin is opened. A new theme:

wells up in grave brass colouring as Amfortas turns to the body, to bid a last farewell to the father of whose death he has been the instrument. No. 16, in the soft wood wind, recalls the modified version of the Faith motive first heard in the opening scene of the opera, when Gurnemanz told the squires how the Saviour's messengers had appeared to Titurel, bringing him the sacred Chalice. Now it is a bitter memory for Amfortas as, to the accompaniment of this No. 16, he implores his father to intercede for him before God's throne: may the life-blood of the brethren be quickened again, but for himself the greatest boon will be death:

"This were the last mercy! That the poison, the wound, the horror may die in me, that my corroded heart may cease to beat! My father, take this my cry to Him on high—'Redeemer, give my son release!'"

39

They press in upon him with a wild cry of "Uncover the Grail! Serve thou thy office!" But he springs up in despair and rushes at the knights, who recoil from him. Mad must they be, he tells them, if they would have him live. As the old motive of his sickness and weariness (No. 9) piles up in a new form in the orchestra he tears open his wound and bids them draw their swords and plunge them into it: "slay ye the sinner and put an end to his woe!"

They fall back again in horror before his delirium. While the confusion has been thus mounting to its climax Parsifal, accompanied by Gurnemanz and Kundry, has entered unobserved. Now he advances, stretches forth the Spear, and touches Amfortas's side with the point of it. "One weapon only serves", he says quietly; "thy wound must be healed by the Spear that dealt it." The face of Amfortas is illumined with ecstasy: he staggers and is upheld by Gurnemanz as No. 9 now winds its way through the orchestral texture in soft colours and transfigured forms. "Be whole, absolved and atoned", says Parsifal, "for I now take on me thy holy office. Blessed be thy suffering, for pity's highest might and wisdom's purest power it taught the tim'rous Fool!" His characteristic motive (No. 20) rises to a new majesty in the orchestra as he steps towards the centre of the stage, holding the Spear high before him. "The holy Spear I bring to you again", he tells the knights, who gaze at the restored symbol in rapture. Motives connected with the Grail and its mysteries of Faith and Love and Hope succeed each other as he bids the squires open the shrine. They do so. Parsifal ascends the altar steps, takes the Grail from the shrine, and breathes a silent prayer before it. The chalice gradually becomes suffused with a soft glow, while darkness slowly descends upon the hall, which in the end is lit only by an illumination that filters down from the heights. The main motives of the prelude to the work are subtly interwoven with each other, a peculiarly mystical effect being obtained by the crossing and re-crossing of the Faith motive (No. 5) in strings, wood wind and harps:

"Wondrous high salvation! Redeemed the Redeemer!" sing the squires and knights in the lines and harmonies of the Pure Fool motive and that of the Love Feast (No. 1), with mystic voices (sopranos and altos) floating down from the middle height and the dome. A ray of light falls upon the Grail, which now glows ardently, and a white dove descends from the dome and hovers over Parsifal's head.[1] Kundry, her enigmatic course through the world completed, her part played to the end in the enlightenment of Parsifal through pity, sinks to the ground lifeless, her last look being turned on him. Amfortas and Gurnemanz kneel in homage before Parsifal, the new King, as he stands aloft among the worshipping brotherhood, waving the Grail from side to side in blessing of them. The harmonic and contrapuntal interweavings shewn in No. 57 become more and more etherealised and mysticised in the orchestra, and the curtain falls to No. 1 rising softly through the texture with a final gentle insistence in the rich tones of trumpet and trombone.

40

In 1871 Wagner thought of writing a symphony of mourning (*Trauersymphonie*) for the German dead in the war of 1870–1.

[1] The spectator should guard against the too common error of identifying Parsifal vaguely with Christ. Any suggestion of that sort angered Wagner. "The idea of making Christ a tenor!" he said: "phew!"

But from official quarters in Berlin he learned that the idea of thus dwelling on the more painful aspects of the conflict was not viewed with favour; so he wrote his *Kaisermarsch* instead. The plan for a *Trauersymphonie* was not given up, however, as is evident from a passage in Cosima's diary in October 1876. (They were in Italy at the time). Cosima had urged him to try to rid his mind of the cares of Bayreuth by writing a new work; "and curiously enough", says her biographer Du Moulin Eckart, "his thoughts were once more turning to the *Trauersymphonie* for those who had fallen in the war; it was to be based on the theme conceived for *Romeo and Juliet*." "He said", Cosima noted in her diary that day, "that he saw the biers being borne into the hall, more and ever more of them, so that the individual grief was always being merged in the suffering of all. Not until after that would come the song of triumph."

Some three and a half years before then he had promised to write for Cosima, Du Moulin informs us, "a composition of a quite peculiar kind, that should in a certain sense constitute a sombre pendant to the *Siegfried Idyll*, a foreshadowing of future destiny—a funeral march from *Romeo and Juliet*."

Evidently this "funeral march from *Romeo and Juliet*" and the projected *Trauersymphonie* of 1871 and 1876 were at bottom much the same. Virtually nothing is known as yet about the plan for a musical work on the Shakespeare subject. In 1943, however, Dr. Otto Strobel, the Wahnfried archivist, published a facsimile of a short sketch found in Wagner's "Brown Book". It consists of thirteen bars of music in the key of A flat minor, originally jotted down in pencil and then inked over at some later date; it is headed "Romeo und Julia", and bears the end-date, in Wagner's hand, "7 May, evening". Dr. Strobel gives the year as 1868.

Not only did this theme, we may conjecture, recur to Wagner in 1873 when he thought of writing "a sombre pendant to the *Idyll*", and again in 1876, in connection with the idea of a *Trauersymphonie*; it apparently became the basis of the funeral music that accompanies the bringing of Titurel's body into the hall of the Grail in the third act of *Parsifal*. The two situations were fundamentally similar—in the one case a succession of biers being carried into a hall amid universal mourning, in the other case a procession of knights bearing the coffin of Titurel. And basically the music is much the same. The sketch of 1868 begins thus:

The dominant figure seen twice in the first bar of this recurs seven times more in the course of the short sketch, and it correlates with the ostinato bass figure that accompanies the greater part of the Titurel procession. (See No. 52). We meet with it again in the opera in the following passage, which is the continuation of our No. 53:

while there is a family likeness between a figure that appears three times in the sketch:

and passages of this type:

in the Titurel music. In the opera, of course, the elaborate tone-picture develops in its own musical way that is also the psychological way of the drama, for Wagner's unique blend of imagination and craftsmanship enabled him to combine the basic elements of the *Romeo and Juliet* sketch with some of the leading motives relevant to the Titurel scene; but there cannot be much doubt that the *Romeo and Juliet* music, the *Trauersymphonie* and the Titurel processional music all stemmed from the same mood within him.

My quotation from the Sketch was taken from the imprint of the latter in Vol. XI of Wagner's *Sämtliche Schriften und Dichtungen*. But after the proofs of this chapter had come through I received from Dr. Otto Strobel a complete facsimile of Wagner's manuscript of the Sketch made for King Ludwig; and in this the parenthesis signs to which I have referred do not appear. If, therefore, they are not Wagner's own my argument is to that extent weakened. But the variants between the manuscript and the imprint are so many and so pronounced that it appears probable that the latter was made from a *draft* of Wagner's for the Ludwig Sketch: the parenthesis signs may therefore have really been in this draft. No hint is anywhere given by the anonymous editor of Vol. XI of the *Sämtliche Schriften* as to the provenance of the documents he is dealing with; and there are many indications that the editorial work has been done in a very slapdash way.

INDEX

Jonathan Cott
**Stockhausen: Conversations
with the Composer** 95p

Jon Cott is an associate editor of *Rolling Stone* magazine and is one
of the most highly respected 'new' journalists in the U.S.

In these conversations with Stockhausen he presents a coherent account
of the composer's techniques and an explanation of his major works as
well as an insight into what makes him tick as a man.

Stockhausen's music is a challenging subject to convey to a general
readership, but Cott writes clearly and simply, transforming what is
potentially obscure and esoteric into a comprehensive philosophy not
only of music but of life itself.

Salvador Dali
The Diary of a Genius £1.00

'Ever since the French Revolution there has been
growing up a vicious, cretinising tendency to consider
a genius as a human being . . . This is false. And if it
is false when applied to me, the genius, it is even
more false when applied to those who, like the almost
divine Raphael, embodied the very genius of the
Renaissance.

'This book will prove that the daily life of a genius,
his sleep, his digestion, his ecstasies, his nails,
his colds, his blood, his life and death are essentially
different from those of the rest of mankind. This book,
then, is the first diary written by a genius.'
From the author's Introduction

A. L. Rowse
The Case Books of Simon Forman £1.25
Sex and society in Shakespeare's age

A. L. Rowse here opens up the Case Books of Simon Forman,
Elizabethan doctor, astrologer, mountebank and compulsive
seducer. They give us the most intimate close-up of Elizabethan
social life, and particularly its sex-life, that we possess.

Forman was consulted by all sorts of people, from that beautiful
poisoner, the Countess of Essex, to Shakespeare's landlady – and also his
Dark Lady – to merchants and actors, to sailors' wives and whores.

'Forman recorded his activities, his thoughts and hopes and fears,
including his sex-life, with veracious accuracy . . . what a portrait,
in depth, of the time ! – what an exposure of the underside . . . the ardours
and passions, the fears and expectations, the sadnesses
and tragedies.' *The Author*

'This new study of the Elizabethan age by this most readable of
historians is written with patent enjoyment of delving into the
private lives of men and woman on all levels of society'
ROGER MANVELL, NEW HUMANIST

You can buy these and other Picador books from booksellers and
newsagents; or direct from the following address:
Pan Books, Cavaye Place, London SW10 9PG
Send purchase price plus 15p for the first book and 5p for
each additional books, to allow for postage and packing
Prices quoted are applicable in UK
While every effort is made to keep prices low, it is sometimes
necessary to increase prices at short notice. Pan Books reserve the
right to show on covers new retail prices which may differ
from those advertised in the text or elsewhere

Selected bestsellers

☐ **Jaws** Peter Benchley 70p
☐ **Let Sleeping Vets Lie** James Herriot 60p
☐ **If Only They Could Talk** James Herriot 60p
☐ **It Shouldn't Happen to a Vet** James Herriot 60p
☐ **Vet in Harness** James Herriot 60p
☐ **Tinker Tailor Soldier Spy** John le Carré 60p
☐ **Alive: The Story of the Andes Survivors** (illus)
   Piers Paul Read 75p
☐ **Gone with the Wind** Margaret Mitchell £1.50
☐ **Mandingo** Kyle Onstott 75p
☐ **Shout at the Devil** Wilbur Smith 70p
☐ **Cashelmara** Susan Howatch £1.25
☐ **Hotel** Arthur Hailey 80p
☐ **The Tower** Richard Martin Stern 70p
   (filmed as *The Towering Inferno*)
☐ **Bonecrack** Dick Francis 60p
☐ **Jonathan Livingston Seagull** Richard Bach 80p
☐ **The Fifth Estate** Robin Moore 75p
☐ **Royal Flash** George MacDonald Fraser 60p
☐ **The Nonesuch** Georgette Heyer 60p
☐ **Murder Most Royal** Jean Plaidy 80p
☐ **The Grapes of Wrath** John Steinbeck 95p

All these books are available at your bookshop or newsagent:
or can be obtained direct from the publisher
Just tick the titles you want and fill in the form below
Prices quoted are applicable in UK

Pan Books, Cavaye Place, London SW10 9PG
Send purchase price plus 15p for the first book and 5p for each
additional book, to allow for postage and packing

Name (block letters) —————————————————————

Address ——————————————————————————

——————————————————————————————

While every effort is made to keep prices low, it is sometimes
necessary to increase prices at short notice. Pan Books reserve the
right to show on covers new retail prices which may differ from
those advertised in the text or elsewhere